TOGAF™

2006 Edition *(Incorporating 8.1.1)*

Copyright 2005-2006, The Open Group

All rights reserved. No part of this publication may be reproduced, stored in a retrieval lsystem, or transmitted, in any form or by any means, electric, mechanical, photocopying, recording or otherwise, without the prior permission of the copyright owners.

TOGAF 2006 Edition (Incorporating TOGAF 8.1.1)

ISBN: 1-931624-62-3
Document Number: G063

Published in the US by The Open Group, August 2006.

Any comments relating to the material contained in this document may be submitted by email to:
OGSpecs@OpenGroup.org

CONTENTS

Foreword

TOGAF Licensing Terms xx
The Development of TOGAF xxi
TOGAF-Related Resources xxi
The Open Group Architecture Forum xxii
Acknowledgements xxii
Referenced Documents xxiii
Trademarks xxv

Part I - INTRODUCTION
Chapter 1: Introduction

1.1 Structure of the TOGAF Document 2
1.2 Downloads 3
    1.2.1 Conditions of Use 3
1.3 Frequently Asked Questions 3

Chapter 2: TOGAF as an Enterprise Architecture Framework

2.1 Introduction 10
2.2 The Role of TOGAF 10
2.3 TOGAF and Architecture Governance 11
2.4 Using TOGAF with Other Frameworks 12
    2.4.1 Overview 12
    2.4.2 The Enterprise Continuum 13
2.5 Summary 13

Part II - ARCHITECTURE DEVELOPMENT METHOD (ADM)
Chapter 3: Introduction to the ADM

3.1 ADM Overview 16
    3.1.1 Relationship to Other Parts of TOGAF 16
    3.1.2 The ADM and the Enterprise Continuum 16
    3.1.3 The ADM and the Resource Base 17
    3.2.1 Key Points 18
    3.2.2 Basic Structure 18
3.3 Adapting the ADM 21
3.4 Architecture Governance 22
3.5 Process Management 22
3.6 Scoping the Architecture 23
    3.6.1 Enterprise Scope/Focus 24
    3.6.2 Architecture Domains 26
    3.6.3 Vertical Scope/Level of Detail 27
    3.6.4 Time Horizon 28
3.7 Architecture Integration 29
3.8 Summary 30

Chapter 4: Preliminary Phase - Framework and Principles

- 4.1 Objectives 33
- 4.2 Approach 33
  - 4.2.1 Principles 33
  - 4.2.2 Framework 34
- 4.3 Inputs 34
- 4.4 Steps 34
- 4.5 Outputs 35

Chapter 5: Phase A - Architecture Vision

- 5.1 Objectives 37
- 5.2 Approach 37
  - 5.2.1 General 37
  - 5.2.2 Creating the Architecture Vision 38
- 5.3 Inputs 39
- 5.4 Steps 39
  - 5.4.1 Business Scenarios 41
- 5.5 Outputs 42

Chapter 6: Phase B - Business Architecture

- 6.1 Objectives 44
- 6.2 Approach 44
  - 6.2.1 General 44
  - 6.2.2 Developing the Baseline Description 45
  - 6.2.3 Business Modeling 46
  - 6.2.4 Enterprise Continuum 47
  - 6.2.5 Gap Analysis 48
- 6.3 Inputs 50
- 6.4 Steps 50
- 6.5 Outputs 53

Chapter 7: Phase C - Information Systems Architectures

- 7.1 Objective 56
- 7.2 Approach 56
  - 7.2.1 Development 56
  - 7.2.2 Implementation 56
- 7.3 Inputs 57
- 7.4 Steps 57
- 7.5 Output 57

Chapter 8: Phase C - Information Systems Architectures - Data Architecture

- 8.1 Objective 59
- 8.2 Approach 59
  - 8.2.1 Enterprise Continuum 59
  - 8.2.2 Gap Analysis 59
- 8.3 Inputs 60
- 8.4 Steps 61
- 8.5 Outputs 65

Chapter 9: Phase C - Information Systems Architectures - Applications Architecture

- 9.1 Objective 66
- 9.2 Approach 66
  - 9.2.1 Enterprise Continuum 66
  - 9.2.2 Gap Analysis 67
- 9.3 Inputs 68
- 9.4 Steps 68
- 9.5 Outputs 73

Chapter 10: Phase D - Technology Architecture

- 10.1 Objective 75
- 10.2 Approach 75
  - 10.2.1 General 75
  - 10.2.2 Architecture Continuum 75
- 10.3 Inputs 75
- 10.4 Steps 76
- 10.5 Outputs 77
- 10.6 Target Technology Architecture - Detail 77
  - 10.6.1 Introduction 77
  - 10.6.2 Overview 77
  - 10.6.3 Step 1 78
    - 10.6.3.1 Objective 78
    - 10.6.3.2 Approach 78
    - 10.6.3.3 Inputs 79
    - 10.6.3.4 Activities 80
    - 10.6.3.5 Outputs 80
  - 10.6.4 Step 2 80
    - 10.6.4.1 Objective 81
    - 10.6.4.2 Approach 81
    - 10.6.4.3 Inputs 81
    - 10.6.4.4 Activities 82
    - 10.6.4.5 Outputs 82
  - 10.6.5 Step 3 83
    - 10.6.5.1 Objective 83
    - 10.6.5.2 Approach 83
    - 10.6.5.3 Inputs 84
    - 10.6.5.4 Activities 84
    - 10.6.5.5 Outputs 85
  - 10.6.6 Step 4 85
    - 10.6.6.1 Objective 85
    - 10.6.6.2 Approach 85
    - 10.6.6.3 Inputs 86
    - 10.6.6.4 Activities 86
    - 10.6.6.5 Outputs 86

        10.6.7 Step 5 86
            10.6.7.1 Objective 86
            10.6.7.2 Approach 86
            10.6.7.3 Inputs 87
            10.6.7.4 Activities 87
            10.6.7.5 Outputs 87
        10.6.8 Step 6 87
            10.6.8.1 Objective 87
            10.6.8.2 Approach 87
            10.6.8.3 Inputs 88
            10.6.8.4 Activities 88
            10.6.8.5 Outputs 88
        10.6.9 Step 7 89
            10.6.9.1 Objective 89
            10.6.9.2 Approach 89
            10.6.9.3 Inputs 90
            10.6.9.4 Activities 90
            10.6.9.5 Outputs 91
        10.6.10 Step 8 91
            10.6.10.1 Objective 91
            10.6.10.2 Approach 91
            10.6.10.3 Inputs 92
            10.6.10.4 Activities 94
            10.6.10.5 Outputs 94
        10.6.11 Postscript 94

Chapter 11: Phase E - Opportunities and Solutions

    11.1 Objectives 96
    11.2 Approach 96
    11.3 Inputs 97
    11.4 Steps 97
    11.5 Outputs 98

Chapter 12: Phase F - Migration Planning

    12.1 Objective 100
    12.2 Approach 100
    12.3 Inputs 102
    12.4 Steps 102
    12.5 Outputs 103

Chapter 13: Phase G - Implementation Governance

    13.1 Objectives 105
    13.2 Approach 105
    13.3 Inputs 105
    13.4 Steps 106
    13.5 Outputs 106

Chapter 14: Phase H - Architecture Change Management

- 14.1 Objective 108
- 14.2 Approach 108
    - 14.2.1 The Drivers for Change 109
    - 14.2.2 The Change Management Process 109
    - 14.2.3 Guidelines for Maintenance versus Architecture Redesign 110
- 14.3 Inputs 111
- 14.4 Steps 111
- 14.5 Outputs 112

Chapter 15: ADM Architecture Requirements Management

- 15.1 Objective 114
- 15.2 Approach 114
    - 15.2.1 Genral 114
    - 15.2.2 Resources 114
        - 15.2.2.1 Business Scenarios 114
        - 15.2.2.2 Volere Requirements Specification Template . . . 115
        - 15.2.2.3 Requirements Tools 115
- 15.3 Inputs 115
- 15.4 Steps 116
    - Notes 117
- 15.4 Outputs 118

Chapter 16: ADM Input and Output Descriptions

- 16.1 Introduction 120
- 16.2 Major Input Descriptions 120
    - 16.2.1 Request for Architecture Work 120
    - 16.2.2 Architecture Principles 121
    - 16.2.3 Re-Usable Architecture Building Blocks 121
    - 16.2.4 Product Information 121
    - 16.2.5 New Technology Reports 121
- 16.3 Major Output Descriptions 121
    - 16.3.1 Statement of Architecture Work 121
    - 16.3.2 Business Scenario/Architecture Vision 122
    - 16.3.3 Business Architecture 122
    - 16.3.4 Technology Architecture 123
    - 16.3.5 Impact Analysis 124
    - 16.3.6 Architecture Contract 124
    - 16.3.7 Requirements Impact Statement 125

Chapter 17: Introduction to the Enterprise Continuum

- 17.1 Overview 128
- 17.2 The Enterprise Continuum and Architecture Re-Use 128
- 17.3 The Enterprise Continuum and the TOGAF ADM 129
- 17.4 Constituents of the Enterprise Continuum 129
- 17.5 Structure of Part III 130

Chapter 18: The Enterprise Continuum in Detail

- 18.1 The Architecture Continuum 131
  - 18.1.1 Introduction 131
  - 18.1.2 Foundation Architecture 132
  - 18.1.3 Common Systems Architectures 133
  - 18.1.4 Industry Architectures 133
  - 18.1.5 Enterprise Architectures 134
- 18.2 The Solutions Continuum 134
  - 18.2.1 Introduction 134
  - 18.2.2 Products and Services 135
  - 18.2.3 Systems Solutions 135
  - 18.2.4 Industry Solutions 136
  - 18.2.5 Enterprise Solutions 136
- 18.3 The Enterprise Continuum and Your Organization 136
  - 18.3.1 Relationships 137
  - 18.3.2 Your Enterprise 138

Chapter 19: Foundation Architecture - Technical Reference Model

- 19.1 Concepts 139
  - 19.1.1 Role of the TRM in the Foundation Architecture 139
  - 19.1.2 TRM Components 139
  - 19.1.3 Other TRMs 140
- 19.2 High-Level Breakdown 140
  - 19.2.1 Overview 141
  - 19.2.2 Portability and Interoperability 141
- 19.3 The TRM in Detail 142
  - 19.3.1 Introduction 143
  - 19.3.2 TRM Entities and Interfaces 143
  - 19.3.3 Application Software 143
    - 19.3.3.1 Business Applications 144
    - 19.3.3.2 Infrastructure Applications 144
  - 19.3.4 Application Platform 145
    - 19.3.4.1 The Platform Concept 145
    - 19.3.4.2 Extending the TRM 146
    - 19.3.4.3 Interfaces Between Services 146
    - 19.3.4.4 Future Developments 146
  - 19.3.5 Communications Infrastructure 147
  - 19.3.6 Application Platform Interface 147
  - 19.3.7 Communications Infrastructure Interface 148
  - 19.3.8 Qualities 148
- 19.4 Application Platform - Taxonomy 148
  - 19.4.1 Basic Principles 149
  - 19.4.2 Application Platform Service Categories 149
    - 19.4.2.1 Object-Oriented Provision of Services 153
  - 19.4.3 Application Platform Service Qualities 153
    - 19.4.3.1 Principles 153
    - 19.4.3.2 Taxonomy of Service Qualities 154

Chapter 20: Detailed Platform Taxonomy

    20.1 Data Interchange Services 156
    20.2 Data Management Services 157
    20.3 Graphics and Imaging Services 159
    20.4 International Operation Services 159
    20.5 Location and Directory Services 160
    20.6 Network Services 161
    20.7 Operating System Services 163
    20.8 Software Engineering Services 164
    20.9 Transaction Processing Services 165
    20.10 User Interface Services 166
    20.11 Security Services 167
    20.12 System and Network Management Services 169
    20.13 Object-Oriented Provision of Services 171

Chapter 21: Foundation Architecture - Standards Information Base

    21.1 Introduction 174
        21.1.1 Role of the SIB 174
            21.1.1.1 What is the SIB? 174
            21.1.1.2 What is it for? 174
            21.1.1.3 How is it Used in Architecture Development? 175
        21.1.2 Accessing the SIB 175
    21.2 The Open Group Standards 175
        21.2.1 Overview 176
        21.2.2 Criteria for Inclusion in the SIB 176
        21.2.3 The Open Group Technical Processes 178
        21.2.4 Product Standards 178
        21.2.5 The Open Brand 179
    21.3 Using the SIB 179
        21.3.1 Introduction 179
        21.3.2 Examples 179
            21.3.2.1 Getting Started 179
            21.3.2.2 Example 1: The Entire SIB 180
            21.3.2.3 Example 2: Referenced Standards 180
            21.3.2.4 Example 3: Open Group Technical Standards 181
            21.3.2.5 Example 4: Open Group Product Standards 182
        21.3.3 Summary of Open Group Databases and Resources 184

Chapter 22: Integrated Information Infrastructure Reference Model

    22.1 Basic Concepts 185
        22.1.1 Background 185
        22.1.2 Components of the Model 185
        22.1.3 Relationship to Other parts of TOGAF 186
        22.1.4 Key Business and Technical Drivers 186
            22.1.4.1 Problem Space: The Need for Boundaryless Information Flow 186
            22.1.4.2 Solution Space: The Need for Integrated Information Infrastructure . . . 187
        22.1.5 Health Warning 188

22.2 High-Level View. 189
   22.2.1 Derivation of the III-RM from the TRM 189
   22.2.2 The High-Level III-RM Graphic 190
   22.2.3 Components of the High-Level III-RM 191
22.3 Detailed Taxonomy 192
   22.3.1 Detailed III-RM Graphic 193
   22.3.2 Business Applications. 193
      22.3.2.1 Information Provider Applications 194
      22.3.2.2 Brokerage Applications 195
      22.3.2.3 Information Consumer Applications 195
   22.3.3 Infrastructure Applications 197
      22.3.3.1 Development Tools 197
      22.3.3.2 Management Utilities 198
   22.3.4 Application Platform 198
      22.3.4.1 Software Engineering Services 199
      22.3.4.2 Security Services 199
      22.3.4.3 Location and Directory Services 199
      22.3.4.4 Human Interaction Services. 200
      22.3.4.5 Data Interchange Services 201
      22.3.4.6 Data Management Services 201
      22.3.4.7 Additional Operating System Services 201
   22.3.5 Qualities 202

Chapter 23: Architecture Board

23.1 Role 204
23.2 Responsibilities 204
23.3 Setting Up the Architecture Board 206
   23.3.1 Triggers 206
   23.3.2 Size of the Board 206
   23.3.3 Board Structure 207
23.4 Operation of the Architecture Board. 207
   23.4.1 General. 208
   23.4.2 Preparation 208
   23.4.3 Agenda 208

Chapter 24: Architecture Compliance

24.1 Introduction 211
24.2 Terminology - The Meaning of Architecture Compliance. 211
24.3 Project Impact Assessments (Project Slices) 212
   24.3.1 Introduction 212
   24.3.2 Sources 213
24.4 Architecture Compliance Reviews 213
   24.4.1 Purpose 213
   24.4.2 Timing 214
   24.4.3 Governance and Personnel Scenarios 215
24.5 Architecture Compliance Review Process 216
   24.5.1 Overview 216

24.5.2 Roles 217
24.5.3 Steps 217
24.6 Architecture Compliance Review Checklists. 219
    24.6.1 Hardware and Operating System Checklist 219
    24.6.2 Software Services and Middleware Checklist 220
    24.6.3 Applications Checklists 222
        24.6.3.1 Infrastructure (Enterprise Productivity) Applications 222
        24.6.3.2 Business Applications 223
        24.6.3.3 Application Integration Approach 224
    24.6.4 Information Management Checklists 224
        24.6.4.1 Data Values 224
        24.6.4.2 Data Definition 224
        24.6.4.3 Security/Protection 224
        24.6.4.4 Hosting, Data Types, and Sharing 225
        24.6.4.5 Common Services 225
        24.6.4.6 Access Method 225
    24.6.5 Security Checklist 225
    24.6.6 System Management Checklist 226
    24.6.7 System Engineering/Overall Architecture Checklists 227
        24.6.7.1 General 227
        24.6.7.2 Processors/Servers/Clients. 228
        24.6.7.3 Client 228
        24.6.7.4 Application Server 229
        24.6.7.5 Data Server 229
        24.6.7.6 COTS (where applicable) 229
    24.6.8 System Engineering/Methods & Tools Checklist 230
24.7 Architecture Compliance Review Guidelines 231
    24.7.1 Guidelines for Tailoring the Checklists 231
    24.7.2 Guidelines for Conducting Architecture Compliance Reviews 231

Chapter 25: Architecture Contracts

25.1 Role 233
25.2 Contents 234
    25.2.1 Statement of Architecture Work. 234
    25.2.2 Contract between Architecture Design and Development Partners 235
    25.2.3 Contract between Architecting Function and Business Users 236
25.3 Relationship to Architecture Governance 236

Chapter 26: Architecture Governance

26.1 Introduction 237
    26.1.1 Levels of Governance within the Enterprise. 237
    26.1.2 The Nature of Governance 238
        26.1.2.1 Governance: A Generic Perspective. 238
        26.1.2.2 The Characteristics of Governance 238
    26.1.3 Technology Governance 239
    26.1.4 IT Governance 239
        26.1.4.1 An IT Governance Framework - COBIT 240

  26.1.5 Architecture Governance: Overview 240
    26.1.5.1 Architecture Governance Characteristics 240
    26.1.5.2 Architecture Governance as a Board-Level Responsibility. 241
    26.1.5.3 TOGAF and Architecture Governance 241
 26.2 Architecture Governance Framework 241
  26.2.1 Architecture Governance Framework - Conceptual Structure 242
    26.2.1.1 Key Concepts 242
    26.2.1.2 Key Architecture Governance Processes 243
  26.2.2 Architecture Governance Framework - Organizational Structure 244
    26.2.2.1 Overview 244
    26.2.2.2 Key Areas 245
    26.2.2.3 Operational Benefits 245
 26.3 Architecture Governance in Practice 247
  26.3.1 Architecture Governance - Key Success Factors. 247
  26.3.2 Elements of an Effective Architecture Governance Strategy 247
    26.3.2.1 Architecture Governance and Corporate Politics 247
    26.3.2.2 Key Strategic Elements 248

Chapter 27: Architecture Maturity Models

 27.1 Overview 249
 27.2 Background 249
 27.3 The US DoC ACMM Framework 251
  27.3.1 Overview 251
  27.3.2 Elements of the ACMM 251
  27.3.3 Example: IT Architecture Process Maturity Levels 252
 27.4 Capability Maturity Models Integration (CMMI) 255
  27.4.1 Introduction 255
  27.4.2 The SCAMPI Method 256
 27.5 Conclusions 256

Chapter 28: Architecture Patterns

 28.1 Introduction 257
  28.1.1 Background. 257
  28.1.2 Content of a Pattern. 258
  28.1.3 Terminology 259
    28.1.3.1 Architecture Patterns and Design Patterns 260
    28.1.3.2 Patterns and the Architecture Continuum 260
    28.1.3.3 Patterns and Views 260
    28.1.3.4 Patterns and Business Scenarios. 260
  28.1.4 Architecture Patterns in Use 261
 28.2 US Treasury Architecture Development Guidance (TADG) 261
  28.2.1 TADG Pattern Content 261
  28.2.2 TADG Architecture Patterns 262
 28.3 IBM Patterns for e-Business 263
 28.4 Some Pattern Resources 264

Chapter 29: Architecture Principles

- 29.1 Introduction 265
- 29.2 Characteristics of Architecture Principles 266
- 29.3 Components of Architecture Principles 266
- 29.4 Developing Architecture Principles 267
  - 29.4.1 Qualities of Principles 267
- 29.5 Applying Architecture Principles 268
- 29.6 Example Set of Architecture Principles 269
  - 29.6.1 Business Principles 269
  - 29.6.2 Data Principles 273
  - 29.6.3 Application Principles 279
  - 29.6.4 Technology Principles 280

Chapter 30: Architecture Skills Framework

- 30.1 Introduction 283
- 30.2 The Need for an IT Architecture Skills Framework 283
  - 30.2.1 Definitional Rigor 283
  - 30.2.2 The Basis of an Internal Architecture Practice 283
- 30.3 Goals/Rationale 285
  - 30.3.1 Enterprise Certification of IT Architects 285
  - 30.3.2 Specific Benefits 285
- 30.4 IT Architecture Role and Skill Categories 286
  - 30.4.1 Overview 286
  - 30.4.2 TOGAF Roles 286
  - 30.4.3 Categories of Skills 287
  - 30.4.4 Proficiency Levels 288
- 30.5 IT Architecture Role and Skill Definitions 288
  - 30.5.1 Generic Skills 288
  - 30.5.2 Business Skills & Methods 289
  - 30.5.3 Enterprise Architecture Skills 289
  - 30.5.4 Program or Project Management Skills 290
  - 30.5.5 IT General Knowledge Skills 290
  - 30.5.6 Technical IT Skills 291
  - 30.5.7 Legal Environment 291
- 30.6 Generic Role and Skills of the IT Architect 291
  - 30.6.1 Generic Role 291
  - 30.6.2 Characterization in Terms of the Enterprise Continuum 293
  - 30.6.3 Key Characteristics of an IT Architect 294
    - 30.6.3.1 Skills and Experience in Producing Designs 294
    - 30.6.3.2 Extensive Technical Breadth, with Technical Depth in One or a Few Disciplines 294
    - 30.6.3.3 Method-Driven Approach to Execution 294
    - 30.6.3.4 Full Project Scope Experience 295
    - 30.6.3.5 Leadership 295
    - 30.6.3.6 Personal and Professional Skills 295
    - 30.6.3.7 Skills and Experience in One or More Industries 295
- 30.7 Conclusions 295

Chapter 31: Developing Architecture Views

- 31.1 The Role of Architecture Views 296
  - 31.1.1 Introduction 296
  - 31.1.2 TOGAF and Standards for IT Architecture Description 296
  - 31.1.3 A Note on Terminology 297
- 31.2 Basic Concepts 298
  - 31.2.1 A Simple Example of a Viewpoint and View 299
- 31.3 Developing Views in the ADM 300
  - 31.3.1 General Guidelines 300
  - 31.3.2 View Creation Process 301
- 31.4 Core Taxonomy of Architecture Views 302
  - 31.4.1 Overview 302
  - 31.4.2 Stakeholders 302
  - 31.4.3 Views/Viewpoints 302
  - 31.4.4 Description 305
- 31.5 Views, Tools, and Languages 307
  - 31.5.1 Overview 307
- 31.6 Views and Viewpoints 307
  - 31.6.1 Example of Views and Viewpoints 307
  - 31.6.2 Views and Viewpoints in Information Systems 308
  - 31.6.3 The Need for a Common Language and Interoperable Tools for Architecture Description 309
- 31.7 Conclusions 309
- 31.8 Developing a Business Architecture View 310
  - 31.8.1 Stakeholder and Concerns 310
  - 31.8.2 Modeling the View 310
  - 31.8.3 Key Issues 311
- 31.9 Developing an Enterprise Security View 312
  - 31.9.1 Stakeholder and Concerns 312
  - 31.9.2 Modeling the View 312
  - 31.9.3 Basic Concepts 312
    - 31.9.3.1 Information Domains 313
    - 31.9.3.2 Strict Isolation 313
    - 31.9.3.3 Absolute Protection 313
  - 31.9.4 Security Generic Architecture View 313
  - 31.9.5 Security Services Allocation 314
    - 31.9.5.1 Operating System Services 315
    - 31.9.5.2 Network Services 315
    - 31.9.5.3 System Security Management Services 316
- 31.10 Developing a Software Engineering View 316
  - 31.10.1 Stakeholders and Concerns 316
    - 31.10.1.1 Development Approach 316
    - 31.10.1.2 Software Modularity and Re-Use 316
    - 31.10.1.3 Portability 317
    - 31.10.1.4 Migration and Interoperability 317
  - 31.10.2 Key Issues 317
    - 31.10.2.1 Data-Intensive Versus Information-Intensive Software Systems 318
    - 31.10.2.2 Achieving Interoperability 318

   31.10.2.3 Software Tiers 319
   31.10.2.4 Some Uses of a Data Access Tier 322
   31.10.2.5 One Possible Instantiation of a Data Access Interface 322
   31.10.2.6 DAIs Enable Flexibility 323
   31.10.2.7 Distribution 324
   31.10.2.8 The Infrastructure Bus 324
  31.10.3 Conclusion 325
 31.11 Developing a System Engineering View 326
  31.11.1 Stakeholder and Concerns 326
  31.11.2 Key Issues. 326
   31.11.2.1 Client/Server Model 327
   31.11.2.2 Master/Slave and Hierarchic Models. 328
   31.11.2.3 Peer-to-Peer Model 329
   31.11.2.4 Distributed Object Management Model 329
 31.12 Developing a Communications Engineering View 332
  31.12.1 Stakeholder and Concerns 333
  31.12.2 Key Issues. 333
   31.12.2.1 Communications Infrastructure 333
   31.12.2.2 Communications Models 334
 31.13 Developing a Data Flow View 337
  31.13.1 Stakeholder and Concerns 337
  31.13.2 Modeling the View 337
  31.13.3 Key Issues. 338
   31.13.3.1 Database Management Systems 338
   31.13.3.2 Data Dictionary/Directory Systems 341
   13.13.3.3 Data Administration 342
   31.13.3.4 Data Security 342
 31.14 Developing an Enterprise Manageability View 343
  31.14.1 Stakeholders and Concerns 343
  31.14.2 Modeling the View 343
  13.14.3 Key Issues. 344
 31.15 Developing an Acquirer's View. 346
  31.15.1 Stakeholders and Concerns 346
  31.15.2 Modeling the View 346
  31.15.3 Key Issues. 346

Chapter 32: Building Blocks

 32.1 Overview 349
 32.2 Introduction to Building Blocks 349
  32.2.1 Overview. 349
  32.2.2 Generic Characteristics. 349
  32.2.3 Architecture Building Blocks 350
   32.2.3.1 Characteristics 350
   32.2.3.2 Specification Content 351
  32.2.4 Solution Building Blocks 351
   32.2.4.1 Characteristics 351
   32.2.4.2 Specification Content 351

        32.3 Building Blocks and the ADM. 352
            32.3.1 Basic Principles. 352
                32.3.1.1 Building Blocks in Architecture Design 352
                32.3.1.2 Building Block Design 352
            32.3.2 Building Block Specification Process in the ADM. 353
            32.3.3 Levels of Modeling 355
                32.3.3.1 Mapping the Modeling Levels to the ADM 356
        32.4 Building Blocks Example 356
            32.4.1 Introduction 356
            32.4.2 Structure 356
            32.4.3 Background to the Example. 357
            32.4.4 Business Process Level (Phase B) 357
            32.4.5 Technical Functionality and Constraints Level (Phases B, C, & D) 362
                32.4.5.1 Assumptions of Required Technical Functionality 364
            32.4.6 Architectural Model Level (Phases B, C, and D) 365
                32.4.6.1 Customer Information System Building Block Specification 373
            32.4.7 Opportunity Identification (Phase E) 375
            32.4.8 Re-Use of Building Blocks in Other Projects (Phases F to G) 375

Chapter 33: Business Process Domain Views

    33.1 Introduction. 378
    33.2 Role 378

Chapter 34: Business Scenarios

    34.1 Introduction 380
    34.2 Benefits of Business Scenarios. 381
    34.3 Creating the Business Scenario 381
        34.3.1 The Overall Process. 381
        34.3.2 Gathering. 382
        34.3.3 Analyzing. 384
        34.3.4 Reviewing 384
    34.4 Contents of a Business Scenario. 384
    34.5 Contributions to the Business Scenario 386
    34.6 Business Scenarios and the TOGAF ADM 387
    34.7 Guidelines on Developing Business Scenarios 388
        34.7.1 General Guidelines. 388
        34.7.2 Questions to Ask for Each Area 388
    34.8 Guidelines on Business Scenario Documentation 391
        34.8.1 Textual Documentation 391
        34.8.2 Business Scenario Models 391
    34.9 Guidelines on Goals and Objectives 392
        34.9.1 The Importance of Goals 392
        34.9.2 The Importance of SMART Objectives .392
        34.9.3 Categories of Goals and Objectives. .393
    34.10 Summary. 397

Chapter 35: Case Studies

- 35.1 The Role of Case Studies 399
- 35.2 Dairy Farm Group (Hong Kong) 399
- 35.3 Department of Social Security (UK) 400
  - 35.3.1 Organizational Context. 400
  - 35.3.2 Existing IT 400
  - 35.3.3 Strategic Objectives 401
  - 35.3.4 The Accord Project 402
  - 35.3.5 The Need for a New Architecture Framework 402
  - 35.3.6 CISITAF Documentation Set 403
  - 35.3.7 Technical Reference Model 404
  - 35.3.8 Standards Information Base 405
  - 35.3.9 Architecture Development Process 406
  - 35.3.10 Architecture Views 406
  - 35.3.11 Model Technical Architecture 407
  - 35.3.12 Using the CISITAF 408
- 35.4 Litton PRC (US) 409
- 35.5 JEDMICS 410
  - 35.5.1 Background 410
  - 35.5.2 Definition of Existing Environment in Existing Terms 410
  - 35.5.3 Restatement of Existing Environment in TOGAF Terms 412
  - 35.5.4 Views, Constraints, and External Environments 414
    - 35.5.4.1 Operations View 414
    - 35.5.4.2 Management View 414
    - 35.5.4.3 Security View 415
    - 34.5.4.4 Constraints 416
    - 35.5.4.5 Goals 417
    - 35.5.4.6 External Environments 418
  - 35.5.5 Target Architecture 418
  - 35.5.6 Migration 420
- 35.6 Ministry of Defence (UK) 420
  - 36.6.1 Executive Summary 420
  - 35.6 2 Laying the Foundations 421
  - 35.6.3 Constructing the Model 421
  - 35.6.4 Building the Framework 422
  - 35.6.5 Defining an Architecture 424
  - 35.6.6 The Way Forward 425
- 35.7 NATO (Belgium) 425
- 35.8 Police IT Organization (UK) 430
  - 35.8.1 Police IT 430
  - 35.8.2 Objectives of NSPIS 431
  - 35.8.3 Purpose 431
  - 35.8.4 NSPIS Technical Architecture Manual 432
  - 35.8.5 Applying the Framework 433
  - 35.8.6 NSPIS Technical Reference Model 436
  - 35.8.7 Interoperability 438
  - 35.8.8 Technical Requirements and Views 438
  - 35.8.9 The Architecture in Action 440

35.9 QA Consulting 441
35.10 Statskonsult (Norway) 441
    35.10.1 Norway Streamlines Government Processes by Going Online. 441
    35.10.2 Working with The Open Group to Plan the Future. 442
    35.10.3 An Internet DialTone Framework as Easy-to-Use as the Telephone. 442
35.11 Westpac (Australia). 443

Chapter 36: Glossary

Chapter 37: Other Architectures and Frameworks

37.1 Introduction 455
37.2 C4ISR Architecture Framework 455
    37.2.1 Overview. 455
    37.2.2 Relationship to TOGAF 456
37.3 CORBA 457
    37.3.1 Overview. 457
    37.3.2 Relationship to TOGAF 457
37.4 Enterprise Architecture Planning (EAP) 458
    37.4.1 Comparison with TOGAF. 459
37.5 Federal Enterprise Architecture: Practical Guide 459
    37.5.1 Overview. 459
    37.5.2 Relationship to TOGAF 461
37.6 FEAF 461
    37.6.1 Overview. 461
    37.6.2 Relationship to TOGAF 461
37.7 ISO/IEC TR 14252 (IEEE Std 1003.0) 463
    37.7.1 Overview. 463
    37.7.2 Relationship to TOGAF 463
37.8 NCR Enterprise Architecture Framework. 463
37.9 ISO RM-ODP 463
    37.9.1 Overview. 463
    37.9.2 Relationship to TOGAF 464
37.10 SPIRIT Platform Blueprint Issue 3.0 465
    37.10.1 Overview. 465
    37.10.2 Relationship to TOGAF 465
37.11 TAFIM 465
    37.11.1 Overview. 465
    37.11.2 Relationship to TOGAF 466
37.12 TEAF 466
    37.12.1 Overview. 466
    37.12.2 Relationship to TOGAF 467
37.13 Zachman Framework. 467
    37.13.1 Relationship to TOGAF 468

Chapter 38: Tools for Architecture Development

38.1 Overview 469
38.2 Issues in Tool Standardization 469
38.3 Evaluation Criteria and Guidelines 470

    38.3.1 Tool Criteria 470
        38.3.1.1 Functionality 470
        38.3.1.2 Architecture of the Tool 471
        38.3.1.3 Full Lifecycle Support. 472
        38.3.1.4 Interoperability Factors 472
        38.3.1.5 Financial Considerations 472
        38.3.1.6 Vendor Factors 473
    38.3.2 General Pointers 473

Chapter 39: ADM and the Zachman Framework

39.1 Introduction. 474
39.2 The Zachman Framework 474
39.3 Mapping TOGAF to the Zachman Framework 476
    39.3.1 Preliminary Phase: Framework and Principles 477
    39.3.2 Phase A: Architecture Vision 477
    39.3.3 Phase B: Business Architecture 479
    39.3.4 Phase C: Informations System Architectures: Data Architecture 481
    39.3.5 Phase C: Informations System Architectures: Applications Architecture 482
    39.3.6 Phase D: Technology Architecture 484

Foreword

It is a great pleasure for me, as Director of The Open Group Architecture Forum, in which TOGAF is developed and evolved, to write this Foreword.

I very much hope that, having read this first professionally published version of TOGAF, the reader will be motivated to use it for architecture work; to feed back to The Open Group the experience of its use; and perhaps also to consider joining the Architecture Forum and contributing to the further evolution of TOGAF, for the benefit of the architecture community at large.

In this Foreword I have three key points:

- To provide some background to TOGAF - how TOGAF originated, and continues to be evolved, within The Open Group Architecture Forum, and how the Forum itself operates
- Secondly, because TOGAF is very much a "live" document, and continues to be evolved, I want to point the reader to information about TOGAF that The Open Group makes freely available on its public web site
- Make clear to the reader the licensing terms under which The Open Group makes TOGAF publicly available

In reverse order, and dispensing with the legalese first.

TOGAF Licensing Terms

There are three main groups of people who download TOGAF from The Open Group web site, and may now purchase this book:

1. Those who are merely curious and interested to read about TOGAF
2. Those who wish to evaluate TOGAF and possibly go on to use it within their own organization
3. Those who wish to use TOGAF for commercial gain (for example, on projects for third parties, or in producing training materials, consultancy, etc.)

All the above are welcome to use TOGAF for their various purposes, including those seeking to use it commercially. However, different licensing terms and conditions apply.

This book is intended to address the needs of the first category above. It does not constitute obtaining a license for use of TOGAF, either within the reader's organization or commercially.

For those seeking to use TOGAF for internal architecture work, The Open Group makes it available under a free, perpetual license.

For those seeking to use TOGAF commercially, a license fee is payable, related to the size of the organization. However, members of The Open Group Architecture Forum may obtain a commercial license for no additional cost over and above their membership fee.

Rather than labor the license details here, the URL where the relevant terms and conditions are set out is:

> www.opengroup.org/architecture/togaf8/index8.htm

The objectives of this licensing policy are twofold.

The Open Group wishes to promote the widespread adoption and use of TOGAF, both for internal architecture work and as the basis of commercial products and services (consultancy, training, information, etc.) in the architecture field.

The Open Group requires a fair and reasonable return for the use of TOGAF for commercial gain, in order to help fund the future development of TOGAF. We owe it to those members who have contributed their time and effort in the past to the work of the Architecture Forum, and to the evolution of TOGAF, to ensure that others make a fair contribution in return.

The Development of TOGAF

TOGAF has come a long way since its inception in 1994, at the instigation of The Open Group User Council (as it then was) – the representatives of the computer user community among The Open Group membership.

The original development of TOGAF was based on the Technical Architecture Framework for Information Management (TAFIM), developed by the US Department of Defense. The DoD gave The Open Group explicit permission and encouragement to create TOGAF by building on the TAFIM, which itself represented hundreds of person-years of development effort and millions of dollars of US government investment

Starting from this sound foundation, the members of The Open Group Architecture Forum have developed successive versions of TOGAF over the years and published them on The Open Group public web site. The present edition of this book is based on TOGAF Version 8.1.1.

TOGAF-Related Resources

Information about the Architecture Forum is available at:

> www.opengroup.org/architecture/index.htm

The complete TOGAF documentation set is available for viewing online.

The Open Group Architecture Forum

The Architecture Forum is one of (currently) nine Forums in which the membership of The Open Group comes together to further the goals of The Open Group as a whole. It meets regularly within the ambit of The Open Group quarterly members' conferences.

Details of these conferences, and thereby details of Architecture Forum meetings, can be found at:

> www.opengroup.org/conference/

Acknowledgements

Although it is invidious to select individuals for specific mention, I do want to take the opportunity of this publication to pay tribute to those past and present members of the Architecture Forum who have served as its officers (Chairs and Vice-Chairs) and Project Leaders over the past decade of its existence. In alphabetical order:

- Christer Askerfjord, Sweden Post
- Terence Blevins, formerly NCR, now The MITRE Corporation
- Simon Dalziel, Architecting-the-Enterprise Limited
- Bill Estrem, Metaplexity Associates
- Hugh Fisher, UK National Health Service
- Chris Greenslade, Frietuna Consultants
- Ed Harrington, Data Access Technologies
- Dave Harrison, Architecting-the-Enterprise Limited
- David Jackson, IBM
- Judith Jones, Architecting-the-Enterprise Limited
- Mike Lambert, The Open Group
- Stuart Macgregor, Real IRM
- Ian McCall, IBM
- Barry Smith, The MITRE Corporation
- Walter Stahlecker, Hewlett-Packard
- Dave van Gelder, Capgemini
- Vish Viswanathan, CC&C Solutions
- Robert Weisman, CGI
- Hal Wilson, Litton PRC

My personal thanks to them all, and to the many other individuals and organizations who have contributed to the development of TOGAF over the years.

John Spencer,
Director, The Open Group Architecture Forum

Referenced Documents

The following documents are referenced in this guide:

- Analysis Patterns – Reusable Object Models. M. Fowler. Addison-Wesley, ISBN: 0-201-89542-0.
- ANSI/IEEE Std 1471-2000, Recommended Practice for Architectural Description of Software-Intensive Systems.
- ANSI/IEEE Std P1471/D5.2, Draft Recommended Practice for Architectural Description.
- A Pattern language: Towns, Buildings, Construction, Christopher Alexander, Oxford University Press, 1979, ISBN: 0-19-501919-9.
- Design Patterns: Elements of Reusable Object-Oriented Software, Erich Gamma, Richard Helm, Ralph Johnson, & John Vlissides, Addison-Wesley, October 1994, ISBN: 0-201-63361-2.
- Enterprise Architecture Planning: Developing a Blueprint for Data, Applications, and Technology, Steven H. Spewak & Steven C. Hill, John Wiley & Sons, 1993, ISBN: 0-47-159985-9.
- Federal Enterprise Architecture Framework (FEAF), Version 1.1, September 1999, US Federal Chief Information Officer (CIO) Council (www.itpolicy.gsa.gov/mke/archplus/fedarch1.pdf).
- Headquarters Air Force Principles for Information Management, US Air Force, June 29, 1998.
- IEEE Std 1003.0-1995 Guide to the POSIX Open System Environment (OSE), identical to ISO/IEC TR 14252 (administratively withdrawn by IEEE).
- IEEE Std 1003.23\(hy1998, Guide for Developing User Organization Open System Environment (OSE) Profiles (administratively withdrawn by IEEE).
- Implementing Enterprise Architecture – Putting Quality Information in the Hands of Oil and Gas Knowledge Workers (SPE 68794), G.A. Cox, R.M. Johnson, SPE, and R. M. Palermo, Area Energy LLC, Copyright 2001, Society of Petroleum Engineers, Inc.
- Interoperable Enterprise Business Scenario, October 2002, (K022), published by The Open Group.
- ISO 10303, Industrial Automation Systems and Integration – Product Data Representation and Exchange.
- ISO/IEC 10746-1:1998, Information Technology – Open Distributed Processing – Reference Model: Overview.
- ISO/IEC 10746-4:1998, Information Technology – Open Distribution Processing – Reference Model: Architectural Semantics.

- ISO/IEC TR 14252:1996, Information Technology – Guide to the POSIX Open System Environment (OSE) (identical to IEEE Std 1003.0).

- OECD Principles of Carporate governance, Organization for Economic Cooperation and Development, December 2001 (www.oecd.org).

- Pattern-Oriented Software Architecture: A System of Patterns, F. Buschmann, R. Meunier, H. Rohnert, P. Sommerlad, & M. Stal, Hohn Wiley & Sons, 1996, ISBN: 0-471-95869-7.

- Patterns and Software: Essential concepts and Terminology, Brad Appleton (www.enteract.com/~bradapp/docs/patterns-intro.html).

- Practical Guide to Federal Enterprise Architecture, Version 1.0, February 2001, US Federal Chief Information Officer (CIO) Council, a cooperative venture with the Gerneral Accounting Office (GAO) and the Office of Management and Budget (OMB).

- The Art of Systems Architecting, Eberhardt Rechtin & Mark W. Maier.

- The Command and Control System Target Architecture (C2STA), Electronic Systems Center (ESC), US Air Force, 2000.

- The Oregon Experiment, Chistopher Alexander, Oxford University Press, 1975, ISBN: 0-19-501824-9.

- The Timeless Way of Building, Christopher Alexander, Oxford University Press, 1979, ISBN: 0-19-502402-8.

- US Treasury Architecture Development Guidance (TADG), formerly known as the Treasury Information System Architecture Framework (TISAF).

The following web sites provide useful reference material:

- IBM Patterns for e-business: www.ibm.com/framework/patterns

- IBM Patterns for e-business Resources (also known as the "Red Books): www.ibm.com/developerworks/patterns/library

- The Patterns Home Page: hillside.net/patterns
  This web site is hosted by The Hillside Group and provides information about patterns, links to online patterns, papers, and books dealing with patterns, and patterns-related mailing lists.

- The Patterns-Discussion FAQ: g.oswego.edu/dl/pd-FAQ.html
  This web site is maintained by Doug Lea and provides a through and highly readable FAQ about patterns.

Trademarks

- Adobe™, Acrobat™, and Acrobat Reader™ are trademarks of Adobe Systems Incorporated.
- Java® is a registered trademark of Sun Microsystems, Inc.
- TOGAF™ and Boundaryless Information Flow™ are trademarks and UNIX® and The Open Group® are registered trademarks of The Open Group in the United States and other countries.
- The following are registered trademarks of the Software engineering Institute (SEI):
    - CMMI® (Capability maturity Model Integration)
    - IPD-CMM® (Integrated Product Development Capability Maturity Model)
    - P-CMM® (People Capability Maturity Model)
    - SA-CMM® (Software Acquisition Capability Maturity Model)
    - SCAMPI® (Standard CMMI Appraisal method for process Improvement)
    - SE-CMM® (Systems Engineering Capability maturity Model)
    - SW-CMM® (Capability maturity Model for Software)

The Open Group acknowledges that there may be other company names and products that might be covered by trademark protection and advises the reader to verify them independently.

PART: I

Introduction

Chapter 1: Introduction

The Open Group Architecture Framework (TOGAF) is a framework - a detailed method and a set of supporting tools - for developing an enterprise architecture. It may be used freely by any organization wishing to develop an enterprise architecture for use within that organization (see Conditions of Use).

TOGAF was developed by members of The Open Group, working within the Architecture Forum (*www.opengroup.org/architecture*). The original development of TOGAF Version 1 in 1995 was based on the Technical Architecture Framework for Information Management (TAFIM), developed by the US Department of Defense (DoD). The DoD gave The Open Group explicit permission and encouragement to create TOGAF by building on the TAFIM, which itself was the result of many years of development effort and many millions of dollars of US Government investment.

Starting from this sound foundation, the members of The Open Group Architecture Forum have developed successive versions of TOGAF each year and published each one on The Open Group public web site.

If you are new to the field of enterprise architecture and/or TOGAF, you may find it worthwhile to read the set of Frequently Asked Questions, where you will find answers to questions such as:

- What is an architecture framework?
- What kind of "architecture" are we talking about?
- How does my organization benefit from using TOGAF?

1.1 Structure of the TOGAF Document

There are four main parts to the TOGAF document:

PART I
(Introduction) This Part provides a high-level introduction to some of the key concepts behind enterprise architecture and in particular the TOGAF approach.

PART II
(Architecture Development Method) This is the core of TOGAF. It describes the TOGAF Architecture Development Method (ADM) - a step-by-step approach to developing an enterprise architecture.

PART III
(Enterprise Continuum) This Part describes the TOGAF Enterprise Continuum, a virtual repository of architecture assets, which includes the TOGAF Foundation Architecture, and the Integrated Information Infrastructure Reference Model (III-RM).

PART IV
(Resources) This Part comprises the TOGAF Resource Base - a set of tools and techniques available for use in applying TOGAF and the TOGAF ADM.

1.2 Downloads

Downloads of the TOGAF documentation, including a printable PDF file, are available under license from the TOGAF information web site (*www.opengroup.org/architecture/togaf*). The license is free to any organization wishing to use TOGAF entirely for internal purposes (for example, to develop an Information Systems Architecture for use within that organization).

1.2.1 Conditions of Use

The TOGAF documentation is freely available for viewing online without a license. Alternatively, the complete TOGAF documentation set may be downloaded and stored under license, as explained on the TOGAF information web site.

In either case, the TOGAF documentation may be used freely by any organization wishing to do so to develop an architecture for use within that organization. No part of it may be reproduced, stored in a retrieval system, or transmitted, in any form or by any means, electronic, mechanical, photocopying, recording, or otherwise, for any other purpose including, but not by way of limitation, any use for commercial gain, without the prior permission of the copyright owners.

1.3 Frequently Asked Questions

What is an enterprise?...

A good definition of "enterprise" in this context is any collection of organizations that has a common set of goals and/or a single bottom line. In that sense, an enterprise can be a government agency, a whole corporation, a division of a corporation, a single department, or a chain of geographically distant organizations linked together by common ownership.

The term "enterprise" in the context of "enterprise architecture" can be used to denote both an entire enterprise, encompassing all of its information systems, and a specific domain within the enterprise. In both cases, the architecture crosses multiple systems, and multiple functional groups within the enterprise.

Confusion also arises from the evolving nature of the term "enterprise". An extended enterprise nowadays frequently includes partners, suppliers, and customers. If the goal is to integrate an extended enterprise, then the enterprise comprises the partners, suppliers, and customers, as well as internal business units.

Large corporations and government agencies may comprise multiple enterprises, and hence there may well be separate enterprise architecture projects. However, there is often much in common about the information systems in each enterprise, and there is usually great potential for gain in the use of a common architecture framework. For example, a common framework can provide a basis for the development of an architecture repository for the integration and re-use of models, designs, and baseline data.

... an architecture?...

The definition of an architecture used in ANSI/IEEE Std 1471-2000 is:

"The fundamental organization of a system, embodied in its components, their relationships to each other and the environment, and the principles governing its design and evolution."

At the present time, TOGAF embraces but does not strictly adhere to ANSI/IEEE Std 1471-2000 terminology. In TOGAF, "architecture" has two meanings depending upon its contextual usage:

- A formal description of a system, or a detailed plan of the system at component level to guide its implementation
- The structure of components, their inter-relationships, and the principles and guidelines governing their design and evolution over time.

In TOGAF we endeavor to strike a balance between promoting the concepts and terminology of ANSI/IEEE Std 1471-2000 - ensuring that our usage of terms defined by ANSI/IEEE Std 1471-2000 is consistent with the standard - and retaining other commonly accepted terminology that is familiar to the majority of the TOGAF readership. For more on terminology, refer to Part IV: Resource Base, Developing Architecture Views.

... an architecture description?...

An architecture description is a formal description of an information system, organized in a way that supports reasoning about the structural properties of the system. It defines the components or building blocks that make up the overall information system, and provides a plan from which products can be procured, and systems developed, that will work together to implement the overall system. It thus enables you to manage your overall IT investment in a way that meets the needs of your business.

... an architecture framework?...

An architecture framework is a tool which can be used for developing a broad range of different architectures. It should describe a method for designing an information system in terms of a set of building blocks, and for showing how the building blocks fit together. It should contain a set of tools and provide a common vocabulary. It should also include a list of recommended standards and compliant products that can be used to implement the building blocks.

Why do I need an enterprise architecture?

The primary reason for developing an enterprise architecture is to support the business by providing the fundamental technology and process structure for an IT strategy. This in turn makes IT a responsive asset for a successful modern business strategy.

Today's CEOs know that the effective management and exploitation of information through IT is the key to business success, and the indispensable means to achieving competitive advantage. An enterprise architecture addresses this need, by providing a strategic context for the evolution of the IT system in response to the constantly changing needs of the business environment.

Furthermore, a good enterprise architecture enables you to achieve the right balance between IT efficiency and business innovation. It allows individual business units to innovate safely in their pursuit of competitive advantage. At the same time, it assures the needs of the organization for an integrated IT strategy, permitting the closest possible synergy across the extended enterprise.

The technical advantages that result from a good enterprise architecture bring important business benefits, which are clearly visible in the bottom line:

- A more efficient IT operation:
    - Lower software development, support, and maintenance costs
    - Increased portability of applications
    - Improved interoperability and easier system and network management
    - Improved ability to address critical enterprise-wide issues like security
    - Easier upgrade and exchange of system components
- Better return on existing investment, reduced risk for future investment:
    - Reduced complexity in IT infrastructure
    - Maximum return on investment in existing IT infrastructure
    - The flexibility to make, buy, or out-source IT solutions
    - Reduced risk overall in new investment, and the costs of IT ownership
- Faster, simpler, and cheaper procurement:
    - Buying decisions are simpler, because the information governing procurement is readily available in a coherent plan.
    - The procurement process is faster - maximizing procurement speed and flexibility without sacrificing architectural coherence.

Why do I need a framework for enterprise architecture?

Using an architecture framework will speed up and simplify architecture development, ensure more complete coverage of the designed solution, and make certain that the architecture selected allows for future growth in response to the needs of the business.

Architecture design is a technically complex process, and the design of heterogeneous, multi-vendor architectures is particularly complex. TOGAF plays an important role in helping to "de-mystify" the architecture development process, enabling IT users to build genuinely open systems-based solutions to their business needs.

Why is this important?

Those IT customers who do not invest in enterprise architecture typically find themselves pushed inexorably to single-supplier solutions in order to ensure an integrated solution. At that point, no matter how ostensibly "open" any single supplier's products may be in terms of adherence to standards, the customer will be unable to realize the potential benefits of truly heterogeneous, multi-vendor open systems.

What specifically would prompt me to develop an architecture?

Typically, an architecture is developed because key people have concerns that need to be addressed by the IT systems within the organization. Such people are commonly referred to as the "stakeholders" in the system. The role of the architect is to address these concerns, by identifying and refining the requirements that the stakeholders have, developing views of the architecture that show how the concerns and the requirements are going to be addressed, and by showing the trade-offs that are going to be made in reconciling the potentially conflicting concerns of different stakeholders.

Without the architecture, it is highly unlikely that all the concerns and requirements will be considered and met.

What is TOGAF?

TOGAF is an architecture framework - The Open Group Architecture Framework. It enables you to design, evaluate, and build the right architecture for your organization.

The key to TOGAF is the Architecture Development Method (ADM) - a reliable, proven method for developing an IT enterprise architecture that meets the needs of your business.

What kind of architecture does TOGAF deal with?

There are four types of architecture that are commonly accepted as subsets of an overall enterprise architecture, all of which TOGAF is designed to support:

- A Business (or Business Process) Architecture - this defines the business strategy, governance, organization, and key business processes.

- A Data Architecture - this describes the structure of an organization's logical and physical data assets and data management resources.
- An Applications Architecture - this kind of architecture provides a blueprint for the individual application systems to be deployed, their interactions, and their relationships to the core business processes of the organization.
- A Technology Architecture - this describes the logical software and hardware capabilities that are required to support the deployment of business, data, and applications services. This includes IT infrastructure, middleware, networks, communications, processing, standards, etc.

Who would benefit from using TOGAF?

Any organization undertaking, or planning to undertake, the design and implementation of an enterprise architecture for the support of mission-critical business applications, using open systems building blocks.

Customers who design and implement enterprise architectures using TOGAF are ensured of a design and a procurement specification that will greatly facilitate open systems implementation, and will enable the benefits of open systems to accrue to their organizations with reduced risk.

What specifically does TOGAF contain?

TOGAF provides a common-sense, practical, prudent, and effective method of developing an enterprise architecture.

TOGAF consists of three main parts:

1. The TOGAF Architecture Development Method (ADM), which explains how to derive an organization-specific enterprise architecture that addresses business requirements. The ADM provides:
   - A reliable, proven way of developing the architecture
   - Architecture views which enable the architect to ensure that a complex set of requirements are adequately addressed
   - Linkages to practical case studies
   - Guidelines on tools for architecture development
2. The Enterprise Continuum, which is a "virtual repository" of all the architecture assets - models, patterns, architecture descriptions, etc. - that exist both within the enterprise and in the IT industry at large, which the enterprise considers itself to have available for the development of architectures. At relevant places throughout the TOGAF ADM, there are reminders to consider which architecture assets from the Enterprise Continuum the architect should use, if any. TOGAF itself provides two reference models for consideration for inclusion in an enterprise's own Enterprise Continuum:

1. The TOGAF Foundation Architecture - an architecture of generic services and functions that provides a foundation on which specific architectures and Architecture Building Blocks (ABBs) can be built. This Foundation Architecture in turn includes:
   - The TOGAF Technical Reference Model (TRM), which provides a model and taxonomy of generic platform services
   - The TOGAF Standards Information Base (SIB), which is a database of open industry standards that can be used to define the particular services and other components of an enterprise-specific architecture
2. The Integrated Information Infrastructure Reference Model (III-RM), which is based on the TOGAF Foundation Architecture, and is specifically aimed at helping the design of architectures that enable and support the vision of Boundaryless Information Flow.
3. The TOGAF Resource Base, which is a set of resources - guidelines, templates, background information, etc. - to help the architect in the use of the ADM.

Just how do you use TOGAF?

TOGAF is published by The Open Group on its public web site, and may be reproduced freely by any enterprise wishing to use it to develop an enterprise architecture for use within that enterprise.

Basically, information about the benefits and constraints of the existing implementation, together with requirements for change, are combined using the methods described in the TOGAF ADM, resulting in a "Target Architecture" or set of Target Architectures.

The SIB provides a database of open industry standards that can be used to define the particular services and components required in the products purchased to implement the developed architecture. The SIB provides a simple and highly effective way to procure against an enterprise architecture.

How much does TOGAF cost?

The Open Group operates as a not-for-profit consortium committed to delivering greater business efficiency by bringing together buyers and suppliers of information systems to lower the barriers of integrating new technology across the enterprise. Its goal is to realize the vision of Boundaryless Information Flow.

TOGAF is a key part of its strategy for achieving this goal, and The Open Group wants TOGAF to be taken up and used in practical architecture projects, and the experience from its use fed back to help improve it.

The Open Group therefore publishes TOGAF on its public web server, and allows and encourages its reproduction and use free-of-charge by any organization wishing to use it internally to develop an enterprise architecture. (There are restrictions on its commercial exploitation, however; see Conditions of Use).

Since TOGAF is freely available, why join The Open Group?

Organizations wishing to reduce the time, cost, and risk of implementing multi-vendor solutions that integrate within and between enterprises need The Open Group as their key partner.

The Open Group brings together the buyers and suppliers of information systems worldwide, and enables them to work together, both to ensure that IT solutions meet the needs of customers, and to make it easier to integrate IT across the enterprise.

The Open Group Architecture Framework is a key enabler in this task.

Yes, TOGAF itself is freely available. But how much will you spend on developing or updating your enterprise architecture using TOGAF? And how much will you spend on procurements based on that architecture?

The price of membership of The Open Group is insignificant in comparison with these amounts.

In addition to the general benefits of membership, as a member of The Open Group you will be eligible to participate in The Open Group Architecture Forum, which is the development program within which TOGAF is evolved, and in which TOGAF users come together to exchange information and feedback.

Members of the Architecture Forum gain:

- Immediate access to the fruits of the current year's TOGAF work program (not publicly available until publication of the next edition of the TOGAF document) - in effect, the latest information on TOGAF, as opposed to information that is up to a year old
- Exchange of experience with other customer and vendor organizations involved in enterprise architecture in general, and networking with architects using TOGAF in significant architecture development projects around the world
- Peer review of specific architecture case study material

Chapter 2:
TOGAF as an Enterprise Architecture Framework

2.1 Introduction

Frequently Asked Questions explains that there are four kinds of "architecture" that are commonly accepted as subsets of an overall enterprise architecture:

- Business Architecture
- Data Architecture
- Applications Architecture
- Technology Architecture

The combination of Data Architecture and Applications Architecture is also referred to as the Information Systems Architecture.

TOGAF was originally designed to support the last of these - the Technology Architecture. Over its years of evolution, however, it has acquired many of the facets of a framework and method for enterprise architecture. As of TOGAF Version 8, these different facets have been integrated, and TOGAF has undergone a major redevelopment, with the result that it is now a fully-fledged enterprise architecture framework.

With Version 8.1, the numbering scheme for successive releases of TOGAF has been modified, to include a major and minor release indicator. Version 8.1 builds on the base established in Version 8, by adding new information in a number of areas.

2.2 The Role of TOGAF

TOGAF in its Enterprise Edition remains what it has always been, namely an architecture framework - a set of methods and tools for developing a broad range of different IT architectures. It enables IT users to design, evaluate, and build the right architecture for their organization, and reduces the costs of planning, designing, and implementing architectures based on open systems solutions.

The key to TOGAF remains a reliable, practical method - the TOGAF Architecture Development Method (ADM) - for defining business needs and developing an architecture that meets those needs, utilizing the elements of TOGAF and other architectural assets available to the organization.

A number of enterprise architecture frameworks already exist and are widely recognized, each of which has its particular advantages and disadvantages - and relevance - for enterprise architecture. They are discussed in Part IV: Resource Base, Other Architectures and Frameworks.

Although a number of enterprise frameworks exist, there is no accepted industry standard method for developing an enterprise architecture. The goal of The Open Group with TOGAF is to work towards making the TOGAF ADM just such an industry standard method, which is neutral towards tools and technologies, and can be used for developing the products associated with any recognized enterprise framework - such as the Zachman Framework, Federal Enterprise Architecture Framework (FEAF), Treasury Enterprise Architecture Framework (TEAF), and C4ISR/DoD Framework - that the architect feels is appropriate for a particular architecture.

The TOGAF ADM therefore does not prescribe any specific set of enterprise architecture deliverables - although it does describe a set by way of example. Rather, TOGAF is designed to be used with whatever set of deliverables the TOGAF user feels is most appropriate. That may be the set of deliverables described in TOGAF itself; or it may be the set associated with another framework, such as the Zachman Framework, FEAF, etc.

In fact, TOGAF has always done this: it does not prescribe a specific set of "architecture views", but describes an example taxonomy of the kinds of views that an architect might consider developing, and why; and it provides guidelines for making the choice, and for developing particular views, if chosen.

With the migration of TOGAF to an enterprise architecture framework, this flexibility becomes even more important. TOGAF is not intended to compete with these other frameworks; rather, it is intended to perform a unique role, in distilling what these other frameworks have to offer, and providing a generic ADM that can be adapted for use with any of these other frameworks.

The Open Group's vision for TOGAF is as a vehicle and repository for practical, experience-based information on how to go about the process of enterprise architecture, providing a generic method with which specific sets of deliverables, specific reference models, and other relevant architectural assets, can be integrated.

2.3 TOGAF and Architecture Governance

As governance has become an increasingly visible requirement for organizational management, the adoption of governance into TOGAF aligns the framework with current business best practice and also ensures a level of visibility, guidance, and control that will support all architecture stakeholder requirements and obligations.

The benefits of architecture governance include:

- Increased transparency of accountability, and informed delegation of authority
- Controlled risk management
- Protection of the existing asset base through maximizing re-use of existing architectural components

- Proactive control, monitoring, and management mechanisms
- Process, concept, and component re-use across all organizational business units
- Value creation through monitoring, measuring, evaluation, and feedback
- Increased visibility supporting internal processes and external parties' requirements

  In particular, increased visibility of decision-making at lower levels ensures oversight at an appropriate level within the enterprise of decisions that may have far-reaching strategic consequences for the organization.

- Greater shareholder value

  In particular, enterprise architecture increasingly represents the core intellectual property of the enterprise.

  Studies have demonstrated a correlation between increased shareholder value and well-governed enterprises.

- Integrates with existing processes and methodologies and complements functionality by adding control capabilities

Further detail on architecture governance is given in Part IV: Resource Base, Architecture Governance.

2.4 Using TOGAF with Other Frameworks

2.4.1 Overview

Two of the key elements of any enterprise architecture framework are:

- A definition of the deliverables that the architecting activity should produce
- A description of the method by which this should be done

With some exceptions, the majority of enterprise architecture frameworks focus on the first of these - the specific set of deliverables - and are relatively silent about the methods to be used to generate them (intentionally so, in some cases).

Because TOGAF is a generic framework, as mentioned above, and intended to be used in a wide variety of environments, it does not prescribe a specific set of deliverables; rather it talks in general terms about the types of deliverable that need to be produced, and focuses instead on the methods by which these should be developed.

As a result, TOGAF may be used either in its own right, with the generic deliverables that it describes; or else these deliverables may be replaced by a more specific set, defined in any other framework that the user architect considers relevant.

In the latter case, the user architect will adapt and build on the TOGAF ADM in order to define a tailored method and process for developing these more specific deliverables.

Guidelines for adapting the TOGAF ADM in such a way are given in Part II: Architecture Development Method (ADM), Adapting the ADM.

As a generic framework and method for enterprise architecture, TOGAF also complements other frameworks that are aimed at specific vertical business domains, specific horizontal technology areas (such as security or manageability), or specific application areas (such as e-Commerce). The concept of leveraging other relevant architectural assets in this way is known within TOGAF as the Enterprise Continuum.

2.4.2 The Enterprise Continuum

TOGAF embodies the concept of the Enterprise Continuum (described in Part III: Enterprise Continuum), to reflect different levels of abstraction in an architecture development process. In this way TOGAF facilitates understanding and cooperation between actors at different levels. It provides a context for the use of multiple frameworks, models, and architecture assets in conjunction with the TOGAF ADM. By means of the Enterprise Continuum, architects are encouraged to leverage all other relevant architectural resources and assets, in addition to the TOGAF Foundation Architecture, in developing an organization-specific IT architecture.

In this context, the TOGAF ADM can be regarded as describing the process of moving from the TOGAF Foundation Architecture to an organization-specific architecture (or set of architectures), leveraging the contents of the Enterprise Continuum along the way, including the TOGAF Foundation Architecture and other relevant architecture frameworks, models, components, and building blocks.

2.5 Summary

TOGAF thus does not seek to compete with or duplicate other frameworks. What TOGAF does seek to provide is a practical, industry standard method of doing enterprise architecture - leveraging all relevant assets in the process - that is freely available and supported by a number of different architecting consultancies, and that is sufficient for an organization to use "as-is" or to adapt as the basis of an enterprise architecture method for other, deliverables-focused frameworks.

PART: II

Architecture Development Method (ADM)

Chapter 3: Introduction to the ADM

This chapter describes the Architecture Development Method (ADM) cycle, adapting the ADM, architecture scope, and architecture integration.

3.1 ADM Overview

The TOGAF ADM is the result of continuous contributions from a large number of architecture practitioners. It describes a method for developing an enterprise architecture, and forms the core of TOGAF. It integrates elements of TOGAF described in this document as well as other available architectural assets, to meet the business and IT needs of an organization.

3.1.1 Relationship to Other Parts of TOGAF

There are two other main parts to TOGAF, besides the ADM:

- The Enterprise Continuum, described in detail in Part III: Enterprise Continuum. This is a "framework-within-a-framework" that provides context for the leveraging of relevant architecture assets and provides navigational help when discussions move between different levels of abstraction.
- The TOGAF Resource Base, described in Part IV: Resource Base. This is a set of resources - guidelines, templates, checklists, and other detailed materials - supporting the TOGAF ADM.

3.1.2 The ADM and the Enterprise Continuum

As mentioned above, the Enterprise Continuum provides a framework and context for the leveraging of relevant architecture assets in executing the ADM. These assets may include architecture descriptions, models, and patterns taken from a variety of sources, as explained in Part III: Enterprise Continuum. At relevant places throughout the ADM, there are reminders to consider which architecture assets from the Enterprise Continuum the architect should use, if any. In some cases - for example, in the development of a Technology Architecture - this may be the TOGAF Foundation Architecture (see Part III: Enterprise Continuum). In other cases - for example, in the development of a Business Architecture - it may be a reference model for e-Commerce taken from the industry at large.

The practical implementation of the Enterprise Continuum will often take the form of a repository that includes reference architectures, models, and patterns that have been accepted for use within the enterprise, and actual architectural work done previously within the enterprise. The architect would seek to re-use as much as possible from the Enterprise Continuum that was relevant to the project at hand. (In addition to the collection of architecture source material, the repository would also contain architecture development work-in-progress.)

The criteria for including source materials in an organization's Enterprise Continuum will typically form part of the organization's IT governance process.

The Enterprise Continuum is thus a framework (a "framework-within-a-framework") for categorizing architectural source material - both the contents of the architecture working repository, and the set of relevant, available reference models in the industry.

In executing the ADM, the architect is not only developing the end result of an organization-specific architecture, but is also populating the organization's own Enterprise Continuum, with all the architectural assets identified and leveraged along the way, including, but not limited to, the resultant enterprise-specific architecture.

Architecture development is an iterative, ongoing process, and in executing the ADM repeatedly over time, the architect gradually populates more and more of the organization's Enterprise Continuum. Although the primary focus of the ADM is on the development of the enterprise-specific architecture, in this wider context the ADM can also be viewed as the process of populating the enterprise's own Enterprise Continuum with relevant re-usable building blocks.

In fact, the first execution of the ADM will often be the hardest, since the architecture assets available for re-use will be relatively few. Even at this stage of development, however, there will be architecture assets available from external sources such as TOGAF, as well as the IT industry at large, that could be leveraged in support of the effort.

Subsequent executions will be easier, as more and more architecture assets become identified, are used to populate the organization's Enterprise Continuum, and are thus available for future re-use.

The ADM is also useful to populate the Foundation Architecture of an enterprise. Business requirements of an enterprise may be used to identify the necessary definitions and selections in the Foundation Architecture. This could be a set of re-usable common models, policy and governance definitions, or even as specific as overriding technology selections (e.g., if mandated by law). Population of the Foundation Architecture follows similar principles as for an enterprise architecture, with the difference that requirements for a whole enterprise are restricted to the overall concerns and thus less complete than for a specific enterprise.

It is important to recognize that existing models from these various sources may not necessarily be integratable into a coherent enterprise architecture. "Integratability" of architecture descriptions is considered in Architecture Integration.

3.1.3 The ADM and the Resource Base

The TOGAF Resource Base is a set of resources - guidelines, templates, checklists, and other detailed materials - that support the TOGAF ADM.

The individual sections of the Resource Base are described separately in Part IV: Resource Base so that they can be referenced from the relevant points in the ADM as necessary, rather than having the detailed text clutter the description of the ADM itself.3.2 The Architecture Development Cycle

3.2.1 Key Points

The following are the key points about the ADM:

- The ADM is iterative, over the whole process, between phases, and within phases. For each iteration of the ADM, a fresh decision must be taken as to:
    - The breadth of coverage of the enterprise to be defined
    - The level of detail to be defined
    - The extent of the time horizon aimed at, including the number and extent of any intermediate time horizons
    - The architectural assets to be leveraged in the organization's Enterprise Continuum, including:
    - Assets created in previous iterations of the ADM cycle within the enterprise
    - Assets available elsewhere in the industry (other frameworks, systems models, vertical industry models, etc.)
- These decisions need to be made on the basis of a practical assessment of resource and competence availability, and the value that can realistically be expected to accrue to the enterprise from the chosen scope of the architecture work.
- As a generic method, the ADM is intended to be used by enterprises in a wide variety of different geographies and applied in different vertical sectors/industry types. As such, it may be, but does not necessarily have to be, tailored to specific needs. For example:
    - It may be used in conjunction with the set of deliverables of another framework, where these have been deemed to be more appropriate for a specific organization. (For example, many US federal agencies have developed individual frameworks that define the deliverables specific to their particular departmental needs.)
    - It may be used in conjunction with the well-known Zachman Framework, which is an excellent classification scheme, but lacks an openly available, well-defined methodology.

These issues are considered in detail in Adapting the ADM.

In addition to the method itself being iterative, there is also iteration within the ADM cycle, both among the individual phases and among the steps within each phase.

3.2.2 Basic Structure

The basic structure of the ADM is shown in Architecture Development Cycle.

Throughout the ADM cycle, there needs to be frequent validation of results against the original expectations, both those for the whole ADM cycle, and those for the particular phase

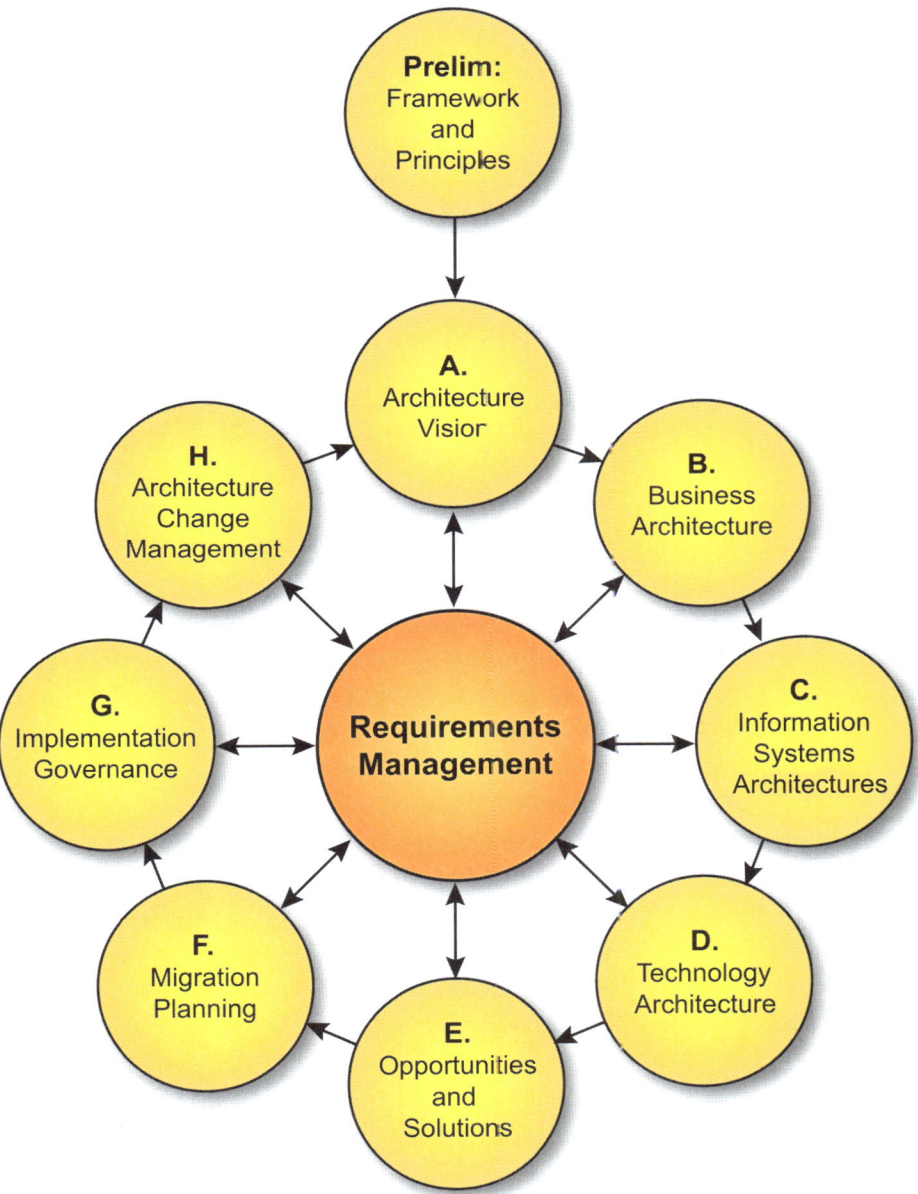

Figure 3.1: Architecture Development Cycle

The phases of the ADM cycle shown in Architecture Development Cycle are further divided into steps, such as the ones depicted by the expansion of the Technology Architecture phase in Architecture Development Cycle - Expansion.

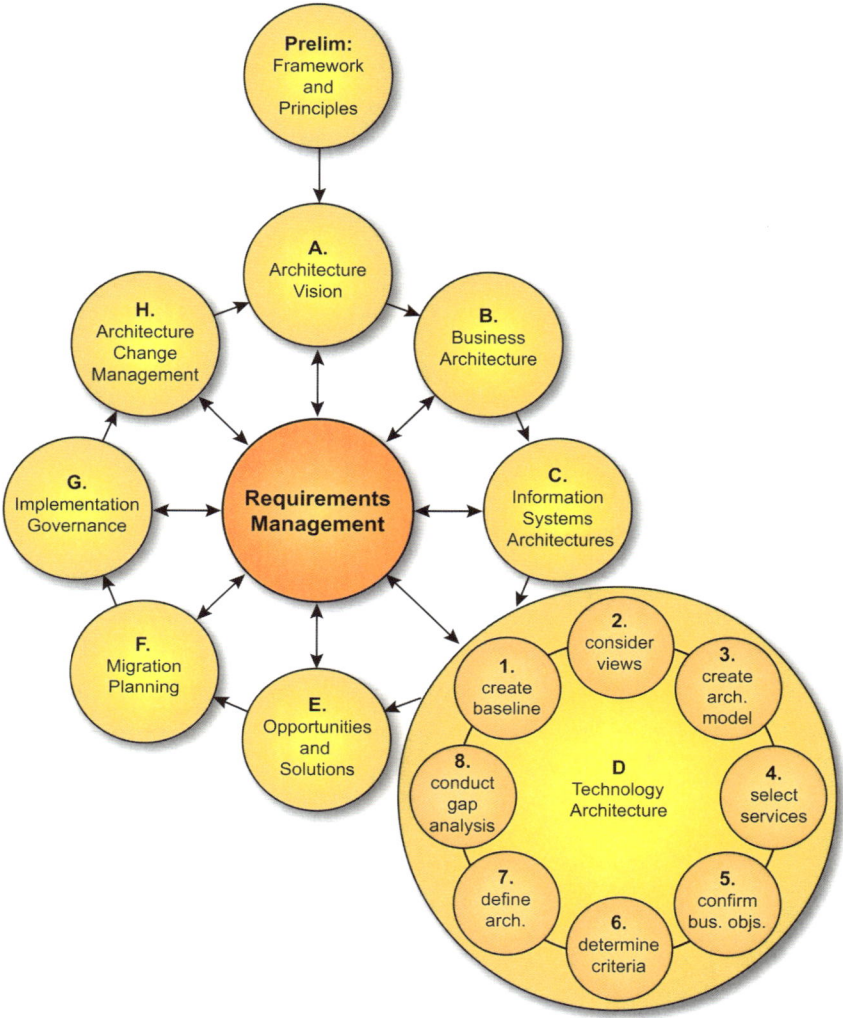

Figure 3.2: Architecture Development Cycle - Expansion

The phases of the cycle are described in detail in the following subsections. Phase D, the creation of a Technology Architecture, is described in greater detail in Phase D: Technology Architecture.

Note that output is generated throughout the process, and that the output in an early phase may be modified in a later phase. The versioning of output is managed through version numbers. In all cases, the ADM numbering scheme is provided as an example. It should be adapted by the architect to meet the requirements of the organization and to work with the architecture tools and repositories employed by the organization.

3.3 Adapting the ADM

The ADM is a generic method for architecture development, which is designed to deal with most system and organizational requirements. However, it will often be necessary to modify or extend the ADM, to suit specific needs. One of the tasks before applying the ADM is to review its components for applicability, and then tailor them as appropriate to the circumstances of the individual enterprise. This activity may well produce an "enterprise-specific" ADM.

One reason for wanting to adapt the ADM, which it is important to stress, is that the order of the phases in the ADM is to some extent dependent on the maturity of the architecture discipline within the enterprise concerned. For example, if the business case for doing architecture at all is not well recognized, then creating an Architecture Vision is almost always essential; and a detailed Business Architecture often needs to come next, in order to underpin the Architecture Vision, detail the business case for remaining architecture work, and secure the active participation of key stakeholders in that work. In other cases a slightly different order may be preferred; for example, a detailed inventory of the baseline environment may be done before undertaking the Business Architecture.

The order of phases may also be defined by the business and architecture principles of an enterprise. For example, the business principles may dictate that the enterprise be prepared to adjust its business processes to meet the needs of a packaged solution, so that it can be implemented quickly to enable fast response to market changes. In such a case, the Business Architecture (or at least the completion of it) may well follow completion of the Information Systems Architecture or the Technology Architecture.

Another reason for wanting to adapt the ADM is if TOGAF is to be integrated with another enterprise framework (as explained in Part I: Introduction, TOGAF as an Enterprise Architecture Framework). For example, an enterprise may wish to use TOGAF and its generic ADM in conjunction with the well-known Zachman Framework, or another enterprise architecture framework that has a defined set of deliverables specific to a particular vertical sector: Government, Defense, e-Business, Telecommunications, etc. The ADM has been specifically designed with this potential integration in mind.

Other possible reasons for wanting to adapt the ADM include:

- The ADM is one of the many corporate processes that make up the corporate governance model. It is complementary to, and supportive of, other standard program management processes, such as those for authorization, risk management, business planning and budgeting, development planning, systems development, and procurement.
- The ADM is to be used as a method for something other than enterprise architecture; for example, as a general program management method.
- The ADM is being mandated for use by a prime or lead contractor in an outsourcing situation, and needs to be tailored to achieve a suitable compromise between the contractor's existing practices and the contracting enterprise's requirements.

- The enterprise is a small-to-medium enterprise, and wishes to use a "cut-down" method more attuned to the reduced level of resources and system complexity typical of such an environment.
- The enterprise is very large and complex, comprising many separate but interlinked "enterprises" within an overall collaborative business framework, and the architecture method needs to be adapted to recognize this. Different approaches to planning and integration may be used in such cases, including the following (possibly in combination):
    - Top-down planning and development - designing the whole interconnected meta-enterprise as a single entity (an exercise that typically stretches the limits of practicality)
    - Development of a "generic" or "reference" architecture, typical of the enterprises within the organization, but not representing any specific enterprise, which individual enterprises are then expected to adapt in order to produce an architecture "instance" suited to the particular enterprise concerned.
    - Replication - developing a specific architecture for one enterprise, implementing it as a proof of concept, and then taking that as a "reference architecture" to be cloned in other enterprises.
- In a vendor or production environment, a generic architecture for a family of related products is often referred to as a "Product Line Architecture", and the analogous process to that outlined above is termed "(Architecture-based) Product Line Engineering". The ADM is targeted primarily at architects in IT user enterprises, but a vendor organization whose products are IT-based might well wish to adapt it as a generic method for a product line architecture development.

3.4 Architecture Governance

The ADM, whether adapted by the organization or used as documented here, is a key process to be managed in the same manner as other architecture artefacts in the Enterprise Continuum. The Architecture Board should be satisfied that the method is being applied correctly across all phases of an architecture development iteration. Compliance with the ADM is fundamental to the governance of the architecture, to ensure that all considerations are made and all required deliverables are produced.

3.5 Process Management

The management of all architectural artefacts, governance, and related processes should be supported by a managed environment. Typically this would be based on one or more repositories supporting versioned object and process control and status.

Governance process management includes repository management, access, communication, training, and accreditation. This section is included to identify the major information areas managed by the governance repository. The repository initially consists of one or more data storage facilities that will contain the following types of information:

- Reference data (collateral from the organization's own repositories/Enterprise Continuum, including external data; e.g., COBIT, ITIL)
- Used for guidance and instruction during project implementation. This includes the details of information outlined above. The reference data includes a description of the governance procedures themselves.
- Process status

    All information regarding the state of any governance processes will be managed; examples of this include outstanding compliance requests, dispensation requests, and compliance assessments investigations.
- Audit information

    This will record all completed governance process actions and will be used to support:
    1. Key decisions and responsible personnel for any architecture project that has been sanctioned by the governance process
    2. A reference for future architectural and supporting process developments, guidance, and precedence

The governance artefacts and process are themselves part of the contents of the Enterprise Continuum.

3.6 Scoping the Architecture

There are many reasons for wanting to limit the scope of the architecture activity to be undertaken, most of which come down to the availability of people, finance, and other resources. The scope chosen for the architecture activity is normally directly dependent on available resources, and in the final analysis is usually a question of feasibility.

Whatever the reasons for wanting or having to limit the scope of the architecture activity, there are four dimensions in which the scope may be defined and limited:

- Enterprise scope or focus: What is the full extent of the enterprise, and how much of that extent should the architecting effort focus on?
    - Many enterprises are very large, effectively comprising a federation of organizational units that could validly be considered enterprises in their own right.
    - The modern enterprise increasingly extends beyond its traditional boundaries, to embrace a fuzzy combination of traditional business enterprise combined with suppliers, customers, and partners.
- Architecture domains: A complete enterprise architecture description should contain all four architecture domains (Business, Data, Applications, Technology), but the realities of resource and time constraints often mean there is not enough time, funding, or resources to build a top-down, all-inclusive architecture description encompassing all four

architecture domains, even if the enterprise scope is chosen to be less than the full extent of the overall enterprise.

- Vertical scope, or level of detail: To what level of detail should the architecting effort go? How much architecture is "enough"? What is the appropriate demarcation between the architecture effort and other, related activities (system design, system engineering, system development)?

- Time horizon: What is the time horizon that needs to be articulated for the Architecture Vision, and does it make sense (in terms of practicality and resources) for the same horizon to be covered in the detailed architecture description? If not, how many intermediate Target Architectures are to be defined, and what are their time horizons?

These aspects are explored in detail below. In each case, particularly in largescale environments where architectures are necessarily developed in a federated manner, there is a danger of architects optimizing within their own scope of activity, instead of at the level of the overall enterprise. It is often necessary to sub-optimize in a particular area, in order to optimize at the enterprise level. The aim should always be to seek the highest level of commonality and focus on scalable and re-usable modules in order to maximize re-use at the enterprise level.

3.6.1 Enterprise Scope/Focus

One of the key decisions is the focus of the architecture effort, in terms of the breadth of overall enterprise activity to be covered (which specific business sectors, functions, organizations, geographical areas, etc.).

One important factor in this context is the increasing tendency for largescale architecture developments to be undertaken in the form of "federated architectures" - independently developed, maintained, and managed architectures that are subsequently integrated within a meta-architecture framework. Such a framework specifies the principles for interoperability, migration, and conformance. This allows specific business units to have architectures developed and governed as stand-alone architecture projects.

Complex architectures are extremely hard to manage, not only in terms of the architecture development process itself, but also in terms of getting buy-in from large numbers of stakeholders. This in turn requires a very disciplined approach to identifying common architectural components, and management of the commonalities between federated components - deciding how to integrate, what to integrate, etc.

There are two basic approaches to federated architecture development:

- The overall enterprise is divided up "vertically", into enterprise "segments", each representing an independent business sector within the overall enterprise, and each having its own enterprise architecture with potentially all four architecture domains (Business, Data, Applications, Technology). These separate, multi-domain architectures can be developed with a view to subsequent integration, but they can also be implemented in their own right, possibly with interim target environments defined, and therefore represent value to the enterprise in their own right.

- The overall enterprise architecture is divided up "horizontally", into architectural "super-domains", in which each architecture domain (Business, Data, Applications, Technology) covering the full extent of the overall enterprise is developed and approved as a major project independently of the others, possibly by different personnel. For example, a Business Architecture for the complete overall enterprise would form one independent architecture project, and the other domains would be developed and approved in separate projects, with a view to subsequent integration.

The US Government, and in particular the US Department of Defense (DoD), has undertaken and published leading work in the field of federated architectures, emphasizing the need for integrated repositories and metamodels to aid integration and ensure interoperability. This work is very much at the leading edge of the state-of-the-art, however, and what works in practice is still very much a matter of debate.

The Introduction section in the Federal Enterprise Architecture Framework (FEAF) published by the US Federal CIO Council explains the choices in approach that faced the US Government in the development of the FEAF:

"In developing the Federal Enterprise Architecture Framework, the CIO Council evaluated three approaches.

- Conventional approach - requires a substantial initial investment in time and dollars. First, a framework must be developed that shows how to prepare an architecture description. Second, the current baseline must be described. Finally, a Target Architecture must be described. Only after these activities are completed, implementing needed architecture changes through design, development, and acquisition of systems can begin. Although this approach appears to be sound, it may result in "paralysis by analysis", because of the complexity of the federal effort.
- Segment approach - promotes the incremental development of architecture segments within a structured enterprise architecture framework. This approach focuses on major business areas (e.g., grants or common financial systems) and is more likely to succeed because the effort is limited to common functions or specific enterprises.
- Status Quo approach - represents business as usual resulting in continued failure to share information and cope with the rapidly changing environment. This approach would result in business rework, decreased productivity, and lost and missed opportunities, as well as failure to comply with Clinger-Cohen Act requirements.

... To mitigate the risk of overreaching with minimal returns, curtail start-up costs for a conventional architecture, and realize returns quickly, the CIO Council selected the segment approach...

The FEAF allows critical parts of the overall federal enterprise, called "architectural segments", to be developed individually, while integrating these segments into the larger enterprise architecture."

The FEAF approach thus seeks to do a "complete" enterprise architecture across a succession of selected individual business domains (or segments), and then to integrate these into a more comprehensive, overarching enterprise architecture.

Conversely, the Practical Guide to Federal Enterprise Architecture, also issued by the US Federal CIO Council, highlights the dangers of selecting too narrow an enterprise scope, particularly at the higher business levels:

> "It is critically important that enterprise architecture development be approached in a top-down, incremental manner, consistent with the hierarchical architecture views that are the building blocks of proven enterprise architecture frameworks.... In doing so, it is equally important that the scope of the higher-level business views of the enterprise architecture span the entire enterprise or agency. By developing this enterprise-wide understanding of business processes and rules, and information needs, flows, and locations, the agency will be positioned to make good decisions about whether the enterprise, and thus the enterprise architecture, can be appropriately compartmentalized. Without doing so, scoping decisions about the enterprise architecture run the risk of promoting "stove-piped" operations and systems environments, and ultimately sub-optimizing enterprise performance and accountability."

Current experience does seem to indicate that, in order to cope with the increasingly broad focus and ubiquity of architectures, it is often necessary to have a number of different architectures existing across an enterprise, focused on particular timeframes, business functions, or business requirements; and this phenomenon would seem to call into question the feasibility of a single enterprise-wide architecture for every business function or purpose. In such cases, the paramount need is to manage and exploit the "federations" of architecture. A good starting point is to adopt a publish-and-subscribe model that allows architecture to be brought under a governance framework. In such a model, architecture developers and architecture consumers in projects (the supply and demand sides of architecture work) sign up to a mutually beneficial framework of governance that ensures that:

1. Architectural material is of good quality, up-to-date, fit-for-purpose, and published (reviewed and agreed to be made public).
2. Usage of architecture material can be monitored, and compliance with standards, models, and principles can be exhibited, via:
   - A compliance assessment process that describes what the user is subscribing to, and assesses their level of compliance
   - A dispensation process that may grant dispensations from adherence to architecture standards and guidelines in specific cases (usually with a strong business imperative).

Publish and subscribe techniques are being developed as part of general IT governance and specifically for the Defense sphere.

3.6.2 Architecture Domains

A complete enterprise architecture should address all four architecture domains (Business,

Data, Applications, Technology), but the realities of resource and time constraints often mean there is not enough time, funding, or resources to build a top-down, all-inclusive architecture description encompassing all four architecture domains.

Architecture descriptions will normally be built with a specific purpose in mind - a specific set of business drivers that drive the architecture development - and clarifying the specific issue(s) that the architecture description is intended to help explore, and the questions it is expected to help answer, is an important part of the initial phase of the ADM.

For example, if the purpose of a particular architecture effort is to define and examine technology options for achieving a particular capability, and the fundamental business processes are not open to modification, then a full Business Architecture may well not be warranted. However, because the Data, Applications, and Technology Architectures build on the Business Architecture, the Business Architecture still needs to be thought through and understood.

While circumstances may sometimes dictate building an architecture description not containing all four architecture domains, it should be understood that such an architecture cannot, by definition, be a complete enterprise architecture. One of the risks is lack of consistency and therefore ability to integrate. Integration either needs to come later - with its own costs and risks - or the risks and trade-offs involved in not developing a complete and integrated architecture need to be articulated by the architect, and communicated to and understood by the enterprise management.

3.6.3 Vertical Scope/Level of Detail

Care should be taken to judge the appropriate level of detail to be captured, based on the intended use of the enterprise architecture and the decisions to be made based on it. It is important that a consistent and equal level of depth be completed in each architecture domain (Business, Data, Applications, Technology) included in the architecture effort. If pertinent detail is omitted, the architecture may not be useful. If unnecessary detail is included, the architecture effort may exceed the time and resources available, and/or the resultant architecture may be confusing or cluttered.

It is also important to predict the future uses of the architecture so that, within resource limitations, the architecture can be structured to accommodate future tailoring, extension, or re-use. The depth and detail of the enterprise architecture needs to be sufficient for its purpose, and no more.

John Zachman advocates developing enterprise-wide architecture at an enormous level of detail, in the same way as an aerospace company needs blueprints for everything down to nuts and bolts. Some regard this as an extreme position in terms of vertical scope, but it can certainly be justified when compared with the lifetime costs of alternatives. Zachman's argument is that information systems are not special. In other industries where very expensive, complex things are built, and where there is an expectation of repair or change, models are kept at an enormous level of detail, with concurrent expense. Aeroplanes, buildings, and cars are built this way. Why are information systems different?

However, it is not necessary to aim to complete a detailed architecture description at the first attempt. Future iterations of the ADM, in a further architecture lifecycle, will build on the artefacts and the competencies created during the current iteration.

The bottom line is that there is a need to document all the models in an enterprise, to whatever level of detail is affordable, within an assessment of the likelihood of change and the concomitant risk, and bearing in mind the need to integrate the components of the different architecture domains (Business, Data, Applications, Technology). The key is to understand the status of the enterprise's architecture work, and what can realistically be achieved with the resources and competencies available, and then focus on identifying and delivering the value that is achievable. Stakeholder value is a key focus: too broad a scope may deter some stakeholders (no return on investment).

3.6.4 Time Horizon

The ADM is described in terms of a single cycle of Architecture Vision, and a set of Target Architectures (Business, Data, Applications, Technology) that enable the implementation of the vision.

However, when the enterprise scope is large, and/or the Target Architectures particularly complex, the development of Target Architecture descriptions may encounter major difficulties, or indeed prove "mission impossible", especially if being undertaken from scratch.

In such cases, a wider view may be taken, whereby an enterprise is represented by several different architecture instances, each representing the enterprise at a particular point in time. One architecture instance will represent the current enterprise state (the "as-is", or baseline). Another architecture instance, perhaps defined only partially, will represent the ultimate target end-state (the "vision"). In-between, intermediate or "Transitional Architecture" instances may be defined, each comprising its own set of Target Architecture descriptions.

By this approach, the Target Architecture work is split into two or more discrete stages:

1. First, develop Target Architecture descriptions for the overall (largescale) system, demonstrating a response to stakeholder objectives and concerns for a relatively distant timeframe (for example, a six-year period).
2. Then develop one or more "Transitional Architecture" descriptions, as increments or plateaus, each in line with and converging on the Target Architecture descriptions, and describing the specifics of the increment concerned.

In such an approach, the Target Architectures are evolutionary in nature, and require periodic review and update according to evolving business requirements and developments in technology, whereas the Transitional Architectures are (by design) incremental in nature, and in principle should not evolve during the implementation phase of the increment, in order to avoid the "moving target" syndrome. This, of course, is only possible if the implementation schedule is under tight control and relatively short (typically less than two years).

The Target Architectures remain relatively generic, and because of that are less vulnerable to obsolescence than the Transitional Architectures. They embody only the key strategic architectural decisions, which should be blessed by the stakeholders from the outset, whereas the detailed architectural decisions in the Transitional Architectures are deliberately postponed as far as possible (i.e., just before implementation) in order to improve responsiveness vis a vis new technologies and products.

The enterprise evolves by migrating to each of these Transitional Architectures in turn. As each Transitional Architecture is implemented, the enterprise achieves a consistent, operational state on the way to the ultimate vision. However, this vision itself is periodically updated to reflect changes in the business and technology environment, and in effect may never actually be achieved, as originally described. The whole process continues for as long as the enterprise exists and continues to change.

Such a breakdown of the architecture description into a family of related architecture products of course requires effective management of the set and their relationships.

3.7 Architecture Integration

There is a need to provide an integration framework that sits above the individual architectures. This can be an "enterprise framework" such as Zachman to position the various domains and artefacts, or it may be a meta-architecture framework (i.e., principles, models, and standards) to allow interoperability, migration, and conformance between federated architectures. The purpose of this meta-architecture framework is to:

1. Allow the architect to understand how components fit into the framework
2. Derive the architectural models that focus on enterprise-level capabilities
3. Define the conformance standards that enable the integration of components for maximum leverage and re-use

As described above, a significant number of scoping decisions need to be taken, in terms of enterprise focus, architecture scope, level of detail, time horizons, and choice of Transitional Architectures, any one of which may result in a less than complete architecture description being developed. A potential way of assessing the gaps in scope or level of detail is to use an enterprise architecture framework (e.g., Zachman) to understand the coverage of the artefacts.

There are varying degrees of architecture description "integratability". At the low end, integratability means that different architecture descriptions (whether prepared by one organizational unit or many) should have a "look and feel" that is sufficiently similar to enable critical relationships between the descriptions to be identified, thereby at least indicating the need for further investigation. At the high end, integratability ideally means that different descriptions should be capable of being combined into a single logical and physical representation.

At the present time, the state of the art is such that architecture integration can be accomplished only at the lower end of the integratability spectrum. Key factors to consider are the granularity and level of detail in each artefact, and the maturity of standards for the interchange of architectural descriptions.

As organizations address common themes (such as service-oriented architecture, and integrated information infrastructure), and universal data models and standard data structures emerge, integration toward the high end of the spectrum will be facilitated. However, there will always be the need for effective standards governance to reduce the need for manual co-ordination and conflict resolution.

3.8 Summary

The TOGAF ADM defines a recommended sequence for the various phases and steps involved in developing an architecture, but it cannot recommend a scope - this has to be determined by the organization itself, bearing in mind that the recommended sequence of development in the ADM process is an iterative one, with the depth and breadth of scope and deliverables increasing with each iteration. Each iteration will add resources to the organization's Architecture Continuum.

The choice of scope is critical to the success of the architecting effort. The key factor here is the sheer complexity of a complete, horizontally and vertically integrated enterprise architecture, as represented by a fully populated instantiation of the Zachman Framework. Very few enterprise architecture developments today actually undertake such an effort in a single development project, simply because it is widely recognized to be at the limits of the state of the art, a fact that John Zachman himself recognizes:

"Some day, you are going to wish you had all these models... However, I am not so altruistic to think that we have to have them all today... or even that we understand how to build and manage them all today. But the very fact that we can identify conceptually where we want to get some day, makes us think more about what we are doing in the current timeframe that might prevent us from getting to where we want to go in the future." (Quote from email correspondence from John Zachman to George Brundage.)

John Zachman himself likes to point out the alternatives available to those who can't countenance the amount of work implied in developing all the models required in his framework. There are only three choices:

1. Trial and error ("knocking down the walls")
2. Starting from new
3. Reverse engineering the architecture from the existing systems

   all of which are risky and/or hugely expensive. What is necessary due to the pace of change is to have a set of readily deployable artifacts and a process for assembling them swiftly.

While such a complete framework is useful (indeed, essential) to have in mind as the ultimate long-term goal, in practice there is a key decision to be made as to the scope of a specific enterprise architecture effort. This being the case, it is vital to understand the basis on which scoping decisions are being made, and to set expectations right for what is the goal of the effort.

The main guideline is to focus on what creates value to the enterprise, and to select horizontal and vertical scope, and time horizons, accordingly. Whether or not this is the first time around, understand that this exercise will be repeated, and that future iterations will build on what is being created in the current effort, adding greater width and depth.

Chapter 4:
Preliminary Phase - Framework and Principles

This chapter describes the architecture framework and the definition of principles.

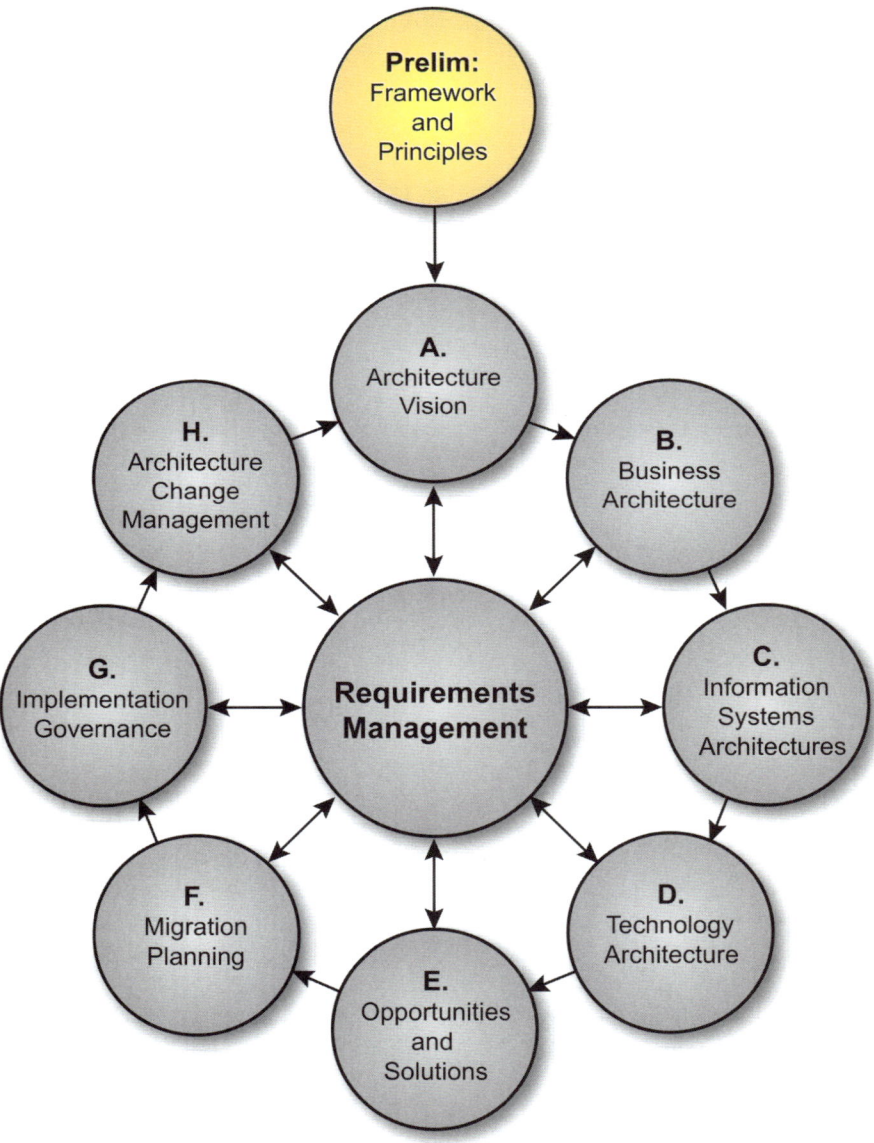

Figure 4.1: Preliminary Phase: Framework and Principles

4.1 Objectives

The objectives of the Preliminary Phase are:

- To ensure that everyone who will be involved in, or benefit from, this approach is committed to the success of the architectural process
- To define the architecture principles that will inform the constraints on any architecture work
- To define the "architecture footprint" for the organization - the people responsible for performing architecture work, where they are located, and their responsibilities
- To define the scope and assumptions (particularly in a federated architecture environment)
- To define the framework and detailed methodologies that are going to be used to develop enterprise architectures in the organization concerned (typically, an adaptation of the generic ADM)
- To set up and monitor a process (normally including a pilot project) to confirm the fitness-for-purpose of the defined framework
- If necessary, to define a set of criteria for evaluating architecture tools (an example set of criteria is given in Part IV: Resource Base), repositories, and repository management processes to be used to capture, publish, and maintain architecture artifacts

4.2 Approach

This Preliminary Phase is about defining "how we do architecture" in the enterprise concerned. There are two main aspects: defining the framework to be used; and defining the architecture principles that will inform any architecture work.

The enterprise's approach to re-use of architecture assets is a key part of both the framework definition and architecture principles. (Typically the principles will state the policy on re-use; and the framework will explain how re-use is effected.)

In federated architectures (see Enterprise Scope/Focus), requirements from a higher-level architecture are often manifested as "principles" in lower-level architectures.

4.2.1 Principles

The Preliminary Phase defines the architecture principles that will form part of the constraints on any architecture work undertaken in the enterprise. The issues involved in this are explained in Part IV: Resource Base, Architecture Principles.

Architecture work is informed by business principles as well as architecture principles. The architecture principles themselves are also normally based in part on business principles. Defining business principles normally lies outside the scope of the architecture function.

However, depending on how such principles are defined and promulgated within the enterprise concerned, it may be possible for the set of architecture principles to also restate, or cross-refer to a set of business principles, business goals, and strategic business drivers defined elsewhere within the enterprise. (Within an architecture project, the architect will normally need to ensure that the definitions of these business principles, goals, and strategic drivers are current, and to clarify any areas of ambiguity.)

The issue of architecture governance is closely linked to that of architecture principles. The body responsible for governance will also normally be responsible for approving the architecture principles, and for resolving architecture issues. This will normally be one of the principles cited. The issues involved in governance are explained in Part IV: Resource Base, Architecture Governance.

4.2.2 Framework

The TOGAF Architecture Development Method (ADM) is a generic method, intended to be used by enterprises in a wide variety of industry types and geographies. It is also designed for use with a wide variety of other enterprise architecture frameworks, if required (although it can be used perfectly well in its own right, without adaptation).

The Preliminary Phase therefore involves doing any necessary work to adapt the ADM to define an organization-specific framework, using either the TOGAF deliverables or the deliverables of another framework. The issues involved in this are discussed in Adapting the ADM.

4.3 Inputs

The inputs to the Preliminary Phase are:

- TOGAF Architecture Development Method (ADM)
- Other architecture framework(s), if required
- Business strategy, business principles, business goals, and business drivers (when pre-existing)
- IT governance strategy, when pre-existing
- Architecture principles (see Architecture Principles), when pre-existing
- Principles that are being subscribed to, arising from other, federated architectures

4.4 Steps

The TOGAF ADM is a generic method, intended to be used by a wide variety of different enterprises, and in conjunction with a wide variety of other architecture frameworks, if required. It is not practical to define specific steps for adapting the ADM to such a wide variety of potential contexts. The issues involved are discussed in detail in Adapting the ADM.

4.5 Outputs

The outputs of the Preliminary Phase are:

- Framework definition
- Architecture principles (see Architecture Principles)
- Restatement of, or reference to, business principles, business goals, and business drivers

Chapter 5: Phase A - Architecture Vision

This chapter defines the architecture scope, how to create the vision, and obtain approvals.

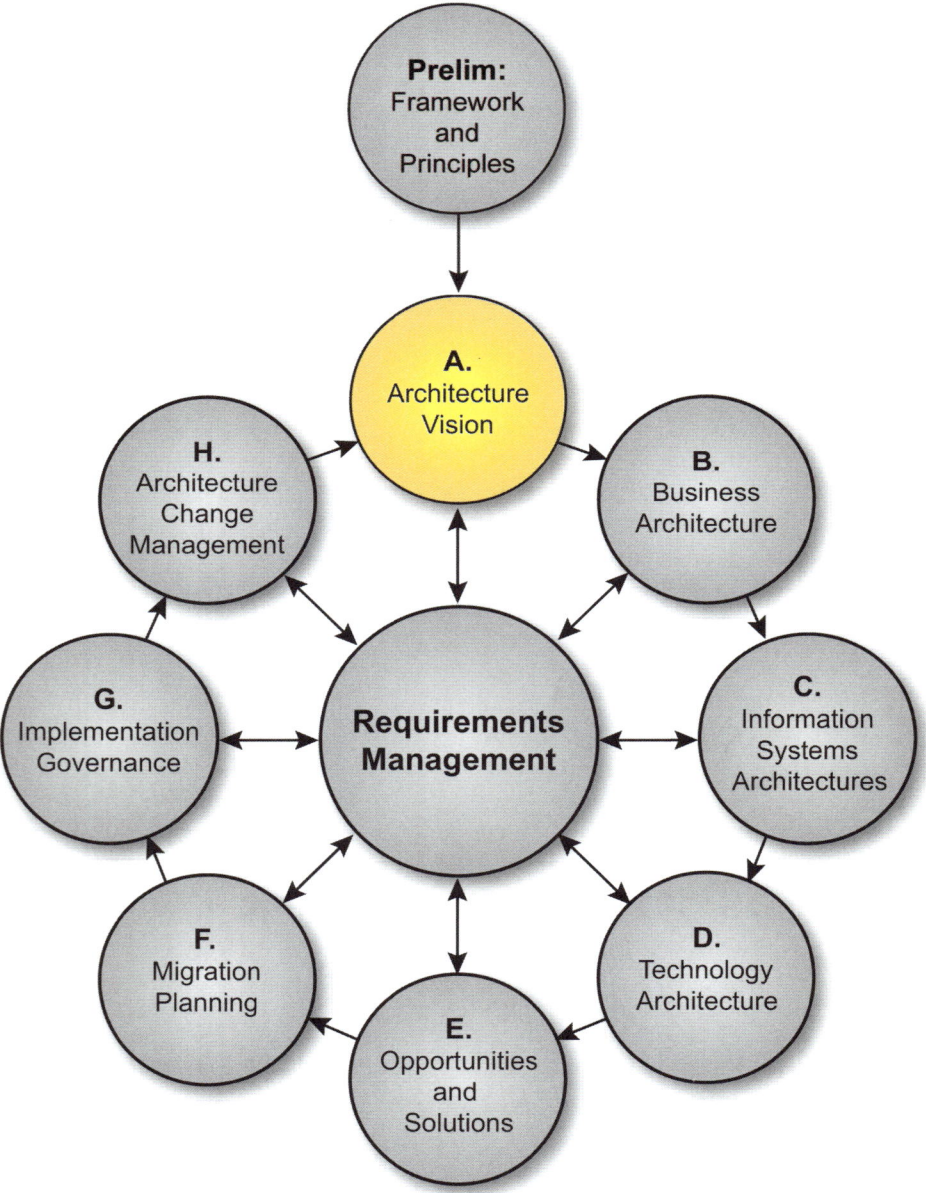

Figure 5.1: Phase A: Architecture Vision

5.1 Objectives

The objectives of Phase A are:

- To ensure that this evolution of the architecture development cycle has proper recognition and endorsement from the corporate management of the enterprise, and the support and commitment of the necessary line management
- To validate the business principles, business goals, and strategic business drivers of the organization
- To define the scope of, and to identify and prioritize the components of, the Baseline Architecture effort
- To define the relevant stakeholders, and their concerns and objectives
- To define the key business requirements to be addressed in this architecture effort, and the constraints that must be dealt with
- To articulate an Architecture Vision that demonstrates a response to those requirements and constraints
- To secure formal approval to proceed
- To understand the impact on, and of, other enterprise architecture development cycles ongoing in parallel

5.2 Approach

5.2.1 General

The phase starts with receipt of a Request for Architecture Work from the sponsoring organization to the architecture organization.

The issues involved in ensuring proper recognition and endorsement from corporate management, and the support and commitment of line management, are discussed in Part IV: Resource Base, IT Governance.

Phase A also defines what is in and what is outside the scope of the architecture effort and the constraints that must be dealt with. Scoping decisions need to be made on the basis of a practical assessment of resource and competence availability, and the value that can realistically be expected to accrue to the enterprise from the chosen scope of architecture work. The issues involved in this are discussed in Scoping the Architecture.

The constraints will normally be informed by the business principles and architecture principles, developed as part of the Preliminary Phase (Preliminary Phase: Framework and Principles).

Normally, the business principles, business goals, and strategic drivers of the organization are already defined elsewhere in the enterprise. If so, the activity in Phase A is involved with ensuring that existing definitions are current, and clarifying any areas of ambiguity. Otherwise, it involves defining these essential items from scratch.

Similarly, the architecture principles that inform the constraints on architecture work will normally have been defined in the Preliminary Phase (Preliminary Phase: Framework and Principles). The activity in Phase A is concerned with ensuring that the existing principles definitions are current, and clarifying any areas of ambiguity. Otherwise, it entails defining the architecture principles from scratch, as explained in Part IV: Resource Base, Architecture Principles.

5.2.2 Creating the Architecture Vision

The Architecture Vision is essentially the architect's "elevator pitch" - the key opportunity to sell the benefits of the proposed development to the decision-makers within the enterprise. The goal is to articulate an Architecture Vision that enables the business goals, responds to the strategic drivers, conforms with the principles, and addresses the stakeholder concerns and objectives.

Clarifying and agreeing the purpose of the architecture effort is one of the key parts of this activity, and the purpose needs to be clearly reflected in the vision that is created. Architecture projects are often undertaken with a specific purpose in mind - a specific set of business drivers that represent the return on investment for the stakeholders in the architecture development. Clarifying that purpose, and demonstrating how it will be achieved by the proposed architecture development, is the whole point of the Architecture Vision.

Normally, key elements of the Architecture Vision - such as the enterprise mission, vision, strategy, and goals - have been documented as part of some wider business strategy or enterprise planning activity that has its own lifecycle within the enterprise. In such cases, the activity in Phase A is concerned with verifying and understanding the documented business strategy and goals, and possibly bridging between the enterprise strategy and goals on the one hand, and the strategy and goals on the part of the enterprise that lies within the scope of the Baseline Architecture project.

In other cases, little or no Business Architecture work may have been done to date. In such cases, there will be a need for the architecture team to research, verify, and gain buy-in to the key business objectives and processes that the architecture is to support. This may be done as a free-standing exercise, either preceding architecture development, or as part of the ADM initiation phase (Preliminary Phase).

The Architecture Vision includes a first-cut, high-level description of the baseline and target environments, from both a business and a technical perspective. These outline descriptions are then built on in subsequent phases.

Business scenarios are an appropriate and useful technique to discover and document business requirements, and to articulate an Architecture Vision that responds to those requirements.

Business scenarios are described in Part IV: Resource Base, Business Scenarios.

Once an Architecture Vision is defined and documented in the Statement of Architecture Work, it is critical to use it to build a consensus, as described in Part IV: Resource Base, IT Governance. Without this consensus it is very unlikely that the final architecture will be accepted by the organization as a whole. The consensus is represented by the sponsoring organization signing the Statement of Architecture Work.

5.3 Inputs

The inputs to Phase A are:

- Request for Architecture Work (see Request for Architecture Work)
- Business strategy, business goals, and business drivers
- Architecture principles (see Architecture Principles), including business principles, when pre-existing
- Enterprise Continuum (see Introduction to the Enterprise Continuum) - existing architectural documentation (framework description, architectural descriptions, existing baseline descriptions, etc.)

5.4 Steps

Key steps in Phase A include:

1. Establish the Project

    Conduct the necessary (enterprise-specific) procedures to secure enterprise-wide recognition of the project, the endorsement of corporate management, and the support and commitment of the necessary line management. Include reference to the IT governance framework for the enterprise, explaining how this project relates to that framework.

2. Identify Business Goals and Business Drivers

    Identify the business goals and strategic drivers of the organization.

    If these have already been defined elsewhere within the enterprise, ensure that the existing definitions are current, and clarify any areas of ambiguity. Otherwise, go back to the originators of the Statement of Architecture Work and work with them to define these essential items from scratch and secure their endorsement by corporate management.

3. Review Architecture Principles, including Business Principles

    Review the principles under which the current architecture is to be developed. Architecture principles are normally based on the business principles developed as part of the Preliminary Phase. They are explained, and an example set given, in Part IV: Resource Base, Architecture Principles. Ensure that the existing definitions are current, and clarify any areas of ambiguity. Otherwise, go back to the body responsible for architecture governance and work with them to define these essential items from scratch and secure their endorsement by corporate management.

4. Define Scope

   Define what is inside and what is outside the scope of the Baseline Architecture effort. The issues involved in this are discussed in Scoping the Architecture. In particular, define:

   - The breadth of coverage of the enterprise
   - The level of detail to be defined
   - The specific architecture domains to be covered (Business, Data, Applications, Technology)
   - The extent of the time horizon aimed at, plus the number and extent of any intermediate time horizons
   - The architectural assets to be leveraged, or considered for use, from the organization's Enterprise Continuum:
     - Assets created in previous iterations of the ADM cycle within the enterprise
     - Assets available elsewhere in the industry (other frameworks, systems models, vertical industry models, etc.)

5. Define Constraints

   Define the constraints that must be dealt with, including enterprise-wide constraints and project-specific constraints (time, schedule, resources, etc.). The enterprise-wide constraints may be informed by the business and architecture principles developed in the Preliminary Phase or clarified as part of Phase A.

6. Identify Stakeholders and Concerns, Business Requirements, and Architecture Vision

   Identify the key stakeholders and their concerns/objectives; define the key business requirements to be addressed in this architecture effort; and articulate an Architecture Vision that will address the requirements, within the defined scope and constraints, and conforming with the business and architecture principles.

   - Business scenarios are an appropriate and useful technique to discover and document business requirements, and to articulate an Architecture Vision that responds to those requirements. Business scenarios may also be used at more detailed levels of the architecture work (e.g., in Phase B, and are described in Part IV: Resource Base, Business Scenarios.
   - This step will generate the first, very high-level definitions of the baseline and target environments, from a business, information systems, and technology perspective, including:
     - Baseline Business Architecture, Version 0.1
     - Baseline Technology Architecture, Version 0.1
     - Baseline Data Architecture, Version 0.1
     - Baseline Applications Architecture, Version 0.1

- Target Business Architecture, Version 0.1
- Target Technology Architecture, Version 0.1
- Target Data Architecture, Version 0.1
- Target Applicaions Architecture, Version 0.1

7. Develop Statement of Architecture Work and Secure Approval

   Based on the purpose, focus, scope, and constraints, determine which architecture domains should be developed, to what level of detail, and which architecture views should be built. Estimate the resources needed, develop a roadmap and schedule for the proposed development, and document all these in the Statement of Architecture Work. Secure formal approval of the Statement of Architecture Work under the appropriate governance procedures.

   A critical evaluation of the architectural starting point - the baseline environment described in the Architecture Vision - may be a key element of such a statement of work, especially for an incremental approach, where neither the architecture development nor the system implementation starts from scratch.

5.4.1 Business Scenarios

The ADM has its own method (a "method-within-a-method") for identifying and articulating the business requirements implied in new business functionality to address key business drivers, and the implied Technology Architecture requirements. This process is known as business scenarios, and is described in detail in Part IV: Rescurce Base, Business Scenarios. The technique may be used iteratively, at different levels of detail in the hierarchical decomposition of the Business Architecture. The generic business scenario process is as follows:

1. Problem

   Identify, document, and rank the problem that is driving the project.

2. Business and Technical Environments

   Document, as high-level architecture models, the business and technical environment where the problem situation is occurring.

3. Objectives and Measures of Success

   Identify and document desired objectives, the results of handling the problems successfully.

4. Human Actors

   Identify human actors and their place in the business model, the human participants, and their roles.

5. Computer Actors

   Identify computer actors and their place in the technology model, the computing elements, and their roles.

6. Roles and Responsibilities

   Identify and document roles, responsibilities, and measures of success per actor, the required scripts per actor, and the desired results of handling the situation properly.

7. Refine

   Check for fitness-for-purpose of inspiring subsequent architecture work, and refine only if necessary.

5.5 Outputs

The outputs of Phase A are:

- Approved Statement of Architecture Work (Major Output Descriptions), including in particular:
    - Scope and constraints
    - Plan for the architectural work
- Refined statements of business goals and strategic drivers
- Architecture principles (see Architecture Principles), including business principles
- Architecture Vision (Business Scenario/Architecture Vision) including:
    - Baseline Business Architecture, Version 0.1
    - Baseline Technology Architecture, Version 0.1
    - Baseline Data Architecture, Version 0.1
    - Baseline Applications Architecture, Version 0.1
    - Target Business Architecture, Version 0.1
    - Target Technology Architecture, Version 0.1
    - Target Data Architecture, Version 0.1
    - Target Applications Architecture, Version 0.1

Note:

Multiple business scenarios may be used to generate a single Architecture Vision. In TOGAF terms, the Architecture Vision may also be referred to as a "conceptual-level architecture".

Chapter 6: Phase B - Business Architecture

This chapter describes the development of a Business Architecture.

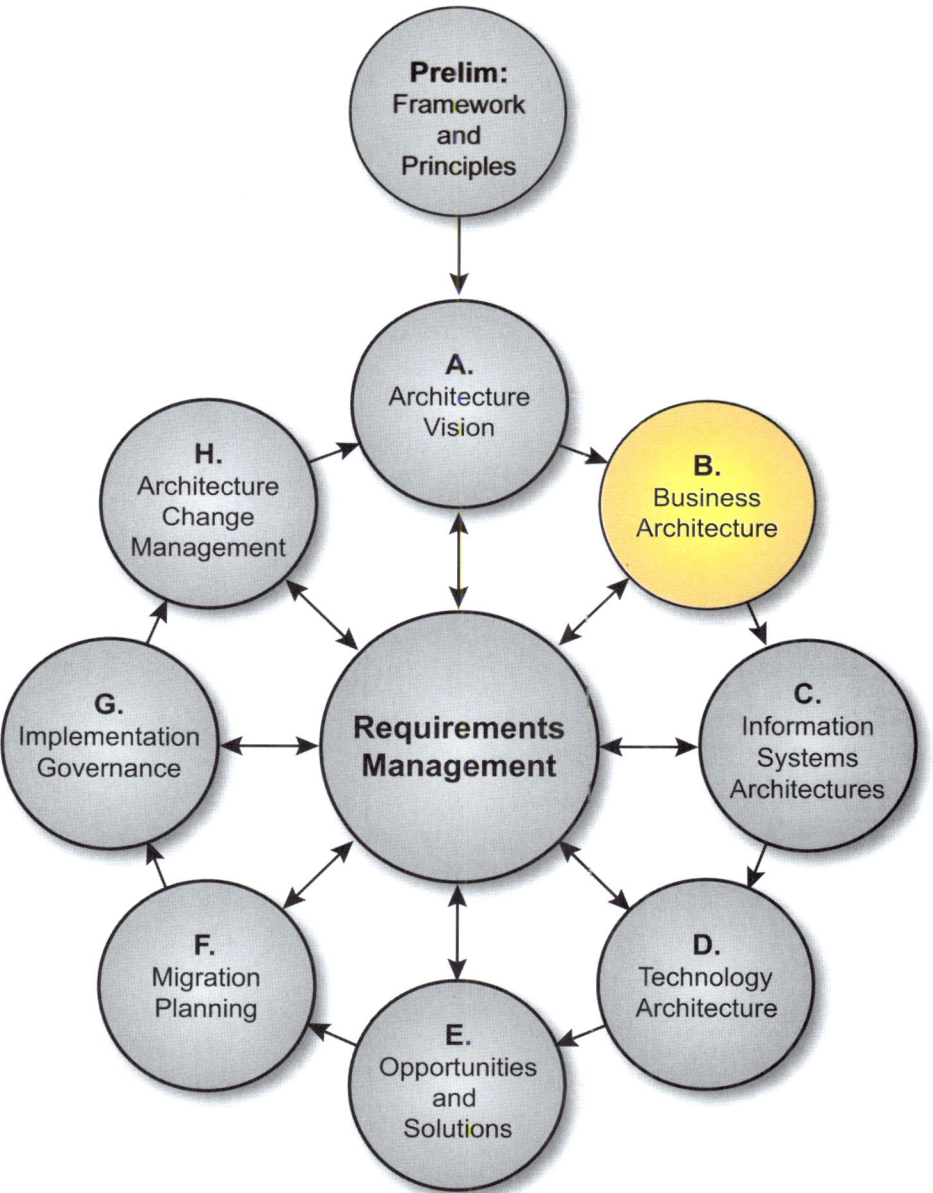

Figure 6.1: Phase B: Business Architecture

6.1 Objectives

The objectives of Phase B are:

- To describe the Baseline Business Architecture
- To develop a Target Business Architecture, describing the product and/or service strategy, and the organizational, functional, process, information, and geographic aspects of the business environment, based on the business principles, business goals, and strategic drivers
- To analyze the gaps between the Baseline and Target Business Architectures
- To select the relevant architecture viewpoints that will enable the architect to demonstrate how the stakeholder concerns are addressed in the Business Architecture
- To select the relevant tools and techniques to be used in association with the selected viewpoints

6.2 Approach

6.2.1 General

A knowledge of the Business Architecture is a prerequisite for architecture work in any other domain (Data, Applications, Technology), and is therefore the first architecture activity that needs to be undertaken, if not catered for already in other organizational processes (enterprise planning, strategic business planning, business process re-engineering, etc.).

In practical terms, the Business Architecture is also often necessary as a means of demonstrating the business value of subsequent Technical Architecture work to key stakeholders, and the return on investment to those stakeholders from supporting and participating in the subsequent work.

The extent of the work in Phase B will depend to a large extent on the enterprise environment. In some cases, key elements of the Business Architecture may be done in other activities; for example, the enterprise mission, vision, strategy, and goals may be documented as part of some wider business strategy or enterprise planning activity that has its own lifecycle within the enterprise.

In such cases, there may be a need to verify and update the currently documented business strategy and plans, and/or to bridge between high-level business drivers, business strategy, and goals on the one hand, and the specific business requirements that are relevant to this architecture development effort. (The business strategy typically defines what to achieve - the goals and drivers, and the metrics for success - but not how to get there. That is role of the Business Architecture.)

In other cases, little or no Business Architecture work may have been done to date. In such cases, there will be a need for the architecture team to research, verify, and gain buy-in to the key business objectives and processes that the architecture is to support. This may be done as a free-standing exercise, either preceding architecture development, or as part of Phase A.

In both of these cases, the business scenario technique (see Business Scenarios) of the TOGAF ADM, or any other method that illuminates the key business requirements and indicates the implied technical requirements for IT architecture, may be used.

A key objective is to re-use existing material as much as possible. In architecturally more mature environments, there will be existing architecture definitions, which (hopefully) will have been maintained since the last architecture development cycle. Where existing architectural descriptions exist, these can be used as a starting point, and verified and updated if necessary; see The Architecture Continuum.

Gather and analyze only that information that allows informed decisions to be made relevant to the scope of this architecture effort. If this effort is focused on the definition of (possibly new) business processes, then Phase B will necessarily involve a lot of detailed work. If the focus is more on the Target Architectures in other domains (data/information, application systems, infrastructure) to support an essentially existing Business Architecture, then it is important to build a complete picture in Phase B without going into unnecessary detail.

6.2.2 Developing the Baseline Description

In architecturally more mature environments, there will be existing architecture definitions, which (hopefully) will have been maintained since the last architecture development cycle. Where existing architectural descriptions exist, they can be used as a starting point, and verified and updated if necessary. Any such existing descriptions will already have been used in Phase A in developing an Architecture Vision, and this work should provide a sound basis for the Baseline Description, and may even be sufficient in itself.

Where no such descriptions exist, information will have to be gathered in whatever format comes to hand.

The normal approach to Target Architecture development is top-down. In the Baseline Description, however, the analysis of the current state often has to be done bottom-up, particularly where little or no existing architecture assets exist. In such a case, the architect simply has to document the working assumptions about high-level architectures, and the process is one of gathering evidence to turn the working assumptions into fact, until the law of diminishing returns sets in.

Business processes that are not to be carried forward have no intrinsic value. However, when developing Baseline Descriptions in other architecture domains, architectural components (principles, models, standards, and current inventory) that are not to be carried forward may still have an intrinsic value, and an inventory may be needed in order to understand the residual value (if any) of those components.

Whatever the approach, the goal should be to re-use existing material as much as possible, and to gather and analyze only that information that allows informed decisions to be made regarding the Target Business Architecture. It is important to build a complete picture without going into unnecessary detail.

6.2.3 Business Modeling

A variety of modeling tools and techniques may be employed, if deemed appropriate (bearing in mind the above caution not to go into unnecessary detail). For example:

- Activity Models (also called Business Process Models) describe the functions associated with the enterprise's business activities, the data and/or information exchanged between activities (internal exchanges), and the data and/or information exchanged with other activities that are outside the scope of the model (external exchanges). Activity models are hierarchical in nature. They capture the activities performed in a business process, and the ICOMs (inputs, controls, outputs, and mechanisms/resources used) of those activities. Activity models can be annotated with explicit statements of business rules, which represent relationships among the ICOMs. For example, a business rule can specify who can do what under specified conditions, the combination of inputs and controls needed, and the resulting outputs. One technique for creating activity models is the IDEF (Integrated Computer Aided Manufacturing (ICAM) DEFinition) modeling technique.

  The Business Process Management Initiative (*www.bpmi.org*) is an organization that is defining standards for business process modeling, including a language with which to specify business processes, their tasks/steps, and the documents produced.

- Use-Case Models can describe either business processes or systems functions, depending on the focus of the modeling effort. A use-case model describes the business processes of an enterprise in terms of use-cases and actors corresponding to business processes and organizational participants (people, organizations, etc.). The use-case model is

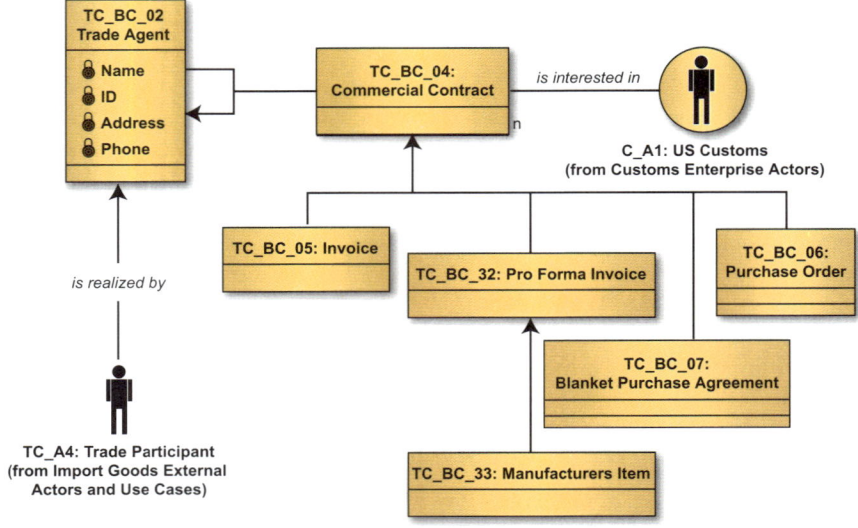

Figure 6.2: UML Business Class Diagram, Trade Class Model (Commercial View)

described in use-case diagrams and use-case specifications.

- Class Models are similar to logical data models. A class model describes static information and relationships between information. A class model also describes informational behaviors. Like many of the other models, it can also be used to model various levels of granularity. Depending on the intent of the model, a class model can represent business domain entities or systems implementation classes. A business domain model represents key business information (domain classes), their characteristics (attributes), their behaviors (methods or operations), and relationships (often referred to as multiplicity, describing how many classes typically participate in the relationship), and cardinality (describes required or optional participation in the relationship). Specifications further elaborate and detail information that cannot be represented in the class diagram.

(UML Business Class Diagram, Trade Class Model (Commercial View) is taken from the Practical Guide to Federal Enterprise Architecture)

All three types of model types above can be represented in Unified Modeling Language (UML), and a variety of tools exist for generating such models.

Certain industry sectors have modeling techniques specific to the sector concerned. For example, the Defense sector uses the following models:

- The Node Connectivity Diagram describes the business locations (nodes), the "needlines" between them, and the characteristics of the information exchanged. Node connectivity can be described at three levels: conceptual, logical, and physical. Each needline indicates the need for some kind of information transfer between the two connected nodes. A node can represent a role (e.g., a CIO); an organizational unit; a business location or facility; and so on. An arrow indicating the direction of information flow is annotated to describe the characteristics of the data or information - for example, its content; media; security or classification level; timeliness; and requirements for information system interoperability.

- The Information Exchange Matrix documents the information exchange requirements for an enterprise architecture. Information exchange requirements express the relationships across three basic entities (activities, business nodes and their elements, and information flow), and focus on characteristics of the information exchange, such as performance and security. They identify who exchanges what information with whom, why the information is necessary, and in what manner.

Although originally developed for use in the Defense sector, these models are finding increasing use in other sectors of government, and may also be considered for use in non-government environments.

6.2.4 Enterprise Continuum

As part of Phase B, the architecture team will need to consider what relevant Business Architecture resources are available from the Enterprise Continuum, in particular:

- Generic business models relevant to the organization's industry sector. (These are "Industry Architectures", in terms of the Enterprise Continuum.) For example:

- The Object Management Group (OMG - *www.omg.org*) has a number of vertical Domain Task Forces developing business models relevant to specific vertical domains such as Healthcare, Transportation, Finance, etc.
- The TeleManagement Forum (TMF - *www.tmforum.org*) has developed detailed business models relevant to the Telecommunications industry.
- Government departments and agencies in different countries have reference models and frameworks mandated for use, intended to promote cross-departmental integration and interoperability. An example is the Federal Enterprise Architecture Business Reference Model (*www.feapmo.gov/feaBrm.htm*), which is a function-driven framework for describing the business operations of the Federal Government independent of the agencies that perform them.

- Business models relevant to common high-level business domains - such as electronic commerce, supply chain management, etc. - that are published within the IT industry. (These are "Common Systems Architectures", in terms of the Enterprise Continuum.) For example:
  - The Resource-Event-Agent (REA) business model was originally created by William E. McCarthy (*www.msu.edu/user/mccarth4*) of Michigan State University, mainly for modeling of accounting systems. It has proved so useful for better understanding of business processes that it has become one of the major modeling frameworks for both traditional enterprises and e-Commerce systems. In particular, it has been extended by Robert Haugen and McCarthy for supply chain management (refer to *www.jeffsutherland.org/oopsla2000/mccarthy/mccarthy.htm*).
  - The STEP Framework (Standard for the Exchange of Product model data) is concerned with product design and supply chain interworking. STEP is an ISO standard (ISO 10303). Implementation of the STEP standard has been led by some large aerospace manufacturers, and has also been taken up in other industries that have a need for complex graphic and process data, such as the construction industry.
  - The Open Applications Group (OAG - *www.openapplications.org*) is focused on defining a framework for allowing heterogeneous business applications to communicate together. Its OAGIS integration model and specification address the needs of traditional Enterprise Resource Planning (ERP) integration, as well as supply chain management and electronic commerce.
  - RosettaNet (*www.rosettanet.org*) is a consortium created by leading companies in the computer, electronic component, and semiconductor manufacturing supply chains. Its mission is to develop a complete set of standard e-Business processes for these supply chains, and to promote and support their adoption and use.

- Enterprise-specific building blocks (process components, business rules, job descriptions, etc.).

6.2.5 Gap Analysis

A key step in validating an architecture is to consider what may have been forgotten. The architecture must support all of the essential information processing needs of the organization.

The most critical source of gaps that should be considered is stakeholder concerns that have not been addressed in prior architectural work.

Other potential sources of gaps:

- People gaps (e.g., cross-training requirements)
- Process gaps (e.g., process inefficiencies)
- Tools gaps (e.g., duplicate or missing tool functionality)
- Information gaps
- Measurement gaps
- Financial gaps
- Facilities gaps (buildings, office space, etc.)

Gap analysis highlights services and/or functions that have been accidentally left out, deliberately eliminated, or are yet to be developed or procured. Gap Analysis Matrix in Phase D illustrates an example of a gap analysis matrix. The suggested steps are as follows:

- Draw up a matrix with all the Business Architecture Building Blocks of the Baseline Architecture on the vertical axis, and all the Business Architecture Building Blocks of the Target Business Architecture on the horizontal axis. In creating the matrix it is imperative to use terminology that is accurate and consistent.
- Add to the Baseline Architecture axis a final row labeled "New Business Architecture Building Blocks", and to the Target Architecture axis a final column labeled "Eliminated Business Architecture Building Blocks".
- Where a Business Architecture Building Block is available in both the Baseline and Target Architectures, record this with "Included" at the intersecting cell.
- Where a Business Architecture Building Block from the Baseline Architecture is missing in the Target Architecture, each must be reviewed. If it was correctly eliminated, mark it as such in the appropriate "Eliminated" cell. If it was not, you have uncovered an accidental omission in your new architecture that must be addressed by reinstating the Business Architecture Building Block in the next iteration of the architecture design - mark it as such in the appropriate "Eliminated" cell.
- Where a Business Architecture Building Block from the Target Architecture cannot be found in the Baseline Architecture, mark it at the intersection with the "New" row, as a gap that needs to be filled, either by developing or procuring the building block.

When the exercise is complete, anything under "Eliminated Services" or "New Services" is a gap, which should either be explained as correctly eliminated, or marked as to be addressed by reinstating or developing/procuring the function.

6.3 Inputs

The inputs to Phase B are:

- Request for Architecture Work (Request for Architecture Work)
- Approved Statement of Architecture Work (Major Output Descriptions)
- Refined statements of business goals and strategic drivers
- Architecture principles (see Architecture Principles), including business principles, when pre-existing
- Enterprise Continuum (as described in Enterprise Continuum)
- Architecture Vision (see Business Scenario/Architecture Vision), including:
    - Baseline Business Architecture, Version 0.1
    - Baseline Technology Architecture, Version 0.1
    - Baseline Data Architecture, Version 0.1
    - Baseline Applications Architecture, Version 0.1
    - Target Business Architecture, Version 0.1
    - Target Technology Architecture, Version 0.1
    - Target Data Architecture, Version 0.1
    - Target Applicaions Architecture, Version 0.1

6.4 Steps

The level of detail addressed in Phase B will depend on the scope and goals of the overall architecture effort.

New business processes being introduced as part of this effort will need to be defined in detail during Phase B. Existing business processes to be carried over and supported in the target environment may already have been adequately defined in previous architectural work; but, if not, they too will need to be defined in Phase B.

Key steps in Phase B include the following:

Note:

The order of the following steps should be adapted to the situation at hand: in particular, determine whether in this situation it is appropriate to do Baseline Description or Target Architecture development first, as described in Introduction to the ADM.

1. Develop Baseline Business Architecture Description

   Develop a Baseline Description of the existing Business Architecture, to the extent necessary to support the Target Business Architecture. The scope and level of detail to be defined will depend on the extent to which existing business elements are likely to be carried over into the Target Business Architecture, and on whether existing architectural descriptions exist, as described in Approach. To the extent possible, identify the relevant Business Architecture building blocks, drawing on the Architecture Continuum.

2. Identify Reference Models, Viewpoints, and Tools:
   i. Select relevant Business Architecture resources (reference models, patterns, etc.) from the Architecture Continuum, on the basis of the business drivers, and the stakeholders and concerns.
   ii. Select relevant Business Architecture viewpoints (e.g., Operations, Management, Financial); i.e., those that will enable the architect to demonstrate how the stakeholder concerns are being addressed in the Business Architecture.
   iii. Identify appropriate tools and techniques to be used for capture, modeling, and analysis, in association with the selected viewpoints. Depending on the degree of sophistication warranted, these may comprise simple documents or spreadsheets, or more sophisticated modeling tools and techniques such as activity models, business process models, use-case models, etc.

3. Create Architecture Model(s):
   i. For each viewpoint, create the model for the specific view required, using the selected tool or method.
   ii. Assure that all stakeholder concerns are covered. If they are not, create new models to address concerns not covered, or augment existing models (see Business Modeling). Business scenarios are a useful technique to discover and document business requirements, and may be used iteratively, at different levels of detail in the hierarchical decomposition of the Business Architecture. Business scenarios are described in Part IV: Resource Base, Business Scenarios. Other techniques may be used, if required. Create models of the following:
      a. Organization structure: document the organization structure, identifying business locations and relating them to organizational units.
      b. Business goals and objectives: document business goals and objectives for each organizational unit.
      c. Business functions: identify and define business functions. This is a detailed, recursive step involving successive decomposition of major functional areas into sub-functions.
      d. Business services: the services that each of the enterprise unit provides to its customers, both internally and externally.
      e. Business processes, including measures and deliverables.
      f. Business roles, including development and modification of skills requirements.

       g. Business data model.
- iii. Information requirements: identify for each business function when, where, how often, and by whom the function is performed; what information is used to perform it, and its source(s); and what opportunities exist for improvements. Include information that needs to be created, retrieved, updated, and deleted. The level of detail to be defined will depend on the scope and focus of the Baseline Architecture effort, as described in Approach. Focus on what will be worthwhile collecting for the purpose at hand.
- iv. Perform trade-off analysis to resolve conflicts (if any) among the different views.

    One method of doing this is CMU/SEI's Architecture Trade-off Analysis (ATA) Method (*www.sei.cmu.edu/ata/ata_method.html*.)
- v. Validate that the models support the principles, objectives, and constraints.
- vi. Note changes to the viewpoint represented in the selected models from the Architecture Continuum, and document.
- vii. Test architecture models for completeness against requirements.

4. Select Business Architecture Building Blocks (e.g., business services)
   - i. Identify required building blocks and check against existing library of building blocks, re-using as appropriate.
   - ii. Where necessary, define new Business Architecture Building Blocks.
5. Conduct Formal Checkpoint Review of Architecture Model and Building Blocks with Stakeholders
6. Review Non-Functional (Qualitative) Criteria (e.g., performance, costs, volumes).
   Use to specify required service levels (for example, via formal Service Level Agreements (SLAs)).
7. Complete Business Architecture:
   - i. Select standards for each of the Architecture Building Blocks, re-using as much as possible from the reference models selected from the Architecture Continuum.
   - ii. Fully document each Architecture Building Block.
   - iii. Final cross-check of overall architecture against business goals. Document rationale for building block decisions in the architecture document.
   - iv. Document final requirements traceability report.
   - v. Document final mapping of the architecture within the Architecture Building Blocks. From the selected architecture building blocks, identify those that might be re-used (working practices, roles, business relationships, job descriptions, etc.), and publish via the architecture repository.
   - vi. Document rationale for building block decisions in the Business Architecture description document.
   - vii. Prepare a Business Architecture Report comprising some or all of:
     - ■ A business footprint (a high-level description of the people and locations

involved with key business functions)
- A detailed description of business functions and their information needs
- A management footprint (showing span of control and accountability)
- Standards, rules, and guidelines showing working practices, legislation, financial measures, etc.
- A skills matrix and set of job descriptions

If appropriate, use reports and/or graphics generated by modeling tools to demonstrate key views of the architecture. Route the Business Architecture document for review by relevant stakeholders, and incorporate feedback.

viii. Checkpoint: check the original motivation for the architecture project and the Statement of Architecture Work against the proposed Business Architecture, asking if it is fit for the purpose of supporting subsequent work in the other architecture domains. Refine the proposed Business Architecture only if necessary.

8. Perform Gap Analysis (see Approach) and Create Report:
   i. Create gap matrix, as described in Gap Analysis.
   ii. Identify building blocks to be carried over, classifying as either changed or unchanged.
   iii. Identify eliminated building blocks.
   iv. Identify new building blocks.
   v. Identify gaps and classify as those that should be developed and those that should be procured.

6.5 Outputs

The outputs of Phase B are:

- Statement of Architecture Work (Major Output Descriptions), updated if necessary
- Validated business principles (Architecture Principles). business goals, and strategic drivers
- Target Business Architecture (Business Architecture), Version 1.0 (detailed), including:
  - Organization structure - identifying business locations and relating them to organizational units
  - Business goals and objectives - for the enterprise and each organizational unit
  - Business functions - a detailed, recursive step involving successive decomposition of major functional areas into sub-functions
  - Business services - the services that the enterprise and each business unit provides to its customers, both internally and externally
  - Business processes, including measures and deliverables

- Business roles, including development and modification of skills requirements
- Business data model
- Correlation of organization and functions - relate business functions to organizational units in the form of a matrix report
- Baseline Business Architecture, Version 1.0 (detailed), if appropriate
- Views corresponding to the selected viewpoints addressing key stakeholder concerns
- Gap analysis results
- Technical requirements - identifying, categorizing, and prioritizing the implications for work in the remaining architecture domains; for example, by a dependency/priority matrix. (For example, guiding trade-off between speed of transaction processing and security.) List the specific models that are expected to be produced (for example, expressed as primitives of the Zachman Framework).
- Business Architecture Report
- Updated business requirements

Chapter 7:
Phase C - Information Systems Architectures

This chapter describes the Information Systems Architecture, including the development of Data and Applications Architectures.

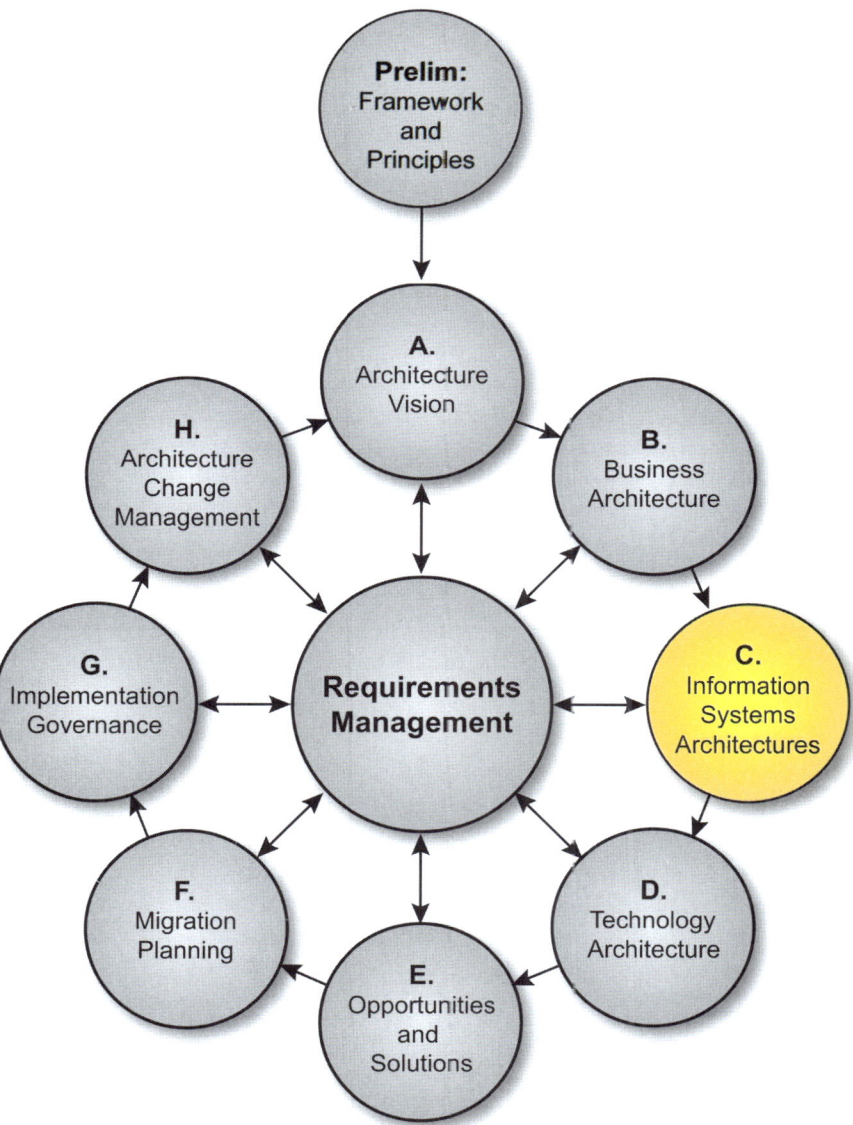

Figure 7.1: Phase C: Information Systems Architectures

7.1 Objective

The objective of Phase C is to develop Target Architectures covering either or both (depending on project scope) of the Data and Application Systems domains.

The scope of the business processes supported in Phase C is limited to those that are supported by IT, and the interfaces of those IT-related processes to non-IT-related processes.

7.2 Approach

7.2.1 Development

Phase C involves some combination of Data and Applications Architecture, in either order. Advocates exist for both sequences. For example, Steven Spewak's Enterprise Architecture Planning (EAP) recommends a data-driven approach.

On the other hand, major applications systems - such as those for Enterprise Resource Planning (ERP), customer relationship management, etc. - often provide a combination of technology infrastructure and business application logic, and some organizations take an application-driven approach, whereby they recognize certain key applications as forming the core underpinning of the mission-critical business processes, and take the implementation and integration of those core applications as the primary focus of architecture effort (the integration issues often constituting a major challenge).

7.2.2 Implementation

Implementation of these architectures may not necessarily follow the same order. For example, one common implementation approach is top-down design and bottom-up implementation:

- Design:
    1. Business Architecture design
    2. Data (or Applications) Architecture design
    3. Applications (or Data) Architecture design
    4. Technology Architecture design
- Implementation:
    1. Technology Architecture implementation
    2. Applications (or Data) Architecture implementation
    3. Data (or Applications) Architecture implementation
    4. Business Architecture implementation

An alternative approach is a data-driven sequence, whereby application systems that create data are implemented first, then applications that process the data, and finally applications that archive data.

7.3 Inputs

Inputs to Phase C are:

- Application principles (Application Principles), if existing
- Data principles (Data Principles), if existing
- Request for Architecture Work (Request for Architecture Work)
- Statement of Architecture Work (Major Output Descriptions)
- Architecture Vision (Business Scenario/Architecture Vision)
- Enterprise Continuum (Introduction to the Enterprise Continuum)
- Baseline Business Architecture, Version 1.0 (detailed), if appropriate
- Target Business Architecture (see Business Architecture), Version 1.0 (detailed)
- Baseline Data Architecture, Version 0.1
- Target Data Architecture, Version 0.1
- Baseline Applications Architecture, Version 0.1
- Target Applications Architecture, Version 0.1
- Relevant technical requirements that will apply to Phase C
- Gap analysis results (from Business Architecture)

7.4 Steps

Detailed steps for Phase C are given separately for each architecture domain:

- Data Architecture (see Data Architecture)
- Applications Architecture (Phase C: Information System Architectures - Applications Architecture)

7.5 Outputs

The main outputs are as follows:

- Statement of Architecture Work (Major Output Descriptions), updated if necessary
- Baseline Data Architecture, Version 1.0
- Target Data Architecture, Version 1.0
- Basline Applications Architecture, Version 1.0
- Target Applications Architecture, Version 1.0

- Data Architecture views corresponding to the selected viewpoints addressing key stakeholder concerns
- Applications Architecture views corresponding to the selected viewpoints addressing key stakeholder concerns
- Data Architecture Report, summarizing what was done and the key findings
- Applications Architecture Report, summarizing what was done and the key findings
- Gap analysis results:
    - Areas where the Business Architecture may need to change to cater for changes in the Data and/or Applications Architecture
    - Constraints on the Technology Architecture about to be designed
- Impact Analysis (see Impact Analysis)
- Updated business requirements (if appropriate)

Chapter 8:
Phase C - Information Systems Architectures - Data Architecture

This chapter describes the Data Architecture part of Phase C.

8.1 Objective

The objective here is to define the major types and sources of data necessary to support the business, in a way that is:

- Understandable by stakeholders
- Complete and consistent
- Stable

It is important to note that this effort is not concerned with database design. The goal is to define the data entities relevant to the enterprise, not to design logical or physical storage systems. (However, linkages to existing files and databases may be developed, and may demonstrate significant areas for improvement.)

8.2 Approach

8.2.1 Enterprise Continuum

As part of this phase, the architecture team will need to consider what relevant Data Architecture resources are available in the organization's Enterprise Continuum; in particular, generic data models relevant to the organization's industry "vertical" sector. For example:

- ARTS has defined a data model for the Retail industry.
- POSC has defined a data model for the Petrotechnical industry.

8.2.2 Gap Analysis

A key step in validating an architecture is to consider what may have been forgotten. The architecture must support all of the essential information processing needs of the organization. The most critical source of gaps that should be considered is stakeholder concerns that have not been addressed in architectural work.

Types of data gap:

- Data not located where it is needed
- Not the data that is needed

- Data not available when needed
- Data not created
- Data not consumed
- Data relationship gaps
- etc.

Gap analysis highlights shortfalls in data services and/or data elements that have been accidentally left out, deliberately eliminated, or are yet to be defined. Gap Analysis Matrix in Phase D illustrates an example of a gap analysis matrix. The suggested steps are as follows:

- Draw up a matrix with all the Data Architecture Building Blocks of the Baseline Architecture on the vertical axis, and all the Data Architecture Building Blocks of the Target Data Architecture on the horizontal axis. In creating the matrix, it is imperative to use terminology that is accurate and consistent.
- Add to the Baseline Architecture axis a final row labeled " New Data Architecture Building Blocks", and to the Target Architecture axis a final column labeled "Eliminated Data Architecture Building Blocks".
- Where a Data Architecture Building Block is available in both the Baseline and Target Architectures, record this with "Included" at the intersecting cell.
- Where a Data Architecture Building Block from the Baseline Architecture is missing in the Target Architecture, each must be reviewed. If it was correctly eliminated, mark it as such in the appropriate "Eliminated" cell. If it was not, you have uncovered an accidental omission in your new architecture that must be addressed by reinstating the Data Architecture building block in the next iteration of the architecture design - mark it as such in the appropriate "Eliminated" cell.
- Where a Data Architecture Building Block from the Target Architecture cannot be found in the Baseline Architecture, mark it at the intersection with the "New" row, as a gap that needs to filled, either by defining or inheriting the building block.

When the exercise is complete, anything under "Eliminated Services" or "New Services" is a gap, which should either be explained as correctly eliminated, or marked as to be addressed by reinstating or developing/procuring the function.

8.3 Inputs

Inputs to this phase are:

- Data principles (Data Principles), if existing
- Request for Architecture Work (Request for Architecture Work)
- Statement of Architecture Work (Major Output Descriptions)
- Architecture Vision (Business Scenario/Architecture Vision)

- Relevant technical requirements that will apply to this phase
- Gap analysis results (from Business Architecture)
- Baseline Business Architecture, Version 1.0 (detailed), if appropriate
- Target Business Architecture (Business Architecture), Version 1.0 (detailed)
- Baseline Data Architecture, Version 0.1, if available
- Target Data Architecture, Version 0.1, if available

8.4 Steps

1. Develop Baseline Data Architecture Description

    Develop a Baseline Description of the existing Data Architecture, to the extent necessary to support the Target Data Architecture. The scope and level of detail to be defined will depend on the extent to which existing data elements are likely to be carried over into the Target Data Architecture, and on whether existing architectural descriptions exist, as described in Approach. To the extent possible, identify the relevant Data Architecture building blocks, drawing on the Architecture Continuum, and review/verify the following primitives from the Zachman Framework:

    - Business data model (entities, attributes, and relationships)

        Entity-relationship diagrams illustrating views of the Data Architecture to address the concerns of stakeholders.

    - Logical data model (logical views of the actual data of interest from the applications point of view)
    - Data management process models, including:
        i Data dissemination view
        ii Data lifecycle view
        iii Data security view
        iv Data model management view
    - Data entity/business function matrix in the Business Architecture

2. Review and Validate Principles, Reference Models, Viewpoints, and Tools

    i. Review and validate (or generate, if necessary) the set of data principles.

        These will normally form part of an overarching set of architecture principles. Guidelines for developing and applying principles, and a sample set of data principles, are given in Part IV: Resource Base, Architecture Principles.

    ii. Select relevant Data Architecture resources (reference models, patterns, etc.) from the Architecture Continuum, on the basis of the business drivers, and the stakeholders and concerns.

iii. Select relevant Data Architecture viewpoints (for example, stakeholders of the data - regulatory bodies, users, generators, subjects, auditors, etc.; various time dimensions - real-time, reporting period, event-driven, etc.; locations; business processes); i.e., those that will enable the architect to demonstrate how the stakeholder concerns are being addressed in the Data Architecture.

iv. Identify appropriate tools and techniques (including forms) to be used for data capture, modeling, and analysis, in association with the selected viewpoints. Depending on the degree of sophistication warranted, these may comprise simple documents or spreadsheets, or more sophisticated modeling tools and techniques such as data management models, data models, etc. Examples of data modeling techniques are:

- IDEF
- Object Role Modeling

3. Create Architecture Model(s)

   i. For each viewpoint, create the model for the specific view required, using the selected tool or method.

   Examples of logical data models are:

   - The C4ISR Architecture Framework Logical Data Model
   - ARTS Data Model for the Retail industry
   - POSC Data Model for the Petrotechnical industry

   ii. Assure that all stakeholder concerns are covered. If they are not, create new models to address concerns not covered, or augment existing models (see above). Model the following:

   a. Business data model (entities, attributes, and relationships)

   Draw entity-relationship diagrams to illustrate views of the Data Architecture to address the concerns of stakeholders.

   b. Logical data model (logical views of the actual data of interest)

   c. Data management process models, including:
   - Data dissemination view
   - Data lifecycle view
   - Data security view
   - Data model management view

   d. Relate data entities to business functions in the Business Architecture, indicating which of the CRUD operations (Create, Reference, Update, and Delete) are performed by which functions.

   - Relate each lowest-level business function in the Business Architecture to the set of data entities, indicating which of the CRUD operations (Create, Reference, Update, and Delete) are performed by the function concerned.

- Generate entity-business function matrices tabulating all the relationships.
- Review and validate the entity-business function matrices, checking that each entity is created by at least one function, and referenced or updated by at least one other function.
- Time permitting, relate entities to the application systems described in the Baseline Applications Architecture Description.

  iii. Ensure that all information requirements in the Business Architecture are met.

  iv. Perform trade-off analysis to resolve conflicts (if any) among the different views.

  One method of doing this is CMU/SEI's Architecture Trade-off Analysis (ATA) Method (refer to *www.sei.cmu.edu/ata/ata_method.html*).

  v. Validate that the models support the principles, objectives, and constraints.

  vi. Note changes to the viewpoint represented in the selected models from the Architecture Continuum, and document.

  vii. Test architecture models for completeness against requirements.

4. Select Data Architecture Building Blocks (e.g., metamodels)

   i. Identify required building blocks and check against existing library of building blocks, re-using as appropriate.

   ii. Where necessary, define new Data Architecture Building Blocks.

5. Conduct Formal Checkpoint Review of Architecture Model and Building Blocks with Stakeholders

   Review the entity-business function matrices generated in Step 3, and the Business Architecture generated in Phase B.

6. Review Qualitative Criteria (e.g., performance, reliability, security, integrity)

   Review the qualitative criteria, providing as many measurable criteria as possible (e.g., costs, minimum tolerable data losses, maximum data volumes at peak times, etc.). Use to specify required service levels for data services (for example, via formal Service Level Agreements (SLAs)).

   The goal here is to guide the Applications and Technology Architecture efforts as to the qualities required in the applications, and the underlying technology, that manage and process the data.

7. Complete Data Architecture

   i. Select standards for each of the Architecture Building Blocks, re-using as much as possible from the reference models selected from the Architecture Continuum.

   ii. Fully document each Architecture Building Block.

   iii. Final cross-check of overall architecture against business requirements. Document rationale for building block decisions in architecture document.

   iv. Document final requirements traceability report.

v. Document final mapping of the architecture within the Architecture Continuum. From the selected Architecture Building Blocks, identify those that might be re-used, and publish via the architecture repository.

vi. Document rationale for building block decisions in architecture document.

vii. Prepare Data Architecture Report. Generate the Data Architecture document, comprising some or all of:
- Business data model
- Logical data model
- Data management process model
- Data entity/business function matrix
- Data interoperability requirements (e.g., XML schema, security policies)

If appropriate, use reports and/or graphics generated by modeling tools to demonstrate key views of the architecture. Route the Data Architecture document for review by relevant stakeholders, and incorporate feedback.

8. Conduct Checkpoint/Impact Analysis

Check the original motivation for the architecture project and the Statement of Architecture Work against the proposed Data Architecture. Conduct an Impact Analysis, to:

i. Identify any areas where the Business Architecture (e.g., business practices) may need to change to cater for changes in the Data Architecture (for example, changes to forms or procedures, application systems, or database systems).

If the impact is significant, this may warrant the Business Architecture being revisited.

ii. Identify any areas where the Applications Architecture (if generated at this point) may need to change to cater for changes in the Data Architecture (or to identify constraints on the Applications Architecture about to be designed).

If the impact is significant, this may warrant the Applications Architecture being revisited, if already developed in this cycle.

iii. Identify any constraints on the Technology Architecture about to be designed.

iv. Refine the proposed Data Architecture only if necessary.

9. Perform Gap Analysis (see Approach) and Create Report

i. Create gap matrix as described above.

ii. Identify building blocks to be carried over, classifying as either changed or unchanged.

iii. Identify eliminated building blocks.

iv. Identify new building blocks.

v. Identify gaps and classify as those that should be defined and those inherited.

8.5 Outputs

The outputs of this phase are:

- Statement of Architecture Work (Major Output Descriptions), updated if necessary
- Baseline Data Architecture, Version 1.0, if appropriate
- Validated data principles (Data Principles), or new data principles (if generated here)
- Target Data Architecture, Version 1.0
    - Business data model
    - Logical data model
    - Data management process models
    - Data entity/business function matrix
    - Data interoperability requirements
- Viewpoints addressing key stakeholder concerns
- Views corresponding to the selected viewpoints; for example:
    - Data dissemination view
    - Data lifecycle view
    - Data security view
    - Data model management view
- Gap analysis results
- Relevant technical requirements that will apply to this evolution of the architecture development cycle
- Data Architecture Report, summarizing what was done and the key findings
- Impact Analysis
    - Areas where the Business Architecture may need to change to cater for changes in the Data Architecture
    - Identify any areas where the Applications Architecture (if generated at this point) may need to change to cater for changes in the Data Architecture
    - Constraints on the Technology Architecture about to be designed
- Updated business requirements, if appropriate

Chapter 9:
Phase C - Information Systems Architectures - Applications Architecture

This chapter describes the Applications Architecture part of Phase C.

9.1 Objective

The objective here is to define the major kinds of application system necessary to process the data and support the business.

It is important to note that this effort is not concerned with applications systems design. The goal is to define what kinds of application systems are relevant to the enterprise, and what those applications need to do in order to manage data and to present information to the human and computer actors in the enterprise.

The applications are not described as computer systems, but as logical groups of capabilities that manage the data objects in the Data Architecture and support the business functions in the Business Architecture. The applications and their capabilities are defined without reference to particular technologies. The applications are stable and relatively unchanging over time, whereas the technology used to implement them will change over time, based on the technologies currently available and changing business needs.

9.2 Approach

9.2.1 Enterprise Continuum

As part of this phase, the architecture team will need to consider what relevant Applications Architecture resources are available in the Enterprise Continuum.

In particular:

- Generic business models relevant to your organization's industry " vertical" sector; for example:
    - The TeleManagement Forum (TMF - www.tmforum.org) has developed detailed applications models relevant to the Telecommunications industry.
    - The Object Management Group (OMG - www.omg.org) has a number of vertical Domain Task Forces developing software models relevant to specific vertical domains such as Healthcare, Transportation, Finance, etc.
- Application models relevant to common high-level business functions, such as electronic commerce, supply chain management, etc.

The Open Group has a Reference Model for Integrated Information Infrastructure (III-RM; see Integrated Information Infrastructure Reference Model) that focuses on the application-level components and services necessary to provide an integrated information infrastructure.

In addition, the ebXML initiative (refer to *www.ebxml.org*) aims to provide an open, XML-based infrastructure enabling global use of electronic business information in an interoperable, secure, and consistent manner. UML is used for modeling aspects and XML for syntax aspects. The initiative was formed as a joint venture by the UN/CEFACT community and the OASIS Consortium, with ANSI X.12 also fully participating.

9.2.2 Gap Analysis

A key step in validating an architecture is to consider what may have been forgotten. The architecture must support all of the essential information processing needs of the organization. The most critical source of gaps that should be considered is stakeholder concerns that have not been addressed in architectural work.

Gap analysis highlights shortfalls in applications services and/or applications components that have been accidentally left out, deliberately eliminated, or are yet to be defined. Gap Analysis Matrix in Phase D illustrates an example of a gap analysis matrix. The suggested steps are as follows:

1. Draw up a matrix with all the applications in the Baseline Applications Architecture on the vertical axis, and all the applications in the Target Applications Architecture on the horizontal axis.
2. Add to the Baseline Architecture axis a final row labeled "New Applications", and to the Target Architecture axis a final column labeled "Eliminated Applications".
3. Where an application exists in both the Baseline and Target Architectures, record this fact with "Retained" at the intersecting cell.
4. Where an application in the Baseline Architecture is missing in the Target Architecture, the Baseline and Target Architectures must be reviewed.
   - If the current application was correctly eliminated, mark it as such in the appropriate "Eliminated Applications" cell.
   - If the current application is to be replaced, wholly or partly, by one or more applications in the Target Architecture, make a note to this effect in the corresponding intersecting cell(s).
   - If the current application was unintentionally eliminated in the Target Architecture, note this fact in the appropriate "Eliminated Applications" cell. The omission will need to be addressed in an iteration of the Target Applications Architecture design.
5. Where an application in the Target Applications Architecture cannot be found in the Baseline Architecture, mark it at the intersection with the "New" row, as a gap that needs to filled, either by developing or procuring the application.

6. When the exercise is complete, anything under "Eliminated Applications" or "New Applications" is a potential gap, which should either be explained as correctly eliminated, or marked as to be addressed, either by reinstating in the Target Architecture, or by developing/procuring the application.
7. Check that the applications gap analysis is complete.

9.3 Inputs

Inputs to this phase are:

- Application principles (Application Principles), if existing
- Request for Architecture Work (Request for Architecture Work)
- Statement of Architecture Work (Major Output Descriptions)
- Architecture Vision (Business Scenario/Architecture Vision)
- Relevant technical requirements that will apply to this phase
- Gap analysis results (from Business Architecture)
- Baseline Business Architecture, Version 1.0 (detailed), if appropriate
- Target Business Architecture (Business Architecture), Version 1.0 (detailed)
- Re-usable building blocks, from organization's Enterprise Continuum (Introduction to the Enterprise Continuum), if available
- Baseline Applications Architecture, Version 0.1, if appropriate and if available
- Target Applications Architecture, Version 0.1, if available

9.4 Steps

1. Develop Baseline Applications Architecture Description

    Develop a Baseline Description of the existing Applications Architecture, to the extent necessary to support the Target Applications Architecture. The scope and level of detail to be defined will depend on the extent to which existing application components are likely to be carried over into the Target Applications Architecture, and on whether existing architectural descriptions exist, as described in Approach. Define for each application:

    - Name (short and long)
    - Who maintains
    - Owner(s)/business unit(s) responsible for requirements
    - Other users
    - Plain language description of what the application does (not how it does it)
    - Status (planned, operational, obsolete)

- Business functions supported
- Organizational units supported
- Hardware/software platform(s) on which it runs
- Networks used
- Precedent and successor applications

To the extent possible, identify the relevant Applications Architecture building blocks, drawing on the Architecture Continuum.

2. Review and Validate Principles, Reference Models, Viewpoints, and Tools
    i. Review and Validate Principles, Reference Models, Viewpoints, and Tools.

       These will normally form part of an overarching set of architecture principles. Guidelines for developing and applying principles, and a sample set of application principles, are given in Part IV: Resource Base, Architecture Principles.

    ii. Select relevant Applications Architecture resources (reference models, patterns, etc.) from the Architecture Continuum, on the basis of the business drivers, and the stakeholders and concerns.

    iii. Select relevant Applications Architecture viewpoints (for example, stakeholders of the applications - viewpoints relevant to functional and individual users of applications, Software Engineering view, Application-to-Application Communication view, Software Distribution view, Enterprise Manageability view, etc.); i.e., those that will enable the architect to demonstrate how the stakeholder concerns are being addressed in the Applications Architecture.

    iv. Identify appropriate tools and techniques to be used for capture, modeling, and analysis, in association with the selected viewpoints. Depending on the degree of sophistication warranted, these may comprise simple documents or spreadsheets, or more sophisticated modeling tools and techniques.

       Consider using platform-independent descriptions of business logic. For example, the OMG's Model-Driven Architecture (MDA) offers an approach to modeling Applications Architectures that preserves the business logic from changes to the underlying platform and implementation technology.

3. Create Architecture Model(s)
    i. For each viewpoint, create the model for the specific view required, using the selected tool or method. Examples of applications models are:
       - The TeleManagement Forum (TMF - www.tmforum.org) has developed detailed applications models relevant to the Telecommunications industry.
       - The Object Management Group (OMG - www.omg.org) has a number of vertical Domain Task Forces developing software models relevant to specific vertical domains such as Healthcare, Transportation, Finance, etc.

    ii. Assure that all stakeholder concerns are covered. If they are not, create new models to address concerns not covered, or augment existing models (see above). Model at least the following:

- Common Applications Services view - both those being consumed, and those being produced for others to consume.
- Applications Interoperability view, assumptions, dependencies, and standards (an example is the LISI Interoperability Model - refer to *www.c3i.osd.mil/org/cio/i3/lisirpt.pdf*). Also, The Open Group has a Reference Model for Integrated Information Infrastructure (III-RM; see Integrated Information Infrastructure Reference Model) that can be used as a basis for this.

iii. Relate the application systems to the business functions in the Business Architecture.
   a. For each application, identify each lowest-level business function that it supports in the Business Architecture.
   b. Generate application-business function matrices tabulating all the relationships.
   c. Review and validate the application-business function matrices. In cases where a business function is supported by more than one application, check for any unnecessary duplication of functionality (and if found, eliminate it by redefining the applications concerned).
   d. Identify any business functions not supported by an application, and rationalize: either provide application support by amending or updating the set of application definitions, iterating Steps 1 to 3; or else document the reason why no application support is warranted.
   e. Use the application-business function matrices generated above, and the business function-to-organizational-unit mappings (business functions cross-linked to the organizational units that perform them) contained in the Business Architecture, to relate the application systems to the organizational units that they support.

iv. Ensure that all information requirements in the Business Architecture are met.

v. Perform trade-off analysis to resolve conflicts (if any) among the different views.

   One method of doing this is CMU/SEI's Architecture Trade-off Analysis (ATA) Method (refer to *www.sei.cmu.edu/ata/ata_method.html*).

vi. Validate that the models support the principles, objectives, and constraints.

vii. Note changes to the viewpoint represented in the selected models from the Architecture Continuum, and document.

viii. Test architecture models for completeness against requirements.

4. Identify Candidate Application Systems

   i. Review the re-usable Architecture Building Blocks and re-usable Solution Building Blocks from the enterprise's Architecture Continuum, the business scenario description, and the Baseline Description, and list all the potential application systems.

ii. If available, review the entity-to-business-function matrices from the Data Architecture, and identify potential applications to perform the required data management functions, and/or to automate particular business functions.

iii. Even if a complete Data Architecture is not available, review whatever lists of data exist.

iv. Develop a user location/applications matrix.

v. Consider other potential application systems based on innovative use of new developments in technology.

vi. Merge all lists into a single, de-duplicated list of candidate application systems, including for each a brief description of business function(s) supported and data/information managed.

vii. Create application definitions for all candidate application systems. For each application:

   a. Assign a unique name and identifier.
   b. Write a brief description of what the application does (not how it works).
   c. Write a brief description of the business benefits arising from the application.
   d. Simplify complicated applications by decomposing them into two or more applications.
   e. Ensure that the set of application definitions is internally consistent, by removing duplicate functionality as far as possible, and combining similar applications into one.
   f. Identify technology requirements and candidate technology building blocks, where this affects the applications design, including re-usable Solution Building Blocks from the Architecture Continuum, and external software packages.
   g. Identify any critical infrastructure dependencies (e.g., operating system and network services required).
   h. Identify any critical application dependencies, and minimize as far as possible.
   i. Time permitting, relate the applications to the files and databases described in the Baseline Description, and/or to the data entities defined in the Data Architecture (if available).
   j. Time permitting, draw simple diagrams to illustrate views of the Applications Architecture relevant to different stakeholders.

5. Conduct Formal Checkpoint Review of the Architecture Model and Building Blocks with Stakeholders.

   Review the application-business function matrices generated in Step 3, and the Business Architecture generated in Phase B.

6. Review Qualitative Criteria (e.g., security, availability, performance, costs)

   Review the qualitative criteria, providing as many measurable criteria as possible (e.g., privacy/confidentiality, reliability, minimum tolerable outages, cycle requirements and transaction volume requirements at peak and mean times, numbers and locations of users, etc.). Use to specify required service levels for applications services (for example, via formal Service Level Agreements (SLAs)).

The goal here is to guide the Data and Technology Architecture efforts as to the qualities required in the data, and the underlying technology, that support and are processed by the application.

7. Complete Applications Architecture
   i. Select standards for each of the Architecture Building Blocks, re-using as much as possible from the reference models selected from the Architecture Continuum.
   ii. Fully document each Architecture Building Block.
   iii. Final cross-check of overall architecture against business requirements. Document rationale for building block decisions in architecture document.
   iv. Document final requirements traceability report.
   v. Document final mapping of the architecture within the Architecture Continuum. From the selected Architecture Building Blocks, identify those that might be re-used, and publish via the architecture repository.
   vi. Document rationale for building block decisions in architecture document.
   vii. Prepare Applications Architecture Report. Generate the Applications Architecture document. If appropriate, use reports and/or graphics generated by modeling tools to demonstrate key views of the architecture. Route the Applications Architecture document for review by relevant stakeholders, and incorporate feedback.
   viii. Checkpoint/Impact Analysis: Check the original motivation for the architecture project and the Statement of Architecture Work against the proposed Applications Architecture. Conduct an Impact Analysis to:
      a. Identify any areas where the Business Architecture (e.g., business practices) may need to change to cater for changes in the Applications Architecture (for example, changes to forms or procedures, application systems, or database systems).

         If the impact is significant, this may warrant the Business Architecture being revisited.

      b. Identify any areas where the Data Architecture (if generated at this point) may need to change to cater for changes in the Applications Architecture (or to identify constraints on the Data Architecture, if about to be designed).

         If the impact is significant, this may warrant the Data Architecture being revisited, if already developed in this cycle).

      c. Identify any constraints on the Technology Architecture about to be designed.
      d. Refine the proposed Applications Architecture only if necessary.

8. Perform Gap Analysis (see Approach) and Create Report
   i. Create gap matrix as described above.
   ii. Identify building blocks to be carried over, classifying as either changed or unchanged.
   iii. Identify eliminated building blocks.
   iv. Identify new building blocks.
   v. Identify gaps and classify as those that should be developed and those inherited.

9.5 Outputs

The outputs of this phase are:

- Statement of Architecture Work (updated if necessary)
- Baseline Applications Architecture, Version 1.0, if appropriate
- Validated application principles, or new application principles (if generated here)
- Target Applications Architecture, Version 1.0
    - Process Systems Model
    - Place Systems Model
    - Time Systems Model
    - People Systems Model
    - Applications interoperability requirements
- Viewpoints addressing key stakeholder concerns
- Views corresponding to the selected viewpoints; for example:
    - Common Applications Services view
    - Applications Interoperability view
    - Applications/Information view
    - Applications/User Locations view
- Gap analysis results
- Applications Architecture Report, summarizing what was done and the key findings
- Impact Analysis
    - Areas where the Business Architecture may need to change to cater for changes in the Applications Architecture
    - Identify any areas where the Data Architecture (if generated at this point) may need to change to cater for changes in the Applications Architecture
    - Constraints on the Technology Architecture about to be designed
- Updated business requirements, if appropriate

Chapter 10: Phase D - Technology Architecture

This chapter describes the development of a Technology Architecture.

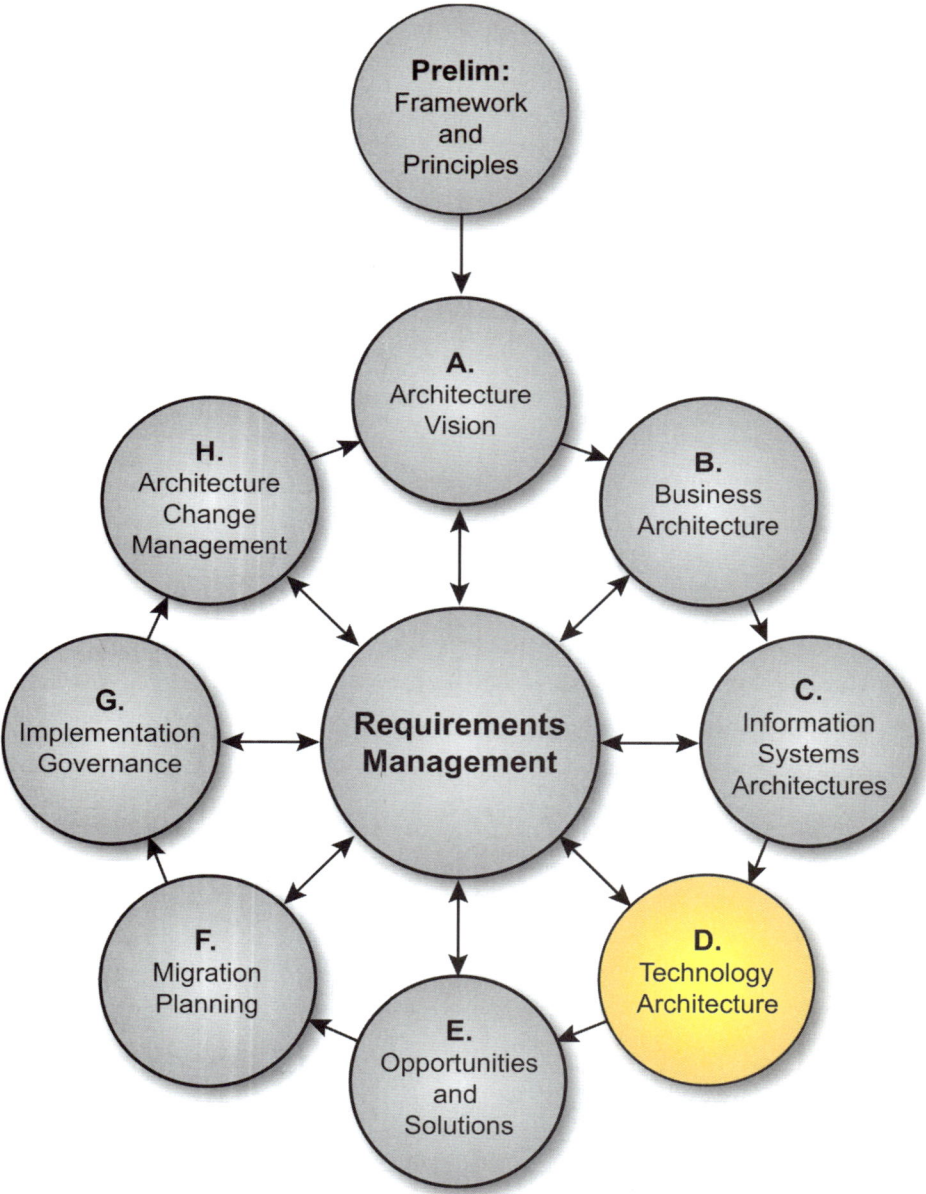

Figure 10.1: Phase D: Technology Architecture

The detailed description of the process to develop the Target Technology Architecture is given in Target Technology Architecture - Detail.

10.1 Objective

The objective of Phase D is to develop a Technology Architecture that will form the basis of the following implementation work.

10.2 Approach

10.2.1 General

Detailed guidelines for Phase D, including Inputs, Steps, and Outputs, are given in Target Technology Architecture - Detail.

10.2.2 Architecture Continuum

As part of Phase D, the architecture team will need to consider what relevant Technology Architecture resources are available in the Architecture Continuum.

In particular:

- The TOGAF Technical Reference Model (TRM)
- Generic technology models relevant to the organization's industry "vertical" sector.

    For example, the TeleManagement Forum (TMF - www.tmforum.org) has developed detailed technology models relevant to the Telecommunications industry.

- Technology models relevant to Common Systems Architectures.

    For example, The Open Group has a Reference Model for Integrated Information Infrastructure (III-RM: see Integrated Information Infrastructure Reference Model) that focuses on the application-level components and underlying services necessary to provide an integrated information infrastructure.

10.3 Inputs

Inputs to Phase D are:

- Technology principles (Technology Principles), if existing
- Request for Architecture Work (Request for Architecture Work)
- Statement of Architecture Work (Major Output Descriptions)

- Architecture Vision (Business Scenario/Architecture Vision)
- Baseline Technology Architecture, Version 0.1 (from Phase A)
- Target Technology Architecture, Version 0.1 (from Phase A)
- Relevant technical requirements from previous phases
- Gap analysis results (from Data Architecture)
- Gap analysis results (from Applications Architecture)
- Baseline Business Architecture, Version 1.0 (detailed), if appropriate
- Baseline Data Architecture, Version 1.0, if appropriate
- Baseline Applications Architecture, Version 1.0, if appropriate
- Target Business Architecture (Business Architecture), Version 1.0 (detailed)
- Re-usable building blocks, from organization's Enterprise Continuum (Introduction to the Enterprise Continuum), if available
- Target Data Architecture, Version 1.0
- Target Applications Architecture, Version 1.0

10.4 Steps

Key steps in Phase D include:

1. Develop Baseline Technology Architecture Description:
    i. Review Baseline Business Architecture, Baseline Data Architecture, and Baseline Applications Architecture, to the degree necessary to inform decisions and subsequent work.
    ii. Develop a Baseline Description of the existing Technology Architecture, to the extent necessary to support the Target Technology Architecture. The scope and level of detail to be defined will depend on the extent to which existing technology components are likely to be carried over into the Target Technology Architecture, and on whether existing architectural descriptions exist, as described in Approach. Define for each major hardware or software platform type:
        - Name (short and long)
        - Physical location
        - Owner(s)
        - Other users
        - Plain language description of what the hardware/software platform is and what it is used for
        - Business functions supported
        - Organizational units supported

- Networks accessed
- Applications and data supported
- System inter-dependencies (for example, fall-back configurations)

iii. To the extent possible, identify and document candidate Technology Architecture Building Blocks (potential re-usable assets).

iv. Draft the Technology Architecture Baseline report: summarize key findings and conclusions, developing suitable graphics and schematics to illustrate baseline configuration(s). If warranted, provide individual Baseline Technology Architecture Descriptions as Annexes.

2. Develope Target Technology Architecture; see detailed steps.

Detailed activities for this step, including Inputs, Activities, and Outputs, are given in Target Technology Architecture - Detail.

10.5 Outputs

The outputs of Phase D are:

- Statement of Architecture Work (Major Output Descriptions), updated if necessary
- Baseline Technology Architecture, Version 1.0, if appropriate
- Validated technology principles, or new technology principles (if generated here)
- Technology Architecture Report, summarizing what was done and the key findings
- Target Technology Architecture (Technology Architecture), Version 1.0
- Technology Architecture, gap report
- Viewpoints addressing key stakeholder concerns
- Views corresponding to the selected viewpoints

10.6 Target Technology Architecture - Detail

10.6.1 Introduction

This is the detailed description of the process to develop the Target Technology Architecture.

10.6.2 Overview

An organization creating or adapting a Technology Architecture may already mandate the use of a list of approved suppliers/products for that organization. The list will be an input to the definition of the organization-specific architecture framework. The architectures can then be used as procurement tools to govern the future growth and development of the organization's IT infrastructure. The key steps are expanded in the following subsections. Note: the order of the following steps should be adapted to the situation as described in Introducton to the ADM (Chapter 3).

10.6.3 Step 1

Step 1 is to create a Baseline Description in the TOGAF format.

10.6.3.1 Objective

The objective of this step is to convert the description of the existing system into services terminology using the organization's Foundation Architecture (e.g., the TOGAF Foundation Architecture's TRM). The rationale behind this is to structure the existing system description in a way which makes it compatible with the breakdown of standards and the descriptions used within your Foundation Architecture.

10.6.3.2 Approach

This step is intended to facilitate moving from product documentation to a service-oriented description. The step will aid in specifying standards for the Target Architecture in Step 4. An additional step, Step 3, oriented to defining building blocks, provides the means to cross-check the architectural definition process in the form of implementation-related decisions.

Additionally, this step captures relevant parts of the existing architecture (using the scope definition established in Phase A) as candidates for re-usable building blocks, along with inhibitors to meeting business requirements using the existing system. The existing architecture is assessed against the Business Architecture, identifying the key inhibitors and opportunities for re-use. Finally, the existing architecture assessment ends with the capture of implied or explicit architecture principles that should be carried forward and imposed on this architecture exercise.

Begin by converting the description of the existing environment into the terms of your organization's Foundation Architecture (e.g., the TOGAF Foundation Architecture's TRM). This will allow the team developing the architecture to gain experience with the model and to understand its component parts. The team may be able to take advantage of a previous architectural definition, but it is assumed that some adaptation may be required to match the architectural definition techniques described as part of this process. Another important task is to set down a list of key questions which can be used later in the development process to measure the effectiveness of the new architecture.

A key process in the creation of a broad architectural model of the target system is the conceptualization of Architectural Building Blocks (ABBs). ABBs are not intended to be solutions, but depictions of how the architecture might be looked on in implementable terms. Their functionality is clearly defined, but without the detail introduced by specific products. The method of defining ABBs, along with some general guidelines for their use in creating an architectural model, is described in Part IV: Resource Base, Building Blocks and the ADM, and illustrated in detail in Building Blocks.

It is recommended that Architecture Building Blocks be documented (e.g., with an architecture description language) and stored (e.g., in a repository or information base), in order to maximize re-use potential.

Applying the ABB method introduces application space into the architectural process. This is the means of linking services, which address functionality that must be considered on an enterprise basis, with applications, which may or may not address global functionality. The building blocks example in Part IV: Resource Base, Building Blocks, provides insight into both application-specific and more global considerations in defining building blocks in order to illustrate this.

10.6.3.3 Inputs

The inputs to Step 1 are:

- Technology principles (Technology Principles), if existing
- Request for Architecture Work (Request for Architecture Work)
- Statement of Architecture Work (Major Output Descriptions)
- Architecture Vision (Business Scenario/Architecture Vision)
- Baseline Technology Architecture, Version 0.1
- Target Technology Architecture, Version 0 1
- Relevant technical requirements from previous phases
- Gap analysis results (from Data Architecture)
- Gap analysis results (from Applications Architecture)
- Baseline Business Architecture, Version 1.0 (detailed), if appropriate
- Baseline Data Architecture, Version 1.0, if appropriate
- Baseline Applicatons Architecture, Version 1.0, if appropriate
- Target Business Architecture (Business Architecture), Version 1.0 (detailed)
- Re-usable building blocks, from organization's Enterprise Continuum (Introduction to the Enterprise Continuum), if available
- Target Data Architecture, Version 1.0
- Target Applications Architecture, Version 1.0
- Re-usable Architecture Building Blocks, from organization's Architecture Continuum (The Architecture Continuum), if available
- Re-usable Solution Building Blocks, from organization's Solutions Continuum (The Solutions Continuum), if available

10.6.3.4 Activities

Key activities in Step 1 include:

1. Collect data on current system
2. Document all constraints
3. Review and validate (or generate, if necessary) the set of Technology Architecture principles

    These will normally form part of an overarching set of architecture principles. Guidelines for developing and applying principles, and a sample set of Technology Architecture principles, are given in Part IV: Resource Base, Architecture Principles
4. List distinct functionality
5. Produce affinity groupings of functionality using TOGAF TRM service groupings (or your business' Foundation Architecture)
6. Analyze relationships between groupings
7. Sanity check functionality to assure all of current system is considered
8. Identify interfaces
9. Produce Technology Architecture model
10. Verify Technology Architecture model
11. Document key questions to test merits of Technology Architecture
12. Document criteria for selection of service portfolio architecture

10.6.3.5 Outputs

The outputs of Step 1 are:

- Technology principles (Technology Principles), if not existing
- Technology Architecture (Technology Architecture), Version 0.1:
    - Technology Architecture - constraints
    - Baseline Technology Architecture (Technology Architecture) Version 1.0
    - Technology Architecture - requirements traceability, key questions list
    - Technology Architecture - requirements traceability, criteria for selection of service portfolio
    - Target Technology Architecture, Version 0.2

10.6.4 Step 2

Step 2 is to consider different architecture reference models, viewpoints, and tools.

10.6.4.1 Objective

The objective of this step is to perform an analysis of the Technology Architecture from a number of different concerns (requirements) or viewpoints and to document each relevant viewpoint. The purpose of considering these viewpoints is to ensure that all relevant stakeholder concerns will have been considered in the final Technology Architecture, so ensuring that the target system will meet all the requirements put on it.

10.6.4.2 Approach

The Business Architecture is used to select the most relevant viewpoints for the project. It is important to recognize that in practice it will be rarely possible to reach 100% coverage of stakeholder concerns.

Pertinent viewpoints are created first from the existing system to identify the salient elements of the current systems requirements that the stakeholders confirm must also be satisfied in the target system. A comprehensive set of stakeholder viewpoints must also be created for the target system. The corresponding views of the existing system will be compared with the views of the target system to identify elements of the existing system that are intended for replacement or improvement.

If a set of viewpoints is carefully chosen, it will expose the most important aspects of the existing architecture and the requirements of the target system.

Several different viewpoints may be useful. Architecture viewpoints and views are described in greater detail in Part IV: Resource Base, Developing Architecture Views. The viewpoints presented there should not be considered an exhaustive set, but simply a starting point. In developing a Technology Architecture, it is very likely that some of the viewpoints given there will not be useful, while others not given there will be essential. Again, use the Business Architecture as a guide in selecting the pertinent viewpoints.

10.6.4.3 Inputs

The inputs to Step 2 are:

- Baseline Technology Architecture (Technology Architecture), Version 1.0
- Target Technology Architecture (Technology Architecture), Version 0.2
- Statement of Architecture Work (Major Output Descriptions)
- Target Business Architecture (Business Architecture), Version 1.0
- Target Technology Architecture (Technology Architecture), Version 0.2

10.6.4.4 Activities

Key activities in Step 2 include:

1. Select relevant Technology Architecture resources (reference models, patterns, etc.) from the Architecture Continuum, on the basis of the business drivers, and the stakeholders and concerns.

2. Select relevant Technology Architecture viewpoints; i.e., those that will enable the architect to demonstrate how the stakeholder concerns are being addressed in the Technology Architecture. (See Part IV: Resource Base, Developing Architecture Views for examples).
   - Document the selected viewpoints, if not already documented.
   - Consider using ANSI/IEEE Std 1471-2000 as a guide for documenting a viewpoint.
   - A primary reference model will be the TOGAF TRM. Other reference models will be taken from the Architecture Continuum.
     - Consider developing at least the following views:
     - Networked Computing/Hardware view
     - Communications view
     - Processing view
     - Cost view
     - Standards view
     - Brainstorm and document technical constraints deriving from analysis of the concerns, and ensure they are covered by the viewpoints.

3. Identify appropriate tools and techniques to be used for capture, modeling, and analysis, in association with the selected viewpoints. Depending on the degree of sophistication warranted, these may comprise simple documents or spreadsheets, or more sophisticated modeling tools and techniques.

4. Perform trade-off analysis to resolve conflicts (if any) among the different viewpoints.
   - One method of doing this is CMU/SEI's Architecture Trade-off Analysis (ATA) Method (refer to *www.sei.cmu.edu/ata/ata_method.html*).

10.6.4.5 Outputs

The outputs of Step 2 are:

- Target Technology Architecture (Technology Architecture), Version 0.3
  - Technology Architecture (Technology Architecture) - architecture viewpoints
  - Networked Computing/Hardware view
  - Communications view
  - Processing view
  - Cost view

- Standards view
- Technology Architecture - constraints

10.6.5 Step 3

Step 3 is to create an architectural model of building blocks.

10.6.5.1 Objective

The reason for selecting viewpoints in Step 2 is to be able to develop views for each of those viewpoints in Step 3. The architectural model created in Step 3 comprises those several views.

The objective of this step is to broadly determine how the services required in the target system will be grouped after considering all pertinent viewpoints of the architecture's use. This differs from Step 1 in that Step 1 dealt mainly with the required functionality of the system, whereas here we are considering many viewpoints that are not expressed explicitly as required functionality.

The rationale behind this is to enable the services required within the system to be selected during the next step, through the creation of an architecture model that clearly depicts the required services.

10.6.5.2 Approach

At Step 3, the purpose of examining different viewpoints in Step 2 becomes clear. The constraints defined and the unique system insights gained through an examination of the viewpoints pertinent to the current system and the target system can be used to validate the ability of the broad architectural model to accommodate the system requirements.

The broad architectural model starts as a TOGAF TRM-based model (or a model based upon the organization's Foundation Architecture), derived from the service-to-function mapping carried out as part of the service examination in Step 1. An architecture based exactly on the TOGAF TRM may not be able to accommodate the stakeholder needs of all organizations. If the examination of different viewpoints identifies architectural features that cannot be expressed in terms of the TOGAF TRM, changes and amendments to the TOGAF TRM should be made to create an organization-specific TRM.

Once the Baseline Description has been established and appropriate views described, it is possible to make decisions about how the various elements of system functionality should be implemented. This should only be in broad terms, to a level of detail which establishes how the major business functions will be implemented; for example, as a transaction processing application or using a client/server model.

Therefore this step defines the future model of building blocks (e.g., collections of functions and services generated from previous steps). It is here that re-use of building blocks from your business' Architecture Continuum is examined carefully, assuring that maximum re-use of existing material is realized.

Once the architecture model of building blocks is created, the model must be tested for coverage and completeness of the required technical functions and services. For each building block decision, completely follow through its impact and note the rationale for decisions, including the rationale for decisions not to do something.

10.6.5.3 Inputs

The inputs to Step 3 are:

- Target Business Architecture (Business Architecture), Version 1.0
- Target Technology Architecture (Technology Architecture), Version 0.3
    - Technology Architecture - viewpoints
    - Technology Architecture - constraints
- Re-usable Architecture Building Blocks, from organization's Architecture Continuum (The Architecture Continuum), if available

10.6.5.4 Activities

Key activities in Step 3 include:

1. To the extent possible, identify the relevant Technology Architecture building blocks, drawing on the Architecture Continuum.
2. For each viewpoint, create the model for the specific view required, using the selected tool or method. Consider developing at least the following views:
    - Networked Computing/Hardware view
    - Communications view
    - Processing view
    - Cost view
    - Standards view
3. Assure that all stakeholder concerns are covered. If they are not, create new models to address concerns not covered, or augment existing models.
4. Ensure that all information requirements in the Business Architecture, Data Architecture, and Applications Architecture are met.
5. Perform trade-off analysis to resolve conflicts (if any) among the different views.

    One method of doing this is CMU/SEI's Architecture Trade-off Analysis (ATA) Method (refer to *www.sei.cmu.edu/ata/ata_method.html*).
6. Validate that the models support the principles, objectives, and constraints.
7. Note changes to the viewpoint represented in the selected models from the Architecture Continuum, and document.
8. Identify Solution Building Blocks that would be used to implement the system, and create a model of building blocks.

9. Check building blocks against existing library of building blocks and re-use as appropriate.
10. Test architecture models for completeness against requirements.
11. Document rationale for building block decisions in the architecture document.

10.6.5.5 Outputs

The outputs of Step 3 are:

- Target Technology Architecture (Technology Architecture), Version 0.4
    - Technology Architecture Model
        - Networked Computing/Hardware view
        - Communications view
        - Processing view
        - Cost view
        - Standards view
    - Technology Architecture - change requests and/or extensions or amendments to be incorporated in an organization-specific Architecture Continuum

10.6.6 Step 4

Step 4 is to select the services portfolio required per building block.

10.6.6.1 Objective

The objective of this step is to select services portfolios for each building block generated in Step 3.

10.6.6.2 Approach

The services portfolios are combinations of basic services from the service categories in the TOGAF TRM that do not conflict. The combination of services are again tested to ensure support for the applications. This is a pre-requisite to the later step of defining the architecture fully.

The constraints output from Step 2 can provide more detailed information about:

- Requirements for organization-specific elements or pre-existing decisions (as applicable)
- Pre-existing and unchanging organizational elements (as applicable)
- Inherited external environment constraints

Where requirements demand definition of specialized services that are not identified in TOGAF, consideration should be given to how these might be replaced if standardized services become available in the future.

For each Architecture Building Block (ABB), build up a service description portfolio as a set of non-conflicting services. The set of services must be tested to ensure that the functionality provided meets application requirements.

10.6.6.3 Inputs

The inputs to Step 4 are:

- Target Business Architecture (Business Architecture), Version 1.0
- Target Technology Architecture (Technology Architecture), Version 0.4
- Technical Reference Model (TRM)
- Standards Information Base (SIB)

10.6.6.4 Activities

Key activities in Step 4 include:

1. Produce affinity grouping of services
2. Cross-check affinity groups against needs
3. Document service description portfolio for each ABB, cross-checking for non-conflicting services
4. Document change requests to architectures in the Architecture Continuum

10.6.6.5 Outputs

The outputs of Step 4 are:

- Target Technology Architecture (Technology Architecture), Version 0.5:
  - Technology Architecture - target services (a description of the service portfolios required also known as an Organization-Specific Framework)
  - Technology Architecture - change requests and/or extensions or amendments to be incorporated in an organization-specific Architecture Continuum

10.6.7 Step 5

Step 5 is to confirm that the business goals and objectives are met.

10.6.7.1 Objective

The objective of this step is to clarify and check the business goals and other objectives of implementing the architecture. This is required as a cross-check that the Technology Architecture meets these objectives.

10.6.7.2 Approach

The key question list is used to pose questions against the architecture model and service description portfolio to test its merit and completeness.

10.6.7.3 Inputs

The inputs to Step 5 are:

- Target Business Architecture (Business Architecture), Version 1.0 (business goals)
- Target Technology Architecture (Technology Architecture), Version 0.5

10.6.7.4 Activities

Key activities in Step 5 include:

1. Conduct a formal checkpoint review of the architecture model and building blocks with stakeholders, validating that business goals are met. Utilizing the key questions list, ensure that the architecture addresses each question.
2. Document findings.

10.6.7.5 Outputs

The outputs of Step 5 are:

- Target Technology Architecture (Technology Architecture), Version 0.6
    - Technology Architecture - requirements traceability (business objectives criteria)

10.6.8 Step 6

Step 6 is to determine criteria for specification selection.

10.6.8.1 Objective

The objective of this step is to develop a set of criteria for choosing specifications and portfolios of specifications.

10.6.8.2 Approach

Choosing the right criteria is vital if the final architecture is to meet its objectives. These criteria will depend on the existing system and the overall objectives for the new architecture. The overall objectives should be developed from the organization's business goals, so it is hard to give specific advice here, but some example objectives are listed in Part IV: Resource Base, Business Scenarios.

Here are some example criteria, selected by a large government organization with the intention of building a stable and widely applicable architecture:

"A standard or specification:

- Must meet the organization's requirements
- Must meet legal requirements
- Should be a publicly available specification
- Should have been developed by a process which sought a high level of consensus from a

wide variety of sources
- Should be supported by a range of readily available products
- Should be complete
- Should be well understood, mature technology
- Should be testable, so that components or products can be checked for conformance
- Should support internationalization
- Should have no serious implications for ongoing support of legacy systems
- Should be stable
- Should be in wide use
- Should have few, if any problems or limitations"

A high level of consensus is often considered the most important factor by large organizations because standards and specifications chosen have to accommodate a wide range of user needs. For example, in determining the level of consensus for standards in their architecture, the Application Portability Profile (APP), the US National Institute for Standards and Technology (NIST) prefers to use international standards for the basis of specifications. The process through which these international standards have evolved requires a very high level of consensus. A number of US Federal Information Processing Standards (FIPS) specified in the APP are based on approved international standards. The use of international standards has significant benefits for any organization which works or trades with organizations in other countries.

10.6.8.3 Inputs

The inputs to Step 6 are:

- Target Business Architecture (Business Architecture), Version 1.0
- Target Technology Architecture (Technology Architecture), Version 0.6
- Standards Information Base (SIB)

10.6.8.4 Activities

Key activities in Step 6 include:

1. Brainstorm criteria for choosing specifications and portfolios of specifications relying on previously used criteria for existing system and extrapolating for new architectural elements.
2. Meet with sponsors and present current state to negotiate a continue request from sponsors.

10.6.8.5 Outputs

The outputs of Step 6 are:

- Target Technology Architecture (Technology Architecture), Version 0.7
    - Technology Architecture - requirements traceability (standards selection criteria)

10.6.9 Step 7

Step 7 is to complete the architecture definition.

10.6.9.1 Objective

The objective of this step is to fully specify the Technology Architecture. This is a complex and iterative process in which the selection of building blocks and interfaces has a big impact on how the original requirements are met. See Part IV: Resource Base, Building Blocks for further details.

10.6.9.2 Approach

Completion of the architecture definition may be achieved in two steps, by defining an intermediate Transitional Architecture in addition to the final Target Architecture, if complexity of migration requires it.

The specification of building blocks as a portfolio of services is an evolutionary process:

- The earliest building block definitions start as relatively abstract ones, defined by standards and services that map most easily to the architecture framework. These building blocks are most probably ABBs.
- At this stage a model and a portfolio of services have been established. The next step is to select the set of specifications that provide the services and that can be combined as required to create the building blocks.
- During this final step in the development of building blocks it must be verified that the organization-specific requirements will be met. The development process must include recognition of dependencies and boundaries for functions and should take account of what products are available in the marketplace. There are architectural and related solution-oriented building blocks.
- An example of how this might be expressed can be seen in the building blocks example (Part IV: Resource Base, Building Blocks). Building blocks can be defined at a number of levels matching the degree of integration that best defines the architecture of the system at any stage.
    - Fundamental functionality and attributes - semantic, unambiguous including security capability and manageability
    - Interfaces - chosen set, supplied (APIs, data formats, protocols, hardware interfaces, standards)
    - Dependent building blocks with required functionality and named used interfaces

- Map to business/organizational entities and policies
■ Finally the building blocks become more implementation-specific as Solution Building Blocks (SBBs) and their interfaces become the detailed architecture specification. SBBs are a means to determine how portions of the Target Architecture might be procured, developed, or re-used. The SBBs architecture should have separate elements for developed, re-used, and procured building blocks, each described in terms of their minimum specification.

A full list of standards and specifications recommended by The Open Group can be found in Part III: Enterprise Continuum, Foundation Architecture: Standards Information Base.

10.6.9.3 Inputs

The inputs to Step 7 are:

■ Target Business Architecture (Business Architecture), Version 1.0
■ Target Technology Architecture (Technology Architecture), Version 0.7
■ Re-usable Architecture Building Blocks, from organization's Architecture Continuum (The Architecture Continuum), if available
■ Standards Information Base (SIB)

10.6.9.4 Activities

Key activities in Step 7 include:

1. Ensure clear documentation of all interfaces for each building block (APIs, data formats, protocols, hardware interfaces).
2. Select standards for each of the Architecture Building Blocks, re-using as much as possible from the reference models selected from the Architecture Continuum.
3. Fully document each Architecture Building Block.
4. Final cross-check of overall architecture against business requirements. Document rationale for building block decisions in the architecture document.
5. Document final requirements traceability reports.
6. Document final mapping of the architecture within the Architecture Continuum. From the selected Architecture Building Blocks, identify those that might be re-used, and publish via the architecture repository.
7. Document rationale for building block decisions in the architecture document.
8. Generate the Technology Architecture document.
9. Prepare the Technology Architecture Report. If appropriate, use reports and/or graphics generated by modeling tools to demonstrate key views of the architecture. Route the Technology Architecture document for review by relevant stakeholders, and incorporate feedback.

10. Checkpoint/Impact Analysis: Check the original motivation for the architecture project and the Statement of Architecture Work against the proposed Technology Architecture. Conduct an Impact Analysis, to:

   a. Identify any areas where the Business Architecture (e.g., business practices) may need to change to cater for changes in the Technology Architecture.

   If the impact is significant, this may warrant the Business Architecture being revisited.

   b. Identify any areas where the Data Architecture may need to change to cater for changes in the Technology Architecture.

   If the impact is significant, this may warrant the Data Architecture being revisited.

   c. Identify any areas where the Applications Architecture may need to change to cater for changes in the Technology Architecture.

   If the impact is significant, this may warrant the Applications Architecture being revisited.

   d. Refine the proposed Technology Architecture only if necessary.

10.6.9.5 Outputs

The outputs of Step 7 are:

- Target Technology Architecture (Technology Architecture), Version 0.8
   - Technology Architecture - architecture specification
   - Technology Architecture - requirements traceability
   - Technology Architecture - mapping of the architectures in the Architecture Continuum
   - Technology Architecture Report

10.6.10 Step 8

Step 8 is to conduct a gap analysis.

10.6.10.1 Objective

The objective of this step is to identify areas of the current and target system for which provision has not been made in the Technology Architecture. This is required in order to identify projects to be undertaken as part of the implementation of the target system.

10.6.10.2 Approach

A key step in validating an architecture is to consider what may have been forgotten. The architecture must support all of the essential information processing needs of the organization, as driven by the required applications. The most critical source of gaps that should be considered is stakeholder concerns that have not been addressed in subsequent architectural work.

Gap analysis highlights services and/or functions that have been accidentally left out, deliberately eliminated, or are yet to be developed or procured:

- Draw up a matrix with all the business functions of the current architecture on the vertical axis, and all the business functions of the Baseline Architecture on the horizontal axis. In creating the matrix, it is imperative to use terminology that is accurate and consistent.
- Add to the Baseline Architecture axis a final row labeled "New Services", and to the Target Architecture axis a final column labeled "Eliminated Services".
- Where a function is available in both the Baseline and Target Architectures, record this with "Included" at the intersecting cell.
- Where a function from the Baseline Architecture is missing in the Target Architecture (in the example, "broadcast services" and "shared screen services"), each must be reviewed. If it was correctly eliminated, mark it as such in the appropriate "Eliminated Services" cell. If it was not, you have uncovered an accidental omission in your new architecture that must be addressed by reinstating the function in the next iteration of the design - mark it as such in the appropriate "Eliminated Services" cell.
- Where a function from the Target Architecture cannot be found in the Baseline Architecture (in the example, "mailing list services"), mark it at the intersection with the "New" row, as a gap that needs to be filled, either by developing or procuring the function.

When the exercise is complete, anything under "Eliminated Services" or "New Services" is a gap, which should either be explained as correctly eliminated, or marked as to be addressed by reinstating or developing/procuring the function.

Gap Analysis Matrix shows an example from the Network Services category when functions from the Baseline Architecture are missing from the Target Architecture.

10.6.10.3 Inputs

The inputs to Step 8 are:

- Target Business Architecture (Business Architecture), Version 1.0
- Target Technology Architecture (Technology Architecture), Version 0.8
- Target Data Architecture, Version 1.0
- Technology Applications Architecture, Version 1.0

Target Architecture → / Baseline Architecture ↓	Video Conferencing Services	Enhanced Telephony Services	Mailing List Services	Eliminated Services ↓
Broadcast Services				Intentionally Eliminated
Video Conferencing Services	Included			
Enhanced Telephony Services		Potential Match		
Shared Screen Services				Unintentionally excluded - a gap in target architecture
New →		Gap: Enhanced services to be developed or produced	Gap: to be developed or produced	

Table 10.1 : Gap Analysis Matrix

Chapter 10: Phase D – Technoloby Architecture

10.6.10.4 Activities

Key activities in Step 8 include:

1. Create gap matrix as described above.
2. Identify building blocks to be carried over, classifying as either changed or unchanged.
3. Identify eliminated building blocks.
4. Identify new building blocks.
5. Identify gaps and classify as those that should be developed, those that should be procured, and those inherited.

10.6.10.5 Outputs

The output of Step 8 is:

- Target Technology Architecture (Technology Architecture), Version 1.0:
    - Technology Architecture - gap report

10.6.11 Postscript

The Technology Architecture development process described above includes iterations. Financial and timing constraints should explicitly limit the number of iterations within Steps 1 through 8, and drive to implementation. After that, a new cycle of architecture evolution may ensue.

Choosing the scope of an architecture development cycle carefully will accelerate the payback. In contrast, an excessively large scope is unlikely to lead to successful implementation.

"How do you eat an elephant? - One bite at a time."

Chapter 11: Phase E - Opportunities and Solutions

This chapter is a checkpoint to verify suitability for implementation.

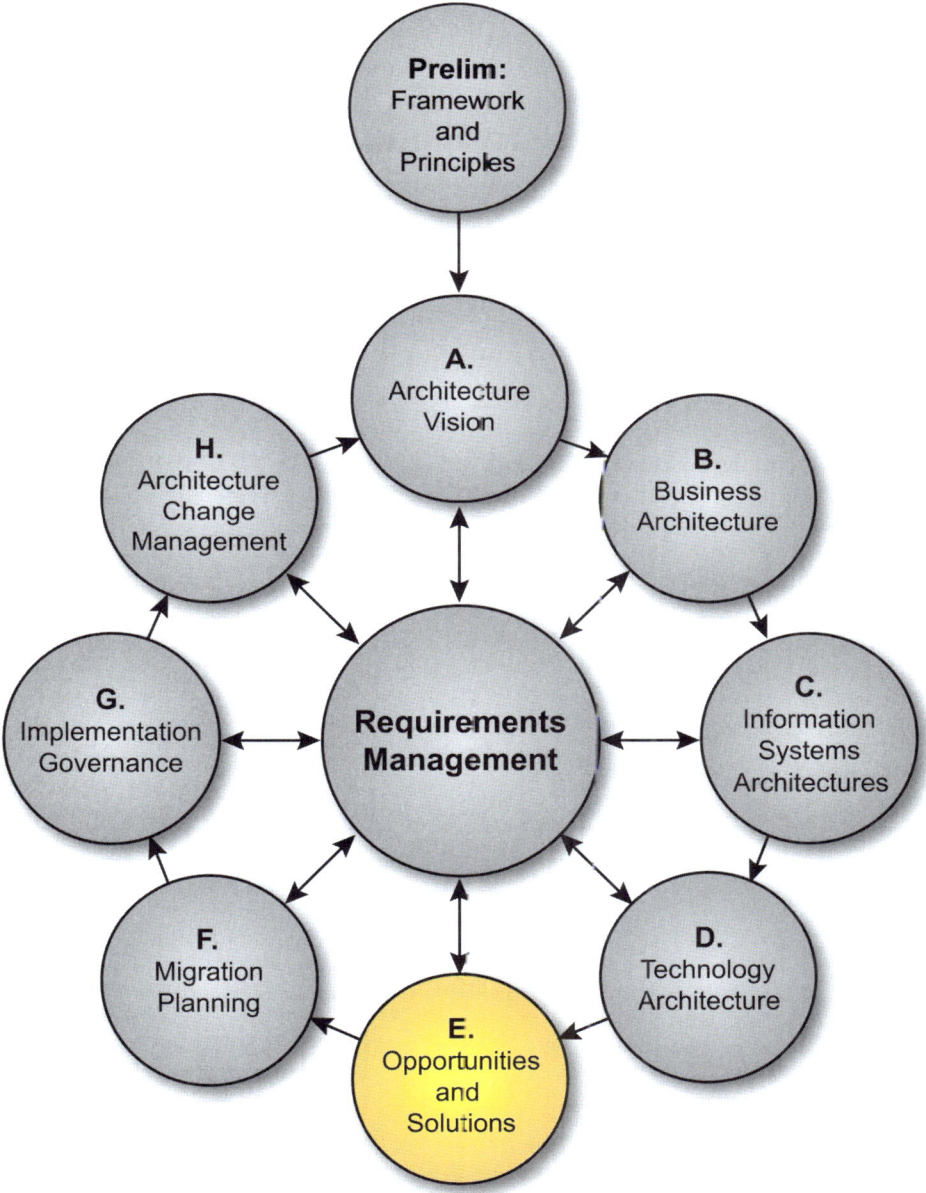

Figure 11.1: Phase E: Opportunities and Solutions

11.1 Objectives

The objectives of Phase E are to:

- Evaluate and select among the implementation options identified in the development of the various Target Architectures (for example, build versus buy versus re-use options, and sub-options within those major options)
- Identify the strategic parameters for change, and the top-level work packages or projects to be undertaken in moving from the current environment to the target
- Assess the dependencies, costs, and benefits of the various projects
- Generate an overall implementation and migration strategy and a detailed Implementation Plan

11.2 Approach

Phase E identifies the parameters of change, the major phases along the way, and the top-level projects to be undertaken in moving from the current environment to the target. The output of Phase E will form the basis of the Implementation Plan required to move to the Target Architecture. This phase also attempts to identify new business opportunities arising from the architecture work in previous phases.

Sometimes the process of identifying implementation opportunities allows a business to identify new applications, and in this case it may be necessary to iterate between Phase E and previous phases. Iteration must be limited by time or money to avoid wasting effort in the search for a perfect architecture.

Phase E is the first phase which is directly concerned with implementation. The task is to identify the major work packages or projects to be undertaken.

An effective way to do this is to use the gap analysis on the business functions between the old environment and the new, created in Phase D. Any functions appearing as "new" items will have to be implemented (developed or purchased and deployed).

Slightly harder to identify are the projects required to update or replace existing functions which must be done differently in the new environment. One of the options to be considered here is leaving an existing system in place and coexisting with the new environment.

During this final step in the specification of building blocks it must be verified that the organization-specific requirements will be met. Key to this is reason checking against the business scenario driving the scope of the project. It is important to note that the ensuing development process must include recognition of dependencies and boundaries for functions and should take account of what products are available in the marketplace. An example of how this might be expressed can be seen in the building blocks example (Part IV: Resource Base, Building Blocks).

Coexistence appears on the surface to be easy. After all, the original system is left in place, largely unchanged. Unfortunately, it is not always as easy as it looks. The main problems with coexistence are:

- User interfaces: combining user interfaces to the old and new applications in a single unit on the users' desks can be difficult, if not impossible.
- Access to data: often the new applications need to share some data with the old applications, and some kind of data sharing must be established. This can be difficult unless the old and new systems use the same database technology.
- Connectivity: this may involve expenditure on software and gateway equipment. In difficult cases, equipment simply may not be available in a useful timescale. Often this happens because the old system is simply too out-of-date for connectivity solutions to be still on the market.

The most successful strategy for Phase E is to focus on projects that will deliver short-term pay-offs and so create an impetus for proceeding with longer-term projects.

11.3 Inputs

Inputs to Phase E are:

- Request for Architecture Work (Request for Architecture Work)
- Statement of Architecture Work (Major Output Descriptions)
- Target Business Architecture (Business Architecture), Version 1.0
- Target Technology Architecture (Technology Architecture), Version 1.0
- Target Data Architecture, Version 1.0
- Target Applications Architecture, Version 1.0
- Re-usable Architecture Building Blocks (from organization's Enterprise Continuum (see Part III: Enterprise Continuum), if available)
- Product information (Product Information)

11.4 Steps

Key steps in Phase E include:

- Identify Key Business Drivers constraining Sequence of Implementation

    Examples are reduction of costs, consolidation of services, introduction of new customer services, etc.
- Review Gap analysis from Phase D
- Brainstorm Technical Requirements from Functional Perspective

- Brainstorm Co-existence and Interoperability Requirements
- Perform Architecture Assessment and Gap Analysis
- Identify Major Work Packages or Projects
    Classify these as new development, purchase opportunity, or re-use of existing system.

11.5 Outputs

The outputs of Phase E are:

- Implementation and migration strategy
- High-level Implementation Plan
- Impact Analysis (see Impact Analysis) - project list

Chapter 12: Phase F - Migration Planning

This chapter addresses migration planning, including work prioritization, selection of major work packages, and development of a Migration Plan.

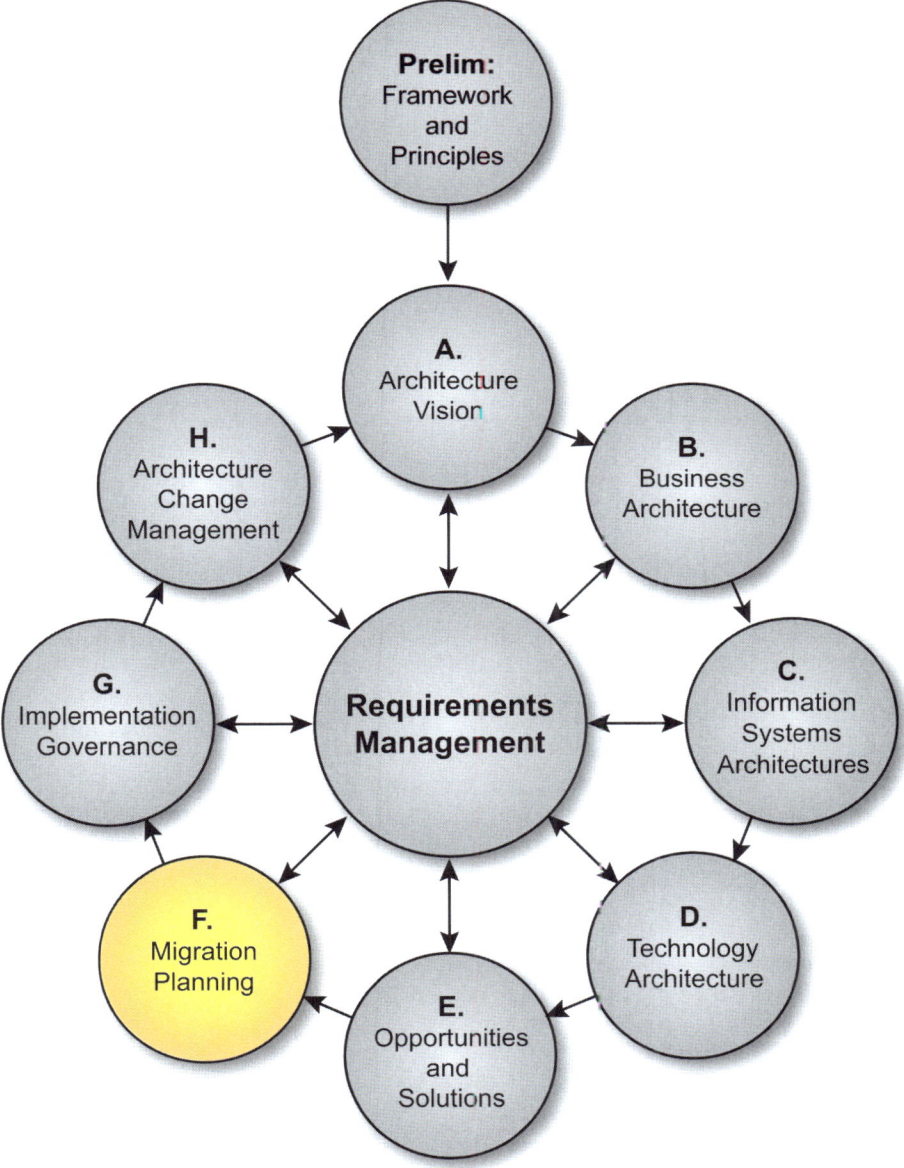

Figure 12.1: Phase F: Migration Planning

12.1 Objective

The objective of Phase F is to sort the various implementation projects into priority order. Activities include assessing the dependencies, costs, and benefits of the various migration projects. The prioritized list of projects will go on to form the basis of the detailed Implementation Plan and Migration Plan.

12.2 Approach

There are some important questions to be asked before embarking on a migration exercise:

- What are the implications of this project on other projects and activities?
- What are the dependencies between this project and other projects and activities?
- What products are needed?
- What components must be developed?
- Does the organization have the resources needed to develop such components?
- What standards are the products or components built on?
- When will they be available?
- Will the products stand the test of time, both because of the technology they use and also because of the viability of the supplier?
- What is the cost of retraining the users?
- What is the likely cultural impact on the user community, and how can it be controlled?
- What is the total cost of the migration, and what benefits will it deliver? It is important to look at actual benefits, and not presumed benefits. Is the funding available?
- Is the migration viable?

Many things affect the answers to these questions, including the current and future architectures, the size of the organization and its complexity, and the value of technology to the core functions of the organization. Other things to consider are the asset value of the current systems, and the level of risk associated with changing the solution and/or the supplier.

Most organizations find that a change of architecture has too much impact on the organization to be undertaken in a single phase. Migration often requires consideration of a number of technical issues, not the least of which are those associated with the means of introducing change to operational systems.

Issues requiring special consideration may include:

- Parallel operations
- Choices of proceeding with phased migration by subsystem or by function

- The impact of geographical separation on migration

The decisions resulting from these considerations should be incorporated in the Implementation Plan.

There are a number of strategies for developing the Migration and Implementation Plan.

The most successful basic strategy is to focus on projects that will deliver short-term pay-offs and so create an impetus for proceeding with longer-term projects.

One common approach is to implement business functions in a data-driven chronological sequence; i.e., create the applications and supporting technology that create data before those that process the data, before those that simply store, archive, or delete data.

For example, the following detailed description of this approach is taken from SPE 68794, Implementing Enterprise Architecture - Putting Quality Information in the Hands of Oil and Gas Knowledge Workers:

1. Determine the future disposition of current systems. Each current system is classified as:
   - Mainstream systems - part of the future information system.
   - Contain systems - expected to be replaced or modified in the planning horizon (next three years).
   - Replace systems - to be replaced in the planning horizon.

   The current system disposition decisions should be made by business people, not IT people.

2. Applications should be combined or split into parts to facilitate sequencing and implementation. This rearrangement of applications creates a number of projects, a project being equivalent to an application or to combinations or parts of applications.

3. Develop the data sequence for the projects as described in the Data Architecture. Using the CRUD (Create/Read/Update/Delete) matrix developed as part of the Data Architecture, sequence the projects such that projects that create data precede projects that read or update that data.

4. Develop an estimated value to the business for each project. To do this, first develop a matrix based on a value index dimension and a risk index dimension. The value index includes the following criteria: principles compliance, which includes financial contribution, strategic alignment, and competitive position. The risk index includes the following criteria: size and complexity, technology, organizational capacity, and impact of a failure. Each of the criteria has an individual weight. The index and its criteria and weighting are developed and approved by senior management early in the project. It is important to establish the decision-making criteria before the options are known.

In addition, there will be key business drivers to be addressed that will also tend to dictate the sequence of implementation, such as:

- Reduction of costs
- Consolidation of services
- Ability to handle change
- A goal to have a minimum of "interim" solutions (they often become long-term/strategic!)

Another, possibly complementary, approach is for the individual projects or work packages to be group-sorted into a series of plateaux, each of which can be achieved in a realistic timescale.

The following description assumes a Target Architecture with only a single time horizon.

12.3 Inputs

Inputs to Phase F are:

- Request for Architecture Work (Request for Architecture Work)
- Statement of Architecture Work (Major Output Descriptions)
- Target Business Architecture (Business Architecture), Version 1.0
- Target Technology Architecture (Technology Architecture), Version 1.0
- Target Data Architecture, Version 1.0
- Target Applications Architecture, Version 1.0
- Impact Analysis (see Impact Analysis) – project list

12.4 Steps

Key steps in Phase F include:

1. Prioritize projects
2. Estimate resource requirements and availability
3. Perform cost/benefit assessment of the various migration projects
4. Perform risk assessment
5. Generate implementation roadmap (timelined)
6. Document the Migration Plan

12.5 Outputs

The output of Phase F is:

- Impact Analysis (see Impact Analysis) - detailed Implementation Plan and Migration Plan (including Architecture Implementation Contract, if appropriate)

Chapter 13: Phase G - Implementation Governance

This chapter provides an architectural oversight of the implementation.

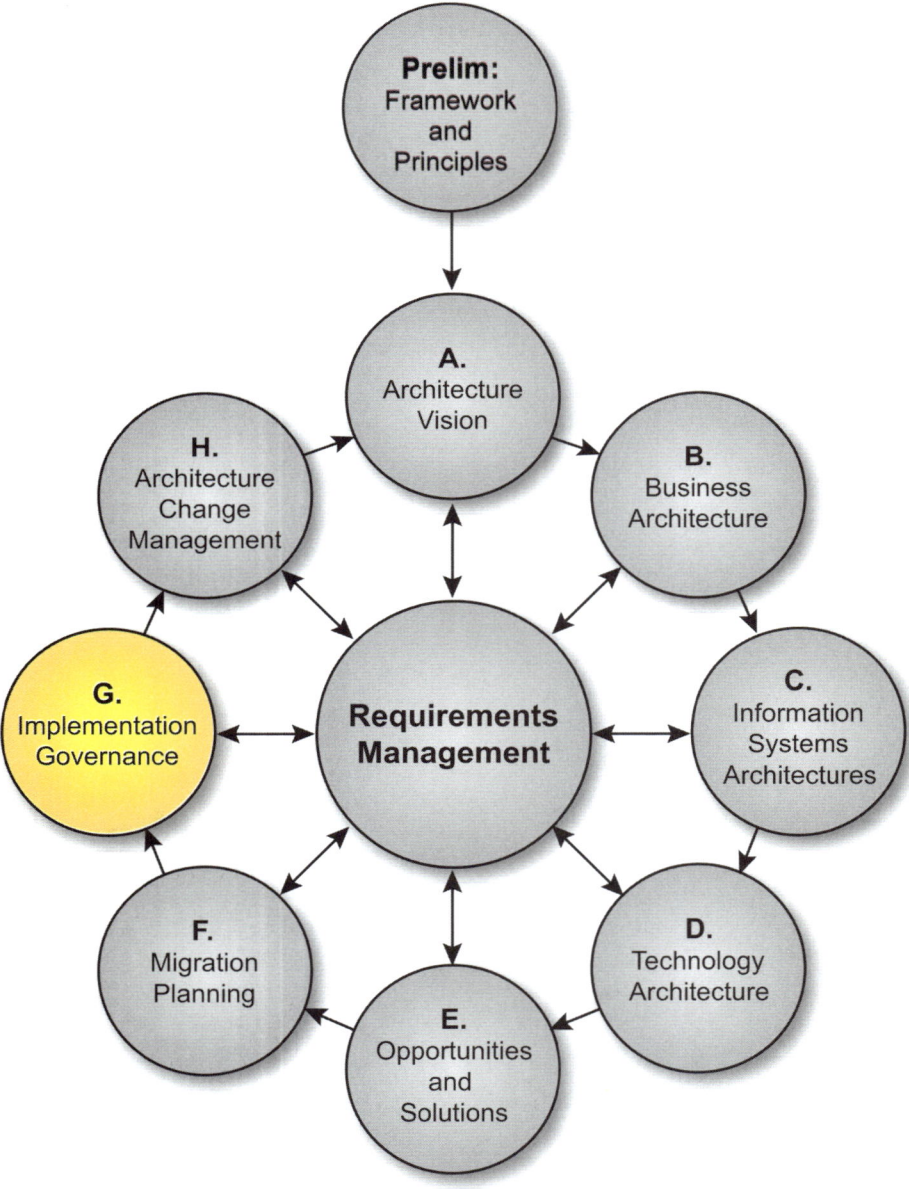

Figure 13.1: Phase G: Implementation Governance

13.1 Objectives

The objectives of Phase G are to:

- Formulate recommendations for each implementation project.
- Construct an Architecture Contract to govern the overall implementation and deployment process.
- Perform appropriate governance functions while the system is being implemented and deployed.
- Ensure conformance with the defined architecture by implementation projects and other projects.

13.2 Approach

It is here that all the information for successful management of the various implementation projects is brought together. Note that in parallel with Phase G there is the execution of an organizational-specific development process, where the actual development happens.

Phase G establishes the connection between architecture and implementation organization, through the Architecture Contract.

Project details are developed, including:

- Name, description, and objectives
- Scope, deliverables, and constraints
- Measures of effectiveness
- Acceptance criteria
- Risks and issues

Implementation governance is closely allied to overall architecture governance, which is discussed in Part IV: Resource Base, Architecture Governance.

A key aspect of Phase G is ensuring compliance with the defined architecture(s), not only by the implementation projects, but also by other ongoing projects within the enterprise. The considerations involved with this are explained in detail in Part IV: Resource Base, Architecture Compliance.

13.3 Inputs

Inputs to Phase G are:

- Request for Architecture Work (Request for Architecture Work)

- Statement of Architecture Work (Major Output Descriptions)
- Re-usable Solution Building Block (from organization's Solutions Continuum (see Part III: Enterprise Continuum), if available)
- Impact Analysis (see Impact Analysis) - detailed Implementation Plan and Migration Plan (including Architecture Implementation Contract, if appropriate)

13.4 Steps

Key steps in Phase G include:

1. Formulate Project Recommendation

   For each separate implementation project do the following:
   - Document scope of individual project in Impact Analysis
   - Document strategic requirements (from the architectural perspective) in Impact Analysis
   - Document change requests (such as support for a standard interface) in Impact Analysis
   - Document rules for conformance in Impact Analysis
   - Document timeline requirements from roadmap in Impact Analysis
2. Document Architecture Contract
   - Obtain signature from all developing organizations and sponsoring organization
3. Review Ongoing Implementation Governance and Architecture Compliance

13.5 Outputs

The outputs of Phase G are:

- Impact Analysis (see Impact Analysis) - implementation recommendations
- Architecture Contract (see Architecture Contract), as recommended in Part IV: Resource Base, Architecture Contracts
- The architecture-compliant implemented system

Note:

The implemented system is actually an output of the development process. However, given the importance of this output, it is stated here as an output of the ADM. The direct involvement of architecture staff in implementation will vary according to organizational policy, as described in Part IV: Resource Base, Architecture Governance.

Chapter 14:
Phase H - Architecture Change Management

This chapter looks at establishing procedures for managing change to the new architecture.

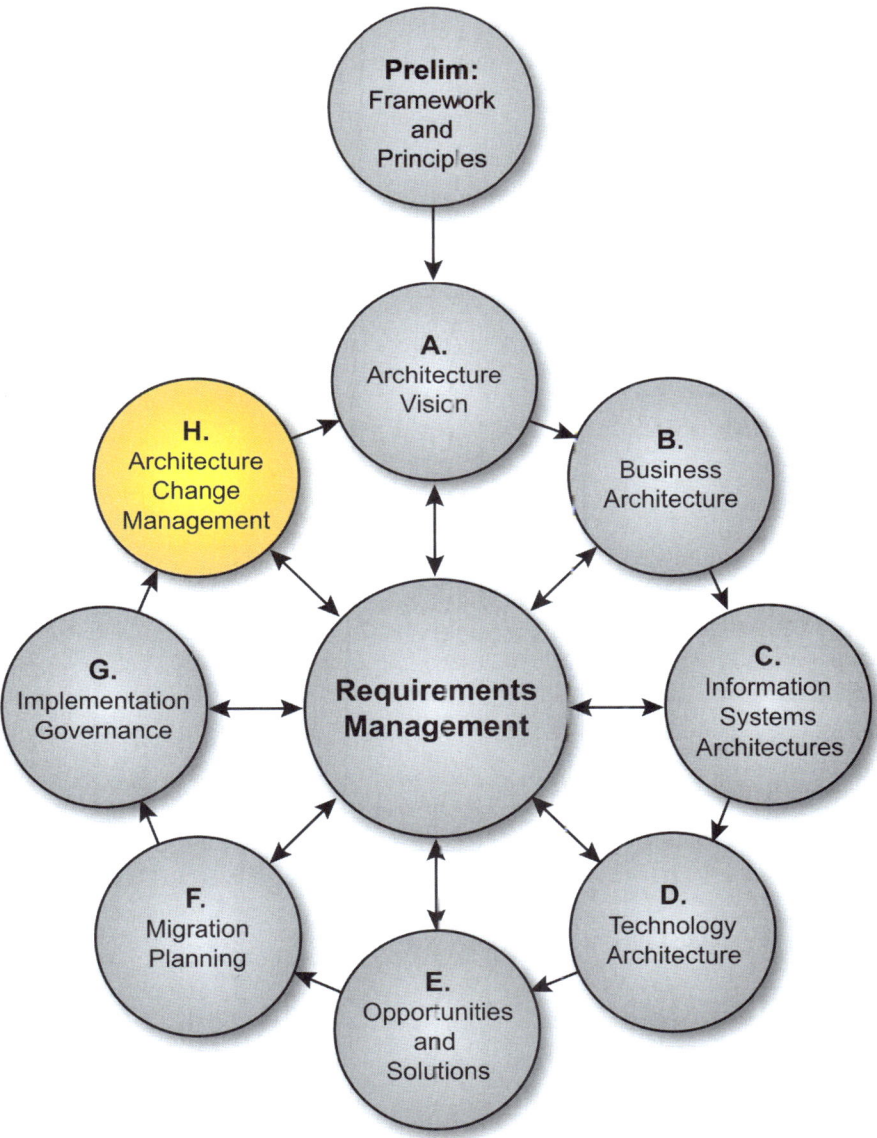

Figure 14.1: Phase H: Architecture Change Management

14.1 Objective

The objective of Phase H is to establish an architecture change management process for the new enterprise architecture baseline that is achieved with completion of Phase G. This process will typically provide for the continual monitoring of such things as new developments in technology and changes in the business environment, and for determining whether to formally initiate a new architecture evolution cycle.

Phase H also provides for changes to the framework and principles set up in the Preliminary Phase.

14.2 Approach

The goal of an architecture change management process is to ensure that changes to the architecture are managed in a cohesive and architected way, and to establish and support the implemented enterprise architecture as a dynamic architecture; that is, one having the flexibility to evolve rapidly in response to changes in the technology and business environment.

The change management process once established will determine:

- The circumstances under which the enterprise architecture, or parts of it, will be permitted to change after implementation, and the process by which that will happen
- The circumstances under which the enterprise architecture development cycle will be initiated again to develop a new architecture

The architecture change management process is very closely related to the architecture governance processes of the enterprise, and to the management of the Architecture Contract (see Architecture Contracts) between the architecture function and the business users of the enterprise.

In Phase H it is critical that the governance body establish criteria to judge whether a change request warrants just an architecture update or whether it warrants starting a new cycle of the Architecture Development Method (ADM). It is especially important to avoid "creeping elegance", and the governance body must continue to look for changes that relate directly to business value.

Guidelines for establishing these criteria are difficult to prescribe, as many companies accept risk differently, but as the ADM is exercised, the maturity level of the governance body will improve, and criteria will become clear for specific needs.

14.2.1 The Drivers for Change

There are many technology-related drivers for architecture change requests. For example:

- New technology reports
- Asset management cost reductions
- Technology withdrawal
- Standards initiatives

This type of change request is normally manageable primarily through an enterprise's change management and architecture governance processes.

In addition there are business drivers for architecture change, including:

- Business-as-usual developments
- Business exceptions
- Business innovations
- Business technology innovations
- Strategic change

This type of change request often results in a complete re-development of the architecture, or at least in an iteration of a part of the architecture development cycle, as explained below.

14.2.2 The Change Management Process

The change management process needs to determine how changes are to be managed, what techniques are to be applied, and what methodologies used. The process also needs a filtering function that determines which phases of the architecture development process are impacted by requirements. For example, changes that affect only migration may be of no interest in the architecture development phases.

There are many valid approaches to change management. and various management techniques and methodologies that can be used to manage change; for example, project management methods such as PRINCE 2, service management methods such as ITIL, management consultancy methods such as Catalyst, and many others. An enterprise that already has a change management process in place in a field other than architecture (for example, in systems development or project management) may well be able to adapt it for use in relation to architecture.

The following describes an approach to change management, aimed particularly at the support of a dynamic enterprise architecture, which may be considered for use if no similar process currently exists.

The approach is based on classifying required architectural changes into one of three categories:

1. Simplification change: A simplification change can normally be handled via change management techniques.
2. Incremental change: An incremental change may be capable of being handled via change management techniques, or it may require partial re-architecting, depending on the nature of the change. See Guidelines for Maintenance versus Architecture Redesign for guidelines.
3. Re-architecting change: A re-architecting change requires putting the whole architecture through the architecture development cycle again.

Another way of looking at these three choices is to say that a simplification change to an architecture is often driven by a requirement to reduce investment; an incremental change, by a requirement to derive additional value from existing investment; and a re-architecting change, by a requirement to increase investment in order to create new value for exploitation.

To determine whether a change is simplification, incremental, or re-architecting, the following activities are undertaken:

1. Registration of all events that may impact the architecture
2. Resource allocation and management for architecture tasks
3. The process or role responsible for architecture resources has to make assessment of what should be done
4. Evaluation of impacts

14.2.3 Guidelines for Maintenance versus Architecture Redesign

A good rule-of-thumb is:

- If the change impacts two stakeholders or more, then it is likely to require an architecture re-design and re-entry to the ADM.
- If the change impacts only one stakeholder, then it is more likely to be a candidate for change management.
- If the change can be allowed under a dispensation, then it is more likely to be a candidate for change management.

For example:

- If the impact is significant for the business strategy, then there may be a need to redo the whole enterprise architecture - thus a re-architecting approach.
- If a new technology or standards emerge, then there may be a need to refresh the Technology Architecture, but not the whole enterprise architecture - thus an incremental change.

- If the change is at an infrastructure level - for example, ten systems reduced or changed to one system - this may not change the architecture above the physical layer, but it will change the Baseline Description of the Technology Architecture. This would be a simplification change handled via change management techniques.

In particular, a refreshment cycle (partial or complete re-architecting) may be required if:

- The Foundation Architecture needs to re-aligned with the business strategy.
- Substantial change is required to components and guidelines for use in deployment of the architecture.
- Significant standards used in the product architecture are changed which have significant end-user impact; e.g., regulatory changes.

If there is a need for a refreshment cycle, then a new Request for Architecture Work must be issued (to move to another cycle).

14.3 Inputs

Inputs to Phase H are:

- Request for Architecture Change - technology changes:
    - New technology reports (New Technology Reports)
    - Asset management cost reduction initiatives
    - Technology withdrawal reports
    - Standards initiatives
- Request for Architecture Change - business changes:
    - Business developments
    - Business exceptions
    - Business innovations
    - Business technology innovations
    - Strategic change developments

14.4 Steps

Key steps in Phase H include:

- Monitor Technology Changes
- Monitor Business Changes
- Assess Changes and Development of Position to Act

- Arrange Meeting of Architecture Board (or other governing council)
  The aim of the meeting is to decide on handling changes (technology and business).

14.5 Outputs

The outputs of Phase H are:

- Architecture updates
- Changes to architecture framework and principles
- New Request for Architecture Work (Request for Architecture Work), to move to another cycle

Chapter 15:
ADM Architecture Requirements Management

This chapter looks at the process of managing architecture requirements throughout the ADM.

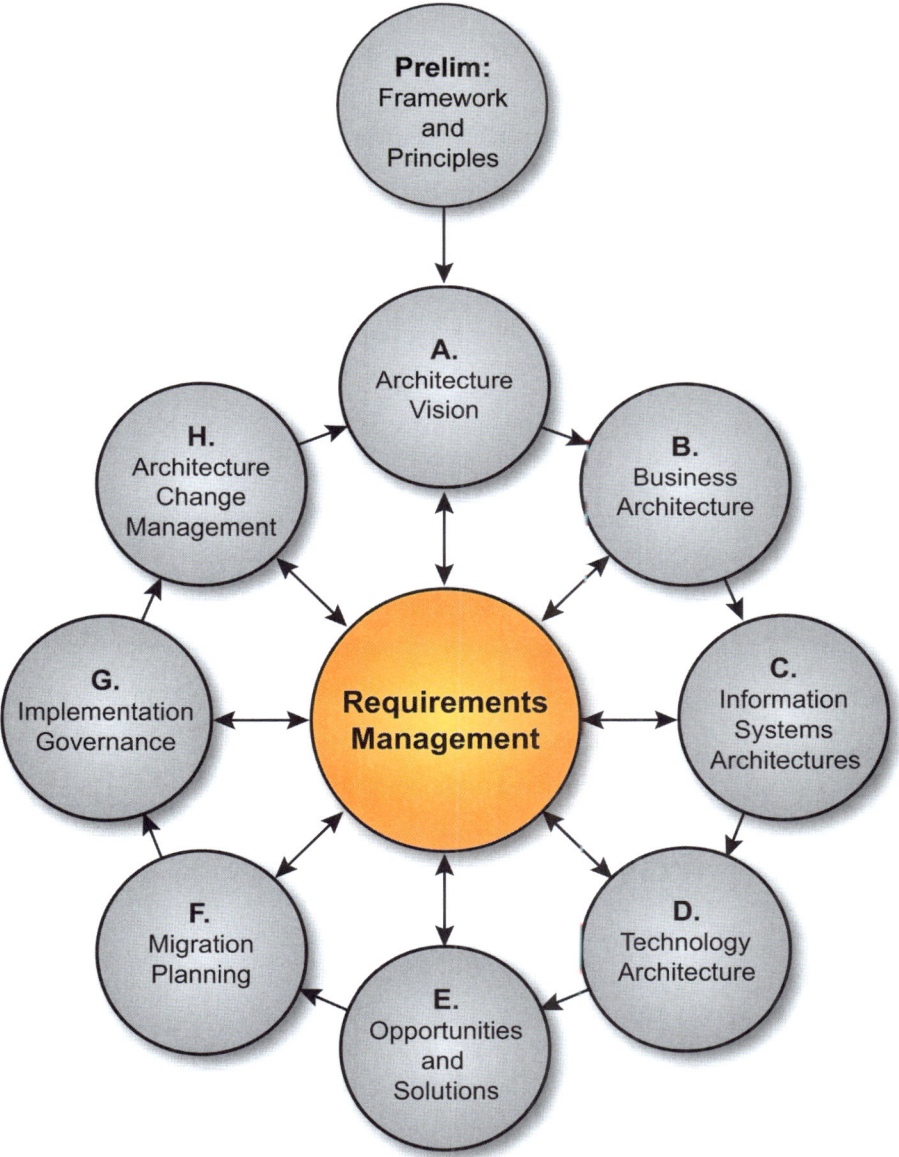

Figure 15.1 : ADM Architecture Requirements Management

15.1 Objective

To define a process whereby requirements for enterprise architecture are identified, stored, and fed into and out of the relevant ADM phases.

15.2 Approach

15.2.1 Genral

As indicated by the "Requirements Management" circle at the center of the ADM graphic, the ADM is continuously driven by the requirements management process.

It is important to note that the Requirements Management circle denotes, not a static set of requirements, but a dynamic process whereby requirements for enterprise architecture and subsequent changes to those requirements are identified, stored, and fed into and out of the relevant ADM phases.

The ability to deal with changes in requirements is crucial. Architecture is an activity that by its very nature deals with uncertainty and change - the "grey area" between what stakeholders aspire to and what can be specified and engineered as a solution. Architecture requirements are therefore invariably subject to change in practice. Moreover, architecture often deals with drivers and constraints, many of which by their very nature are beyond the control of the enterprise (changing market conditions, new legislation, etc.), and which can produce changes in requirements in an unforeseen manner.

Note also that the requirements management process itself does not dispose of, address, or prioritize any requirements: this is done within the relevant phase of the ADM. It is merely the process for managing requirements throughout the overall ADM.

15.2.2 Resources

The world of requirements engineering is rich with emerging recommendations and processes for requirements management. TOGAF does not mandate or recommend any specific process or tool; it simply states what an effective requirements management process should achieve (i.e., the "requirements for requirements", if you like).

15.2.2.1 Business Scenarios

One effective technique that is described in TOGAF itself is business scenarios, which are an appropriate and useful technique to discover and document business requirements, and to articulate an architectural vision that responds to those requirements. Business scenarios are described in detail in Part IV: Resource Base, Business Scenarios.

15.2.2.2 Volere Requirements Specification Template

Architecture requirements is very much a niche area within the overall requirements field. One useful resource is the Volere Requirements Specification Template, available from Volere (*www.volere.co.uk/template.htm*)[1]. While not designed with architecture requirements in mind, this is a very useful requirements template, which is freely available and may be modified or copied (for internal use, provided the copyright is appropriately acknowledged).

One interesting item in this template is the "waiting room", which is a hold-all for requirements in waiting. There are often requirements identified which, as a result of the prioritization activity that forms part of the requirements management process (see below), are designated as beyond the planned scope, or the time available, for the current iteration of the architecture. The waiting room is a repository of future requirements. Having the ability to store such requirements helps avoid the perception that they are simply being discarded, while at the same time helping to manage expectations about what will be delivered.

15.2.2.3 Requirements Tools

There is a large, and increasing, number of Commercial Off-The-Shelf (COTS) tools available for the support of requirements management, albeit not necessarily designed for architecture requirements. The Volere web site has a very useful list of leading requirements tools (*www.volere.co.uk/tools.htm*).

15.3 Inputs

The inputs to the requirements management process are the requirements-related outputs from each ADM phase.

The first high-level requirements are articulated as part of the Architecture Vision, generated by means of the business scenario or analogous technique.

Each architecture domain then generates detailed design requirements specific to that domain, and potentially to other domains (for example, areas where already designed architecture domains may need to change to cater for changes in this architecture domain; constraints on other architecture domains still to be designed.)

Deliverables in later ADM phases also contain mappings to the design requirements, and may also generate new types of requirements (for example, conformance requirements, time windows for implementation).

---

1. The Volere web site is hosted by the Atlantic Systems Guild (*www.systemsguild.com*).

15.4 Steps

Key steps in the requirements management process include:

	Requirements Management Steps	ADM Phase Steps
1		Identify/document requirements - use business scenarios, or an analogous technique.
2	Baseline requirements: a Determine priorities arising from current phase of ADM. b Confirm stakeholder buy-in to resultant priorities. c Record requirements priorities and place in requirements repository.	
3	Monitor baseline requirements	
4		Identify changed requirement: a Remove or re-assess priorities. b Add requirements and re-assess priorities. c Modify existing requirements.
5	Identify changed requirement and record priorities: a Identify changed requirements and ensure the requirements are prioritized by the architect(s) responsible for the current phase, and by the relevant stakeholders. b Record new priorities. c Ensure that any conflicts are identified and managed through the phases to a successful conclusion and prioritization. d Generate Requirements Impact Statement (see Requirements Impact Statement) for steering the architecture team.	

Requirements Management Steps	ADM Phase Steps
	Notes ■ Changed requirements can come in through any route. To ensure that the requirements are properly assessed requirements are properly assessed and prioritized, this process needs to direct the ADM phases and record the decisions related to the requirements. ■ The requirements management phase needs to determine stakeholder satisfaction with the decisions. Where there is dissatisfaction, the phase remains accountable to ensure the resolution of the issues and determine next steps.
6	a Assess impact of changed requirements on current (active) phase. b Assess impact of changed requirements on previous phases. c Determine whether to implement change. or defer to later ADM cycle. If decision is to implement, assess timescale for change management implementation. d Issue Requirements Impact Statement, Version n+1.
7	Implement requirements arising from Phase H. The architecture can be changed through its lifecycle by the architecture change management phase (Phase H). The requirements management process ensures that new or changing requirements that are derived from Phase H are managed accordingly.

	Requirements Management Steps	ADM Phase Steps
8	Update the requirements repository with information relating to the changes requested, including stakeholder views affected.	
9		Implement change in the current phase.
10		Assess and revise gap analysis for past phases. The gap analysis in the ADM Phases B through D identifies the gaps between Baseline and Target Architectures. Certain types of gap can give rise to gap requirements. The ADM describes two kinds of gap: 1 Something that is present in the baseline, but not in the target (i.e., eliminated - by accident or design) 2 Something not in the baseline, but present in the target (i.e., new) A "gap requirement" is anything that has been eliminated by accident, and therefore requires a change to the Target Architecture. If the gap analysis generates gap requirements, then this step will ensure that they are addressed, documented, and recorded in the requirements repository, and that the Target Architecture is revised accordingly.

15.4 Outputs

The output of the requirements management process itself is:

- A structured requirements statement, including:
    - Changed requirements
    - Requirements Impact Statement

The requirements repository contains the current requirements for the Target Architecture. When new requirements arise, or existing ones are changed, a Requirements Impact Statement is generated, which identifies the phases of the ADM that need to be revisited to address the changes. The statement goes through various iterations until the final version, which includes the full implications of the requirements (e.g., costs, timescales, business metrics) on the architecture development.

Chapter 16: ADM Input and Output Descriptions

This chapter provides descriptions of input and output items referenced in the Architecture Development Method (ADM).

16.1 Introduction

This section provides example descriptions of input and output items referenced in the ADM.

Note that not all the content described here need be contained in a particular input or output. Rather, it is recommended that external references be used where possible; for example, the strategic plans should not be copied into the Request for Architecture Work, but rather the title of the strategic plans should be referenced.

Also, it is not suggested that these descriptions should be followed to the letter. However, each element should be considered carefully; ignoring any input or output item may cause problems downstream.

Finally, note that versioning is used to indicate that input or output items may undergo change as the ADM is executed. As an input or output item is updated, a new version may be produced. In all cases, the TOGAF ADM numbering scheme is provided as an example. It should be adapted by the architect to meet the requirements of the organization and to work with the architecture tools and repositories employed by the organization.

16.2 Major Input Descriptions

16.2.1 Request for Architecture Work

- Organization sponsors
- Organization's mission statement
- Business goals (and changes)
- Strategic plans of the business
- Time limits
- Changes in the business environment
- Organizational constraints
- Budget information, financial constraints
- External constraints, business constraints
- Current business system description
- Current architecture/IT system description

- Description of developing organization
- Description of resources available to developing organization

16.2.2 Architecture Principles

See Part IV: Resource Base, Architecture Principles for guidelines and a detailed set of generic architecture principles, including:

- Business principles (Business Principles)
- Data principles (Data Principles)
- Application principles (Application Principles)
- Technology principles (Technology Principles)

16.2.3 Re-Usable Architecture Building Blocks

- Architecture documentation and models from the enterprise's Architecture Continuum

16.2.4 Product Information

- Functional descriptions of products that are candidates for the implementation
- Architectural descriptions of elements that are candidates for the implementation

16.2.5 New Technology Reports

- New developments in potentially relevant technology

16.3 Major Output Descriptions

16.3.1 Statement of Architecture Work

- Statement of work title
- Project request and background
- Project description and scope
- Architecture vision
- Managerial approach
- Change of scope procedures
- Responsibilities and deliverables
- Acceptance criteria and procedures
- Project plan and schedule
- Support of the Enterprise Continuum

- Signature approvals

16.3.2 Business Scenario/Architecture Vision

- Problem description
    - Purpose of scenario
- Detailed objectives
- Environment and process models
    - Process description
    - Process steps mapped to environment
    - Process steps mapped to people
    - Information flow
- Actors and their roles and responsibilities
    - Human actors and roles
    - Computer actors and roles
    - Requirements
- Resulting architecture model
    - Constraints
    - IT principles
    - Architecture supporting the process
    - Requirements mapped to architecture

16.3.3 Business Architecture

- Baseline Business Architecture
- Business goals, objectives, and constraints
    - Business requirements and key system and architecture drivers
    - Business return given required changes
    - Assumptions (e.g., business, financial, organizational, or required technical functionality)
    - Business Architecture principles
- Business Architecture models
    - Organization structure
    - Business functions
    - Business roles
    - Correlation of organization and functions
    - Business Architecture Building Blocks list (e.g., business services)

- Business Architecture Building Blocks models
- Candidate Solution Building Blocks list
- Candidate Solution Building Blocks models
- Relevant business process descriptions, including measures and deliverables
- Technical requirements (drivers for other architecture work)

16.3.4 Technology Architecture

- Baseline Technology Architecture
- Objectives and constraints
  - Technology requirements and key system and architecture drivers
  - Assumptions (e.g., business, financial, organizational, or required technical functionality)
- Technology Architecture model(s)
  - Architecture Building Block models of views (minimally model of functions and a model of services)
  - Architecture Building Block models of service portfolios (enterprise-specific framework)
- Technology Architecture specification
  - Per-Architecture Building Block:
    - Details of the technical functionality
    - Fully defined list of all the standards
    - Description of building block at the levels necessary to support implementation, enterprise-wide strategic decision-making, and further iterations of the architectural definition process
    - Rationale for decisions taken that relate to the building block, including rationales for decisions not to do something
    - Specification identifying the interworking with other building blocks and how they do so
    - Guidelines for procuring
  - Standards summary list
- Requirements traceability
  - Acceptance criteria
  - Criteria for choosing specifications
  - Criteria for selection of portfolios of specifications
  - Criteria to test merits of architecture (key question list)
  - Report on cost/benefit analyses

- Report on how the proposed architecture meets the business goals and objectives
- Criteria response answers to key question list to test merits of architecture
■ Gap report
    - Report on gap analysis
    - Report of gap analysis matrix
■ Mapping of the architectures in the Enterprise Continuum
    - Change requests for extensions or amendments to related architectures

16.3.5 Impact Analysis

■ Project list
    - Name, description, and objectives of each impacted project
    - Prioritized list of impacted projects to implement the proposed architecture
■ Time-oriented Migration Plan
    - Benefits of migration, determined (including mapping to business requirements)
    - Estimated costs of migration options
■ Implementation recommendations
    - Criteria measures of effectiveness of projects
    - Risks and issues
    - Solution Building Blocks - description and model

16.3.6 Architecture Contract

Typical contents of an Architecture Design and Development Contract are:

- Introduction and background
- The nature of the agreement
- Scope of the architecture
- Architecture and strategic principles and requirements
- Conformance requirements
- Architecture development and management process and roles
- Target architecture measures
- Defined phases of deliverables
- Prioritized joint workplan
- Time window(s)
- Architecture delivery and business metrics

Typical contents of a Business Users' Architecture Contract are:

- Introduction and background
- The nature of the agreement
- Scope
- Strategic requirements
- Conformance requirements
- Architecture adopters
- Time window
- Architecture business metrics
- Service architecture (includes Service Level Agreement (SLA))

This contract is also used to manage changes to the enterprise architecture in Phase H (see Phase H: Architecture Change Management).

16.3.7 Requirements Impact Statement

- Reference to specific requirements
- Stakeholder priority of the requirements to date
- Phases to be revisited
- Phase to lead on requirements prioritization
- Results of phase investigations and revised priorities
- Recommendations on management of requirements
- Repository reference number

PART: III

Enterprise Continuum

Chapter 17: Introduction to the Enterprise Continuum

17.1 Overview

This section introduces the concept of the Enterprise Continuum, which sets the broader context for TOGAF, by explaining the different types and scopes of the architecture artifacts and assets that can be derived from it, and leveraged during its use.

The Enterprise Continuum is an important aid to communication and understanding, both within individual enterprises, and between customer enterprises and vendor organizations. Without an understanding of "where in the continuum you are", people discussing architecture can often talk at cross purposes because they are referencing different points in the continuum at the same time, without realizing it.

Any architecture is context-specific; for example, there are architectures that are specific to individual customers, industries, subsystems, products, and services. Architects, on both the buy side and supply side, must have at their disposal a consistent language to effectively communicate the differences between architectures. Such a language will enable engineering efficiency and the effective leveraging of Commercial Off-The-Shelf (COTS) product functionality. The Enterprise Continuum provides that consistent language.

Not only does the Enterprise Continuum represent an aid to communication, it represents an aid to organizing re-usable architecture and solution assets. This is explained further below.

17.2 The Enterprise Continuum and Architecture Re-Use

The simplest way of thinking of the Enterprise Continuum is as a "virtual repository" of all the architecture assets - models, patterns, architecture descriptions, and other artifacts - that exist both within the enterprise and in the IT industry at large, which the enterprise considers itself to have available for the development of architectures for the enterprise.

Examples of "assets within the enterprise" are the deliverables of previous architecture work, which are available for re-use. Examples of "assets in the IT industry at large" are the wide variety of industry reference models and architecture patterns that exist, and are continually emerging, including those that are highly generic (such as TOGAF's own Technical Reference Model (TRM)); those specific to certain aspects of IT (such as a web services architecture, or a generic manageability architecture); those specific to certain types of information processing, such as e-Commerce, supply chain management, etc.; and those specific to certain vertical industries, such as the models generated by vertical consortia like TMF (in the Telecommunications sector), ARTS (Retail), POSC (Petrotechnical), etc.

The decision as to which architecture assets a specific enterprise considers part of its own Enterprise Continuum will normally form part of the overall architecture governance function within the enterprise concerned.

17.3 The Enterprise Continuum and the TOGAF ADM

The TOGAF Architecture Development Method (ADM) describes the process of moving from the TOGAF Foundation Architecture to an enterprise-specific architecture (or set of architectures). This process leverages the elements of the TOGAF Foundation Architecture and other relevant architectural assets, components, and building blocks along the way.

At relevant places throughout the TOGAF ADM, there are reminders to consider which architecture assets from the Enterprise Continuum the architect should use, if any. In some cases - for example in the development of a Technology Architecture - this may be TOGAF's own Foundation Architecture (see below). In other cases - for example, in the development of a Business Architecture - it may be a reference model for e-Commerce taken from the industry at large.

TOGAF itself provides two reference models for consideration for inclusion in an organization's Enterprise Continuum:

- The TOGAF Foundation Architecture, which comprises a TRM of generic services and functions that provides a firm foundation on which more specific architectures and architectural components can be built; and a Standards Information Base (SIB) - an information base of relevant specifications and standards.
- The Integrated Information Infrastructure Reference Model (III-RM), which is based on the TOGAF Foundation Architecture, and is specifically designed to help the realization of architectures that enable and support the Boundaryless Information Flow vision

However, in developing architectures in the various domains within an overall enterprise architecture, the architect will need to consider the use and re-use of a wide variety of different architecture assets, and the Enterprise Continuum provides a framework (a "framework within a framework", if you like) for categorizing and communicating these different assets.

17.4 Constituents of the Enterprise Continuum

The "Enterprise Continuum" is a phrase that denotes the combination of two complementary concepts: the Architecture Continuum and the Solutions Continuum:

- The Architecture Continuum (The Architecture Continuum) offers a consistent way to define and understand the generic rules, representations, and relationships in an information system. The Architecture Continuum represents a structuring of re-usable architecture assets. The Architecture Continuum is directly supported by the Solutions Continuum (see below). The Architecture Continuum shows the relationships among foundational frameworks (such as TOGAF), common systems architectures (such as the III-RM), industry architectures, and enterprise architectures. The Architecture Continuum is a useful tool to discover commonality and eliminate unnecessary redundancy.

- The Solutions Continuum (The Solutions Continuum) provides a consistent way to describe and understand the implementation of the Architecture Continuum. The Solutions Continuum defines what is available in the organizational environment as re-usable Solutions Building Blocks (SBBs). The solutions are the results of agreements, between customers and business partners, that implement the rules and relationships defined in the architecture space. The Solutions Continuum addresses the commonalities and differences among the products, systems, and services of implemented systems.

The Enterprise Continuum in Detail provides greater detail about the Enterprise Continuum. It first outlines the Architecture Continuum and Solutions Continuum separately, and then explains how they come together to form the Enterprise Continuum.

17.5 Structure of Part III

Part III is structured as follows:

- Introduction (this section)
- The Enterprise Continuum in Detail
    - The Architecture Continuum
    - The Solutions Continuum
    - The Enterprise Continuum and your organization
- TOGAF Foundation Architecture: Technical Reference Model (TRM)
    - TRM Concepts
    - High-level breakdown
    - TRM in detail
    - Detailed platform taxonomy (Detailed Platform Taxonomy)
- TOGAF Foundation Architecture: Standards Information Base (SIB)
    - Introduction
    - Open Group standards
    - Using the SIB and linked resources
- TOGAF Integrated Information Infrastructure Reference Model (III-RM)
    - Basic concepts
    - High-level view
    - Detailed taxonomy

Chapter 18: The Enterprise Continuum in Detail

This chapter describes a framework for architecture re-use.

18.1 The Architecture Continuum

18.1.1 Introduction

There is a continuum of architectures, Architecture Building Blocks (ABBs), and architectural models that are relevant to the task of constructing an enterprise-specific architecture.

The Architecture Continuum, and the relative positioning of different types of architectures within it, is illustrated in The Architecture Continuum.

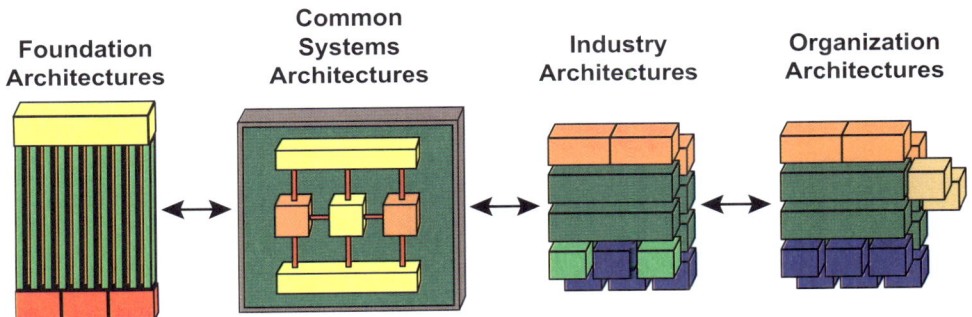

Figure 18.1: The Architecture Continuum

The Architecture Continuum illustrates how architectures are developed across a continuum ranging from Foundation Architectures such as TOGAF's, through common systems architectures, and industry-specific architectures, to an enterprise's own individual architectures.

The arrows in The Architecture Continuum represent the bi-directional relationship that exists between the different architectures in the Architecture Continuum. The leftwards direction focuses on meeting enterprise needs and business requirements, while the rightwards direction focuses on leveraging architectural components and building blocks.

The enterprise needs and business requirements are addressed in increasing detail from left to right. The architect will typically look to find re-usable architectural elements toward the left of the continuum. When elements are not found, the requirements for the missing elements are passed to the left of the continuum for incorporation. Those implementing architectures within their own organizations can use the same continuum models specialized for their business.

The four particular architectures illustrated in The Architecture Continuum are intended to indicate the range of different types of architecture that may be developed at different points in the continuum; they are not fixed stages in a process. Many different types of architecture may occur at points in-between those illustrated in The Architecture Continuum.

Although the continuum illustrated in The Architecture Continuum does not represent a formal process, it does represent a progression, which occurs at several levels:

- Logical to physical
- Horizontal (IT-focused) to vertical (business-focused)
- Generalization to specialization
- Taxonomy to complete and specific architecture specification

At each point in the continuum, an architecture is designed in terms of the design concepts and building blocks available and relevant to that point.

The four architectures illustrated in The Architecture Continuum represent main classifications of potential architectures, and will be relevant and familiar to many architects. They are analyzed in detail in the following subsections.

18.1.2 Foundation Architecture

A Foundation Architecture is an architecture of building blocks and corresponding standards that supports all the common systems architectures and, therefore, the complete computing environment.

For The Open Group, this Foundation Architecture is the Technical Reference Model (TRM) and Standards Information Base (SIB). The TOGAF ADM explains how to get from that Foundation Architecture to an enterprise-specific one.

The TOGAF TRM and SIB describe a fundamental architecture upon which other, more specific architectures can be based. The TOGAF Foundation Architecture contains many alternatives in each of the ABBs. Other characteristics of the TOGAF Foundation Architecture include the following:

- Reflects general computing requirements
- Reflects general building blocks
- Defines technology standards for implementing these building blocks
- Provides direction for products and services
- Reflects the function of a complete, robust computing environment that can be used as a foundation
- Provides open system standards, directions, and recommendations
- Reflects directions and strategies

18.1.3 Common Systems Architectures

Common Systems Architectures guide the selection and integration of specific services from the Foundation Architecture to create an architecture useful for building common (i.e., re-usable) solutions across a wide number of relevant domains.

Examples of Common Systems Architectures include: a Security Architecture, a Management Architecture, a Network Architecture, etc. Each is incomplete in terms of overall information system functionality, but is complete in terms of a particular problem domain (security, manageability, networking, etc.), so that solutions implementing the architecture constitute re-usable building blocks for the creation of functionally complete information systems.

Other characteristics of Common Systems Architectures include:

- Reflects requirements specific to a generic problem domain
- Defines building blocks specific to a generic problem domain
- Defines technology standards for implementing these building blocks
- Provides building blocks for easy re-use and lower costs

The TOGAF Integrated Information Infrastructure Reference Model (III-RM; see Integrated Information Infrastructure Reference Model) is a Common Systems Architecture that focuses on the requirements, building blocks, and standards relating to the vision of Boundaryless Information Flow.

18.1.4 Industry Architectures

Industry Architectures guide the integration of common systems components with industry-specific components, and guide the creation of industry solutions for targeted customer problems within a particular industry.

A typical example of an industry-specific component is a data model representing the business functions and processes specific to a particular vertical industry, such as the Retail industry's "Active Store" architecture, or an Industry Architecture that incorporates the Petrotechnical Open Software Corporation (POSC) (*www.posc.org*) data model.

Other characteristics of Industry Architectures include the following:

- Reflects requirements and standards specific to a vertical industry
- Defines building blocks specific to a generic problem domain
- Contains industry-specific logical data and process models
- Contains industry-specific applications and process models, as well as industry-specific business rules
- Provides guidelines for testing collections of systems
- Encourages levels of interoperability throughout the industry

18.1.5 Enterprise Architectures

Enterprise architectures are the most relevant to the IT customer community, since they describe and guide the final deployment of user-written or third-party components that constitute effective solutions for a particular enterprise or enterprises that have a need to share information.

IEEE Std 1003.23, Guide for Developing User Organization Open System Environment (OSE) Profiles[2], provides a method for identifying and documenting an organization's operational requirements, the IT and IS services needed to support those requirements, and the standards, standards options, interim solutions, and products that will provide the needed services.

There may be a continuum of enterprise architectures that are needed to effectively cover the organization's requirements by defining the enterprise architecture in increasing levels of detail. Alternatively, this might result in several more detailed enterprise architectures for specific entities within the global enterprise.

The enterprise architecture guides the final customization of the solution, and has the following characteristics:

- Provides a means to communicate and manage the IT environment
- Reflects requirements specific to a particular enterprise
- Defines building blocks specific to a particular enterprise
- Contains organization-specific physical data, applications, and process models, as well as business rules
- Provides a means to encourage implementation of appropriate IT to meet business needs
- Provides the criteria to measure and select appropriate products, solutions, and services
- Provides an evolutionary path to support growth and new business needs

18.2 The Solutions Continuum

18.2.1 Introduction

The Solutions Continuum represents the implementations of the architectures at the corresponding levels of the Architecture Continuum. At each level, the Solutions Continuum is a population of the architecture with reference building blocks - either purchased products or built components - that represent a solution to the enterprise's business need expressed at that level. A populated Solutions Continuum can be regarded as a solutions inventory or re-use library, which can add significant value to the task of managing and implementing improvements to the IT environment.

---

2. Note that this standard is administratively withdrawn by IEEE.

The Solutions Continuum is illustrated in The Solutions Continuum.

In the Architecture Continuum in The Architecture Continuum, the arrows represent bi-directional relationships that exist between the different architectures in the Architecture Continuum (the leftwards direction focused on meeting customer needs and business requirements, the rightwards direction on leveraging architectural components and building blocks).

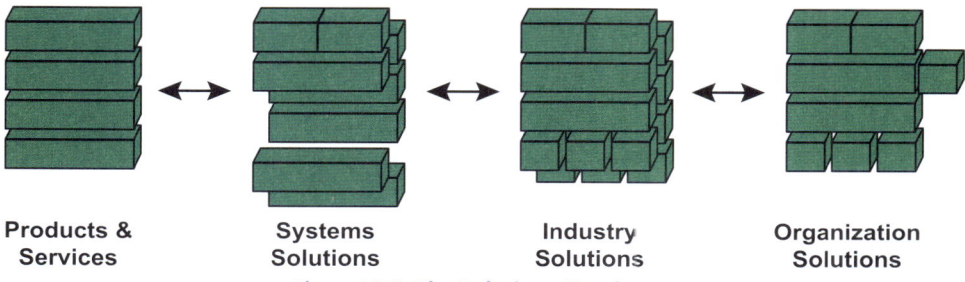

Figure18.2: The Solutions Continuum

A similar concept applies to the bi-directional arrows underlying the Solutions Continuum in The Solutions Continuum. The rightwards direction of the arrows is focused on providing solutions value (i.e., Products and Services provide value in creating systems solutions; systems solutions value is used to create industry solutions; and industry solutions are used to create customer solutions). The leftwards direction is focused on addressing enterprise needs.

These two viewpoints are significant for a company attempting to focus on its needs while maximizing the use of its internal resources through leverage

The following subsections describe each of the solution types within the Solutions Continuum.

18.2.2 Products and Services

Products are separately procurable hardware, software, or service entities. Products are the fundamental providers of capabilities.

Services include professional services - such as training and consulting services - that ensure the maximum investment value from solutions in the shortest possible time; and support services - such as Help Desk - that ensure the maximum possible value from solutions (services that ensure timely updates and upgrades to the products and systems).

18.2.3 Systems Solutions

A "system solution" is an implementation of a Common Systems Architecture comprised of a set of products and services, which may be certified or branded. It represents the highest common denominator for one or more solutions in the industry segments that the system solution supports.

System solutions represent collections of common requirements and capabilities, rather than those specific to a particular customer or industry. System solutions provide organizations with operating environments specific to operational and informational needs, such as high availability transaction processing and scaleable data warehousing systems. Examples of systems solutions include: an enterprise management system product or a security system product.

Computer systems vendors are the primary provider of systems solutions.

18.2.4 Industry Solutions

An "industry solution" is an implementation of an Industry Architecture, which provides re-usable packages of common components and services specific to an industry.

Fundamental components are provided by system solutions and/or products and services, and are augmented with industry-specific components. Examples include: a physical database schema or an industry-specific point-of-service device.

Industry solutions are industry-specific, aggregate procurements that are ready to be tailored to an individual organization's requirements.

In some cases an industry solution may include not only an implementation of the Industry Architecture, but also other solution elements, such as specific products, services, and systems solutions that are appropriate to that industry.

18.2.5 Enterprise Solutions

An "enterprise solution" is an implementation of the enterprise architecture that provides the required business functions. Because solutions are designed for specific business operations, they contain the highest amount of unique content in order to accommodate the varying people and processes of specific organizations.

Building enterprise solutions on industry solutions, systems solutions, and products and services is the primary purpose of connecting the Architecture Continuum to the Solutions Continuum, as guided by the architects within an enterprise.

18.3 The Enterprise Continuum and Your Organization

The preceding sections have described both the Architecture Continuum and the Solutions Continuum. As explained in Introduction to the Enterprise Continuum, the combination of these two complementary concepts constitutes the Enterprise Continuum, illustrated in The Enterprise Continuum.

18.3.1 Relationships

The relationship between the Architecture Continuum and the Solutions Continuum is one of guidance, direction, and support.

For example, the Foundation Architecture guides the creation or selection of products and services. The products and services support the Foundation Architecture by helping to realize the architecture defined in the Architecture Continuum. The Foundation Architecture also guides development of products and services, by providing descriptions of required functions to build open computing systems, and the rationale for those functions. A similar relationship exists between the other elements of the Enterprise Continuum.

The Enterprise Continuum presents mechanisms to help improve productivity through leverage. The Solutions Continuum offers a consistent way to understand the different products, systems, services, and solutions required. The Architecture Continuum offers a consistent way to understand the different architectures and their components.

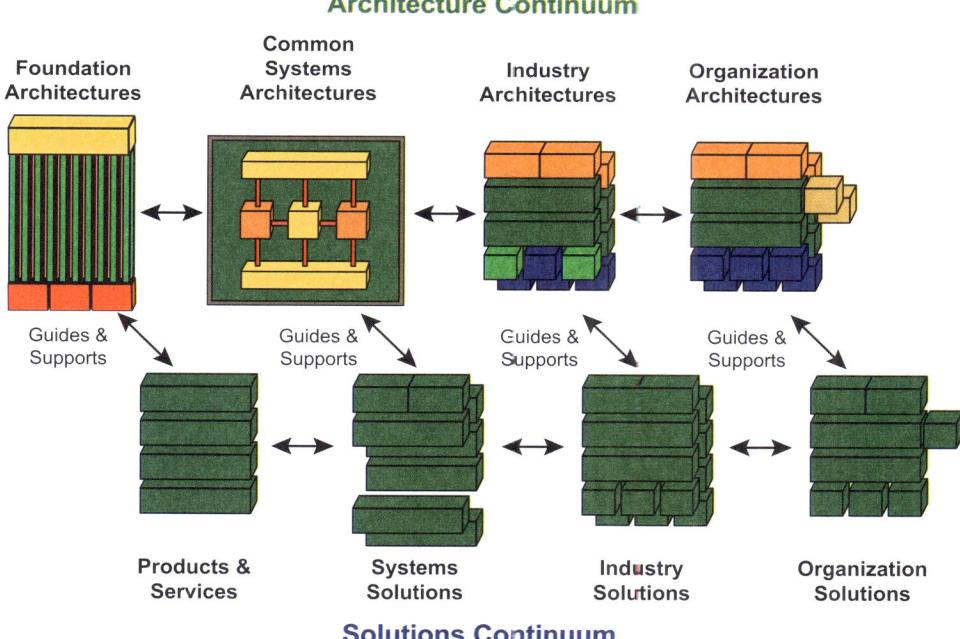

Figure 18.3: The Enterprise Continuum

The Enterprise Continuum should not be interpreted as representing strictly chained relationships. Enterprise Architectures could have components from a Common Systems Architecture, and enterprise solutions could contain a product or service. The relationships depicted in The Enterprise Continuum are a best case for the ideal leveraging of architecture and solution components.

Finally, it is worth emphasizing that the beginning and the end of the Enterprise Continuum lie in a Foundation Architecture, which serves as a tool chest or repository of re-usable guidelines and standards. For The Open Group, this Foundation Architecture is the Technical Reference Model (TRM) and Standards Information Base (SIB).

18.3.2 Your Enterprise

TOGAF provides a method for you to "architect" the IT systems in your enterprise. Your architecture organization will have to deal with each type of architecture described above. For example, it is recommended that you have your own Foundation Architecture that governs all of your IT systems. You should also have your own Common Systems Architectures that govern major shared infrastructure systems - such as the networking system or management system. You may have your own industry-specific architectures that govern the way your IT systems must behave within your industry. Finally, any given department or organization within your business may need its own individual enterprise architecture to govern the IT systems within that department. All-in-all this implies that your architecture organization is responsible for maintaining your business' Architecture Continuum.

Your architecture organization will either adopt or adapt existing architectures, or will develop its own architectures from ground up. In either case, TOGAF represents a tool to help. It provides a method to assist you in generating/maintaining any type of architecture within the Architecture Continuum while leveraging architecture assets already defined, internal or external to your organization. The TOGAF Architecture Development Method (ADM) helps you to re-use architecture assets, making your architecture organization more efficient and effective.

Chapter 19:
Foundation Architecture - Technical Reference Model

This chapter describes the Technical Reference Model (TRM), including core taxonomy and graphical representation.

The detailed platform taxonomy is described in Detailed Platform Taxonomy.

19.1 Concepts

This section describes the role of the TRM, the components of the TRM, and using other TRMs.

19.1.1 Role of the TRM in the Foundation Architecture

The TOGAF Foundation Architecture is an architecture of generic services and functions that provides a foundation on which more specific architectures and architectural components can be built. This Foundation Architecture has two main elements:

1. The **Technical Reference Model** (TRM), which provides a model and taxonomy of generic platform services
2. The **Standards Information Base** (SIB), which provides a database of standards that can be used to define the particular services and other components of an organization-specific architecture that is derived from the TOGAF Foundation Architecture

The TRM is universally applicable and, therefore, can be used to build any system architecture.

The list of standards and specifications in the SIB is designed to facilitate choice by concentrating on open standards, so that architectures derived from the framework will have good characteristics of interoperability and software portability, but the TOGAF Architecture Development Method (ADM) specifically includes extending the list of specifications to allow for coexistence with or migration from other architectures.

19.1.2 TRM Components

Any TRM has two main components:

1. A **taxonomy**, which defines terminology, and provides a coherent description of the components and conceptual structure of an information system
2. An associated **TRM graphic**, which provides a visual representation of the taxonomy, as an aid to understanding

The objective of the TOGAF TRM is to provide a widely accepted core taxonomy, and an appropriate visual representation of that taxonomy. The TRM graphic is illustrated in The TRM in Detail, and the taxonomy is explained in Application Platform - Taxonomy.

19.1.3 Other TRMs

One of the great difficulties in developing an architecture framework is in choosing a TRM that works for everyone.

The TOGAF TRM was originally derived from the Technical Architecture Framework for Information Management (TAFIM) TRM (which in turn was derived from the IEEE 1003.0 model - see Part IV: Resource Base, ISO/IEC TR 14252 (IEEE Std 1003.0) for details). This TRM is "platform-centric": it focuses on the services and structure of the underlying platform necessary to support the use and re-use of applications (i.e., on application portability). In particular, it centers on the interfaces between that platform and the supported applications, and between the platform and the external environment.

The current TOGAF TRM is an amended version of the TAFIM TRM, which aims to emphasize the aspect of interoperability as well as that of portability.

The objective of the TRM is to enable structured definition of the standardized Application Platform and its associated interfaces. The other entities, which are needed in any specific architecture, are only addressed in the TRM insofar as they influence the application platform. The underlying aim in this approach is to ensure that the higher-level building blocks which make up business solutions have a complete, robust platform on which to run.

Other architectural models - taxonomies and/or graphics - not only are possible, but may be preferable for some enterprises. For example, such an enterprise-specific model could be derived by extension or adaptation of the TOGAF TRM. Alternatively, a different taxonomy may be embodied in the legacy of previous architectural work by an enterprise, and the enterprise may prefer to perpetuate use of that taxonomy. Similarly, an enterprise may prefer to represent the TOGAF taxonomy (or its own taxonomy) using a different form of graphic, which better captures legacy concepts and proves easier for internal communication purposes.

Apart from the need to recognize that the structure embodied in the taxonomy is reflected in the structure of the SIB (so any enterprise adopting a different taxonomy will need to reflect its taxonomy in its own SIB), there is no problem with using other architectural taxonomies and/or graphics with TOGAF. The core of TOGAF is its ADM: the TRM and the SIB are tools used in applying the ADM in the development of specific architectures. Provided consistency between TRM and SIB are maintained, the TOGAF ADM is valid whatever the choice of specific taxonomy, TRM graphic, or SIB toolset.

19.2 High-Level Breakdown

This section describes the major elements of the TRM.

19.2.1 Overview

The coarsest breakdown of the TRM is shown in Technical Reference Model - High-Level View, which shows three major entities (Application Software, Application Platform, and Communications Infrastructure) connected by two interfaces (Application Platform Interface and Communications Infrastructure Interface).

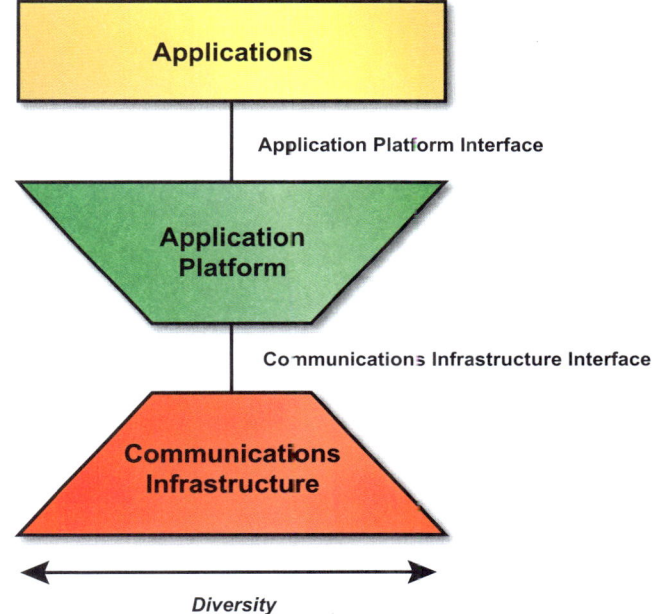

Figure 19.1: Technical Reference Model - High-Level View

The diagram says nothing about the detailed relationships between the entities; only that they exist.

Each of the elements in this diagram is discussed in detail in The TRM in Detail.

19.2.2 Portability and Interoperability

The high-level TRM seeks to emphasize two major common architectural objectives:

1. **Application Portability**, via the Application Platform Interface - identifying the set of services that are to be made available in a standard way to applications via the platform
2. **Interoperability**, via the Communications Infrastructure Interface - identifying the set of Communications Infrastructure services that are to be leveraged in a standard way by the platform

Both of these goals are essential to enable integration within the enterprise and trusted interoperability on a global scale between enterprises.

Chapter 19: Foundation Architecture – Technical Reference Model

In particular, the high-level model seeks to reflect the increasingly important role of the Internet as the basis for inter- and intra-enterprise interoperability.

The horizontal dimension of the model in Technical Reference Model - High-Level View represents diversity, and the shape of the model is intended to emphasize the importance of minimum diversity at the interface between the Application Platform and the Communications Infrastructure.

This in turn means focusing on the core set of services that can be guaranteed to be supported by every IP-based network, as the foundation on which to build today's interoperable enterprise computing environments.

19.3 The TRM in Detail

This section describes the TRM in detail, including platform service categories and external environment sub-entities.

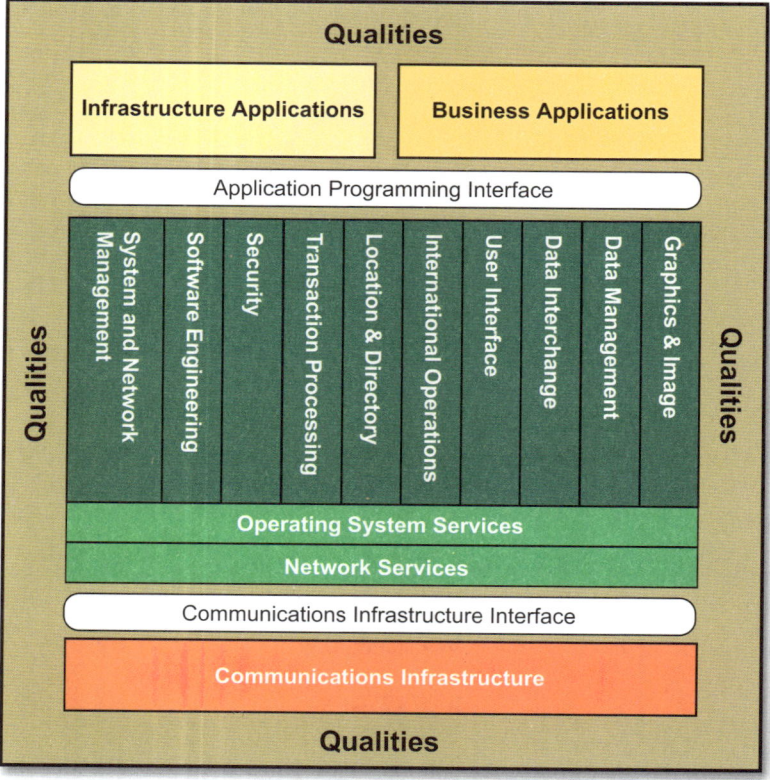

Figure 19.2: Detailed Technical Reference Model
(Showing Service Categories)

19.3.1 Introduction

Detailed Technical Reference Model (Showing Service Categories) expands on Technical Reference Model - High-Level View to present the service categories of the Application Platform and the two categories of Application Software.

Detailed Technical Reference Model (Showing Service Categories) is only a depiction of the TRM entities: it neither implies nor inhibits inter-relationships among them.

IT architectures derived from TOGAF may differ greatly depending on the requirements of the information system. In practice, many architectures will not include all of the services discussed here, and many will include additional services to support Application Software that is specific to the organization or to its vertical industry.

In building an architecture, users of TOGAF should assess their own requirements and select the services, interfaces, and standards that satisfy their own business needs.

19.3.2 TRM Entities and Interfaces

The following sections discuss in detail each element of the TRM illustrated in Detailed Technical Reference Model (Showing Service Categories). They are dealt with in the following order:

- The three entities:
    - Application Software (Application Software)
    - Application Platform (Application Platform)
    - Communications Infrastructure (Communications Infrastructure)
- The two interfaces:
    - Application Platform Interface (Application Platform Interface)
    - Communications Infrastructure Interface (Communications Infrastructure Interface)

19.3.3 Application Software

The detailed TRM recognizes two categories of Application Software:

1. **Business Applications**, which implement business processes for a particular enterprise or vertical industry. The internal structure of business applications relates closely to the specific application software configuration selected by an organization.
2. **Infrastructure Applications**, which provide general-purpose business functionality, based on infrastructure services.

During development of the Technology Architecture, business applications and infrastructure applications are important sources of requirements for Technology Architecture services, and the selection of standards for the Application Platform will be influenced strongly by the Application Software configuration to be supported.

19.3.3.1 Business Applications

Business applications are applications that are specific to a particular enterprise or vertical industry. Such applications typically model elements of an enterprise's domain of activity or business processes. Examples of business applications might include:

- Patient record management services used in the Medical industry
- Inventory management services used in the Retail industry
- Geological data modeling services used in the Petroleum industry

Over time, particular business applications may become infrastructure applications, if they become sufficiently ubiquitous, interoperable, and general-purpose to be potentially useful to a broad range of enterprise IT users.

19.3.3.2 Infrastructure Applications

Infrastructure applications are applications that have all, or nearly all, of the following characteristics:

- Widespread availability as Commercial Off-The-Shelf (COTS) software means that it is uneconomic to consider custom implementation.
- User interaction is an important part of the application's function.
- Implementations are based on infrastructure services.
- Implementations may include significant extensions beyond that needed to use the underlying infrastructure services.
- Interoperability is a strong requirement.

Examples of applications in this category include:

- Electronic payment and funds transfer services
- Electronic mail client services
- Publish and subscribe
- Intelligent agents
- Calendaring and scheduling services
- Groupware services
- Workflow services
- Spreadsheets
- Presentation software
- Document editing and presentation
- Management applications, performing general-purpose system and network management functions for the system administrator

- Software engineering tools, providing software development functions for systems development staff

Infrastructure applications have strong dependencies on lower-level services in the architecture. For example, a workflow application may use platform services such as messaging or transaction processing to implement the flow of work among tasks. Similarly, a groupware application is likely to make extensive use of both data and communication services for the structure of documents, as well as the mechanics of storing and accessing them.

Infrastructure applications by definition are applications that are considered sufficiently ubiquitous, interoperable, and general-purpose within the enterprise to be effectively considered as part of the IT infrastructure. Just as business applications may over time come to be regarded as infrastructure applications, so infrastructure applications are normally candidates for inclusion as infrastructure services in future versions of an IT architecture.

19.3.4 Application Platform

19.3.4.1 The Platform Concept

The term "platform" is used in many different ways within the IT industry today. Because of the different usages, the term is often qualified; for example, "application platform", "standardized" and "proprietary platforms", "client" and "server platforms", "distributed computing platform", "portability platform". Common to all these usages is the idea that someone needs a set of services provided by a particular kind of platform, and will implement a "higher-level" function that makes use of those services.

The TOGAF TRM focuses on the Application Platform, and the "higher-level function" is the set of Application Software, running on top of the Application Platform, that is needed to address the enterprise's business requirements.

It is important to recognize that the Application Platform in the TOGAF TRM is a single, generic, conceptual entity. From the viewpoint of the TOGAF TRM, the Application Platform contains all possible services. In a specific Target Architecture, the Application Platform will contain only those services needed to support the required functions.

Moreover, the Application Platform for a specific Target Architecture will typically not be a single entity, but rather a combination of different entities for different, commonly required functions, such as desktop client, file server, print server, application server, Internet Server, database server, etc., each of which will comprise a specific, defined set of services necessary to support the specific function concerned.

It is also important to recognize that many of the real-world IT systems that are procured and used today to implement a Technology Architecture come fully equipped with many advanced services, which are often taken for granted by the purchaser. For example, a typical desktop computer system today comes with software that implements services from most if not all of the service categories of the TOGAF TRM. Since the purchaser of such a system often does not consider anything "smaller" than the total bundle of services that comes with the system, that service bundle can very easily become the "platform". Indeed, in the absence of a Technology Architecture to guide the procurement process, this is invariably what happens. As this process is repeated across an enterprise, different systems purchased for similar functions (such as desktop client, print server, etc.) can contain markedly different bundles of services.

Service bundles are represented in a Technology Architecture in the form of "building blocks". One of the key tasks of the IT architect in going from the conceptual Application Platform of the TRM to an enterprise-specific Technology Architecture is to look beyond the set of real-world platforms already in existence in the enterprise. The IT architect must analyze the services actually needed in order to implement an IT infrastructure that meets the enterprise's business requirements in the optimal manner, and define the set of optimal Solution Building Blocks (SBBs) - real-world "platforms" - to implement that architecture.

19.3.4.2 Extending the TRM

The TOGAF TRM identifies a generic set of platform services, and provides a taxonomy in which these platform services are divided into categories of like functionality. A particular organization may need to augment this set with additional services or service categories which are considered to be generic in its own vertical market segment.

The set of services identified and defined for the Application Platform will change over time. New services will be required as new technology appears and as application needs change.

19.3.4.3 Interfaces Between Services

In addition to supporting Application Software through the Application Platform Interface (API), services in the Application Platform may support each other, either by openly specified interfaces which may or may not be the same as the API, or by private, unexposed interfaces. A key goal of architecture development is for service modules to be capable of replacement by other modules providing the same service functionality via the same service API. Use of private, unexposed interfaces among service modules may compromise this ability to substitute. Private interfaces represent a risk that should be highlighted to facilitate future transition.

19.3.4.3 Future Developments

The TRM deals with future developments in the Application Platform in two ways. Firstly, as interfaces to services become standardized, functionality which previously formed part of the Application Software entity migrates to become part of the Application Platform. Secondly, the TRM may be extended with new service categories as new technology appears.

Examples of functional areas which may fall into Application Platform service categories in the future include:

- Spreadsheet functions, including the capability to create, manipulate, and present information in tables or charts; this capability should include fourth generation language-like capabilities that enable the use of programming logic within spreadsheets

- Decision support functions, including tools that support the planning, administration, and management of projects
- Calculation functions, including the capability to perform routine and complex arithmetic calculations
- Calendar functions, including the capability to manage projects and co-ordinate schedules via an automated calendar

A detailed taxonomy of the Application Platform is given in Application Platform - Taxonomy.

19.3.5 Communications Infrastructure

The Communications Infrastructure provides the basic services to interconnect systems and provide the basic mechanisms for opaque transfer of data. It contains the hardware and software elements which make up the networking and physical communications links used by a system, and of course all the other systems connected to the network. It deals with the complex world of networks and the physical Communications Infrastructure, including switches, service providers, and the physical transmission media.

A primary driver in enterprise-wide Technology Architecture in recent years has been the growing awareness of the utility and cost-effectiveness of the Internet as the basis of a Communications Infrastructure for enterprise integration. This is causing a rapid increase in Internet usage and a steady increase in the range of applications linking to the network for distributed operation.

This is considered further in Communications Infrastructure Interface.

19.3.6 Application Platform Interface

The Application Platform Interface (API) specifies a complete interface between the Application Software and the underlying Application Platform across which all services are provided. A rigorous definition of the interface results in application portability, provided that both platform and application conform to it. For this to work, the API definition must include the syntax and semantics of not just the programmatic interface, but also all necessary protocol and data structure definitions.

Portability depends on the symmetry of conformance of both applications and the platform to the architected API. That is, the platform must support the API as specified, and the application must use no more than the specified API.

The API specifies a complete interface between an application and one or more services offered by the underlying Application Platform. An application may use several APIs, and may even use different APIs for different implementations of the same service.

19.3.7 Communications Infrastructure Interface

The Communications Infrastructure Interface is the interface between the Application Platform and the Communications Infrastructure.

Technical Reference Model - High-Level View seeks to reflect the increasingly important role of the Internet as the basis for inter- and intra-enterprise interoperability. The horizontal dimension of the model in Technical Reference Model - High-Level View represents diversity, and the shape of the model is specifically intended to emphasize minimum diversity at the interface between the Application Platform and the Communications Infrastructure.

In particular, the model emphasizes the importance of focusing on the core set of services that can be guaranteed to be supported by every IP-based network, as the foundation on which to build today's interoperable enterprise computing environments.

19.3.8 Qualities

Besides the set of components making up the TRM, there is a set of attributes or qualities that are applicable across the components. For example, for the management service to be effective, manageability must be a pervasive quality of all platform services, applications, and Communications Infrastructure services.

Detailed Technical Reference Model (Showing Service Categories) captures this concept by depicting the TRM components sitting on a backplane of qualities.

Another example of a service quality is security. The proper system-wide implementation of security requires not only a set of Security services, corresponding to the security services category shown in the platform, but also the support (i.e., the "security awareness") of software in other parts of the TRM. Thus, an application might use a security service to mark a file as read-only, but it is the correct implementation of the security quality in the operating system services which prevents write operations on the file. Security and operating system services must co-operate in making the file secure.

Qualities are specified in detail during the development of a Target Architecture. Some qualities are easier than others to describe in terms of standards. For instance, support of a set of locales can be defined to be part of the specification for the international operation quality. Other qualities can better be specified in terms of measures rather than standards. An example would be performance, for which standard APIs or protocols are of limited use.

19.4 Application Platform - Taxonomy

This section describes the Application Platform taxonomy, including basic principles and a summary of services and qualities.

19.4.1 Basic Principles

The TOGAF TRM has two main components:

1. A **taxonomy**, which defines terminology, and provides a coherent description of the components and conceptual structure of an information system
2. An associated **TRM graphic**, which provides a visual representation of the taxonomy, as an aid to understanding

This section describes in detail the taxonomy of the TOGAF TRM. The aim is to provide a core taxonomy that provides a useful, consistent, structured definition of the Application Platform entity and is widely acceptable.

No claims are made that the chosen categorization is the only one possible, or that it represents the optimal choice.

Indeed, it is important to emphasize that the use of TOGAF, and in particular the TOGAF ADM, is in no way dependent on use of the TOGAF TRM taxonomy. Other taxonomies are perfectly possible, and may be preferable for some organizations.

For example, a different taxonomy may be embodied in the legacy of previous architectural work by an organization, and the organization may prefer to perpetuate use of that taxonomy. Alternatively, an organization may decide that it can derive a more suitable, organization-specific taxonomy by extending or adapting the TOGAF TRM taxonomy.

In the same way, an organization may prefer to depict the TOGAF taxonomy (or its own taxonomy) using a different form of TRM graphic, which better captures legacy concepts and proves easier for internal communication purposes.

However, a consideration to bear in mind in deciding which taxonomy to use, is that the taxonomy of the TOGAF TRM is used in structuring the TOGAF SIB, the database of all industry standards endorsed by The Open Group which is available for populating an architecture. Any differences from the TOGAF TRM taxonomy would need to be catered for when using the TOGAF SIB. (This typically represents an additional overhead, but not a major obstacle.)

19.4.2 Application Platform Service Categories

The major categories of services defined for the Application Platform are listed below.

Note that "Object Services" does not appear as a category in the TRM taxonomy. This is because all the individual object services are incorporated into the relevant main service categories. However, the various descriptions are also collected into a single subsection (Object-Oriented Provision of Services) in order to provide a single point of reference which shows how object services relate to the main service categories.

- Data Interchange Services (Data Interchange Services):
    - Document generic data typing and conversion services

- Graphics data interchange services
- Specialized data interchange services
- Electronic data interchange services
- Fax services
- Raw graphics interface functions
- Text processing functions
- Document processing functions
- Publishing functions
- Video processing functions
- Audio processing functions
- Multimedia processing functions
- Media synchronization functions
- Information presentation and distribution functions
- Hypertext functions

■ Data Management Services (Data Management Services):
  - Data dictionary/repository services
  - Database Management System (DBMS) services
  - Object-Oriented Database Management System (OODBMS) services
  - File management services
  - Query processing functions
  - Screen generation functions
  - Report generation functions
  - Networking/concurrent access functions
  - Warehousing functions

■ Graphics and Imaging Services (Graphics and Imaging Services):
  - Graphical object management services
  - Drawing services
  - Imaging functions

■ International Operation Services (International Operation Services):
  - Character sets and data representation services
  - Cultural convention services
  - Local language support services

■ Location and Directory Services (Location and Directory Services):
  - Directory services

- Special-purpose naming services
- Service location services
- Registration services
- Filtering services
- Accounting services

■ Network Services (Network Services):
- Data communications services
- Electronic mail services
- Distributed data services
- Distributed file services
- Distributed name services
- Distributed time services
- Remote process (access) services
- Remote print spooling and output distribution services
- Enhanced telephony functions
- Shared screen functions
- Video conferencing functions
- Broadcast functions
- Mailing list functions

■ Operating System Services (Operating System Services):
- Kernel operations services
- Command interpreter and utility services
- Batch processing services
- File and directory synchronization services

■ Software Engineering Services (Software Engineering Services):
- Programming language services
- Object code linking services
- Computer-aided software engineering (CASE) environment and tools services
- Graphical user interface (GUI) building services
- Scripting language services
- Language binding services
- Run-time environment services
- Application binary interface services

■ Transaction Processing Services (Transaction Processing Services):

- Transaction manager services
- User Interface Services (User Interface Services):
    - Graphical client/server services
    - Display objects services
    - Window management services
    - Dialogue support services
    - Printing services
    - Computer-based training and online help services
    - Character-based services
- Security Services (Security Services):
    - Identification and authentication services
    - System entry control services
    - Audit services
    - Access control services
    - Non-repudiation services
    - Security management services
    - Trusted recovery services
    - Encryption services
    - Trusted communication services
- System and Network Management Services (System and Network Management Services):
    - User management services
    - Configuration management (CM) services
    - Performance management services
    - Availability and fault management services
    - Accounting management services
    - Security management services
    - Print management services
    - Network management services
    - Backup and restore services
    - Online disk management services
    - License management services
    - Capacity management services
    - Software installation services
    - Trouble ticketing services

19.4.2.1 Object-Oriented Provision of Services

A detailed description of each of these service categories is given in Object-Oriented Provision of Services.

- Object Request Broker (ORB) Services:
    - Implementation repository services
    - Installation and activation services
    - Interface repository services
    - Replication services
- Common Object Services:
    - Change management services
    - Collections services
    - Concurrency control services
    - Data interchange services
    - Event management services
    - Externalization services
    - Licensing services
    - Lifecycle services
    - Naming services
    - Persistent object services
    - Properties services
    - Query services
    - Relationship services
    - Security services
    - Start-up services
    - Time services
    - Trading services
    - Transaction services

19.4.3 Application Platform Service Qualities

19.4.3.1 Principles

Besides the platform service categories delineated by functional category, service qualities affect Information Systems Architectures. A service quality describes a behavior such as adaptability or manageability. Service qualities have a pervasive effect on the operation of most or all of the functional service categories.

In general a requirement for a given level of a particular service quality requires one or more functional service categories to co-operate in achieving the objective. Usually this means that the software building blocks that implement the functional services contain software which contributes to the implementation of the quality.

For the quality to be provided properly, all relevant functional services must have been designed to support it. Service qualities may also require support from software in the Application Software entity and the External Environment as well as the Application Platform.

In some cases, a service quality affects each of the service categories in a similar fashion, while in other cases, the service quality has a unique influence on one particular service category. For instance, international operation depends on most of the service categories in the same way, both providing facilities and needing their co-operation for localization of messages, fonts, and other features of a locale, but it may have a more profound effect on the software engineering services, where facilities for producing internationalized software may be required.

During the process of architecture development, the architect must be aware of the existence of qualities and the extent of their influence on the choice of software building blocks used in implementing the architecture. The best way of making sure that qualities are not forgotten is to create a quality matrix, describing the relationships between each functional service and the qualities that influence it.

19.4.3.2 Taxonomy of Service Qualities

The service qualities presently identified in the TRM taxonomy are:

- **Availability** (the degree to which something is available for use), including:
    - **Manageability**, the ability to gather information about the state of something and to control it
    - **Serviceability**, the ability to identify problems and take corrective action, such as to repair or upgrade a component in a running system
    - **Performance**, the ability of a component to perform its tasks in an appropriate time
    - **Reliability,** or resistance to failure
    - **Recoverability,** or the ability to restore a system to a working state after an interruption
    - **Locatability,** the ability of a system to be found when needed
- **Assurance**, including:
    - **Security**, or the protection of information from unauthorized access
    - **Integrity**, or the assurance that data has not been corrupted
    - **Credibility**, or the level of trust in the integrity of the system and its data
- **Usability**, or ease-of-operation by users, including:
    - **International Operation**, including multi-lingual and multi-cultural abilities

- Adaptability, including:
    - **Interoperability**, whether within or outside the organization (for instance, interoperability of calendaring or scheduling functions may be key to the usefulness of a system)
    - **Scalability**, the ability of a component to grow or shrink its performance or capacity appropriately to the demands of the environment in which it operates
    - **Portability**, of data, people, applications, and components
    - **Extensibility**, or the ability to accept new functionality
    - The ability to offer access to services in new paradigms such as object-orientation

Chapter 20: Detailed Platform Taxonomy

This chapter provides a detailed taxonomy of platform services and qualities.

20.1 Data Interchange Services

Data interchange services provide specialized support for the interchange of information between applications and the external environment. These services are designed to handle data interchange between applications on the same platform and applications on different (heterogeneous) platforms. An analogous set of services exists for object-oriented data interchange, which can be found under Data Interchange services and Externalization services in Object-Oriented Provision of Services.

- **Document Generic Data Typing and Conversion** services are supported by specifications for encoding the data (e.g., text, pictures, numerics, special characters) and both the logical and visual structures of electronic documents, including compound documents.

- **Graphics Data Interchange** services are supported by device-independent descriptions of picture elements for vector-based graphics and descriptions for raster-based graphics.

- **Specialized Data Interchange** services are supported by specifications that describe data used by specific vertical markets. Markets where such specifications exist include the Medical, Library, Dental, Assurance, and Oil industries.

- **Electronic Data Interchange** services are used to create an electronic (paperless) environment for conducting commerce and achieving significant gains in quality, responsiveness, and savings afforded by such an environment. Examples of applications that use electronic commerce services include: vendor search and selection; contract award; product data; shipping, forwarding, and receiving; customs; payment information; inventory control; maintenance; tax-related data; and insurance-related data.

- **Fax** services are used to create, examine, transmit, and/or receive fax images.

The following functional areas are currently supported mainly by Application Software, but are progressing towards migration into the Application Platform:

- **Raw Graphics Interface** functions support graphics data file formats such as TIFF, JPEG, GIF, and CGM.

- **Text Processing** functions, including the capability to create, edit, merge, and format text.

- **Document Processing** functions, including the capability to create, edit, merge, and format documents. These functions enable the composition of documents that incorporate graphics, images, and even voice annotation, along with stylized text. Included are advanced formatting and editing functions such as style guides, spell checking, use of multiple columns, table of contents generation, headers and footers, outlining tools, and support for scanning images into bit-mapped formats. Other capabilities include compression and decompression of images or whole documents.

- **Publishing** functions, including incorporation of photographic quality images and color graphics, and advanced formatting and style features such as wrapping text around graphic objects or pictures and kerning (i.e., changing the spacing between text characters). These functions also interface with sophisticated printing and production equipment. Other capabilities include color rendering and compression and decompression of images or whole documents.

- **Video Processing** functions, including the capability to capture, compose, edit, compress, and decompress video information using formats such as MPEG. Still graphics and title generation functions are also provided.

- **Audio Processing** functions, including the capability to capture, compose, edit, compress, and decompress audio information.

- **Multimedia Processing** functions, including the capability to store, retrieve, modify, sort, search, and print all or any combination of the above-mentioned media. This includes support for microfilm media, optical storage technology that allows for storage of scanned or computer produced documents using digital storage techniques, a scanning capability, and data compression and decompression.

- **Media Synchronization** functions allow the synchronization of streams of data such as audio and video for presentation purposes.

- **Information Presentation and Distribution** functions are used to manage the distribution and presentation of information from batch and interactive applications. These functions are used to shield business area applications from how information is used. They allow business area applications to create generic pools of information without embedding controls that dictate the use of that information. Information distribution and presentation functions include the selection of the appropriate formatting functions required to accomplish the distribution and presentation of information to a variety of business area applications and users. Information presentation and distribution functions also include the capability to store, archive, prioritize, restrict, and recreate information.

- **Hypertext** functions support the generation, distribution, location, search, and display of text and images either locally or globally. These functions include searching and browsing, hypertext linking, and the presentation of multimedia information.

20.2 Data Management Services

Central to most systems is the management of data that can be defined independently of the processes that create or use it, maintained indefinitely, and shared among many processes. Data management services include:

- **Data Dictionary/Repository** services allow data administrators and information engineers to access and modify data about data (i.e., metadata). Such data may include internal and external formats, integrity and security rules, and location within a distributed system. Data dictionary and repository services also allow end users and applications to define and obtain data that is available in the database. Data administration defines the standardization and registration of individual data element types to meet the requirements for data sharing and interoperability among information systems throughout the enterprise. Data administration functions include procedures, guidelines, and methods for effective data planning, analysis, standards, modeling, configuration management, storage, retrieval, protection, validation, and documentation. Data dictionaries are sometimes tied to a single Database Management System (DBMS), but heterogeneous data dictionaries will support access to different DBMSs. Repositories can contain a wide variety of information including Management Information Bases (MIB) or CASE-related information. Object-oriented systems may provide repositories for objects and interfaces, described under Implementation Repository services and Interface Repository services in Object-Oriented Provision of Services.

- **Database Management System (DBMS)** services provide controlled access to structured data. To manage the data, the DBMS provides concurrency control and facilities to combine data from different schemas. Different types of DBMS support different data models, including relational, hierarchical, network, object-oriented, and flat-file models. Some DBMSs are designed for special functions such as the storage of large objects or multimedia data. DBMS services are accessible through a programming language interface, an interactive data manipulation language interface (such as SQL), or an interactive/fourth-generation language interface. Look-up and retrieval services for objects are described separately under Query services in Object-Oriented Provision of Services. For efficiency, DBMSs often provide specific services to create, populate, move, backup, restore, recover, and archive databases, although some of these services could be provided by the general file management capabilities described in Operating System Services or a specific backup service. Some DBMSs support distribution of the database, including facilities for remotely updating records, data replication, locating and caching data, and remote management.

- **Object-Oriented Database Management System (OODBMS)** services provide storage for objects and interfaces to those objects. These services may support the Implementation Repository, Interface Repository, and Persistent Object services in Object-Oriented Provision of Services.

- **File Management** services provide data management through file access methods including indexed sequential (ISAM) and hashed random access. Flat file and directory services are described in Operating System Services.

The following functional areas are currently supported mainly by Application Software, but are progressing towards migration into the Application Platform:

- **Query Processing** functions that provide for interactive selection, extraction, and formatting of stored information from files and databases. Query processing functions are invoked via user-oriented languages and tools (often referred to as fourth generation languages), which simplify the definition of searching criteria and aid in creating effective presentation of the retrieved information (including use of graphics).

- **Screen Generation** functions that provide the capability to define and generate screens that support the retrieval, presentation, and update of data.
- **Report Generation** functions that provide the capability to define and generate hardcopy reports composed of data extracted from a database.
- **Networking/Concurrent Access** functions that manage concurrent user access to Database Management System (DBMS) functions.
- **Warehousing** functions provide the capability to store very large amounts of data - usually captured from other database systems - and to perform online analytical processing on it in support of ad hoc queries.

20.3 Graphics and Imaging Services

Graphics services provide functions required for creating, storing, retrieving, and manipulating images. These services include:

- **Graphical Object Management** services, including defining multi-dimensional graphic objects in a form that is independent of output devices, and managing hierarchical structures containing graphics data. Graphical data formats include two- and three-dimensional geometric drawings as well as images.
- **Drawing** services support the creation and manipulation of images with software such as GKS, PEX, PHIGS, or OpenGL.

The following functional areas are currently supported mainly by Application Software, but are progressing towards migration into the Application Platform:

- **Imaging** functions providing for the scan, creation, edit, compression, and decompression of images in accordance with recognized image formatting standards; for example, PIKS/IPI, OpenXIL, or XIE.

20.4 International Operation Services

As a practice, information system developers have generally designed and developed systems to meet the requirements of a specific geographic or linguistic market segment, which may be a nation or a particular cultural market. To make that information system viable, or marketable, to a different segment of the market, a full re-engineering process was usually required. Users or organizations that needed to operate in a multi-national or multi-cultural environment typically did so with multiple, generally incompatible information processing systems.

International operation provides a set of services and interfaces that allow a user to define, select, and change between different culturally-related application environments supported by the particular implementation. In general, these services should be provided in such a way that internationalization issues are transparent to the application logic.

- **Character Sets and Data Representation** services include the capability to input, store, manipulate, retrieve, communicate, and present data independently of the coding scheme used. This includes the capability to maintain and access a central character set repository of all coded character sets used throughout the platform. Character sets will be uniquely identified so that the end user or application can select the coded character set to be used. This system-independent representation supports the transfer (or sharing) of the values and syntax, but not the semantics, of data records between communicating systems. The specifications are independent of the internal record and field representations of the communicating systems. Also included is the capability to recognize the coded character set of data entities and subsequently to input, communicate, and present that data.

- **Cultural Convent**ion services provide the capability to store and access rules and conventions for cultural entities maintained in a cultural convention repository called a locale. Locales should be available to all applications. Locales typically include date and currency formats, collation sequences, and number formats. Standardized locale formats and APIs allow software entities to use locale information developed by others.

- **Local Language Support** services provide the capability to support more than one language concurrently on a system. Messages, menus, forms, and online documentation can be displayed in the language selected by the user. Input from keyboards that have been modified locally to support the local character sets can be correctly interpreted.

The proper working of international operation services depends on all the software entities involved having the capability to:

- Use locales
- Switch between locales as required
- Maintain multiple active locales
- Access suitable fonts

This requires software entities to be written to a particular style and to be designed from the outset with internationalization in mind.

20.5 Location and Directory Services

Location and directory services provide specialized support for locating required resources and for mediation between service consumers and service providers.

The World Wide Web, based on the Internet, has created a need for locating information resources, which currently is mainly satisfied through the use of search engines. Advancements in the global Internet, and in heterogeneous distributed systems, demand active mediation through broker services that include automatic and dynamic registration, directory access, directory communication, filtration, and accounting services for access to resources.

- **Directory** services provide services for clients to establish where resources are, and by extension how they can be reached. "Clients" may be humans or computer programs, and "resources" may be a wide variety of things, such as names, email addresses, security certificates, printers, web pages, etc.

- **Special-Purpose Naming** services provide services that refer names (ordered strings of printable characters) to objects within a given context (namespaces). Objects are typically hierarchically organized within namespaces. Examples are:
  - File systems
  - Security databases
  - Process queues
- **Service Location** services provide access to "Yellow Pages" services in response to queries based on constraints.
- **Registration** services provide services to register identity, descriptions of the services a resource is providing, and descriptions of the means to access them.
- **Filtering** services provide services to select useful information from data using defined criteria.
- **Accounting** services provide services such as account open, account update, account balance, account detail, account close, account discounts, account bill/usage tally, account payment settlement based on message traffic, and/or connection time, and/or resource utilization, and/or broker-specific (e.g., value-based).

20.6 Network Services

Network services are provided to support distributed applications requiring data access and applications interoperability in heterogeneous or homogeneous networked environments.

A network service consists of both an interface and an underlying protocol.

- Data Communications, which include interfaces and protocols for reliable, transparent, end-to-end data transmission across communications networks. Data communications services include both high-level functions (such as file transfer, remote login, remote process execution, or PC integration services) and low-level functions (such as a sockets API) giving direct access to communications protocols.
- Electronic Mail services include the capability to send, receive, forward, store, display, retrieve, prioritize, authenticate, and manage messages. This includes the capability to append files and documents to messages. Messages may include any combination of data, text, audio, graphics, and images and should be capable of being formatted into standard data interchange formats. This service includes the use of directories and distribution lists for routing information, the ability to assign priorities, the use of pre-formatted electronic forms, and the capability to trace the status of messages. Associated services include a summarized listing of incoming messages, a log of messages received and read, the ability to file or print messages, and the ability to reply to or forward messages.
- Distributed Data services provide access to, and modification of, data/metadata in remote

or local databases. In a distributed environment, data not available on the local database is fetched from a remote data server at the request of the local client.

- Distributed File services provide for transparent remote file access. Applications have equivalent access to data regardless of the data's physical location. Ancillary services for this function can include transparent addressing, cached data, data replication, file locking, and file logging.

- Distributed Name services provide a means for unique identification of resources within a distributed computing system. These services are available to applications within the network and provide information that can include resource name, associated attributes, physical location, and resource functionality. Note that all system resources should be identifiable, in all information systems, by the distributed name. This permits physical location to change, not only to accommodate movement, but also load balancing, system utilization, scaling (adding processors and moving resources to accommodate the increased resources), distributed processing, and all aspects of open systems. Distributed name services include directory services such as X.500 and network navigation services. Distributed name services include ways to locate data objects both by name and by function. Object-Oriented Provision of Services describes equivalent services under Naming services and Trading services, respectively.

- Distributed Time services provide synchronized time co-ordination as required among distributed processes in different timezones. An equivalent service is described under Time services in Object-Oriented Provision of Services.

- Remote Process (Access) services provide the means for dispersed applications to communicate across a computer network. These services facilitate program-to-program communications regardless of their distributed nature or operation on heterogeneous platforms. Remote process services including remote procedure call (RPC) and asynchronous messaging mechanisms underpin client/server applications.

- Remote Print Spooling and Output Distribution services provide the means for printing output remotely. The services include management of remote printing including printer and media selection, use of forms, security, and print queue management.

The following functional areas are currently supported mainly by Application Software, but are progressing towards migration into the Application Platform:

- Enhanced Telephony functions, including call set-up, call co-ordination, call forwarding, call waiting, programmed directories, teleconferencing, automatic call distribution (useful for busy customer service categories), and call detail recording.

- Shared Screen functions that provide audio teleconferencing with common workstation windows between two or more users. This includes the capability to refresh windows whenever someone displays new material or changes an existing display. Every user is provided with the capability to graphically annotate or modify the shared conference window.

- Video-Conferencing functions that provide two-way video transmission between different sites. These functions include call set-up, call co-ordination, full motion display of events and participants in a bi-directional manner, support for the management of directing the cameras, ranging from fixed position, to sender directed, to receiver directed, to automated sound pickup.

- Broadcast functions that provide one-way audio or audio/video communications functions between a sending location and multiple receiving locations or between multiple sending and receiving locations.

- Mailing List functions that allow groups to participate in conferences. These conferences may or may not occur in real time. Conferees or invited guests can drop in or out of conferences or subconferences at will. The ability to trace the exchanges is provided. Functions include exchange of documents, conference management, recording facilities, and search and retrieval capabilities.

20.7 Operating System Services

Operating system services are responsible for the management of platform resources, including the processor, memory, files, and input and output. They generally shield applications from the implementation details of the machine. Operating system services include:

- **Kernel Operations** provide low-level services necessary to:
    - Create and manage processes and threads of execution
    - Execute programs
    - Define and communicate asynchronous events
    - Define and process system clock operations
    - Implement security features
    - Manage files and directories
    - Control input/output processing to and from peripheral devices

Some kernel services have analogues described in Object-Oriented Provision of Services, such as concurrency control services.

- **Command Interpreter and Utility** services include mechanisms for services at the operator level, such as:
    - Comparing, printing, and displaying file contents
    - Editing files
    - Searching patterns
    - Evaluating expressions
    - Logging messages
    - Moving files between directories
    - Sorting data

- Executing command scripts
- Local print spooling
- Scheduling signal execution processes
- Accessing environment information

■ **Batch Processing** services support the capability to queue work (jobs) and manage the sequencing of processing based on job control commands and lists of data. These services also include support for the management of the output of batch processing, which frequently includes updated files or databases and information products such as printed reports or electronic documents. Batch processing is performed asynchronously from the user requesting the job.

■ File and Directory Synchronization services allow local and remote copies of files and directories to be made identical. Synchronization services are usually used to update files after periods of offline working on a portable system.

20.8 Software Engineering Services

The functional aspect of an application is embodied in the programming languages used to code it. Additionally, professional system developers require tools appropriate to the development and maintenance of applications. These capabilities are provided by software engineering services, which include:

■ **Programming Language** services provide the basic syntax and semantic definition for use by a software developer to describe the desired Application Software function. Shell and executive script language services enable the use of operating system commands or utilities rather than a programming language. Shells and executive scripts are typically interpreted rather than compiled, but some operating systems support compilers for executive scripts. In contrast, some compilers produce code to be interpreted at runtime. Other tools in this group include source code formatters and compiler compilers.

■ **Object Code Linking** services provide the ability for programs to access the underlying application and operating system platform through APIs that have been defined independently of the computer language. It is used by programmers to gain access to these services using methods consistent with the operating system and specific language used. Linking is operating system-dependent, but language-independent.

■ **Computer-Aided Software Engineering (CASE) Environment and Tools** services include systems and programs that assist in the automated development and maintenance of software. These include, but are not limited to, tools for requirements specification and analysis, for design work and analysis, for creating, editing, testing, and debugging program code, for documenting, for prototyping, and for group communication. The interfaces among these tools include services for storing and retrieving information about systems and exchanging this information among the various components of the system development environment. An adjunct to these capabilities is the ability to manage and control the configuration of software components, test data, and libraries to record changes to source code or to access CASE repositories. Other language tools include code generators and translators, artificial intelligence tools and tools like the UNIX system command make, which uses knowledge of the interdependencies between modules to recompile and link only those parts of a program which have changed.

- **Graphical User Interface (GUI) Building** services assist in the development of the Human Computer Interface (HCI) elements of applications. Tools include services for generating and capturing screen layouts, and for defining the appearance, function, behavior, and position of graphical objects.

- **Scripting Language** services provide interpreted languages which allow the user to carry out some complicated function in a simple way. Application areas served by special-purpose scripting languages include calculation, graphical user interface development, and development of prototype applications.

- **Language Binding** services provide mappings from interfaces provided by programming languages onto the services provided by the Application Platform. In many cases the mapping is straightforward since the platform supplies analogous services to those expected by the application. In other cases the language binding service must use a combination of Application Platform services to provide a fully functional mapping.

- **Run-Time Environment** services provide support for Application Software at run time. This support includes locating and connecting dynamically linked libraries, or even emulation of an operating environment other than the one which actually exists.

- **Application Binary Interface** services provide services that make the Application Platform comply with defined application binary interface standards.

20.9 Transaction Processing Services

Transaction Processing (TP) services provide support for the online processing of information in discrete units called transactions, with assurance of the state of the information at the end of the transaction. This typically involves predetermined sequences of data entry, validation, display, and update or inquiry against a file or database. It also includes services to prioritize and track transactions. TP services may include support for distribution of transactions to a combination of local and remote processors.

A transaction is a complete unit of work. It may comprise many computational tasks, which may include user interface, data retrieval, and communications. A typical transaction modifies shared resources. Transactions must also be able to be rolled back (that is, undone) if necessary, at any stage. When a transaction is completed without failure, it is committed. Completion of a transaction means either commitment or rollback.

Typically a TP service will contain a transaction manager, which links data entry and display software with processing, database, and other resources to form the complete service.

The sum of all the work done anywhere in the system in the course of a single transaction is called a global transaction. Transactions are not limited to a single Application Platform.

- **Transaction Manager** services, which allow an application to demarcate transactions, and direct their completion. Transaction manager services include:
  - Starting a transaction
  - Co-ordination of recoverable resources involved in a transaction
  - Committing or rolling back transactions
  - Controlling timeouts on transactions
  - Chaining transactions together
  - Monitoring transaction status

Some transaction manager services have equivalents described in Object-Oriented Provision of Services, under Transaction services.

20.10 User Interface Services

User interface services define how users may interact with an application. Depending on the capabilities required by users and the applications, these interfaces may include the following:

- Graphical Client/Server services that define the relationships between client and server processes operating graphical user interface displays, usually within a network. In this case, the program that controls each display unit is a server process, while independent user programs are client processes that request display services from the server.

- Display Objects services that define characteristics of display elements such as color, shape, size, movement, graphics context, user preferences, font management, and interactions among display elements.

- Window Management services that define how windows are created, moved, stored, retrieved, removed, and related to each other.

- Dialogue Support services translate the data entered for display to that which is actually displayed on the screen (e.g., cursor movements, keyboard data entry, external data entry devices).

- Printing services support output of text and/or graphical data, including any filtering or format conversion necessary. Printing services may include the ability to print all or part of a document, to print and collate more than one copy, to select the size and orientation of output, to choose print resolution, colors, and graphical behavior, and to specify fonts and other characteristics.

- Computer-Based Training and Online Help services provide an integrated training environment on user workstations. Training is available on an as-needed basis for any application available in the environment. Electronic messages are provided at the stroke of a key from anywhere within the application. This includes tutorial training on the application in use and the availability of offline, on-site interactive training.

- Character-Based services, which deal with support for non-graphical terminals. Character-based services include support for terminal type-independent control of display attributes, cursor motions, programmable keys, audible signals, and other functions.

The services associated with a window system include the visual display of information on a screen that contains one or more windows or panels, support for pointing to an object on the screen using a pointing device such as a mouse or touch-screen, and the manipulation of a set of objects on the screen through the pointing device or through keyboard entry. Other user interfaces included are industrial controls and virtual reality devices.

20.11 Security Services

Security services are necessary to protect sensitive information in the information system. The appropriate level of protection is determined based upon the value of the information to the business area end users and the perception of threats to it.

To be effective, security needs to be made strong, must never be taken for granted, and must be designed into an architecture and not bolted on afterwards. Whether a system is standalone or distributed, security must be applied to the whole system. It must not be forgotten that the requirement for security extends not only across the range of entities in a system but also through time.

In establishing a security architecture, the best approach is to consider what is being defended, what value it has, and what the threats to it are. The principal threats to be countered are:

- Loss of confidentiality of data
- Unavailability of data or services
- Loss of integrity of data
- Unauthorized use of resources

Counters to these threats are provided by the following services:

- **Identification and Authentication** services provide:
    - Identification, accountability, and audit of users and their actions
    - Authentication and account data
    - Protection of authentication data
    - Active user status information
    - Password authentication mechanisms
- **System Entry Control** services provide:
    - Warning to unauthorized users that the system is security-aware
    - Authentication of users
    - Information, displayed on entry, about previous successful and unsuccessful login attempts

- User-initiated locking of a session preventing further access until the user has been re-authenticated
- **Audit** services provide authorized control and protection of the audit trail, recording of detailed information security-relevant events, and audit trail control, management, and inspection.
- **Access Control** services provide:
    - Access control attributes for subjects (such as processes) and objects (such as files)
    - Enforcement of rules for assignment and modification of access control attributes
    - Enforcement of access controls
    - Control of object creation and deletion, including ensuring that re-use of objects does not allow subjects to accidentally gain access to information previously held in the object

    Access control services also appear under Security services in Object-Oriented Provision of Services.
- **Non-Repudiation** services provide proof that a user carried out an action, or sent or received some information, at a particular time. Non-repudiation services also appear under Security services in Object-Oriented Provision of Services.
- **Security Management** services provide secure system set-up and initialization, control of security policy parameters, management of user registration data, and system resources and restrictions on the use of administrative functions.
- **Trusted Recovery** services provide recovery facilities such as restoring from backups in ways that do not compromise security protection.
- **Encryption** services provide ways of encoding data such that it can only be read by someone who possesses an appropriate key, or some other piece of secret information. As well as providing data confidentiality for trusted communication, encryption services are used to underpin many other services including identification and authentication, system entry control, and access control services.
- **Trusted Communication** services provide:
    - A secure way for communicating parties to authenticate themselves to each other without the risk of an eavesdropper subsequently masquerading as one of the parties
    - A secure way of generating and verifying check values for data integrity
    - Data encipherment and decipherment for confidentiality and other purposes
    - A way to produce an irreversible hash of data for support of digital signature and non-repudiation functions
    - Generation, derivation, distribution, storage, retrieval, and deletion of cryptographic keys

Security services require other software entities to co-operate in:

- Access control for resources managed by the entity

- Accounting and audit of security-relevant events
- The import and export of data
- Potentially all other security services depending on the particular implementation approach

Security services are one category where a wide view is particularly important, as a chain is only as strong as its weakest link. This is one category of services where the external environment has critical implications on the Application Platform. For instance, the presence of a firewall may provide a single point of access onto a network from the outside world, making it possible to concentrate access control in one place and relax requirements behind the firewall.

20.12 System and Network Management Services

Information systems are composed of a wide variety of diverse resources that must be managed effectively to achieve the goals of an open system environment. While the individual resources (such as printers, software, users, processors) may differ widely, the abstraction of these resources as managed objects allows for treatment in a uniform manner. The basic concepts of management - including operation, administration, and maintenance - may then be applied to the full suite of information system components along with their attendant services.

System and network management functionality may be divided in several different ways; one way is to make a division according to the management elements that generically apply to all functional resources. This division reduces as follows:

- **User Management** services provide the ability to maintain a user's preferences and privileges.
- **Configuration Management (CM)** services address four basic functions:
    - Identification and specification of all component resources
    - Control, or the ability to freeze configuration items, changing them only through agreed processes
    - Status accounting of each configuration item
    - Verification through a series of reviews to ensure conformity between the actual configuration item and the information recorded about it

    These services include: Processor CM, Network CM, Distributed System CM, Topology CM, and Application CM. Processor CM takes a platform-centric approach. Network CM and Distributed System CM services allow remote systems to be managed and monitored including the interchange of network status. Topology CM is used to control the topology of physical or logical entities that are distributed. Application CM focuses on applications. Configuration management also appears as Change Management services in Object-Oriented Provision of Services.

- **Performance Management** services monitor performance aspects of hardware, platform and application software, and network components and provide ways to tune the system to meet performance targets.
- **Availability and Fault Management** services allow a system to react to the loss or incorrect operation of system components including hardware, platform software, and application software.
- **Accounting Management** services provide the ability to cost services for charging and reimbursement.
- **Security Management** services control the security services in accordance with applicable security policies.
- **Print Management** services provide the ability to manage both local and remote print spooling services.
- **Network Management** services comprise elements of all the services described above, but are often treated as a separate service.
- **Backup and Restore** services provide a multi-level storage facility to ensure continued data security in case of component or subsystem failure.
- **Online Disk Management** services manage the utilization of disk storage against threshold values and invoke corrective action.
- **License Management** services support the effective enforcement of software license agreements. Licensing services for objects are described under Licensing services in Object-Oriented Provision of Services.
- **Capacity Management** services address three basic functions:
    - Capacity management analyzing current and historic performance and capacity
    - Workload management to identify and understand applications that use the system
    - Capacity planning to plan required hardware resources for the future
- **Software Installation** services support distribution, installation, removal, relocation, activation, and automatic update of software or data packages from transportable media or over networks. Similar services for objects are described under Installation and Activation services in Object-Oriented Provision of Services.

The following functional areas are currently supported mainly by Application Software, but are progressing towards migration into the Application Platform:

- **Trouble Ticketing** services support the generation, processing, and tracking of problem reports. Trouble ticketing is a term originating in the telecommunications world, referring to the ability to pass fault reports both within and between telecommunications service providers. In this environment, faults are often found by a customer of one provider, while the cause of the problem lies within the administrative domain of another provider. Trouble ticketing is a common service that may be useful to an increasing range of applications if the necessary work is done to extend it from telecommunications into wider areas of distributed applications such as email.

This breakout of system and network management services parallels the breakout of emerging OSI network management, thereby presenting an overall coherent framework that applies equally to whole networks and the individual nodes of the networks.

One important consideration of the standards supporting the services in this category is that they should not enforce specific management policies, but rather enable a wide variety of different management policies to be implemented, selected according to the particular needs of the end-user installations.

System and network management services require the co-operation of other software entities in:

- Providing status information
- Notifying events
- Responding to management instructions

20.13 Object-Oriented Provision of Services

This section shows how services are provided in an object-oriented manner. "Object Services" does not appear as a category in the Technical Reference Model (TRM) since all the individual object services are incorporated as appropriate in the given service categories.

An object is an identifiable, encapsulated entity that provides one or more services that can be requested by a client. Clients request a service by invoking the appropriate method associated with the object, and the object carries out the service on the client's behalf. Objects provide a programming paradigm that can lead to important benefits, including:

- Increased modularity
- A reduction in errors
- Ease of debugging

Object management services provide ways of creating, locating, and naming objects, and allowing them to communicate in a distributed environment. The complete set of object services identified so far is listed below for the sake of completeness. Where a particular object service is part of a more generally applicable service category, a pointer to the other service category is given. Object services include:

- **Object Request Broker (ORB)** services, which enable objects to transparently make and receive requests and responses in a distributed environment. ORB services include:
    - **Implementation Repository** services support the location and management of object implementations. The services resemble those provided by the Data Dictionary/Repository services in Data Management Services.
    - **Installation and Activation** services provide ways to distribute, install, activate, and relocate objects. This corresponds to the Software Installation services in System and

Network Management Services.

- **Interface Repository** services support the storage and management of information about interfaces to objects. The services resemble those provided by the Data Dictionary/Repository services in Data Management Services.
- **Replication** services support replication of objects in distributed systems, including management of consistency between the copies.

■ **Common Object services**, which provide basic functions for using and implementing objects. These are the services necessary to construct any distributed application. Common object services include:

- **Change Management** services provide for version identification and configuration management of object interfaces, implementations, and instances. This corresponds to the Configuration Management services described in System and Network Management Services.
- **Collections** services provide operations on collections of objects, such as lists, trees, stacks, or queues. Services include establishing, adding objects to or removing them from collections, testing set membership, forming unions and intersections of sets, and so on.
- **Concurrency Control** services enable multiple clients to co-ordinate their access to shared resources. Synchronization like this is normally provided using the Kernel services provided in Operating System Services.
- **Data Interchange** services support the exchange of visible state information between objects. Depending on the kind of object involved, this corresponds to one or more of the services provided in Data Interchange Services.
- **Event Management** services provide basic capabilities for the management of events, including asynchronous events, event "fan-in", notification "fan-out", and reliable event delivery.
- **Externalization** services define protocols and conventions for externalizing and internalizing objects. Externalizing means recording the object state in a stream of data, and internalizing means recreating an object state from a data stream. This is one example of the Information Presentation and Distribution functions in Data Interchange Services.
- **Licensing** services support policies for object licensing, and measurement and charging for object use. This corresponds to the License Management services in System and Network Management Services.
- **Lifecycle** services define conventions for creating, deleting, copying, and moving objects. The creation of objects is defined in terms of factory objects, which are objects that create other objects.
- **Naming** services provide the ability to bind a name to an object, and to locate an object by its name. This is analogous to the Distributed Name service described in Network Services.

- **Persistent Object** services provide common interfaces for retaining and managing the persistent state of objects. Objects are often stored in an OODBMS, described as one of the services in Data Management Services.
- **Properties** services support the creation, deletion, assignment, and protection of dynamic properties associated with objects.
- **Query** services support indexing and query operations on collections of objects that return a subset of the collection. This is similar to database lookup, a part of the DBMS functions in Data Management Services.

- **Relationship** services allow relationships between objects (such as ownership or containment) to be explicitly represented as objects.
- **Security** services support access control on objects and non-repudiation of operations on objects. Access control is defined as a security service (see Security Services). Non-repudiation, which is also a Security service, provides proof that an action was carried out by a particular user at a particular time.
- **Start-Up** services support automatic start-up and termination of object services at ORB start-up or termination.
- **Time** services support synchronization of clocks in a distributed system. This is the same as the Distributed Time service in Network Services.
- **Trading** services allow clients to locate objects by the services the objects provide, rather than by name. This is similar to the Distributed Name service in Network Services.
- **Transaction** services provide facilities for grouping operations into atomic units, called transactions, with the certainty that a transaction will be carried out in its entirety or not at all. This corresponds to some of the Transaction Manager services in Transaction Processing Services.

Chapter 21:
Foundation Architecture - Standards Information Base

This chapter describes the Standards Information Base (SIB), the database of industry standards for populating an architecture.

21.1 Introduction

This section describes the role of the SIB, and how to access it.

21.1.1 Role of the SIB

Previous sections of Part III: Enterprise Continuum have set the TOGAF Foundation Architecture in context to the Architecture Continuum, and described in detail one part of it, the TOGAF Technical Reference Model (TRM). This section describes the other part of the TOGAF Foundation Architecture, the Standards Information Base (SIB).

21.1.1.1 What is the SIB?

The SIB is a database of facts and guidance about information systems standards. The standards to which it refers come from many sources: from formal standards bodies such as ISO or IEEE; from authoritative standards makers such as the Internet Society; and from other consortia, like the World Wide Web Consortium (*www.w3.org*) and the Object Management Group (*www.omg.org*).

21.1.1.2 What is it for?

The SIB has three main uses:

1. Architecture Development

   For an organization that is creating an architecture for its information systems, the SIB provides a valuable source of information about standards that may be used to populate the architecture.

2. Acquisition/Procurement

   An organization that is planning a procurement (whether or not based on an architecture) will find that the SIB can help ensure that the procurement gives a clear statement of technical requirements, with an assurance of conformance.

3. General Information

   Finally, it can simply be a source of information about relevant IT standards, for use by anyone at any time.

The standards listed in the various tables are all Open Group standards; that is, standards endorsed by The Open Group as fit-for-purpose in architecture specification and procurement. They have been approved by the members of The Open Group as appropriate for use in architecture and procurement.

21.1.1.3 How is it Used in Architecture Development?

The entries in the SIB are linked either to other Open Group databases and resources (in particular those relating to Product Standards and Registered Products) or, where relevant, to the web sites of other organizations.

In this way, the SIB provides the architect with a gateway to a uniquely powerful set of tools for defining the standards that an architecture is to mandate, and for checking the availability in the marketplace of products guaranteed to conform to those standards.

In the context of TOGAF, the SIB can be used to dynamically generate lists, structured according to the TOGAF TRM taxonomy, of the standards endorsed by The Open Group for use in open systems architectures.

For a detailed explanation of how the standards generated in this way are used, refer to Part II: Architecture Development Method (ADM), which describes how to use the complete TOGAF Foundation Architecture as a basis for defining (by service) all the standards that make up the Target Technology Architecture, and all the Software Building Blocks (SBBs) that will be used to implement it.

21.1.2 Accessing the SIB

Originally held as part of the TOGAF document set, the SIB is now held in a database with web-enabled user access:

- The SIB home page (*www.opengroup.org/sib*) is the usual starting point. You may want to bookmark the home page after following the hyperlink. It contains the two direct links shown below, plus a link to the detailed explanation on Using the SIB (see Using the SIB).
- You can access the SIB selectively through a search interface (*www.opengroup.org/cgi-bin/dbcgi?TPL=search_sib*) according to your own defined criteria.
- Alternatively, you can view the entire SIB (*www.opengroup.org/sib*).

21.2 The Open Group Standards

This section looks at The Open Group standards, including technical processes, Product Standards, and the Open Brand.

21.2.1 Overview

Besides the fact that they are structured and made accessible in the SIB, using The Open Group standards to populate an architecture has a number of distinct advantages for the architect, and for the architect's organization:

- Individual Open Group standards are developed by proven technical processes (see The Open Group Technical Processes) that establish strong industry consensus behind a standard.

- The Open Group adds value to individual standards by integrating them into sets, known as Product Standards (see Product Standards), which are designed to be used together.

- The Open Group Product Standards are supported by a unique brand - the Open Brand (see The Open Brand) - which in turn is supported by an extensive set of conformance tests, and which guarantees the conformance to a Product Standard of real products available in the market.

Information on the different types of Open Group standards and publications is available from The Open Group Bookstore (*www.opengroup.org/bookstore*).

The Open Group makes all of its standards published since January 1997 freely available in PDF and/or HTML. It also maintains a current list of The Open Group standards and other Open Group publications that are accessible in this way (*www.opengroup.org/bookstore/catalog/web.htm*).

21.2.2 Criteria for Inclusion in the SIB

The content of the SIB is determined by a consensus technical process (see The Open Group Technical Processes). In order to be included in the SIB, a standard needs to be recommended by a Program Group that has responsibility in the relevant technical area. At the same time, confirmation is sought that each new entry acceptably meets the criteria listed below.

Criterion	Explanation
Non-discriminatory Implementation	If the specification is taken from an existing product source licensable from a single vendor only, then implementations should be available to all companies on a non-discriminatory basis. This includes pricing and licensing conditions.
Availability of Dependencies	If an implementation requires other products or services to be usable (e.g., protocols), the complementary products or services must be publicly available, specified by The Open Group, or obtainable from multiple sources.
Availability of Implementations	Commercial availability of implementations.

Criterion	Explanation
Completeness of Specification	The interfaces to be adopted must be specified sufficiently that a conformant product may be implemented (and usable) using only: ■ The specification itself ■ Products or services (e.g., protocols) that are publicly available or obtainable from multiple sources on a non-discriminatory basis ■ Formal standards from accredited standards development organizations ■ Other Open Group originated or adopted specifications ■ Other freely available information
Freedom to Develop	Freedom for anyone to develop a practical product which either supports or utilizes the same specification, subject to the need to license any predisclosed patents.
Future Access	The contributor to give The Open Group access to all future versions of the material with no obligation on The Open Group to adopt them.
Immunity from Liability	An assurance that a person developing a product in accordance with the specification is immune from any liability to the contributor of the material in respect of the use by him or his customers of such material, other than through failure to properly license predisclosed patents.
Market Need	Evidence that there is a market need for the interface. For example: ■ Customer requirement ■ Requirement derived from The Open Group's product management activities ■ Vendor submitted evidence
No Proprietary Lock-in	The interfaces to be adopted are complete, in that it is not necessary to use any additional interfaces, retained as proprietary, in order to create commercially usable products.
Non-discriminatory Patents	If the interfaces to be adopted are covered by patents, such patents must be licensed by their owners on a reasonable and non-discriminatory basis
Other Activities	Understanding of activities in this area in other consortia and official standards bodies.

Criterion	Explanation
Specification Availability	The availability of a high-quality specification upon which The Open Group activities can be based.
Test Suite Availability	The availability of a test suite which could be used as the basis for conformance testing.

21.2.3 The Open Group Technical Processes

The technical processes by which The Open Group produces its standards are long established and widely accepted throughout the industry.

They are also central to The Open Group's mission of delivering greater business efficiency by making it easier to integrate IT across the enterprise.

By means of these processes, The Open Group:

- Defines the industry consensus standards necessary to support the deployment of interoperable infrastructures and business applications
- Promotes the availability in the marketplace of products that conform to those standards

As a result, enterprise architects can design, and customer organizations procure, multi-vendor IT solutions that both meet the business needs, and integrate within and between enterprises, with reduced time, cost, and risk.

More information about The Open Group technical processes is available at *www.opengroup.org/tech/procedures*.

21.2.4 Product Standards

All individual standards adopted through The Open Group's technical processes are known as Open Group Standards, and are documented in its SIB.

The Open Group adds value to the standards in its SIB by integrating related standards into sets, known as Product Standards (analogous to Solution Building Blocks (SBBs) in TOGAF terms, or "technical profiles" in the formal standards world[3]), which are designed to be used together.

This is a recursive process, the goal being the definition of "procurement-ready" Product Standards, whose functionality is strongly related to the needs of customers, and whose scope and structure is strongly related to real products that can be procured in the open market.

More information about Open Group Product Standards is available at *www.opengroup.org/onlinepubs/7501899/file4.htm*.

21.2.5 The Open Brand

The Open Brand is signified by the green " X" Device. It can be associated with, and used in relation to, IT systems that have been registered with The Open Group as being fully conformant with one or more Product Standards.

Anyone wishing to register a product, or products, and use the "X" Device, must first sign the Open Brand Trademark License Agreement and thereby " warrant and represent" that any products they register will fully conform to the identified Product Standard(s), and continue to do so.

Thus the Open Brand, when associated with a vendor's product, communicates clearly and unambiguously to a procurer that the software bearing the brand correctly implements the corresponding Open Group Product Standard.

Customers specifying the Open Brand in their procurements can therefore be certain that the branded products they buy will conform to the Product Standard at the time of purchase, and will continue to do so for as long as the product remains registered.

21.3 Using the SIB

This section covers how to use the SIB, including examples and a list of URLs.

21.3.1 Introduction

The database entries in the SIB are linked either to other Open Group databases and resources - in particular those relating to Product Standards and Registered Products - or, where relevant, to the web sites of other de facto and de jure standards organizations.

In this way, the SIB provides the architect with a gateway to a uniquely powerful set of tools for defining the standards that an architecture is to mandate, and for checking the availability in the marketplace of products guaranteed to conform to those standards.

21.3.2 Examples

21.3.2.1 Getting Started

First, go to the SIB home page (*www.opengroup org/sib*). (It opens in a new window, to enable you to keep these instructions visible.) You may want to bookmark the home page after following the hyperlink.

---
3. For example, as defined in ISO/IEC TR 14252 (IEEE Std 1003.0) and IEEE Std 1003.23.

The home page provides four hyperlinks:

1. Search it - generates a form to guide the search for specific standards or sets of standards.
2. View it - generates a full summary listing of the entire SIB, structured according to the TOGAF TRM taxonomy.
3. Help - links to an explanatory page giving information on the structure of an entry in the SIB.
4. Learn more about it - links to this page, giving an overview.

The following examples are intended to provide an initial guide through the different resources available, and to provide readers with an understanding of the wide range of information available, starting from the SIB home page.

The examples are far from exhaustive, and readers are encouraged to investigate further for themselves after following the examples.

21.3.2.2 Example 1: The Entire SIB

From the SIB home page (*www.opengroup.org/sib*), click the 'View it' hyperlink.

The result is a full summary listing of the SIB, represented as a series of tables, one for each of the major service categories in the TOGAF TRM taxonomy. The hyperlinks at the head of the page provide links to the start of each service category table.

Note: If you want to, save this page for off-line viewing later. (Size is ~200K.)

As you can see, the SIB contains hyperlinks to the web sites of many different standards organizations, both de jure and de facto.

The standards listed in the various tables are all standards adopted by The Open Group; that is, standards endorsed by The Open Group as fit-for-purpose in architecture specification and procurement.

21.3.2.3 Example 2: Referenced Standards

Many of the standards listed in the SIB have been developed and published by The Open Group itself. There are also many Referenced Standards - standards developed and published by other organizations, and referenced from the SIB.

Data Interchange in particular is an area where The Open Group has elected not to duplicate the excellent work done in other organizations, and instead has adopted from those organizations the relevant standards with demonstrated industry consensus.

1. From the SIB home page (*www.opengroup.org/sib*), click the 'Search it' hyperlink. The search form appears, which allows you to specify several criteria to help you find what you want.

2. From the 'Service Category' drop-down box, select the 'Data Interchange Services' category (but don't click the 'Search' button just yet).

3. Click the 'Service' drop-down box. You will see that it now lists all the individual services within the 'Data Interchange' category.

4. Select 'Hypertext', and then click the 'Search' button.

5. When the search results appear, look under the 'Reference and Status' column and locate the 'HTML 4..0' entry. Click on 'Details' in the 'Other Views' column. This displays the full SIB entry for HTML 4..0.

6. In the full SIB entry, click the hyperlink shown against 'URL' (you could also have clicked the HTML 4..0 hyperlink in the previous page). This takes you to the HTML 4..0 Specification on the W3C public web site.

7. Go back to The Open Group web site, and go back again to the search results for 'Hypertext '.

8. Locate the entry for IETF RFC 2068 and click the 'Details' link. This displays the full SIB entry for IETF RFC 2068. The full entry explains the relationship of HTTP/1..1. to HTTP/1..0, and (under See Also) gives a link to the SIB entry for the corresponding IETF RFC (1945).

9. Again, click the hyperlink shown against 'URL' . This takes you to the text of the HTTP/1..1. specification as approved by the Internet Engineering Task Force.

10. Go back to The Open Group web site, and go back again to the search results for 'Hypertext ' . Browse the remaining links at your leisure. Note that all organizations whose standards are referenced from the SIB make the full text freely available.

21.3.2.4 Example 3: Open Group Technical Standards

Now we will look at the facilities available in the SIB for the Technical Standards developed and published by The Open Group itself.

1. From the SIB home page (*www.opengroup.org/sib*), click the 'Search it' hyperlink.

2. When the search form appears, under 'Service Category' select 'System and Network Management Services' (but don't click the 'Search' button just yet).

3. Click the 'Service' drop-down box. You will see that it now lists all the individual services within the 'System and Network Management' category.

4. Leave the 'Any' entry in place under 'Service ', and press the 'Search' button. The table displayed as a result shows all the standards in the SIB under the 'System and Network Management Services' category.

5. Search down the table under the 'Reference and Status' column to locate the entry for C701(XDSA). This is the Systems Management: Distributed Software Administration (XDSA) Technical Standard. This time, click on the 'C701' hyperlink.

6. This links to The Open Group Publications database (a separate database from the SIB). The next table displayed shows full publication details of the Technical Standard, and

links to a range of further information. Options at this point:

i. Press the 'Systems Management' hyperlink. This provides a page of structured hyperlinks to all Open Group Systems Management publications (not just standards).

ii. Go back to the previous page. The two hyperlinks under 'Availability' offer two different ways of obtaining a copy of the standard, including free access to an HTML version; and an order form for a hard copy version. Investigate these links at your leisure.

21.3.2.5 Example 4: Open Group Product Standards

This time we will look at the facilities for the Product Standards developed and published by The Open Group.

1. From the SIB home page (*www.opengroup.org/sib*), click the 'Search it' hyperlink.
2. When the search form appears, under 'Service Category' select 'Operating System Services', and press the 'Search' button.
3. The table displayed as a result shows all the standards in the SIB under the 'Operating System Services' category. As you can see, there are a lot!
4. Search down the table under the 'Reference and Status' column to locate the entry 'X/Open XX'. This is the UNIX 98 Product Standard. Click on the 'X/Open XX' hyperlink.
5. The next table displayed shows all the products registered as conformant to the UNIX 98 Product Standard, organized by vendor. Select a vendor's registered product and click on the hyperlink.
6. The next table shows details of the product registration, and links to a range of further information. Options at this point:

    i. Click the vendor's company name to go the vendor's own web site, either for general information on the vendor, or for information on the specific registered product.

    ii. Click the 'Brand Certificate' link to display a copy of the actual Brand Certificate (in PDF).

    iii. Click the 'Go to the Completed Conformance Statement' hyperlink. (The Conformance Statement is a document, compiled from the answers to a Conformance Statement Questionnaire (CSQ), that the vendor supplies as part of the registration process, giving full details of the conformance of the product to the relevant Product Standard.)

    - The resultant table offers three levels of detail, available from the three icons in the left-hand column. (If required, click on the 'Help' button for an explanation of the icons, in addition to other help information; then return to this table.) Click one of the icons.

    - The next table shows the Conformance Statement for the overall Product Standard, most of which is effectively a compilation of the Conformance Statements for each of the individual Open Group standards that the Product Standard comprises. Select a particular question, and click on an icon.

- The final table shows the full details of the Conformance Statement for that Open Group standard.

iv. Click the 'Manual Search of the CSQ System' hyperlink.

- The resultant search form provides access to the complete Conformance Statement Library.
- Clicking the 'Search the Completed Conformance Statements' hyperlink enables you to search the complete library by individual Product Standard and/or by vendor, and to select how you want the results organized, and the level of detail displayed. Options now:
- Select a particular Product Standard, and leave the vendor column as 'Any', to show all the vendor products registered as conforming to that Product Standard.
- Select a particular vendor, and leave the Product Standard column as 'Any', to show all the Product Standards for which that vendor has registered a conforming product.
- Select a particular Product Standard, and a particular vendor, to show whether that vendor has a product registered as conforming to that Product Standard.
- Click the 'Select Here for an Extended Selection' hyperlink for an even more detailed search form, allowing selection of individual vendor products as well as Product Standards and vendors.
- Clicking the 'View the Conformance Statement Questionnaires' hyperlink provides access to a complete list of (blank) Conformance Statement Questionnaires, so you can see the questions that vendors have to answer as part of the product registration process.

v. Click the 'More Information about UNIX 98' hyperlink to display details of the UNIX 98 Product Standard, including:

- The full text of the Product Standard definition
- A list of all the component standards
- Links to each of the individual specifications
- Links to the corresponding Conformance Statement Questionnaires
- Links to information on the test suites used as the indicator of compliance

As you can see, there is a wealth of information underpinning the entries for standards developed by The Open Group, particularly the Product Standards.

For this reason, Open Group Product Standards should be the first point of departure when considering open industry standards for architecture specifications and procurements.

Where Open Group Product Standards do not exist, individual Open Group standards will often be the next best thing.

21.3.3 Summary of Open Group Databases and Resources

A summary of URLs to key Open Group resources relevant to the architect is given below.

www.opengroup.org/sib	Starting Point: the SIB home page.
www.opengroup.org/sib.htm	Direct link to the full listing of the SIB.
www.opengroup.org/sib2/search_sib.tpl	Direct link to the SIB search facility.
www.opengroup.org/togaf	The TOGAF public information home page.
www.opengroup.org/bookstore	Catalog of Specifications and Other Publications.
www.opengroup.org/testing	Testing Technology information.

Chapter 22:
Integrated Information Infrastructure Reference Model

This chapter describes the Integrated Information Infrastructure Reference Model (III-RM), in terms of its concepts, an overview, and taxonomy.

22.1 Basic Concepts

This section looks at the basic concepts of the III-RM, including background, components, and drivers.

22.1.1 Background

With the emergence of Internet-based technologies in recent years, for many organizations the main focus of attention, and the main return on investment in architecture effort, has shifted from the Application Platform space to the Application Software space. (Indeed, this has been one of the drivers behind the migration of TOGAF itself from a framework and method for Technology Architecture to one for overall enterprise architecture.)

The TOGAF Technical Reference Model (TRM) described in Foundation Architecture: Technical Reference Model focuses on the Application Platform space, and it is what the Enterprise Continuum terms a " Foundation Architecture".

This section describes another reference model, one that focuses on the Application Software space, and one that is a " Common Systems Architecture" in Enterprise Continuum terms. This is the Integrated Information Infrastructure Reference Model (III-RM).

The III-RM is a subset of the TOGAF TRM in terms of its overall scope, but it also expands certain parts of the TRM - in particular, the business applications and infrastructure applications parts - in order to provide help in addressing one of the key challenges facing the enterprise architect today: the need to design an integrated information infrastructure to enable Boundaryless Information Flow. These concepts are explained in detail below.

This introductory section examines the concept of Boundaryless Information Flow; why an integrated information infrastructure is necessary to enable it; and how the III-RM can help the architect in designing an integrated information infrastructure for their enterprise.

22.1.2 Components of the Model

Like the TOGAF TRM, the III-RM has two main components:

1. A **taxonomy**, which defines terminology, and provides a coherent description of the components and conceptual structure of an integrated information infrastructure

2. An associated **III-RM graphic**, which provides a visual representation of the taxonomy, and the inter-relationship of the components, as an aid to understanding

The model assumes the underlying existence of a computing and network platform, as described in the TRM; these are not depicted in the model.

22.1.3 Relationship to Other parts of TOGAF

The relationship of the III-RM to the TRM is explained above.

Although the III-RM is intended as a useful tool in the execution of the TOGAF Architecture Development Method (ADM), it is important to emphasize that the ADM is in no way dependent on use of the III-RM (any more than it is dependent on use of the TRM). Other taxonomies and reference models exist in this space that can be used in conjunction with the ADM, and indeed may be preferable for some organizations.

22.1.4 Key Business and Technical Drivers

22.1.4.1 Problem Space: The Need for Boundaryless Information Flow

The Boundaryless Information Flow problem space is one that is shared by many customer members of The Open Group, and by many similar organizations worldwide. It is essentially the problem of getting information to the right people at the right time in a secure, reliable manner, in order to support the operations that are core to the extended enterprise.

In General Electric, Jack Welch invented the term " the Boundaryless Organization", not to imply that there are no boundaries, but that they should be made permeable.

Creating organizational structures that enabled each individual department to operate at maximum efficiency was for a long time accepted as the best approach to managing a large enterprise. Among other benefits, this approach fostered the development of specialist skills in staff, who could apply those skills to specific aspects of an overall activity (such as a manufacturing process), in order to accomplish the tasks involved better, faster, and cheaper.

As each overall activity progressed through the organization, passing from department to department (for example, from Design to Production to Sales), each department would take inputs from the previous department in the process, apply its own business processes to the activity, and send its output to the next department in line.

In today's world where speed, flexibility, and responsiveness to changing markets make all the difference between success and failure, this method of working is no longer appropriate. Organizations have been trying for some time to overcome the limitations imposed by traditional organization structures. Many business process re-engineering efforts have been undertaken and abandoned because they were too ambitious, while others cost far more in both time and money than originally intended.

However, organizations today recognize that they need not abandon functional or departmental organization altogether. They can enable the right people to come together in cross-functional teams so that all the skills, knowledge, and expertise can be brought to bear on any specific problem or business opportunity.

But this in turn poses it own challenges. CIOs are under enormous pressure to provide access to information to each cross-functional team on an as-required basis, and yet the sources of this data can be numerous and the volumes huge.

Even worse, the IT systems, which have been built over a period of 20 or 30 years at a cost of many billions of dollars, and are not about to be thrown out or replaced wholesale, were built for each functional department. So although it may be possible to get people to work together effectively (no minor achievement in itself), the IT systems they use are designed to support the old-style thinking. The IT systems in place today do not allow for information to flow in support of the boundaryless organization. When they do, then we will have Boundaryless Information Flow.

22.1.4.2 Solution Space: The Need for Integrated Information Infrastructure

The Open Group's Interoperable Enterprise Business Scenario[4] originally published in 2001, crystallizes this need for Boundaryless Information Flow and describes the way in which this need drives IT customers' deployment of their information infrastructure.

In this scenario, the customer's problem statement says that I (as the customer enterprise) could gain significant operational efficiencies and improve the many different business processes of the enterprise - both internal processes, and those spanning the key interactions with suppliers, customers, and partners - if only I could provide my staff with:

- **Integrated information** so that different and potentially conflicting pieces of information are not distributed throughout different systems
- **Integrated access** to that information so that staff can access all the information they need and have a right to, through one convenient interface

The infrastructure that enables this vision is termed the "integrated information infrastructure".

As an example, one current approach to integrated information infrastructure is to provide "enterprise portals" that allow integrated access to information from different applications systems enterprise-wide, via a convenient, web-enabled interface (one of the colored segments in the ends of the cylinder in An approach to Boundaryless Information Flow (Enterprise Portals)).

One of the key challenges for the architect in today's enterprise is to work out, and then communicate to senior management, how far technologies such as web services, application integration services, etc., can go toward achieving an integrated information

---

4. Available at *www.opengroup.org/bookstore/catalog/k022.htm*.

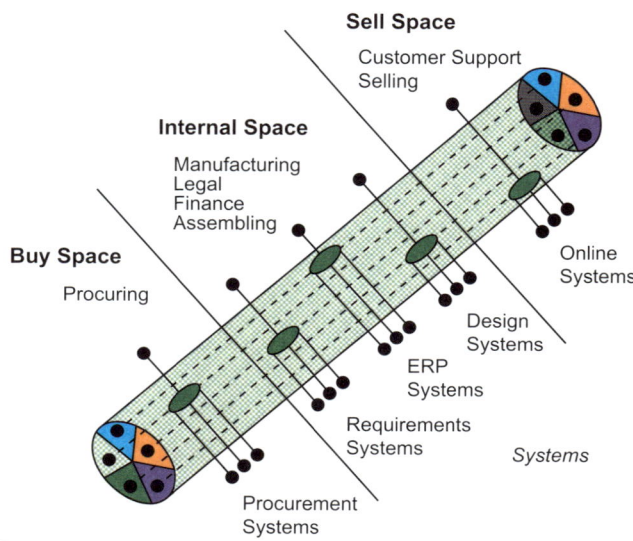

Figure 22.1 : An approach to Boundaryless Information Flow (Enterprise Portals)

infrastructure, and realizing the vision of Boundaryless Information Flow, in the enterprise concerned.

The Open Group's follow-up analysis of the Interoperable Enterprise Business Scenario has resulted in the development of an integrated information infrastructure model (the III-RM), which depicts the major components required to address the Boundaryless Information Flow problem space, and can help the architect in this task.

The III-RM thus provides insights related to customer needs for Boundaryless Information Flow in enterprise environments. The model also points to rules and standards to assist in leveraging solutions and products within the value chain.

The following subsections discuss the model in detail.

22.1.5 Health Warning

The III-RM is documented as it stands today, and is by no means considered a finished article. However, it is a model that has been developed and approved by the members of The Open Group as a whole, in response to the Interoperable Enterprise Business Scenario, which itself was developed in response to an urgent need articulated by the customer members of The Open Group for assistance in this field.

The Business Scenario and the Reference Model thus represent a problem and a solution approach that The Open Group membership as a whole fully endorses.

It is hoped that publication of the model as part of TOGAF will encourage its widespread adoption and use, and provide a channel of communication whereby experience with use of the model can be fed back, improvement points assimilated, and the model refined and republished as necessary.

22.2 High-Level View

This section provides a high-level view of the III-RM, including derivation of the model, high-level graphic, and components.

22.2.1 Derivation of the III-RM from the TRM

The III-RM is a model of the major component categories for developing, managing, and operating an integrated information infrastructure. It is a model of a set of applications that sits on top of an Application Platform. This model is a subset of the TOGAF TRM, and it uses a slightly different orientation.

Consider TOGAF TRM Orientation Views where two views of the TOGAF TRM are presented. The left side is the familiar view of the TOGAF TRM; it is a side view, where we look at the model as if looking at a house from the side, revealing the contents of the "floors". The top-down view on the right-hand side depicts what one might see if looking at a house from the "roof" down.

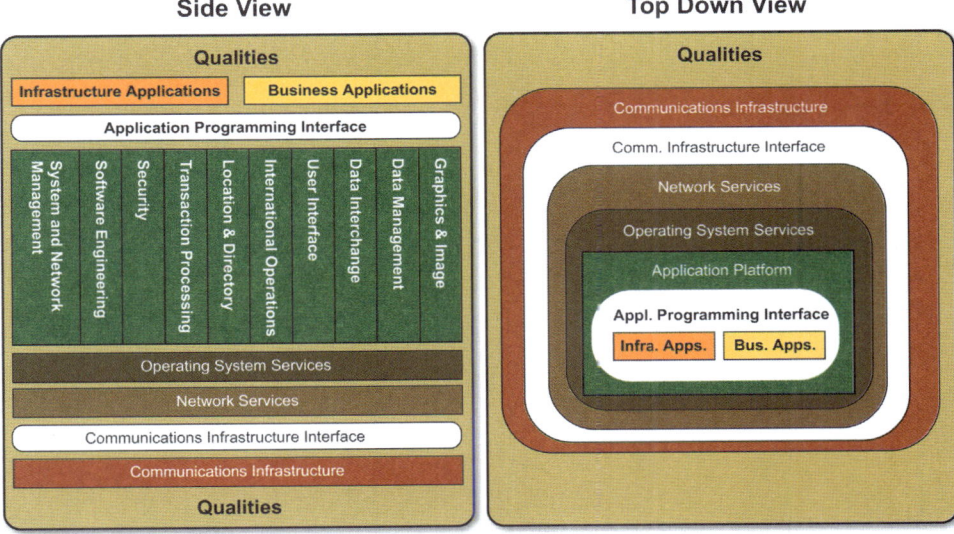

Figure 22.2: TOGAF TRM Orientation Views

The subset of the TRM that comprises the III-RM is depicted in Focus of the III-RM, in which those parts of the TRM not relevant to the III-RM are "greyed out".

Focus of the III-RM illustrates that the focus is on the Application Software, Application Platform, and qualities subset of the TOGAF TRM.

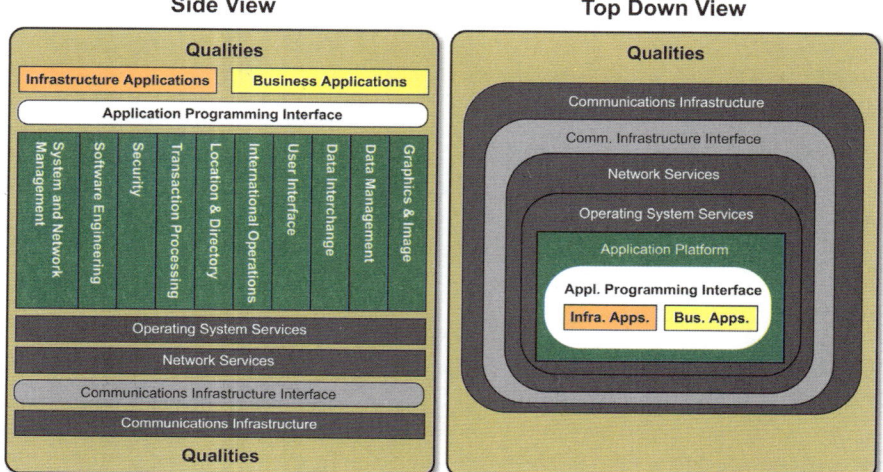

Figure 22.3 : Focus of the III-RM

22.2.2 The High-Level III-RM Graphic

The resulting III-RM itself is depicted in III-RM - High-Level . It is fundamentally an Applications Architecture reference model - a model of the application components and application services software essential for an integrated information infrastructure. (There are more business applications and infrastructure applications than these in the environment, of course, but these are the subsets relevant to the Boundaryless Information Flow problem space.)

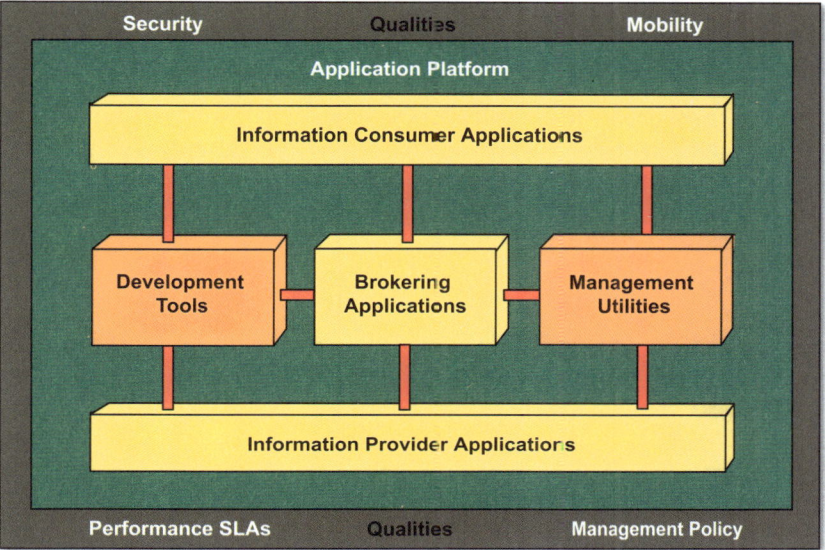

Figure 22.4: III-RM - High-Level

As explained above, the model assumes the underlying existence of a computing and network platform, and does not depict them explicitly.

Although the computing and network platform are not depicted, there may be requirements on them that must be met, in addition to requirements on the components of the III-RM, in order to fully address the Boundaryless Information Flow problem space.

22.2.3 Components of the High-Level III-RM

The III-RM has the following core components:

- **Business Applications**, denoted by the light-brown boxes in the high-level model (corresponding to the light-brown " Business Applications" box in the TRM graphic). There are three types of Business Application in the model:
    - **Brokering Applications**, which manage the requests from any number of clients to and across any number of Information Provider Applications
    - **Information Provider Applications**, which provide responses to client requests and rudimentary access to data managed by a particular server
    - **Information Consumer Applications**, which deliver content to the user of the system, and provide services to request access to information in the system on the user's behalf

- **Infrastructure Applications**, denoted by the dark-brown boxes in the high-level model (corresponding to the dark-brown " Infrastructure Applications" box in the TRM graphic). There are two types of Infrastructure Application in the model:
  - **Development Tools**, which provide all the necessary modeling, design, and construction capabilities to develop and deploy applications that require access to the integrated information infrastructure, in a manner consistent with the standards of the environment
  - **Management Utilities**, which provide all the necessary utilities to understand, operate, tune, and manage the run-time system in order to meet the demands of an ever-changing business, in a manner consistent with the standards of the environment
- An **Application Platform**, which provides supporting services to all the above applications - in areas such as location, directory, workflow, data management, data interchange, etc. - and thereby provides the ability to locate, access, and move information within the environment. This set of services constitutes a subset of the total set of services of the TRM Application Platform, and is denoted by the dark green underlay in the high-level model (corresponding to the dark green of the Application Platform in the TRM graphic).
- The **Interfaces** used between the components. Interfaces include formats and protocols, Application Program Interfaces (APIs), switches, data values, etc. Interfaces among components at the application level are colored brown. Interfaces between any application-level components and their supporting services in the Application Platform are colored white (corresponding to the white of the API box in the TRM graphic).
- The **Qualities** backplane, denoted by the beige underlay in the high-level model (corresponding to the beige of the Qualities backplane in the TRM graphic). The Application Software and Application Platform must adhere to the policies and requirements depicted by the qualities backplane.

22.3 Detailed Taxonomy

This section provides a detailed taxonomy of the III-RM, including detailed graphic, platform service categories, and external environment sub-entities.

22.3.1 Detailed III-RM Graphic

The detailed III-RM is depicted in III-RM - Detailed .

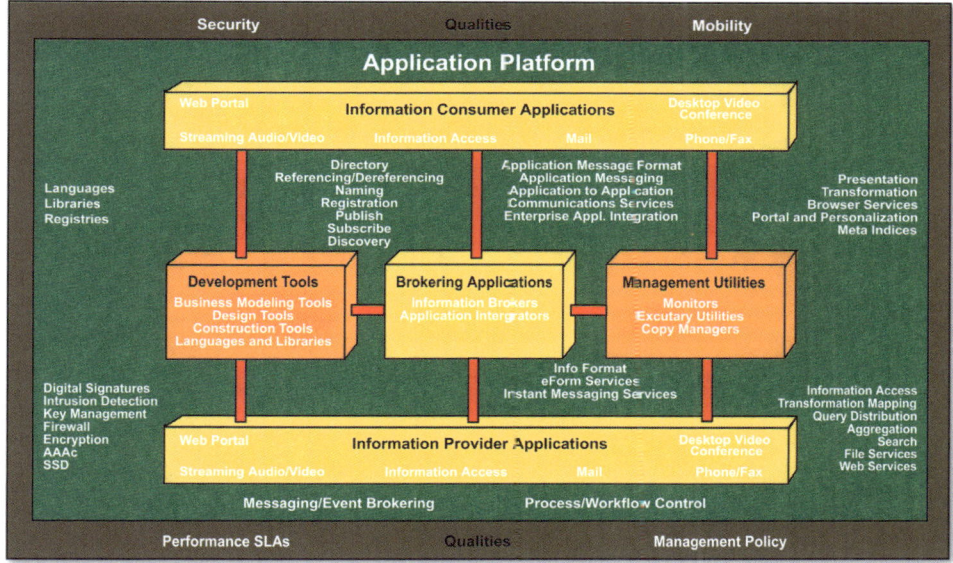

Figure 22.5: III-RM - Detailed

The remaining subsections expand on the taxonomy/component detail shown in III-RM - Detailed .

22.3.2 Business Applications

There are three types of business application in the model:

- **Information Provider Applications**, which provide responses to client requests and rudimentary access to data managed by a particular server
- **Brokering Applications**, which manage the requests from any number of clients to and across any number of service providers
- **Information Consumer Applications**, which deliver content to the user of the system, and provide services to request access to information in the system on the user's behalf

The overall set of Information Provider, Information Consumer, and Brokerage Applications collectively creates an environment that provides a rich set of end-user services for transparently accessing heterogeneous systems, databases, and file systems.

22.3.2.1 Information Provider Applications

To the extent that information today can be regarded as being " held hostage", as depicted in Liberate Data Silos to Meet Information Needs of Cross-Functional Enterprise Teams , Information Provider Applications are those applications that " liberate" data from their silos.

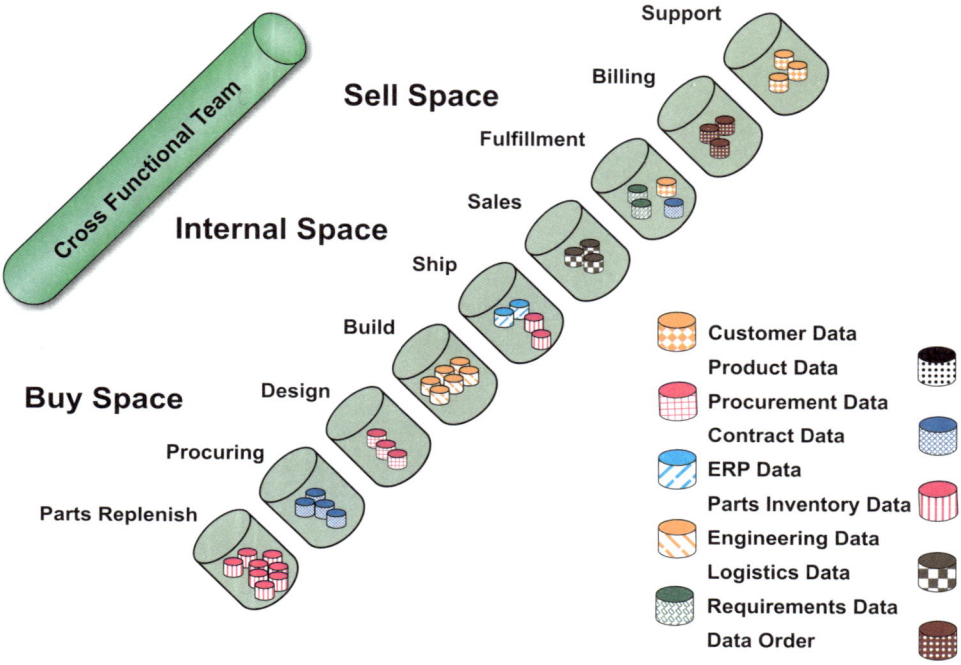

Figure 22.6 : Liberate Data Silos to Meet Information Needs of Cross-Functional Enterprise Teams

Information Provider Applications achieve this by providing an open interface to a potentially proprietary silo interface, as illustrated in Information Provider Applications Liberate Data by Providing Open Interfaces to Data Silos , where the interfaces on the left of the Information Provider Applications are open interfaces and the interfaces between the Information Provider Applications and silo data are proprietary interfaces.

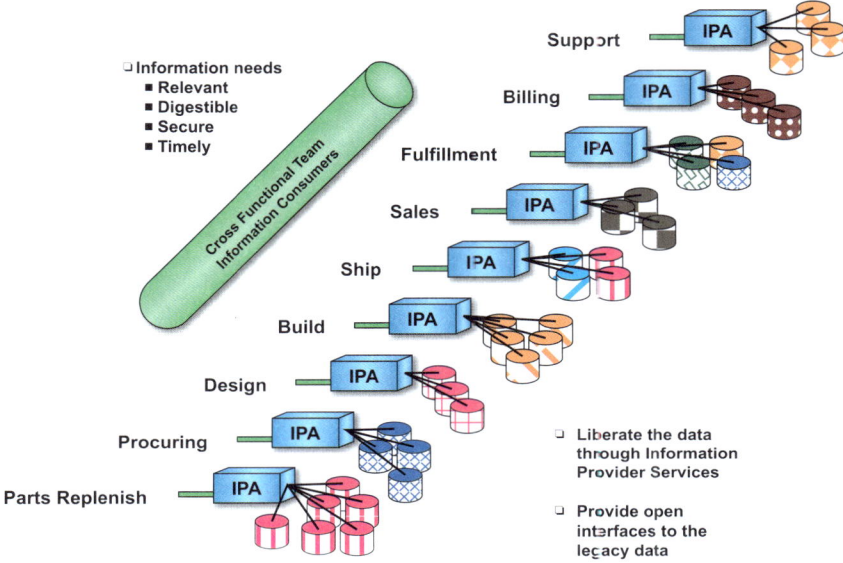

Figure 22.7: Information Provider Applications Liberate Data by Providing Open Interfaces to Data Silos

22.3.2.2 Brokerage Applications

Brokerage Applications serve up single requests that require access to multiple information sources. A Brokerage Application breaks down such a request, distributes the request to multiple information sources, collects the responses, and sends a single response back to the requesting client.

Brokerage Applications access Information Provider Applications using the open interfaces provided by the Information Provider Applications (as described above); they integrate information from multiple Information Provider Applications and pass the integrated information to Information Consumer Applications using open interfaces.

Brokerage Applications also enable access to information within the enterprise by strategic partners.

22.3.2.3 Information Consumer Applications

Information Consumer Applications provide information to end users in the form in which they need it, when they need it, and in a secured manner. This includes providing the information in text, video, audio, English, German, etc.

Information Consumer Applications communicate with Brokerage Applications or Information Provider Applications using the open interfaces that the Brokerage and Information Provider Applications provide. Security is provided through the firewalls and/or security services. Information Consumer Applications Communicate using Open Interfaces depicts the Information Consumer Applications with the security services depicted as the brick pattern.

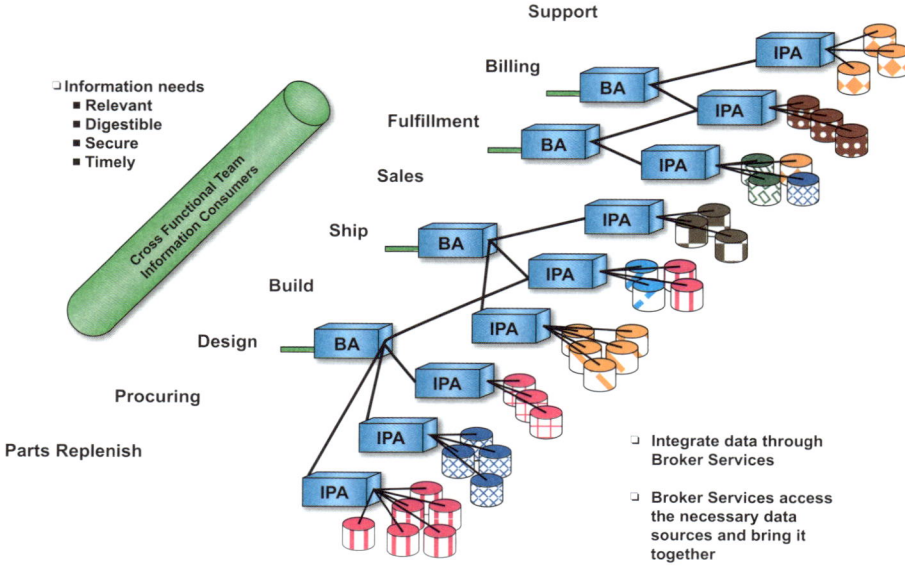

Figure 22.8: Brokerage Applications Integrate Information from Information Provider Applications

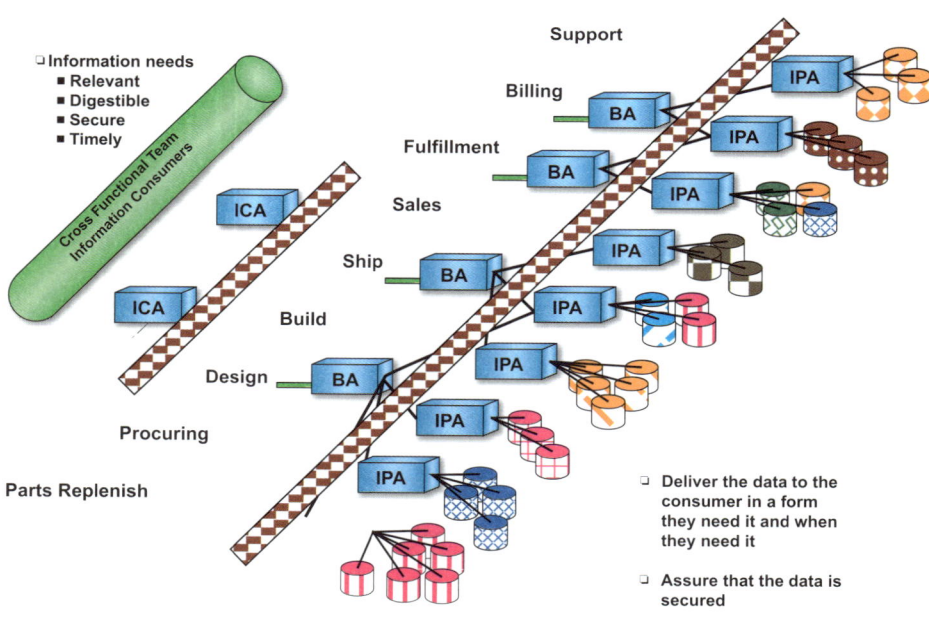

Figure 22.9 : Information Consumer Applications Communicate using Open Interfaces

22.3.3 Infrastructure Applications

There are two types of Infrastructure Application in the model:

- **Development Tools**, which provide all the necessary modeling, design, and construction capabilities to develop and deploy applications that require access to the integrated information infrastructure, in a manner consistent with the standards of the environment
- **Management Utilities**, which provide all the necessary utilities to understand, operate, tune, and manage the run-time system in order to meet the demands of an ever-changing business, in a manner consistent with the standards of the environment

22.3.3.1 Development Tools

The Development Tools component of the model comprises applications that take the form of tools for modeling, designing, and constructing the integrated information infrastructure. Specifically, it includes tools for business, process, and data modeling, as well as the traditional application construction tools that transform the business model into software that automates the business processes revolving around information.

Note that each set of tools will be logically connected through a directory, allowing one tool to be driven by data from another. The following sections describe the requirements for components of Development Tools. The tool set also includes a repository.

Business Modeling Tools

This category covers tools for the modeling of business rules and business process rules.

Business modeling describes and documents the business in a comprehensive knowledge base. It establishes a consensus among general management of the business direction, organization, processes, information requirements, and the current environment of the business. Perhaps most importantly, this understanding is documented in a common, business-oriented format to be utilized for subsequent enhancement.

Design Modeling Tools

This category covers tools for designing, defining, and documenting the most pertinent IT elements of the business based upon the business and business process rules. Examples of elements to be designed include: connections between people, organizations, workflows and computers; data and object models; physical data translation and translation rules; and constraints.

Implementation and Construction Tools

Implementation tools enable timely development of re-usable processes, applications, and application services. Such tools include intelligent browsers, data manipulation language compilers and optimizers, distributed application compilers and debuggers, heterogeneous client and server development tools, policy definition tools, and workflow script generation tools.

Data Modeling Tools

Deployment Tools

Deployment tools are necessary to move implemented software from the development environment into the operational environment.

Libraries

This component includes re-usable libraries of software that use the standards of the operational environment.

22.3.3.2 Management Utilities

This category covers applications that take the form of utilities for operations, administration, and systems management, and for the management of data based on availability and cost requirements. Such utilities may execute in an attended or an unattended environment.

Operations, Administration, and Management (OA&M) Utilities

The OA&M component covers traditional systems management and administration utilities that manage business rules and information objects. Examples include: utilities for installation, copyright and license management; and miscellaneous administration, configuration, and registration functions. Additionally there are utilities for the control of service billing, service triggering, and account management.

Quality of Service Manager Utilities

These include health monitoring and management utilities.

Copy Management Utilities

Copy Management utilities are those that manage data movement from any given operational system to necessary distribution points in the enterprise, in order to ensure the maximum leverage of operational systems data. They also include tools that detect and flag poor quality data.

Storage Management Utilities

These are utilities that provide least-cost data storage management. Storage management utilities support the wide variety of storage mechanisms and are connected to file, object, and database systems.

22.3.4 Application Platform

All the different types of application described above are built on top of the services provided by the Application Platform.

The Application Platform component of the III-RM comprises a subset of all the services defined in the TOGAF TRM, the subset that pertains to integrated information infrastructure. Specifically, it comprises all those services in the TRM Application Platform that allow applications to focus on understanding and processing the information required, rather than understanding the form, format, and/or location of the information.

The services of the Application Platform component can be used to support conventional applications as well as Brokerage, Information Consumer, and Information Provider applications. When used as part of an overall Applications Architecture in this way, such an approach enables maximum leverage of a single operational environment that is designed to ensure effective and consistent transfer of data between processes, and to support fast and efficient development, deployment, and management of applications.

The Application Platform component comprises the following categories of service.

22.3.4.1 Software Engineering Services

- Languages
- Libraries
- Registries

22.3.4.2 Security Services

- Authentication, authorization, and access control
- Single sign-on
- Digital signature
- Firewall
- Encryption
- Intrusion detection
- Identity management
- Key management

22.3.4.3 Location and Directory Services

Location and directory services provide access facilities for name, location, description, and relationship data that describes the integrated information infrastructure.

Directory services support the deployment and enterprise-wide availability of an integrated information infrastructure directory. The data in the directory is made available to all other components in the architecture model.

Juxtaposition of Location and Directory Services to Other Components depicts the juxtaposition of location and directory services to the other components.

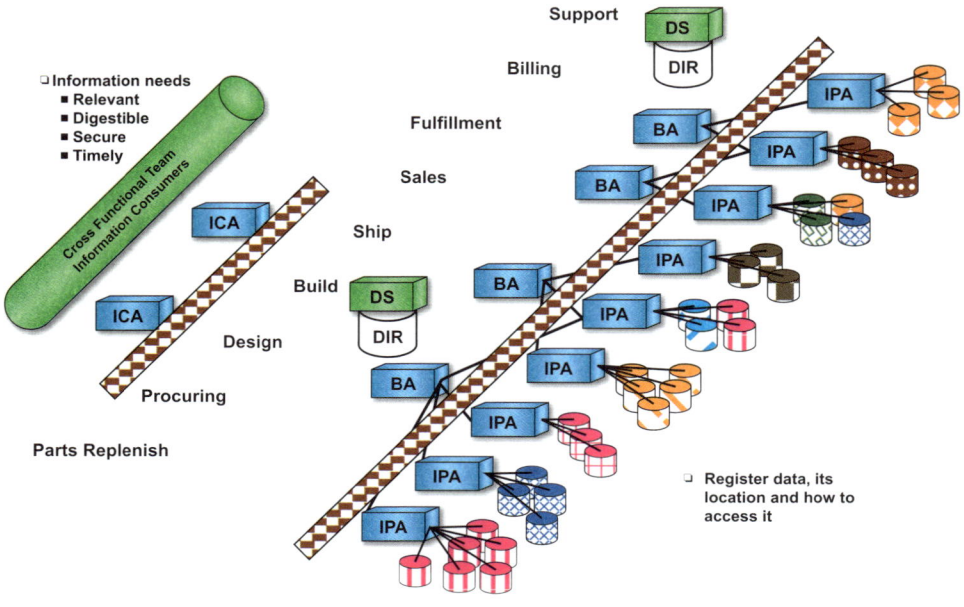

**Figure 22.10:
Juxtaposition of Location and Directory Services to Other Components**

Specific services include:

- Directory
- Registration
- Publish/subscribe
- Discovery
- Naming
- Referencing/dereferencing

22.3.4.4 Human Interaction Services

Human Interaction services provide the means to consistently present data to the end user in the appropriate format. They comprise services that assist in the formulation of customer data requests and enable visualization and presentation of the data accessed.

Specific services include:

- Presentation
- Transformation
- Browser

- Meta indices
- Portal and personalization

22.3.4.5 Data Interchange Services

Specific services include:

- Information format
- eForm
- Instant messaging
- Application messaging
- Application-to-application communications
- Enterprise application integration

22.3.4.6 Data Management Services

Specific services include:

- Information and data access
- Transformation mapping
- Query distribution
- Aggregation
- Search
- File

Information access services provide the ability for an application to access an integrated view of data, regardless of whether the data exists in a mainframe system or in a distributed system. The information access services ensure that data integrity is maintained among multiple databases, and also provide online data cleansing (whereby data is checked against data rules for each access).

Data access services provide open interfaces to legacy data, provide new applications standard database access services to vast amounts of existing data, and provide standard access services to new data types.

22.3.4.7 Additional Operating System Services

Specific services include:

- Event brokering
- Workflow

These additional services enable the flow of information, as depicted in Workflow Services Enable Information Flow .

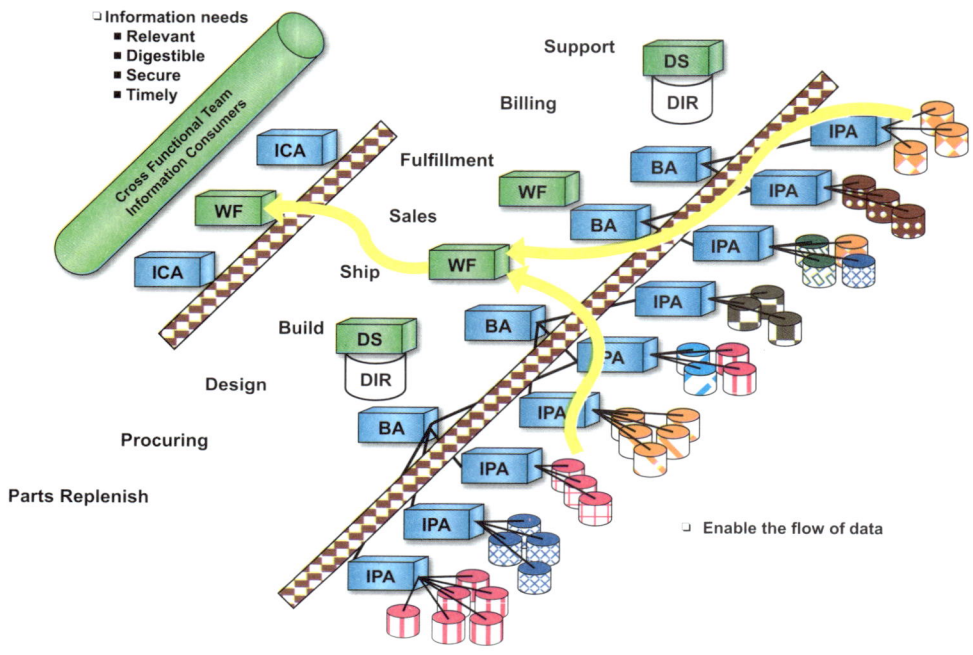

Figure 22.11: Workflow Services Enable Information Flow

Workflow denotes the concept of automating processes by facilitating user interactions and executing applications according to a process map. Workflow services enable integration of enterprise applications, resulting in applications of extended value.

Workflow services also address the needs of managing an environment where legacy systems are prevalent.

Workflow services also provide a means to encapsulate existing applications, thereby supporting customer needs for leverage of existing assets.

22.3.5 Qualities

The qualities component of the model is supported by quality of service services, including the various services required to maintain the quality of the system as specified in Service Level Agreements (SLAs).

Included in this are the services to post conditions to, and react to requests from, the Quality of Service Manager.

PART: IV

Resource Base

Chapter 23: Architecture Board

This chapter provides guidelines for establishing and operating an Enterprise Architecture Board.

23.1 Role

A key element in a successful architecture governance strategy (see Architecture Governance) is a cross-organization Architecture Board to oversee the implementation of the strategy. This body should be representative of all the key stakeholders in the architecture, and will typically comprise a group of executives responsible for the review and maintenance of the overall architecture.

The costs of establishing and operating an Architecture Board are more than offset by the savings that accrue as a result of preventing one-off solutions and unconstrained developments across the enterprise, which invariably lead to:

- High costs of development
- High costs of operation and support:
    - Numerous run-time environments
    - Numerous implementation languages
    - Numerous interfaces and protocols ...
- Lower quality
- Higher risk
- Difficulty in replicating and re-using solutions

Architecture Boards may have global, regional, or business line scope. Particularly in larger enterprises, Architecture Boards typically comprise representatives from the organization at a minimum of two levels:

- Local (domain experts, line responsibility)
- Global (organization-wide responsibility)

In such cases, each board will be established with identifiable and articulated:

- Responsibilities and decision-making capabilities
- Remit and authority limits

23.2 Responsibilities

The Architecture Board is typically made responsible, and accountable, for achieving some or all of the following goals:

- Consistency between sub-architectures
- Identifying re-usable components
- Flexibility of enterprise architecture:
    - To meet changing business needs
    - To leverage new technologies
- Enforcement of Architecture Compliance
- Improving the maturity level of architecture discipline within the organization
- Ensuring that the discipline of architecture-based development is adopted
- Providing the basis for all decision-making with regard to changes to the architectures
- Supporting a visible escalation capability for out-of-bounds decisions

Further responsibilities from an operational perspective should include:

- All aspects of monitoring and control of the Architecture Contract
- Meeting on a regular basis
- Ensuring the effective and consistent management and implementation of the architectures
- Resolving ambiguities, issues, or conflicts that have been escalated
- Providing advice, guidance, and information
- Ensuring compliance with the architectures, and granting dispensations that are in keeping with the technology strategy and objectives
- Considering policy (schedule, Service Level Agreements (SLAs), etc.) changes where similar dispensations are requested and granted; e.g., new form of service requirement
- Ensuring that all information relevant to the implementation of the Architecture Contract is published under controlled conditions and made available to authorized parties
- Validation of reported service levels, cost savings, etc.

From a governance perspective, the Architecture Board is also responsible for:

- The production of usable governance material and activities
- Providing a mechanism for the formal acceptance and approval of architecture through consensus and authorized publication
- Providing a fundamental control mechanism for ensuring the effective implementation of the architecture
- Establishing and maintaining the link between the implementation of the architecture, the architectural strategy and objectives embodied in the enterprise architecture, and the strategic objectives of the business

- Identifying divergence from the architecture and planning activities for realignment through dispensations or policy updates

23.3 Setting Up the Architecture Board

23.3.1 Triggers

One or more of the following occurrences typically triggers the establishment of an Architecture Board:

- New CIO
- Merger or acquisition
- Consideration of a move to newer forms of computing
- Recognition that IT is poorly aligned to business
- Desire to achieve competitive advantage via technology
- Creation of an enterprise architecture program
- Significant business change or rapid growth
- Requirement for complex, cross-functional solutions

In many companies, the executive sponsor of the initial architecture effort is the CIO (or other senior executive). However, to gain broad corporate support, a sponsoring body has more influence. This sponsoring body is here called an Architecture Board, but the title is not important. Whatever the name, it is the executive-level group responsible for the review and maintenance of the strategic architecture and all of its sub-architectures.

The Architecture Board is the sponsor of the architecture within the enterprise, but the Architecture Board itself needs an executive sponsor from the highest level of the corporation. This commitment must span the planning process and continue into the maintenance phase of the architecture project. In many companies that fail in an architecture planning effort, there is a notable lack of executive participation and encouragement for the project.

A frequently overlooked source of Architecture Board members is the company's Board of Directors. These individuals invariably have diverse knowledge about the business and its competition. Because they have a significant impact on the business vision and objectives, they may be successful in validating the alignment of IT strategies to business objectives.

23.3.2 Size of the Board

The recommended size for an Architecture Board is four or five (and no more than ten) permanent members.

In order to keep the Architecture Board to a reasonable size, while ensuring enterprise-wide representation on it over time, membership of the Architecture Board may be rotated, giving decision-making privileges and responsibilities to various senior managers. This may be required in any case, due to some Architecture Board members finding that time constraints prevent long-term active participation.

However, some continuity must exist on the Architecture Board, to prevent the corporate architecture from varying from one set of ideas to another. One technique for ensuring rotation with continuity is to have set terms for the members, and to have the terms expire at different times.

In the ongoing architecture process following the initial architecture effort, the Architecture Board may be re-chartered. The executive sponsor will normally review the work of the Architecture Board and evaluate its effectiveness; if necessary, the Architecture Compliance review process is updated or changed.

23.3.3 Board Structure

The TOGAF Architecture Governance Framework (see Architecture Governance Framework) provides a generic organizational framework that positions the Architecture Board in the context of the broader governance structures of the enterprise. This structure identifies the major organizational groups and responsibilities, as well as the relationship between each group. This is a best practice structure, and may be subject to change depending on the organization's form and existing structures.

Consideration must be given to the size of the organization, its form, and how the IT functions are implemented. This will provide the basis for designing the Architecture Board structure within the context of the overall governance environment. In particular, consideration should be given to the concept of global ownership and local implementation, and the integration of new concepts and technologies from all areas implementing against architectures.

The structure of the Architecture Board should reflect the form of the organization. The architecture governance structure required may well go beyond the generic structures outlined in the TOGAF Architecture Governance Framework (see Architecture Governance Framework). The organization may need to define a combination of the IT governance process in place and the existing organizational structures and capabilities, which typically include the following types of body:

- Global governance board
- Local governance board
- Design authorities
- Working parties

23.4 Operation of the Architecture Board

This section describes the operation of the Architecture Board particularly from the governance perspective.

23.4.1 General

Architecture Board meetings should be conducted within clearly identified agendas with explicit objectives, content coverage, and defined actions. In general, board meetings will be aligned with best practice, such as given in the COBIT framework (see An IT Governance Framework - COBIT).

These meetings will provide key direction in:

- Supporting the production of quality governance material and activities
- Providing a mechanism for formal acceptance through consensus and authorized publication
- Providing a fundamental control mechanism for ensuring the effective implementation of the architectures
- Establishing and maintaining the link between the implementation of the architectures and the stated strategy and objectives of the organization (business and IT)
- Identifying divergence from the contract and planning activities to realign with the contract through dispensations or policy updates

23.4.2 Preparation

Each participant will receive an agenda and any supporting documentation - e.g., dispensation requests, performance management reports, etc. - and will be expected to be familiar with the contents of each.

Where actions have been allocated to an individual, it is that person's responsibility to report on progress against these.

Each participant must confirm their availability and attendance at the Architecture Board meeting.

23.4.3 Agenda

This section outlines the contents of a Architecture Board meeting agenda. Each agenda item is described in terms of its content only.

Minutes of Previous Meeting

Minutes contain the details of previous Architecture Board meeting as per standard organizational protocol.

Requests for Change

Items under this heading are normally change requests for amendments to architectures, principles, etc., but may also include business control with regard to Architecture Contracts; e.g., ensure that voice traffic to premium numbers, such as weather reports, are barred and data traffic to certain web sites is controlled.

Any request for change is made within agreed authority levels and parameters defined by the Architecture Contract.

Dispensations

The dispensation is the mechanism used to request a change to the existing architectures, contracts, principles, etc. outside of normal operating parameters; e.g., exclude provision of service to a subsidiary, request for unusual service levels for specific business reasons, deploy non-standard technology or products to support specific business initiatives.

Dispensations are granted for a given time period and set of identified services and operational criteria that must be enforced during the lifespan of the dispensation. Dispensations are not granted indefinitely, but are used as a mechanism to ensure that service levels and operational levels, etc. are met while providing a level flexibility in their implementation and timing. The time-bound nature of dispensations ensures that they are a trigger to the Architecture Compliance activity.

Compliance Assessments

Compliance is assessed against SLAs, Operational Level Agreements (OLAs), cost targets, and required architecture refreshes. These assessments will be reviewed and either accepted or rejected depending on the criteria defined within the Architecture Governance Framework. The Architecture Compliance assessment report will include details as described.

Dispute Resolution

Disputes that have not been resolved through the Architecture Compliance and dispensation processes are identified here for further action and are documented through the Architecture Compliance assessments and dispensation documentation.

Architecture Strategy and Direction Documentation

This describes the architecture strategies, direction, and priorities and will only be formulated by the global Architecture Board. It should take the form of standard architecture documentation.

Actions Assigned

This is a report on the actions assigned at previous Architecture Board meetings. An action tracker is used to document and keep the status of all actions assigned during the Architecture Board meetings and should consist of at least the following information:

- Reference
- Priority
- Action description
- Action owner
- Action details

- Date raised
- Due date
- Status
- Type
- Resolution date

Contract Documentation Management

This is a formal acceptance of updates and changes to architecture documentation for onward publication as versioned Adobe Acrobat PDF files (see *www.adobe.com*).

Any Other Business (AOB)

Description of issues not directly covered under any of the above. These may not be described in the agenda but should be raised at the beginning of the meeting. Any supporting documentation must be managed as per all architecture governance documentation.

Schedule of Meetings

All meeting dates detail should be detailed and published.

Chapter 24: Architecture Compliance

This chapter provides guidelines for ensuring project compliance to the architecture.

24.1 Introduction

Ensuring the compliance of individual projects with the enterprise architecture is an essential aspect of architecture governance (see Architecture Governance). To this end, the IT governance function within an enterprise will normally define two complementary processes:

- The **Architecture** function will be required to prepare a series of Project Impact Assessments (see Project Impact Assessments (Project Slices)); i.e., project-specific views of the enterprise architecture that illustrate how the enterprise architecture impacts on the major projects within the organization. (These are sometimes referred to as project slices through the architecture.)
- The **IT Governance** function will define a formal Architecture Compliance review process (see Architecture Compliance Reviews) for reviewing the compliance of projects to the enterprise architecture.

Apart from defining formal processes, the architecture governance (see Architecture Governance) function may also stipulate that the architecture function should extend beyond the role of architecture definition and standards selection, and participate also in the technology selection process, and even in the commercial relationships involved in external service provision and product purchases. This may help to minimize the opportunity for misinterpretation of the enterprise architecture, and maximize the value of centralized commercial negotiation.

24.2 Terminology - The Meaning of Architecture Compliance

A key relationship between the architecture and the implementation lies in the definitions of the terms "conformant", "compliant", etc. While terminology usage may differ between organizations, the concepts of levels of conformance illustrated in Levels of Architecture Conformance should prove useful in formulating an IT compliance strategy.

The phrase "In accordance with" in Levels of Architecture Conformance means:

- Supports the stated strategy and future directions
- Adheres to the stated standards (including syntax and semantic rules specified)
- Provides the stated functionality
- Adheres to the stated principles; for example:
    - Open wherever possible and appropriate

- Re-use of component building blocks wherever possible and appropriate

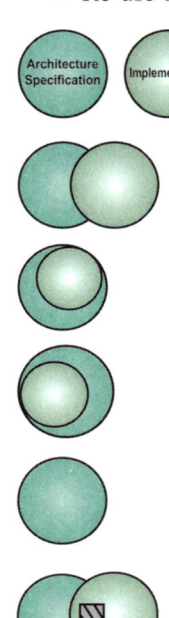

Irrelevant:
The implementation has no features in common with the architecture specification (so the question of conformance does not arise).

Consistent:
The implementation has some features in common with the architecture specification, and those common features are implemented in accordance with the specification. However, some features in the architecture specification are not implemented, and the implementation has other features that are not covered by the specification.

Compliant:
Some features in the architecture specification are not implemented, but all features implemented are covered by the specification, and in accordance with it.

Conformant:
All the features in the architecture specification are implemented in accordance with the specification, but some more features are implemented that are not in accordance with it.

Fully Conformant:
There is full correspondence between architecture specification and implementation. All specified features are implemented in accordance with the specification, and there are no features implemented that are not covered by the specification.

Non-Conformant:
Any of the above in which some features in the architecture specification are implemented not in accordance with the specification.

Figure 24.1: Levels of Architecture Conformance

24.3 Project Impact Assessments (Project Slices)

24.3.1 Introduction

A "project slice" is a project-specific subset of the enterprise architecture. It is written in order to illustrate how the enterprise architecture impacts on the major projects within the organization.

The structure of the description for each project is:

Introduction	Describes the project's business objectives, the applications being deployed, the major service qualities required for the project, and the assumptions and constraints.
Target Architecture(s) Mapping	Shows the business domain and Target Architecture coverage of the project, provides a system schematic, breaks down the application into its logical partitioning and its physical topology, and (if relevant) provides a product table.

Project Development Process Overview	Provides the project's key milestones, release schedule, and a roles, responsibilities, and contacts table.
Future Directions	Briefly outlines known future directions for the project.
References	Lists appropriate project documentation for further detail.

24.3.2 Sources

Much of this information will normally come from the projects themselves, and is not originated by the architect.

Project Impact Assessments will normally be developed as an output of Phase E of Part II: Architecture Development Method (ADM).

It is important to note that, besides the ADM, an organization will often have other relevant methodologies - in particular, for project management - that will have an input here.

There is also an important link to the architecture governance strategy (see Architecture Governance). Defining a Project Impact Assessment is only worthwhile if project managers take notice of the impact!

24.4 Architecture Compliance Reviews

An Architecture Compliance review is a scrutiny of the compliance of a specific project against established architectural criteria, spirit, and business objectives. A formal process for such reviews normally forms the core of an enterprise Architecture Compliance strategy.

24.4.1 Purpose

The goals of an Architecture Compliance review include some or all of the following:

- First and foremost, catch errors in the project architecture early, and thereby reduce the cost and risk of changes required later in the lifecycle. This in turn means that the overall project time is shortened, and that the business gets the bottom-line benefit of the architecture development faster.
- Ensure the application of best practices to architecture work.
- Provide an overview of the compliance of an architecture to mandated enterprise standards.
- Identify where the standards themselves may require modification.
- Identify services that are currently application-specific but might be provided as part of the enterprise infrastructure.
- Document strategies for collaboration, resource sharing, and other synergies across multiple architecture teams.

- Take advantage of advances in technology.
- Communicate to management the status of technical readiness of the project.
- Identify key criteria for procurement activities (e.g., for inclusion in Commercial Off-The-Shelf (COTS) product RFI/RFP documents).
- Identify and communicate significant architectural gaps to product and service providers.

Apart from the generic goals related to quality assurance outlined above, there are additional, more politically-oriented motivations for conducting Architecture Compliance reviews, which may be relevant in particular cases:

- The Architecture Compliance review can be a good way of deciding between architectural alternatives, since the business decision-makers typically involved in the review can guide decisions in terms of what is best for the business, as opposed to what is technically more pleasing or elegant.
- The output of the Architecture Compliance review is one of the few measurable deliverables to the CIO to assist in decision-making.
- Architecture reviews can serve as a way for the architecture organization to engage with development projects that might otherwise proceed without involvement of the architecture function.
- Architecture reviews can demonstrate rapid and positive support to the enterprise business community:
    - The enterprise architecture and Architecture Compliance helps ensure the alignment of IT projects with business objectives.
    - Architects can sometimes be regarded as being deep into technical infrastructure and far removed from the core business.
    - Since an Architecture Compliance review tends to look primarily at the critical risk areas of a system, it often highlights the main risks for system owners.

While compliance to architecture is required for development and implementation, non-compliance also provides a mechanism for highlighting:

1. Areas to be addressed for realignment
2. Areas for consideration for integration into the architectures as they are uncovered by the compliance processes

The latter point identifies the ongoing change and adaptability of the architectures to requirements that may be driven by indiscipline, but also allows for changes to be registered by faster moving changes in the operational environment. Typically dispensations (see IT Governance) will be used to highlight these changes and set in motion a process for registering, monitoring, and assessing the suitability of any changes required.

24.4.2 Timing

Timing of compliance activities should be considered with regard to the development of the architectures themselves.

Compliance reviews are held at appropriate project milestones or checkpoints in the project's lifecycle. Specific checkpoints should be included as follows:

- Development of the architecture itself (ADM compliance)
- Implementation of the architecture(s) (architecture compliance)

Architecture project timings for assessments should include:

- Project initiation
- Initial design
- Major design changes
- Ad hoc

The Architecture Compliance review is typically targeted for a point in time when business requirements and the enterprise architecture are reasonably firm, and the project architecture is taking shape, well before its completion.

The aim is to hold the review as soon as practical, at a stage when there is still time to correct any major errors or shortcomings, with the obvious proviso that there needs to have been some significant development of the project architecture in order for there to be something to review.

Inputs to the Architecture Compliance review may come from other parts of the standard project lifecycle, which may have an impact on timing.

24.4.3 Governance and Personnel Scenarios

In terms of the governance and conduct of the Architecture Compliance review, and the personnel involved, there are various possible scenarios:

- For smaller-scale projects, the review process could simply take the form of a series of questions that the project architect or project leader poses to him or herself, using the checklists provided below, perhaps collating the answers into some form of project report to management. The need to conduct such a process is normally included in overall enterprise-wide IT governance policies.
- Where the project under review has not involved a practicing or full-time architect to date (for example, in an application-level project), the purpose of the review is typically to bring to bear the architectural expertise of an enterprise architecture function. In such a case, the enterprise architecture function would be organizing, leading, and conducting the review, with the involvement of business domain experts. In such a scenario, the review is not a substitute for the involvement of architects in a project, but it can be a supplement or a guide to their involvement. It is probable that a database will be necessary to manage the volume of data that would be produced in the analysis of a large system or set of systems.
- In most cases, particularly in larger-scale projects, the architecture function will have

been deeply involved in, and perhaps leading, the development project under review. (This is the typical TOGAF scenario.) In such cases, the review will be co-ordinated by the Lead Architect, who will assemble a team of business and technical domain experts for the review, and compile the answers to the questions posed during the review into some form of report. The questions will typically be posed during the review by the business and technical domain experts. Alternatively, the review might be led by a representative of an Architecture Board or some similar body with enterprise-wide responsibilities.

In all cases, the Architecture Compliance review process needs the backing of senior management, and will typically be mandated as part of corporate architecture governance policies (see Architecture Governance). Normally, the enterprise CIO or enterprise Architecture Board (see Architecture Board) will mandate architecture reviews for all major projects, with subsequent annual reviews.

24.5 Architecture Compliance Review Process

24.5.1 Overview

The Architecture Compliance review process is illustrated in Architecture Compliance Review Process .

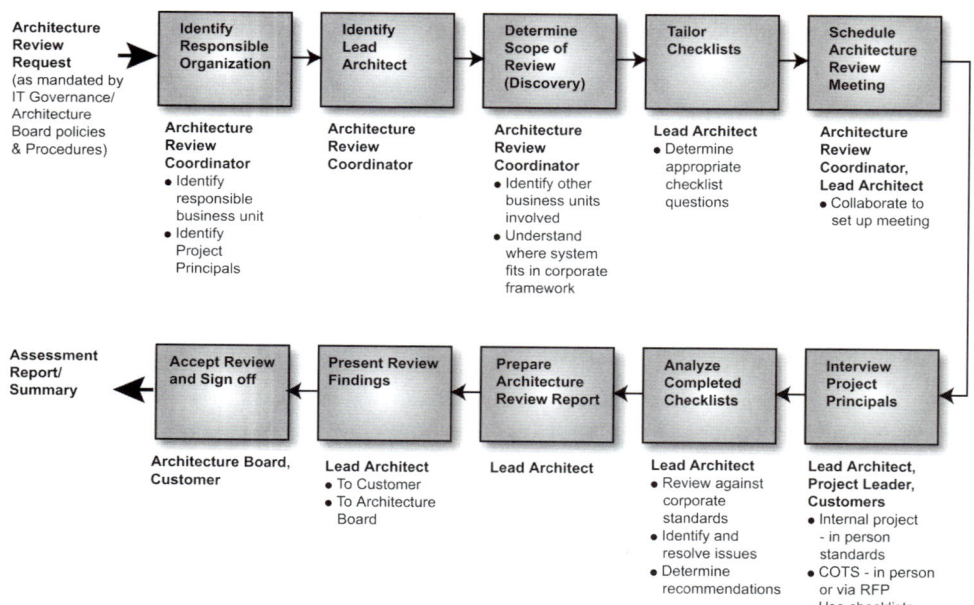

Figure 24.2: Architecture Compliance Review Process

24.5.2 Roles

The main roles in the process are tabulated below.

No.	Role	Responsibilities	Notes
1.	Architecture Board	To ensure that IT architectures are consistent and support overall business needs.	Sponsor and monitor architecture activities.
2.	Project Leader (or Project Board)	Responsible for the whole project.	
3.	Architecture Review Co-ordinator	To administer the whole architecture development and review process.	More likely to be business-oriented than technology-oriented.
4.	Lead Architect	To ensure that the architecture is technically coherent and future-proof.	An IT architecture specialist.
5.	Architect	One of the Lead Architect's technical assistants.	
6.	Customer	To ensure that business requirements are clearly expressed and understood.	Manages that part of the organization that will depend on the success of the IT described in the architecture.
7.	Business Domain Expert	To ensure that the processes to satisfy the business requirements are justified and understood.	Knows how the business domain operates; may also be the customer.
8.	Project Principals	To ensure that the architects have a sufficiently detailed understanding of the customer department's processes. They can provide input to the business domain expert or to the architects.	Members of the customer's organization who have input to the business requirements that the architecture is to address.

24.5.3 Steps

The main steps in the process are tabulated on the following page.

No.	Action	Notes	Who
1.	Request architecture review	As mandated by IT governance policies and procedures.	Anyone, whether IT or business-oriented, with an interest in or responsibility for the business area affected.
2.	Identify responsible part of organization and relevant project principals.		Architecture Review Co-ordinator
3.	Identify Lead Architect and other architects.		Architecture Review Co-ordinator
4.	Determine scope of review	Identify which other business units/departments are involved. Understand where the system fits in the corporate architecture framework.	Architecture Review Co-ordinator
5.	Tailor checklists.	To address the business requirements.	Lead Architect
6.	Schedule Architecture Review Meeting		Architecture Review Co-ordinator with collaboration of Lead Architect.
7.	Interview project principals	To get background and technical information:1 For internal project: in personl For COTS: in person or via RFP Use checklists.	Lead Architect and/or Architect, Project Leader, and Customers
8.	Analyze completed checklists	Review against corporate standards. Identify and resolve issues. Determine recommendations.	Lead Architect
9.	Prepare Architecture Compliance review report	May involve supporting staff.	Lead Architect
10.	Present review findings	To Customer To Architecture Board	Lead Architect
11.	Accept review and sign off		Architecture Board and Customer

No.	Action	Notes	Who
12.	Send assessment report/summary to Architecture Review Co-ordinator		Lead Architect

24.6 Architecture Compliance Review Checklists

The following review checklists provide a wide range of typical questions that may be used in conducting Architecture Compliance reviews, relating to various aspects of the architecture. The organization of the questions includes the basic disciplines of system engineering, information management, security, and systems management. The checklists are based on material provided by a member of The Open Group, and are specific to that organization. Other organizations could use the following checklists with other questions tailored to their own particular needs.

The checklists provided contain too many questions for any single review: they are intended to be tailored selectively to the project concerned (see Architecture Compliance Review Guidelines). The checklists actually used will typically be developed/selected by subject matter experts. They are intended to be updated annually by interest groups in those areas.

Some of the checklists include a brief description of the architectural principle that provokes the question, and a brief description of what to look for in the answer. These extensions to the checklist are intended to allow the intelligent re-phrasing of the questions, and to give the user of the checklist a feel for why the question is being asked.

Occasionally the questions will be written, as in RFPs, or in working with a senior project architect. More typically they are expressed orally, as part of an interview or working session with the project.

The checklists provided here are designed for use in individual architecture projects, not for business domain architecture or for architecture across multiple projects. (Doing an architecture review for a larger sphere of activity, across multiple business processes and system projects, would involve a similar process, but the checklist categories and their contents would be different.)

24.6.1 Hardware and Operating System Checklist

1. What is the project's lifecycle approach?
2. At what stage is the project in its lifecycle?
3. What key issues have been identified or analyzed that the project believes will drive evaluations of hardware and operating systems for networks, servers, and end-user devices?

4. What system capabilities will involve high-volume and/or high-frequency data transfers?
5. How does the system design impact or involve end-user devices?
6. What is the quantity and distribution (regional and global) of usage, data storage, and processing?
7. What applications are affinitized with your project by similarities in data, application services, etc? To what defree is data affinitized with your project?
9. What hardware and operating system choices have been made before functional design of key elements of the system?
10. If hardware and operating system decisions were made outside of the project's control:
    - What awareness does the project have of the rationale for those decisions?
    - How can the project influence those decisions as system design takes shape?
11. If some non-standards have been chosen:
    - What are the essential business and technical requirements for not using corporate standards?
    - Is this supported by a business case?
    - Have the assumptions in the business case been subject to scrutiny?
12. What is your process for evaluating full lifecycle costs of hardware and operating systems?
13. How has corporate financial management been engaged in evaluation of lifecycle costs?
14. Have you performed a financial analysis of the supplier?
15. Have you made commitments to any supplier?
16. Do you believe your requirements can be met by only one supplier?

24.6.2 Software Services and Middleware Checklist

1. Describe how error conditions are defined, raised, and propagated between application components.
2. Describe the general pattern of how methods are defined and arranged in various application modules.
3. Describe the general pattern for how method parameters are defined and organized in various application modules. Are [in], [in/out], [out] parameters always specified in the same order? Do Boolean values returned by modules have a consist outcome?
4. Describe the approach that is used to minimize the number of round-trips between client and server calls, particularly for out-of-process calls, and when complex data structures are involved.
5. Describe the major data structures that are passed between major system components.
6. Describe the major communication protocols that are used between major system components.

7. Describe the marshaling techniques that are used between various system components. Describe any specialized marshaling arrangements that are used.
8. Describe to what extent the system is designed with stateful and stateless components.
9. Describe how and when state is saved for both stateful and stateless components.
10. Describe the extent to which objects are created, used, and destroyed versus re-used through object pooling.
11. Describe the extent to which the system relies on threading or critical section coding.
12. Describe the approach and the internal documentation that is used internally in the system to document the methods, methods arguments, and method functionality.
13. Describe the code review process that was used to build the system.
14. Describe the unit testing that has been used to test the system components.
15. Describe the pre and post-condition testing that is included in various system modules.
16. Describe the assertion testing that is included with the system.
17. Do components support all the interface types they need to support or are certain assumptions made about what types of components will call other components either in terms of language bindings or other forms of marshaling?
18. Describe the extent to which big endian or little endian data format problems need to be handled across different platforms.
19. Describe if numbers or strings need to be handled differently across different platforms.
20. Describe whether the software needs to check for floating-point round-off errors.
21. Describe how time and data functions are Year 2000-compliant.
22. Describe what tools or processes have been used to test the system for memory leaks, reachability, or general robustness.
23. Describe the layering of the systems services software. Describe the general number of links between major system components. Is the system composed of a lot of point-to-point interfaces or are major messaging backbones used instead?
24. Describe to what extent the system components are either loosely coupled or tightly coupled.
25. What requirements does the system need from the infrastructure in terms of shared libraries, support for communication protocols, load balancing, transaction processing, system monitoring, naming services, or other infrastructure services?
26. Describe how the system and system components are designed for refactoring.
27. Describe how the system or system components rely on common messaging infrastructure versus a unique point-to-point communication structure.

24.6.3 Applications Checklists

24.6.3.1 Infrastructure (Enterprise Productivity) Applications

1. Is there need for capabilities that are not provided through the enterprise's standard infrastructure application products? For example:
    - Collaboration
        - Application sharing
        - Video conferencing
        - Calendaring
        - Email
    - Workflow management
    - Publishing/word processing applications
        - HTML
        - SGML and XML
        - Portable document format
        - Document processing (proprietary format)
        - Desktop publishing
    - Spreadsheet applications
    - Presentation applications
        - Business presentations
        - Image
        - Animation
        - Video
        - Sound
        - CBT
        - Web browsers
    - Data management applications
        - Database interface
        - Document management
        - Product data management
        - Data warehouses/mart
    - Program management applications
        - Project management
        - Program visibility

2. Describe the business requirements for enterprise infrastructure application capabilities that are not met by the standard products.

24.6.3.2 Business Applications

1. Are any of the capabilities required provided by standard products supporting one or more line-of-business applications? For example:
   - Business Acquisition applications
     - Sales and marketing
   - Engineering applications
     - Computer-aided design
     - Computer aided engineering
     - Mathematical and statistics analysis
   - Supplier management applications
     - Supply chain management
     - Customer relationship management
   - Manufacturing applications
     - Enterprise Resource Planning (ERP) applications
     - Manufacturing execution systems
     - Manufacturing quality
     - Manufacturing process engineering
     - Machine and adaptive control
   - Customer support applications
     - Airline logistics support
     - Maintenance engineering
   - Finance applications
   - People applications
   - Facilities applications
   - Information systems applications
     - Systems engineering
     - Software engineering
     - Web developer tools
     - Integrated development environments
     - Lifecycle categories
     - Functional categories
     - Specialty categories
   - Computer-aided manufacturing
   - e-Business enablement
   - Business process engineering

- Statistical quality control

2. Describe the process requirements for business application capabilities that are not met by the standard products.

24.6.3.3 Application Integration Approach

1. What integration points (business process/activity, application, data, computing environment) are targeted by this architecture?
2. What application integration techniques will be applied (common business objects [ORBs], standard data definitions [STEP, XML, etc], common user interface presentation/desktop)?

24.6.4 Information Management Checklists

24.6.4.1 Data Values

1. What are the processes that standardize the management and use of the data?
2. What business process supports the entry and validation of the data? Use of the data?
3. What business actions correspond to the creation and modification of the data?
4. What business actions correspond to the deletion of the data and is it considered part of a business record?
5. What are the data quality requirements required by the business user?
6. What processes are in place to support data referential integrity and/or normalization?

24.6.4.2 Data Definition

1. What are the data model, data definitions, structure, and hosting options of purchased applications (COTS)?
2. What are the rules for defining and maintaining the data requirements and designs for all components of the information system?
3. What shareable repository is used to capture the model content and the supporting information for data?
4. What is the physical data model definition (derived from logical data models) used to design the database?
5. What software development and data management tools have been selected?
6. What data owners have been identified to be responsible for common data definitions, eliminating unplanned redundancy, providing consistently reliable, timely, and accurate information, and protecting data from misuse and destruction?

24.6.4.3 Security/Protection

1. What are the data entity and attribute access rules which protect the data from unintentional and unauthorized alterations, disclosure, and distribution?

2. What are the data protection mechanisms to protect data from unauthorized external access?
3. What are the data protection mechanisms to control access to data from external sources that temporarily have internal residence within the enterprise?

24.6.4.4 Hosting, Data Types, and Sharing

1. What is the discipline for managing sole-authority data as one logical source with defined updating rules for physical data residing on different platforms?
2. What is the discipline for managing replicated data, which is derived from operational sole-authority data?
3. What tier data server has been identified for the storage of high or medium-critical operational data?
4. What tier data server has been identified for the storage of type C operational data?
5. What tier data server has been identified for the storage of decision support data contained in a data warehouse?
6. What Database Management Systems (DBMSs) have been implemented?

24.6.4.5 Common Services

1. What are the standardized distributed data management services (e.g., validation, consistency checks, data edits, encryption, and transaction management) and where do they reside?

24.6.4.6 Access Method

1. What are the data access requirements for standard file, message, and data management?
2. What are the access requirements for decision support data?
3. What are the data storage and the application logic locations?
4. What query language is being used?

24.6.5 Security Checklist

1. **Security Awareness:** Have you ensured that the corporate security policies and guidelines to which you are designing are the latest versions? Have you read them? Are you aware of all relevant computing security compliance and risk acceptance processes? (Interviewer should list all relevant policies and guidelines.)
2. **Identification/Authentication:** Diagram the process flow of how a user is identified to the application and how the application authenticates that the user is who they claim to be. Provide supporting documentation to the diagram explaining the flow from the user interface to the application/database server(s) and back to the user. Are you compliant with corporate policies on accounts, passwords, etc?
3. **Authorization:** Provide a process flow from beginning to end showing how a user requests access to the application, indicating the associated security controls and

separation of duties. This should include how the request is approved by the appropriate data owner, how the user is placed into the appropriate access-level classification profile, how the user ID, password, and access is created and provided to the user. Also include how the user is informed of their responsibilities associated with using the application, given a copy of the access agreement, how to change password, who to call for help, etc.

4. **Access Controls:** Document how the user IDs, passwords, and access profiles are added, changed, removed, and documented. The documentation should include who is responsible for these processes.

5. **Sensitive Information Protection:** Provide documentation that identifies sensitive data requiring additional protection. Identify the data owners responsible for this data and the process to be used to protect storage, transmission, printing, and distribution of this data. Include how the password file/field is protected. How will users be prevented from viewing someone else's sensitive information? Are there agreements with outside parties (partners, suppliers, contractors, etc.) concerning the safeguarding of information? If so, what are the obligations?

6. **Audit Trails and Audit Logs:** Identify and document group accounts required by the users or application support, including operating system group accounts. Identify and document individual accounts and/or roles that have superuser type privileges, what these privileges are, who has access to these accounts, how access to these accounts are controlled, tracked, and logged, and how password change and distribution are handled, including operating system accounts. Also identify audit logs, who can read the audit logs, who can modify the audit logs, who can delete the audit logs, and how the audit logs are protected and stored. Is the user ID obscured in the audit trails?

7. **External Access Considerations:** Will the application be used internally only? If not, are you compliant with corporate external access requirements?

24.6.6 System Management Checklist

1. What is the frequency of software changes that must be distributed?
2. What tools are used for software distribution?
3. Are multiple software and/or data versions allowed in production?
4. What is the user data backup frequency and expected restore time?
5. How are user accounts created and managed?
6. What is the system license management strategy?
7. What general system administration tools are required?
8. What specific application administration tools are required?
9. What specific service administration tools are required?
10. How are service calls received and dispatched?
11. Describe how the system is uninstalled.

12. Describe the process or tools available for checking that the system is properly installed.
13. Describe tools or instrumentation that are available that monitor the health and performance of the system.
14. Describe the tools or process in place that can be used to determine where the system has been installed.
15. Describe what form of audit logs are in place to capture system history, particularly after a mishap.
16. Describe the capabilities of the system to dispatch its own error messages to service personnel.

24.6.7 System Engineering/Overall Architecture Checklists

24.6.7.1 General

1. What other applications and/or systems require integration with yours?
2. Describe the integration level and strategy with each.
3. How geographically distributed is the user base?
4. What is the strategic importance of this system to other user communities inside or outside the enterprise?
5. What computing resources are needed to provide system service to users inside the enterprise? Outside the enterprise and using enterprise computing assets? Outside the enterprise and using their own assets?
6. How can users outside the native delivery environment access your applications and data?
7. What is the life expectancy of this application?
8. Describe the design that accommodates changes in the user base, stored data, and delivery system technology.
9. What is the size of the user base and their expected performance level?
10. What performance and stress test techniques do you use?
11. What is the overall organization of the software and data components?
12. What is the overall service and system configuration?
13. How are software and data configured and mapped to the service and system configuration?
14. What proprietary technology (hardware and software) is needed for this system?
15. Describe how each and every version of the software can be reproduced and re-deployed over time.
16. Describe the current user base and how that base is expected to change over the next three to five years.

17. Describe the current geographic distribution of the user base and how that base is expected to change over the next three to five years.
18. Describe the how many current or future users need to use the application in a mobile capacity or who need to work off-line.
19. Describe what the application generally does, the major components of the application, and the major data flows.
20. Describe the instrumentation included in the application that allows for the health and performance of the application to be monitored.
21. Describe the business justification for the system.
22. Describe the rationale for picking the system development language over other options in terms of initial development cost versus long-term maintenance cost.
23. Describe the systems analysis process that was used to come up with the system architecture and product selection phase of the system architecture.
24. Who besides the original customer might have a use for or benefit from using this system?
25. What percentage of the users use the system in browse mode versus update mode?
26. What is the typical length of requests that are transactional?
27. Do you need guaranteed data delivery or update, or does the system tolerate failure?
28. What are the up-time requirements of the system?
29. Describe where the system architecture adheres or does not adhere to standards.
30. Describe the project planning and analysis approach used on the project.

24.6.7.2 Processors/Servers/Clients

1. Describe the client/server Applications Architecture.
2. Annotate the pictorial to illustrate where application functionality is executed.

24.6.7.3 Client

1. Are functions other than presentation performed on the user device?
2. Describe the data and process help facility being provided.
3. Describe the screen-to-screen navigation technique.
4. Describe how the user navigates between this and other applications.
5. How is this and other applications launched from the user device?
6. Are there any inter-application data and process sharing capabilities? If so, describe what is being shared and by what technique/technology.
7. Describe data volumes being transferred to the client.
8. What are the additional requirements for local data storage to support the application?

9. What are the additional requirements for local software storage/memory to support the application?
10. Are there any known hardware/software conflicts or capacity limitations caused by other application requirements or situations which would affect the application users?
11. Describe how the look-and-feel of your presentation layer compares to the look-and-feel of the other existing applications.
12. Describe to what extent the client needs to support asynchronous and/or synchronous communication.
13. Describe how the presentation layer of the system is separated from other computational or data transfer layers of the system.

24.6.7.4 Application Server

1. Can/do the presentation layer and application layers run on separate processors?
2. Can/do the application layer and data access layer run on separate processors?
3. Can this application be placed on an application server independent of all other applications? If not, explain the dependencies
4. Can additional parallel application servers be easily added? If so, what is the load balancing mechanism?
5. Has the resource demand generated by the application been measured and what is the value? If so, has the capacity of the planned server been confirmed at the application and aggregate levels?

24.6.7.5 Data Server

1. Are there other applications, which must share the data server? If so, please identify them and describe the data and data access requirements.
2. Has the resource demand generated by the application been measured and what is the value? If so, has the capacity of the planned server been confirmed at the application and aggregate levels?

24.6.7.6 COTS (where applicable)

1. Is the vendor substantial and stable?
2. Will the enterprise receive source code upon demise of the vendor?
3. Is this software configured for the enterprise's usage?
4. Is there any peculiar A&D data or processes that would impede the use of this software?
   - Is this software currently available?
5. Has it been used/demonstrated for volume/availability/service-level requirements similar to those of the enterprise?
   - Describe the past financial and market share history of the vendor.

24.6.8 System Engineering/Methods & Tools Checklist

1. Do metrics exist for the current way of doing business?
2. Has the system owner created evaluation criteria that will be used to guide the project? Describe how the evaluation criteria will be used.
3. Has research of existing architectures been done to leverage existing work? Describe the method used to discover and understand. Will the architectures be integrated? If so, explain the method that will be used.
4. Describe the methods that will be used on the project:
    - For defining business strategies
    - For defining areas in need of improvement
    - For defining as-is and to-be business processes
    - For defining transition processes
    - For managing the project
    - For team communication
    - For knowledge management, change management, and configuration management
    - For software development
    - For referencing standards and statements of direction
    - For quality assurance of deliverables
    - For design reviews and deliverable acceptance
    - For capturing metrics
5. Are the methods documented and distributed to each team member?
6. To what extent are team members familiar with these methods?
7. What processes are in place to ensure compliance with the methods?
8. Describe the infrastructure that is in place to support the use of the methods through the end of the project and anticipated releases.
    - How is consultation and trouble-shooting provided?
    - How is training coordinated?
    - How are changes and enhancements incorporated and cascaded?
    - How are lessons learned captured and communicated?
9. What tools are being used on the project? (Please specify versions and platforms). To what extent are team members familiar with these tools?
10. Describe the infrastructure that is in place to support the use of the tools through the end of the project and anticipated releases?
    - How is consultation and trouble-shooting provided?
    - How is training coordinated?

- How are changes and enhancements incorporated and cascaded?
- How are lessons learned captured and communicated?

11. Describe how the project will promote the re-use of its deliverables and deliverable content.
12. Will the architecture designs "live" after the project has been implemented? Describe the method that will be used to incorporate changes back into the architecture designs.
13. Were the current processes defined?
14. Were issues documented, rated, and associated to current processes? If not, how do you know you are fixing something that is broken?
15. Were existing/planned process improvement activities identified and associated to current processes? If not, how do you know this activity is not in conflict with or redundant to other Statements of Work?
16. Do you have current metrics? Do you have forecasted metrics? If not, how do you know you are improving something?
17. What processes will you put in place to gather, evaluate, and report metrics?
18. What impacts will the new design have on existing business processes, organizations, and information systems? Have they been documented and shared with the owners?

24.7 Architecture Compliance Review Guidelines

24.7.1 Guidelines for Tailoring the Checklists

- Focus on:
    - High risk areas
    - Expected (and emergent) differentiators
- For each question in the checklist, understand:
    - The question itself
    - The principle behind it
    - What to look for in the responses
- Ask subject experts for their views
- Fix the checklists questions for your use
- Bear in mind the need for feedback to the Architecture Board

24.7.2 Guidelines for Conducting Architecture Compliance Reviews

- Understand clearly the objectives of those soliciting the review; and stay on track and deliver what was asked for. For example, they typically want to know what is right or wrong with the system being architected; not what is right or wrong with the development methodology used, their own management structure, etc. It is easy to get off-track and discuss subjects that are interesting and perhaps worthwhile, but not what was solicited. If you can shed light and insight on technical approaches, but the discussion is not necessary for the review, volunteer to provide it after the review.

- If it becomes obvious during the discussion that there are other issues that need to be addressed, which are outside the scope of the requested review, bring it up with the meeting chair afterwards. A plan for addressing the issues can then be developed in accordance with their degree of seriousness.
- Stay "scientific". Rather than: "We like to see large databases hosted on ABC rather than XYZ.", say things like: "The downtime associated with XYZ database environments is much greater than on ABC database environments. Therefore we don't recommend hosting type M and N systems in an XYZ environment."
- Ask "open" questions; i.e., questions that do not presume a particular answer.
- There are often "hidden agendas" or controversial issues among those soliciting a review, which you probably won't know up-front. A depersonalized approach to the discussions may help bridge the gaps of opinion rather than exacerbate them.
- Treat those being interviewed with respect. They may not have built the system "the way it should be", but they probably did the best they could under the circumstances they were placed in.
- Help the exercise become a learning experience for you and the presenters.
- Reviews should include detailed assessment activities against the architectures and should ensure that the results are stored in the Enterprise Continuum.

Chapter 25: Architecture Contracts

This chapter provides guidelines for defining and using Architecture Contracts.

25.1 Role

Architecture Contracts are the joint agreements between development partners and sponsors on the deliverables, quality, and fitness-for-purpose of an architecture. Successful implementation of these agreements will be delivered through effective architecture governance (see Architecture Governance). By implementing a governed approach to the management of contracts, the following will be ensured:

- A system of continuous monitoring to check integrity, changes, decision-making, and audit of all architecture-related activities within the organization
- Adherence to the principles, standards, and requirements of the existing or developing architectures
- Identification of risks in all aspects of the development and implementation of the architecture(s) covering the internal development against accepted standards, policies, technologies, and products as well as the operational aspects of the architectures such that the organization can continue its business within a resilient environment
- A set of processes and practices that ensure accountability, responsibility, and discipline with regard to the development and usage of all architectural artefacts.

The traditional Architecture Contract is an agreement between the sponsor and the architecture function or IS department. However, increasingly more services are being provided by systems integrators, applications providers, and service providers, co-ordinated through the architecture function or IS department. There is therefore a need for an Architecture Contract to establish joint agreements between all parties involved in the architecture development and delivery.

Architecture Contracts may occur at various stages of the Architecture Development Method (ADM); for example:

- The Statement of Work created in Phase A of Part II: Architecture Development Method (ADM) is effectively an Architecture Contract between the architecting organization and the sponsor of the enterprise architecture (or the IT governance function).
- The development of one or more architecture domains (Business, Data, Applications, Technology), and in some cases the oversight of the overall enterprise architecture, may be contracted out to systems integrators, applications providers, and/or service providers. Each of these arrangements will normally be governed by an Architecture Contract that defines the deliverables, quality, and fitness-for-purpose of the developed architecture, and the processes by which the partners in the architecture development will work

together.

- At the beginning of Phase G (the implementation governance phase), between the architecture function and the function responsible for implementing the enterprise architecture defined in the preceding ADM phases. Typically, this will be either the in-house systems development function, or a major contractor to whom the work is outsourced.
    - What is being "implemented" in Phase G of the ADM is the overall enterprise architecture. This will typically include the technology infrastructure (from Phase D), and also those enterprise applications and data management capabilities that have been defined in the Applications Architecture and Data Architecture (from Phase C), either because they are enterprise-wide in scope, or because they are strategic in business terms, and therefore of enterprise-wide importance and visibility. However, it will typically not include non-strategic business applications, which business units will subsequently deploy on top of the technology infrastructure that is implemented as part of the enterprise architecture.
    - In larger-scale implementations, there may well be one Architecture Contract per implementation team in a program of implementation projects.
- When the enterprise architecture has been implemented (at the end of Phase G), the ADM defines an Architecture Contract between the architecting function (or the IT governance function, subsuming the architecting function) and the business users who will subsequently build and deploy business unit-specific application systems in conformance with the architected environment.

It is important to bear in mind in all these cases that the ultimate goal is not just an enterprise architecture, but a dynamic enterprise architecture; i.e., one that allows for flexible evolution in response to changing technology and business drivers, without unnecessary constraints. The Architecture Contract is crucial to enabling a dynamic enterprise architecture.

Typical contents of these three kinds of Architecture Contract are explained below.

25.2 Contents

25.2.1 Statement of Architecture Work

The Statement of Architecture Work is created as a deliverable of Phase A, and is effectively an Architecture Contract between the architecting organization and the sponsor of the enterprise architecture (or the IT governance function, on behalf of the enterprise).

Typical contents of a Statement of Architecture Work are:

- Statement of work title
- Project request and background
- Project description and scope
- Architecture vision
- Managerial approach

- Change of scope procedures
- Responsibilities and deliverables
- Acceptance criteria and procedures
- Project plan and schedule
- Support of the Enterprise Continuum
- Signature approvals

25.2.2 Contract between Architecture Design and Development Partners

This is a signed statement of intent on designing and developing the enterprise architecture, or significant parts of it, from partner organizations, including systems integrators, applications providers, and service providers.

Increasingly the development of one or more architecture domains (Business, Data, Applications, Technology) may be contracted out, with the enterprise's architecture function providing oversight of the overall enterprise architecture, and co-ordination and control of the overall effort. In some cases even this oversight role may be contracted out, although most enterprises prefer to retain that core responsibility in-house.

Whatever the specifics of the contracting-out arrangements, the arrangements themselves will normally be governed by an Architecture Contract that defines the deliverables, quality, and fitness-for-purpose of the developed architecture, and the processes by which the partners in the architecture development will work together.

Typical contents of an Architecture Design and Development Contract are:

- Introduction and background
- The nature of the agreement
- Scope of the architecture
- Architecture and strategic principles and requirements
- Conformance requirements
- Architecture development and management process and roles
- Target architecture measures
- Defined phases of deliverables
- Prioritized joint workplan
- Time window(s)
- Architecture delivery and business metrics

The template for this contract will normally be defined as part of the Preliminary Phase of the ADM, if not existing already, and the specific contract will be defined at the appropriate stage of the ADM, depending on the particular work that is being contracted out.

25.2.3 Contract between Architecting Function and Business Users

This is a signed statement of intent to conform with the enterprise architecture, issued by enterprise business users. When the enterprise architecture has been implemented (at the end of Phase G), an Architecture Contract will normally be drawn up between the architecting function (or the IT governance function, subsuming the architecting function) and the business users who will subsequently be building and deploying application systems in the architected environment.

Typical contents of a Business Users' Architecture Contract are:

- Introduction and background
- The nature of the agreement
- Scope
- Strategic requirements
- Architecture deliverables that meet the business requirements
- Conformance requirements
- Architecture adopters
- Time window
- Architecture business metrics
- Service architecture (includes Service Level Agreement (SLA))

This contract is also used to manage changes to the enterprise architecture in Phase H.

25.3 Relationship to Architecture Governance

The Architecture Contract document produced in Phase G of the ADM figures prominently in the area of architecture governance, as explained in Part IV: Resource Base, Architecture Governance .

In the context of architecture governance, the Architecture Contract is often used as a means of driving architecture change.

In order to ensure that the Architecture Contract is effective and efficient, the following aspects of the governance framework may need to be introduced into Phase G:

- Simple processes
- People-centered authority
- Strong communication
- Timely responses and an effective escalation process
- Supporting organizational structures

Chapter 26: Architecture Governance

This chapter provides a framework and guidelines for architecture governance.

26.1 Introduction

This section describes the nature of governance, and the levels of governance.

26.1.1 Levels of Governance within the Enterprise

Architecture governance is the practice and orientation by which enterprise architectures and other architectures are managed and controlled at an enterprise-wide level.

Architecture governance typically does not operate in isolation, but within a hierarchy of governance structures, which, particularly in the larger enterprise, can include all of the following as distinct domains with their own disciplines and processes:

- Corporate governance
- Technology governance
- IT governance
- Architecture governance

Each of these domains of governance may exist at multiple geographic levels - global, regional, and local - within the overall enterprise.

Corporate governance is thus a broad topic, beyond the scope of an enterprise architecture framework such as TOGAF.

This and related subsections are focused on architecture governance; but they describe it in the context of enterprise-wide governance, because of the hierarchy of governance structures within which it typically operates, as explained above.

In particular, this and following sections aim to:

- Provide an overview of the nature of governance as a discipline in its own right
- Describe the governance context in which architecture governance typically functions within the enterprise
- Describe an Architecture Governance Framework that can be adapted and applied in practice, both for enterprise architecture and for other forms of IT architecture

26.1.2 The Nature of Governance

26.1.2.1 Governance: A Generic Perspective

Governance is essentially about ensuring that business is conducted properly. It is less about overt control and strict adherence to rules, and more about guidance and effective and equitable usage of resources to ensure sustainability of an organization's strategic objectives.

The following outlines the basic principles of corporate governance, as identified by the Organization for Economic Co-operation and Development (OECD):

- Focuses on the rights, roles, and equitable treatment of shareholders
- Disclosure and transparency and the responsibilities of the board
- Ensures:
    - Sound strategic guidance of the organization
    - Effective monitoring of management by the board
    - Board accountability for the company and to the shareholders
- Board's responsibilities:
    - Reviewing and guiding corporate strategy
    - Setting and monitoring achievement of management's performance objectives

Supporting this, the OECD considers a traditional view of governance as: "... the system by which business corporations are directed and controlled. The corporate governance structure specifies the distribution of rights and responsibilities among different participants in the corporation - such as the board, managers, shareholders, and other stakeholders - and spells out the rules and procedures for making decisions on corporate affairs. By doing this, it also provides the structure through which the company objectives are set, and the means of attaining those objectives and monitoring performance" [OECD (1999)].

26.1.2.2 The Characteristics of Governance

The following characteristics have been adapted from Naidoo (2002) and are positioned here to highlight both the value and necessity for governance as an approach to be adopted within organizations and their dealings with all involved parties:

Discipline	All involved parties will have a commitment to adhere to procedures, processes, and authority structures established by the organization.
Transparency	All actions implemented and their decision support will be available for inspection by authorized organization and provider parties.
Independence	All processes, decision-making, and mechanisms used will be established so as to minimize or avoid potential conflicts of interest.

Accountability	Identifiable groups within the organization - e.g., governance boards who take actions or make decisions - are authorized and accountable for their actions.
Responsibility	Each contracted party is required to act responsibly to the organization and its stakeholders.
Fairness	All decisions taken, processes used, and their implementation will not be allowed to create unfair advantage to any one particular party.

26.1.3 Technology Governance

Technology governance is a key capability, requirement, and resource for most organizations because of the pervasiveness of technology across the organizational spectrum.

Recent studies have shown that many organizations have a balance in favor of intangibles rather than tangibles that require management. Given that most of these intangibles are informational and digital assets, it is evident that businesses are becoming more reliant on IT: and the governance of IT - IT governance - is therefore becoming an even more important part of technology governance.

These trends also highlight the dependencies of businesses on not only the information itself but also the processes, systems, and structures that create deliver, and consume it. As the shift to increasing value through intangibles increases in many industry sectors, so risk management must be considered as key to understanding and moderating new challenges, threats, and opportunities.

Not only are organizations increasingly dependent on IT for their operations and profitability, but also their reputation, brand, and ultimately their value are also dependent on that same information and the supporting technology.

26.1.4 IT Governance

IT governance provides the framework and structure that links IT resources and information to enterprise goals and strategies. Furthermore, IT governance institutionalizes best practices for planning, acquiring, implementing, and monitoring IT performance, to ensure that the enterprise's IT assets support its business objectives.

In recent years, IT governance has become integral to the effective governance of the modern enterprise. Businesses are increasingly dependent on IT to support critical business functions and processes; and to successfully gain competitive advantage, businesses need to manage effectively the complex technology that is pervasive throughout the organization, in order to respond quickly and safely to business needs.

In addition, regulatory environments around the world are increasingly mandating stricter enterprise control over information, driven by increasing reports of information system disasters and electronic fraud. The management of IT-related risk is now widely accepted as a key part of enterprise governance.

It follows that an IT governance strategy, and an appropriate organization for implementing the strategy, must be established with the backing of top management, clarifying who owns the enterprise's IT resources, and, in particular, who has ultimate responsibility for their enterprise-wide integration.

26.1.4.1 An IT Governance Framework - COBIT

As with corporate governance, IT governance is a broad topic, beyond the scope of an enterprise architecture framework such as TOGAF. A good source of detailed information on IT governance is the COBIT framework (Control OBjectives for Information and related Technology). This is an open standard for control over IT, developed and promoted by the IT Governance Institute, and published by the Information Systems Audit and Control Foundation (ISACF).

COBIT also provides a generally accepted standard for good IT security and control practices to support the needs of enterprise management in determining and monitoring the appropriate level of IT security and control for their organizations.

The IT Governance Institute has also developed and built into the COBIT framework a set of Management Guidelines for COBIT, which consist of Maturity Models, Critical Success Factors (CFSs), Key Goal Indicators (KGIs), and Key Performance Indicators (KPIs). The framework responds to management's need for control and measurability of IT, by providing management with tools to assess and measure their organization's IT environment against the IT processes that COBIT identifies.

26.1.5 Architecture Governance: Overview

26.1.5.1 Architecture Governance Characteristics

Architecture governance is the practice and orientation by which enterprise architectures and other architectures are managed and controlled at an enterprise-wide level. It includes the following:

- Implementing a system of controls over the creation and monitoring of all architectural components and activities, to ensure the effective introduction, implementation, and evolution of architectures within the organization
- Implementing a system to ensure compliance with internal and external standards and regulatory obligations
- Establishing processes that support effective management of the above processes within agreed parameters
- Developing practices that ensure accountability to a clearly identified stakeholder community, both inside and outside the organization

26.1.5.2 Architecture Governance as a Board-Level Responsibility

As mentioned above, IT governance has recently become a board responsibility as part of overall business governance. The governance of an organization's architectures is a key factor in effective IT/business linkage, and is therefore increasingly becoming a key board-level responsibility in its own right.

This section aims to provide the impetus for opening up IT and architecture governance so that the business responsibilities associated with architecture activities and artefacts can be elucidated and managed.

26.1.5.3 TOGAF and Architecture Governance

Phase G of the TOGAF ADM (see Part II: Architecture Development Method (ADM), Phase G: Implementation Governance) is dedicated to implementation governance, which concerns itself with the realization of the architecture through change projects. implementation governance is just one aspect of architecture governance, which covers the management and control of all aspects of the development and evolution of enterprise architectures and other architectures within the enterprise.

Architecture governance needs to be supported by an Architecture Governance Framework (described in detail in Architecture Governance Framework) which assists in identifying effective processes so that the business responsibilities associated with architecture governance can be elucidated, communicated, and managed effectively.

26.2 Architecture Governance Framework

This section describes a conceptual and organizational framework for architecture governance.

As previously explained, Phase G of the TOGAF ADM (see Part II: Architecture Development Method (ADM), Phase G: Implementation Governance) is dedicated to implementation governance, which concerns itself with the realization of the architecture through change projects.

Implementation governance is just one aspect of architecture governance, which covers the management and control of all aspects of the development and evolution of enterprise architectures and other architectures within the enterprise.

Architecture governance needs to be supported by an Architecture Governance Framework, described in detail below. The governance framework described is a generic framework that can be adapted to the existing governance environment of an enterprise. It is intended to assist in identifying effective processes and organizational structures, so that the business responsibilities associated with architecture governance can be elucidated, communicated, and managed effectively.

26.2.1 Architecture Governance Framework - Conceptual Structure

26.2.1.1 Key Concepts

Conceptually, architecture governance is an approach, a series of processes, a cultural orientation, and set of owned responsibilities that ensure the integrity and effectiveness of the organization's architectures.

The key concepts are illustrated in Architecture Governance Framework - Conceptual Structure .

The split of process, content, and context are key to the support of the architecture governance initiative, by allowing the introduction of new governance material (legal, regulatory, standards-based, or legislative) without unduly impacting the processes. This content-agnostic approach ensures that the framework is flexible. The processes are typically independent of the content and implement a proven best practice approach to active governance.

The Architecture Governance Framework is integral to the Enterprise Continuum, and manages all content relevant both to the architecture itself and to architecture governance processes.

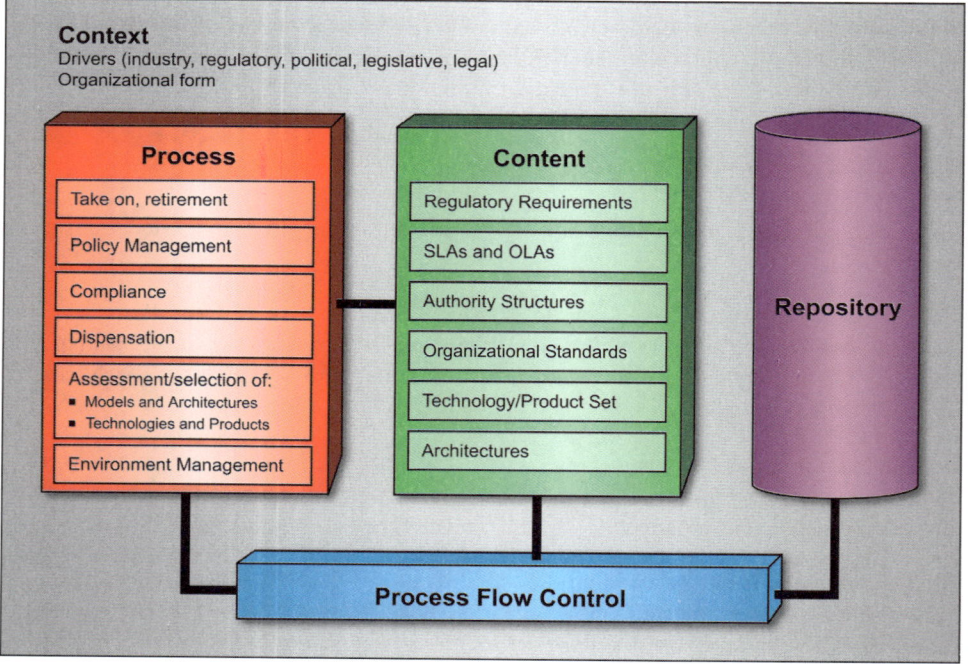

Figure 26.1: Architecture Governance Framework - Conceptual Structure

26.2.1.2 Key Architecture Governance Processes

Governance processes are required to identify, manage, audit, and disseminate all information related to architecture management, contracts, and implementation. These governance processes will be used to ensure that all architecture artefacts and contracts, principles, and operational-level agreements are monitored on an ongoing basis with clear auditability of all decisions made.

Policy Management and Take-On

All architecture amendments, contracts, and supporting information must come under governance through a formal process in order to register, validate, ratify, manage, and publish new or updated content. These processes will ensure the orderly integration with existing governance content such that all relevant parties, documents, contracts, and supporting information are managed and audited.

Compliance

Compliance assessments against Service Level Agreements (SLAs), Operational Level Agreements (OLAs), standards, and regulatory requirements will be implemented on an ongoing basis to ensure stability, conformance, and performance monitoring. These assessments will be reviewed and either accepted or rejected depending on the criteria defined within the governance framework.

Dispensation

A Compliance Assessment can be rejected where the subject area (design, operational, service level, or technology) are not compliant. In this case the subject area can:

1. Be adjusted or realigned in order to meet the compliance requirements
2. Request a dispensation

Where a Compliance Assessment is rejected, an alternate route to meeting interim conformance is provided through dispensations. These are granted for a given time period and set of identified service and operational criteria that must be enforced during the lifespan of the dispensation. Dispensations are not granted indefinitely, but are used as a mechanism to ensure that service levels and operational levels are met while providing a level flexibility in their implementation and timing. The time-bound nature of dispensations ensures that they are a major trigger in the compliance cycle.

Monitoring and Reporting

Performance management is required to ensure that both the operational and service elements are managed against an agreed set of criteria. This will include monitoring against service and operational-level agreements, feedback for adjustment, and reporting.

Internal management information will be considered in Environment Management .

Business Control

Business Control relates to the processes invoked to ensure compliance with the organization's business policies.

Environment Management

This identifies all the services required to ensure that the repository-based environment underpinning the governance framework is effective and efficient. This includes the physical and logical repository management, access, communication, training, and accreditation of all users.

All architecture artefacts, service agreements, contracts, and supporting information must come under governance through a formal process in order to register, validate, ratify, manage, and publish new or updated content. These processes will ensure the orderly integration with existing governance content such that all relevant parties, documents, contracts, and supporting information are managed and audited.

The governance environment will have a number of administrative processes defined in order to effect a managed service and process environment. These processes will include user management, internal SLAs (defined in order to control its own processes), and management information reporting.

26.2.2 Architecture Governance Framework - Organizational Structure

26.2.2.1 Overview

Architecture governance is the practice and orientation by which enterprise architectures and other architectures are managed and controlled. In order to ensure that this control is effective within the organization, it is necessary to have the correct organizational structures established to support all governance activities.

An architecture governance structure for effectively implementing the approach described in this section will typically include the following levels, which may in practice involve a combination of existing IT governance processes, organizational structures, and capabilities. They will typically include the following:

- Global governance board
- Local governance board
- Design authorities
- Working parties

The architecture organization illustrated in Architecture Governance Framework - Organizational Structure highlights the major structural elements required for an architecture governance initiative. While each enterprise will have differing requirements, it is expected that the basics of the organizational design shown in Architecture Governance Framework

- Organizational Structure will be applicable and implementable in a wide variety of organizational types.

26.2.2.2 Key Areas

Architecture Governance Framework - Organizational Structure identifies three key areas of architecture management: Develop, Implement, and Deploy. Each of these is the responsibility of one or more groups within the organization, while the Enterprise Continuum is shown to support all activities and artefacts associated with the governance of the architectures throughout their lifecycle.

The Develop responsibilities, processes, and structures are usually linked to the TOGAF ADM and its usage, while the Implement responsibilities, processes, and structures are typically linked to Phase G (see Part II: Architecture Development Method (ADM), Phase G: Implementation Governance).

As mentioned above, the Architecture Governance Framework is integral to the Enterprise Continuum, and manages all content relevant both to the architectures themselves and to architecture governance processes.

26.2.2.3 Operational Benefits

As illustrated in Architecture Governance Framework - Organizational Structure , the governance of the organization's architectures provides not only direct control and guidance of their development and implementation, but also extends into the operations of the implemented architectures.

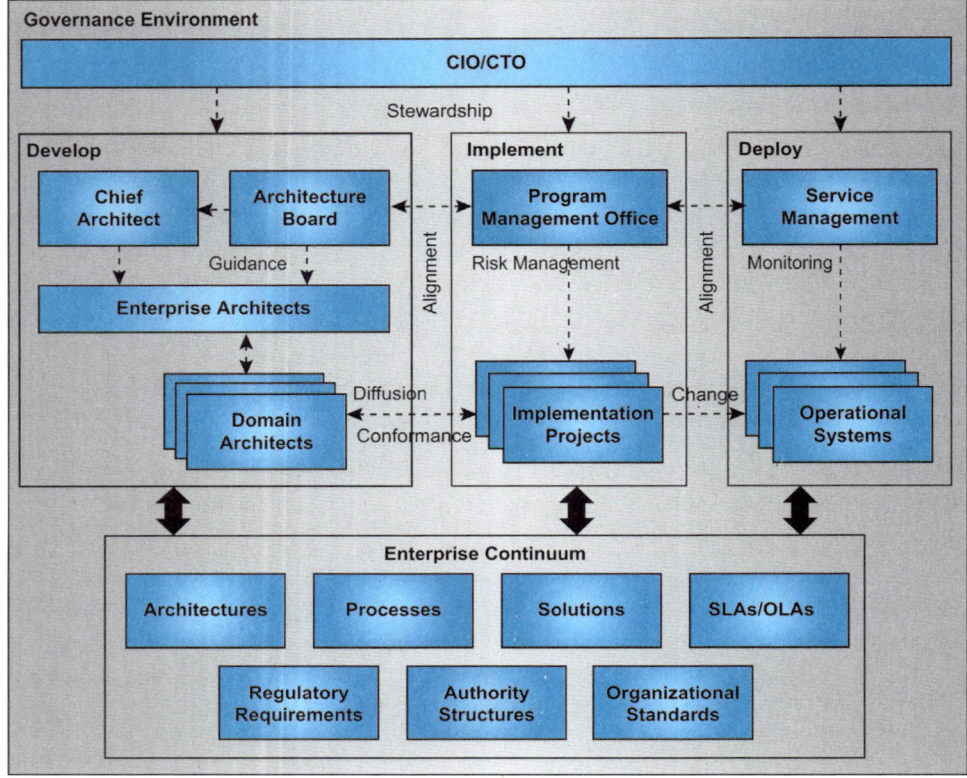

Figure 26.2 : Architecture Governance Framework - Organizational Structure

The following benefits have been found to be derived through the continuing governance of architectures:

- Links IT processes, resources, and information to organizational strategies and objectives
- Integrates and institutionalizes IT best practices
- Aligns with industry frameworks such as COBIT (planning and organizing, acquiring and implementing, delivering and supporting, and monitoring IT performance)
- Enables the organization to take full advantage of its information, infrastructure, and hardware and software assets
- Protects the underlying digital assets of the organization
- Supports regulatory and best practice requirements such as auditability, security, responsibility, and accountability
- Promotes visible risk management

These benefits position the TOGAF Architecture Governance Framework as an approach, a series of processes, a cultural orientation, and a set of owned responsibilities, that together ensure the integrity and effectiveness of the organization's architectures.

26.3 Architecture Governance in Practice

This section provides practical guidelines for the effective implementation of architecture governance.

26.3.1 Architecture Governance - Key Success Factors

It is important to consider the following to ensure a successful approach to architecture governance, and to the effective management of the Architecture Contract:

- Establishment and operation of best practices for the submission, adoption, re-use, reporting, and retirement of architecture policies, procedures, roles, skills, organizational structures, and support services
- Establishment of the correct organizational responsibilities and structures to support the architecture governance processes and reporting requirements
- Integration of tools and processes to facilitate the take-up of the processes, both procedurally and culturally
- Management of criteria for the control of the architecture governance processes, dispensations, compliance assessments, SLAs, and OLAs
- Meeting the internal and external requirements for the effectiveness, efficiency, confidentiality, integrity, availability, compliance, and reliability of all architecture governance-related information, services, and processes

26.3.2 Elements of an Effective Architecture Governance Strategy

26.3.2.1 Architecture Governance and Corporate Politics

There is a similarity between enterprise architecture and architecture in the physical world, in that politics has an important role to play in the acceptance of both architectures. In the real world, it is the dual politics of the environment and commerce, while in the world of enterprise architecture a consideration of corporate politics is critical.

An enterprise architecture imposed without appropriate political backing is bound to fail. In order to succeed, the enterprise architecture must reflect the needs of the organization. Enterprise architects, if they are not involved in the development of business strategy, must at least have a fundamental understanding of it and of the prevailing business issues facing the organization. It may even be necessary for them to be involved in the system deployment process and to ultimately own the investment and product selection decisions arising from the implementation of the Technology Architecture.

26.3.2.2 Key Strategic Elements

There are three important elements of architecture governance strategy that relate particularly to the acceptance and success of architecture within the enterprise. While relevant and applicable in their own right apart from their role in governance, and therefore described separately, they also from an integral part of any effective architecture governance strategy:

- A cross-organizational Architecture Board (see Architecture Board) must be established with the backing of top management to oversee the implementation of the IT governance strategy.

- A comprehensive set of architecture principles (Architecture Principles) should be established, to guide, inform, and support the way in which an organization sets about fulfilling its mission through the use of IT.

- An Architecture Compliance (see Architecture Compliance) strategy should be adopted - specific measures (more than just a statement of policy) to ensure compliance with the architecture, including Project Impact Assessments, a formal Architecture Compliance review process, and possibly including the involvement of the architecture team in product procurement.

Chapter 27: Architecture Maturity Models

This chapter provides techniques for evaluating and quantifying an organization's maturity in enterprise architecture.

27.1 Overview

Organizations that can manage change effectively are generally more successful than those that cannot. Many organizations know that they need to improve their IT-related development processes in order to successfully manage change, but don't know how. Such organizations typically either spend very little on process improvement, because they are unsure how best to proceed; or spend a lot, on a number of parallel and unfocussed efforts, to little or no avail.

Capability Maturity Models (CMMs) address this problem by providing an effective and proven method for an organization to gradually gain control over and improve its IT-related development processes. Such models provide the following benefits:

- They describe the practices that any organization must perform in order to improve its processes.
- They provide a yardstick against which to periodically measure improvement.
- They constitute a proven framework within which to manage the improvement efforts.

The various practices are typically organized into five levels, each level representing an increased ability to control and manage the development environment.

An evaluation of the organization's practices against the model - called an assessment - determines the level at which the organization currently stands. It indicates the organization's maturity in the area concerned, and the practices on which the organization needs to focus in order to see the greatest improvement and the highest return on investment.

The benefits of capability maturity models are well documented for software and systems engineering. Their application to enterprise architecture has been a recent development, stimulated by the increasing interest in enterprise architecture in recent years, combined with the lack of maturity in this discipline.

This section introduces into TOGAF the topic of capability maturity models and their associated methods and techniques, as a widely used industry standard that is mature enough to consider for use in relation to enterprise architecture.

27.2 Background

The Software Engineering Institute (SEI),[5] a federally funded research and development

---

5. Refer to *www.sei.cmu.edu/sei-home.html*.

center sponsored by the US Department of Defense and operated by Carnegie Mellon University, developed the original capability maturity model - SW-CMM, Capability Maturity Model for Software - in the early 1990s, which is still widely used today.

Capability maturity models have gained widescale acceptance over the last decade. These models and their associated methods were originally applied to IT solutions, particularly software solutions, but a number of IT-related disciplines have developed capability maturity models to support process improvement in areas such as:

- People - the P-CMM (People Capability Maturity Model), and the IDEAL Life Cycle Model for Improvement
- Systems Engineering - the SE-CMM (Systems Engineering Capability Maturity Model)
- Software Acquisition - the SA-CMM (Software Acquisition Capability Maturity Model)
- CMMI (Capability Maturity Model Integration)

The models have been adopted by large organizations, including the US Department of Commerce, the US DoD, the UK Government, and a number of large services organizations, to assess competencies.

The increasing interest in applying these techniques to the IT architecture and enterprise architecture fields has resulted in a series of template tools which assess:

- The state of the IT architecture process
- The IT architecture
- The organization's buy-in to both

The main issues addressed by US and UK Government use of these models include:

- eCommerce maturity
- Process implementation and audit
- Quality measurements
- People competencies
- Investment management

They involve use of a multiplicity of models, and focus in particular on measuring business benefits and return on investment.

Another key driver is the increasing use of outsourcing. Recent analyst projections indicate that around 75 percent of IS organizations are refocusing their role on brokering resources and facilitating business-driven demands, rather than on being direct providers of IT services. The capability maturity model is increasingly the standard by which outsourcers are being evaluated.

This section reviews the state of development in such techniques.

A closely related topic is that of the Architecture Skills Framework (see Architecture Skills Framework), which can be used to plan the target skills and capabilities required by an organization to successfully deliver an enterprise architecture, and to determine the training and development needs of individuals.

27.3 The US DoC ACMM Framework

27.3.1 Overview

As an example of the trend towards increased interest in applying capability maturity model techniques to IT architecture, all US federal agencies are now expected to provide maturity models and ratings as part of their IT investment management and audit requirements.

In particular, the US Department of Commerce (DoC) has developed an IT Architecture Capability Maturity Model (ACMM)[6] to aid in conducting internal assessments. The ACMM provides a framework that represents the key components of a productive IT architecture process. The goal is to enhance the overall odds for success of IT architecture by identifying weak areas and providing a defined evolutionary path to improving the overall architecture process.

The ACMM comprises three sections:

1. The IT architecture maturity model
2. IT architecture characteristics of operating units' processes at different maturity levels
3. The IT architecture capability maturity model scorecard

The first two sections explain the architecture capability maturity levels and the corresponding IT architecture characteristics for each maturity level to be used as measures in the assessment process. The third section is used to derive the architecture capability maturity level that is to be reported to the DoC Chief Information Officer (CIO).

27.3.2 Elements of the ACMM

The DoC ACMM consists of six levels and nine architecture characteristics. The six levels are:

0	None
1	Initial
2	Under development
3	Defined
4	Managed
5	Measured

---

6. Refer to *secure.cio.noaa.gov/hpcc/docita/files/*.

The nine IT architecture characteristics are:

- IT architecture process
- IT architecture development
- Business linkage
- Senior management involvement
- Operating unit participation
- Architecture communication
- IT security
- Architecture governance
- IT investment and acquisition strategy

Two complementary methods are used in the ACMM to calculate a maturity rating. The first method obtains a weighted mean IT architecture maturity level. The second method shows the percent achieved at each maturity level for the nine architecture characteristics.

27.3.3 Example: IT Architecture Process Maturity Levels

The following example shows the detail of the IT architecture maturity levels as applied to the first of the nine characteristics, IT architecture process.

Level 0: None

No IT architecture program. No IT architecture to speak of.

Level 1: Initial

Informal IT architecture process underway.

1. Processes are ad hoc and localized. Some IT architecture processes are defined. There is no unified architecture process across technologies or business processes. Success depends on individual efforts.
2. IT architecture processes, documentation, and standards are established by a variety of ad hoc means and are localized or informal.
3. Minimal, or implicit linkage to business strategies or business drivers.
4. Limited management team awareness or involvement in the architecture process.
5. Limited operating unit acceptance of the IT architecture process.
6. The latest version of the operating unit's IT architecture documentation is on the web. Little communication exists about the IT architecture process and possible process improvements.
7. IT security considerations are ad hoc and localized.

8. No explicit governance of architectural standards.
9. Little or no involvement of strategic planning and acquisition personnel in the enterprise architecture process. Little or no adherence to existing standards.

Level 2: Under Development

IT architecture process is under development.

1. Basic IT architecture process is documented based on OMB Circular A-130 and Department of Commerce IT Architecture Guidance. The architecture process has developed clear roles and responsibilities.
2. IT vision, principles, business linkages, baseline, and Target Architecture are identified. Architecture standards exist, but not necessarily linked to Target Architecture. Technical Reference Model (TRM) and Standards Profile framework established.
3. Explicit linkage to business strategies.
4. Management awareness of architecture effort.
5. Responsibilities are assigned and work is underway.
6. The DoC and operating unit IT architecture web pages are updated periodically and are used to document architecture deliverables.
7. IT security architecture has defined clear roles and responsibilities.
8. Governance of a few architectural standards and some adherence to existing Standards Profile.
9. Little or no formal governance of IT investment and acquisition strategy. Operating unit demonstrates some adherence to existing Standards Profile.

Level 3: Defined

Defined IT architecture including detailed written procedures and TRM.

1. The architecture is well defined and communicated to IT staff and business management with operating unit IT responsibilities. The process is largely followed.
2. Gap analysis and migration plan are completed. Fully developed TRM and Standards Profile. IT goals and methods are identified.
3. IT architecture is integrated with capital planning and investment control.
4. Senior management team aware of and supportive of the enterprise-wide architecture process. Management actively supports architectural standards.
5. Most elements of operating unit show acceptance of or are actively participating in the IT architecture process.
6. Architecture documents updated regularly on DoC IT architecture web page.
7. IT security architecture Standards Profile is fully developed and is integrated with IT architecture.

8. Explicit documented governance of majority of IT investments.
9. IT acquisition strategy exists and includes compliance measures to IT enterprise architecture. Cost benefits are considered in identifying projects.

Level 4: Managed

Managed and measured IT architecture process.

1. IT architecture process is part of the culture. Quality metrics associated with the architecture process are captured.
2. IT architecture documentation is updated on a regular cycle to reflect the updated IT architecture. Business, Data, Applications, and Technology Architectures defined by appropriate de jure and de facto standards.
3. Capital planning and investment control are adjusted based on the feedback received and lessons learned from updated IT architecture. Periodic re-examination of business drivers.
4. Senior management team directly involved in the architecture review process.
5. The entire operating unit accepts and actively participates in the IT architecture process.
6. Architecture documents are updated regularly, and frequently reviewed for latest architecture developments/standards.
7. Performance metrics associated with IT security architecture are captured.
8. Explicit governance of all IT investments. Formal processes for managing variances feed back into IT architecture.
9. All planned IT acquisitions and purchases are guided and governed by the IT architecture.

Level 5: Optimizing

Continuous improvement of IT architecture process.

1. Concerted efforts to optimize and continuously improve architecture process.
2. A standards and waivers process is used to improve architecture development process.
3. Architecture process metrics are used to optimize and drive business linkages. Business involved in the continuous process improvements of IT architecture.
4. Senior management involvement in optimizing process improvements in architecture development and governance.
5. Feedback on architecture process from all operating unit elements is used to drive architecture process improvements.
6. Architecture documents are used by every decision-maker in the organization for every IT-related business decision.

7. Feedback from IT security architecture metrics are used to drive architecture process improvements.
8. Explicit governance of all IT investments. A standards and waivers process is used to make governance-process improvements.
9. No unplanned IT investment or acquisition activity.

27.4 Capability Maturity Models Integration (CMMI)

27.4.1 Introduction

The capability models that the SEI is currently involved in developing, expanding, or maintaining include the following:

- CMMI (Capability Maturity Model Integration)
- IPD-CMM (Integrated Product Development Capability Maturity Model)
- P-CMM (People Capability Maturity Model)
- SA-CMM (Software Acquisition Capability Maturity Model)
- SE-CMM (Systems Engineering Capability Maturity Model)
- SW-CMM (Capability Maturity Model for Software)

As explained in Architecture Maturity Models , in recent years the industry has witnessed significant growth in the area of maturity models. The multiplicity of models available has led to problems of its own, in terms of how to integrate all the different models to produce a meaningful metric for overall process maturity.

In response to this need, the SEI has developed a Framework called Capability Maturity Model Integration (CMMI), to provide a means of managing the complexity.

According to the SEI, the use of the CMMI models improves on the best practices of previous models in many important ways, in particular enabling organizations to:

- More explicitly link management and engineering activities to business objectives
- Expand the scope of and visibility into the product lifecycle and engineering activities to ensure that the product or service meets customer expectations
- Incorporate lessons learned from additional areas of best practice (e.g., measurement, risk management, and supplier management)
- Implement more robust high-maturity practices
- Address additional organizational functions critical to its products and services
- More fully comply with relevant ISO standards

CMMI is being adopted worldwide.

27.4.2 The SCAMPI Method

The Standard CMMI Appraisal Method for Process Improvement (SCAMPI) is the appraisal method associated with CMMI. The SCAMPI appraisal method is used to identify strengths, weaknesses, and ratings relative to CMMI reference models. It incorporates best practices found successful in the appraisal community, and is based on the features of several legacy appraisal methods. It is applicable to a wide range of appraisal usage modes, including both internal process improvement and external capability determinations.

The SCAMPI method definition document[7] describes the requirements, activities, and practices associated with each of the processes that compose the SCAMPI method.

27.5 Conclusions

This section has sought to introduce into TOGAF the topic of capability maturity model-based methods and techniques, as a widely used industry standard that is mature enough to consider for use in relation to enterprise architecture.

The benefits of capability maturity models are well documented for software and systems engineering. Their application to enterprise architecture has been a more recent development, stimulated by the increasing interest in enterprise architecture, combined with the lack of maturity in the discipline of enterprise architecture.

Future versions of TOGAF will seek to build on this base, as more experience is gained on the use of these methods and techniques specifically relating to enterprise architecture.

---

7. Available at www.sei.cmu.edu/publications/documents/01.reports/01hb001.html.

Chapter 28: Architecture Patterns

This chapter provides guidelines for using architecture patterns.

28.1 Introduction

Patterns for system architecting are very much in their infancy. They have been introduced into TOGAF essentially to draw them to the attention of the systems architecture community as an emerging important resource, and as a placeholder for hopefully more rigorous descriptions and references to more plentiful resources in future versions of TOGAF.

They have not (as yet) been integrated into TOGAF. However, in the following, we attempt to indicate the potential value to TOGAF, and to which parts of the TOGAF Architecture Development Method (ADM) they might be relevant.

28.1.1 Background

A "pattern" has been defined as: "an idea that has been useful in one practical context and will probably be useful in others" [archetecture patterns - Reusable Object Models].

In TOGAF, patterns are considered to be a way of putting building blocks into context; for example, to describe a re-usable solution to a problem. Building blocks are what you use: patterns can tell you how you use them, when, why, and what trade-offs you have to make in doing so.

Patterns offer the promise of helping the architect to identify combinations of Architecture and/or Solution Building Blocks (ABBs/SBBs) that have been proven to deliver effective solutions in the past, and may provide the basis for effective solutions in the future.

Pattern techniques are generally acknowledged to have been established as a valuable architectural design technique by Christopher Alexander, a buildings architect, who described this approach in his book The Timeless Way of Building, published in 1979. This book provides an introduction to the ideas behind the use of patterns, and Alexander followed it with two further books (A Pattern Language and The Oregon Experiment) in which he expanded on his description of the features and benefits of a patterns approach to architecture.

Software and buildings architects have many similar issues to address, and so it was natural for software architects to take an interest in patterns as an architectural tool. Many papers and books have been published on them since Alexander's 1979 book, perhaps the most renowned being Design Patterns: Elements of Reusable Object-Oriented Software. This book describes simple and elegant solutions to specific problems in object-oriented software design.

28.1.2 Content of a Pattern

Several different formats are used in the literature for describing patterns, and no single format has achieved widespread acceptance. However, there is broad agreement on the types of things that a pattern should contain. The headings which follow are taken from Pattern-Oriented Software Architecture: A System of Patterns. The elements described below will be found in most patterns, even if different headings are used to describe them.

Name	A meaningful and memorable way to refer to the pattern, typically a single word or short phrase.
Problem	A description of the problem indicating the intent in applying the pattern - the intended goals and objectives to be reached within the context and forces described below (perhaps with some indication of their priorities).
Context	The preconditions under which the pattern is applicable - a description of the initial state before the pattern is applied.
Forces	A description of the relevant forces and constraints, and how they interact/conflict with each other and with the intended goals and objectives. The description should clarify the intricacies of the problem and make explicit the kinds of trade-offs that must be considered. (The need for such trade-offs is typically what makes the problem difficult, and generates the need for the pattern in the first place.) The notion of "forces" equates in many ways to the "qualities" that architects seek to optimize, and the concerns they seek to address, in designing architectures. For example:l Security, robustness, reliability, fault-tolerancel Manageabilityl Efficiency, performance, throughput, bandwidth requirements, space utilizationl Scalability (incremental growth on-demand)l Extensibility, evolvability, maintainabilityl Modularity, independence, re-usability, openness, composability (plug-and-play), portabilityl Completeness and correctnessl Ease-of-constructionl Ease-of-usel etc., ...
Solution	A description, using text and/or graphics, of how to achieve the intended goals and objectives. The description should identify both the solution's static structure and its dynamic behavior - the people and computing actors, and their collaborations. The description may include guidelines for implementing the solution. Variants or specializations of the solution may also be described.

Resulting Context	The post-conditions after the pattern has been applied. Implementing the solution normally requires trade-offs among competing forces. This element describes which forces have been resolved and how, and which remain unresolved. It may also indicate other patterns that may be applicable in the new context. (A pattern may be one step in accomplishing some larger goal.) Any such other patterns will be described in detail under Related Patterns.
Examples	One or more sample applications of the pattern which illustrate each of the other elements: a specific problem, context, and set of forces; how the pattern is applied; and the resulting context.
Rationale	An explanation/justification of the pattern as a whole, or of individual components within it, indicating how the pattern actually works, and why - how it resolves the forces to achieve the desired goals and objectives, and why this is "good". The Solution element of a pattern describes the external structure and behavior of the solution: the Rationale provides insight into its internal workings.
Related Patterns	The relationships between this pattern and others. These may be predecessor patterns, whose resulting contexts correspond to the initial context of this one; or successor patterns, whose initial contexts correspond to the resulting context of this one; or alternative patterns, which describe a different solution to the same problem, but under different forces; or co-dependent patterns, which may/must be applied along with this pattern.
Known Uses	Known applications of the pattern within existing systems, verifying that the pattern does indeed describe a proven solution to a recurring problem. Known Uses can also serve as Examples.

Patterns may also begin with an Abstract providing an overview of the pattern and indicating the types of problems it addresses. The Abstract may also identify the target audience and what assumptions are made of the reader.

28.1.3 Terminology

Although design patterns have been the focus of widespread interest in the software industry for several years, particularly in the object-oriented and component-based software fields, it is only recently that there has been increasing interest in architecture patterns - extending the principles and concepts of design patterns to the architecture domain.

The technical literature relating to this field is complicated by the fact that many people in the software field use the term "architecture" to refer to software, and many patterns described as "architecture patterns" are high-level software design patterns. This simply makes it all the more important to be precise in use of terminology.

28.1.3.1 Architecture Patterns and Design Patterns

The term "design pattern" is often used to refer to any pattern which addresses issues of software architecture, design, or programming implementation. In Pattern-Oriented Software Architecture: A System of Patterns, the authors define these three types of patterns as follows:

- An Architecture Pattern expresses a fundamental structural organization or schema for software systems. It provides a set of predefined subsystems, specifies their responsibilities, and includes rules and guidelines for organizing the relationships between them.
- A Design Pattern provides a scheme for refining the subsystems or components of a software system, or the relationships between them. It describes a commonly recurring structure of communicating components that solves a general design problem within a particular context.
- An Idiom is a low-level pattern specific to a programming language. An idiom describes how to implement particular aspects of components or the relationships between them using the features of the given language.

These distinctions are useful, but it is important to note that architecture patterns in this context still refers solely to software architecture. Software architecture is certainly an important part of the focus of TOGAF, but it is not its only focus.

In this section we are concerned with patterns for enterprise system architecting. These are analogous to software architecture and design patterns, and borrow many of their concepts and terminology, but focus on providing re-usable models and methods specifically for the architecting of enterprise information systems - comprising software, hardware, networks, and people - as opposed to purely software systems.

28.1.3.2 Patterns and the Architecture Continuum

Although architecture patterns have not (as yet) been integrated into TOGAF, each of the first four main phases of the ADM (Phases A through D) gives an indication of the stage at which relevant re-usable architecture assets from the enterprise's Architecture Continuum should be considered for use. Architecture patterns are one such asset.

An enterprise that adopts a formal approach to use and re-use of architecture patterns will normally integrate their use into the enterprise's Architecture Continuum.

28.1.3.3 Patterns and Views

Architecture views are selected parts of one or more models representing a complete system architecture, focusing on those aspects that address the concerns of one or more stakeholders. Patterns can provide help in designing such models, and in composing views based on them.

28.1.3.4 Patterns and Business Scenarios

Relevant architecture patterns may well be identified in the work on business scenarios.

28.1.4 Architecture Patterns in Use

Two examples of architecture patterns in use are outlined in the following subsections, one from the domain of an IT customer enterprise's own architecture framework, and the other from a major system vendor who has done a lot of work in recent years in the field of architecture patterns.

- The US Treasury Architecture Development Guidance (TADG) document (see US Treasury Architecture Development Guidance (TADG)) provides a number of explicit architecture patterns, in addition to explaining a rationale, structure, and taxonomy for architectural patterns as they relate to the US Treasury.

- The IBM Patterns for e-Business web site (see IBM Patterns for e-Business) gives a series of architecture patterns that go from the business problem to specific solutions, firstly at a generic level and then in terms of specific IBM product solutions. A supporting resource is IBM's set of Red Books.

The following material is intended to give the reader pointers to some of the places where architecture patterns are already being used and made available, in order to help readers make their own minds up as to the usefulness of this technique for their own environments.

28.2 US Treasury Architecture Development Guidance (TADG)

The US Treasury Architecture Development Guidance (TADG) document - formerly known as the Treasury Information System Architecture Framework (TISAF) - provides a number of explicit architecture patterns.

Section 7 of the TADG document describes a rationale, structure, and taxonomy for architecture patterns, while the patterns themselves are formally documented in Appendix D. The architecture patterns presented embrace a larger set of systems than just object-oriented systems. Some architecture patterns are focused on legacy systems, some on concurrent and distributed systems, and some on real-time systems.

28.2.1 TADG Pattern Content

The content of an architecture pattern as defined in the TADG document contains the following elements:

Name	Each architecture pattern has a unique, short descriptive name. The collection of architecture pattern names can be used as a vocabulary for describing, verifying, and validating Information Systems Architectures.
Problem	Each architecture pattern contains a description of the problem to be solved. The problem statement may describe a class of problems or a specific problem.

Rationale	The rationale describes and explains a typical specific problem that is representative of the broad class of problems to be solved by the architecture pattern. For a specific problem, it can provide additional details of the nature of the problem and the requirements for its resolution.
Assumptions	The assumptions are conditions that must be satisfied in order for the architecture pattern to be usable in solving the problem. They include constraints on the solution and optional requirements that may make the solution more easy to use.
Structure	The architecture pattern is described in diagrams and words in as much detail as is required to convey to the reader the components of the pattern and their responsibilities.
Interactions	The important relationships and interactions among the components of the pattern are described and constraints on these relationships and interactions are identified.
Consequences	The advantages and disadvantages of using this pattern are described, particularly in terms of other patterns (either required or excluded) as well as resource limitations that may arise from using it.
Implementation	Additional implementation advice that can assist designers in customizing this architectural design pattern for the best results.

28.2.2 TADG Architecture Patterns

The TADG document contains the following patterns.

Architectural Design Pattern Name	Synopsis
Client-Proxy Server	Acts as a concentrator for many low-speed links to access a server.
Customer Support	Supports complex customer contact across multiple organizations.
Reactor	Decouples an event from its processing.
Replicated Servers	Replicates servers to reduce burden on central server.
Layered Architecture	A decomposition of services such that most interactions occur only between neighboring layers.
Pipe and Filter Architecture	Transforms information in a series of incremental steps or processes.
Subsystem Interface	Manages the dependencies between cohesive groups of functions (subsystems).

28.3 IBM Patterns for e-Business

The IBM Patterns for e-Business web site (*www.ibm.com/framework/patterns*) provides a group of re-usable assets aimed at speeding the process of developing e-Business applications. A supporting IBM web site is Patterns for e-Business Resources (*www.ibm.com/developerworks/patterns/library*). This is also known as the "Red Books".

The rationale for IBM's provision of these patterns is to:

- Provide a simple and consistent way to translate business priorities and requirements into technical solutions
- Assist and speed up the solution development and integration process by facilitating the assembly of a solution and minimizing custom one-of-a-kind implementations
- Capture the knowledge and best practices of experts and make it available for use by less experienced personnel
- Facilitate the re-use of intellectual capital such as reference architectures, frameworks, and other architecture assets

IBM's patterns are focused specifically on solutions for e-Business; i.e., those which allow an organization to leverage web technologies in order to re-engineer business processes, enhance communications, and lower organizational boundaries with:

- Customers and shareholders (across the Internet)
- Employees and stakeholders (across a corporate Intranet)
- Vendors, suppliers, and partners (across an Extranet)

They are intended to address the following challenges encountered in this type of environment:

- High degree of integration with legacy systems within the enterprise and with systems outside the enterprise
- The solutions need to reach users faster; this does not mean sacrificing quality, but it does mean coming up with better and faster ways to develop these solutions
- Service Level Agreements (SLAs) are critical
- Need to adapt to rapidly changing technologies and dramatically reduced product cycles
- Address an acute shortage of the key skills needed to develop quality solutions

IBM defines five types of pattern:

- Business Patterns, which identify the primary business actors, and describe the interactions between them in terms of different archetypal business interactions such as:
    - Service (a.k.a. user-to-business) - users accessing transactions on a 24x7 basis
    - Collaboration (a.k.a. user-to-user) - users working with one another to share data and information

- Information Aggregation (a.k.a. user-to-data) - data from multiple sources aggregated and presented across multiple channels
- Extended Enterprise (a.k.a. business-to-business) - integrating data and processes across enterprise boundaries

■ Integration Patterns, which provide the "glue" to combine business patterns to form solutions. They characterize the business problem, business processes/rules, and existing environment to determine whether front-end or back-end integration is required.

- Front-end integration (a.k.a. access integration) - focused on providing seamless and consistent access to business functions. Typical functions provided include single sign-on, personalization, transcoding, etc.
- Back-end integration (a.k.a. application integration) - focused on connecting, interfacing, or integrating databases and systems. Typical integration can be based on function, type of integration, mode of integration, and by topology.

■ Composite Patterns, which are previously identified combinations and selections of business and integration patterns, for previously identified situations such as: electronic commerce solutions, (public) enterprise portals, enterprise intranet portal, collaboration ASP, etc.

■ Application Patterns. Each business and integration pattern can be implemented using one or more application patterns. An application pattern characterizes the coarse-grained structure of the application - the main application components, the allocation of processing functions and the interactions between them, the degree of integration between them, and the placement of the data relative to the applications.

■ Runtime Patterns. Application patterns can be implemented by run-time patterns, which demonstrate non-functional, service-level characteristics, such as performance, capacity, scalability, and availability. They identify key resource constraints and best practices.

The IBM web site also provides specific (IBM) product mappings for the run-time patterns, indicating specific technology choices for implementation.

28.4 Some Pattern Resources

- The Patterns Home Page (hillside.net/patterns) hosted by the Hillside Group provides information about patterns, links to online patterns, papers, and books dealing with patterns, and patterns-related mailing lists.
- The Patterns-Discussion FAQ (g.oswego.edu/dl/pd-FAQ/pd-FAQ.html) maintained by Doug Lea provides a very thorough and highly readable FAQ about patterns.
- Patterns and Software: Essential Concepts and Terminology by Brad Appleton (*www. enteract.com/ ~bradapp/docs/patterns-intro.html*) provides another thorough and readable account of the patterns field.

Chapter 29: Architecture Principles

This chapter provides principles for the use and deployment of IT resources across the enterprise.

This chapter builds on work done by the US Air Force in establishing its Headquarters Air Force Principles for Information Management (June 29, 1998), with the addition of other input materials.

29.1 Introduction

Principles are general rules and guidelines, intended to be enduring and seldom amended, that inform and support the way in which an organization sets about fulfilling its mission.

In their turn, principles may be just one element in a structured set of ideas that collectively define and guide the organization, from values through to actions and results.

Depending on the organization, principles may be established at any or all of three levels:

- Enterprise principles provide a basis for decision-making throughout an enterprise, and inform how the organization sets about fulfilling its mission. Such enterprise-level principles are commonly found in governmental and not-for-profit organizations, but are encountered in commercial organizations also, as a means of harmonizing decision-making across a distributed organization. In particular, they are a key element in a successful architecture governance strategy (see Architecture Governance).
- Information Technology (IT) principles provide guidance on the use and deployment of all IT resources and assets across the enterprise. They are developed in order to make the information environment as productive and cost-effective as possible.
- Architecture principles are a subset of IT principles that relate to architecture work. They reflect a level of consensus across the enterprise, and embody the spirit and thinking of the enterprise architecture. Architecture principles can be further divided into:
    - Principles that govern the architecture process, affecting the development, maintenance, and use of the enterprise architecture
    - Principles that govern the implementation of the architecture, establishing the first tenets and related guidance for designing and developing information systems

These sets of principles form a hierarchy, in that IT principles will be informed by, and elaborate on, the principles at the enterprise level; and architecture principles will likewise be informed by the principles at the two higher levels.

The remainder of this section deals exclusively with architecture principles.

29.2 Characteristics of Architecture Principles

Architecture principles define the underlying general rules and guidelines for the use and deployment of all IT resources and assets across the enterprise. They reflect a level of consensus among the various elements of the enterprise, and form the basis for making future IT decisions.

Each architecture principle should be clearly related back to the business objectives and key architecture drivers.

29.3 Components of Architecture Principles

It is useful to have a standard way of defining principles. In addition to a definition statement, each principle should have associated rationale and implications statements, both to promote understanding and acceptance of the principles themselves, and to support the use of the principles in explaining and justifying why specific decisions are made.

A recommended template is given in Recommended Format for Defining Principles .

Name	Should both represent the essence of the rule as well as be easy to remember. Specific technology platforms should not be mentioned in the name or statement of a principle. Avoid ambiguous words in the Name and in the Statement such as: "support", "open", "consider", and for lack of good measure the word "avoid", itself, be careful with "manage(ment)", and look for unnecessary adjectives and adverbs (fluff).
Statement	Should succinctly and unambiguously communicate the fundamental rule. For the most part, the principles statements for managing information are similar from one organization to the next. It is vital that the principles statement be unambiguous.
Rationale	Should highlight the business benefits of adhering to the principle, using business terminology. Point to the similarity of information and technology principles to the principles governing business operations. Also describe the relationship to other principles, and the intentions regarding a balanced interpretation. Describe situations where one principle would be given precedence or carry more weight than another for making a decision.
Implications	Should highlight the requirements, both for the business and IT, for carrying out the principle - in terms of resources, costs, and activities/tasks. It will often be apparent that current systems, standards, or practices would be incongruent with the principle upon adoption. The impact to the business and consequences of adopting a principle should be clearly stated. The reader should readily discern the answer to: "How does this affect me?" It is important not to oversimplify, trivialize, or judge the merit of the impact. Some of the implications will be identified as potential impacts only, and may be speculative rather than fully analyzed.

Table 29.1: Recommended Format for Defining Principles

An example set of architecture principles following this template is given in Example Set of Architecture Principles .

29.4 Developing Architecture Principles

Architecture principles are typically developed by the Lead Architect, in conjunction with the enterprise CIO, Architecture Board, and other key business stakeholders.

Appropriate policies and procedures must be developed to support the implementation of the principles.

Architecture principles will be informed by overall IT principles and principles at the enterprise level, if they exist. They are chosen so as to ensure alignment of IT strategies with business strategies and visions. Specifically, the development of architecture principles is typically influenced by the following:

- Enterprise mission and plans: the mission, plans, and organizational infrastructure of the enterprise.
- Enterprise strategic initiatives: the characteristics of the enterprise - its strengths, weaknesses, opportunities, and threats - and its current enterprise-wide initiatives (such as process improvement and quality management).
- External constraints: market factors (time-to-market imperatives, customer expectations, etc.); existing and potential legislation.
- Current systems and technology: the set of information resources deployed within the enterprise, including systems documentation, equipment inventories, network configuration diagrams, policies, and procedures.
- Computer industry trends: predictions about the usage, availability, and cost of computer and communication technologies, referenced from credible sources along with associated best practices presently in use.

29.4.1 Qualities of Principles

Merely having a written statement that is called a principle does not mean that the principle is good, even if everyone agrees with it.

A good set of principles will be founded in the beliefs and values of the organization and expressed in language that the business understands and uses. Principles should be few in number, future-oriented, and endorsed and championed by senior management. They provide a firm foundation for making architecture and planning decisions, framing policies, procedures, and standards, and supporting resolution of contradictory situations. A poor set of principles will quickly become disused, and the resultant architectures, policies, and standards will appear arbitrary or self-serving, and thus lack credibility. Essentially, principles drive behavior.

There are five criteria that distinguish a good set of principles:

- Understandable: the underlying tenets can be quickly grasped and understood by individuals throughout the organization. The intention of the principle is clear and unambiguous, so that violations, whether intentional or not, are minimized.
- Robust: enable good quality decisions about architectures and plans to be made, and enforceable policies and standards to be created. Each principle should be sufficiently definitive and precise to support consistent decision-making in complex, potentially controversial situations.
- Complete: every potentially important principle governing the management of information and technology for the organization is defined. The principles cover every situation perceived.
- Consistent: strict adherence to one principle may require a loose interpretation of another principle. The set of principles must be expressed in a way that allows a balance of interpretations. Principles should not be contradictory to the point where adhering to one principle would violate the spirit of another. Every word in a principle statement should be carefully chosen to allow consistent yet flexible interpretation.
- Stable: principles should be enduring, yet able to accommodate changes. An amendment process should be established for adding, removing, or altering principles after they are ratified initially.

29.5 Applying Architecture Principles

Architecture principles are used to capture the fundamental truths about how the enterprise will use and deploy IT resources and assets. The principles are used in a number of different ways:

1. To provide a framework within which the enterprise can start to make conscious decisions about IT
2. As a guide to establishing relevant evaluation criteria, thus exerting strong influence on the selection of products or product architectures in the later stages of managing compliance to the IT architecture
3. As drivers for defining the functional requirements of the architecture
4. As an input to assessing both existing IS/IT systems and the future strategic portfolio, for compliance with the defined architectures. These assessments will provide valuable insights into the transition activities needed to implement an architecture, in support of business goals and priorities
5. The Rationale statements (see below) highlight the value of the architecture to the enterprise, and therefore provide a basis for justifying architecture activities
6. The Implications statements (see below) provide an outline of the key tasks, resources, and potential costs to the enterprise of following the principle; they also provide valuable inputs to future transition initiative and planning activities

7. Support the architecture governance activities in terms of:
   - Providing a "back-stop" for the standard Architecture Compliance assessments where some interpretation is allowed or required
   - Supporting the decision to initiate a dispensation request where the implications of a particular architecture amendment cannot be resolved within local operating procedure

Principles are inter-related, and need to be applied as a set.

Principles will sometimes compete; for example, the principles of "accessibility" and "security" tend towards conflicting decisions. Each principle must be considered in the context of "all other things being equal".

At times a decision will be required as to which information principle will take precedence on a particular issue. The rationale for such decisions should always be documented.

A common reaction on first reading of a principle is "this is motherhood", but the fact that a principle seems self-evident does not mean that the principle is actually observed in an organization, even when there are verbal acknowledgements of the principle.

Although specific penalties are not prescribed in a declaration of principles, violations of principles generally cause operational problems and inhibit the ability of the organization to fulfil its mission.

29.6 Example Set of Architecture Principles

Too many principles can reduce the flexibility of the architecture. Many organizations prefer to define only high-level principles, and to limit the number to between 10 and 20.

The following example illustrates both the typical content of a set of architecture principles, and the recommended format for defining them, as explained above.

Another example of architecture principles is contained in the US Government's Federal Enterprise Architecture Framework (FEAF - see FEAF).

29.6.1 Business Principles

Principle 1: **Primacy of Principles**

Statement: These principles of information management apply to all organizations within the enterprise.

Rationale: The only way we can provide a consistent and measurable level of quality information to decision-makers is if all organizations abide by the principles.

Implications:
- without this principle, exclusions, favoritism, and inconsistency would rapidly undermine the management of information.
- Information management initiatives will not begin until they are examined for compliance with the principles.
- A conflict with a principle will be resolved by changing the framework of the initiative.

Principle 2: **Maximize Benefit to the Enterprise**

Statement: Information management decisions are made to provide maximum benefit to the enterprise as a whole.

Rationale: This principle embodies "service above self". Decisions made from an enterprise-wide perspective have greater long-term value than decisions made from any particular organizational perspective. Maximum return on investment requires information management decisions to adhere to enterprise-wide drivers and priorities. No minority group will detract from the benefit of the whole. However, this principle will not preclude any minority group from getting its job done.

Implications:
- Achieving maximum enterprise-wide benefit will require changes in the way we plan and manage information. Technology alone will not bring about this change.
- Some organizations may have to concede their own preferences for the greater benefit of the entire enterprise.
- Application development priorities must be established by the entire enterprise for the entire enterprise.
- Applications components should be shared across organizational boundaries.
- Information management initiatives should be conducted in accordance with the enterprise plan. Individual organizations should pursue information management initiatives which conform to the blueprints and priorities established by the enterprise. We will change the plan as we need to.
- As needs arise, priorities must be adjusted. A forum with comprehensive enterprise representation should make these decisions.

Principle 3: **Information Management is Everybody's Business**

Statement: All organizations in the enterprise participate in information management decisions needed to accomplish business objectives.

Rationale:	Information users are the key stakeholders, or customers, in the application of technology to address a business need. In order to ensure information management is aligned with the business, all organizations in the enterprise must be involved in all aspects of the information environment. The business experts from across the enterprise and the technical staff responsible for developing and sustaining the information environment need to come together as a team to jointly define the goals and objectives of IT
Implications:	■ To operate as a team, every stakeholder, or customer, will need to accept responsibility for developing the information environment.
	■ Commitment of resources will be required to implement this principle.

Principle 4: Business Continuity

Statement:	Enterprise operations are maintained in spite of system interruptions.
Rationale:	As system operations become more pervasive we become more dependent on them; therefore, we must consider the reliability of such systems throughout their design and use. Business premises throughout the enterprise must be provided with the capability to continue their business functions regardless of external events. Hardware failure, natural disasters, and data corruption should not be allowed to disrupt or stop enterprise activities. The enterprise business functions must be capable of operating on alternative information delivery mechanisms.
Implications:	■ Dependency on shared system applications mandates that the risks of business interruption must be established in advance and managed. Management includes but is not limited to periodic reviews, testing for vulnerability and exposure, or designing mission-critical services to assure business function continuity through redundant or alternative capabilities.
	■ Recoverability, redundancy, and maintainability should be addressed at the time of design.
	■ Applications must be assessed for criticality and impact on the enterprise mission, in order to determine what level of continuity is required and what corresponding recovery plan is necessary.

Principle 5: Common Use Applications

Statement:	Development of applications used across the enterprise is preferred over the development of similar or duplicative applications which are only provided to a particular organization.
Rationale:	Duplicative capability is expensive and proliferates conflicting data.

Implications:	■ Organizations which depend on a capability which does not serve the entire enterprise must change over to the replacement enterprise-wide capability. This will require establishment of and adherence to a policy requiring this.
	■ Organizations will not be allowed to develop capabilities for their own use which are similar/duplicative of enterprise-wide capabilities. In this way, expenditures of scarce resources to develop essentially the same capability in marginally different ways will be reduced.
	■ Data and information used to support enterprise decision-making will be standardized to a much greater extent than previously. This is because the smaller, organizational capabilities which produced different data (which was not shared among other organizations) will be replaced by enterprise-wide capabilities. The impetus for adding to the set of enterprise-wide capabilities may well come from an organization making a convincing case for the value of the data/information previously produced by its organizational capability, but the resulting capability will become part of the enterprise-wide system, and the data it produces will be shared across the enterprise.

Principle 6:   Compliance with Law

Statement:	Enterprise information management processes comply with all relevant laws, policies, and regulations.
Rationale:	Enterprise policy is to abide by laws, policies, and regulations. This will not preclude business process improvements that lead to changes in policies and regulations.
Implications:	■ The enterprise must be mindful to comply with laws, regulations, and external policies regarding the collection, retention, and management of data.
	■ Education and access to the rules. Efficiency, need, and common sense are not the only drivers. Changes in the law and changes in regulations may drive changes in our processes or applications.

Principle 7:   IT Responsibility

Statement:	The IT organization is responsible for owning and implementing IT processes and infrastructure that enable solutions to meet user-defined requirements for functionality, service levels, cost, and delivery timing.
Rationale:	Effectively align expectations with capabilities and costs so that all projects are cost-effective. Efficient and effective solutions have reasonable costs and clear benefits.

Implications:
- A process must be created to prioritize projects.
- The IT function must define processes to manage business unit expectations.
- Data, application, and technology models must be created to enable integrated quality solutions and to maximize results.

Principle 8: **Protection of Intellectual Property**

Statement: The enterprise's Intellectual Property (IP) must be protected. This protection must be reflected in the IT architecture, implementation, and governance processes.

Rationale: A major part of an enterprise's IP is hosted in the IT domain.

Implications:
- While protection of IP assets is everybody's business, much of the actual protection is implemented in the IT domain. Even trust in non-IT processes can be managed by IT processes (email, mandatory notes, etc.).
- A security policy, governing human and IT actors, will be required that can substantially improve protection of IP. This must be capable of both avoiding compromises and reducing liabilities.
- Resources on such policies can be found at the SANS Institute (*www.sans.org/newlook/home.php*).

29.6.2 Data Principles

Principle 9: **Data is an Asset**

Statement: Data is an asset that has value to the enterprise and is managed accordingly.

Rationale: Data is a valuable corporate resource; it has real, measurable value. In simple terms, the purpose of data is to aid decision-making. Accurate, timely data is critical to accurate, timely decisions. Most corporate assets are carefully managed, and data is no exception. Data is the foundation of our decision-making, so we must also carefully manage data to ensure that we know where it is, can rely upon its accuracy, and can obtain it when and where we need it.

Implications:
- This is one of three closely-related principles regarding data: data is an asset; data is shared; and data is easily accessible. The implication is that there is an education task to ensure that all organizations within the enterprise understand the relationship between value of data, sharing of data, and accessibility to data.
- Stewards must have the authority and means to manage the data for which they are accountable.
- We must make the cultural transition from "data ownership" thinking to "data stewardship" thinking.
- The role of data steward is critical because obsolete, incorrect, or inconsistent data could be passed to enterprise personnel and adversely affect decisions across the enterprise.
- Part of the role of data steward, who manages the data, is to ensure data quality. Procedures must be developed and used to prevent and correct errors in the information and to improve those processes that produce flawed information. Data quality will need to be measured and steps taken to improve data quality - it is probable that policy and procedures will need to be developed for this as well.
- A forum with comprehensive enterprise-wide representation should decide on process changes suggested by the steward.
- Since data is an asset of value to the entire enterprise, data stewards accountable for properly managing the data must be assigned at the enterprise level.

Principle 10: Data is Shared

Statement: Users have access to the data necessary to perform their duties; therefore, data is shared across enterprise functions and organizations.

Rationale: Timely access to accurate data is essential to improving the quality and efficiency of enterprise decision-making. It is less costly to maintain timely, accurate data in a single application, and then share it, than it is to maintain duplicative data in multiple applications. The enterprise holds a wealth of data, but it is stored in hundreds of incompatible stovepipe databases. The speed of data collection, creation, transfer, and assimilation is driven by the ability of the organization to efficiently share these islands of data across the organization.

Shared data will result in improved decisions since we will rely on fewer (ultimately one virtual) sources of more accurate and timely managed data for all of our decision-making. Electronically shared data will result in increased efficiency when existing data entities can be used, without re-keying, to create new entities.

Implications:	■ This is one of three closely-related principles regarding data: data is an asset; data is shared; and data is easily accessible. The implication is that there is an education task to ensure that all organizations within the enterprise understand the relationship between value of data, sharing of data, and accessibility to data.
	■ To enable data sharing we must develop and abide by a common set of policies, procedures, and standards governing data management and access for both the short and the long term.
	■ For the short term, to preserve our significant investment in legacy systems, we must invest in software capable of migrating legacy system data into a shared data environment.
	■ We will also need to develop standard data models, data elements, and other metadata that defines this shared environment and develop a repository system for storing this metadata to make it accessible.
	■ For the long term, as legacy systems are replaced, we must adopt and enforce common data access policies and guidelines for new application developers to ensure that data in new applications remains available to the shared environment and that data in the shared environment can continue to be used by the new applications.
	■ For both the short term and the long term we must adopt common methods and tools for creating, maintaining, and accessing the data shared across the enterprise.
	■ Data sharing will require a significant cultural change.
	■ This principle of data sharing will continually "bump up against" the principle of data security. Under no circumstances will the data sharing principle cause confidential data to be compromised.
	■ Data made available for sharing will have to be relied upon by all users to execute their respective tasks. This will ensure that only the most accurate and timely data is relied upon for decision-making. Shared data will become the enterprise-wide "virtual single source" of data.

Principle 11:	**Data is Accessible**
Statement:	Data is accessible for users to perform their functions.
Rationale:	Wide access to data leads to efficiency and effectiveness in decision-making, and affords timely response to information requests and service delivery. Using information must be considered from an enterprise perspective to allow access by a wide variety of users. Staff time is saved and consistency of data is improved.

Implications:	■ This is one of three closely-related principles regarding data: data is an asset; data is shared; and data is easily accessible. The implication is that there is an education task to ensure that all organizations within the enterprise understand the relationship between value of data, sharing of data, and accessibility to data.
	■ Accessibility involves the ease with which users obtain information.
	■ The way information is accessed and displayed must be sufficiently adaptable to meet a wide range of enterprise users and their corresponding methods of access.
	■ Access to data does not constitute understanding of the data. Personnel should take caution not to misinterpret information.
	■ Access to data does not necessarily grant the user access rights to modify or disclose the data. This will require an education process and a change in the organizational culture, which currently supports a belief in "ownership" of data by functional units.

Principle 12: **Data Trustee**

Statement: Each data element has a trustee accountable for data quality.

Rationale: One of the benefits of an architected environment is the ability to share data (e.g., text, video, sound, etc.) across the enterprise. As the degree of data sharing grows and business units rely upon common information, it becomes essential that only the data trustee makes decisions about the content of data. Since data can lose its integrity when it is entered multiple times, the data trustee will have soleresponsibility for data entry which eliminates redundant human effort and data storage resources.

Note: A trustee is different than a steward - a trustee is responsible for accuracy and currency of the data, while responsibilities of a steward may be broader and include data standardization and definition tasks.

Implications: ■ Real trusteeship dissolves the data "ownership" issues and allows the data to be available to meet all users' needs. This implies that a cultural change from data "ownership" to data "trusteeship" may be required.

■ The data trustee will be responsible for meeting quality requirements levied upon the data for which the trustee is accountable.

- It is essential that the trustee has the ability to provide user confidence in the data based upon attributes such as "data source".

- It is essential to identify the true source of the data in order that the data authority can be assigned this trustee responsibility. This does not mean that classified sources will be revealed nor does it mean the source will be the trustee.

- Information should be captured electronically once and immediately validated as close to the source as possible. Quality control measures must be implemented to ensure the integrity of the data.

- As a result of sharing data across the enterprise, the trustee is accountable and responsible for the accuracy and currency of their designated data element(s) and, subsequently, must then recognize the importance of this trusteeship responsibility.

Principle 13: Common Vocabulary and Data Definitions

Statement: Data is defined consistently throughout the enterprise, and the definitions are understandable and available to all users.

Rationale: The data that will be used in the development of applications must have a common definition throughout the Headquarters to enable sharing of data. A common vocabulary will facilitate communications and enable dialogue to be effective. In addition, it is required to interface systems and exchange data.

Implications:
- We are lulled into thinking that this issue is adequately addressed because there are people with "data administration" job titles and forums with charters implying responsibility. Significant additional energy and resources must be committed to this task. It is key to the success of efforts to improve the information environment. This is separate from but related to the issue of data element definition, which is addressed by a broad community - this is more like a common vocabulary and definition.

- The enterprise must establish the initial common vocabulary for the business. The definitions will be used uniformly throughout the enterprise

- Ambiguities resulting from multiple parochial definitions of data must give way to accepted enterprise-wide definitions and understanding.

- Multiple data standardization initiatives need to be co-ordinated.

- Functional data administration responsibilities must be assigned.

Principle 14: **Data Security**

Statement: Data is protected from unauthorized use and disclosure. In addition to the traditional aspects of national security classification, this includes, but is not limited to, protection of pre-decisional, sensitive, source selection-sensitive, and proprietary information.

Rationale: Open sharing of information and the release of information via relevant legislation must be balanced against the need to restrict the availability of classified, proprietary, and sensitive information.

Existing laws and regulations require the safeguarding of national security and the privacy of data, while permitting free and open access. Pre-decisional (work-in-progress, not yet authorized for release) information must be protected to avoid unwarranted speculation, misinterpretation, and inappropriate use.

Implications:
- Aggregation of data, both classified and not, will create a large target requiring review and de-classification procedures to maintain appropriate control. Data owners and/or functional users must determine whether the aggregation results in an increased classification level. We will need appropriate policy and procedures to handle this review and de-classification. Access to information based on a need-to-know policy will force regular reviews of the body of information.

- The current practice of having separate systems to contain different classifications needs to be rethought. Is there a software solution to separating classified and unclassified data? The current hardware solution is unwieldy, inefficient, and costly. It is more expensive to manage unclassified data on a classified system. Currently, the only way to combine the two is to place the unclassified data on the classified system, where it must remain.

- In order to adequately provide access to open information while maintaining secure information, security needs must be identified and developed at the data level, not the application level

- Data security safeguards can be put in place to restrict access to "view only", or "never see". Sensitivity labeling for access to pre-decisional, decisional, classified, sensitive, or proprietary information must be determined..

- Security must be designed into data elements from the beginning; it cannot be added later. Systems, data, and technologies must be protected from unauthorized access and manipulation. Headquarters information must be safeguarded against inadvertent or unauthorized alteration, sabotage, disaster, or disclosure.

- Need new policies on managing duration of protection for pre-decisional information and other works-in-progress, in consideration of content freshness.

29.6.3 Application Principles

Principle 15: Technology Independence

Statement: Applications are independent of specific technology choices and therefore can operate on a variety of technology platforms.

Rationale: Independence of applications from the underlying technology allows applications to be developed, upgraded, and operated in the most cost-effective and timely way. Otherwise technology, which is subject to continual obsolescence and vendor dependence, becomes the driver rather than the user requirements themselves.

Realizing that every decision made with respect to IT makes us dependent on that technology, the intent of this principle is to ensure that Application Software is not dependent on specific hardware and operating systems software.

Implications:
- This principle will require standards which support portability.

- For Commercial Off-The-Shelf (COTS) and Government Off-The-Shelf (GOTS) applications, there may be limited current choices, as many of these applications are technology and platform-dependent.

- Application Program Interfaces (APIs) will need to be developed to enable legacy applications to interoperate with applications and operating environments developed under the enterprise architecture.

- Middleware should be used to decouple applications from specific software solutions.

- As an example, this principle could lead to use of Java, and future Java-like protocols, which give a high degree of priority to platform-independence.

Principle 16: Ease-of-Use

Statement: Applications are easy to use. The underlying technology is transparent to users, so they can concentrate on tasks at hand.

Rationale:	The more a user has to understand the underlying technology, the less productive that user is. Ease-of-use is a positive incentive for use of applications. It encourages users to work within the integrated information environment instead of developing isolated systems to accomplish the task outside of the enterprise's integrated information environment. Most of the knowledge required to operate one system will be similar to others. Training is kept to a minimum, and the risk of using a system improperly is low. Using an application should be as intuitive as driving a different car.
Implications:	■ Applications will be required to have a common "look and feel" and support ergonomic requirements. Hence, the common look and feel standard must be designed and usability test criteria must be developed. ■ Guidelines for user interfaces should not be constrained by narrow assumptions about user location, language, systems training, or physical capability. Factors such as linguistics, customer physical infirmities (visual acuity, ability to use keyboard/mouse), and proficiency in the use of technology have broad ramifications in determining the ease-of-use of an application.

29.6.4 Technology Principles

Principle 17: Requirements-Based Change

Statement:	Only in response to business needs are changes to applications and technology made.
Rationale:	This principle will foster an atmosphere where the information environment changes in response to the needs of the business, rather than having the business change in response to IT changes. This is to ensure that the purpose of the information support - the transaction of business - is the basis for any proposed change. Unintended effects on business due to IT changes will be minimized. A change in technology may provide an opportunity to improve the business process and, hence, change business needs.

Implications:	■ Changes in implementation will follow full examination of the proposed changes using the enterprise architecture.
	■ We don't fund a technical improvement or system development unless a documented business need exists.
	■ Change management processes conforming to this principle will be developed and implemented.
	■ This principle may bump up against the responsive change principle. We must ensure the requirements documentation process does not hinder responsive change to meet legitimate business needs. The purpose of this principle is to keep us focused on business, not technology needs - responsive change is also a business need.

Principle 18: **Responsive Change Management**

Statement: Changes to the enterprise information environment are implemented in a timely manner.

Rationale: If people are to be expected to work within the enterprise information environment, that information environment must be responsive to their needs.

Implications:
- We have to develop processes for managing and implementing change that do not create delays.
- A user who feels a need for change will need to connect with a "business expert" to facilitate explanation and implementation of that need.
- If we are going to make changes, we must keep the architectures updated.
- Adopting this principle might require additional resources.
- This will conflict with other principles (e g., maximum enterprise-wide benefit, enterprise-wide applications, etc.).

Principle 19: **Control Technical Diversity**

Statement: Technological diversity is controlled to minimize the non-trivial cost of maintaining expertise in and connectivity between multiple processing environments.

Rationale:	There is a real, non-trivial cost of infrastructure required to support alternative technologies for processing environments. There are further infrastructure costs incurred to keep multiple processor constructs interconnected and maintained.
	Limiting the number of supported components will simplify maintainability and reduce costs.
	The business advantages of minimum technical diversity include: standard packaging of components; predictable implementation impact; predictable valuations and returns; redefined testing; utility status; and increased flexibility to accommodate technological advancements. Common technology across the enterprise brings the benefits of economies of scale to the enterprise. Technical administration and support costs are better controlled when limited resources can focus on this shared set of technology.
Implications:	• Policies, standards, and procedures that govern acquisition of technology must be tied directly to this principle.
	• Technology choices will be constrained by the choices available within the technology blueprint. Procedures for augmenting the acceptable technology set to meet evolving requirements will have to be developed and emplaced.
	• We are not freezing our technology baseline. We welcome technology advances and will change the technology blueprint when compatibility with the current infrastructure, improvement in operational efficiency, or a required capability has been demonstrated.

Principle 20: **Interoperability**

Statement:	Software and hardware should conform to defined standards that promote interoperability for data, applications, and technology.
Rationale:	Standards help ensure consistency, thus improving the ability to manage systems and improve user satisfaction, and protect existing IT investments, thus maximizing return on investment and reducing costs. Standards for interoperability additionally help ensure support from multiple vendors for their products, and facilitate supply chain integration.
Implications:	• Interoperability standards and industry standards will be followed unless there is a compelling business reason to implement a non-standard solution.
	• A process for setting standards, reviewing and revising them periodically, and granting exceptions must be established.
	• The existing IT platforms must be identified and documented.

Chapter 30: Architecture Skills Framework

This chapter provides a set of role, skill, and experience norms for staff undertaking enterprise architecture work.

30.1 Introduction

Skills frameworks provide a view of the competency levels required for specific roles. They define:

- The roles within a work area
- The skills required by each role
- The depth of knowledge required to fulfil the role successfully

They are relatively common for defining the skills required for a consultancy and/or project management assignment, to deliver a specific project or work package. They are also widely used by recruitment and search agencies to match candidates and roles.

Their value derives from their ability to provide a means of rapidly identifying skill matches and gaps. Successfully applied, they can ensure that candidates are fit for the jobs assigned to them.

Their value in the context of enterprise architecture arises from the immaturity of the enterprise architecture discipline, and the problems that arise from this.

30.2 The Need for an IT Architecture Skills Framework

30.2.1 Definitional Rigor

"IT Architecture" and "IT Architect" are widely used but poorly defined terms in the IT industry today. They are used to denote a variety of practices and skills applied in a wide variety of IT domains. There is a need for better classification to enable more implicit understanding of what type of architect/architecture is being described.

This lack of uniformity leads to difficulties for organizations seeking to recruit or assign/promote staff to fill positions in the architecture field. Because of the different usages of terms, there is often misunderstanding and miscommunication between those seeking to recruit for, and those seeking to fill, the various roles of the architect.

30.2.2 The Basis of an Internal Architecture Practice

Despite the lack of uniform terminology, architecture skills are in increasing demand, as the discipline of architecture gains increasing attention within the IT industry.

Many enterprises have set up, or are considering setting up, an IT architecture practice, as a means of fostering development of the necessary skills and experience among in-house staff to undertake the various architecting tasks required by the enterprise.

An IT architecture practice is a formal program of development and certification, by which an enterprise formally recognizes the skills of its practicing IT architects, as demonstrated by their work. Such a program is essential in order to ensure the alignment of staff skills and experience with the IT architecture tasks that the enterprise wishes to be performed.

The role and skill definitions on which such a program needs to be based are also required, by both recruiting and supplying organizations, in cases where external personnel are to be engaged to perform architecture work (for example, as part of a consultancy engagement).

An IT architecture practice is both difficult and costly to set up. It is normally built around a process of peer review, and involves the time and talent of the strategic technical leadership of an enterprise. Typically it involves establishment of a peer review board, and documentation of the process, and of the requirements for internal certification. Time is also required of candidates to prepare for peer review, by creating a portfolio of their work to demonstrate their skills, experiences, and contributions to the profession.

The TOGAF Architecture Skills Framework attempts to address this need by providing definitions of the architecting skills and proficiency levels required of personnel, internal or external, who are to perform the various architecting roles defined within the TOGAF Framework.

Because of the complexity, time, and cost involved, many enterprises do not have an internal IT architect certification program, preferring instead to simply interview and recruit architecture staff on an ad hoc basis. There are serious risks associated with this approach:

- Communication between recruiting organizations, consultancies, and employment agencies is very difficult.
- Time is wasted interviewing staff who may have applied in all good faith, but still lack the skills and/or experience required by the employer.
- Staff who are capable of filling architecture roles may be overlooked, or may not identify themselves with advertised positions and hence not even apply.
- There is increased risk of unsuitable personnel being employed or engaged, through no-one's fault, and despite everyone involved acting in good faith. This in turn can:
    - Increase personnel costs, through the need to rehire or reassign staff
    - Adversely impact the time, cost, and quality of operational IT systems, and the projects that deliver them

30.3 Goals/Rationale

30.3.1 Enterprise Certification of IT Architects

The main purpose behind an enterprise setting up an internal IT architect certification program are twofold:

- To formally recognize the skill of its practicing IT architects, as part of the task of establishing and maintaining a professional IT architecting organization
- To ensure the alignment of necessary staff skills and experience with the IT architecture tasks that the enterprise wishes to be performed, whether these are to be performed internally to the enterprise or externally; for example, as part of a consultancy engagement

30.3.2 Specific Benefits

Specific benefits anticipated from use of the TOGAF Architecture Skills Framework include:

- Reduced time, cost, and risk in training, hiring, and managing IT architecture professionals, both internal and external:
    - Simplifies communication between recruiting organizations, consultancies, and employment agencies
    - Avoids wasting time interviewing staff who may have applied in all good faith, but still lack the skills and/or experience required by the employer
    - Avoids staff who are capable of filling IT architecture roles being overlooked, or not identifying themselves with advertised positions and hence not even applying
- Reduced time and cost to set up an internal IT architecture practice:
    - Many enterprises do not have an internal IT architecture practice due to the complexity involved in setting one up, preferring instead to simply interview and recruit architecture staff on an ad hoc basis.
    - By providing definitions of the architecting skills and proficiency levels required of personnel who are to perform the various architecting roles defined within TOGAF, the Architecture Skills Framework greatly reduces the time, cost, and risk of setting up a practice from scratch, and avoids "re-inventing wheels".
    - Enterprises that already have an internal IT architecture practice are able to set enterprise-wide norms, but still experience difficulties as outlined above in recruiting staff, or engaging consultants, from external sources, due to the lack of uniformity between different enterprises. By aligning its existing skills framework with the industry-accepted definitions provided by The Open Group, an enterprise can greatly simplify these problems.
- Reduced time and cost to implement an IT architect practice helps reduce the time, cost, and risk of overall IT development:

- Enterprises that do not have an internal IT architecture practice run the risk of unsuitable personnel being employed or engaged, through no-one's fault, and despite everyone involved acting in good faith. The resultant time and cost penalties far outweigh the time and cost of having an internal IT architecture practice:
    - Personnel costs are increased, through the occasional need to rehire or reassign staff.
    - Even more important is the adverse impact on the time, cost, and quality of operational IT systems, and the projects to deliver them, resulting from poor staff assignments.

30.4 IT Architecture Role and Skill Categories

30.4.1 Overview

This section describes the role of an IT architect, the fundamental skills required, and some possible disciplines in which an IT architect might specialize.

TOGAF Version 8 delivers an enterprise architecture, and therefore requires both business and IT-trained professionals to develop the enterprise architecture.

The TOGAF Architecture Skills Framework provides a view of the competency levels for specific roles within the enterprise architecture team. The Framework defines:

- The roles within an enterprise architecture work area
- The skills required by those roles
- The depth of knowledge required to fulfil each role successfully

The value is in providing a rapid means of identifying skills and gaps. Successfully applied, the Framework can be used as a measure for:

- Staff development
- Ensuring that the right person does the right job

30.4.2 TOGAF Roles

A typical IT architecture team undertaking the development of an enterprise architecture as described in TOGAF would comprise the following roles:

- Architecture Board Members
- Architecture Sponsor
- IT Architecture Manager
- IT Architects for:
    - Enterprise Architecture

- Business Architecture
- Data Architecture
- Applications Architecture
- Technology Architecture
- Program and/or Project Managers
- IT Designer
- And many others ...

The tables that follow show, for each of these roles, the skills required and the desirable level of proficiency in each skill.

Of all the roles listed above, the one that needs particularly detailed analysis and definition is of course the central role of IT architect. As explained above, "IT Architecture" and "IT Architect" are terms that are very widely used but very poorly defined in the IT industry today, denoting a wide variety of practices and skills applied in a wide variety of IT domains. There is often confusion between the role of an IT architect and that of an IT designer or IT builder. Many of the skills required by an IT architect are also required by the IT designer, who delivers the solutions. While their skills are complimentary, those of the IT designer are primarily technology focussed and translate the architecture into deliverable components.

The final subsection below therefore explores in some detail the generic characteristics of the role of IT architect, and the key skill requirements, whatever the particular IT domain (Enterprise Architecture, Business Architecture, Data Architecture, Applications Architecture, Technology Architecture, etc.).

30.4.3 Categories of Skills

The TOGAF team skill set will need to include the following main categories of skills:

- **Generic Skills:** - typically comprising leadership, teamworking, inter-personal skills, etc.
- **Business Skills and Methods:** - typically comprising business cases, business process, strategic planning, etc.
- **Enterprise Architecture Skills:** - typically comprising modeling, building block design, applications and role design, systems integration, etc.
- **Program or Project Management Skills:** - typically comprising managing business change, project management methods and tools, etc.
- **IT General Knowledge Skills:** - typically comprising brokering applications, asset management, migration planning, SLAs, etc.
- **Technical IT Skills:** - typically comprising software engineering, security, data interchange, data management, etc.
- **Legal Environment:** - typically comprising data protection laws, contract law, procurement law, fraud, etc.

The tables that follow illustrate each of these categories of skills.

The tables that follow show, for each of these skills, the roles to which they are relevant and the desirable level of proficiency in each skill.

30.4.4 Proficiency Levels

The TOGAF Architecture Skills Framework identifies four levels of knowledge or proficiency in any area:

Level	Achievement	Description
1	Background	Not a required skill though should be able to define and manage skill if required.
2	Awareness	Understands the background, issues, and implications sufficiently to be able to understand how to proceed further and advise client accordingly.
3	Knowledge	Detailed knowledge of subject area and capable of providing professional advice and guidance. Ability to integrate capability into architecture design.
4	Expert	Extensive and substantial practical experience and applied knowledge on the subject.

30.5 IT Architecture Role and Skill Definitions

30.5.1 Generic Skills

IT Architect Roles	Architecture Board Member	Architecture Sponsor	IT Architecture Manager	IT Architecture Technology	IT Architecture Data	IT Architecture Application	IT Architecture Business	Program or Project Manager	IT Designer
Framework Skills Areas									
Generic Skills									
Leadership	4	4	4	3	3	3	3	4	1
Team Work	3	3	4	4	4	4	4	4	2
Inter-personal Skills	4	4	4	4	4	4	4	4	2
Oral Communications	3	3	4	4	4	4	4	4	2
Written Communications	3	3	4	4	4	4	4	3	3
Logical Analysis	2	2	4	4	4	4	4	3	3
Stakeholder Management	4	3	4	3	3	3	3	4	2
Risk Management	3	3	4	3	3	3	3	4	1

30.5.2 Business Skills & Methods

IT Architect Roles	Architecture Board Member	Architecture Sponsor	IT Architecture Manager	IT Architecture Technology	IT Architecture Data	IT Architecture Application	IT Architecture Business	Program or Project Manager	IT Designer
Business Skills & Methods									
Business Case	3	4	4	4	4	4	4	4	2
Business Scenario	2	3	4	4	4	4	4	3	2
Organization	3	3	4	3	3	3	4	3	2
Business Process	3	3	4	4	4	4	4	3	2
Strategic Planning	2	3	3	3	3	3	4	3	1
Budget Management	3	3	3	3	3	3	3	4	3
Visioning	3	3	4	3	3	3	4	3	2
Business Metrics	3	4	4	4	4	4	4	4	3
Business Culture	4	4	4	3	3	3	3	3	1
Legacy Investments	4	4	3	2	2	2	2	3	2
Business Functions	3	3	3	3	4	4	4	3	2

30.5.3 Enterprise Architecture Skills

IT Architect Roles	Architecture Board Member	Architecture Sponsor	IT Architecture Manager	IT Architecture Technology	IT Architecture Data	IT Architecture Application	IT Architecture Business	Program or Project Manager	IT Designer
Enterprise Architecture Skills									
Business Modelling	2	2	4	3	3	4	4	2	2
Business Process Design	1	1	4	3	3	4	4	2	2
Role Design	2	2	4	3	3	4	4	2	2
Organization Design	2	2	4	3	3	4	4	2	2
Data Design	1	1	3	3	4	3	3	2	3
Application Design	1	1	3	3	3	4	3	2	3
Systems Integration	1	1	4	4	3	3	3	2	2
IT Industry Standards	1	1	4	4	4	4	3	2	3
Services Design	2	2	4	4	3	4	3	2	2
Architecture Principles Design	2	2	4	4	4	4	4	2	2
Architecture Views & Viewpoints Design	2	2	4	4	4	4	4	2	2
Building Block Design	1	1	4	4	4	4	4	2	3
Solutions Modelling	1	1	4	4	4	4	4	2	3
Benefits Analysis	2	2	4	4	4	4	4	4	2
Business Inter-working	3	3	4	3	3	4	4	3	1
Systems Behavior	1	1	4	4	4	4	3	3	2
Project Management	1	1	3	3	3	3	3	4	2

30.5.4 Program or Project Management Skills

IT Architect Roles	Architecture Board Member	Architecture Sponsor	IT Architecture Manager	IT Architecture Technology	IT Architecture Data	IT Architecture Application	IT Architecture Business	Program or Project Manager	IT Designer
Program or Project Management									
Program Management	1	2	3	3	3	3	3	4	2
Project Management	1	2	3	3	3	3	3	4	2
Managing Business Change	3	3	4	3	3	3	4	4	2
Change Management	3	3	4	3	3	3	4	3	2
Value Management	4	4	4	3	3	3	4	3	2

30.5.5 IT General Knowledge Skills

IT Architect Roles	Architecture Board Member	Architecture Sponsor	IT Architecture Manager	IT Architecture Technology	IT Architecture Data	IT Architecture Application	IT Architecture Business	Program or Project Manager	IT Designer
IT Knowledge Skills									
IT Application Development Methodologies & Tools	2	2	3	4	4	4	2	3	3
Programming Languages	1	1	3	4	4	4	2	2	3
Brokering Applications	1	1	3	3	4	4	3	2	3
Information Consumer Applications	1	1	3	3	4	4	3	2	3
Information Provider Applications	1	1	3	3	4	4	3	2	3
Storage Management	1	1	3	4	4	2	2	2	3
Networks	1	1	3	4	3	2	2	2	3
Web-Based Services	1	1	3	3	4	4	2	2	3
IT Infrastructure	1	1	3	4	3	2	2	2	3
Asset Management	1	1	4	4	3	3	3	2	3
Service Level Agreements	1	1	4	4	3	4	3	2	3
Systems	1	1	3	4	3	3	2	2	3
COTS	1	1	3	4	3	4	2	2	3
Enterprise Continuums	1	1	4	4	4	4	4	2	3
Migrations Planning	1	1	4	3	4	3	3	2	3
Management Utilities	1	1	3	2	4	4	2	2	3
Infrastructure	1	1	3	4	3	4	2	2	3

30.5.6 Technical IT Skills

IT Architect Roles	Architecture Board Member	Architecture Sponsor	IT Architecture Manager	IT Architecture Technology	IT Architecture Data	IT Architecture Application	IT Architecture Business	Program or Project Manager	IT Designer
Technical IT Skills									
Software Engineering	1	1	3	3	4	4	3	2	3
Security	1	1	3	4	3	4	3	2	3
Systems & Network Managment	1	1	3	4	3	3	3	2	3
Transaction Processing	1	1	3	4	3	4	3	2	3
Location & Directory	1	1	3	4	4	3	3	2	3
User Interface	1	1	3	4	4	4	3	2	3
International Operations	1	1	3	4	3	3	2	2	2
Data Interchange	1	1	3	4	4	3	2	2	3
Data Management	1	1	3	4	4	3	2	2	3
Graphics and Image	1	1	3	4	3	3	2	2	3
Operating Systems Services	1	1	3	4	3	3	2	2	3
Network Services	1	1	3	4	3	3	2	2	3
Communications Infrastructure	1	1	3	4	3	3	2	2	3

30.5.7 Legal Environment

IT Architect Roles	Architecture Board Member	Architecture Sponsor	IT Architecture Manager	IT Architecture Technology	IT Architecture Data	IT Architecture Application	IT Architecture Business	Program or Project Manager	IT Designer
Legal Environment									
Contract Law	2	2	2	2	2	2	2	3	1
Data Protection Laws	3	3	4	3	3	3	3	2	2
Procurement Law	3	2	2	2	2	2	2	4	1
Fraud	3	3	3	3	3	3	3	3	1
Commercial Law	3	3	2	2	2	2	3	3	1

30.6 Generic Role and Skills of the IT Architect

Of all the roles listed above, the one that needs particularly detailed analysis and definition is, of course, the central role of IT architect. As explained above, "IT Architecture" and "IT Architect" are terms that are very widely used but very poorly defined in the IT industry today, denoting a wide variety of practices and skills applied in a wide variety of IT domains.

This section therefore explores in some detail the generic characteristics of the role of IT architect, and some key skill requirements, whatever the particular IT domain (Enterprise Architecture, Business Architecture, Data Architecture, Applications Architecture, Technology Architecture, etc.).

30.6.1 Generic Role

IT architects are visionaries, coaches, team leaders, business-to-technical liaisons, computer scientists, and industry experts.

The following is effectively a job description for an IT architect:

"The architect has a responsibility for ensuring the completeness (fitness-for-purpose) of the architecture, in terms of adequately addressing all the pertinent concerns of its stakeholders; and the integrity of the architecture, in terms of connecting all the various views to each other, satisfactorily reconciling the conflicting concerns of different stakeholders, and showing the trade-offs made in so doing (as between security and performance, for example).

The choice of which particular architecture views to develop is one of the key decisions that the IT architect has to make. The choice has to be constrained by considerations of practicality, and by the principal of fitness-for-purpose (i.e., the architecture should be developed only to the point at which it is fit-for-purpose, and not reiterated ad infinitum as an academic exercise)."

The role of the IT architect is more like that of a city planner than that of a building architect, and the product of the IT architect is more aptly characterized as a planned community (as opposed to an unconstrained urban sprawl), rather than as a well-designed building or set of buildings.

An IT architect does not create the technical vision of the enterprise, but has professional relationships with executives of the enterprise to gather and articulate the technical vision, and to produce the strategic plan for realizing it. This plan is always tied to the business plans of the enterprise, and design decisions are traceable to the business plan.

The strategic plan of the IT architect is tied to the architecture governance process (see Architecture Governance) for the enterprise, so design decisions are not circumvented for tactical convenience.

The IT architect produces documentation of design decisions for application development teams or product implementation teams to execute.

An architect is involved in the entire process, beginning with working with the customer to understand real needs, as opposed to wants, and then throughout the process to translate those needs into capabilities verified to meet the needs. Additionally, the architect may present different models to the customer that communicate how those needs may be met, and is therefore an essential participant in the consultative selling process.

However, the architect is not the builder, and must remain at a level of abstraction necessary to ensure s/he does not get in the way of practical implementation.

The following excerpt from The Art of Systems Architecting depicts this notion:

"It is the responsibility of the architect to know and concentrate on the critical few details and interfaces that really matter, and not to become overloaded with the rest."

The architect's focus is on understanding what it takes to satisfy the client, where qualitative worth is used more than quantitative measures. The architect uses more inductive skills than the deductive skills of the builder. The architect deals more with guidelines, rather than rules that builders use as a necessity.

It also must be clear that the role of an architect may be performed by an engineer. A goal of this document is to describe the role - what should be done, regardless of who is performing it.

Thus, the role of the architect can be summarized as to:

- **Understand and interpret requirements:** probe for information, listen to information, influence people, facilitate consensus building, synthesize and translate ideas into actionable requirements, articulate those ideas to others. Identify use or purpose, constraints, risks, etc. The architect participates in the discovery and documentation of the customer's business scenarios that are driving the solution. The architect is responsible for requirements understanding and embodies that requirements understanding in the architecture specification.
- **Create a useful model:** take the requirements and develop well-formulated models of the components of the solution, augmenting the models as necessary to fit all of the circumstances. Show multiple views through models to communicate the ideas effectively. The architect is responsible for the overall architecture integrity and maintaining the vision of the offering from an architectural perspective. The architect also ensures leverage opportunities are identified, using building blocks, and is a liaison between the functional groups (especially development and marketing) to ensure that the leverage opportunities are realized. The architect provides and maintains these models as a framework for understanding the domain(s) of development work, guiding what should be done within the organization, or outside the organization. The architect must represent the organization view of the architecture by understanding all the necessary business components.
- **Validate, refine, and expand the model:** verify assumptions, bring in subject matter experts, etc. in order to improve the model and to further define it, adding as necessary new ideas to make the result more flexible and more tightly linked to current and expected requirements. The architect additionally should assess the value of solution-enhancing developments emanating from field work and incorporate these into the architecture models as appropriate.
- **Manage the architecture:** continuously monitor the models and update them as necessary to show changes, additions, and alterations. Represent architecture and issues during development and decision points of the program. The architect is an "agent of change", representing that need for the implementation of the architecture. Through this development cycle, the architect continuously fosters the sharing of customer, architecture, and technical information between organizations.

30.6.2 Characterization in Terms of the Enterprise Continuum

Under certain circumstances, the complexity of a solution may require additional architects to support the architecture effort. The different categories of architects are described below, but as they are architects, they all perform the tasks described above. Any combination of foundation, systems, solutions, and customer architects may be utilized, as a team. In such cases each member may have a specific focus, if not specific roles and responsibilities, within the phases of the development process. In cases where a team of architects is deemed necessary, a Lead Architect should be assigned to manage and lead the team members.

- The **Foundation Architect** has the responsibility for architectural design and documentation at a technical reference model level. The Foundation Architect often leads a group of the System and/or Industry Architects related to a given program. The focus of the Foundation Architect is on enterprise-level business functions required.
- The **System Architect** has the responsibility for architectural design and documentation at a system or subsystem level, such as management or security. A System Architect may shield the Foundation Architect from the unnecessary details of the systems, products, and/or technologies. The focus of the System Architect is on system technology solutions; for example, a component of a solution such as enterprise data warehousing.
- The **Industry Architect** has the responsibility for architectural design and documentation at an industry level. The focus of the Industry Architect is on industry problems and solutions; for example, Petrochemical solutions, Banking solutions, Retail solutions.
- The **Organization Architect** has the responsibility for architectural design and documentation of specific organizations. An Organization Architect re-uses the output from all other architects. The focus of the Organization Architect is on enterprise-level business solutions in a given domain, such as finance, human resources, sales, etc.

30.6.3 Key Characteristics of an IT Architect

30.6.3.1 Skills and Experience in Producing Designs

An IT architect must be proficient in the techniques that go into producing designs of complex IT systems, including requirements discovery and analysis, formulation of solution context, identification of solution alternatives and their assessment, technology selection, and design configuration.

30.6.3.2 Extensive Technical Breadth, with Technical Depth in One or a Few Disciplines

An IT architect should possess an extensive technical breadth through experience in the IT industry. This breadth should be in areas of application development and deployment, and in the areas of creation and maintenance of the infrastructure to support the complex application environment. Current IT environments are heterogeneous by nature, and the experienced IT architect will have skills across multiple platforms, including distributed systems and traditional mainframe environments. IT architects will have, as a result of their careers, skills in at least one discipline that is considered to be at the level of a subject matter expert.

30.6.3.3 Method-Driven Approach to Execution

The IT architect approaches his or her job through the consistent use of recognized design methods such as the TOGAF Architecture Development Method (ADM). The IT architect should have working knowledge of more than one design method and be comfortable deploying parts of methods appropriate to the situation in which s/he is working. This should be seen in the body of design work the IT architect has produced through repeated successful use of more than one design method. Proficiency in methodology use is in knowing what parts of methods to use in a given situation, and what methods not to use.

30.6.3.4 Full Project Scope Experience

While the IT architect is responsible for design and hand-off of the project to implementors, it is vital that s/he have experience with all aspects of a project from design through development, testing, implementation, and production. This scope of experience will serve to keep IT architects grounded in the notion of fitness-for-purpose and the practical nature of system implementation. The impact of full project scope experience should lead the IT architect to make better design decisions, and better inform the trade-offs made in those decisions.

30.6.3.5 Leadership

Communication and team building are key to the successful role of the IT architect. The mix of good technical skill and the ability to lead are crucial to the job. S/he should be viewed as a leader in the enterprise by the IT organization, the clients they serve, and management.

30.6.3.6 Personal and Professional Skills

The IT architect must have strong communications and relationship skills. A major task of the IT architect is to communicate complex technical information to all stakeholders of the project, including those who do not have a technical background. Strong negotiation and problem-solving skills are also required. The IT architect must work with the project management team to make decisions in a timely manner to keep projects on track.

30.6.3.7 Skills and Experience in One or More Industries

Industry skill and experience will make the task of gathering requirements and deciding priorities easier and more effective for the IT architect. The IT architect must understand the business processes of the enterprise in which he works, and how those processes work with other peer enterprises in the industry. S/he should also be able to spot key trends and correct flawed processes, giving the IT organization the capability to lead the enterprise, not just respond to requests. The mission of the IT architect is strategic technical leadership.

30.7 Conclusions

The TOGAF Architecture Skills Framework provides an assessment of the skills required to deliver a successful enterprise architecture.

It is hoped that the provision of this Architecture Skills Framework will help reduce the time, cost, and risk involved in training, recruiting, and managing IT architecture professionals, and at the same time enable and encourage more organizations to institute an internal IT architecture practice, hopefully based on (or at least leveraging) the role and skill definitions provided

Chapter 31: Developing Architecture Views

This chapter describes the role and taxonomy of architecture views.

Note that some of the material in this section is from The Command and Control System Target Architecture (C2STA), which was developed by the Electronic Systems Center (ESC) of the US Air Force between 1997 and 2000.

31.1 The Role of Architecture Views

31.1.1 Introduction

Architecture views are representations of the overall architecture that are meaningful to one or more stakeholders in the system. The architect chooses and develops a set of views that will enable the architecture to be communicated to, and understood by, all the stakeholders, and enable them to verify that the system will address their concerns.

An architecture is usually represented by means of one or more architecture models that together provide a coherent description of the system's architecture. A single, comprehensive model is often too complex to be understood and communicated in its most detailed form, showing all the relationships between the various business and technical components. As with the architecture of a building, it is normally necessary to develop multiple views of the architecture of an information system, to enable the architecture to be communicated to, and understood by, the different stakeholders in the system.

For example, just as a building architect might create wiring diagrams, floor plans, and elevations to describe different facets of a building to its different stakeholders (electricians, owners, planning officials), so an IT architect might create physical and security views of an IT system for the stakeholders who have concerns related to these aspects.

31.1.2 TOGAF and Standards for IT Architecture Description

An important recent development in IT architecture practice has been the emergence of standards for architecture description, principally through the adoption by ANSI and the IEEE of ANSI/IEEE Std 1471-2000, Recommended Practice for Architectural Description of Software-Intensive Systems. One of the aims of this standard is to promote a more consistent, systematic approach to the creation of views.

At the present time, TOGAF encourages but does not mandate the use of ANSI/IEEE Std 1471-2000.

Organizations that have incorporated, or plan to incorporate, ANSI/IEEE Std 1471-2000 into their IT architecture practice should find that none of the key concepts in TOGAF is incompatible with this standard, although some of the terminology used is not completely consistent with it.

In TOGAF we endeavor to strike a balance between promoting the concepts and terminology of ANSI/IEEE Std 1471-2000 - ensuring that our usage of terms defined by ANSI/IEEE Std 1471-2000 is consistent with the standard - and retaining other commonly accepted terminology that is familiar to the majority of the TOGAF readership.

An example of common terminology retained in TOGAF is the use of the terms "Business Architecture", "Technology Architecture", etc. These terms reflect common usage, but are at variance with ANSI/IEEE Std 1471-2000 (in which "architecture" is a property of a thing, not a thing in its own right). This situation will be reviewed in future versions of TOGAF. The process of gradual convergence between TOGAF and relevant standards for architecture description will continue as ANSI/IEEE Std 1471-2000 gains increased acceptance within the industry.

More general information about ANSI/IEEE Std 1471-2000 can be obtained from the IEEE Architecture Working Group (see *www.pithecanthropus.com/~awg*).

31.1.3 A Note on Terminology

It is arguable that the term "architecture" in this document should be replaced with the term "view", in accordance with ANSI/IEEE Std 1471-2000 recommended practice. There are practical problems with this.

Firstly, there is common usage. Typically an overall enterprise architecture comprising all four "architectures" (Business, Data, Applications, Technology) will not be undertaken as a single project. Rather each "architecture" - and in some cases, subsets of them - will be undertaken as individual projects. The ultimate deliverable of such a project is commonly referred to as an "... architecture" (for example, a Business Architecture). Within such an architecture there will very likely be views, in the true ANSI/IEEE Std 1471-2000 sense.

Secondly, such individual projects - leading to a "Business Architecture", or an "Applications Architecture", etc. - are often undertaken without any intent to develop all four "architectures" and integrate them into an overall enterprise architecture. (Or at least, there may be a long-term strategic goal to develop all four, but the initial development may be intended as a free-standing architecture and not a view of some larger entity.)

In summary, therefore, choice of terminology will depend largely on the extent to which the enterprise concerned regards each of the above as a part of a larger enterprise architecture.

For the present, TOGAF retains the terminology of "Business Architecture", "Technology Architecture", etc., since the terminology associated with ANSI/IEEE Std 1471-2000 recommended practice is still relatively new to the industry and not yet in widespread use. This situation will be reviewed in future versions of TOGAF.

31.2 Basic Concepts

The following concepts are central to the topic of views. These concepts have been adapted from more formal definitions contained in ANSI/IEEE Std 1471-2000.

A *system* is a collection of components organized to accomplish a specific function or set of functions.

The *architecture* of a system is the system's fundamental organization, embodied in its components, their relationships to each other and to the environment, and the principles guiding its design and evolution.

An *architecture description* is a collection of artifacts that document an architecture. In TOGAF, architecture views are the key artifacts in an architecture description.

Stakeholders are people who have key roles in, or concerns about, the system; for example, as users, developers, or managers. Different stakeholders with different roles in the system will have different concerns. Stakeholders can be individuals, teams, or organizations (or classes thereof).

Concerns are the key interests that are crucially important to the stakeholders in the system, and determine the acceptability of the system. Concerns may pertain to any aspect of the system's functioning, development, or operation, including considerations such as performance, reliability, security, distribution, and evolvability.

A *view* is a representation of a whole system from the perspective of a related set of concerns.

In capturing or representing the design of a system architecture, the architect will typically create one or more architecture models, possibly using different tools. A view will comprise selected parts of one or more models, chosen so as to demonstrate to a particular stakeholder or group of stakeholders that their concerns are being adequately addressed in the design of the system architecture.

A *viewpoint* defines the perspective from which a view is taken. More specifically, a viewpoint defines: how to construct and use a view (by means of an appropriate schema or template); the information that should appear in the view; the modeling techniques for expressing and analyzing the information; and a rationale for these choices (e.g., by describing the purpose and intended audience of the view).

- A view is what you see. A viewpoint is where you are looking from - the vantage point or perspective that determines what you see.
- Viewpoints are generic, and can be stored in libraries for re-use. A view is always specific to the architecture for which it is created.
- Every view has an associated viewpoint that describes it, at least implicitly. ANSI/IEEE Std 1471-2000 encourages architects to define viewpoints explicitly. Making this distinction between the content and schema of a view may seem at first to be an

unnecessary overhead, but it provides a mechanism for re-using viewpoints across different architectures.

In summary, then, architecture views are representations of the overall architecture in terms meaningful to stakeholders. They enable the architecture to be communicated to and understood by the stakeholders, so they can verify that the system will address their concerns.

> Note: The terms "concern" and "requirement" are not synonymous. A concern is an area of interest. So, system reliability might be a concern/area of interest for some stakeholders. The reason why architects should identify concerns and associate them with viewpoints, is to ensure that those concerns will be addressed in some fashion by the models of the architecture. For example, if the only viewpoint selected by an architect is a structural viewpoint, then reliability concerns are almost certainly not being addressed, since they cannot be represented in a structural model. Within theat concern, stakeholders may have many distinct requirements: different classes of users may have very different reliability requirements for different capabilities of the system.
>
> Concerns are the root of the process of decomposition into requirements. Concerns are represented in the architecture by these requirements. Requirements should be SMART (e.g., specific metrics).

31.2.1 A Simple Example of a Viewpoint and View

For many architectures, a useful viewpoint is that of business domains, which can be illustrated by an example from The Open Group itself.

The viewpoint is specified as follows:

Viewpoint Element	Description
Stakeholders	Management Board, Chief Information Officer
Concerns	Show the top-level relationships between geographical sites and business functions.
Modeling technique	Nested boxes diagram.
	Blue = locations; brown = business functions.
	Semantics of nesting = functions performed in the locations.

The corresponding view of The Open Group (in 2001) is shown in Example View - The Open Group Business Domains in 2001 .

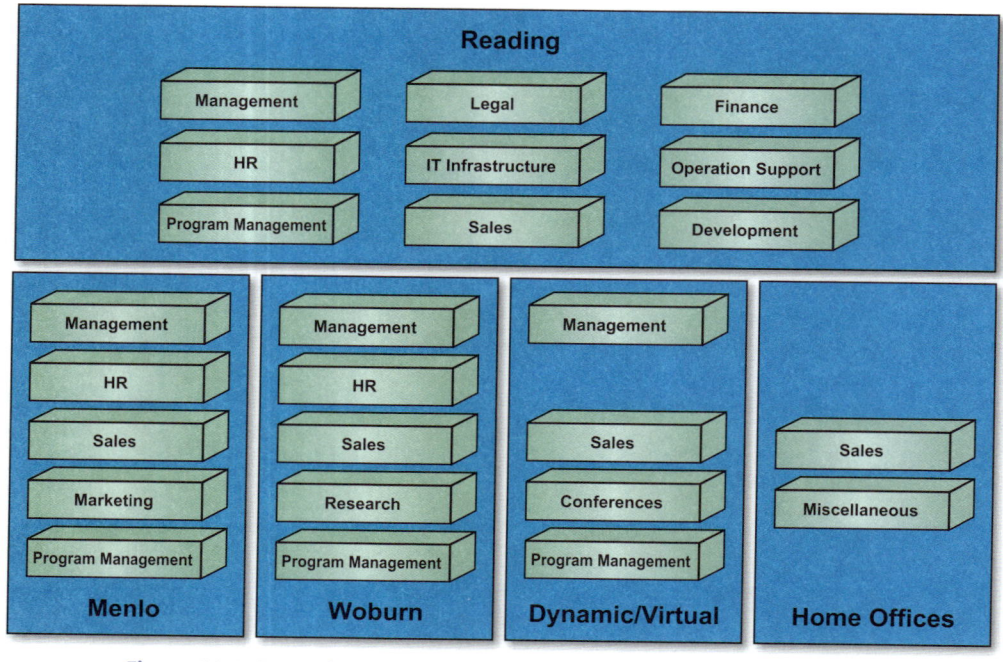

Figure 31.1: Example View - The Open Group Business Domains in 2001

31.3 Developing Views in the ADM

31.3.1 General Guidelines

The choice of which particular architecture views to develop is one of the key decisions that the architect has to make.

The architect has a responsibility for ensuring the completeness (fitness-for-purpose) of the architecture, in terms of adequately addressing all the pertinent concerns of its stakeholders; and the integrity of the architecture, in terms of connecting all the various views to each other, satisfactorily reconciling the conflicting concerns of different stakeholders, and showing the trade-offs made in so doing (as between security and performance, for example).

The choice has to be constrained by considerations of practicality, and by the principle of fitness-for-purpose (i.e., the architecture should be developed only to the point at which it is fit-for-purpose, and not reiterated ad infinitum as an academic exercise).

As explained in Part II: Architecture Development Method (ADM), the development of architecture views is an iterative process. The typical progression is from business to technology, using a technique such as business scenarios (see Business Scenarios) to properly identify all pertinent concerns; and from high-level overview to lower-level detail, continually referring back to the concerns and requirements of the stakeholders throughout the process.

Moreover, each of these progressions has to be made for two distinct environments: the existing environment (referred to as the baseline in the ADM) and the target environment. The architect must develop pertinent Business and Technology Architecture views of both the existing system and the target system. This provides the context for the gap analysis at the end of Phase C of the ADM, which establishes which elements of the current system must be carried forward and which must be removed or replaced.

This whole process is explained in Part II: Architecture Development Method (ADM), Step 2 .

31.3.2 View Creation Process

As mentioned above, at the present time TOGAF encourages but does not mandate the use of ANSI/IEEE Std 1471-2000. The following description therefore covers both the situation where ANSI/IEEE Std 1471-2000 has been adopted and where it has not.

ANSI/IEEE Std 1471-2000 itself does not require any specific process for developing viewpoints or creating views from them. Where ANSI/IEEE Std 1471-2000 has been adopted and become well-established practice within an organization, it will often be possible to create the required views for a particular architecture by following these steps:

1. Refer to an existing library of viewpoints.
2. Select the appropriate viewpoints (based on the stakeholders and concerns that need to be covered by views).
3. Generate views of the system by using the selected viewpoints as templates.

This approach can be expected to bring the following benefits:

- Less work for the architects (because the viewpoints have already been defined and therefore the views can be created faster)
- Better comprehensibility for stakeholders (because the viewpoints are already familiar)
- Greater confidence in the validity of the views (because their viewpoints have a known track record)

However, situations can always arise in which a view is needed for which no appropriate viewpoint has been pre-defined. This is also the situation, of course, when an organization has not yet incorporated ANSI/IEEE Std 1471-2000 into its architecture practice and established a library of viewpoints.

In each case, the architect may choose to develop a new viewpoint that will cover the outstanding need, and then generate a view from it. (This is the ANSI/IEEE Std 1471-2000 recommended practice.) Alternatively, a more pragmatic approach can be equally successful: the architect can create an ad hoc view for a specific system and later consider whether a generalized form of the implicit viewpoint should be defined explicitly and saved in a library, so that it can be re-used. (This is one way of establishing a library of viewpoints initially.)

Whatever the context, the architect should be aware that every view has a viewpoint, at least implicitly, and that defining the viewpoint in a systematic way (as recommended by ANSI/

IEEE Std 1471-2000) will help in assessing its effectiveness (i.e., does the viewpoint cover the relevant stakeholder concerns?).

31.4 Core Taxonomy of Architecture Views

31.4.1 Overview

TOGAF's core taxonomy of architecture views defines the minimum set of views that should be considered in the development of an architecture.

Since in ANSI/IEEE Std 1471-2000 every view has an associated viewpoint that defines it, this taxonomy may also be regarded as a taxonomy of viewpoints by those organizations that have adopted ANSI/IEEE Std 1471-2000.

31.4.2 Stakeholders

The minimum set of stakeholders for a system that should be considered in the development of architecture viewpoints and views is:

- Users
- System and Software Engineers
- Operators, Administrators, and Managers
- Acquirers

31.4.3 Views/Viewpoints

The architecture views, and corresponding viewpoints, that may be created to support each of these stakeholders fall into the following categories. (As mentioned above, this taxonomy may be regarded as a taxonomy of viewpoints by those organizations that have adopted ANSI/IEEE Std 1471-2000.)

- Business Architecture views, which address the concerns of the users of the system, and describe the flows of business information between people and business processes
- Data Architecture views, which address the concerns of database designers and database administrators, and system engineers responsible for developing and integrating the various database components of the system
- Applications Architecture views, which address the concerns of system and software engineers responsible for developing and integrating the various Application Software components of the system
- Technology Architecture views, which address the concerns of acquirers (procurement personnel responsible for acquiring the Commercial Off-The-Shelf (COTS) software and hardware to be included in the system), operations staff, systems administrators, and systems managers

Examples of specific views that may be created in each category are tabulated below, and explained in detail in the following subsection.

To address the concerns of the following stakeholders...			
Users, Planners, Business Management	**Database Designers and Administrators, System Engineers**	**System and Software Engineers**	**Acquirers, Operators, Administrators, & Managers**
... the following views may be developed			
Business Architecture Views	**Data Architecture Views**	**Applications Architecture Views**	**Technology Architecture Views**
Business Function View	Data Entity View	Software Engineering View	Networked Computing/ Hardware View
Business Services View			
Business Process View			
Business Information View			Communications Engineering View
Business Locations View			
Business Logistics View	Data Flow View (Organization Data Use)	Applications Interoperability View	
People View (Organization Chart)			Processing View
Workflow View			
Usability View			
Business Strategy and Goals View	Logical Data View	Software Distribution View	Cost View
Business Objectives View			
Business Rules View			Standards View
Business Events View			
Business Performance View			
	System Engineering View		
Enterprise Security View			
Enterprise Manageability View			
Enterprise Quality of Service View			
Enterprise Mobility View			

Table 31.1: Example Taxonomy of Architecture Views

A mapping of these views to the schema of the well-known Zachman Framework is illustrated below.

	Stakeholder	Data	Function	Network	People	Time	Motivation
Scope	Planner	Data Entity View (Class Model)	Business Function View	Business Locations View	People View (org chart)	Business Events View	Business Strategy and Goals View
			Business Services View	Enterprise Mobility View		Enterprise Quality of Service View	
Enterprise Model	Owner	Data Flow View (Organization Data Use)	Business Services View	Business Logistics View (Business-to-Location Mapping)	Workflow View	Business Performance View (Master Schedule)	Business Objectives View (SMART objectives from Business Scenario)
			Business Process View	Enterprise Mobility View		Enterprise Quality of Service View	
System Model	Designer	System Engineering View	System Engineering View	System Engineering View	Usability View	System Engineering View	Business Rules View
		Logical Data View	System Engineering View	Standards View		Processing View	
		Standards View	Application-to-Application Communication View	Enterprise Mobility View	Standards View	Standards View	Cost View
			Standards View			Enterprise Quality of Service View	
Technology Constrained Model	Builder	Physical Data View (out of TOGAF scope)	Software Distribution View	Networked Computing/Hardware View	Usability View	Control Structure (out of TOGAF scope)	Business Logic (Rules) Design (out of TOGAF scope)
				Communications Engineering View			
Detailed Representations	Subcontractor	Data Definitions (out of TOGAF scope)	Application Program Code (out of TOGAF scope)	(out of TOGAF scope)	(out of TOGAF scope)	Timing Definitions (out of TOGAF scope)	Application Program (Rules Specification) (out of TOGAF scope)
Functioning Enterprise		Enterprise Security View	Enterprise Security View	Enterprise Security View	Enterprise Security View	Enterprise Security View	Enterprise Security View
		Enterprise Mobility View	Enterprise Mobility View	Enterprise Mobility View	Enterprise Mobility View	Enterprise Mobility View	Enterprise Mobility View
		Enterprise Quality of Service View	Enterprise Quality of Service View	Enterprise Quality of Service View	Enterprise Quality of Service View	Enterprise Quality of Service View	Enterprise Quality of Service View
		Enterprise Manageability View	Enterprise Manageability View	Enterprise Manageability View		Enterprise Manageability View	

Table 31.2: Mapping of Example Taxonomy of Architecture Views to Zachman Framework

31.4.4 Description

The following description explains some of the views listed above. A more detailed description of each view, and guidelines for developing it, can be obtained by following the relevant hyperlink in the following.

1. Business Architecture views (see Developing a Business Architecture View) address the concerns of users, planners, and business managers, and focus on the functional aspects of the system from the perspective of the users of the system; that is, on what the new system is intended to do, including performance, functionality, and usability. These can be built up from an analysis of the existing environment and of the requirements and constraints affecting the new system.

   - The People view focuses on the human resource aspects of the system. It examines the human actors involved in the system.
   - The Business Process view deals with the user processes involved in the system.
   - The Business Function view deals with the functions required to support the processes.
   - The Business Information view deals with the information required to flow in support of the processes.
   - The Usability view considers the usability aspects of the system and its environment.
   - The Business Performance view considers the performance aspects of the system and its environment.

2. Data Architecture views and Applications Architecture views address the concerns of the database designers and administrators, and the system and software engineers of the system. They focus on how the system is implemented from the perspective of different types of engineers (security, software, data, computing components, communications), and how that affects its properties. Systems and software engineers are typically concerned with modifiability, re-usability, and availability of other services.

   - The Data Flow view (see Developing a Data Flow View) deals with the architecture of the storage, retrieval, processing, archiving, and security of data. It looks at the flow of data as it is stored and processed, and at what components will be required to support and manage both storage and processing.
   - The Software Engineering view (see Developing a Software Engineering View) deals with aspects of interest to software developers. It considers what software development constraints and opportunities exist in the new system, and looks at how development can be carried out, both in terms of technology and resources. The software engineering view is particularly important in that it provides a reference for selection of building blocks related to elements of the existing system that may be re-used in the Target Architecture.
   - The System Engineering view (see Developing a System Engineering View) presents a number of different ways in which software and hardware components can be assembled into a working system. To a great extent the choice of model determines the properties of the final system. It looks at technology which already exists in

the organization, and what is available currently or in the near future. This reveals areas where new technology can contribute to the function or efficiency of the new architecture, and how different types of processing platform can support different parts of the overall system.

3. Technology Architecture views address the concerns of the acquirers, operators, communications engineers, administrators, and managers of the system.

- The Communications Engineering view (see Developing a Communications Engineering View) addresses the concerns of the communications engineers. It examines various ways of structuring communications facilities to simplify the business of network planning and design. It examines the networking elements of the architecture in the light of geographic constraints, bandwidth requirements, and so on.
- Acquirer's views (see Developing an Acquirer's View) address the needs of an acquirer or procurer, providing appropriate guidance for purchasing components that "fit" the architecture. Acquirer's views of the architecture are primarily concerned with costs, and standards that must be adhered to; for example:
  - The Cost View
  - The Standards View

  These views typically depict building blocks of the architecture that can be purchased, and the standards that the building blocks must adhere to in order for the building block to be most useful.

4. Composite views:

- The Enterprise Manageability view (see Developing an Enterprise Manageability View) addresses the concerns of the operations, administration, and management of the system, and concentrates more on the details of location, type, and power of the equipment and software in order to manage the health and availability of the system. It covers issues such as initial deployment, upgrading, availability, security, performance, asset management, fault and event management of system components, from the management perspective of the following subject matters:
  - Security
  - Software
  - Data
  - Computing/Hardware
  - Communications
- The Enterprise Security view (see Developing an Enterprise Security View) focuses on the security aspects of the system for the protection of information within the organization. It examines the system to establish what information is stored and processed, how valuable it is, what threats exist, and how they can be addressed.

Architects also have concerns of their own which basically define the fitness-for-purpose of an effort. Architects must understand completeness, where completeness includes considering all relevant views, the relationships between those views, and dealing with the conflicts that arise from those different views. Architects also must deal with viability of the architecture: if the architecture is not capable of being implemented, then its value is in doubt.

31.5 Views, Tools, and Languages

The need for architecture views, and the process of developing them following the Architecture Development Method (ADM), are explained above. This subsection describes the relationships between architecture views, the tools used to develop and analyze them, and a standard language enabling interoperability between the tools.

31.5.1 Overview

In order to achieve the goals of completeness and integrity in an architecture, architecture views are usually developed, visualized, communicated, and managed using a tool.

In the current state of the market, different tools normally have to be used to develop and analyze different views of the architecture. It is highly desirable that an architecture description be encoded in a standard language, to enable a standard approach to the description of architecture semantics and their re-use among different tools.

A viewpoint is also normally developed, visualized, communicated, and managed using a tool, and it is also highly desirable that standard viewpoints (i.e., templates or schemas) be developed, so that different tools that deal in the same views can interoperate, the fundamental elements of an architecture can be re-used, and the architecture description can be shared among tools.

Issues relating to the evaluation of tools for architecture work are discussed in detail in Tools for Architecture Development .

31.6 Views and Viewpoints

31.6.1 Example of Views and Viewpoints

To illustrate the concepts of views and viewpoints, consider the example of a very simple airport system with two different stakeholders, the pilot and the air traffic controller.

The pilot has one view of the system, and the air traffic controller has another. Neither view represents the whole system, because the perspective of each stakeholder constrains (and reduces) how each sees the overall system.

The view of the pilot comprises some elements not viewed by the controller, such as passengers and fuel, while the view of the controller comprises some elements not viewed by the pilot, such as other planes. There are also elements shared between the views, such as the communication model between the pilot and the controller, and the vital information about the plane itself.

A viewpoint is a model (or description) of the information contained in a view. In our example, one viewpoint is the description of how the pilot sees the system, and the other viewpoint is how the controller sees the system.

Pilots describe the system from their perspective, using a model of their position and vector toward or away from the runway. All pilots use this model, and the model has a specific language that is used to capture information and populate the model.

Controllers describe the system differently, using a model of the airspace and the locations and vectors of aircraft within the airspace. Again, all controllers use a common language derived from the common model in order to capture and communicate information pertinent to their viewpoint.

Fortunately, when controllers talk with pilots, they use a common communication language. (In other words, the models representing their individual viewpoints partially intersect.) Part of this common language is about location and vectors of aircraft, and is essential to safety.

So in essence each viewpoint is an abstract model of how all the stakeholders of a particular type - all pilots, or all controllers - view the airport system.

Tools exist to assist stakeholders, especially when they are interacting with complex models such as the model of an airspace, or the model of air flight.

The interface to the human user of a tool is typically close to the model and language associated with the viewpoint. The unique tools of the pilot are fuel, altitude, speed, and location indicators. The main tool of the controller is radar. The common tool is a radio.

To summarize from the above example, we can see that a view can subset the system through the perspective of the stakeholder, such as the pilot versus the controller. This subset can be described by an abstract model called a viewpoint, such as an air flight versus an air space model. This description of the view is documented in a partially specialized language, such as "pilot-speak" versus "controller-speak". Tools are used to assist the stakeholders, and they interface with each other in terms of the language derived from the viewpoint ("pilot-speak" versus' "controller-speak").

When stakeholders use common tools, such as the radio contact between pilot and controller, a common language is essential.

31.6.2 Views and Viewpoints in Information Systems

Now let us map this example to Information Systems Architecture. Consider two stakeholders in a new small computing system: the users and the developers.

The users of the system have a view of the system, and the developers of the system have a different view. Neither view represents the whole system, because each perspective reduces how each sees the system.

The view of the user is comprised of all the ways in which s/he interacts with the system, not seeing any details such as applications or Database Management Systems (DBMS).

The view of the developer is one of productivity and tools, and doesn't include things such as actual live data and connections with consumers.

However, there are things that are shared, such as descriptions of the processes that are enabled by the system and/or communications protocols set up for users to communicate problems directly to development.

In this example, one viewpoint is the description of how the user sees the system, and the other viewpoint is how the developer sees the system. Users describe the system from their perspective, using a model of availability, response time, and access to information. All users of the system use this model, and the model has a specific language.

Developers describe the system differently than users, using a model of software connected to hardware distributed over a network, etc. However, there are many types of developers (database, security, etc.) of the system, and they do not have a common language derived from the model.

31.6.3 The Need for a Common Language and Interoperable Tools for Architecture Description

Tools exist for both users and developers. Tools such as online help are there specifically for users, and attempt to use the language of the user. Many different tools exist for different types of developers, but they suffer from the lack of a common language that is required to bring the system together. It is difficult, if not impossible, in the current state of the tools market to have one tool interoperate with another tool.

Issues relating to the evaluation of tools for architecture work are discussed in detail in Tools for Architecture Development .

31.7 Conclusions

This section attempts to deal with views in a structured manner, but this is by no means a complete treatise on views.

In general, TOGAF embraces the concepts and definitions presented in ANSI/IEEE Std 1471-2000, specifically the concepts that help guide the development of a view and make the view actionable. These concepts can be summarized as:

- Selecting a key stakeholder
- Understanding their concerns and generalizing/documenting those concerns
- Understanding how to model and deal with those concerns

In the following subsections TOGAF presents some recommended views, some or all of which may be appropriate in a particular architecture development. This is not intended as an exhaustive set of views, but simply as a starting point. Those described may be supplemented by additional views as required. These TOGAF subsections on views should be considered as guides for the development and treatment of a view, not as a full definition of a view.

Each subsection describes the stakeholders related to the view, their concerns, and the entities modeled and the language used to depict the view (the viewpoint). The viewpoint provides architecture concepts from the different perspectives, including components, interfaces, and allocation of services critical to the view. The viewpoint language, analytical methods, and modeling methods associated with views are typically applied with the use of appropriate tools.

31.8 Developing a Business Architecture View

The Business Architecture view is concerned with addressing the concerns of users.

31.8.1 Stakeholder and Concerns

This view should be developed for the users. It focuses on the functional aspects of the system from the perspective of the users of the system.

Addressing the concerns of the users includes consideration of the following:

People	The human resource aspects of the system. It examines the human actors involved in the system.
Process	Deals with the user processes involved in the system.
Function	Deals with the functions required to support the processes.
Business Information	Deals with the information required to flow in support of the processes.
Usability	Considers the usability aspects of the system and its environment.
Performance	Considers the performance aspects of the system and its environment.

31.8.2 Modeling the View

Business scenarios (see Business Scenarios) are an important technique that may be used prior to, and as a key input to, the development of the Business Architecture view, to help identify and understand business needs, and thereby to derive the business requirements and constraints that the architecture development has to address. Business scenarios are an extremely useful way to depict what should happen when planned and unplanned events occur. It is highly recommended that business scenarios be created for planned change, and for unplanned change.

The following paragraphs describe some of the key issues that the architect might consider when constructing business scenarios.

31.8.3 Key Issues

The Business Architecture view considers the functional aspects of the system; that is, what the new system is intended to do. This can be built up from an analysis of the existing environment and of the requirements and constraints affecting the new system.

The new requirements and constraints will appear from a number of sources, possibly including:

- Existing internal specifications and lists of approved products
- Business goals and objectives
- Business process re-engineering activities
- Changes in technology

What should emerge from the Business Architecture view is a clear understanding of the functional requirements for the new architecture, with statements like: "Improvements in handling customer enquiries are required through wider use of computer/telephony integration".

The Business Architecture view considers the usability aspects of the system and its environment. It should also consider impacts on the user such as skill levels required, the need for specialized training, and migration from current practice. When considering usability the architect should take into account:

- The ease-of-use of the user interface, and how intuitive it is
- Whether or not there is transparent access to data and applications, irrespective of location
- Ease-of-management of the user environment by the user
- Application interoperability through means such as drag-and-drop
- Online help facilities
- Clarity of documentation
- Security and password aspects, such as avoiding the requirement for multiple sign-on and password dialogues
- Access to productivity applications such as mail or a spreadsheet

Note that, although security and management are thought about here, it is from a usability and functionality point of view. The technical aspects of security and management are considered in the enterprise security view (see Developing an Enterprise Security View) and the enterprise manageability view (see Developing an Enterprise Manageability View).

31.9 Developing an Enterprise Security View

The enterprise security view is concerned with the security aspects of the system.

31.9.1 Stakeholder and Concerns

This view should be developed for security engineers of the system. It focuses on how the system is implemented from the perspective of security, and how security affects the system properties. It examines the system to establish what information is stored and processed, how valuable it is, what threats exist, and how they can be addressed.

Major concerns for this view are understanding how to ensure that the system is available to only those that have permission, and how to protect the system from unauthorized tampering.

31.9.2 Modeling the View

The subjects of the general architecture of a "security system" are components that are secured, or components that provide security services. Additionally Access Control Lists (ACLs) and security schema definitions are used to model and implement security.

31.9.3 Basic Concepts

This section presents basic concepts required for an understanding of information system security.

The essence of security is the controlled use of information. The purpose of this section is to provide a brief overview of how security protection is implemented in the components of an information system. Doctrinal or procedural mechanisms, such as physical and personnel security procedures and policy, are not discussed here in any depth.

Abstract Security Architecture View depicts an abstract view of an Information Systems Architecture, which emphasizes the fact that an information system from the security perspective is either part of a Local Subscriber Environment (LSE) or a Communications Network (CN). An LSE may be either fixed or mobile. The LSEs by definition are under the control of the using organization. In an open system distributed computing implementation, secure and non-secure LSEs will almost certainly be required to interoperate.

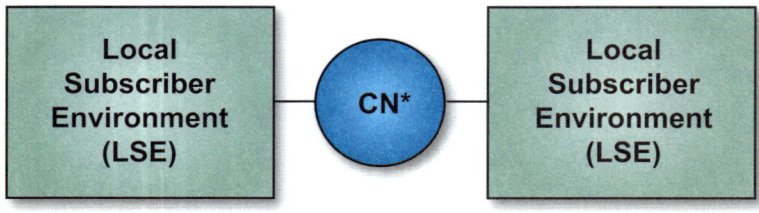

*CN = Communications Network

Figure 31.2 : Abstract Security Architecture View

31.9.3.1 Information Domains

The concept of an information domain provides the basis for discussing security protection requirements. An information domain is defined as a set of users, their information objects, and a security policy. An information domain security policy is the statement of the criteria for membership in the information domain and the required protection of the information objects. Breaking an organization's information down into domains is the first step in reducing the task of security policy development to a manageable size.

The business of most organizations requires that their members operate in more than one information domain. The diversity of business activities and the variation in perception of threats to the security of information will result in the existence of different information domains within one organization security policy. A specific activity may use several information domains, each with its own distinct information domain security policy.

Information domains are not necessarily bounded by information systems or even networks of systems. The security mechanisms implemented in information system components may be evaluated for their ability to meet the information domain security policies.

31.9.3.2 Strict Isolation

Information domains can be viewed as being strictly isolated from one another. Information objects should be transferred between two information domains only in accordance with established rules, conditions, and procedures expressed in the security policy of each information domain.

31.9.3.3 Absolute Protection

The concept of "absolute protection" is used to achieve the same level of protection in all information systems supporting a particular information domain. It draws attention to the problems created by interconnecting LSEs that provide different strengths of security protection. This interconnection is likely because open systems may consist of an unknown number of heterogeneous LSEs. Analysis of minimum security requirements will ensure that the concept of absolute protection will be achieved for each information domain across LSEs.

31.9.4 Security Generic Architecture View

Generic Security Architecture View shows a generic architecture view which can be used to discuss the allocation of security services and the implementation of security mechanisms. This view identifies the architectural components within an LSE. The LSEs are connected by CNs. The LSEs include end systems, relay systems, and Local Communications Systems (LCSs), described below.

- Relay System (RS): The component of an LSE, the functionality of which is limited to information transfer and is only indirectly accessible by users (e.g., router, switch, multiplexor, Message Transfer Agent (MTA)). It may have functionality similar to an end system, but an end user does not use it directly. Note that relay system functions may be provided in an end system.

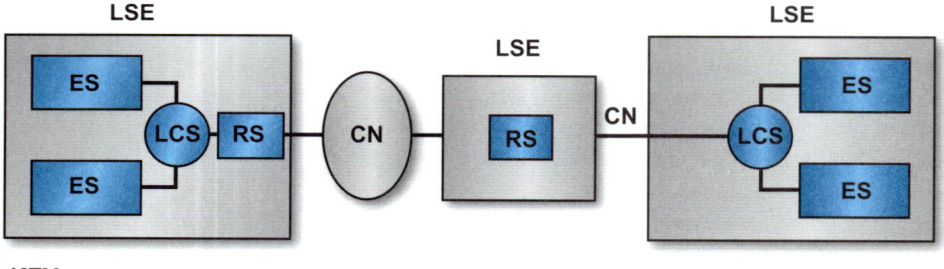

KEY

CN   Communications Network
ES   End System
LCS   Local Communications System
LSE   Local Subscriber Environment
RS   Relay System

Figure 31.3: Generic Security Architecture View

- Local Communication System (LCS): A network that provides communications capabilities between LSEs or within an LSE with all of the components under control of an LSE.

- Communications Network (CN): A network that provides inter-LSE communications capabilities, but is not controlled by LSEs (e.g., commercial carriers).

The end system and the relay system are viewed as requiring the same types of security protection. For this reason, a discussion of security protection in an end system generally also applies to a relay system. The security protections in an end system could occur in both the hardware and software.

31.9.5 Security Services Allocation

Security protection of an information system is provided by mechanisms implemented in the hardware and software of the system and by the use of doctrinal mechanisms. The mechanisms implemented in the system hardware and software are concentrated in the end system or relay system. This focus for security protection is based on the open system, distributed computing approach for information systems. This implies use of commercial common carriers and private common-user communications systems as the CN provider between LSEs. Thus, for operation of end systems in a distributed environment, a greater degree of security protection can be assured from implementation of mechanisms in the end system or relay system.

However, communications networks should satisfy the availability element of security in order to provide appropriate security protection for the information system. This means that CNs must provide an agreed level of responsiveness, continuity of service, and resistance to accidental and intentional threats to the communications service availability.

Implementing the necessary security protection in the end system occurs in three system service areas of TOGAF. They are operating system services, network services, and system management services.

Most of the implementation of security protection is expected to occur in software. The hardware is expected to protect the integrity of the end-system software. Hardware security mechanisms include protection against tampering, undesired emanations, and cryptography.

31.9.5.1 Operating System Services

A "security context" is defined as a controlled process space subject to an information domain security policy. The security context is therefore analogous to a common operating system notion of user process space. Isolation of security contexts is required. Security contexts are required for all applications (e.g., end-user and security management applications). The focus is on strict isolation of information domains, management of end-system resources, and controlled sharing and transfer of information among information domains. Where possible, security-critical functions should be isolated into relatively small modules that are related in well-defined ways.

The operating system will isolate multiple security contexts from each other using hardware protection features (e.g., processor state register, memory mapping registers) to create separate address spaces for each of them. Untrusted software will use end-system resources only by invoking security-critical functions through the separation kernel. Most of the security-critical functions are the low-level functions of traditional operating systems.

31.9.5.2 Network Services

Two basic classes of communications are envisioned for which distributed security contexts may need to be established. These are interactive and staged (store and forward) communications.

The concept of a "security association" forms an interactive distributed security context. A security association is defined as all the communication and security mechanisms and functions that extend the protections required by an information domain security policy within an end system to information in transfer between multiple end systems. The security association is an extension or expansion of an OSI application layer association. An application layer association is composed of appropriate application layer functions and protocols plus all of the underlying communications functions and protocols at other layers of the OSI model. Multiple security protocols may be included in a single security association to provide for a combination of security services.

For staged delivery communications (e.g., email), use will be made of an encapsulation technique (termed "wrapping process") to convey the necessary security attributes with the data being transferred as part of the network services. The wrapped security attributes are intended to permit the receiving end system to establish the necessary security context for processing the transferred data. If the wrapping process cannot provide all the necessary security protection, interactive security contexts between end systems will have to be used to ensure the secure staged transfer of information.

31.9.5.3 System Security Management Services

Security management is a particular instance of the general information system management functions discussed in earlier chapters. Information system security management services are concerned with the installation, maintenance, and enforcement of information domain and information system security policy rules in the information system intended to provide these security services. In particular, the security management function controls information needed by operating system services within the end system security architecture. In addition to these core services, security management requires event handling, auditing, and recovery. Standardization of security management functions, data structures, and protocols will enable interoperation of Security Management Application Processes (SMAPs) across many platforms in support of distributed security management.

31.10 Developing a Software Engineering View

The software engineering view is concerned with the development of new software systems.

31.10.1 Stakeholders and Concerns

Building a software-intensive system is both expensive and time-consuming. Because of this, it is necessary to establish guidelines to help minimize the effort required and the risks involved. This is the purpose of the software engineering view, which should be developed for the software engineers who are going to develop the system.

Major concerns for these stakeholders are:

- Development approach
- Software modularity and re-use
- Portability
- Migration and interoperability

31.10.1.1 Development Approach

There are many lifecycle models defined for software development (waterfall, prototyping, etc.). A consideration for the architect is how best to feed architectural decisions into the lifecycle model that is going to be used for development of the system.

31.10.1.2 Software Modularity and Re-Use

As a piece of software grows in size, so the complexity and inter-dependencies between different parts of the code increase. Reliability will fall dramatically unless this complexity can be brought under control.

Modularity is a concept by which a piece of software is grouped into a number of distinct and logically cohesive sub-units, presenting services to the outside world through a well-defined interface. Generally speaking, the components of a module will share access to common data, and the interface will provide controlled access to this data. Using modularity, it becomes possible to build a software application incrementally on a reliable base of pre-tested code.

A further benefit of a well-defined modular system is that the modules defined within it may be re-used in the same or on other projects, cutting development time dramatically by reducing both development and testing effort.

In recent years, the development of object-oriented programming languages has greatly increased programming language support for module development and code re-use. Such languages allow the developer to define "classes" (a unit of modularity) of objects that behave in a controlled and well-defined manner. Techniques such as inheritance - which enables parts of an existing interface to an object to be changed - enhance the potential for re-usability by allowing predefined classes to be tailored or extended when the services they offer do not quite meet the requirement of the developer.

If modularity and software re-use are likely to be key objectives of new software developments, consideration must be given to whether the component parts of any proposed architecture may facilitate or prohibit the desired level of modularity in the appropriate areas.

31.10.1.3 Portability

Software portability - the ability to take a piece of software written in one environment and make it run in another - is important in many projects, especially product developments. It requires that all software and hardware aspects of a chosen Technology Architecture (not just the newly developed application) be available on the new platform. It will, therefore, be necessary to ensure that the component parts of any chosen architecture are available across all the appropriate target platforms.

31.10.1.4 Migration and Interoperability

Interoperability is always required between the component parts of a new architecture. It may also, however, be required between a new architecture and parts of an existing legacy system; for example, during the staggered replacement of an old system. Interoperability between the new and old architectures may, therefore, be a factor in architectural choice.

31.10.2 Key Issues

- Data-intensive versus information-intensive software systems
- Achieving interoperability
- Software tiers
- Uses of a data access tier
- Distribution

31.10.2.1 Data-Intensive Versus Information-Intensive Software Systems

This view considers two general categories of software systems. First, there are those systems that require only a user interface to a database, requiring little or no business logic built into the software. These systems can be called data-intensive. Second, there are those systems that require users to manipulate information that might be distributed across multiple databases, and to do this manipulation according to a predefined business logic. These systems can be called information-intensive.

Data-intensive systems can be built with reasonable ease through the use of 4GL tools. In these systems, the business logic is in the mind of the user; i.e., the user understands the rules for manipulating the data and uses those rules while doing his work.

Information-intensive systems are different. Information is defined as "meaningful data"; i.e., data in a context that includes business logic. Information is different from data. Data is the tokens that are stored in databases or other data stores. Information is multiple tokens of data combined to convey a message. For example, "3" is data, but "3 widgets" is information. Typically, information reflects a model. Information-intensive systems also tend to require information from other systems and, if this path of information passing is automated, usually some mediation is required to convert the format of incoming information into a format that can be locally used. Because of this, information-intensive systems tend to be more complex than others, and require the most effort to build, integrate, and maintain.

This view is concerned primarily with information-intensive systems. In addition to building systems that can manage information, though, systems should also be as flexible as possible. This has a number of benefits. It allows the system to be used in different environments; for example, the same system should be usable with different sources of data, even if the new data store is a different configuration. Similarly, it might make sense to use the same functionality but with users who need a different user interface. So information systems should be built so that they can be reconfigured with different data stores or different user interfaces. If a system is built to allow this, it enables the enterprise to re-use parts (or components) of one system in another.

31.10.2.2 Achieving Interoperability

The word "interoperate" implies that one processing system performs an operation on behalf of or at the behest of another processing system. In practice, the request is a complete sentence containing a verb (operation) and one or more nouns (identities of resources, where the resources can be information, data, physical devices, etc.). Interoperability comes from shared functionality.

Interoperability can only be achieved when information is passed, not when data is passed. Most information systems today get information both from their own data stores and other information systems. In some cases the web of connectivity between information systems is quite extensive. The US Air Force, for example, has a concept known as "A5 Interoperability". This means that the required data is available Anytime, Anywhere, by Anyone, who is Authorized, in Any way. This requires that many information systems are architecturally linked and provide information to each other.

There must be some kind of physical connectivity between the systems. This might be a Local Area Network (LAN), a Wide Area Network (WAN), or, in some cases, it might simply be the passing of a disk or CD between systems.[8] Assuming a network connects the systems, there must be agreement on the protocols used. This enables the transfer of bits.

When the bits are assembled at the receiving system, they must be placed in the context that the receiving system needs. In other words, both the source and destination systems must agree on an information model. The source system uses this model to convert its information into data to be passed, and the destination system uses this same model to convert the received data into information it can use.

This usually requires an agreement between the architects and designers of the two systems. In the past, this agreement was often documented in the form of an Interface Control Document (ICD). The ICD defines the exact syntax and semantics that the sending system will use so that the receiving system will know what to do when the data arrives. The biggest problem with ICDs is that they tend to be unique solutions between two systems. If a given system must share information with n other systems, there is the potential need for n2 ICDs. This extremely tight integration prohibits flexibility and the ability of a system to adapt to a changing environment. Maintaining all these ICDs is also a challenge.

New technology such as eXtensible Markup Language (XML) has the promise of making data "self describing". Use of new technologies such as XML, once they become reliable and well documented, might eliminate the need for an ICD. Further, there would be Commercial Off-The-Shelf (COTS) products available to parse and manipulate the XML data, eliminating the need to develop these products in-house. It should also ease the pain of maintaining all the interfaces.

Another approach is to build "mediators" between the systems. Mediators would use metadata that is sent with the data to understand the syntax and semantics of the data and convert it into a format usable by the receiving system. However, mediators do require that well-formed metadata be sent, adding to the complexity of the interface.

31.10.2.3 Software Tiers

Typically, software architectures are either two-tier or three-tier.[9]

Each tier typically presents at least one capability.

---

8. At usable Ethernet speeds (usually about 4 mb/s), it takes about 33 minutes to transfer a 1GB file. Today, many databases are considerably larger than 1GB, and the fastest way to transfer these extremely large databases might well be to put them on CDs and send them by an overnight courier.

9. These are different from two and three-tiered system architectures in which the middle tier is usually middleware. In the approach being presented here, middleware is seen as an enabler for the software components to interact with each other. See The Infrastructure Bus for more details.

Two-Tier

In a two-tier architecture, the user interface and business logic are tightly coupled while the data is kept independent. This gives the advantage of allowing the data to reside on a dedicated data server. It also allows the data to be independently maintained. The tight coupling of the user interface and business logic assure that they will work well together, for this problem in this domain. However, the tight coupling of the user interface and business logic dramatically increases maintainability risks while reducing flexibility and opportunities for re-use.

Three-Tier

A three-tier approach adds a tier that separates the business logic from the user interface. This in principle allows the business logic to be used with different user interfaces as well as with different data stores. With respect to the use of different user interfaces, users might want the same user interface but using different COTS presentation servers; for example, Java Virtual Machine (JVM) or Common Desktop Environment (CDE).[10] Similarly, if the business logic is to be used with different data stores, then each data store must use the same data model[11] (data standardization), or a mediation tier must be added above the data store (data encapsulation).

Five-Tier

To achieve maximum flexibility, software should utilize a five-tier scheme for software which extends the three-tier paradigm (see The Five-Tier Organization). The scheme is intended to provide strong separation of the three major functional areas of the architecture. Since there are client and server aspects of both the user interface and the data store, the scheme then has five tiers.[12]

The presentation tier is typically COTS-based. The presentation interface might be an X Server, Win32, etc. There should be a separate tier for the user interface client. This client establishes the look-and-feel of the interface; the server (presentation tier) actually performs the tasks by manipulating the display. The user interface client hides the presentation server from the application business logic.

The application business logic (e.g., a scheduling engine) should be a separate tier. This tier is called the "application logic" and functions as a server for the user interface client. It interfaces to the user interface typically through callbacks. The application logic tier also functions as a client to the data access tier.

If there is a user need to use an application with multiple databases with different schema, then a separate tier is needed for data access. This client would access the data stores using the appropriate COTS interface[13] and then convert the raw data into an abstract data type

---

10. This allows for the same user interface to be run on PCs, workstations, and mainframes, for example.

11. If, for example, SQL statements are to be embedded in the business logic.

12. Note that typical "layered" architectures require each layer to be a client of the layer below it and a server to the layer above it. The scheme presented here is not compliant with this description and therefore we have used the word "tier" instead of "layer".

13. The interface to the data store might utilize embedded SQL. A more flexible way would be to use the Distributed Relational Database Architecture (DRDA) or ODBC since either of these standards would enable an application to

representing parts of the information model. The interface into this object network would then provide a generalized Data Access Interface (DAI) which would hide the storage details of the data from any application that uses that data.

Each tier in this scheme can have zero or more components. The organization of the components within a tier is flexible and can reflect a number of different architectures based on need. For example, there might be many different components in the application logic tier (scheduling, accounting, inventory control, etc.) and the relationship between them can reflect whatever architecture makes sense, but none of them should be a client to the presentation server.

This clean separation of user interface, business logic, and information will result in maximum flexibility and componentized software that lends itself to product line development practices. For example, it is conceivable that the same functionality should be built once and yet be usable by different presentation servers (e.g., on PCs or UNIX system boxes), displayed with different looks and feels depending on user needs, and usable with multiple legacy databases. Moreover, this flexibility should not require massive rewrites to the software whenever a change is needed.

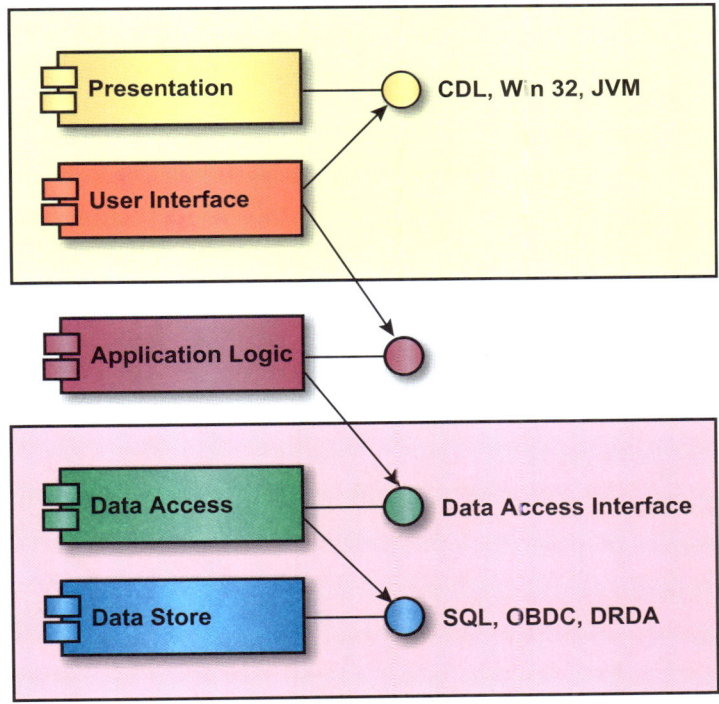

Figure 31.4: The Five-Tier Organization

Chapter 31: Developing Architecture Views

31.10.2.4 Some Uses of a Data Access Tier

The data access tier provides a standardized view of certain classes of data, and as such functions as a server to one or more application logic tiers. If implemented correctly, there would be no need for application code to "know" about the implementation details of the data. The application code would only have to know about an interface that presents a level of abstraction higher than the data. This interface is called the Data Access Interface (DAI).

For example, should a scheduling engine need to know what events are scheduled between two dates, that query should not require knowledge of tables and joins in a relational database. Moreover, the DAI could provide standardized access techniques for the data. For example, the DAI could provide a Publish and Subscribe (P&S) interface whereby systems which require access to data stores could register an interest in certain types of data, perhaps under certain conditions, and the DAI would provide the required data when those conditions occur.

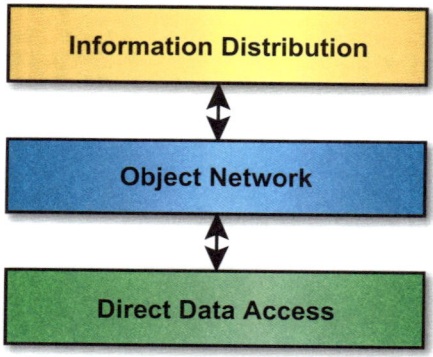

Figure 31.5 : Data Access Interface (DAI)

31.10.2.5 One Possible Instantiation of a Data Access Interface

One means to instantiate a data access component is with three layers, as is shown in Data Access Interface (DAI) . This is not the only means to build a DAI, but is presented as a possibility.

Whereas the Direct Data Access layer contains the implementation details of one or more specific data stores, the Object Network and the Information Distribution layer require no such knowledge. Instead, the upper two layers reflect the need to standardize the interface for a particular domain. The Direct Data Access layer spans the gap between the Data Access tier and the Data Store tier, and therefore has knowledge of the implementation details of the data. SQL statements, either embedded or via a standard such as DRDA or ODBC, are located here.

The Object Network layer is the instantiation in software of the information model. As such, it is an efficient means to show the relationships that hold between pieces of data. The translation of data accesses to objects in the network would be the role of the Direct Data Access layer.

Within the Information Distribution layer lies the interface to the "outside world". This interface typically uses a data bus to distribute the data (see below).[14] It could also contain various information-related services; for example, a P&S registry and publication service or an interface to a security server for data access control.[15] The Information Distribution layer might also be used to distribute applications or applets required to process distributed information. Objects in the object network would point to the applications or applets, allowing easy access to required processing code.

31.10.2.6 DAIs Enable Flexibility

The DAI enables a very flexible architecture. Multiple raw capabilities can access the same or different data stores all through the same DAI. Each DAI might be implemented in many ways, according to the specific needs of the raw capabilities using it. Multiple Uses of a Data Access Interface (DAI) illustrates a number of possibilities, including multiple different DAIs in different domains accessing the same database, a single DAI accessing multiple databases, and multiple instantiations of the same DAI access the same database.

It is not always clear that a DAI is needed, and it appears to require additional work during all phases of development. However, should a database ever be redesigned, or if an application is to be re-used and there is no control over how the new data is implemented, using a DAI saves time in the long run.

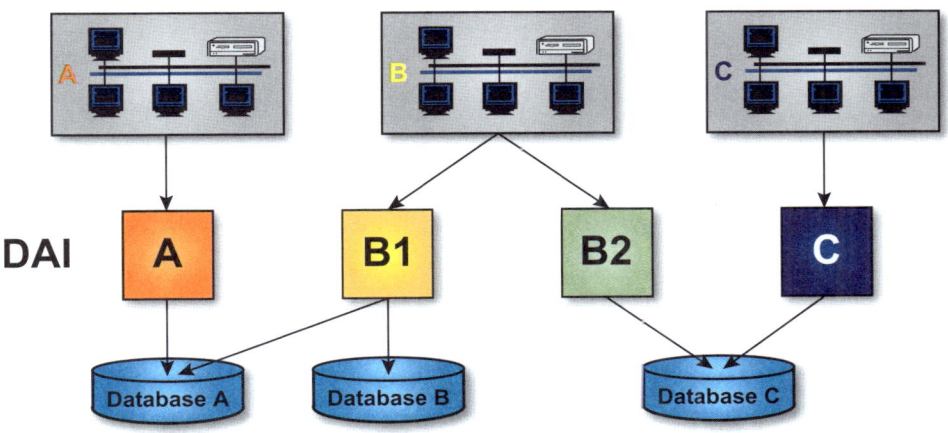

Figure 31.6: Multiple Uses of a Data Access Interface (DAI)

---

14. Although it could use other mechanisms. For example, the DAI could be built as a shared library to be linked with the application logic at compile time.

15. The security server itself would use a five-tier architecture. The security application logic tier would interface with the DAI of other systems to provide data access control.

31.10.2.7 Distribution

The ISO Reference Model for Open Distributed Processing (RM-ODP) offers a meta-standard that is intended to allow more specific standards to emerge. The RM-ODP Reference Model defines a set of distribution transparencies that are applicable to the TOGAF software engineering view.

Transparency	Definition
Access	Masks differences in data representation and invocation mechanisms to enable interworking between objects. This transparency solves many of the problems of interworking between heterogeneous systems, and will generally be provided by default.
Failure	Masks from an object the failure and possible recovery of other objects (or itself) to enable fault tolerance. When this transparency is provided, the designer can work in an idealized world in which the corresponding class of failures does not occur.
Location	Masks the use of information about location in space when identifying and binding to interfaces. This transparency provides a logical view of naming, independent of actual physical location.
Migration	Masks from an object the ability of a system to change the location of that object. Migration is often used to achieve load balancing and reduce latency.
Relocation	Masks relocation of an interface from other interfaces bound to it. Relocation allows system operation to continue even when migration or replacement of some objects creates temporary inconsistencies in the view seen by their users.
Replication	Masks the use of a group of mutually behaviorally compatible objects to support an interface. Replication is often used to enhance performance and availability.
Transaction	Masks coordination of activities amongst a configuration of objects to achieve consistency.

Table 31.3: RM-ODP Distribution Transparencies

31.10.2.8 The Infrastructure Bus

The Infrastructure Bus represents the middleware that establishes the client/server relationship. This commercial software is like a backplane onto which capabilities can be plugged. A system should adhere to a commercial implementation of a middleware standard. This is to ensure that capabilities using different commercial implementations of the standard can interoperate. If more than one commercial standard is used (e.g., COM and CORBA),

---

16. For example, many people believe that the user interface should be built on COM while the data access tiers should be built on CORBA.

then the system should allow for interoperability between implementations of these standards via the use of commercial bridging software.[16] Wherever practical, the interfaces should be specified in the appropriate Interface Description Language (IDL). Taken this way, every interface in the five-tier scheme represents an opportunity for distribution.

Clients can interact with servers via the Infrastructure Bus. In this interaction, the actual network transport (TCP/IP, HTTP, etc.), the platform/vendor of the server, and the operating system of the server are all transparent.

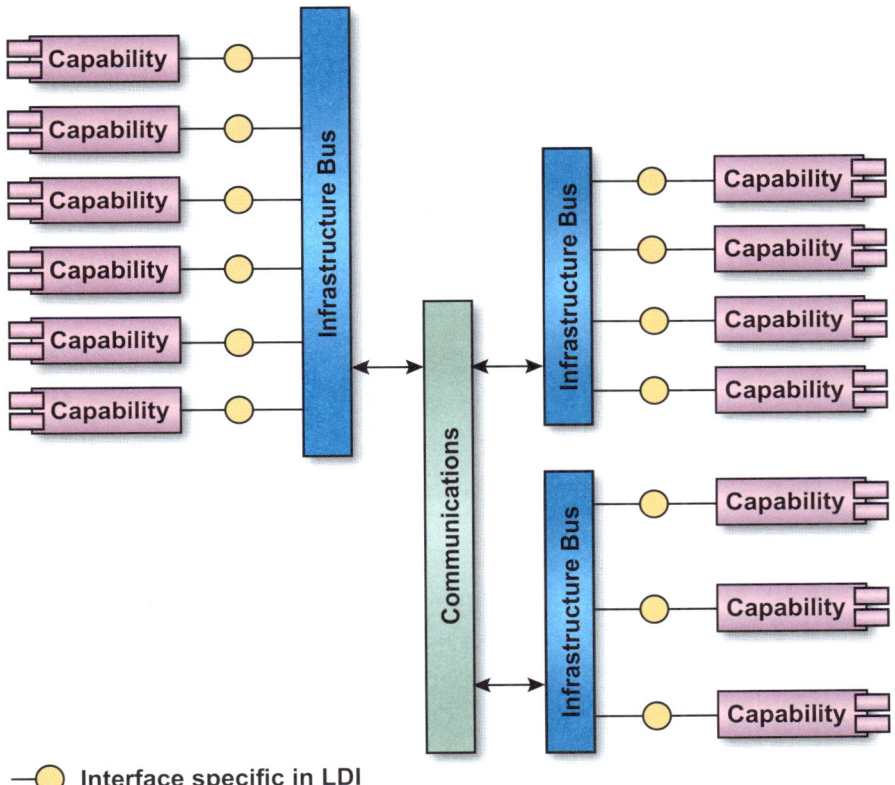

Figure 31.7: Notional Distribution Model

31.10.3 Conclusion

The software engineering view gives guidance on how to structure software in a very flexible manner. By following these guidelines, the resulting software will be componentized. This enables the re-use of components in different environments. Moreover, through the use of an infrastructure bus and clean interfaces, the resulting software will be location-independent, enabling its distribution across a network.

31.11 Developing a System Engineering View

The system engineering view is concerned with assembling software and hardware components into a working system.

31.11.1 Stakeholder and Concerns

This view should be developed for the systems engineering personnel of the system, and should focus on how the system is implemented from the perspective of hardware/software and networking.

Systems engineers are typically concerned with location, modifiability, re-usability, and availability of all components of the system. The system engineering view presents a number of different ways in which software and hardware components can be assembled into a working system. To a great extent the choice of model determines the properties of the final system. It looks at technology which already exists in the organization, and what is available currently or in the near future. This reveals areas where new technology can contribute to the function or efficiency of the new architecture, and how different types of processing platform can support different parts of the overall system.

Major concerns for this view are understanding the system requirements. In general these stakeholders are concerned with assuring that the appropriate components are developed and deployed within the system in an optimal manner.

Developing this view assists in the selection of the best configurations for the system.

31.11.2 Key Issues

This view of the architecture focuses on computing models that are appropriate for a distributed computing environment. To support the migration of legacy systems, this section also presents models that are appropriate for a centralized environment. The definitions of many of the computing models (e.g., host-based, master/slave, and three-tiered) historically preceded the definition of the client/server model, which attempts to be a general-purpose model. In most cases the models have not been redefined in the computing literature in terms of contrasts with the client/server model. Therefore, some of the distinctions of features are not always clean. In general, however, the models are distinguished by the allocation of functions for an information system application to various components (e.g., terminals, computer platforms). These functions that make up an information system application are presentation, application function, and data management.

31.11.2.1 Client/Server Model

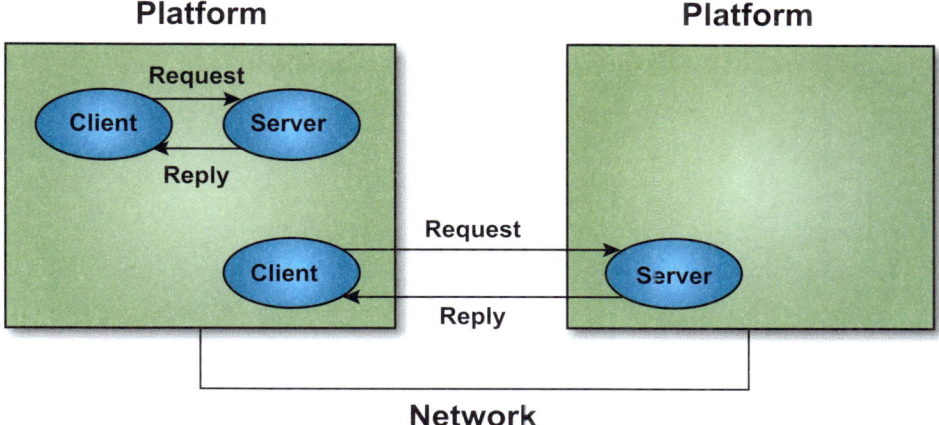

Figure 31.8: Basic Client/Server Model

Client/server processing is a special type of distributed computing termed co-operative processing because the clients and servers co-operate in the processing of a total application (presentation, functional processing, data management). In the model, clients are processes that request services, and servers are processes that provide services. Clients and servers can be located on the same processor, different multi-processor nodes, or on separate processors at remote locations. The client typically initiates communications with the server. The server typically does not initiate a request with a client. A server may support many clients and may act as a client to another server. Basic Client/Server Model depicts a basic client/server model, which emphasizes the request-reply relationships. Reference Model Representation of Client/Server Model shows the same model drawn following the TOGAF Technical Reference Model (TRM), showing how the various entities and interfaces can be used to support a client/server model, whether the server is local or remote to the client. In these representations, the request-reply relationships would be defined in the API.

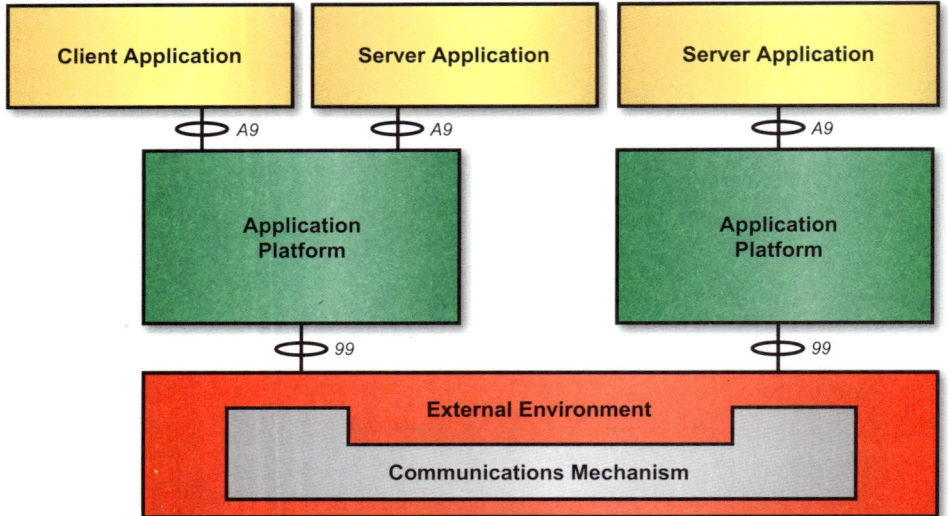

Figure 31.9: Reference Model Representation of Client/Server Model

Clients tend to be generalized and can run on one of many nodes. Servers tend to be specialized and run on a few nodes. Clients are typically implemented as a call to a routine. Servers are typically implemented as a continuous process waiting for service requests (from clients). Many client/server implementations involve remote communications across a network. However, nothing in the client/server model dictates remote communications, and the physical location of clients is usually transparent to the server. The communication between a client and a server may involve a local communication between two independent processes on the same machine.

An application program can be considered to consist of three parts:
- Data handling
- Application function
- Presentation

In general, each of these can be assigned to either a client or server application, making appropriate use of platform services. This assignment defines a specific client/server configuration.

31.11.2.2 Master/Slave and Hierarchic Models

In this model, slave computers are attached to a master computer. In terms of distribution, the master/slave model is one step up from the host-based model. Distribution is provided in one direction - from the master to the slaves. The slave computers perform application processing only when directed to by the master computer. In addition, slave processors can perform limited local processing, such as editing, function key processing, and field validation. A typical configuration might be a mainframe as the master with PCs as the slaves acting as intelligent terminals, as illustrated in Host-Based, Master/Slave, and Hierarchic Models .

The hierarchic model is an extension of the master/slave model with more distribution capabilities. In this approach, the top layer is usually a powerful mainframe, which acts as a server to the second tier. The second layer consists of LAN servers and clients to the first layer as well as servers to the third layer. The third layer consists of PCs and workstations. This model has been described as adding true distributed processing to the master/slave model. Host-Based, Master/Slave, and Hierarchic Models shows an example hierarchic model in the third configuration, and below, Hierarchic Model using the Reference Model shows the hierarchic model represented in terms of the entities and interfaces of the TRM.

31.11.2.3 Peer-to-Peer Model

In the peer-to-peer model there are co-ordinating processes. All of the computers are servers in that they can receive requests for services and respond to them; and all of the computers are clients in that they can send requests for services to other computers. In current implementations, there are often redundant functions on the participating platforms.

Attempts have been made to implement the model for distributed heterogeneous (or federated) database systems. This model could be considered a special case of the client/server model, in which all platforms are both servers and clients. Peer-to-Peer and Distributed Object Management Models (A) shows an example peer-to-peer configuration in which all platforms have complete functions.

31.11.2.4 Distributed Object Management Model

In this model the remote procedure calls typically used for communication in the client/server and other distributed processing models are replaced by messages sent to objects. The services provided by systems on a network are treated as objects. A requester need not know the details of how the object is configured. The approach requires:

- A mechanism to dispatch messages
- A mechanism to co-ordinate delivery of messages
- Applications and services that support a messaging interface

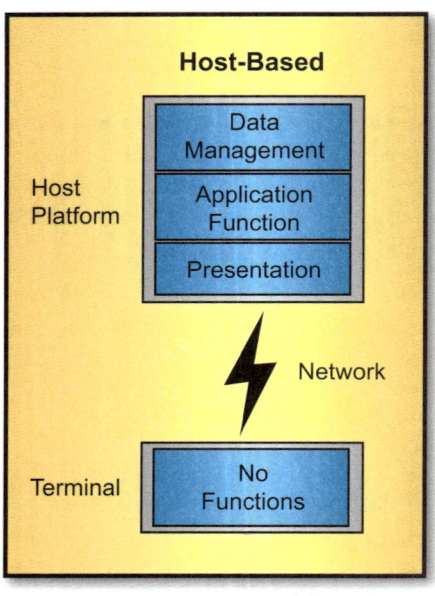
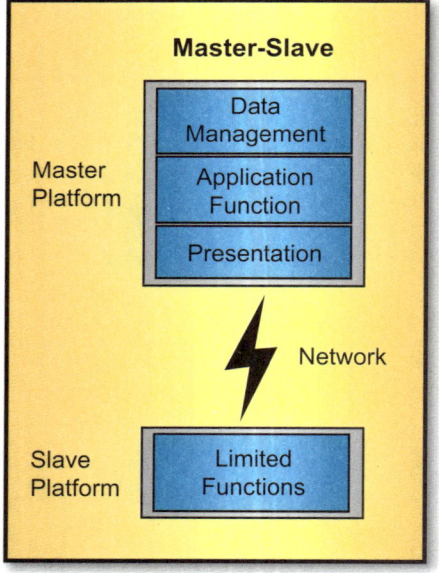
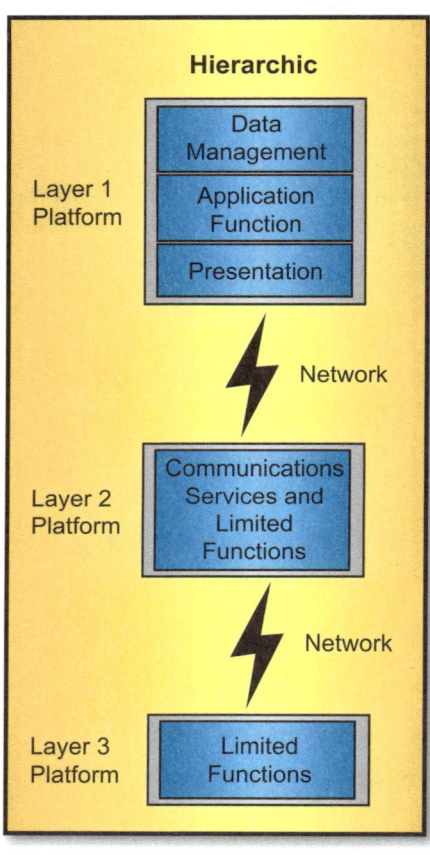

Figure 31.10: Host-Based, Master/Slave, and Hierarchic Models

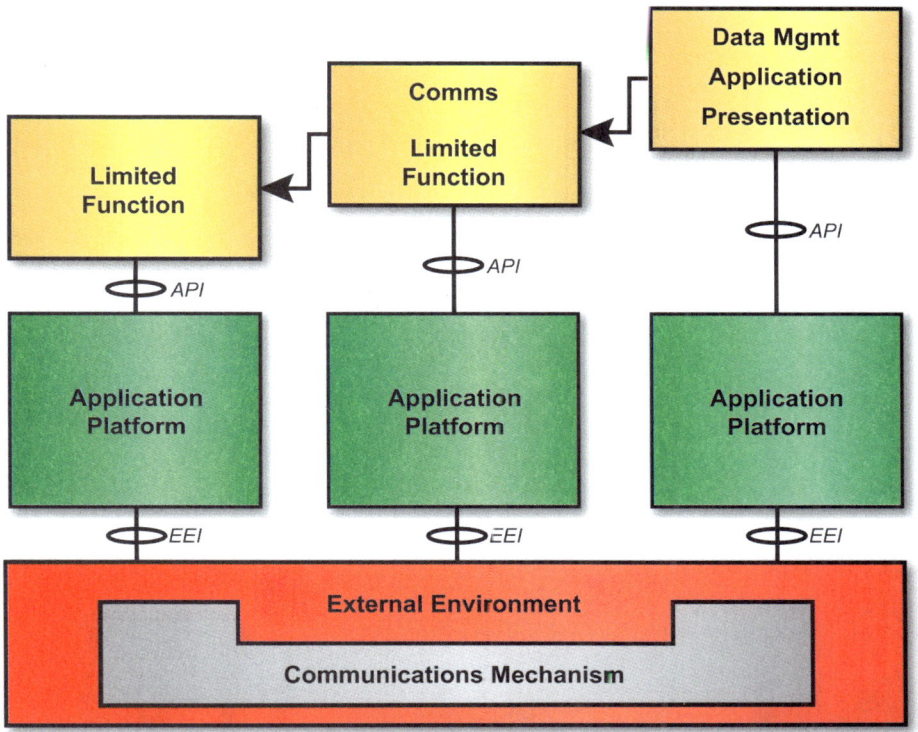

Figure 31.11: Hierarchic Model using the Reference Model

This approach does not contrast with client/server or peer-to-peer models but specifies a consistent interface for communicating between co-operating platforms. It is considered by some as an implementation approach for client/server and peer-to-peer models. Peer-to-Peer and Distributed Object Management Models presents two distributed object model examples. Example B shows how a client/server configuration would be altered to accommodate the distributed object management model. Example C shows how a peer-to-peer model would be altered to accomplish distributed object management.

The Object Management Group (OMG), a consortium of industry participants working toward object standards, has developed an architecture - the Common Object Request Broker Architecture (CORBA) - which specifies the protocol a client application must use to communicate with an Object Request Broker (ORB), which provides services. The ORB specifies how objects can transparently make requests and receive responses. In addition, Microsoft's Object Linking and Embedding (OLE) standard for Windows is an example of an implementation of distributed object management, whereby any OLE-compatible application can work with data from any other OLE-compatible application.

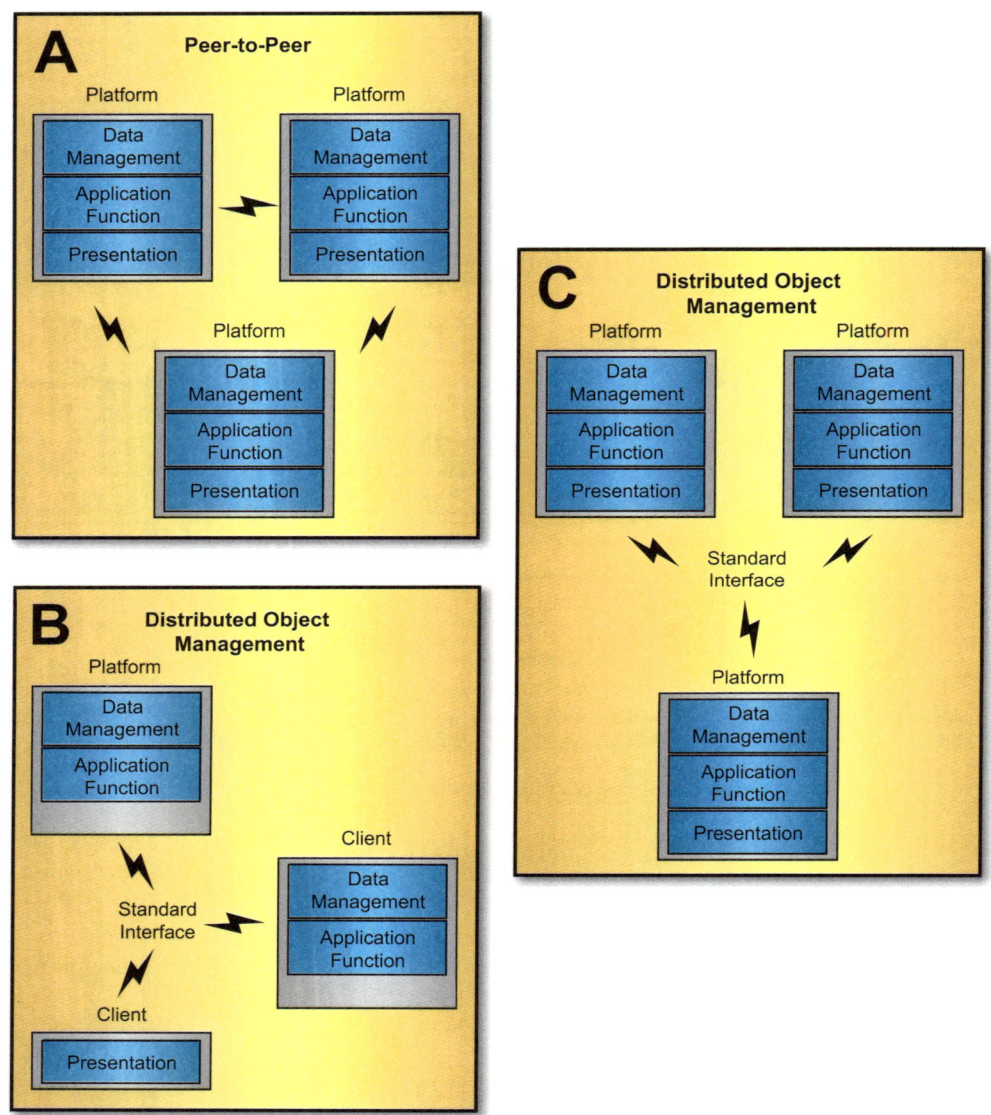

Figure 31.12: Peer-to-Peer and Distributed Object Management Models

31.12 Developing a Communications Engineering View

The communications engineering view is concerned with structuring communications and networking elements to simplify network planning and design.

31.12.1 Stakeholder and Concerns

This view should be developed for the communications engineering personnel of the system, and should focus on how the system is implemented from the perspective of the communications engineer.

Communications engineers are typically concerned with location, modifiability, re-usability, and availability of communications and networking services. Major concerns for this view are understanding the network and communications requirements. In general these stakeholders are concerned with assuring that the appropriate communications and networking services are developed and deployed within the system in an optimal manner.

Developing this view assists in the selection of the best model of communications for the system.

31.12.2 Key Issues

Communications networks are constructed of end devices (e.g., printers), processing nodes, communication nodes (switching elements), and the linking media that connect them. The communications network provides the means by which information is exchanged. Forms of information include data, imagery, voice, and video. Because automated information systems accept and process information using digital data formats rather than analogue formats, the TOGAF communications concepts and guidance will focus on digital networks and digital services. Integrated multimedia services are included.

The communications engineering view describes the communications architecture with respect to geography, discusses the Open Systems Interconnection (OSI) reference model, and describes a general framework intended to permit effective system analysis and planning.

31.12.2.1 Communications Infrastructure

The Communications Infrastructure may contain up to three levels of transport - local, regional/metropolitan, and global, as shown in Communications Infrastructure . The names of the transport components are based on their respective geographic extent, but there is also a hierarchical relationship among them. The transport components correspond to a network management structure in which management and control of network resources are distributed across the different levels.

The local components relate to assets that are located relatively close together geographically. This component contains fixed communications equipment and small units of mobile communications equipment. LANs, to which the majority of end devices will be connected, are included in this component. Standard interfaces will facilitate portability, flexibility, and interoperability of LANs and end devices.

Regional and Metropolitan Area Networks (MANs) are geographically dispersed over a large area. A regional or metropolitan network could connect local components at several fixed bases or connect separate remote outposts. In most cases, regional and metropolitan networks are used to connect local networks. However, shared databases, regional processing platforms, and network management centers may connect directly or through a LAN. Standard interfaces will be provided to connect local networks and end devices.

Global or Wide Area Networks (WANs) are located throughout the world, providing connectivity for regional and metropolitan networks in the fixed and deployed environment. In addition, mobile units, shared databases, and central processing centers can connect directly to the global network as required. Standard interfaces will be provided to connect regional and metropolitan networks and end devices.

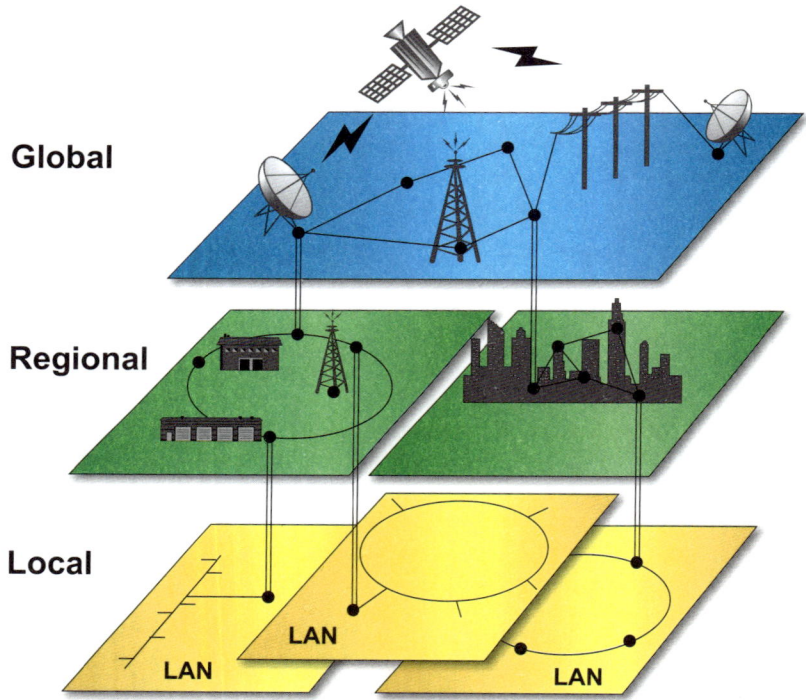

Figure 31.13: Communications Infrastructure

31.12.2.2 Communications Models

The geographically divided infrastructure described above forms the foundation for an overall communications framework. These geographic divisions permit the separate application of different management responsibilities, planning efforts, operational functions, and enabling technologies to be applied within each area. Hardware and software components and services fitted to the framework form the complete model.

The following sections describe the OSI Reference Model and a grouping of the OSI layers that facilitates discussion of interoperability issues.

The OSI Reference Model

The Open Systems Interconnection (OSI) Reference Model, portrayed in OSI Reference Model, is the model used for data communications in TOGAF. Each of the seven layers in the model represents one or more services or protocols (a set of rules governing communications between systems), which define the functional operation of the communications between user and network elements. Each layer (with the exception of the top layer) provides services for the layer above it. This model aims at establishing open systems operation and implies standards-based implementation. It strives to permit different systems to accomplish complete interoperability and quality of operation throughout the network.

The seven layers of the OSI model are structured to facilitate independent development within each layer and to provide for changes independent of other layers. Stable international standard protocols in conformance with the OSI Reference Model layer definitions have been published by various standards organizations. This is not to say that the only protocols which fit into TOGAF are OSI protocols. Other protocol standards such as SNA or TCP/IP can be described using the OSI seven layer model as a reference.

Support and business area applications, as defined in TOGAF, are above the OSI Reference Model protocol stack and use its services via the applications layer.

Communications Framework

A communications system based on the OSI Reference Model includes services in all the relevant layers, the support and business area application software which sits above the application layer of the OSI Reference Model, and the physical equipment carrying the data. These elements may be grouped into architectural levels that represent major functional capabilities, such as switching and routing, data transfer, and the performance of applications.

These architectural levels are:

- The Transmission level (below the physical layer of the OSI Reference Model) provides all of the physical and electronic capabilities, which establish a transmission path between functional system elements (wires, leased circuits, interconnects, etc.).
- The Network Switching level (OSI layers 1 through 3) establishes connectivity through the network elements to support the routing and control of traffic (switches, controllers, network software, etc.).
- The Data Exchange level (OSI layers 4 through 7) accomplishes the transfer of information after the network has been established (end-to-end, user-to-user transfer) involving more capable processing elements (hosts, workstations, servers, etc.).

In the TRM, OSI application layer services are considered to be part of the Application Platform entity, since they offer standardized interfaces to the application programming entity.

- The Applications Program level (above the OSI) includes the support and business area applications (non-management application programs).

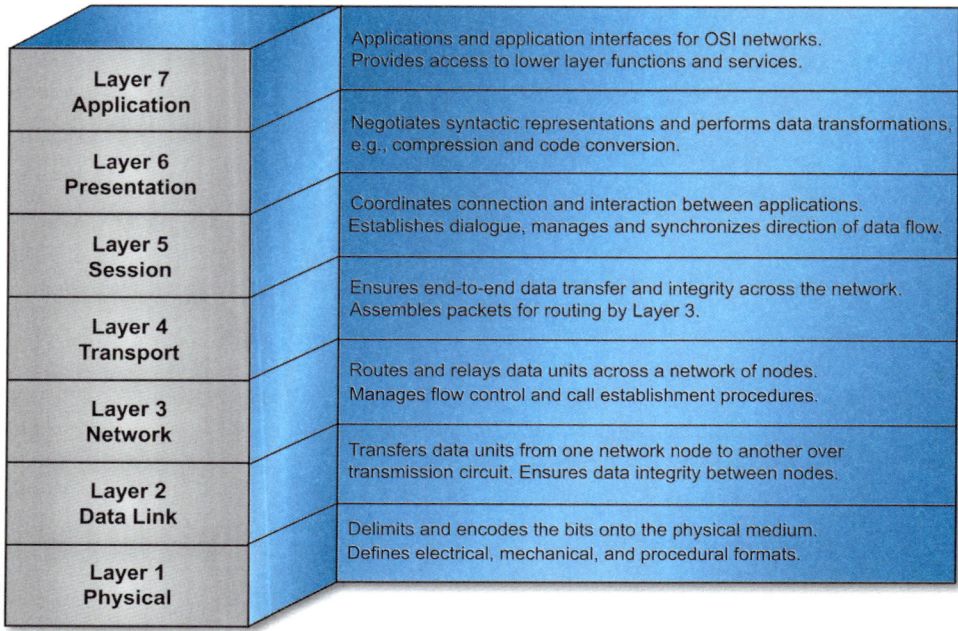

Figure 31.14: OSI Reference Model

The communications framework is defined to consist of the three geographical components of the Communications Infrastructure (local, regional, and global) and the four architectural levels (Transmission, Network Switching, Data Exchange, and Applications Program), and is depicted in Communications Framework . Communications services are performed at one or more of these architectural levels within the geographical components. Communications Framework shows computing elements (operating at the Applications Program level) with supporting Data Exchange elements, linked with each other through various switching elements (operating at the Network Switching level), each located within its respective geographical component. Communications Framework also identifies the relationship of TOGAF to the communication architecture.

Allocation of Services to Components

The Communications Infrastructure consists of the local, regional, and global transport components. The services allocated to these components are identical to the services of the Application Program, Data Exchange, Network Switching, or Transmission architectural levels that apply to a component. Data Exchange and Network Switching level services are identical to the services of the corresponding OSI Reference Model layers. Typically, only Network Switching and Transmission services are allocated to the regional and global components, which consist of communications nodes and transmission media. All services may be performed in the local component, which includes end devices, processing nodes, communications nodes, and linking media. Transmission, switching, transport, and applications are all performed in this component.

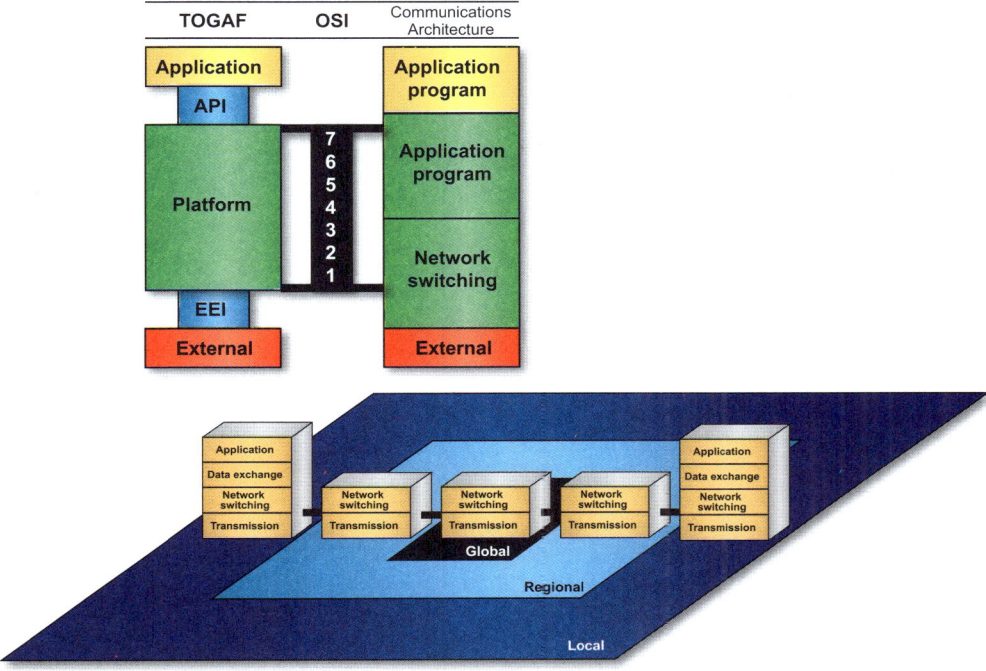

Figure 31.15: Communications Framework

31.13 Developing a Data Flow View

The data flow view is concerned with storage, retrieval, processing, archiving, and security of data.

31.13.1 Stakeholder and Concerns

This view should be developed for database engineers of the system.

Major concerns for this view are understanding how to provide data to the right people and applications with the right interfaces at the right time. This view deals with the architecture of the storage, retrieval, processing, archiving, and security of data. It looks at the flow of data as it is stored and processed, and at what components will be required to support and manage both storage and processing. In general these stakeholders are concerned with assuring ubiquitous access to high quality data.

31.13.2 Modeling the View

The subjects of the general architecture of a "database system" are database components or components that provide database services.

The modeling of a "database" is typically done with entity-relationship diagrams and schema definitions, including document type definitions.

31.13.3 Key Issues

Data management services may be provided by a wide range of implementations. Some examples are:

- Mega-centers providing functionally-oriented corporate databases supporting local and remote data requirements
- Distributed DBMSs that support the interactive use of partitioned and partially replicated databases
- File systems provided by operating systems, which may be used by both interactive and batch processing applications

Data management services include the storage, retrieval, manipulation, backup, restart/recovery, security, and associated functions for text, numeric data, and complex data such as documents, graphics, images, audio, and video. The operating system provides file management services, but they are considered here because many legacy databases exist as one or more files without the services provided by a DBMS.

Major components that provide data management services that are discussed in this section are:

- Database Management Systems (see Database Management Systems)
- Data Dictionary/Directory Systems (see Data Dictionary/Directory Systems)
- Data Administration (see Data Administration)
- Data Security (see Data Security)

These are critical aspects of data management for the following reasons. The DBMS is the most critical component of any data management capability, and a data dictionary/directory system is necessary in conjunction with the DBMS as a tool to aid the administration of the database. Data security is a necessary part of any overall policy for security in information processing.

31.13.3.1 Database Management Systems

A Database Management System (DBMS) provides for the systematic management of data. This data management component provides services and capabilities for defining the data, structuring the data, accessing the data, as well as security and recovery of the data. A DBMS performs the following functions:

- Structures data in a consistent way
- Provides access to the data
- Minimizes duplication

- Allows reorganization; that is, changes in data content, structure, and size
- Supports programming interfaces
- Provides security and control

A DBMS must provide:

- Persistence; the data continues to exist after the application's execution has completed
- Secondary storage management
- Concurrency
- Recovery
- Data Definition/Data Manipulation Language (DDL/DML), which may be a graphical interface

Database Models

The logical data model that underlies the database characterizes a DBMS. The common logical data models are as follows:

- The Relational Model

    A Relational Database Management System (RDBMS) structures data into tables that have certain properties:

    - Each row in the table is distinct from every other row.
    - Each row contains only atomic data; that is, there is no repeating data or such structures as arrays.
    - Each column in the relational table defines named data fields or attributes.

    A collection of related tables in the relational model makes up a database. The mathematical theory of relations underlies the relational model - both the organization of data and the languages that manipulate the data. Edgar Codd, then at IBM, developed the relational model in 1973. It has been popular, in terms of commercial use, since the early 1980s.

- The Hierarchical Model

    The hierarchical data model organizes data in a tree structure. There is a hierarchy of parent and child data segments. This structure implies that a record can have repeating information, generally in the child data segments. For example, an organization might store information about an employee, such as name, employee number, department, salary. The organization might also store information about an employee's children, such as name and date of birth. The employee and children data forms a hierarchy, where the employee data represents the parent segment and the children data represents the child segment. If an employee has three children, then there would be three child segments associated with one employee segment. In a hierarchical database the parent-child relationship is one-to-many. This restricts a child segment to having only one parent segment. Hierarchical DBMSs were popular from the late 1960s, with the introduction of IBM's Information Management System (IMS) DBMS, through the 1970s.

- **The Network Model**

  The popularity of the network data model coincided with the popularity of the hierarchical data model. Some data was more naturally modeled with more than one parent per child. So, the network model permitted the modeling of many-to-many relationships in data. In 1971, the Conference on Data Systems Languages (CODASYL) formally defined the network model. The basic data modeling construct in the network model is the set construct. A set consists of an owner record type, a set name, and a member record type. A member record type can have that role in more than one set, hence the multi-parent concept is supported. An owner record type can also be a member or owner in another set. The CODASYL network model is based on mathematical set theory.

- **The Object-Oriented Model**

  An Object-Oriented Database Management System (OODBMS) must be both a DBMS and an object-oriented system. As a DBMS it must provide the capabilities identified above. OODBMSs typically can model tabular data, complex data, hierarchical data, and networks of data. The following are important features of an object-oriented system:

  - Complex objects: e.g., objects may be composed of other objects.
  - Object identity: each object has a unique identifier external to the data.
  - Encapsulation: an object consists of data and the programs (or methods) that manipulate it.
  - Types or classes: a class is a collection of similar objects.
  - Inheritance: subclasses inherit data attributes and methods from classes.
  - Overriding with late binding: the method particular to a subclass can override the method of a class at run time.
  - Extensibility: e.g., a user may define new objects.
  - Computational completeness: a general-purpose language (such as Ada, C, or C++) is computationally complete. The special-purpose language SQL is not. Most OODBMSs incorporate a general-purpose programming language.

- **Flat Files**

  A flat file system is usually closely associated with a storage access method. An example is IBM's Indexed Sequential Access Method (ISAM). The models discussed earlier in this section are logical data models; flat files require the user to work with the physical layout of the data on a storage device. For example, the user must know the exact location of a data item in a record. In addition, flat files do not provide all of the services of a DBMS, such as naming of data, elimination of redundancy, and concurrency control. Further, there is no independence of the data and the application program. The application program must know the physical layout of the data.

Distributed DBMSs

A distributed DBMS manages a database that is spread over more than one platform. The database can be based on any of the data models discussed above (except the flat file). The database can be replicated, partitioned, or a combination of both. A replicated database is one in which full or partial copies of the database exist on the different platforms. A partitioned database is one in which part of the database is on one platform and parts are on other platforms. The partitioning of a database can be vertical or horizontal. A vertical partitioning puts some fields and the associated data on one platform and some fields and the associated data on another platform. For example, consider a database with the following fields: employee ID, employee name, department, number of dependents, project assigned, salary rate, tax rate. One vertical partitioning might place employee ID, number of dependents, salary rate, and tax rate on one platform and employee name, department, and project assigned on another platform. A horizontal partitioning might keep all the fields on all the platforms but distribute the records. For example, a database with 100,000 records might put the first 50,000 records on one platform and the second 50,000 records on a second platform.

Whether the distributed database is replicated or partitioned, a single DBMS manages the database. There is a single schema (description of the data in a database in terms of a data model; e.g., relational) for a distributed database. The distribution of the database is generally transparent to the user. The term "distributed DBMS" implies homogeneity.

Distributed Heterogeneous DBMSs

A distributed, heterogeneous database system is a set of independent databases, each with its own DBMS, presented to users as a single database and system. "Federated" is used synonymously with "distributed heterogeneous". The heterogeneity refers to differences in data models (e.g., network and relational), DBMSs from different suppliers, different hardware platforms, or other differences. The simplest kinds of federated database systems are commonly called gateways. In a gateway, one vendor (e.g., Oracle) provides single-direction access through its DBMS to another database managed by a different vendor's DBMS (e.g., IBM's DB2). The two DBMSs need not share the same data model. For example, many RDBMS vendors provide gateways to hierarchical and network DBMSs.

There are federated database systems both on the market and in research that provide more general access to diverse DBMSs. These systems generally provide a schema integration component to integrate the schemas of the diverse databases and present them to the users as a single database, a query management component to distribute queries to the different DBMSs in the federation, and a transaction management component, to distribute and manage the changes to the various databases in the federation.

31.13.3.2 Data Dictionary/Directory Systems

The second component providing data management services, the Data Dictionary/Directory System (DD/DS), consists of utilities and systems necessary to catalog, document, manage, and use metadata (data about data). An example of metadata is the following definition: a six-character long alphanumeric string, for which the first character is a letter of the alphabet and each of the remaining five characters is an integer between 0 and 9; the name for the string is "employee ID" . The DD/DS utilities make use of special files that contain the database schema. (A schema, using metadata, defines the content and structure of a database.) This schema is represented by a set of tables resulting from the compilation of Data Definition Language (DDL) statements. The DD/DS is normally provided as part of a DBMS but is sometimes available from alternate sources. In the management of distributed data, distribution information may also be maintained in the network directory system. In this case, the interface between the DD/DS and the network directory system would be through the API of the network services component on the platform.

In current environments, data dictionaries are usually integrated with the DBMS, and directory systems are typically limited to a single platform. Network directories are used to expand the DD/DS realms. The relationship between the DD/DS and the network directory is an intricate combination of physical and logical sources of data.

13.13.3.3 Data Administration

Data administration properly addresses the Data Architecture, which is outside the scope of TOGAF. We discuss it briefly here because of areas of overlap. It is concerned with all of the data resources of an enterprise, and as such there are overlaps with data management, which addresses data in databases. Two specific areas of overlap are the repository and database administration, which are discussed briefly below.

Repository

A repository is a system that manages all of the data of an enterprise, which includes data and process models and other enterprise information. Hence, the data in a repository is much more extensive than that in a DD/DS, which generally defines only the data making up a database.

Database Administration

Data administration and database administration are complementary processes. Data administration is responsible for data, data structure, and integration of data and processes. Database administration, on the other hand, includes the physical design, development, implementation, security, and maintenance of the physical databases. Database administration is responsible for managing and enforcing the enterprise's policies related to individual databases.

31.13.3.4 Data Security

The third component providing data management services is data security. This includes procedures and technology measures implemented to prevent unauthorized access, modification, use, and dissemination of data stored or processed by a computer system. Data security also includes data integrity (i.e., preserving the accuracy and validity of the data), and protecting the system from physical harm (including preventive measures and recovery procedures).

Authorization control allows only authorized users to have access to the database at the appropriate level. Guidelines and procedures can be established for accountability, levels of control, and type of control. Authorization control for database systems differs from that in traditional file systems because, in a database system, it is not uncommon for different users to have different rights to the same data. This requirement encompasses the ability to specify subsets of data and to distinguish between groups of users. In addition, decentralized control of authorizations is of particular importance for distributed systems.

Data protection is necessary to prevent unauthorized users from understanding the content of the database. Data encryption, as one of the primary methods for protecting data, is useful for both information stored on disk and for information exchanged on a network.

31.14 Developing an Enterprise Manageability View

The enterprise manageability view is concerned with operations, administration, and management of the system.

31.14.1 Stakeholders and Concerns

This view should be developed for the operations, administration, and management personnel of the system.

Major concerns for these stakeholders are understanding how the system is managed as a whole, and how all components of the system are managed. The key concern is managing change in the system and predicting necessary preventative maintenance.

In general these stakeholders are concerned with assuring that the availability of the system does not suffer when changes occur. Managing the system includes managing components such as:

- Security components
- Data assets
- Software assets
- Hardware assets
- Networking assets

31.14.2 Modeling the View

Business scenarios are an extremely useful way to depict what should happen when planned and unplanned events occur. It is highly recommended that business scenarios be created for planned change, and for unplanned change.

The following paragraphs describe some of the key issues that the architect might consider when constructing business scenarios.

31.14.3 Key Issues

The enterprise manageability view acts as a check and balance on the difficulties and day-to-day running costs of systems built within the new architecture. Often, system management is not considered until after all the important purchasing and development decisions have been taken, and taking a separate management view at an early stage in architecture development is one way to avoid this pitfall. It is good practice to develop the enterprise manageability view with close consideration of the system engineering view, since in general management is difficult to retrofit into an existing design.

Key elements of the enterprise manageability view are:

- The policies, procedures, and guidelines that drive your management requirements (such as a policy to restrict downloading software from the Internet)
- How your shop measures system availability
- The management services and utilities required
- The likely quantity, quality, and location of management and support personnel
- The ability of users to take on system management tasks, such as password maintenance
- The manageability of existing and planned components in each of the component categories
- Whether management should be centralized or distributed
- Whether security is the responsibility of system managers or a separate group, bearing in mind any legal requirements

Key technical components categories that are the subject of the enterprise manageability view deal with change, either planned upgrades, or unplanned outages. The following table lists specific concerns for each component category.

Component Category	Planned Change Considerations	Unplanned Change Considerations
Security Components	How is a security change propagated throughout the system? Who is responsible for making changes; end users, or security stewards?	What should happen when security is breached? What should happen if a security component fails?
Data Assets	How are new data elements added? How is data imported/exported or loaded/unloaded? How is backup managed while running continuously? How is data change propagated in a distributed environment?	What are the backup procedures and are all the system capabilities there to backup in time?
Software Assets	How is a new application introduced into the systems? What procedures are there to control software quality? How are application changes propagated in a distributed environment? How is unwanted software introduction restricted given the Internet?	What do you want to happen when an application fails? What do you want to happen when a resource of the application fails?
Hardware Assets	How do you assess the impact of new hardware on the system, especially network load?	What do you want to happen when hardware outages occur?
Networking Assets	How do you assess the impact of new networking components?	How do you optimize your networking components?

31.15 Developing an Acquirer's View

The Acquirer's view is concerned with acquiring Commercial Off-The-Shelf (COTS) software and hardware.

31.15.1 Stakeholders and Concerns

This view should be developed for personnel involved in the acquisition of any components of the subject architecture.

Major concerns for these stakeholders are understanding what building blocks of the architecture can be bought, and what constraints (or rules) exist that are relevant to the purchase. The acquirer will shop with multiple vendors looking for the best cost solution while adhering to the constraints (or rules) applied by the architecture, such as standards.

The key concern is to make purchasing decisions that fit the architecture, and thereby to reduce the risk of added costs arising from non-compliant components.

31.15.2 Modeling the View

The Acquirer's view is normally represented as an architecture of Solution Building Blocks (SBBs), supplemented by views of the standards to be adhered to by individual building blocks.

31.15.3 Key Issues

The acquirer typically executes a process similar to the one below. Within the step descriptions we can see the concerns and issues that the acquirer faces.

Procurement Process Steps	Step Description and Output
Acquisition Planning	Creates the plan for the purchase of some component. For IT systems the following considerations are germane to building blocks. This step requires access to Architecture Building Blocks (ABBs) and Solution Building Blocks (SBBs). • The procurer needs to know what ABBs apply constraints (standards) for use in assessment and for creation of RFP/RFIs. • The procurer needs to know what candidate SBBs adhere to these standards. • The procurer also needs to know what suppliers provide accepted SBBs and where they have been deployed. • The procurer needs to know what budget this component was given relative to the overall system cost.
Concept Exploration	In this step the procurer looks at the viability of the concept. Building blocks give the planner a sense of the risk involved; if many ABBs or SBBs exist that match the concept, the risk is lower. This step requires access to ABBs and SBBs. The planner needs to know what ABBs apply constraints (standards), and needs to know what candidate SBBs adhere to these standards.
Concept Demonstration and Validation	In this step, the procurer works with development to prototype an implementation. The procurer recommends the re-usable SBBs based upon standards fit, and past experience with suppliers.\\ This step requires access to re-usable SBBs.
Development	In this step the procurer works with development to manage the relationship with the vendors supplying the SBBs. Building blocks that are proven to be fit-for-purpose get marked as approved. This step requires an update of the status to "procurement approved" of an SBB.

Procurement Process Steps	Step Description and Output
Production	In this step, the procurer works with development to manage the relationship with the vendors supplying the SBBs. Building blocks that are put into production get marked appropriately

This step requires an update of the status to "in production" of SBBs, with the system identifier of where the building block is being developed.. |
| Deployment | In this step, the procurer works with development to manage the relationship with the vendors supplying the SBBs. Building blocks that are fully deployed get marked appropriately.

This step requires an update of the status to "deployed" of SBBs, with the system identifier of where the building block was deployed. |

Chapter 32: Building Blocks

This chapter explains the concept of building blocks and contains a fictional example illustrating building blocks in architecture.

32.1 Overview

This section is intended to explain and illustrate the concept of building blocks in architecture.

Following this overview, there are three main parts.

- The first part, Introduction to Building Blocks (Introduction to Building Blocks), discusses the general concepts of building blocks, and explains the differences between Architecture Building Blocks (ABBs) and Solution Building Blocks (SBBs).
- The second, Building Blocks and the ADM (Building Blocks and the ADM), summarizes the stages at which building block design and specification occurs within the TOGAF Architecture Development Method (ADM).
- The third part, Building Blocks Example (see Building Blocks Example), comprises a series of separate subsections that together provide a detailed worked example showing how building block context is captured, how building blocks are identified, and how building blocks are defined when executing the major steps of the ADM.

32.2 Introduction to Building Blocks

This section is an introduction to the concept of building blocks.

32.2.1 Overview

This subsection describes the characteristics of building blocks. The use of building blocks in the ADM is described separately in Building Blocks and the ADM.

32.2.2 Generic Characteristics

Building blocks have generic characteristics as follows:

- A building block is a package of functionality defined to meet the business needs across an organization.
- A building block has published interfaces to access the functionality.
- A building block may interoperate with other, inter-dependent, building blocks.
- A good building block has the following characteristics:
    - It considers implementation and usage, and evolves to exploit technology and standards.

- It may be assembled from other building blocks.
- It may be a subassembly of other building blocks.
- Ideally a building block is re-usable and replaceable, and well. specified.

■ A building block may have multiple implementations but with different inter-dependent building blocks.

A building block is therefore simply a package of functionality defined to meet business needs. The way in which functionality, products, and custom developments are assembled into building blocks will vary widely between individual architectures. Every organization must decide for itself what arrangement of building blocks works best for it. A good choice of building blocks can lead to improvements in legacy system integration, interoperability, and flexibility in the creation of new systems and applications.

Systems are built up from collections of building blocks, so most building blocks have to interoperate with other building blocks. Wherever that is true, it is important that the interfaces to a building block are published and reasonably stable.

Building blocks can be defined at various levels of detail, depending on what stage of architecture development has been reached.

For instance, at an early stage, a building block can simply consist of a grouping of functionality such as a customer database and some retrieval tools. Building blocks at this functional level of definition are described in TOGAF as Architecture Building Blocks (ABBs). Later on, real products or specific custom developments replace these simple definitions of functionality, and the building blocks are then described as Solution Building Blocks (SBBs).

More detail on each of these aspects of building blocks is given below.

32.2.3 Architecture Building Blocks

Architecture Building Blocks (ABBs) relate to the Architecture Continuum (The Architecture Continuum), and are defined or selected as a result of the application of the ADM.

32.2.3.1 Characteristics

ABBs:

- Define what functionality will be implemented
- Capture business and technical requirements
- Are technology aware
- Direct and guide the development of SBBs

32.2.3.2 Specification Content

ABB specifications include the following as a minimum:

- Fundamental functionality and attributes: semantic, unambiguous, including security capability and manageability
- Interfaces: chosen set, supplied (APIs, data formats, protocols, hardware interfaces, standards)
- Dependent building blocks with required functionality and named user interfaces
- Map to business/organizational entities and policies

32.2.4 Solution Building Blocks

Solution Building Blocks (SBBs) relate to the Solutions Continuum (The Solutions Continuum), and may be either procured or developed.

32.2.4.1 Characteristics

SBBs:

- Define what products and components will implement the functionality
- Define the implementation
- Fulfil business requirements
- Are product or vendor-aware

32.2.4.2 Specification Content

SBB specifications include the following as a minimum:

- Specific functionality and attributes
- Interfaces; the implemented set
- Required SBBs used with required functionality and names of the interfaces used
- Mapping from the SBBs to the IT topology and operational policies
- Specifications of attributes shared across the environment (not to be confused with functionality) such as security, manageability, localizability, scalability
- Performance, configurability
- Design drivers and constraints, including the physical architecture
- Relationships between SBBs and ABBs

32.3 Building Blocks and the ADM

32.3.1 Basic Principles

This section focuses on the use of building blocks in the ADM. General considerations and characteristics of building blocks are described in Introduction to Building Blocks .

32.3.1.1 Building Blocks in Architecture Design

An architecture is a set of building blocks depicted in an architectural model, and a specification of how those building blocks are connected to meet the overall requirements of an information system.

The various building blocks in an architecture specify the services required in an enterprise-specific system.

There are some general principles underlying the use of building blocks in the design of specific architectures:

- An architecture need only contain building blocks to implement those services that it requires.
- Building blocks may implement one, more than one, or only part of a service identified in the architecture framework.
- Building blocks should conform to standards relevant to the services they implement.

32.3.1.2 Building Block Design

The process of identifying building blocks includes looking for collections of functions which require integration to draw them together or make them different:

- Consider three classes of building blocks:
    - Re-usable building blocks such as legacy items
    - Building blocks to be the subject of development, such as new applications
    - Building blocks to be the subject of purchase; i.e., Commercial Off-The-Shelf (COTS) applications
- Use the desired level of integration to bind or combine functions into building blocks. For instance, legacy elements could be treated as large building blocks to avoid breaking them apart.

In the early stages and during views of the highest-level enterprise, the building blocks are often kept at a broad integration definition. It is during these exercises that the services definitions can often be best viewed. As implementation considerations are addressed, more detailed views of building blocks can often be used to address implementation decisions, focus on the critical strategic decisions, or aid in assessing the value and future impact of commonality and re-usability.

32.3.2 Building Block Specification Process in the ADM

The process of building block definition takes place gradually as the ADM is followed, mainly in Phases A, B, C, and D. It is an iterative process because as definition proceeds, detailed information about the functionality required, the constraints imposed on the architecture, and the availability of products may affect the choice and the content of building blocks.

The key parts of the ADM at which building blocks are designed and specified are summarized below.

The major work in these steps consists of identifying the ABBs required to meet the business goals and objectives. The selected set of ABBs is then refined in an iterative process to arrive at a set of SBBs which can either be bought off-the-shelf or custom developed.

The specification of building blocks using the ADM is an evolutionary and iterative process. The key phases and steps of the ADM at which building blocks are evolved and specified are summarized below, and illustrated in Key Phases/Steps of ADM at which Building Blocks are Evolved/Specified .

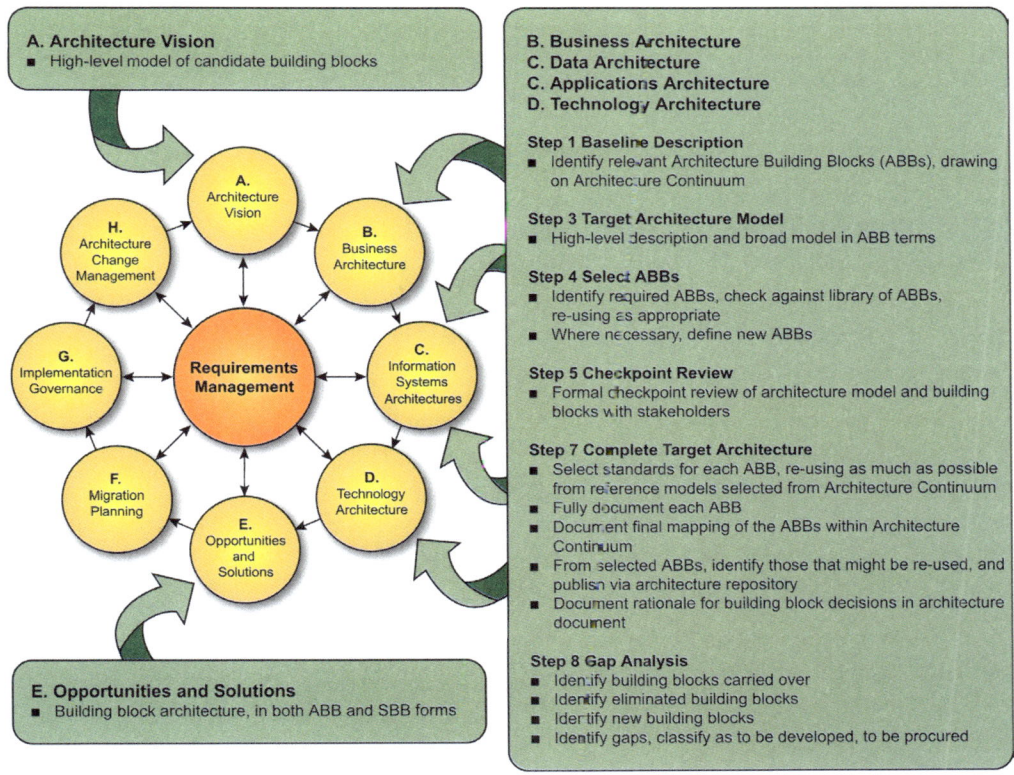

Figure 32.1:
Key Phases/Steps of ADM at which Building Blocks are Evolved/Specified

In Phase A the earliest building block definitions start as relatively abstract entities within the Architecture Vision.

In Phases B, C, and D building blocks within the Business, Data, Applications, and Technology Architectures are evolved to a common pattern of steps:

- Step 1, Baseline Description produces:
    - A list of candidate building blocks, from the analysis of the baseline
- Step 3, Target Architecture Model, takes this list and high-level model as inputs, and evolves them iteratively into a definition of the Target Architecture, specified in terms of ABBs. Specifically, Step 3 produces:
    - A high-level description and broad model of the target system in terms of ABBs
    - A rationale for each building block decision
- Step 4, Services Portfolio, produces:
    - For each ABB, a service description portfolio, built up as a set of non-conflicting services
- Step 5, Business Goals and Objectives, produces:
    - A confirmation of the merit and completeness of the model and service description portfolio, and a description of how the emerging Target Architecture meets the objectives of the architecture development
- Step 7, Architecture Definition, produces:
    - A Target Architecture, fully specified in terms of ABBs
    - A fully defined (by service) list of all the standards that make up the Target Architecture, and all the ABBs that will be used to implement it
    - A diagrammatic depiction of the building blocks at the levels needed to describe the strategic and implementation aspects of the architecture
- Step 8, Gap Analysis, produces:
    - A gap analysis of eliminated building blocks, carried over building blocks, and new building blocks

Finally, in Phase E the building blocks become more implementation-specific as SBBs, and their interfaces become the detailed architecture specification. The output of Phase E is the building block architecture, both in ABB (i.e., functionally defined) and SBB (i.e., product-specific) forms.

The minimum contents of an ABB specification and a SBB specification are described in Introduction to Building Blocks .

32.3.3 Levels of Modeling

Defining and developing the context for a set of building blocks takes place at two levels:

- The business process level (colored green in the diagrams in this section). This deals only at the highest level with what has to happen for a business process to be carried out.
- The technical functionality and constraints level (colored blue in the diagrams). This level deals with the component activities that form part of the business process and whether they can be supported or not.

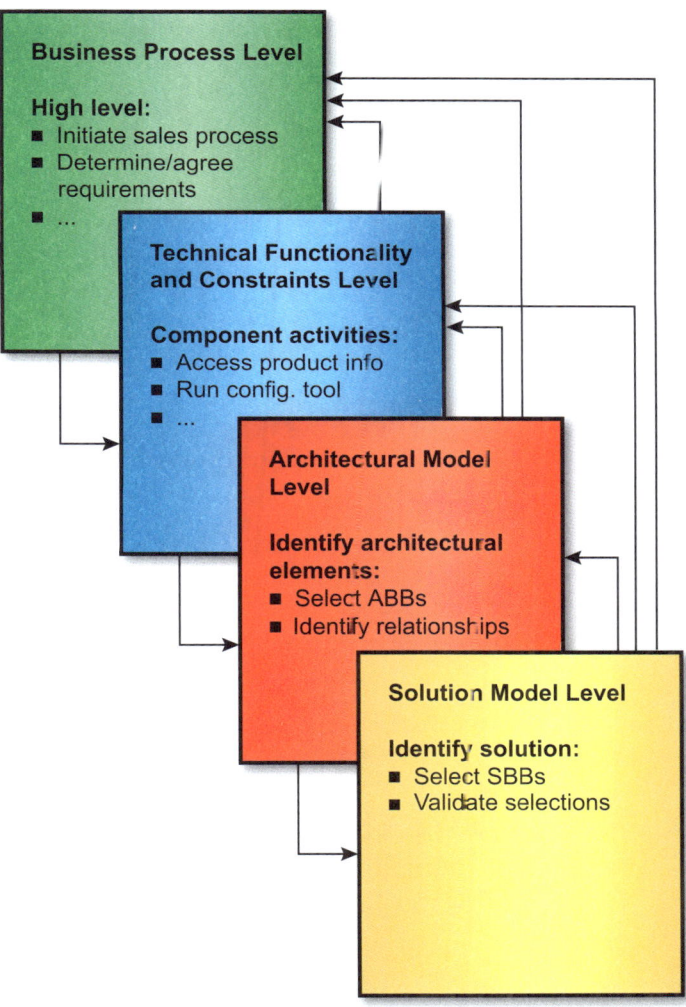

Figure 32.2: Iteration between the Four Levels of Modeling

Defining and developing an actual set of building blocks also takes place at two levels:

- The architectural model level (colored red in the diagrams). This level identifies the systems and components that will implement the technical functionality and expresses the relationships between them. This level introduces the idea of a notation to describe the architectural elements and relationships.
- The solution model level (colored black in the diagrams). This is the level where the individual products and/or product components that will implement the architecture are identified.

Working through the four levels is an iterative process. Iteration between the Four Levels of Modeling shows how considerations at any level can result in change at any or all of the other levels.

32.3.3.1 Mapping the Modeling Levels to the ADM

The Business Process level of definition takes place in Phases A and B of the ADM.

The Technical Functionality and Constraints level work happens early in Phases B, C, and D, once the characteristics of the current system have been established. At that stage it is possible to identify the constraints imposed on new architecture work by the legacy of the old system (the baseline).

The Architectural Model and Solution Model levels consist of work done later in Phases B, C, and D, the Target Architecture steps of each phase, and Phase E. The Architectural Model work is mostly done when taking different views of the architecture, and the Solution Model work in Phase E, where selection of products and projects takes place.

To show how building block definition happens in practice, the remainder of this chapter consists of a fictional worked example. In this fictional example much detail has been left out in order to emphasize the process.

32.4 Building Blocks Example

32.4.1 Introduction

This and the following sections provide a detailed worked example showing how building block context is captured, how building blocks are identified, and how building blocks are defined when executing the major steps of the ADM.

32.4.2 Structure

The levels of modeling within the ADM are explained in Building Blocks and the ADM , and the example follows the structure of modeling explained there:

- Background to the Example (Background to the Example)

- The Business Process level (Business Process Level (Phase B))
- The Technical Functionality and Constraints level (Technical Functionality and Constraints Level (Phases B, C, & D))
- The Architectural Model level (Architectural Model Level (Phases B, C, and D))
- The Opportunity Identification level (Opportunity Identification (Phase E))
- The Building Block Re-use level (Re-Use of Building Blocks in Other Projects (Phases F to G))

32.4.3 Background to the Example

In this example, a fictional company called XYZ Manufacturing has decided to improve the efficiency of its mobile sales force by replacing paper-based configuration and ordering systems with an IT solution.

The XYZ team have already done the preliminary stages of describing their existing system and reviewing it from a number of different viewpoints, and as a result have established a number of goals and objectives for the new system.

The principal goal is to give the sales force in the field direct access to the sales process back at base. This will allow sales staff to create and verify the product configuration, to check the price and availability of the goods, and to place the order while actually with the customer.

Other stages of the sales process - such as initiating the sale and determining the customer requirements - are considered to be outside the scope of this example.

32.4.4 Business Process Level (Phase B)

The inputs to ADM Phase B are:

- Request for Architecture Work
- Statement of Architecture Work
- Business principles, business goals, and strategic drivers
- Architecture principles
- Architecture Continuum
- Architecture Vision

The outputs of this step are:

- Statement of Architecture Work (updated if necessary)
- Validated principles, business goals, and strategic drivers
- Target Business Architecture
- Baseline Business Architecture

- Views corresponding to the selected viewpoints addressing key stakeholder concerns
- Gap analysis results
- Technical requirements (drivers for the Technology Architecture work)
- Business Architecture Report
- Updated business requirements

As a preliminary to this step it is necessary to define the scope of activity, including what is in scope, what is out of scope, what the limits are, and what the financial envelope is. Within this step fall defining the business process, recording the assumptions made, and developing any new requirements. The information collected is used to gauge the current system and to determine the return on investment of potential changes. Use-cases are a useful tool in this step to describe the business processes and they can be used to do a sanity check against the resulting architecture.

The business goals driving improvements in the sales process were:

- To improve the quality of the sales process
- To reduce the number of errors in the sales process
- To speed up the sales process

In this example, financial and time constraints and business return have not been dealt with in detail, but normally these constraints would be used to guide the process along the entire way to avoid over-engineering or "creeping elegance". The architect should especially look at these constraints whenever iterating between steps. Also not shown in this example are the use-case scenarios. However, the process described below does include participants, or actors, of the use-case with brief descriptions of their roles in Use-Case Table of Sales Process .

For the sake of brevity in this example, it is assumed that the scope of the architectural work would not extend beyond the sales arena, and that the proposed solutions fit within the financial and time constraints imposed by XYZ.

The assumptions made by the XYZ architect during Phase B are:

- To support the mission of the business, it is desired to have the sales person and the customer meet and interact face-to-face at the customer location.
- The model for such a customer visit should be two persons interacting using a shared PC.
- The sales person needs to be able to close the deal on-site, and then synchronize with information held at the sales base.
- There is a clearly-defined product set subject of the sales process; e.g., there is a car to buy.

The relevant business process in scope of this example in the XYZ company is the customer-facing portion of the sales process and the supporting systems. This sales process consists of the following steps:

1. Initiate the sales process with the customer:
    1.1. Sales Person
    1.2. Customer
2. Discuss the customer requirements:
    2.1. Customer
    2.2. Sales Person
3. Work with the customer to create a product configuration:
    3.1. Sales Person
    3.1. Sales Person's Laptop
    3.3. Sales Person's Local (LIPR) and Central (CIPR) Information Process Resources
    3.4. Product Configurator
    3.5. Customer
4. Verify that the desired configuration can be delivered:
    4.1. Sales Person
    4.2. Sales Person's Laptop
    4.3. Inventory Control System
    4.4. Scheduling System
    4.5. Customer Accepts or Rejects
5. Determine the price of the requested configuration:
    5.1. Sales Person
    5.2. Sales Person's Laptop
    5.3. Pricing System
6. Confirm the desire to purchase with the customer:
    6.1. Sales Person
    6.2. Customer
7. Place an order:
    7.1. Sales Person
    7.2. Sales Person's Laptop with Printer (for Fax)
    7.3. Order System
    7.4. Customer
8. Customer acceptance:
    8.1. Sales Person
    8.2. Customer

The following use-case table represents participants (sometimes referred to as "actors" in use-cases) in the rows, steps of the business process in the columns, and roles in the cells. Note that this is an example, and it is not intended to be accurate, but rather demonstrative. Constructing a use-case table is a comparatively small effort that will ultimately enhance the speed and quality of the resulting architecture.

The meanings of the various acronyms used in the table, and in subsequent figures, are listed below:

CIPR	Central Information Processing Resource
ICSys	Inventory Control System
LIPR	Local Information Processing Resource
OrdSys	Order Processing/Information System
ProdConfig	Product Configurator System
ProdSys	Product Information System
SchSys	Scheduling System
$Sys	Pricing Information System

	1:Initiate	2:Discuss Reqmts	3:Create Config	4:Verify Config	5:Price	6:Confirm	7: Order	8:Accept
Sales Person	Greets customer.	Listens.	Represents options with different capabilities.	Accesses ICSys and SchSys and presents availability to customer.	Accesses price system and presents price to customer.	Presents offer.	Accesses order system.	Presents contract.
Customer	Accepts sales person.	Discusses problems/desires.	Listens and decides on options based on capabilities.	Accepts or rejects.		Accepts or rejects.		Signs or rejects.
Sales Person's Laptop			Interacts with configurator.	Interacts with ICSys and SchSys.	Interacts with price system.		Interacts with order system and receives fax response.	
Sales Person's CIPR			Provides central information processing.					
Sales Person's LIPR			Provides local information processing					

ProdConfig			Presents configs to sales person per needs, providing capabilities.					
ICSys				Provides availability.				
SchSys				Provides delivery date.				
$Sys					Provides price information on a config.			
OrderSys							Processes order and sends fax of order to sales person's laptop.	

Table 32.1: Use-Case Table of Sales Process

Steps 1, 2, 6, and 8 are not within scope of the architecture work since the only participants involved are humans. The other steps are considered within scope since there are computing components involved in supporting the sales process. Note the computing participants are the first set of identified candidate building blocks - Business Process-Driven List.

During Phase A, the business goals were developed into more detailed business requirements, and these were:

- To improve on the current turnaround time of 48 hours for order processing
- To reduce the number of errors in orders by a factor of three

A very simplified view of the candidate building blocks required to support the business process with an idea of location is provided below. This model was built from elements of the above table.

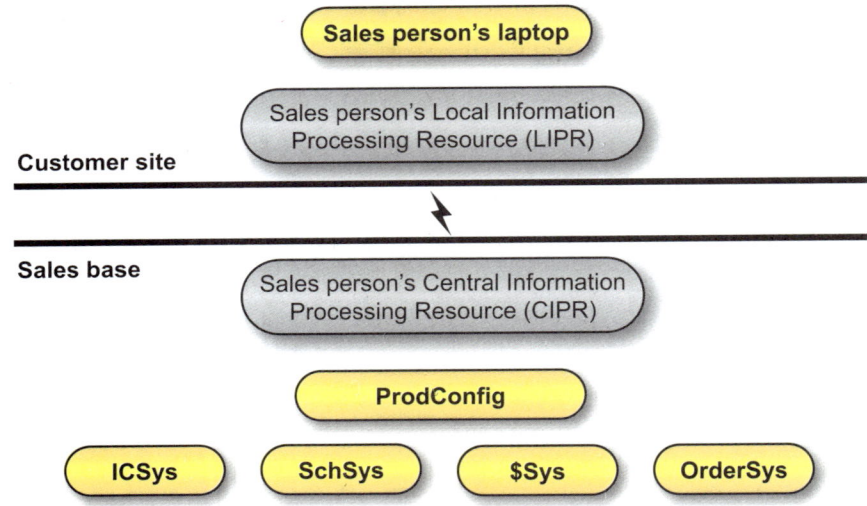

Figure 32.3: Model of the Candidate Building Blocks: Business Process-Driven List

32.4.5 Technical Functionality and Constraints Level (Phases B, C, & D)

The objective of the first step in Phases B, C, and D of the ADM is to build a high-level description of the characteristics of the current system, re-usable building blocks from the current system, the technical functionality needed to address the business problem, and to identify additional constraints. This is necessary as the description documents the starting point for architectural development and lists the interoperability issues that the final architecture will have to take into account. Potential re-usable building blocks may be contained in the existing environment. They are identified in this step.

The best approach is to describe the system in terms already used within the organization. A reliable picture can be built up of the business functions served and the platforms which support those functions. Gather and analyze only that information that allows informed decisions to be made regarding the Target Architecture.

The inputs to this step are:

- Descriptions of the current system
- Information on the existing architecture
- Model of candidate building blocks

The essential outputs from this activity are:

- A clear description of the current system and its functions
- A statement of the constraints imposed by the internal organization
- A statement of the constraints imposed by the business or external environments

- Architecture principles embodied in the current system
- Assumptions of required technical functionality
- Candidate building blocks - Baseline-Driven List
- Model of candidate building blocks (see Candidate Building Blocks from the Baseline-Driven List)

The key input to this step is the existing architecture. In this example, a depiction of an existing architecture is shown in XYZ Existing Architecture . Additionally depicted in this architecture model are pointers to existing problems with the existing architecture. These pointers are used by the architect to determine where existing components are failing, and where existing systems can be re-used.

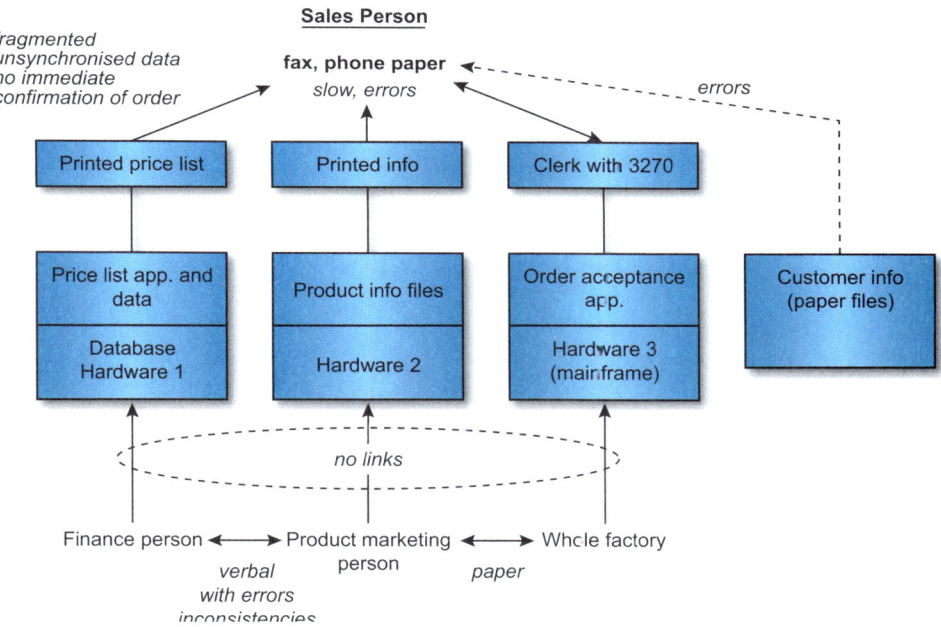

Figure 32.4: XYZ Existing Architecture

It is necessary to record existing strategic decisions about the existing architectural and technological issues such as:

- The existing architecture is founded on the mainframe.
- Databases are tied to application logic.
- Security is embedded in the application.

The next step consists of restating the business process, considering what functionality will be required, and deciding what constraints apply. Decisions at this stage are not definitive, but act as input for the following steps and iterations.

The architects of XYZ identified the following pieces of technical functionality as necessary to support the business processes. This list was produced using standard brainstorming techniques.

32.4.5.1 Assumptions of Required Technical Functionality

- Access to central functions
- Application support for simultaneous access by multiple sales persons through multiple connections
- Execution of local functions at the point-of-sale
- Access to product information
- Entering and checking the required product configuration
- Access to customer information
- Access to price information
- Order entry
- Order acceptance
- Delivery of confirmation of order to the customer
- The process must be secured

Also in the brainstorming session, some assumptions were made and therefore must be documented as they should be used throughout the process:

- Initiation of the sales process and determination/agreement of the customer requirements were outside the scope of the current work.
- Functionality could be distributed between the point-of-sale and a central base.
- Closure of the order should take place at the central location.
- The price list and product information could be made available electronically.
- Access could be provided to the acceptance and confirmation of order systems.
- The ordering, product information, and price information systems could be linked together.

One constraint was put on the development because XYZ already had systems in place to support the sales process:

- Existing systems should be used to support product information, order placement, and customer information.

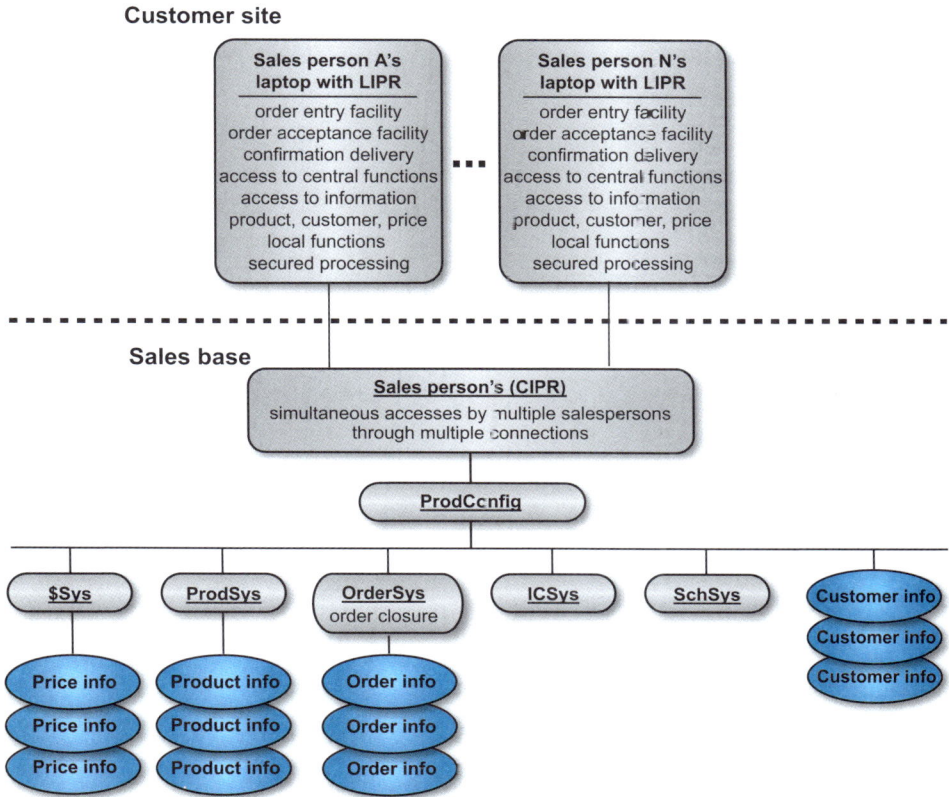

Figure 32.5:
Model of Candidate Building Blocks Augmented with Technical Functionality

The above model is scrutinized and questions are asked about the functionality that could be provided by the existing system. Candidate Building Blocks from the Baseline-Driven List depicts the set of candidate building blocks from the existing system, resulting from this question.

32.4.6 Architectural Model Level (Phases B, C, and D)

In Phases B, C, and D a number of different architecture views are considered and used to build up a model of the new architecture. At XYZ, the Architectural Model level was developed in the following steps:

1. A Baseline Description in the TOGAF format
2. Consider different architecture views
3. Create an architectural model of building blocks
4. Select the services portfolio required per building block

5. Confirm that the business goals and objectives are met
6. Determine criteria for specification selection
7. Complete the architecture definition
8. Conduct a gap analysis

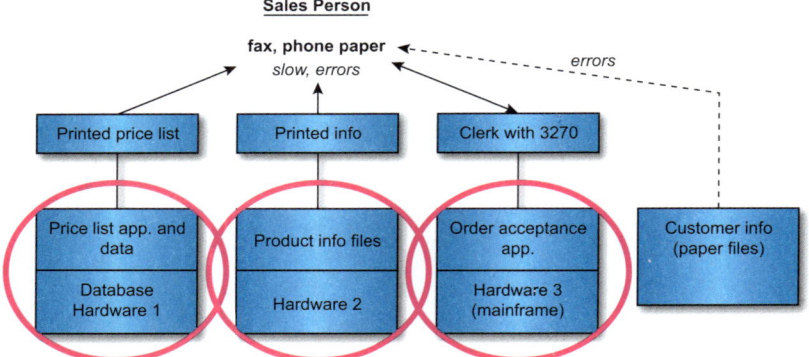

Figure 32.6: Candidate Building Blocks from the Baseline-Driven List

In executing Step 1, the existing architecture was assessed:

- To describe the architecture principles of the existing architecture
- To describe the existing architecture in TOGAF terms
- To identify new requirements, inhibitors, and opportunities

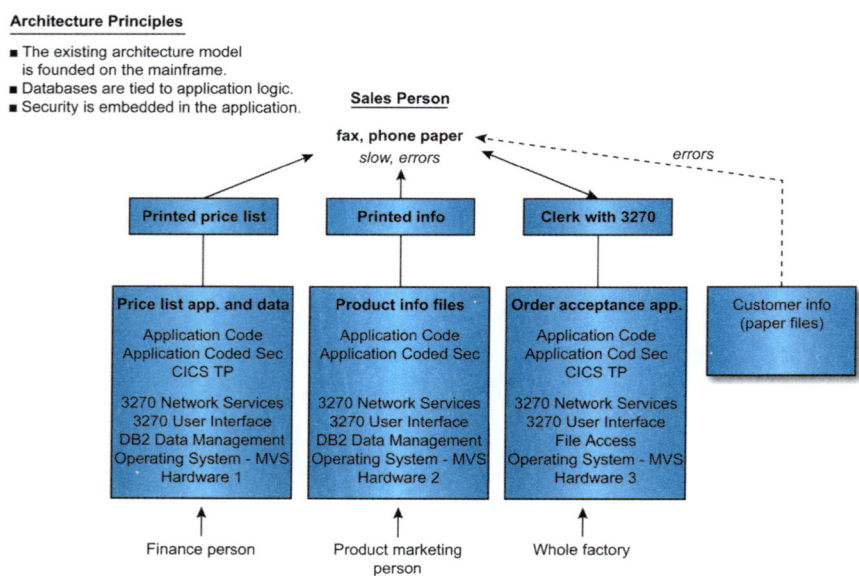

Figure 32.7: Existing Architecture in TOGAF Terms

Notice how in Existing Architecture in TOGAF Terms and Future Architecture of Functions the legacy systems supporting the price list, product info, and order acceptance applications are easy to handle as monolithic building blocks. Augmented Future Architecture of Functions , Representation of XYZ SOAP System , and Services Map show they can be connected to new building blocks using adapters.

In Step 2, the function view was examined based upon what the system was intended to do, and how it should behave. The function view is depicted in Future Architecture of Functions . Note that the inventory control and scheduling system are not covered.

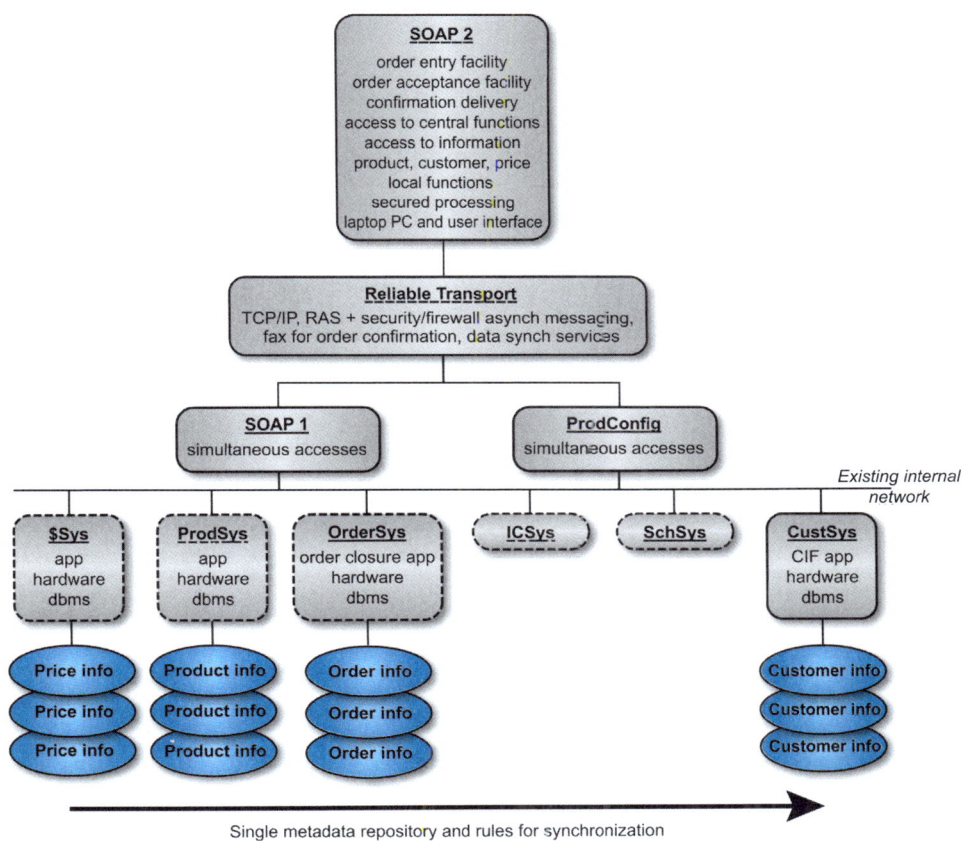

Figure 32.8: Future Architecture of Functions

In executing Step 2, a view of the future architecture was created by processing the technical functionality that must be provided and by:

- Identifying obvious additions
- Identifying what would be carried forward from the old system
- Determining the return on investment for various options, allowing them to be ranked

- Assessing the risk of the various changes
- Checking the coverage of the technical functionality
- Adding technical functionality required for completeness, checking against the TOGAF Technical Reference Model (TRM)
- Updating and clarifying the business requirements and technical functionality
- Iteratively adding precision and detail to the future architecture
- For each architectural decision, completely following through the impact of it
- Noting the rationale for each decision whether the answer was yes or no, so as to avoid reopening old issues later

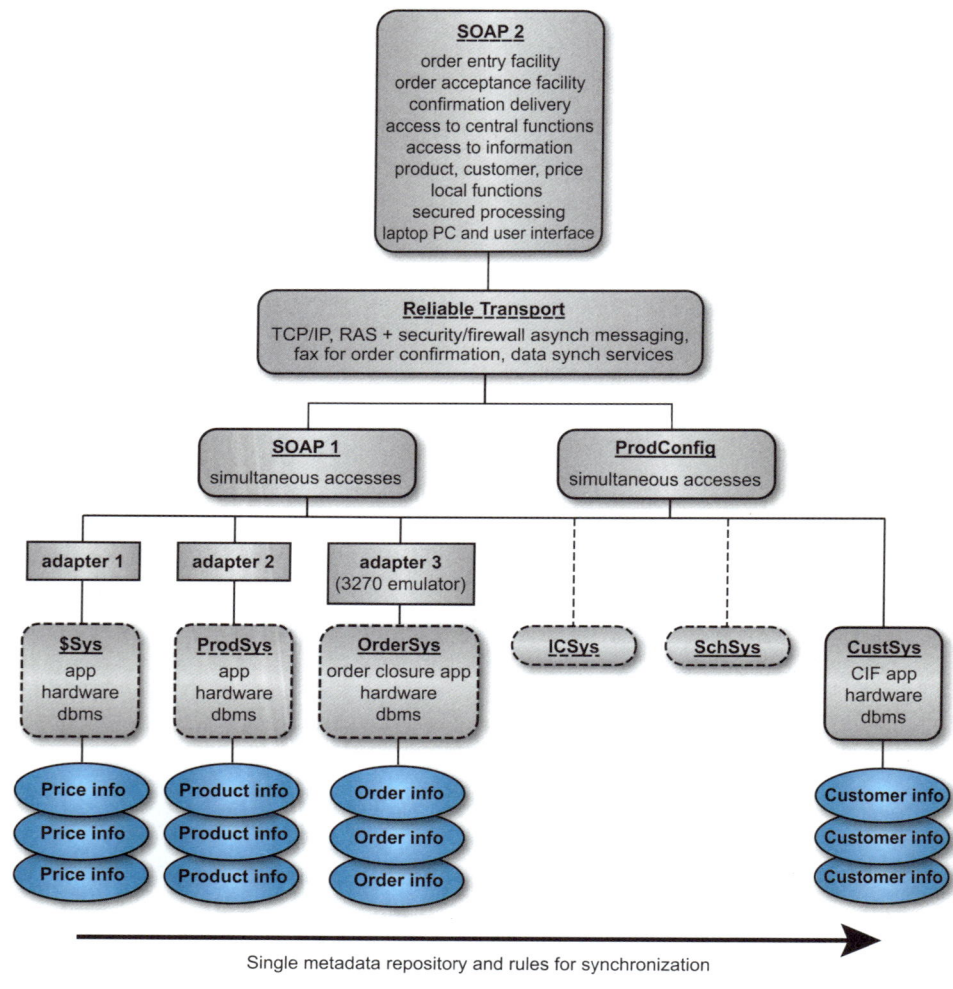

Figure 32.9: Augmented Future Architecture of Functions

Augmented Future Architecture of Functions shows how the constraints identified in the earlier technical functionality and constraints work have been incorporated. It was necessary to retain the existing systems for order handling and product information. The initial constraint list also included retaining the existing system for customer information, but this was overridden by the need to improve the quality of the sales process and a new system is proposed to deal with this. Return on investment is the driving force behind the decision to retain the existing system for price data. Quality problems with the price system highlighted in XYZ Existing Architecture will be resolved through a single metadata definition and rules for synchronization as shown in Future Architecture of Functions . These legacy systems are integrated into the new SOAP (Sales Order Application) by developing adapter software. The following describes the SOAP application.

- SOAP consists of two parts. SOAP1 runs at the central site, and SOAP2 on a portable system carried by the sales person. Communication between the two is carried by a reliable transport (TCP/IP and RAS), and includes security provided by a firewall. Asynchronous messaging is also provided. Fax services are required at the central site so as to provide the customer with written confirmation of acceptance of the order. Data synchronization services are needed to keep the sales person's portable systems and the central systems up-to-date with each other. Iteration of the architecture development process to validate the results against the business requirements is helped by considering detailed "use-cases". For instance, consider the activity of verifying an entered configuration.
- Entry is handled by SOAP2, running on the sales person's portable system. SOAP2 must deal with:
    - Establishment of the link to SOAP1:
        - Physical link
        - Protocols
    - Security check
    - Direct information request to the proper database
- Then, at the central site:
    - SOAP1 contacts the configurator.
    - The configurator:
        - Reacts to the named request
        - Gets information from the price, product information, customer information, and production systems
        - Determines the yes or no result
        - Returns to SOAP1
    - SOAP1 returns the result to SOAP2.
- All of the separate elements in the use-case must be supplied by the Solution Architecture. Another way of refining the developing architectural model is to use the

architecture views:

- The Computing view is often the default.
- The Data Management view is often useful.
- The Security and Management views are of growing importance.
- Performance is an important consideration both on the existing architecture to discover the underlying assumptions and on the future architecture to document the assumptions and provide a basis for change in performance limits. Performance should be addressed in a number of views, including the Computing, Communications, and Builder's views.

To ensure that building blocks are as re-usable as possible, detailed information is needed about the building block. For this reason it is helpful to take views of individual building blocks and not just of the complete system. For the maximum benefit, it may be necessary to take views of both ABBs and SBBs.

It is the responsibility of the architect to foresee the integration of any application with the rest of the enterprise regardless of the isolated position of the application today. This future integration is facilitated by complete definition of building blocks. It is the responsibility of the business unit to implement in accordance with the rules of the architecture.

Step 3 consists of creating an architecture model of building blocks. Augmented Future Architecture of Functions depicts a future architecture model of functions, but does not express the relationships and interfaces between the elements in the architecture model. As the architectural development process continues, it becomes important to define a manageable granularity for building blocks and to fully define their linkages. Without this work there is no guarantee of interoperability between the various building blocks chosen.

We have identified two lists of candidate building blocks in the above steps. Prior to building a model of building blocks, these lists are processed and some candidates become recommended building blocks.

Candidate Building Blocks:	Candidate Building Blocks:
Business Process-Driven List	Baseline-Driven List
Sales person's laptop	Price list application, data, and platform
Sales person's CIPR	Product information and platform
Sales person's LIPR	Order acceptance application, data, and platform
ProdConfig	
ICSys	
SchSys	
$Sys	
OrderSys	

Table 32.2: Candidate Building Blocks - Lists

The process of identifying building blocks includes looking for collections of functions which require integration to draw them together or make them different.

First, it is recommended that the candidate building blocks from list B be selected as building blocks because they are re-usable legacy items. With these, a building block containing all the adapters is identified given the affinity of similar logic; e.g., providing the network adapter functionality on behalf of all the legacy applications.

Next a network building block appears to be required as it is a new network that must be built or purchased and is independent of the applications implemented. It itself can be a re-usable building block for other applications.

The laptop with the SOAP2 application is identified as a building block because it is a modular pack of functionality specially built with applications and data tightly integrated for the mobile sales force. However, a RAS-capable firewall was also identified as a separable building block.

The new customer information system is also identified as a re-usable building block given its applicability across applications past, new, and future. The SOAP1 and configuration systems were identified as two additional building blocks.

We depict the ABBs at a high-level in Representation of XYZ SOAP System .

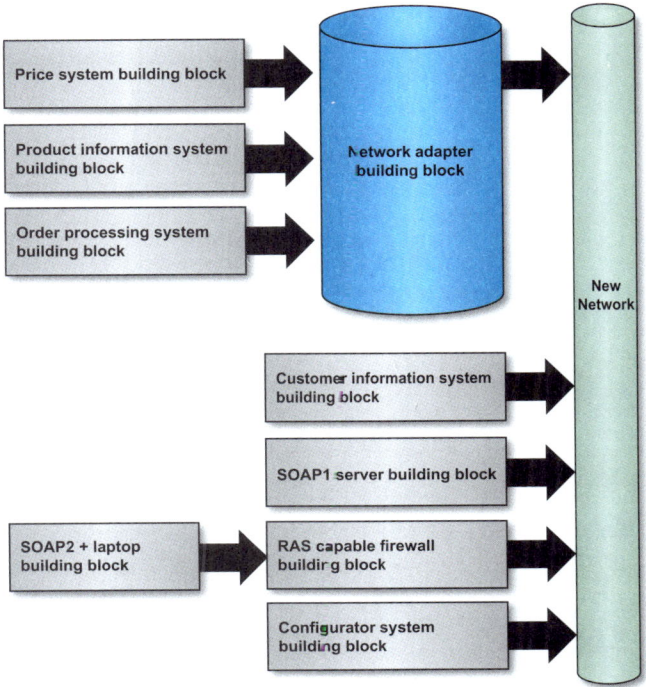

Figure 32.10: Representation of XYZ SOAP System

Representation of XYZ SOAP System presents a relationship view of the system. Compare this with Augmented Future Architecture of Functions , a functional view, to see how different diagrammatic views of the same system can be used to show different things.

In executing Step 3, the future architecture was created by processing the technical functionality that must be provided and:

- Diagrams of larger systems drawn with this notation quickly show what interfaces are needed between building blocks and which ones need to be identical to realize interoperability benefits.

- Representation of XYZ SOAP System clearly shows where and how glue software is required to bind the legacy systems to the new network.

Step 4 is to select the services portfolio required per building block. Services Map depicts the services mapped to component in the architecture model.

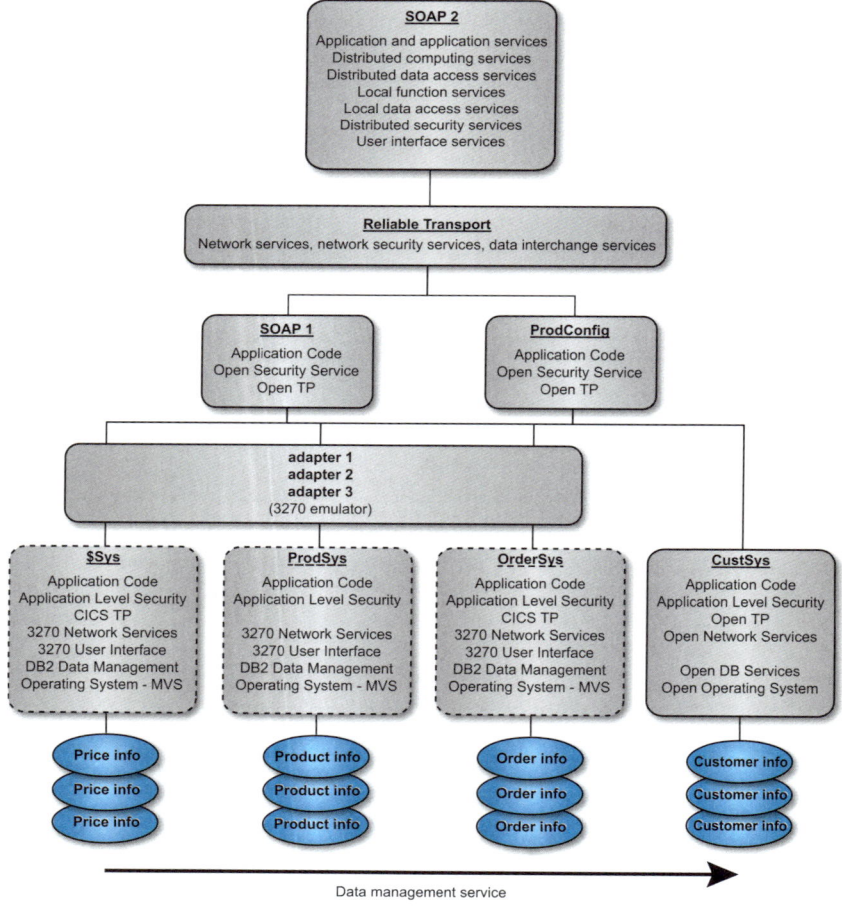

Figure 32.11: Services Map

Step 5 in the process is to confirm that the architecture supports the business goals and objectives. This is a relatively subjective task of answering the questions developed in Step 1. In this example, we did not establish a set of questions that would be used to test the architecture, but such questions (and how to pose them in light of the architecture) could easily be envisioned. For example, one question could be: "Does the architecture prohibit the immediate processing of an order by a customer?" which would be answered "no" in our case above.

The use-cases developed earlier are a handy tool to test the completeness and applicability of the architecture and its building blocks.

Building block specifications should be recorded in detail. An example of a building block specification document is given in Customer Information System Building Block Specification .

Where an enterprise architecture exists or is being developed, it may be valuable at this point to review the new set of building blocks. Anything of benefit to the wider enterprise should be abstracted back to an architectural level and then fed back into the enterprise architecture development process.

Step 8 is to conduct a gap analysis, and is not covered in this example.

32.4.6.1 Customer Information System Building Block Specification

Description

This system is put in place of the existing paper-based customer information system to support the goal of improving the speed and quality of order closure. It shields the database from the complexity of the many applications looking at it but it contains an architectural break-point which could be used later on to make the database itself accessible to other applications.

The interfaces selected must go through an internal approval process modeled on the interface adoption criteria of The Open Group. This means that all specifications must be or become part of the corporate Standards Information Base (SIB).

Functionality Category	Functionality	Interfaces - APIs, Formats, & Protocols	Product or Project
CIF Application Code	Respects metadata repository spec	User-defined	User-defined
	Implements business rules	User-defined	User-defined
	Has remote access by SOAP and configurator	DCE RPC	See SIB
	Uses SQL	ANSI SQL CLI	
	Uses UNIX	UNIX 95	
Open DB Services	Relational	Codd	
	Supports concurrent access	Codd	
	Offers SQL	ANSI SQL	
Open Security Services	Single sign-on		
	Authorization	DCE	
	Authentication	DCE	
	Integrity		
	Audit	DCE	
	Non-repudiation		
Open Operating System	UNIX	UNIX 95	
Network Services	Existing internal network	User-defined	User-defined
Open TP	Multiple concurrent access	The Open Group XA	
	Load leveling		
+Performance	50 enquiries per second		
+Manageability	Online software update		
	Service-level data provision	DMTF Spec	
	Integration into enterprise management system	TBD	
+Availability	24 by 7 by 52		

Mandated Building Blocks

Building Block Name	Required Functionality	Owner	Named Used Interfaces
Enterprise Management System	Corporate IT	Service-level data handling Integration - TBD	
Enterprise Network	Corporate IT		
CIF System	Marketing		

Map to Business Organization Entities and Policies

Policy	Entity	Remarks
Security	Corporate admin	
Audit	Corporate admin	
Development and deployment	Corporate IT	
Metadata definition	Corporate IT	
Data quality	Corporate IT	
IT architecture	Corporate IT	
Corporate SIB	Corporate IT	This is linked to The Open Group SIB.

32.4.7 Opportunity Identification (Phase E)

This is the step where projects are identified, ranked, and selected.

The steps illustrated above have laid the foundation for this analysis. Augmented Future Architecture of Functions , for instance, shows the SOAP applications, the reliable transport, the adapters, and the new customer information system as potential projects.

32.4.8 Re-Use of Building Blocks in Other Projects (Phases F to G)

In ADM Phases F to G, the choice of building blocks may be affected by outside events, such as a change in the availability of products. They can also affect and be affected by issues such as the cost of retraining users during migration from one product to another. Perhaps the most important impact though is the effect that building block choice can have on other work in progress within an organization. This section shows how a diagrammatic representation of the building blocks in a system can be used to identify or prioritize future projects.

An important benefit of defining the building blocks and their linkages is that it becomes possible to pick out re-usable components in the architecture. The best way to do this is to draw up a matrix of the building blocks used in an architecture and the applications that use them. Such a matrix for a simple subset of the XYZ case is shown in Simple Component/Application Matrix .

Careful ordering of the building blocks in the left-hand column allows the architect to identify subsets of functionality common to a number of applications. Identifying Common Functionality shows such a subset. In this case the subset of platform, network, and customer information database gives a strong indication that the configurator, SOAP1, and customer information applications should be hosted on the same platform.

Such identifiable subsets of building blocks also serve another purpose, which is that they can draw attention to opportunities for component re-use. If in the future XYZ decides to implement a customer care system, adding that into the matrix reveals that there would be significant advantages to building the customer care system on the same building blocks used for the configurator, SOAP1, and customer information applications.

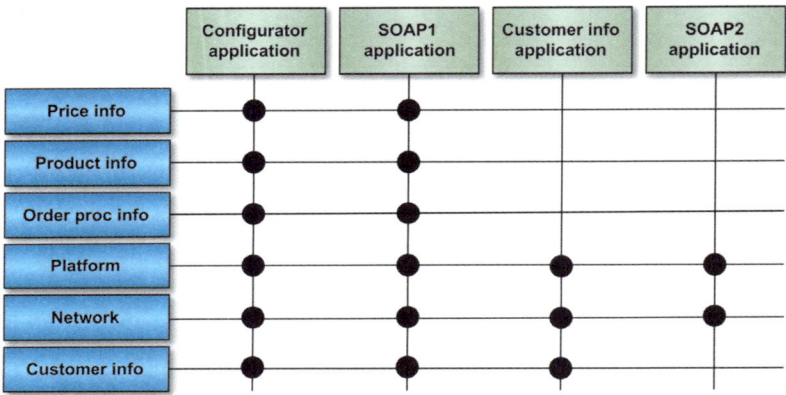

Figure 32.12: Simple Component/Application Matrix

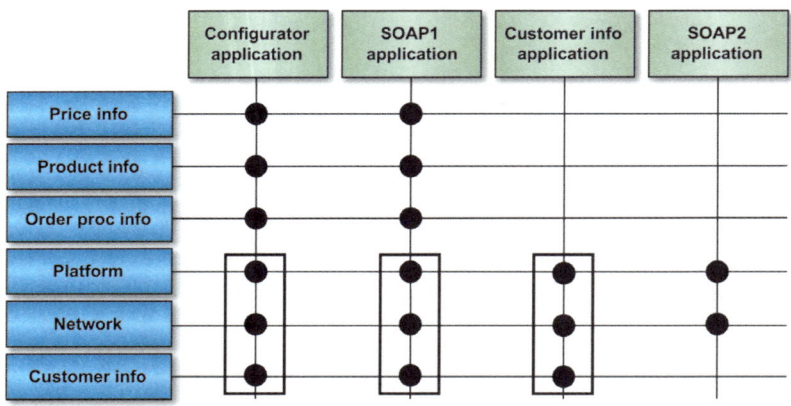

Figure 32.13: Identifying Common Functionality

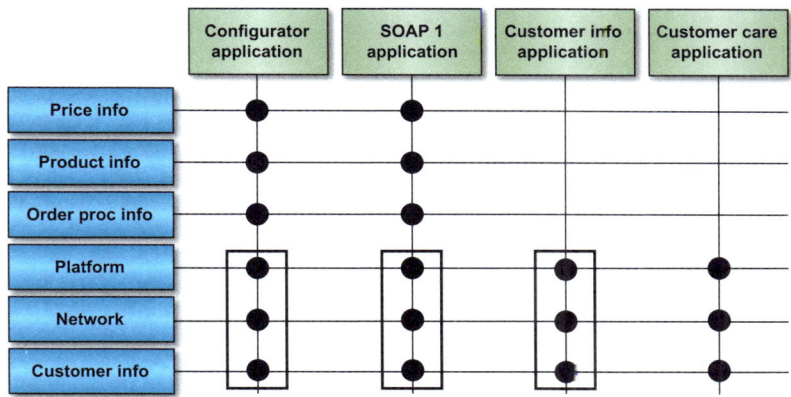

Figure 32.14: Using the Matrix to Steer Future Procurement

The key to success in working with building blocks is to establish a useful level of granularity. Too much detail in the chosen set of building blocks will make the architecture unworkable, while too coarse a level of detail will make the work valueless.

Chapter 33: Business Process Domain Views

This chapter presents a set of function views aligned with the business process structure of the enterprise.

33.1 Introduction

A business process domain is a logical grouping of business systems dedicated to a common purpose. Such systems may be geographically co-located, thus emphasizing their purpose; or they may be grouped by some other constraint, such as a common systems availability target.

In order to demonstrate the responsiveness of the enterprise architecture to the business needs of the organization, among the various architecture views that are developed, a business process domain view may be used. This describes the enterprise architecture from the perspective of the enterprise's key business process domains.

33.2 Role

A business process domain view is a set of function views, aligned with the business process structure of the enterprise.

Business process domain views are used during architecture development as a means of verifying, and demonstrating, that the architecture being developed is addressing the business requirements.

Thorough and detailed application of the business scenario technique (see Business Scenarios) in the early stages of architecture development should provide an excellent foundation for a set of business process domain views.

Each business process domain view addresses components, interfaces, and allocation of services critical to the view. A typical structure is shown below.

Introduction	A description of the domain, its key applications, and attributes that characterize the applications within the domain.
Business Problem Statement	A short description of the important business problems relating to the domain, and how they are addressed in the Target Architecture.
Applications Deployed within the Business Process Domain	A table listing currently deployed applications.

Assumptions, Constraints, and Guidelines	General guidelines for developers, implementors, and system suppliers.
Domain Structure	Target architecture/business process domain mapping: a table highlighting the services and building blocks applicable to this domain. Application topology: a figure showing the relationships between the major application elements within this domain.
Domain Service Qualities	A description of the service qualities (see Application Platform Service Qualities) that are important for each business process domain, and how they are achieved in the Target Architecture.
Deployment Guidance Strategy	Lessons learnt with respect to deployment. The migration strategy for implementing the Target Architecture, as it applies to this business process domain Also any guidance for the implementation team responsible for deployment.
Future Directions	Any important directions identified for systems within the domain.
References	Pointers to reference material.

Table 33.1: Business Process Domain Views - Description Structure

Chapter 34: Business Scenarios

This chapter describes a method for deriving business requirements for architecture and the implied technical requirements.

34.1 Introduction

A key factor in the success of an enterprise architecture is the extent to which it is linked to business requirements, and demonstrably supporting and enabling the enterprise to achieve its business objectives.

Business scenarios are an important technique that may be used at various stages of the enterprise architecture, principally the Architecture Vision and the Business Architecture, but in other architecture domains as well, if required, to derive the characteristics of the architecture directly from the high-level requirements of the business. They are used to help identify and understand business needs, and thereby to derive the business requirements that the architecture development has to address.

A business scenario describes:

- A business process, application, or set of applications that can be enabled by the architecture
- The business and technology environment
- The people and computing components (called "actors") who execute the scenario
- The desired outcome of proper execution

A good business scenario is representative of a significant business need or problem, and enables vendors to understand the value to the customer organization of a developed solution.

A good business scenario is also "SMART":

- Specific, by defining what needs to be done in the business
- Measurable, through clear metrics for success
- Actionable, by:
    - Clearly segmenting the problem
    - Providing the basis for determining elements and plans for the solution
- Realistic, in that the problem can be solved within the bounds of physical reality, time, and cost constraints
- Time-bound, in that there is a clear statement of when the solution opportunity expires

Guidelines on Goals and Objectives provides detailed examples on objectives that could be considered. Whatever objectives you use, the idea is to make those objectives SMART.

34.2 Benefits of Business Scenarios

A business scenario is essentially a complete description of a business problem, both in business and in architectural terms, which enables individual requirements to be viewed in relation to one another in the context of the overall problem. Without such a complete description to serve as context:

- There is a danger of the architecture being based on an incomplete set of requirements that do not add up to a whole problem description, and that can therefore misguide architecture work.
- The business value of solving the problem is unclear.
- The relevance of potential solutions is unclear.

Also, because the technique requires the involvement of business line management and other stakeholders at an early stage in the architecture project, it also plays an important role in gaining the buy-in of these key personnel to the overall project and its end-product - the enterprise architecture.

An additional advantage of business scenarios is in communication with vendors. Most architecture nowadays is implemented by making maximum use of Commercial Off-The-Shelf (COTS) software solutions, often from multiple vendors, procured in the open market. The use of business scenarios by an IT customer can be an important aid to IT vendors in delivering appropriate solutions. Vendors need to ensure that their solution components add value to an open solution and are marketable. Business scenarios provide a language with which the vendor community can link customer problems and technical solutions. Besides making obvious what is needed, and why, they allow vendors to solve problems optimally, using open standards and leveraging each other's skills.

34.3 Creating the Business Scenario

34.3.1 The Overall Process

Creating a business scenario involves the following, as illustrated in Creating a Business Scenario :

1. Identifying, documenting, and ranking the problem driving the scenario
2. Identifying the business and technical environment of the scenario and documenting it in scenario models
3. Identifying and documenting desired objectives (the results of handling the problems successfully); get "SMART"
4. Identifying the human actors (participants) and their place in the business model
5. Identifying computer actors (computing elements) and their place in the technology model

6. Identifying and documenting roles, responsibilities, and measures of success per actor; documenting the required scripts per actor, and the results of handling the situation
7. Checking for "fitness-for-purpose" and refining only if necessary

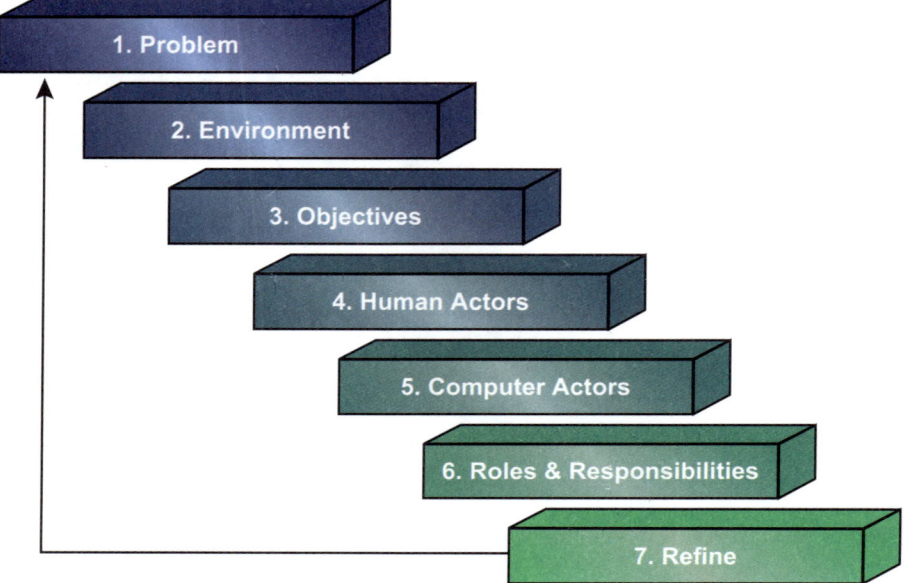

Figure 34.1: Creating a Business Scenario

A business scenario is developed over a number of iterative phases of Gathering, Analyzing, and Reviewing the information in the business scenario.

In each phase, each of the areas above is successively improved. The refinement step involves deciding whether to consider the scenario complete and go to the next phase, or whether further refinement is necessary. This is accomplished by asking whether the current state of the business scenario is fit for the purpose of carrying requirements downstream in the architecture process.

The three phases of developing a business scenario are described in detail below, and depicted in Phases of Developing Business Scenarios .

34.3.2 Gathering

The Gathering phase is where information is collected on each of the areas in Creating a Business Scenario . If information gathering procedures and practices are already in place in an organization - for example, to gather information for strategic planning - they should be used as appropriate, either during business scenario workshops or in place of business scenario workshops.

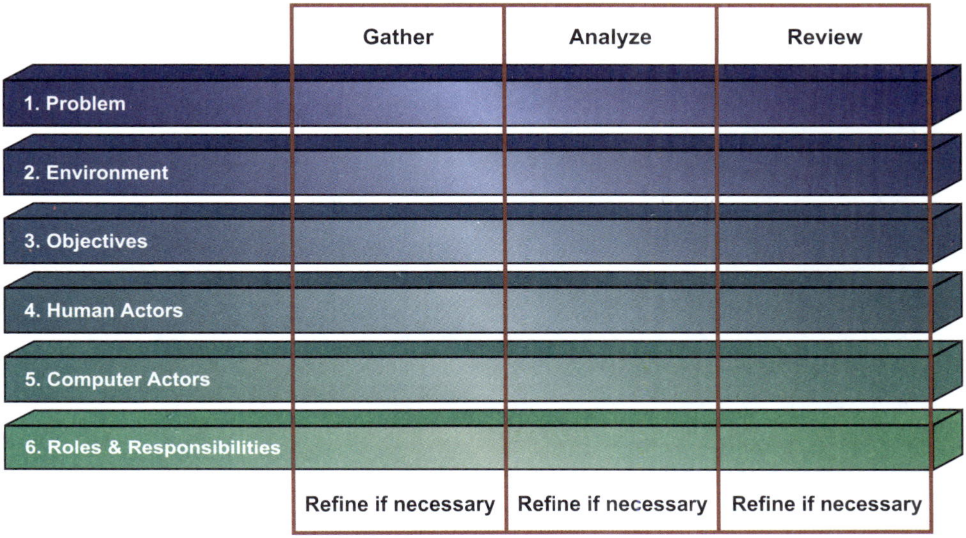

	Gather	Analyze	Review
1. Problem			
2. Environment			
3. Objectives			
4. Human Actors			
5. Computer Actors			
6. Roles & Responsibilities			
	Refine if necessary	Refine if necessary	Refine if necessary

Figure 34.2: Phases of Developing Business Scenarios

Multiple techniques may be used in this phase, such as information research, qualitative analysis, quantitative analysis, surveys, requests for information, etc. As much information as possible should be gathered and preprocessed "off-line" prior to any face-to-face workshops (described below). For example, a request for information may include a request for strategic and operational plans. Such documents typically provide great insights, but the information that they contain usually requires significant preprocessing. The information may be used to generate an initial draft of the business scenario prior to the workshop, if possible. This will increase the understanding and confidence of the architect, and the value of the workshop to its participants.

A very useful way to gather information is to hold business scenario workshops, whereby a business scenario consultant leads a select and small group of business representatives through a number of questions to elicit the information surrounding the problem being addressed by the architecture effort. The workshop attendees must be carefully selected from high levels in the business and technical sides of the organization. It is important to get people that can and will provide information openly and honestly Where a draft of the business scenario already exists - for example, as a result of preprocessing information gathered during this phase, as described above - the workshop may also be used to review the state of the business scenario draft.

Sometimes it is necessary to have multiple workshops: in some cases, to separate the gathering of information on the business side from the gathering of information on the technical side; and in other cases simply to get more information from more people.

When gathering information, the architect can greatly strengthen the business scenario by obtaining "real-world examples"; i.e., case studies to which the reader can easily relate. When citing real-world examples, it is important to maintain a level of anonymity of the parties involved, to avoid blame.

34.3.3 Analyzing

The Analyzing phase is where a great deal of real Business Architecture work is actually done. This is where the information that is gathered is processed and documented, and where the models are created to represent that information, typically visually.

The Analyzing phase takes advantage of the knowledge and experience of the business scenario consultant using past work and experience to develop the models necessary to depict the information captured. Note that the models and documentation produced are not necessarily reproduced verbatim from interviews, but rather filtered and translated according to the real underlying needs.

In the Analyzing phase it is important to maintain linkages between the key elements of the business scenario. One technique that assists in maintaining such linkages is the creation of matrices that are used to relate business processes to each of:

- Constituencies
- Human Actors
- Computer Actors
- Issues
- Objectives

In this way, the business process becomes the binding focal point, which makes a great deal of sense, since in most cases it is business process improvement that is being sought.

34.3.4 Reviewing

The Reviewing phase is where the results are fed back to the sponsors of the project to ensure that there is a shared understanding of the full scope of the problem, and the potential depth of the technical impact.

Multiple business scenario workshops or "readout" meetings with the sponsors and involved parties are recommended. The meetings should be set up to be open and interactive. It is recommended to have exercises built into meeting agendas, in order to test attendees' understanding and interest levels, as well as to test the architect's own assumptions and results.

This phase is extremely important, as the absence of shared expectations is in many cases the root cause of project failures.

34.4 Contents of a Business Scenario

The documentation of a business scenario should contain all the important details about the scenario. It should capture, and sequence, the critical steps and interactions between actors that address the situation. It should also declare all the relevant information about all actors, specifically: the different responsibilities of the actors; the key pre-conditions that have to be met prior to proper system functionality; and the technical requirements for the service to be of acceptable quality.

There are two main types of content: graphics (models), and descriptive text. Both have a part to play.

- Business Scenario Models capture business and technology views in a graphical form, to aid comprehension. Specifically, they relate actors and interactions, and give a starting point to confirm specific requirements.

- Business Scenario Descriptions capture details in a textual form. A typical contents list for a business scenario is given below.

Table of Contents

PREFACE
  EXECUTIVE SUMMARY
  DOCUMENT ROADMAP
BUSINESS SCENARIO
 BUSINESS SCENARIO OVERVIEW
      BACKGROUND OF SCENARIO
      PURPOSE OF SCENARIO
      DEFINITIONS/DESCRIPTIONS OF TERMS USED
  VIEWS OF ENVIRONMENTS AND PROCESSES
    BUSINESS ENVIRONMENT
      Constituencies
    PROCESS DESCRIPTIONS
      Process "a"
      etc. ...
    TECHNICAL ENVIRONMENT
      Technical environment "a"
      etc. ...
    ACTORS AND THEIR ROLES AND RESPONSIBILITIES
    COMPUTER ACTORS AND ROLES
    RELATIONSHIP OF COMPONENTS AND PROCESSES
    HUMAN ACTORS AND ROLES
    RELATIONSHIP OF HUMANS AND PROCESSES
    INFORMATION FLOW ANALYSIS
    PRINCIPLES AND CONSTRAINTS
      IT Principles
      Constraints

— continued on next page —

> — *continued from previous page* —
>
> REQUIREMENTS
> BUSINESS SCENARIO ANALYSIS
>
> PROBLEM SUMMARY
> Issues
> Objectives
>
> SUMMARY
>
> APPENDIXES
>
> APPENDIX A: BUSINESS SCENARIOS - ADDITIONAL INFORMATION
> APPENDIX B-n: BUSINESS SCENARIO WORKSHOP NOTES

34.5 Contributions to the Business Scenario

It is important to realize that the creation of a business scenario is not solely the province of the architect. As mentioned previously, business line management and other stakeholders in the enterprise are involved, to ensure that the business goals are accurately captured. In addition, depending on the relationship that an organization has with its IT vendors, the latter also may be involved, to ensure that the roles of technical solutions are also accurately captured, and to ensure communication with the vendors.

Typically, the involvement of the business management is greatest in the early stages, while the business problems are being explored and captured, while the involvement of the architect is greatest in the later stages, and when architectural solutions are being described. Similarly, if vendors are involved in the business scenario process, the involvement of the customer side (business management plus enterprise architects) is greatest in the early stages, while that of the vendors is greatest in the later stages, when the role of specific technical solutions is being explored and captured. This concept is illustrated in Relative Contributions to a Business Scenario .

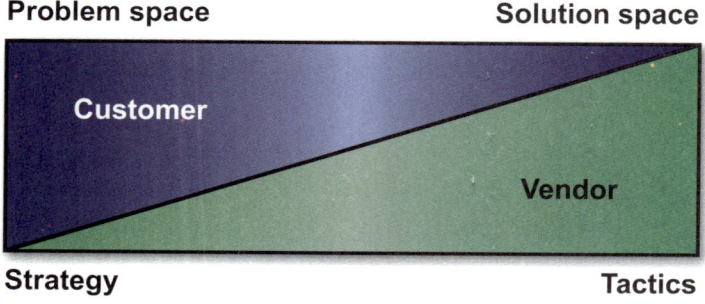

Figure 34.3: Relative Contributions to a Business Scenario

Vendor IT architects might be able to assist enterprise IT architects with integration of the vendors' products into the enterprise architecture. This assistance most probably falls in the middle of the timeline in Relative Contributions to a Business Scenario.

34.6 Business Scenarios and the TOGAF ADM

Business scenarios figure most prominently in the initial phase of the Architecture Development Method (ADM), Architecture Vision, when they are used to define relevant business requirements, and to build consensus with business management and other stakeholders.

However, the business requirements are referred to throughout all phases of the ADM lifecycle, as illustrated in Relevance of Requirements Throughout the ADM.

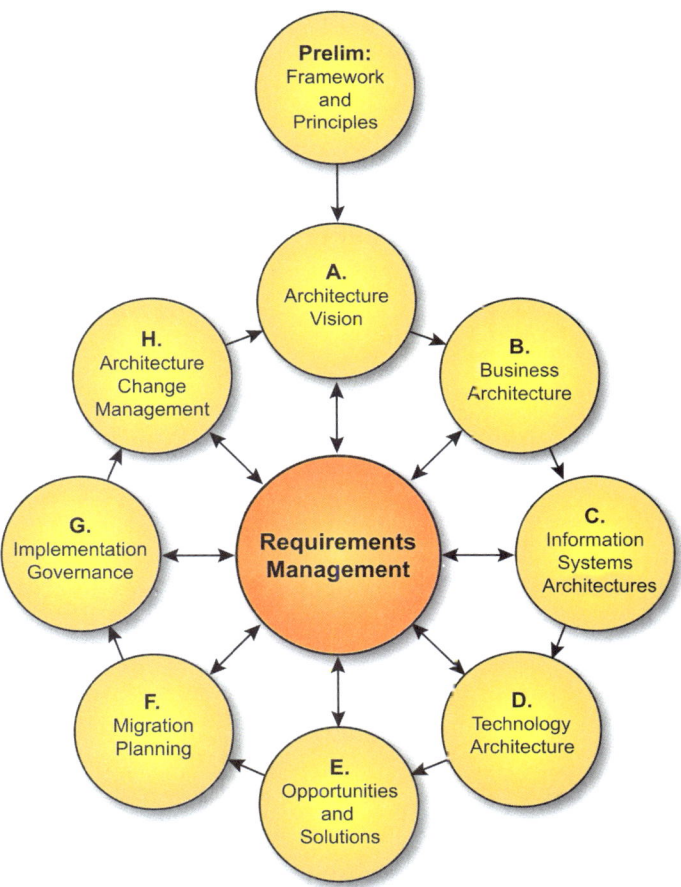

Figure 34.5: Relevance of Requirements Throughout the ADM

Because business requirements are important throughout all phases of the ADM lifecycle, the business scenario technique has an important role to play in the TOGAF ADM, by ensuring that the business requirements themselves are complete and correct.

34.7 Guidelines on Developing Business Scenarios

34.7.1 General Guidelines

The stakeholders (e.g., business managers, end users) will tell you what they want, but as an architect you must still gain an understanding of the business, so you must know the most important actors in the system. If the stakeholders do not know what they want:

- Take time, observe, and record how they are working today
- Structure information in such a way that it can be used later
- Uncover critical business rules from domain experts
- Stay focused on what needs to be accomplished, and how it is to be accomplished

This effort provides the anchor for a chain of reason from business requirements through to technical solutions. It will pay off later to be diligent and critical at the start.

34.7.2 Questions to Ask for Each Area

The business scenario workshops mentioned above in the Gathering phase are really structured interviews. While there is no single set of appropriate questions to ask in all situations, the following provides some guidance to help business scenario consultants in asking questions.

Identifying, Documenting, and Ranking the Problem

Is the problem described as a statement of what needs to be accomplished, like steps in a process, and not how (with technology "push")?

If the problem is too specific or a "how":

- Raise a red flag
- Ask "Why do you need to do it that way?" questions

If the problem is too vague or unactionable:

- Raise a red flag
- Ask "What is it you need to do, or will be able to do if this problem is solved?" questions

Ask questions that help to identify where and when the problem exists:

- Where are you experiencing this particular problem? In what business process?
- When do you encounter these issues? During the beginning of the process, the middle, the end?

Ask questions that help to identify the costs of the problem:

- Do you account for the costs associated with this problem? If so, what are they?
- Are there hidden costs? If so, what are they?
- Is the cost of this problem covered in the cost of something else? If so, what and how much?
- Is the problem manifested in terms of poor quality or a perception of an ineffective organization?

Identifying the Business & Technical Environment, and Documenting in Models

Questions to ask about the business environment:

- What key process suffers from the issues? What are the major steps that need to be processed?
- Location/scale of internal business departments?
- Location/scale of external business partners?
- Any specific business rules and regulations related to the situation?

Questions to ask about the current technology environment:

- What technology components are already presupposed to be related to this problem?
- Are there any technology constraints?
- Are there any technology principles that apply?

Identifying and Documenting Objectives

Is the "what" sufficiently backed up with the rationale for "why"? If not, ask for measurable rationale in the following areas:

- Return on investment
- Scalability
- Performance needs
- Compliance to standards
- Ease-of-use measures

Identifying Human Actors and their Place in the Business Model

An actor represents anything that interacts with or within the system. This can be a human, or a machine, or a computer program. Actors initiate activity with the system, for example:

- Computer user with the computer
- Phone user with the telephone
- Payroll clerk with the payroll system
- Internet subscriber with the web browser

An actor represents a role that a user plays; i.e., a user is someone playing a role while using the system (e.g., John (user) is a dispatcher (actor)). Each actor uses the system in different ways (otherwise they should be the same actor). Ask about the humans that will be involved, from different viewpoints, such as:

- Developer
- Maintainer
- Operator
- Administrator
- User

Identifying Computer Actors and their Place in the Technology Model

Ask about the computer components likely to be involved, again from different points of view. What must they do?

Documenting Roles, Responsibilities, Measures of Success, Required Scripts

When defining roles, ask questions like:

- What are the main tasks of the actor?
- Will the actor have to read/write/change any information?
- Will the actor have to inform the system about outside changes?
- Does the actor wish to be informed about unexpected changes?

Checking for Fitness-for-Purpose, and refining if necessary

Is there enough information to identify who/what could fulfill the requirement? If not, probe more deeply.

Is there a description of when, and how often, the requirement needs to be addressed? If not, ask about timing.

34.8 Guidelines on Business Scenario Documentation

34.8.1 Textual Documentation

Effective business scenario documentation requires a balance between ensuring that the detail is accessible, and preventing it from overshadowing the results and overwhelming the reader. To this end, the business scenario document should have the main findings in the body of the document and the details in appendices.

In the appendices:

- Capture all the important details about a business scenario.
    - Situation description and rationale
    - All measurements
    - All actor roles and sub-measurements
    - All services required
- Capture the critical steps between actors that address the situation, and sequence the interactions
- Declare relevant information about all actors
    - Partition the responsibility of the actors
    - List pre-conditions that have to be met prior to proper system functionality
    - Provide technical requirements for the service to be of acceptable quality

In the main body of the business scenario:

- Generalize all the relevant data from the detail in the appendices

34.8.2 Business Scenario Models

- Remember the purpose of using models:
    - Capture business and technology views in a graphical form
    - Help comprehension
    - Give a starting point to confirm requirements
    - Relate actors and interactions
- Keep drawings clear and neat:
    - Do not put too much into one diagram
    - Simpler diagrams are easier to understand
- Number diagrams for easy reference:
    - Maintain a catalog of the numbers to avoid duplicates

34.9 Guidelines on Goals and Objectives

34.9.1 The Importance of Goals

One of the first steps in the development of an architecture is to define the overall goals and objectives for the development. The objectives should be derived from the business goals of the organization, and the way in which IT is seen to contribute to meeting those goals.

Every organization behaves differently in this respect, some seeing IT as the driving force for the enterprise and others seeing IT in a supporting role, simply automating the business processes which already exist. The essential thing is that the architectural objectives should be very closely aligned with the business goals and objectives of the organization.

34.9.2 The Importance of SMART Objectives

Not only must goals be stated in general terms, but also specific measures need to be attached to them to make them SMART, as described above.

The amount of effort spent in doing this will lead to greater clarity for the sponsors of the architecture evolution cycle. It will pay back by driving proposed solutions much more closely toward the goals at each step of the cycle. It is extremely helpful for the different stakeholders inside the organization, as well as for suppliers and consultants, to have a clear yardstick for measuring fitness-for-purpose. If done well, the ADM can be used to trace specific decisions back to criteria, and thus yield their justification.

The goals below have been adapted from those given in previous versions of TOGAF. These are categories of goals, each with a list of possible objectives. Each of these objectives should be made SMART with specific measures and metrics for the task. However, since the actual work to be done will be specific to the architecture project concerned, it is not possible to provide a list of generic SMART objectives that will relate to any project.

Instead, we provide here some example SMART objectives.

Example of Making Objectives SMART

Under the general goal heading "Improve User Productivity" below, there is an objective to provide a "Consistent User Interface" and it is described as follows:

"A consistent user interface will ensure that all user-accessible functions and services will appear and behave in a similar, predictable fashion regardless of application or site. This will lead to better efficiency and fewer user errors, which in turn may result in lower recovery costs."

To make this objective SMART, we ask whether the objective is specific, measurable, actionable, realistic, and time-bound, and then augment the objective appropriately.

The following captures an analysis of these criteria for the stated objective:

- Specific: The objective of providing "a consistent user interface that will ensure all user accessible functions and services will appear and behave in a similar, predictable fashion regardless of application or site". is pretty specific. However, the measures listed in the second sentence could be more specific ...

- Measurable: As stated above, the objective is measurable, but could be more specific. The second sentence could be amended to read (for example): "This will lead to 10% greater user efficiency and 20% fewer order entry user errors, which in turn may result in 5% lower order entry costs".

- Actionable: The objective does appear to be actionable. It seems clear that consistency of the user interface must be provided, and that could be handled by whoever is responsible for providing the user interface to the user device.

- Realistic: The objective of providing "a consistent user interface that will ensure all user accessible functions and services will appear and behave in a similar, predictable fashion regardless of application or site" might not be realistic. Considering the use today of PDAs at the user end might lead us to augment this objective to assure that the downstream developers don't unduly create designs that hinder the use of new technologies. The objective could be re-stated as "a consistent user interface, across user interface devices that provide similar functionality, that will ensure ..." etc.

- Time-bound: The objective as stated is not time-bound. To be time-bound the objective could be re-stated as "By the end of Q3, provide a consistent ...".

The above results in a SMART objective that looks more like this (again remember this is an example):

"By the end of Q3, provide a consistent user interface across user interface devices that provide similar functionality to ensure all user accessible functions and services appear and behave in a similar way when using those devices in a predictable fashion regardless of application or site. This will lead to 10% greater user efficiency and 20% fewer order entry user errors, which in turn may result in 5% lower order entry costs."

34.9.3 Categories of Goals and Objectives

Although every organization will have its own set of goals, some examples may help in the development of an organization-specific list. The goals given below are categories of goals, each with a list of possible objectives, which have been adapted from the goals given in previous versions of TOGAF.

Each of the objectives given below should be made SMART with specific measures and metrics for the task involved, as illustrated in the example above. However, the actual work to be done will be specific to the architecture project concerned, and it is not possible to provide a list of generic SMART objectives that will relate to any project.

Goal: Improve Business Process Performance

Business process improvements can be realized through the following objectives:

- Increased process throughput
- Consistent output quality
- Predictable process costs
- Increased re-use of existing processes
- Reduced time of sending business information from one process to another process

Goal: Decrease Costs

Cost improvements can be realized through the following objectives:

- Lower levels of redundancy and duplication in assets throughout the enterprise
- Decreased reliance on external IT service providers for integration and customization
- Lower costs of maintenance

Goal: Improve Business Operations

Business operations improvements can be realized through the following objectives:

- Increased budget available to new business features
- Decreased costs of running the business
- Decreased time-to-market for products or services
- Increased quality of services to customers
- Improved quality of business information

Goal: Improve Management Efficacy

Management efficacy improvements can be realized through the following objectives:

- Increased flexibility of business
- Shorter time to make decisions
- Higher quality decisions

Goal: Reduce Risk

Risk improvements can be realized through the following objectives:

- Ease of implementing new processes
- Decreased errors introduced into business processes through complex and faulty systems
- Decreased real-world safety hazards (including hazards that cause loss of life)

Goal: Improve Effectiveness of IT Organization

IT organization effectiveness can be realized through the following objectives:

- Increased rollout of new projects
- Decreased time to rollout new projects
- Lower cost in rolling out new projects
- Decreased loss of service continuity when rolling out new projects
- Common development: applications that are common to multiple business areas will be developed or acquired once and re-used rather than separately developed by each business area.
- Open systems environment: a standards-based common operating environment, which accommodates the injection of new standards, technologies, and applications on an organization-wide basis, will be established. This standards-based environment will provide the basis for development of common applications and facilitate software re-use.
- Use of products: as far as possible, hardware-independent, off-the-shelf items should be used to satisfy requirements in order to reduce dependence on custom developments and to reduce development and maintenance costs.
- Software re-use: for those applications that must be custom developed, development of portable applications will reduce the amount of software developed and add to the inventory of software suitable for re-use by other systems.
- Resource sharing: data processing resources (hardware, software, and data) will be shared by all users requiring the services of those resources. Resource sharing will be accomplished in the context of security and operational considerations.

Goal: Improve User Productivity

User productivity improvements can be realized through the following objectives:

- Consistent user interface: a consistent user interface will ensure that all user-accessible functions and services will appear and behave in a similar, predictable fashion regardless of application or site. This will lead to better efficiency and fewer user errors, which in turn may result in lower recovery costs
- Integrated applications: applications available to the user will behave in a logically consistent manner across user environments, which will lead to the same benefits as a consistent user interface.
- Data sharing: databases will be shared across the organization in the context of security and operational considerations, leading to increased ease-of-access to required data.

Goal: Improve Portability and Scalability

The portability and scalability of applications will be through the following objectives:

- Portability: applications that adhere to open systems standards will be portable, leading to increased ease-of-movement across heterogeneous computing platforms. Portable applications can allow sites to upgrade their platforms as technological improvements occur, with minimal impact on operations.
- Scalability: applications that conform to the model will be configurable, allowing operation on the full spectrum of platforms required.

Goal: Improve Interoperability

Interoperability improvements across applications and business areas can be realized through the following objectives:

- Common infrastructure: the architecture should promote a communications and computing infrastructure based on open systems and systems transparency including, but not limited to, operating systems, database management, data interchange, network services, network management, and user interfaces.
- Standardization: by implementing standards-based platforms, applications will be provided with and will be able to use a common set of services that improve the opportunities for interoperability.

Goal: Increase Vendor Independence

Vendor independence will be increased through the following objectives:

- Interchangeable components: only hardware and software that have standards-based interfaces will be selected, so that upgrades or the insertion of new products will result in minimal disruption to the user's environment.
- Non-proprietary specifications: capabilities will be defined in terms of non-proprietary specifications that support full and open competition and are available to any vendor for use in developing commercial products.

Goal: Reduce Lifecycle Costs

Lifecycle costs can be reduced through most of the objectives discussed above. In addition, the following objectives directly address reduction of lifecycle costs:

- Reduced duplication: replacement of isolated systems and islands of automation with interconnected open systems will lead to reductions in overlapping functionality, data duplication, and unneeded redundancy because open systems can share data and other resources.

- Reduced software maintenance costs: reductions in the quantity and variety of software used in the organization will lead to reductions in the amount and cost of software maintenance. Use of standard off-the-shelf software will lead to further reductions in costs since vendors of such software distribute their product maintenance costs across a much larger user base.

- Incremental replacement: common interfaces to shared infrastructure components allow for phased replacement or upgrade with minimal operational disturbance.

- Reduced training costs: common systems and consistent Human Computer Interfaces (HCIs) will lead to reduced training costs.

Goal: Improve Security

Security can be improved in the organization's information through the following objectives:

- Consistent security interfaces for applications: consistent security interfaces and procedures will lead to fewer errors when developing applications and increased application portability. Not all applications will need the same suite of security features, but any features used will be consistent across applications.

- Consistent security interfaces for users: a common user interface to security features will lead to reduced learning time when moving from system to system.

- Security independence: application deployment can use the security policy and mechanisms appropriate to the particular environment if there is good layering in the architecture.

- A 25% reduction in calls to the help desk relating to security issues.

- A 20% reduction in "false positives" detected in the network (a false positive is an event that appears to be an actionable security event, but in fact is a false alarm).

Goal: Improve Manageability

Management improvement can be realized through the following objectives:

- Consistent management interface: consistent management practices and procedures will facilitate management across all applications and their underlying support structures. A consistent interface can simplify the management burden, leading to increased user efficiency.

- Reduced operation, administration, and maintenance costs: operation, administration, and maintenance costs may be reduced through the availability of improved management products and increased standardization of the objects being managed.

34.10 Summary

Business scenarios help address one of the most common issues facing IT executives: aligning IT with the business.

The success of any major IT project is measured by the extent to which it is linked to business requirements, and demonstrably supports and enables the enterprise to achieve its business objectives. Business scenarios are an important technique that may be used at various stages of defining enterprise architecture, or any other major IT project, to derive the characteristics of the architecture directly from the high-level requirements of the business. Business scenarios are used to help identify and understand business needs, and thereby to derive the business requirements that the architecture development, and ultimately the IT, has to address.

However, it is important to remember that business scenarios are just a tool, not the objective. They are a part of, and enable, the larger process of architecture development. The architect should use them, but not get lost it them. The key is to stay focused - watch out for "feature creep", and address the most important issues that tend to return the greatest value.

Chapter 35: Case Studies

35.1 The Role of Case Studies

One of the goals of The Open Group Architecture Forum is to provide a forum within which both customer and vendor organizations can exchange feedback and experience in the use of TOGAF.

All of this feedback is considered in the ongoing evolution of TOGAF within the Architecture Forum, and indeed much of it has already been incorporated in this current version of TOGAF.

It is important to emphasize that no case study can provide a complete blueprint for how another organization should go about using TOGAF. All organizations are different, and each organization should understand what TOGAF has to offer, and adopt and adapt the parts that are useful for its needs.

Nevertheless, over the years of its existence as an architecture framework, TOGAF has been used by a variety organizations around the world in major architecture developments, both in its entirety, and in an adapted form.

It is hoped that the case studies presented here will provide useful guidance to organizations intending to use TOGAF or considering using it to develop an enterprise IT architecture.

The formats of the case studies vary, between normal descriptive text, through presentations, and in some cases video.

The following case studies show TOGAF in use in a variety of situations.

35.2 Dairy Farm Group (Hong Kong)

The Dairy Farm Group Case Study[17] illustrates extensive use of TOGAF as the basis of an enterprise-wide IT architecture to integrate many disparate business units.

The Dairy Farm Group (DFG) is a holding company in the Retail sector. It has a very strong presence in the Asia/Pacific region, and is the 71st largest retailing company worldwide.

DFG has a corporate goal to be the largest, most successful retailer in Asia/Pacific in its chosen markets. To support this goal, DFG has restructured from a federation to a unified group of companies, with a single corporate purpose business focus, and a single IT infrastructure.

The DFG Technical Program Architecture Group (TAPG) was chartered to develop a Technical Architecture for DFG, and chose TOGAF and its supporting methodology as the

---

17 Available at *www.opengroup.org/public/member/q498/DFG/dfg_frame.htm*.

basis. Using TOGAF, the TAPG was able, in a very short period of time (from July through October 1998) to develop a world-class technical architecture.

It was particularly helpful to be able to point key suppliers to a published version of TOGAF, so that they could see an explanation of the methodology and refer to the TOGAF Standards Information Base (SIB).

This Case Study has its own web site at: *www.opengroup.org/public/member/q498/DFG/dfg_frame.htm*.

35.3 Department of Social Security (UK)

The DSS Case Study illustrates the use of TOGAF, both as the basis of a new architecture framework, and as a key tool in managing the outsourcing of service delivery, in that vendors and integrators were required to use TOGAF as the basis for their tenders, and to use it subsequently in the ongoing management of the IT architecture.

35.3.1 Organizational Context

The UK Department of Social Security (DSS) is responsible for the development, maintenance, and delivery of the UK's social security program and of the UK Government's policy for child support. The DSS currently employs around 90,000 staff and utilizes the largest civilian computer operation in Europe to provide services to its executive agencies, other government bodies, and various Independent Statutory Bodies. One of those executive agencies, the Information Technology Services Agency (ITSA), is responsible for providing the necessary IT systems and services, either internally or through contracts with the private sector.

Social Security spending is approaching £100 billion a year (1999), making it the biggest single spending department in government. At any given time, 70% of the population are in contact with the DSS. In 1998 the Department:

- Dealt with 15 million benefit claims, and 33 million changes of circumstances
- Made nearly a billion payments (a great deal of which were handled electronically)
- Handled upwards of 160 million telephone enquires

35.3.2 Existing IT

Departmental IT systems have tended to be product-based rather than customer-centered. There are separate systems for each DSS agency. In the case of the Benefits Agency, there are separate systems for each benefit. Each benefit system has evolved as a series of processes, supported by its own IS/IT. These "Benefit Chimneys" support their own individual processes, and hold their own information. The consequence is unnecessary duplication and inefficiency, between processes and functions that are, or could be, common. This is especially the case in the way that the Department uses the information it holds. This belies the fact that these systems have data and functions in common.

35.3.3 Strategic Objectives

Recognizing the problems inherent in a product-based approach, a Corporate IS/IT (CISIT) Strategy was developed to support government objectives for a modern, more responsive social security service. IS and IT are crucial, not just to change the Welfare State, but to fundamentally change, for the better, the way that the DSS delivers services. Within the IS/IT arena the changes have shifted the focus to the definition, and purchase, of services rather than products, and promotes a new sourcing strategy. Private sector service providers are expected to a play a greater role in the development of the Department's new IS/IT systems to capitalize on their experience, expertise, and self-financing abilities.

The welfare system must be an active system. It must be simpler, more efficient, transparent, and easier to use. It must be better geared towards the needs of the people who actually use it, be they the general public or the Department's staff. IS and IT will have a key part in enabling these changes, in that any services must be:

- More accessible and easier to use than they are now
- More efficient and effective
- More accurate and less vulnerable to fraud
- Simpler and more flexible than they are now

Central to the Corporate IS/IT Strategy is the provision of a single logical data repository capable of supporting all of the Department's core business activities. This will reduce duplication of stored data and, thus costs to the taxpayer and the potential for fraudulent claims. It will also ensure that information common to different benefits only needs to be captured once, so providing an improved service to the public.

The data will be complemented by a set of shared systems which will carry out common functions which need to be consistent, such as capturing information, calculating entitlements, and making payments. Ultimately such functions are also expected to be shared, with the intention that they maximize flexibility for, and responsiveness to, policy changes.

Greater freedom is permitted in local business practices. but local systems are required to work with the common services to provide cohesive end-to-end support of social security administration.

The UK Government as a whole is looking to new technology to improve the way government services are delivered: the Prime Minister has pledged to increase the number of opportunities for customers to access DSS services electronically. Using its Corporate IS/IT Strategy, the DSS intends to position itself to optimize its use of new technologies in order to provide better, simpler services for DSS customers and staff alike.

It is also the intention of the DSS to modernize the links that exist with other government departments and other relevant organizations, such as Local Authorities. What is needed to be achieved in social security - flexible, easy-to-use and efficient services, based on common information - needs to be achieved across government. This is known as "joined up" government and is focussed around delivering the goals of government as a whole in a seamless, integrated way. This will enable staff to concentrate on delivering a better service to clients, whilst improving efficiency and effectiveness through IT support.

35.3.4 The Accord Project

Realizing the Department's IS/IT Strategy will be a large and complex task that will be delivered in stages, over a number of years. These strategic aims are being taken forward by a major procurement project - the ACcess to CORporate Data (ACCORD) project. Three private sector consortia (composed of major international companies) satisfied the criteria for participation in this procurement and all have been awarded IS/IT Services Agreements under which a range of IS/IT services may be purchased. These IS/IT services may be allocated for different time periods, at the end of which time the services must be capable of being recompeted and provided by a different service provider. The DSS, therefore, is required to manage multiple service providers. It must also ensure that their services, which may run in heterogeneous environments, are capable of interacting.

Given the scale of DSS operations, the transition to CISIT-compliant systems will take place on an incremental basis over a number of years. Thus, legacy and the new IS/IT systems will be required to run in parallel and interoperate.

35.3.5 The Need for a New Architecture Framework

Despite the importance of ACCORD IT developments, other initiatives, both sourced from within ITSA and via external procurement routes, will inevitably occur. This dictates the need for Departmental control and the setting of a context for any development. The Department will retain strategic and management control of its architecture via the use of an architecture framework. It is intended that this framework will:

- Provide a classification and structuring scheme within which IT applications can be placed
- Identify those architectural components which can be used, as required, in various combinations to construct operational (sub)systems
- Provide the reference documentation for the architecture(s) of CISIT systems
- Provide the vehicle whereby the principles and standards of the architecture(s) are described along with their dependencies/interdependencies
- Provide a process for developing the architecture/solutions throughout the lifetime of CISIT systems
- Document the different perspectives of the CISIT systems
- Support the specification of requirements and evaluation of supplier bids
- Support the development and monitoring of contractual milestones

- Facilitate, through the documentation of the CISIT systems:
  - Better integration and interoperation of systems
  - Subsequent developments
  - Support re-competition (over time)
  - Change/contract management

The Department's legacy systems had been developed according to an in-house architecture framework. Rather than extend that framework, it was decided that a new architecture framework was required that more closely met the needs of the CISIT Strategy. The Department's Corporate IS/IT Architecture Framework (CISITAF) has been based on that produced by The Open Group, The Open Group Architecture Framework (TOGAF) because:

- It provides a common set of vendor-independent terminologies for documenting the Department's technical requirements.
- It has been widely accepted within the IT industry. Due to the nature of the Departmental context, this was seen as a key advantage of using TOGAF. All SPs would have their own preference for an architecture framework; e.g., ICL would utilize Open/Framework whilst IBM would prefer Open/Blueprint. However, TOGAF is vendor-neutral having been developed with input from many leading IT companies and cognizant of the other major frameworks.
- It complements the architecture framework upon which the Department's legacy systems are based.

35.3.6 CISITAF Documentation Set

It would not be practical to document the whole CISIT architecture framework within a single document. The documents that will eventually comprise the CISITAF (they will be developed along different time lines) are shown in the following diagram.

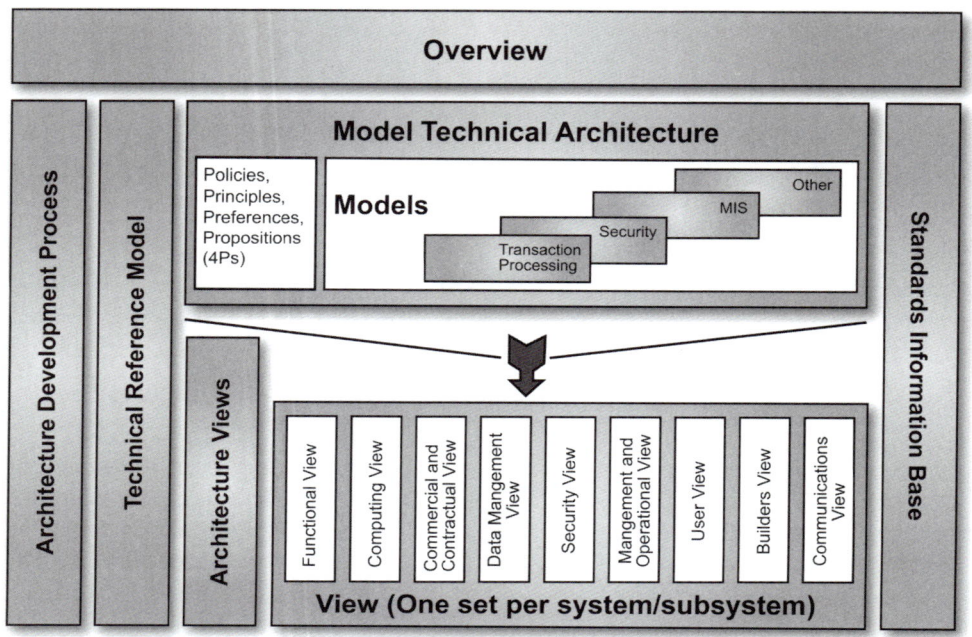

Figure 35.1: CISITAF Documentation Set

Although the CISITAF tends to place a different emphasis on the elements, it includes all of those in the TOGAF base set, namely:

- A Technical Reference Model (TRM)
- A Standards Information Base (SIB)
- An Architecture Development Process

supported by descriptions of the architecture from different views.

These have been supplemented by a new framework component: the Model Technical Architecture.

35.3.7 Technical Reference Model

Development of the CISITAF commenced with the definition of a Technical Reference Model (TRM). Use of the TRM aimed to ensure completeness of the architectural definition, by providing a taxonomy of common terms and definitions.

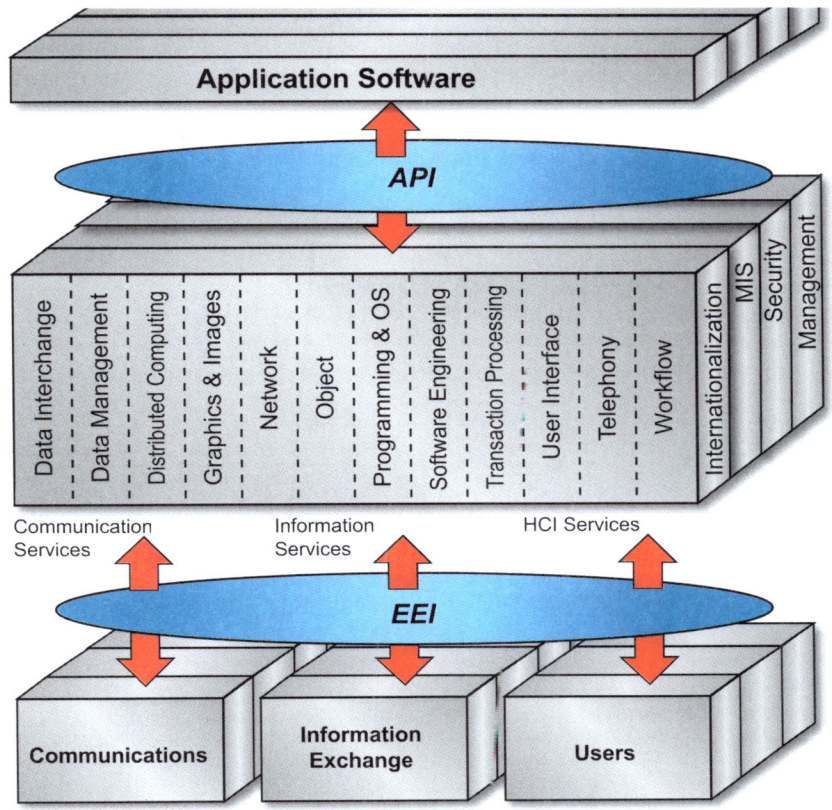

Figure 35.2: CISITAF Technical Reference Model

It identifies the IT infrastructure services that may be required on one or a number of application platforms within the CISIT architecture.

The set of services shown is based upon the TOGAF TRM with additions to reflect DSS-specific requirements. The additional services are telephony services and workflow services.

Conformance to this model does not mean that an application will implement all or only these named services without any additional facilities. The set of services used in any situation will be tailored to meet specific business needs.

35.3.8 Standards Information Base

The Standards Information Base (SIB) within TOGAF comprises a comprehensive list of the standards adopted by The Open Group.

The CISITAF SIB has the same aims of promoting interoperability and software portability. However, it will focus upon Departmental technical policies and standards, together with relationships between them, which may be used to assist in the selection of standards and products.

This document will be populated incrementally as appropriate standards are identified and agreed.

35.3.9 Architecture Development Process

The Architecture Development Process (ADP) will describe how the CISITAF will be developed and maintained. It will also outline the stages to be followed, roles and responsibilities of relevant parties, and the products to be produced throughout the process.

Documentation of the ADP is pending the resolution of various organizational and technical issues. It is intended that it will be progressed through an Architecture Control Service.

35.3.10 Architecture Views

The Architecture Views describe an IT system/subsystem from different perspectives to satisfy the requirements of diverse interest groups. The CISITAF makes use of the following Views:

- Functional View
- Management and Operational View
- Security View
- Builder's View
- Data Management View
- User View
- Commercial and Contractual View
- Computing View
- Communications View

Essentially, these views are the same as those recommended by TOGAF, with two principal differences:

- A consideration of operational aspects has been added to the Management View
- A Commercial and Contractual View has been defined.

The Commercial and Contractual View is a necessary addition given that the DSS intends to implement the CISIT Strategy using a number of services/systems, potentially supplied by different service providers. It provides the perspective which concentrates on those metrics and processes that are required to support a (sub)system's commercial and contractual aspects and interface it successfully with (sub)systems provided by other service providers.

35.3.11 Model Technical Architecture

The CISITAF Model Technical Architecture (MTA) constitutes an addition to the standard TOGAF approach. It is complementary to the TRM in that it focuses on providing a number of models for features which may be implemented on one, or a number of application platforms. In addition, the models may be implemented by one or more IT infrastructure services on each application platform, which would reflect the TRM taxonomy.

The MTA describes the goal technical architecture for systems, which will be developed within the CISIT Strategy. Each architectural aspect is defined within a separate chapter, supported by what have been termed the "four Ps":

- Policies are statements that (once agreed) must be adhered to in any specification, construction, and operation of a system within the CISITAF. Any proposal or bid will be assessed as to its ability to meet all of the policies.
- Principles are the engineering principles that should be adhered to. Like all principles there are implementation options, but the underlying spirit of the principles must be adhered to.
- Preferences are areas where the Department would prefer a particular mechanism, style, methodology, product, etc. The adoption of alternatives by service providers is possible, but convincing reasons for the adoption of any alternatives will need to be provided.
- Propositions collect the hypotheses and ideas raised in the various areas of the model architecture. Service providers are required to consider the propositions and adopt them or articulate alternatives together with convincing reasons for the alternative.

Where more detail is required, there may be an architectural model, held as a separate document, giving more information regarding the architectural aspect, including the description, objectives, and rationale for that particular architecture. Aspects meriting such treatment include:

- Component architecture
- Transaction management
- Data management
- Security
- Interoperation with legacy systems
- Management Information Systems (MIS)
- Directory services
- Workflow management
- Output services
- Event management
- Data networks

In addition, the MTA specifies a number of general engineering principles, or qualities, that must be exhibited by all CISIT deliverables:

- Scalability
- Resilience
- Security
- Serviceability
- Availability
- Manageability
- Auditability
- Interoperability
- Flexibility
- Suitability

35.3.12 Using the CISITAF

The ACCORD procurement has proceeded in a number of stages and the CISITAF has been used, to varying degrees, in all of them.

The specification of the technical requirements has been informed by the policies and principles detailed in the MTA. In their responses, service providers have been required to commit to adhering to all the policies and principles in the CISITAF. They have had to describe how their proposed solutions satisfy the general engineering principles.

In ascertaining the capabilities of different service providers, during the initial bidding stages of the procurement, to deliver ACCORD services, Architecture Views have provided the Department with a means of eliciting full and comparable descriptions of proposed solutions. These views also provided a concise description of the technical proposals that were invaluable in allowing staff not directly involved in the procurement to quickly gain of overview of the solutions. To assist the Department in carrying out technical compliance and technical assurance, a matrix had to be provided for each product used, which detailed how that product supports the CISITAF engineering principles.

From those consortia awarded an ACCORD IS/IT Services Agreement, one, Affinity, was selected to take the lead role in delivering the initial implementations of IS/IT services. At this stage, the service provider was required to be more explicit about their proposed solutions. The CISITAF is coming to the fore in finalizing the detailed technical requirements. The MTA and its subordinate models have been used as the basis for informed, detailed consultation with the service provider. These discussions have resulted in the production of the Technical Solution Statement within which the Architecture Views are being used to document the agreed system architecture.

Continuing use of the CISITAF has been assured for the duration of the ACCORD IS/IT Services Agreements. All Service Providers, who have signed such agreements, have committed themselves to using and assisting in the development of the CISITAF so that it encompasses changes in business and IS/IT strategy.

The Department has determined that the principal way in which this will be achieved is through an Architecture Control Service (ACS), operated jointly by the Department and lead service provider, with other service providers in supporting roles. In addition to the ACCORD initiative, there are also a number of other IS/IT developments planned or currently underway. The ACS will be the authority responsible for ensuring that all providers of CISIT services, including ITSA, comply with the CISITAF standards. This is intended to facilitate the integration and interoperation of systems from different sources and maintain flexibility in the choice of supply channels.

The Department has instituted an organizational structure in order to obtain senior commitment to the ACS. An Architecture Board has been established made up of senior officers representing both the Department's IS and IT and the Department's private sector partners. The IS/IT Architecture Board will drive the strategic IS/IT Architecture activities of the Department, maintaining very close links with the business vision via the involvement of the Modern Services Team. The DSS Architecture Board is supported by an Architecture Control Team that will carry out the day-to-day activities of the ACS, including:

- Maintenance of the Architecture Vision
- Communication of the vision
- Co-ordination of the architecture definition
- Input into the process of control; e.g., liaison between the architecture board and architecture working groups
- Supporting services; e.g., secretariat and architects-R-US (selling architects into projects)

The aim of this team is not to try and create a single architecture team, but to control the architecture via the co-ordination of the other Departmental groups. This will be achieved by the establishment of architecture working groups that will carry out the detailed technical work with the support of the architecture control team and with the authority of the Architecture Board.

Amongst the initial activities of the ACS will be the agreement and documentation of the CISITAF architectural development process and the identification of IS/IT systems to support the ACS. It is envisaged that the CISITAF standards information base will emerge from the latter piece of work.

35.4 Litton PRC (US)

Litton PRC chose the TOGAF Architecture Development Method (ADM) as a basis for its revamped internal Architecture Design Process. The Litton PRC Case Study[18] reviews the use of TOGAF within Litton PRC, and explains why TOGAF was chosen.

ailable at *www.opengroup.org/architecture/togaf8-doc/arch/p4/cases/prc2/wilson.pdf.*

35.5 JEDMICS

The Joint Engineering Data Management Information and Control System (JEDMICS) Case Study illustrates the early stages of the ADM in use on a specific project.

35.5.1 Background

The JEDMICS, formerly known as EDMICS before the "joint" services status was added, is designed to provide a modern means of storing and retrieving engineering drawings and data in electronic repositories through the use of various optical, digital and magnetic mass storage devices, digitizing scanners, graphics hard copy devices, graphics display workstations, and communications devices. JEDMICS addresses the needs of the primary and secondary engineering repositories for the US Armed Services and the Defense Logistics Agency, including activities such as Navy Shipyards, Naval Aviation Depots, and Army and Air Force maintenance depots.

A key element of JEDMICS is the conversion of repositories for engineering data - which include both drawings and documents - into digital format and storing the data on optical disk to support changes in depot maintenance processes. These repositories will store 190 million engineering drawings and 500,000 technical publications. Such an extensive amount of data in JEDMICS repositories represents an enormous investment in labor and in the establishment of workflow processes to utilize that data. It is, therefore, critically important that the JEDMICS investment be kept technologically fresh. This puts tremendous emphasis on platform and software interchange and interoperability.

35.5.2 Definition of Existing Environment in Existing Terms

JEDMICS can be viewed as several subsystems: Input, Data Integrity, Index, Optical Storage, Graphics Display Workstation, and Output. The functional view of the JEDMICS architecture is shown in Functional View of Existing JEDMICS Environment .

The Input Subsystem is the primary entry point for scanning drawings, aperture cards, and documents into JEDMICS. The major hardware components include large-format scanners, dual-sided page scanners, and high-speed aperture card scanners.

The Data Integrity Subsystem provides for the processing of scanned images that temporarily reside on magnetic storage while awaiting quality assurance on Data Integrity Control workstations.

The Index Subsystem provides for the inquiry and access of image-related index information upon being scanned into the JEDMICS system.

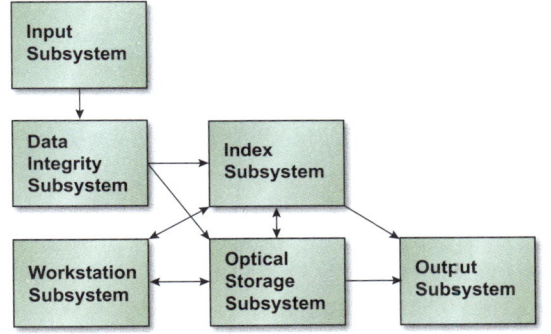

Figure 35.3: Functional View of Existing JEDMICS Environment

The Optical Storage Subsystem provides for the storage of image data on both multiple disk autochangers, "jukeboxes", and standalone single-disk devices. The stand-alone units provide backup for the jukebox and, in addition, are a means for exchanging data between sites.

The Remote Output (Workstation) Subsystem provides the capability to access image and index data that resides in the Data Integrity Control and Optical Storage Subsystems. The Multifunction Graphics Display Workstation provides the ability to view an image and direct output to a hardcopy output device. The multifunction capability of this workstation allows the site to access different systems from the same hardware platform. The Engineering Graphics Display Workstation provides a true raster editing capability.

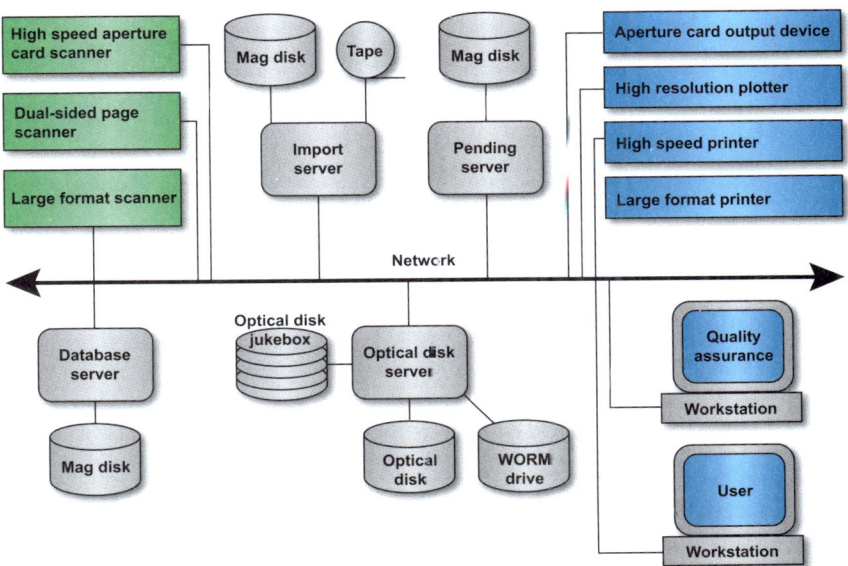

Figure 35.4: Existing Hardware Topology

The Output Subsystem provides for a variety of output devices and media types for JEDMICS engineering data. Output capabilities include aperture card production, high-resolution hardcopy plotting, large-format printing, and high-speed printing.

The topology of the existing JEDMICS is shown in Existing Hardware Topology .

35.5.3 Restatement of Existing Environment in TOGAF Terms

The existing JEDMICS environment follows a distributed computing architectural model. A client JEDMICS application on a workstation communicates with server applications on the Index Server and Optical Data Management Server to retrieve engineering data and display it at the workstation. The Input Subsystem works as a client communicating with the Data Integrity Subsystem server to enter engineering data into JEDMICS. The data, once subjected to quality control checks, is then transferred from the Data Integrity (Pending) Server to the Index and Optical Data Management Servers to be entered into JEDMICS permanent storage.

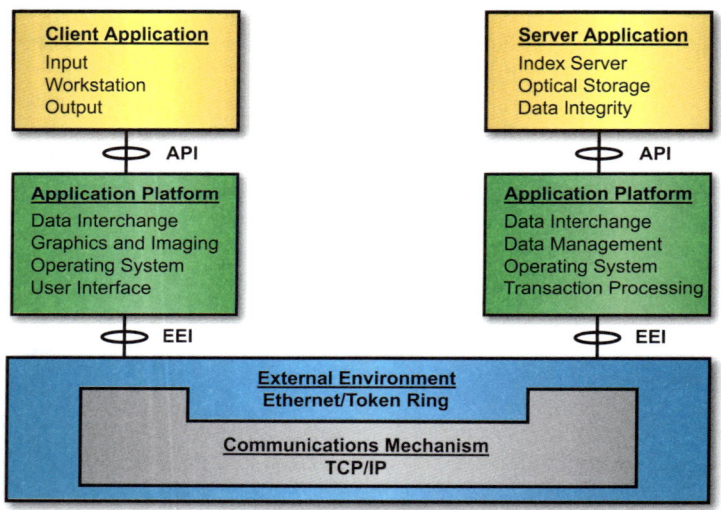

Figure 35.5: JEDMICS Distributed Computing Architecture

The Output Subsystem also acts as a client to the Index and Optical Data Management Servers to output JEDMICS data. Requests for output are initiated by the Workstation client and communicated to the Output Subsystem. The Output client application requests the data from the Index and Optical Data Management Servers and outputs it to aperture cards, tapes, printers, plotters, CD-ROMs, or any other output device available to JEDMICS.

The general diagram for the JEDMICS distributed computing model is shown in JEDMICS Distributed Computing Architecture .

The existing environment can be restated in TOGAF terms using Mapping of Services to Existing Architecture that maps the existing JEDMICS components into the standard application platform services.

	Input	Data Integrity	Index	Optical Storage	Output	Workstation
Data Interchange	●	●			●	
Data Management		●	●	●		
Graphics & Imaging	●				●●	
Network	●	●	●	●	●	●
Object			●	●		
Operating System	●	●	●	●	●	●
Software Engineering						
Transaction Processing			●			
User Interface	●					●

Table 35.1: Mapping of Services to Existing Architecture

The standard application platform services provided in JEDMICS perform the following specific functions:

- Data Interchange: In JEDMICS, drawings are input to the system and output from the system in C4 format, which is a tiled, CCITT Group IV bitmap encoding format service. The Data Interchange services convert the bitmap from various scanned formats into C4 format and convert from C4 format to bitmap data that can be sent to common data output devices like printers and CRT screens.

- Data Management: These services are satisfied by an Oracle Relational Database Management System (RDBMS) for the index data and Kodak KOSI optical disk management software.

- Graphics and Imaging: Scanners and compression software services are used in the Input Subsystem and decompression software and imaging and drawing services are used by the Workstation and Output Subsystems.

- Network: In JEDMICS all of the components use the functions provided by the TCP/IP protocol stack working over either an Ethernet or Token Ring network (depending on the user installation).

- Object: The Index and Optical Storage Subsystems manage the drawing objects in JEDMICS and make use of Object Services.

- Operating System: The Operating System Services are found on all of the JEDMICS subsystems.

- Software Engineering: Although programming language compilers and GUI builders are used to develop JEDMICS, no Software Engineering Services map into existing subsystems.

- Transaction Processing: The ORACLE RDBMS used by the Index subsystem provides these services.

- User Interface: These functions are provided at the Input Subsystem and at the Workstation subsystem.

35.5.4 Views, Constraints, and External Environments

35.5.4.1 Operations View

In the Operations view, the key operational aspect of the system is the storage of engineering data and the retrieval by users of that data. JEDMICS is designed to be the authoritative repository for all DoD engineering data. The majority of the engineering data to be stored is in the form of drawings. Drawings consist of sheets and frames of data and can have accompanying documents associated with them. Drawings and drawing sheets can be revised and the coherent basis for each set of revisions among the drawings and drawing sheets must be made. Additionally, sets of drawings or individual sheets may be associated with each other to create sets that can be used for procurement, manufacturing, and maintenance of objects described by the drawings.

Because the JEDMICS is to serve as the authoritative repository of engineering data, strict quality controls are placed on all data entering the system. This quality control function is exercised by staging input to interim magnetic storage first, and then migrating the data to optical disk for permanent storage once it has been checked. Data placed in permanent storage may be accessed by local and remote users and viewed or printed as needed. Each piece of data in the system must be able to be accessed by drawing number, manufacturer, description, and weapon system.

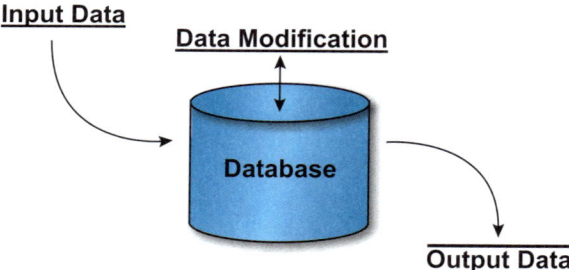

Figure 35.6: Operations View

35.5.4.2 Management View

The management view of the system is that the user has a role in the system according to the function that they are performing. This view partitions the users of the system into the following categories:

- System Supervisors: Control the operation of the system and assign privileges to other users.
- Scanner Operators: Input data to the system.

- Quality Assurance Operators: Check the quality of input data and edit as necessary.
- Engineers: Edit the data and create new data.
- Users: View and print the data but do not modify the data. Users can create their own associations of existing data for maintenance and procurement activities.

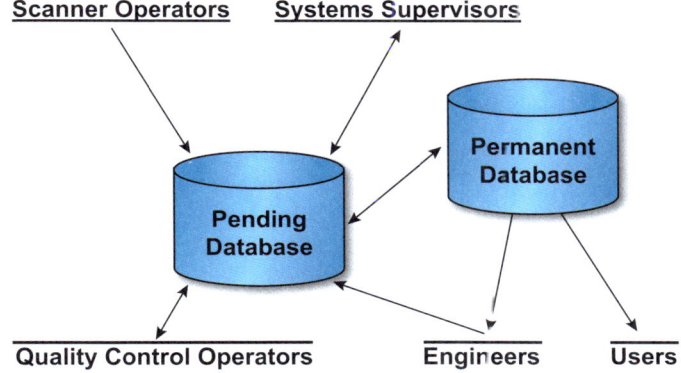

Figure 35.7: Management View

35.5.4.3 Security View

The security view has two types of security mechanisms. Each user has a unique user ID and password that allows him or her access to certain categories of data. In addition, each hardware device capable of inputting or outputting data has restrictions on the category of data on which it can operate. Data can be input, viewed, printed, and output only if both the user and the input/output device have the prerequisite access authority to the required categories.

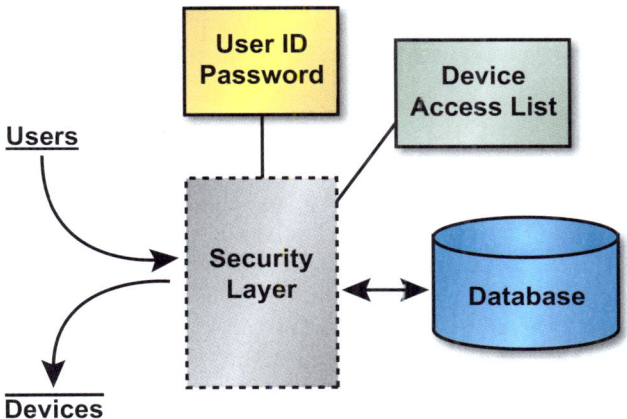

Figure 35.8: Security View

34.5.4.4 Constraints

JEDMICS provides the means for the acquisition, storage, management, and distribution of engineering technical data as well as the wide variety of other published material related to the operation and maintenance of ships, airplanes, and weapons systems in the Services. With JEDMICS, this information is received, stored, accessed, and transferred digitally on optical disk.

The optical disk technology in JEDMICS is the cornerstone of the weapons system acquisition process improvements anticipated through CALS. The repositories of drawings maintained in JEDMICS are the source for the efficient distribution and sharing of the large volume of complex engineering drawings and technical data.

JEDMICS has replaced the current manual and semi-automated aperture card-based repository functions with a fully automated optical disk-based system that will enhance access, timeliness, and product quality for the primary government users of engineering drawings.

The current JEDMICS was constructed using an open systems approach to software development, the integration of commercial off-the-shelf (COTS) hardware/software, training, maintenance, site surveys, and system design plans. The JEDMICS contract included a technology refreshment clause that allowed for the incorporation of new technology as it became available. The system was initially deployed with VAX computers as the Index Server, Sun Sparc 1+ computer workstations for Editing Workstations, and Zenith 286 computers for the User Workstations. Because open system principles were adhered to during the JEDMICS design, the system has evolved to SGI Challenge POSIX index servers, Sun Sparc 5 Editing Workstations, and Pentium User Workstations. The latest software version fielded for the 36 systems in use supports both of these configurations (original VAX and current SGI), plus intermediate technical refresh configurations. Only minor software differences exist, and only because of the operating system differences between the VAX (non-POSIX compliant VMS operating system) and the SGI (POSIX-compliant IRIX operating system). A uniform software baseline is supported across all installations.

The major constraint is that the Target Architecture should be compatible with the existing hardware suite already fielded to users. COTS software already purchased and fielded with the earlier version of the JEDMICS software should also be retained in the Target Architecture. Specifically, the ORACLE RDBMS represents a significant investment and must be retained. COTS drawing viewers and editors as well as special-purpose hardware devices are not subject to redesign. The workstations and server computers have been refreshed periodically with new technology, but the current assets represent too large an investment to replace. Similarly, all of the data entered into existing JEDMICS sites must be transformed, with no loss of information, to a new Target Architecture.

The other constraints associated with the existing base of hardware and software are:

- Existing large-format scanners which can scan paper, vellum, and mylar drawings
- Existing dual-sided page scanners which can scan 8.5 x 11" documents at an effective

rate of 1,200 pages per hour

- High-speed aperture card scanners which scan at an effective rate of 350 cards per hour
- All input scan devices capable of surpassing the contract-specified minimum resolution of 200 dots per inch, and support 512 x 512 tiling and software image compression based on CCITT Group IV algorithms
- A magnetic disk storage system that temporarily holds scanned images while awaiting quality assurance on Data Integrity Control workstations - the primary processing steps include quality assurance verification of image and hollerith index data, and the migration of images to permanent optical storage
- A COTS relational database and forms processing software used for the Index Subsystem
- Optical Storage Subsystems used to hold image data on both multiple disk autochangers, jukeboxes (14-inch platters), and standalone single-disk devices (14" and 5.25"). The jukebox is capable of handling the storage for up to 6 million JEDMICS images. The stand-alone units provide backup for the jukebox and, in addition, are a means for exchanging data between sites.
- Existing Workstation Subsystems that are used to edit and quality control scanned images - the multifunction capability of this workstation allows the site to access different systems from the same hardware platform; existing Engineering Graphics Display Workstations provide a true raster editing capability
- Output devices that include aperture card production, high-resolution hardcopy plotting, large-format printing, and high-speed printing - the Aperture Card Plotters collectively have the capability to produce 200 aperture cards per hour from images stored on JEDMICS; the main feature of the high-Resolution plotter is the capability to output drawing sizes A through K

A final business process constraint is that the old and new software systems must coexist during the transition period of all 36 sites.

35.5.4.5 Goals

Besides the constraints that the existing COTS hardware and software impose, certain business goals and objectives also affect the Target Architecture. As part of the most recent change in system specifications, the JEDMICS customer has specified that the software be redesigned using object-oriented programming models and the DOD-STD-2167A lifecycle methodology. (The DOD-STD-2167A lifecycle is a formal "waterfall" software development model designed to produce maintainable, complete, and correct software systems). The motivation for using object-oriented programming models was the desire to increase the maintainability of the software in the future and to provide sufficient isolation layers to allow the system to evolve as a repository. Because of the aging base of fielded weapon systems, engineering data contained in JEDMICS repositories will still be providing long-term support to users well into the next century.

35.5.4.6 External Environments

The network used at each JEDMICS site is part of the local environment and, as such, the existing JEDMICS coexists with other networked systems and equipment. The new Target Architecture will also be required to fit into existing external environments without disruption of the site's other missions. JEDMICS, within certain limits, also must be portable to user provided workstations and other equipment such as printers and plotters. The data created using the existing JEDMICS software must be transferable to the new JEDMICS Target Architecture without any data loss and with a minimum of disruption.

35.5.5 Target Architecture

The Target Architecture for the new JEDMICS software followed a number of goals:

1. Make maximum use of existing equipment
2. Follow open system precepts for portability, interoperability, and vendor-independence
3. Use object-oriented database techniques to isolate specific technology choices
4. Use COTS software to lower conversion costs

Based on the analysis of the user functional requirements, the new JEDMICS subsystems were partitioned along object-oriented boundaries. The subsystems in the Target Architecture are:

1. Session Management subsystem - handles all user-level interaction in a consistent manner.
2. Distributed Object Management subsystem - manages all of the engineering data contained in JEDMICS regardless of specific location.
3. Drawing Management subsystem - maintains all of the special relationships associated with drawings, drawing sheets, drawing revision, and accompanying documents.
4. Input and Output subsystem - handles all input and output of data to JEDMICS in a uniform and consistent manner.

The target JEDMICS environment still follows a distributed computing architectural model. A client JEDMICS Session Management application on a workstation communicates with the Distributed Object Management server application to enter and retrieve engineering data on the Index Server and Optical Data Management Server. This engineering data is displayed at the workstation. The Session Management application can also communicate with the Drawing Management application to request or set the various drawing management relationships. The Input and Output application works as a client communicating with the Distributed Object Management server application to enter engineering data into JEDMICS. The Distributed Object Management server application makes use of an RDBMS (Oracle - existing) and a network data object manager (SQL*NET - new) to store data in JEDMICS.

The Input and Output Subsystem also acts as a client to the Distributed Object Management server application to output JEDMICS data. Requests for output are initiated by the Session Management application client and communicated to the Input and Output Subsystem. The

Input and Output client application requests the data from the Distributed Object Management server application and outputs it to aperture cards, tapes, printers, plotters, CD-ROMs, or any other output device available to JEDMICS.

The general diagram for the new JEDMICS distributed computing model is shown in The New Distributed Computing Architecture .

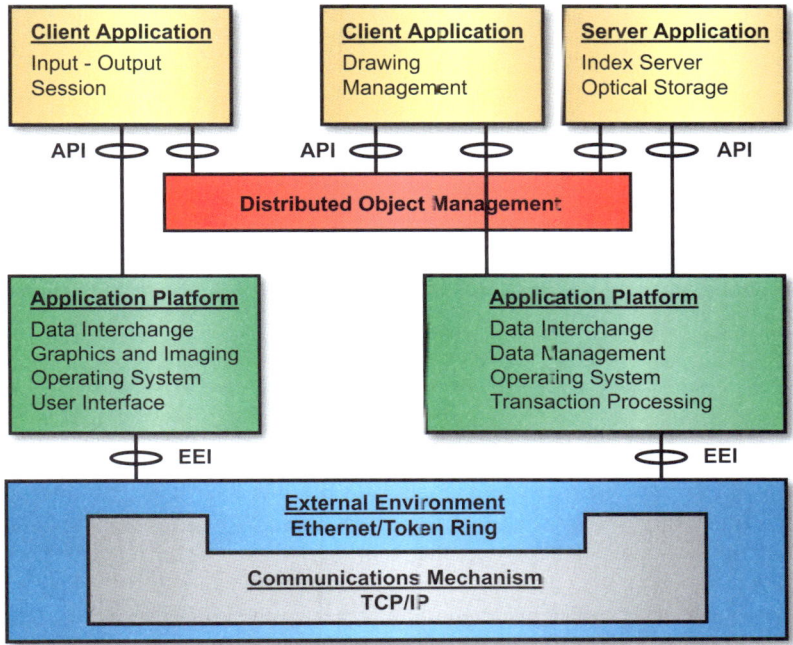

Figure 35.9: The New Distributed Computing Architecture

The functional components of the new JEDMICS system architecture are shown in The New JEDMICS Functional Architecture .

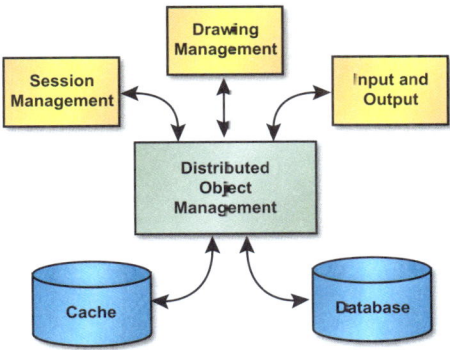

Figure 35.10: The New JEDMICS Functional Architecture

Using object-oriented methodology, the functional architecture becomes simpler and more direct. The Target Architecture will use these standards for each of the Application Platform Services:

Service	Standard	Description
Data Interchange	MIL-STD-1840B, MIL-STD-28002	CALS data interchange
Data Management	ISO/IEC 9075	SQL data definition
Graphics & Imaging	MIL-STD-28002	CALS raster image format
Network		TCP/IP, TFTP
Object	X/Open G302	Object definition and registration
Operating System	IEEE Std 1003.1-1990	POSIX
Software Engineering	ISO/IEC 9899	Programming languages - C
Transaction Processing		
User Interface	X/Open C150, C160, C320	X Windows and Motif API

35.5.6 Migration

The migration phase will require moving the 36 sites from their old system to their new Target Architecture. One of the elements that will simplify the transition is the decision to maintain all of the drawing images saved on optical media in their current raster format. While images remain the same, the index structure in the Oracle database will be radically changed. This will necessitate the transfer and conversion of all currently entered drawing index data into the new object-oriented database structure. A separate conversion effort will address these activities. The implementation of the conversion will require that both the old and new software architectures will be briefly run in the same user environment.

New software COTS products will be installed at the sites during migration, and translation software will be in operation to allow interoperability between sites running the old and new architectures.

35.6 Ministry of Defence (UK)

The UK Ministry of Defence (MoD) Case Study shows how the ADM can be used to develop an organization-specific architecture framework, allowing independent operating divisions to develop their own architectures while ensuring that they share a common core operating environment.

36.6.1 Executive Summary

The UK MoD recognizes the value of a standards-based approach to achieving interoperability between defense communications and information systems (CIS). It has established a CIS standards organization comprising the Defence CIS Standards Executive Group (DCISSEG), the Defence CIS Standards Committee (DCISSC), and the Defence CIS Systems Board (DCISB). The DCISSEG includes members from all the MoD sectors and formulates standards recommendations and guidelines based on achieving business goals of interoperability and reducing costs.

The DCISSEG has defined a Defence CIS Technical Reference Model (TRM) which is based on the NATO Open Systems Environment Technical Reference Model (NATO OSE TRM). The DCIS TRM meets the MoD's CIS requirements, and at the same time is open, aligned with the marketplace, and in a position to incorporate future developments in technology. Population of the DCIS TRM with appropriate open system standards has generated the Defence CIS Framework for Standards, Profiles, and Products (DCISF) which provides the basis for the design of all future MoD CISs.

The DCISF has been applied in the procurement of an operational system for the RAF. A standards-based architecture was derived from the DCISF and written into the project procurement specification. This proved to be effective in ensuring that the future system would be compliant with the DCISF. The approach was rather ad hoc, however, and highlighted the need to define architectures that could be used for communities of CISs. Such architectures are called Common Operating Environments (COEs) and the MoD is in the process of defining an initial COE that will be applicable to all operational CISs.

35.6 2 Laying the Foundations

The first step along the road to achieving communication and information system (CIS) interoperability in the MoD involved two key activities:

1. Providing motivation for the work: The MoD recognized the need for a common reference model and standards framework for guiding CIS projects, with the aim of improving interoperability, portability, scalability, and cost-effectiveness of procurements. In order to exploit its emerging common user infrastructure, the MoD had to make use of COTS products based on open system standards.
2. Creating a CIS architecture and standards organization within MoD: The Defence CIS Standards Executive Group (DCISSEG) and its parent bodies, the Defence CIS Standards Committee (DCISSC) and the Defence CIS Systems Board (DCISB), were charged with delivering the required reference model and standards framework. The core personnel were drawn from all MoD sectors, including the Procurement Executive, Navy, Army, and Air Force sectors. They provided the necessary seniority, experience, technical authority, and ability to communicate with a wide range of interested parties including potential users, project managers, policy-makers, and technical experts outside the group.

35.6.3 Constructing the Model

The next step was to define a DCIS TRM. A TRM is a model representing an abstraction of an IT system. It assists in understanding and identifying the basic building blocks of an IT system but is not populated with standards and does not contain guidance on application. The benefits arising from the use of a TRM include the following:

1. It enables the technical strategy for future purchases and migration to be set out.
2. It simplifies system procurement since it provides a ready-made structure for specifying CIS requirements.
3. It exposes the interfaces between the building blocks of a system, leading to improved interoperability, application portability and software development, re-use, and maintenance.
4. It provides a coherent view of the whole system, leading to a better understanding of issues such as security and management which are pervasive throughout the system.
5. It permits existing systems to be described clearly and in a standard way.

There were several existing TRMs on which the DCIS TRM could have been based. The choice of TRM was guided by the following considerations:

1. The TRM should be open, widely supported, and aligned with the marketplace.
2. It should be capable of meeting the majority of military requirements.
3. There should be a commitment by the "owners" of the TRM to maintain it and allow future developments in technology to be incorporated.

The above considerations led to the adoption of the NATO Open Systems Environment (OSE) TRM as the basis for the DCIS TRM. The NATO OSE TRM aligns well with The Open Group TRM, thus ensuring that the first of the above criteria is met. At the same time, the NATO OSE TRM has been developed within an international military context. Finally, NATO is committed to maintaining the TRM and keeping it in step with changing technology.

The following amendments were made to the NATO OSE TRM in order to meet with the UK MoD's requirements:

1. A Physical Environment component was added, mainly to meet the needs of the Army sector.
2. Elements within the Application Software Entity were re-grouped, in order to reflect MoD's view of support applications.

The DCIS TRM is represented in figure 35.11.

Further information about the definition of the DCIS TRM can be found in Volume 2 of the DCIS Standards Guides.

35.6.4 Building the Framework

This step involved the population of the DCIS TRM with relevant open system standards wherever possible. The resulting framework is the Defence CIS Framework for Standards, Profiles, and Products (DCISF) as detailed in Volume 3 of the DCIS Standards Guides.

Population of the DCIS TRM required suitable standards to be identified and placed within each of the IT Service components of the TRM. The standards selected were intended to be neither exhaustive nor unique. A relevant standard would be included in the DCISF if it was judged to meet the following selection criteria (as applicable):

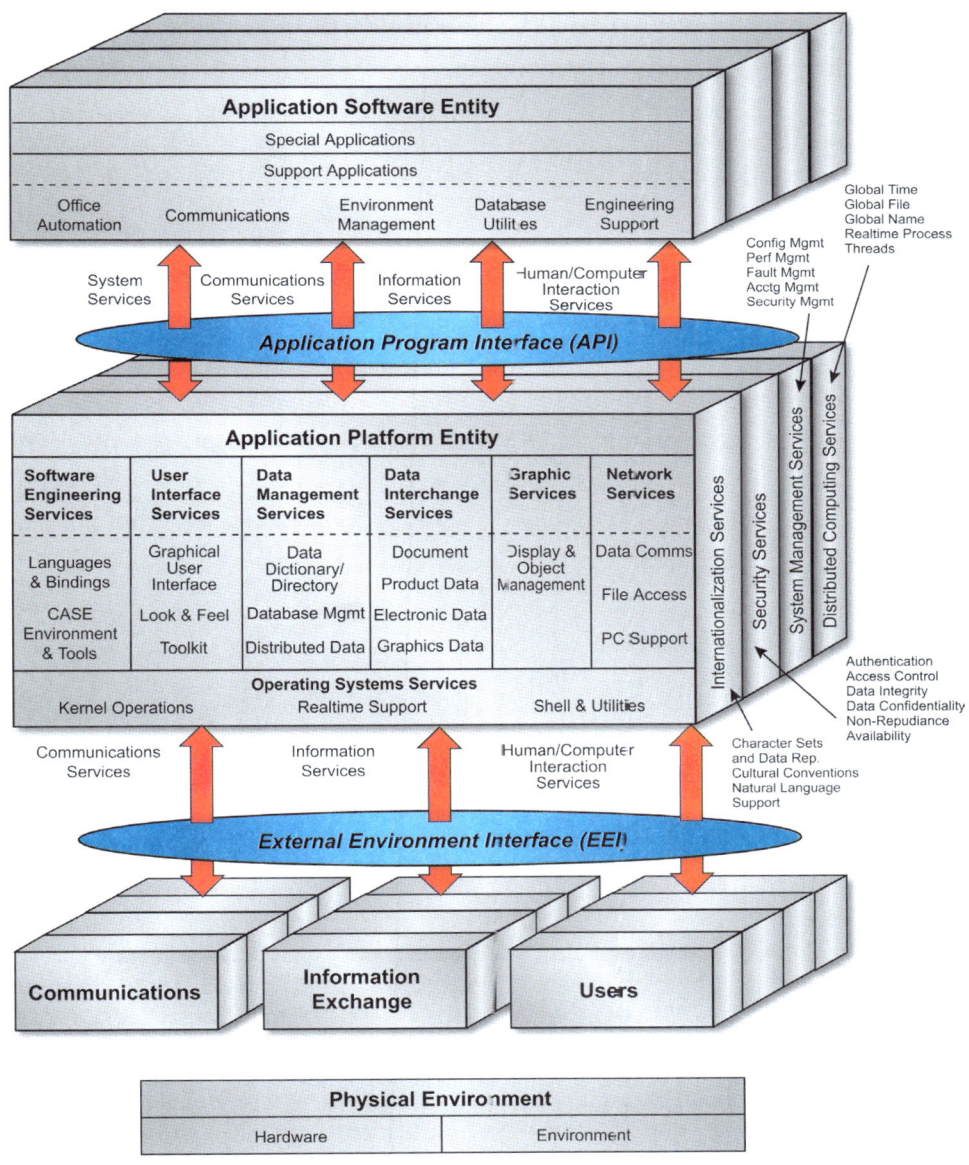

Figure 35.11: DCIS TRM

1. Promotes interoperability
2. Enables people portability
3. Enables application portability
4. Has market support
5. Is technically consistent with the DCIS TRM and other DCIS standards
6. Is consistent with other relevant MoD initiatives

The standards were categorized according to their status. For example, "Recommended" standards were assessed to meet the relevant selection criteria in full; "Emerging" standards met most of the selection criteria, but represent a higher risk, owing to their lack of maturity and stability.

The population of the TRM with open system standards was based on a consensus within the MoD CIS community. This consensus was achieved through a series of technical workshops held by DCISSEG, attended by representatives from each of the MoD sectors.

35.6.5 Defining an Architecture

This step involved the application of the DCISF to an MoD project. The purpose of this was two-fold:

1. To offer the relevant project the benefits of using the DCIS TRM and DCISF
2. To validate the DCISF through its application to a real project

The general benefits that are brought to a CIS procurement from the use of the DCIS TRM and DCISF include the following:

1. Greater clarity and quality of the architecture and standards sections of the Invitation to Tender and the tenders
2. Ease of tender assessment since a standard structure is adopted
3. Improved technical communication with industry since a standard vocabulary is adopted

The project concerns an operational CIS being procured for the RAF. The project team sought advice from the RAF Sector Interoperability Authority (SIA) on the specification of technical standards for the system. The RAF SIA is the focus for IT architectures, standards, and interoperability within the RAF Sector and provides RAF representation within the DCISSEG. The RAF SIA were ideally placed, therefore, to apply the RAF Sector Technical Architecture Framework (RAF STAF), which is based closely on the emerging DCISF, to the project.

Key features of the system technical architecture are its graphical and geographical services, its interfaces with external systems, and its security requirements. The system standards specification was prepared by the RAF SIA in close consultation with the project team. The structure of the standards specification is aligned with the structure of the DCIS TRM, and the technical standards constitute a profile of standards from the DCISF, tailored to meet the system's requirements. The standards define an implementable and system-specific architecture, derived from the overarching DCIS standards framework. Thus, the system will be able to interoperate with future systems that are also compliant with the DCISF.

In conclusion, the application of the DCISF in defining a system-specific architecture for a real CIS project proved to be effective. The approach used was rather ad hoc, however, and this points to a requirement for a more systematic way of defining standards-based architectures for CIS. The answer is to define Common Operating Environments (COEs). A COE is an agreed specification derived from a framework of open standards which is applicable to CIS within a particular community. A COE is defined once, and applied many times, as CISs within a particular community are procured. The MoD is in the process of defining COEs, starting with an operational COE.

35.6.6 The Way Forward

The following future MoD CIS interoperability activities are identified:

1. Maintain the DCIS TRM.
2. Maintain the DCISF in line with MoD business requirements and market developments in CIS standards and products.
3. Continue to apply the DCISF to CIS projects in the near-term, using the initial application to an operational CIS as a model.
4. Complete the definition of the operational COE and begin to define other COEs as required. In particular, there is a requirement for an overall Defence COE, the Defence Interoperability Environment (DIE), which will provide Intranet-type services such as wide area networking and messaging to the vast majority of MoD CISs.
5. Apply the MoD COEs to future projects.

35.7 NATO (Belgium)

NATO's example illustrates the development of Target and Transitional Architectures in the context of overall enterprise architecture.

Within NATO the two Strategic Commands (ACE and ACLANT) are equipped with different C2-systems: basically Allied Command Europe - Automated Command and Control System (ACE-ACCIS) for ACE and Maritime Command and Control System (MCCIS) for ACLANT.

In reaction to the NATO Washington Summit (April 1999) a double convergence between ACE and ACLANT on the one hand and between the Command and Control Systems and the Management Information Systems (MIS) on the other hand has been initiated in order to improve the interoperability and the cost-efficiency of these systems. As the combination of the C2-services and MIS-services is called Automated Information System (AIS), the common system target between the two Strategic Commands is therefore called Bi-SC AIS.

In practice the convergence is envisaged incrementally, whereas the first implementation target revolves around a common "core capability". Such a concept is close to The Open Group's Boundaryless Information Flow initiative and consists of harmonizing/standardizing the foundation IT services throughout the two command structures and also implementing common applications where possible.

The applications are categorized into:

- Core applications, which are general-purpose applications that are built on the basis of "off-the-shelf" packages (typical examples are Military Message Handling, Document Management, or Enterprise Management)
- Functional applications, which are business-specific applications in support of the military functions (typical examples are OPS-, INTEL-, or LOG- applications in support of operation control, intelligence, or logistics)

The breakdown of the overall AIS target into "implementation segments", the articulation of these segments, and the planning and management of their implementation, are of course many issues which cannot be successfully addressed without a sound and comprehensive architecture of the system targeted.

In order to avoid a "big-bang" development of such a Target Architecture, which would be almost mission impossible at this scale, the architectural process has been divided into two parallel development activities with different objectives and scopes, namely:

- A high-level Target Architecture, describing the key objectives of the system for the next six years. Its development is mainly top-down out of the strategic objectives of the commands or the operational and policy requirements.
- A Transitional Architecture, describing the services targeted for the near term and the transitions from the existing system baseline. Such a Transitional Architecture is developed as an extension to the previous architecture but also accommodates a bottom-up approach, in order to capture the migration constraints and the lessons learned from the fielded baseline.

The respective customers of these two kinds of architectures are the "stakeholders" on the one hand and the end users and implementors on the other hand.

As explained in Time Horizon : "In such an approach, the Target Architecture is evolutionary in nature, and requires periodic review and update according to evolving business requirements and developments in technology, whereas the Transitional Architectures are (by design) incremental in nature, and in principle should not evolve during the implementation phase of the increment, in order to avoid the "moving target" syndrome. This of course is only possible if the implementation schedule is under tight control and relatively short (typically less than two years)."

An Implementation Plan, which both considers the operational priorities and the architectural constraints, and consequently defines the optimal implementation sequence, is required to transition from an agreed high-level Target Architecture to a Transitional Architecture dedicated to the first implementation target.

The following figure illustrates the above considerations and stresses the role of the Architects, who mediate between the stakeholders and implementors and are supposed to maintain the consistency of the whole edifice. They typically aim to reduce the latent gap or lack of understanding between stakeholders and implementors that is caused by the increasing complexity of their respective activities.

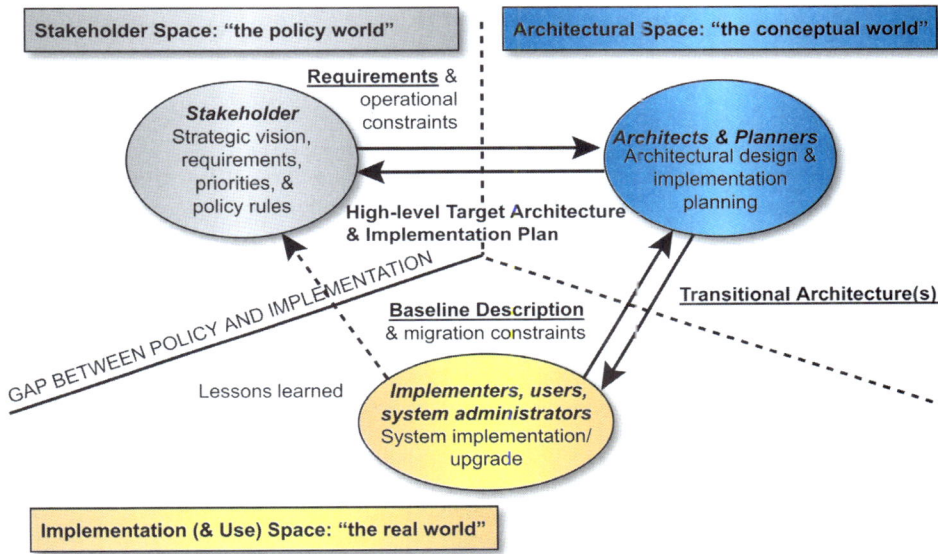

Figure 35.12: Role of Architects vis-à-vis the Stakeholders and Implementors

The high-level Target Architecture of the Bi-SC AIS has been developed and endorsed in the years 2001 and 2002, and has entered a maintenance process, whereas the Transitional Architecture for the first Bi-SC AIS implementation target has been initiated.

The architectural consistency of these two architectures is largely based on the following factors:

- They both use the same "NATO Architecture Framework" which is in fact a customization of the US-C4ISR (also described in C4ISR Architecture Framework) to the NATO context. The breakdown of the architectural descriptions into "operational", "system", and "technical" views, combined with the development of standard "architectural templates", establishes a common language between the architects and a sound means of communication with the stakeholders.
- They also make use of the same "NATO C3 Technical Architecture". This is an architectural design and implementation guidance for the development of System and Technical Views of C3 (Command, Control, and Communications) systems. It includes a detailed TRM, an inventory of standards, and guidelines/directives to develop

"interoperability profiles", implement system building blocks, and eventually select software products. The NC3TA is based on the US DoD TRM and DII COE, but has evolved to incorporate the needs of NATO nations as well as Australia and New Zealand.

- Last but not least, there is a tight collaboration between the architects involved.

The adoption/customization of a comprehensive architectural methodology, which would formally relate all the architectural tasks and make the linkage with the implementation projects, is still an issue. There is still some risk for a Target Architecture to be misinterpreted by implementors, whereas its traceability with the strategic objectives and mapping with the operational requirements remain both critical.

The TOGAF ADM is considered as a valuable starting point for the methodology, due to its adaptability and comprehensiveness. The concept of system "building blocks" is perceived as crucial to manage the interdependency between the aforementioned Target Architectures and to communicate with the users and implementors. Moreover, the latest release of the ADM (Version 8) explicitly supports an incremental approach and makes use of the IEEE Std 1471 concepts (stakeholders, views and viewpoints, etc.) which are fully applicable to a large organization like NATO.

The current architectural development is based on the following paradigms.

The architectural description is broken down into three views:

- Operation view (equivalent to the Business Architecture, in TOGAF terms)
- System view (the combination of the Applications and Data Architecture)
- Technical view (equivalent to the Technology Architecture)

The three architecture views are described in three distinct levels of abstraction (conceptual, logical, and physical) which enables a progressive development and facilitates the validation/exploitation of the architectural description. It is indeed no use developing a logical description of a view if the underlying concepts are not clear or agreed. The same way, a detailed physical description of a view, which deals with the site characteristics, is only possible when a common logical description is agreed.

The following figures describe the expected properties of the architectural rows and columns.

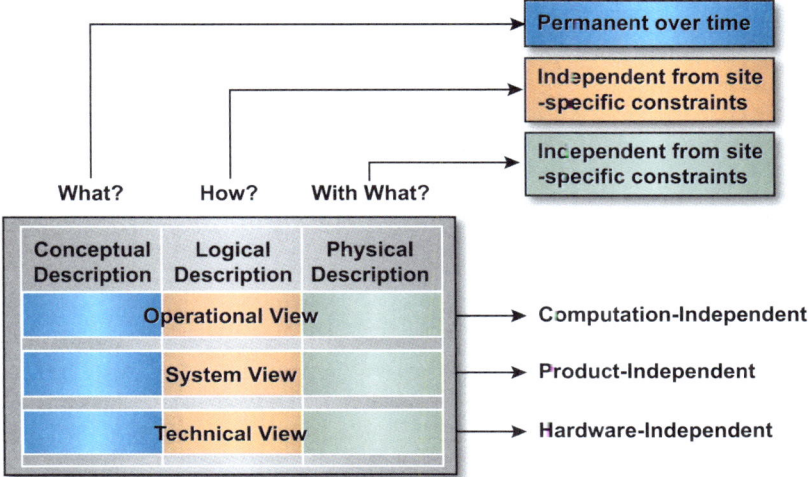

Figure 35.13: Expected Properties of the Architectural Model

Such a model, based on a 3-by-3 matrix, is also likely to facilitate the maintenance of the architectural descriptions and the consistency of the whole architectural process. A detailed mapping of this model with the aforementioned (NATO or US-C4ISR) "architectural templates" is available but exceeds the scope of this Case Study and is replaced by the following figure, which gives an overview of the internal structuring of the architectural description.

	Conceptual Description	Logical Description	Physical Description
Operational View			
	Business/ organization model	Node connectivity model	Information flow diagram
System View			
	System conceptual model	System logical model	System physical model
Technical View			
	Software component model	Integration model	Implementation model

Figure 35.14: Overview of the Structuring of the Architectural Description

The linkage of architecture with its environment is perceived as follows.

Some underlying "principles and objectives", derived from the stakeholders' views, pertain to the whole architectural model, whereas the operational context, the feedback from the fielded baseline, the "state-of-the art", or the user or system requirements apply to the model as follows:

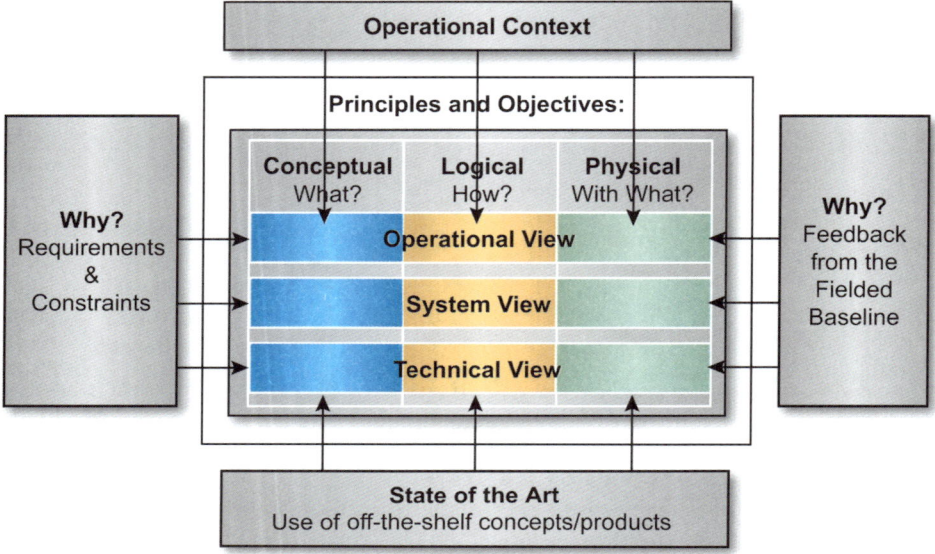

Figure 35.15: Linkage of the Architectural Description with its Environment

35.8 Police IT Organization (UK)

The UK Police IT Organization (PITO) used TOGAF as the basis for the Technical Architecture for its National Strategy for Police Information Systems (NSPIS).

The NSPIS Case Study includes a comprehensive approach to architecture views, and a methodology for ensuring interoperability between the building blocks of the final architecture.

35.8.1 Police IT

The UK has some 43 police forces. Each one has a different way of doing basically the same job and the authority to purchase what it likes, when it likes, and from who it likes. It is not surprising therefore that there is a whole variety of IT solutions to meet the business need. In addition there are national systems and networks that connect to the local force systems. The most notable is the Police National Computer connected over a facilities managed Police National Network.

35.8.2 Objectives of NSPIS

- Interoperability
- Openness
- Scalability
- Rationalize Data Structures
- Effective Pricing
- Modularity
- Future Proofing

The police business has identified 38 varied application areas. The NSPIS applications include personnel, accounting, invoicing, case preparation, command & control, crime & incident reporting, custody, etc. The applications can be grouped into business domains. These domains or business groups are likely to contain some commonality of architecture and application functionality which distinguishes them from other domains. It is acknowledged that over time each domain will change due to new additions and re-arrangements of the current set.

In bringing solutions to market, we need to be aware of the high degree of interoperability demanded by the business, both between forces and between applications, both intra and inter-force in order to reduce cross-boundary effects. In order to move forward, the Home Office is not in a position to dictate how things should be. In essence there must be a local and central partnership, together with a commitment at all levels to support the formal strategy agreement. In order to achieve this, we must promote all aspects of the strategy not only to the local forces as the prime users, but to the suppliers who will need to be taken on board during application procurement.

35.8.3 Purpose

The purpose of the technical architecture is to:

- Provide the format and documentation standards for the technical constraints applied to the NSPIS application procurements
- Assist the application procurement process by describing an advocated set of technical development and software procurement options in a standard fashion
- Describe the products and standards used by each NSPIS application

The NSPIS technical architecture is also intended as an aid to discussions with suppliers when it is important to ensure that:

- Parties are clear on what constitutes conformance to the NSPIS technical architecture.
- Queries on NSPIS technical issues and other requests are handled uniformly.
- An appropriate level of liaison and negotiating presence is provided.

- Change control records are kept and maintained.

The NSPIS technical architecture advocates services (i.e., components and products) that support the policy laid down by the technical design authority. Currently the architecture must conform to the following properties:

- Multi-tiered client/server
- Distributed
- Modular/re-usable components-based
- Based on common APIs
- Able to interwork with other NSPIS systems/components
- Multi-vendor; i.e., open and heterogeneous

The NSPIS technical architecture is based on The Open Group Architecture Framework Reference Model with additions made to reflect the set of services required by the NSPIS recommended applications.

The NSPIS technical architecture is, in principle, the optimum way to achieve the objectives of interoperable, portable, scalable systems by means of an advocated set of services using open architecture standards. However, practical consideration should also be given to each architecture components:

- Degree of completeness - how tried and tested is the service?
- Degree of certainty - how mature is the service?
- Likely longevity - what is the predicted future market position of the service?
- Cost - what is the life-time cost across the range of applications?

To provide a complete, cost-effective architecture, it may be necessary to pursue a "shades of openness" policy that includes the pragmatic use of proprietary products with an awareness of "lock-in" issues. Wherever possible, the NSPIS technical architecture will recommend a single choice of component with the lowest predicted obsolescence factor. Where a single recommendation is not possible, a range of advocated options that conform to the technical architecture may be given instead. Procured applications are required to adhere to the NSPIS technical architecture recommendations and standards profile outlined within this document. Furthermore, the framework will be used to assist in the development and evolution of all future NSPIS applications services requirements.

35.8.4 NSPIS Technical Architecture Manual

The NSPIS technical architecture is described in three volumes:

- Volume 1: Overview has the rules and guidelines and defines the platform services. It covers the principles which form the basis of the NSPIS technical architecture and the way in which it is intended to be used and maintained. The appendix has a profile of available services and standards and contains general NSPIS requirements and a methodology for selection and conformance.

- Volume 2: Generic Architecture contains the mandated platform services and the range of allowable standards. Also, the architectural requirements to satisfy the user requirements and the conformance criteria. This document is the technical architecture requirements and constraints for NSPIS application procurement.

- Volume 3: Application-Specific Architecture is the supplier's response to the user and technical requirement and contains a complete list of platform services and the relationship between the components chosen, together with a description of the hardware and communication environment required to deliver the performance and scalability. The application-specific architecture describes the complete architecture for each application and forms the basis of the subsequent configuration management. There will be an application-specific architecture associated with each NSPIS application and it will contain all the elements recommended to implement the service provided under the NSPIS framework agreement. The supplier's application-specific architecture forms the basis of the technical evaluation and the conformance test quote. It informs the evaluation of future generic components and helps define acceptance and conformance tests.

The technical architecture documents are intended for use by members of the NSPIS community in NSPIS projects, and in any subsequent implementations including the maintenance and operations of NSPIS products. The NSPIS community includes:

- IT Managers
- Project Managers
- NSPIS Program/Project Teams
- Procurement and Contract Managers
- Suppliers
- Technical User Group
- In-house Development Teams
- Configuration Managers

Additionally, this framework may also be referenced by individual purchasers at force level. Teams using the NSPIS framework should remember that these guidelines are a coherent and integrated framework that should be used in their entirety. To use the criteria in an ad hoc fashion like a "pick-list" will represent non-compliance and compromise interoperability.

35.8.5 Applying the Framework

The NSPIS technical architecture is a set of components and a specification of how these components are connected to meet the overall requirements of NSPIS. The following are a set of principles for the application of a component-based approach:

- The architecture need only contain components to implement those framework services that it requires.

- Components may implement one, more than one, or only part of a service identified in the framework.
- Components should conform to standards relevant to the services they implement.

At least four complementary and simultaneous mechanisms are seen as contributing to the definition of the components making up the overall NSPIS Architecture Framework, and each application-specific architecture.

These mechanisms are:

- By theoretical debate, evaluation, and choice
- Competitive procurement through infrastructure projects
- Evaluation and selection of options provided by the application procurement process
- Selection of components and APIs during application system build.

Under this arrangement, potential components and APIs of the technical infrastructure could be in one of the following states of procurement:

| NSPIS Generic Architecture Components | Undefined | Optional | Mandated |
| NSPIS Application-Specific Components | Undefined | Optional | Mandated |

At the award of contract we would expect to see the application-specific component being mandated but not necessarily immutable; i.e.:

| NSPIS Generic Architecture Components | Mandated | Mandated | Mandated |
| NSPIS Application-Specific Components | Mandated | Mandated | Mandated |

At system build, final decisions would be taken with reference to those components initially allowed freedom of choice (i.e., not defined or optional) and decisions made whether to embrace any of them in the NSPIS Generic Application Platform. At conformance testing, performance testing, and live running, a formal evaluation of the future status of all components would be made to update in particular the generic application component services by addition, subtraction, or substitution. Each procurement process will generate new releases of the technical architecture and each application system build and test will influence future changes. An overview of the role of the technical architecture in the procurement process is shown in the figure below.

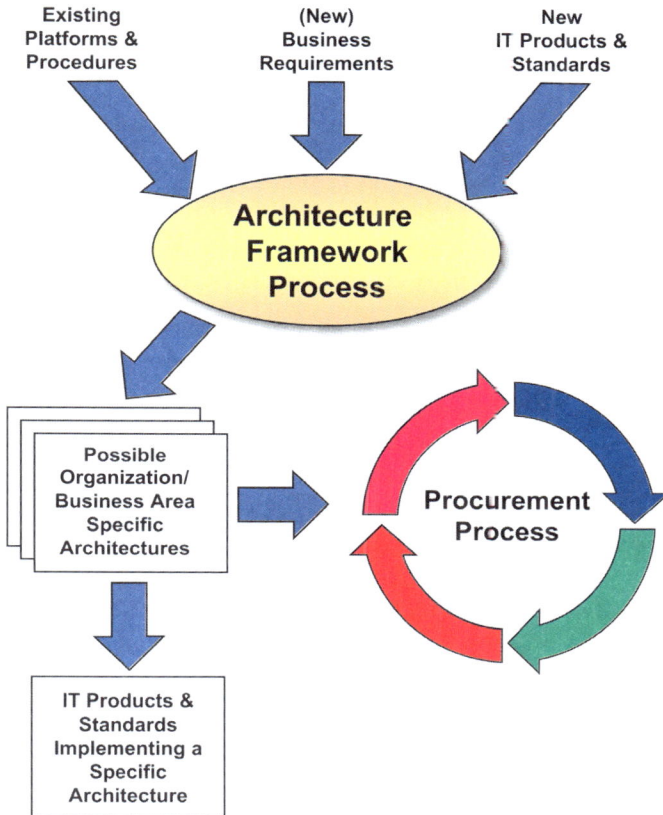

Figure 35.16: Technical Architecture & Procurement Process Overview

All suppliers who respond to procurements are given the opportunity, indeed are required, to submit their application-specific architectures. This allows the opportunity to refine, further develop, and recommend alternatives or substitutes to the Generic Architecture.

There are four basic migration models that can be defined:

- The Gateway Model

    A Force has two environments, a Force-specific environment and its NSPIS environment, and it gateways between these two environments.

    This model is applicable when the Force's current environment has no reasonable evolution to the NSPIS world, and the investment in current systems mean that a radical change to build a complete Force environment conforming to the NSPIS technical architecture is untenable.

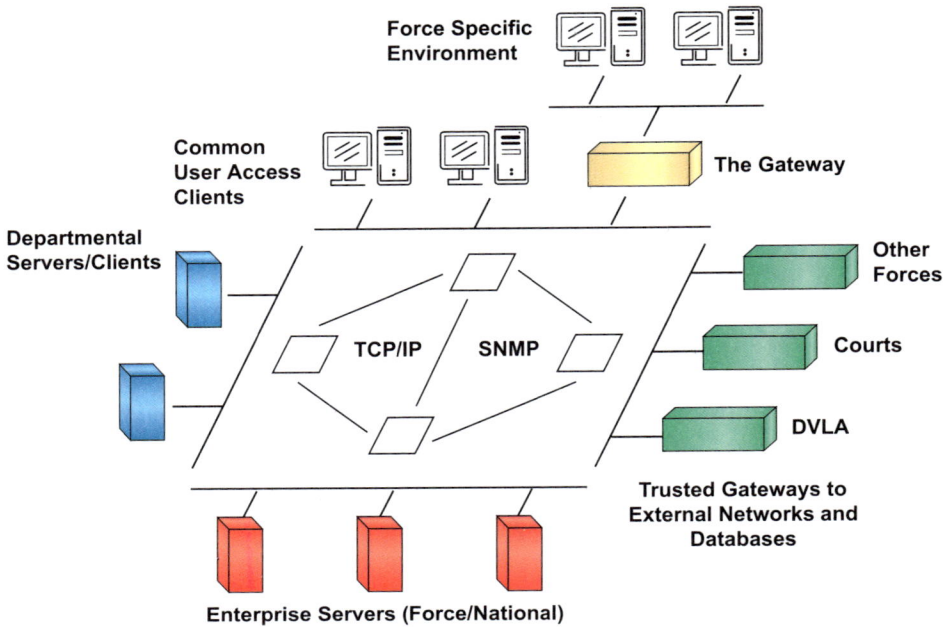

Figure 35.17: The Gateway Model

- The NSPIS Environment Model

    A Force has an environment based on NSPIS-compatible operating systems and networks - e.g., UNIX and TCP/IP - but has NSPIS and legacy applications working on a variety of platforms at the middleware level within this environment.

- The Application Platform Model

    A Force has not only an NSPIS-compatible environment, but conforms at the application platform level, with services and components compatible and based on the NSPIS technical architecture at the middleware level.

- The Legacy Integration Model

    Force either modifies existing legacy applications or acquires non-NSPIS applications which use or replace interfaces defined within implemented NSPIS applications.

35.8.6 NSPIS Technical Reference Model

This section contains descriptions of the Application Platform component complete with approved or contender standard, service, and product names.

This section describes the Technical Reference Model (TRM), a more detailed view of the Logical Framework. The purpose of the TRM is to allow components of an existing or planned information system and the relationships between components to be recorded in a consistent manner.

The following diagram shows the TRM complete with the classes or types of services within the recommended categories on the Application Platform.

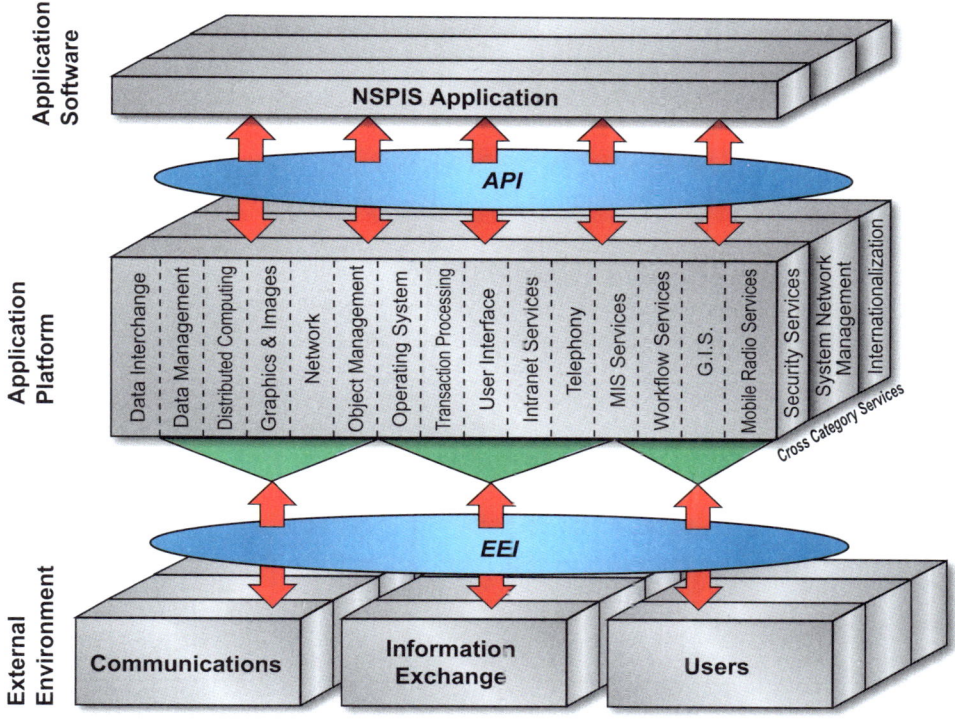

Figure 35.18: NSPIS Technical Reference Model

The set of services shown here is based upon TOGAF TRM with additions to reflect NSPIS-specific requirements. The additional NSPIS-specific services are Intranet Services, Telephony, MIS Services, Workflow Services, GIS, and Mobile Radio Services. These are services which would normally exist in more than one service category and/or in the Application Software tier. At this level of detail the framework depicts entities, interfaces, and service areas only and does not imply inter-relationships between the service areas.

Conforming to the model does not mean that each application will implement all or only these named services without any additional facilities. The intention of the NSPIS TRM is that applications will use a set of services tailored to their specific business area needs.

Each service within the application platform is described under four headings:

- Mandated Components
- Approved Components
- Interoperable Components

- Illustrative Components

The component definitions and standards profile are maintained as a reference as standard definitions for NSPIS suppliers and Police IT community. Inclusion does not imply selection. Conforming to the model does not mean that each application will implement all or only these named services without any additional facilities. The intention of the NSPIS TRM is that applications will use a set of services tailored to their specific business area needs.

35.8.7 Interoperability

It is important that the components on the application platform are able to interoperate and do not mutually interfere one with the other. To this end, suppliers fill in an interoperability matrix which contains rows of all the application-specific components and columns of all the application-specific components, other generic components, and any other components used by other NSPIS applications which are not already included. (See table below.)

		Application-Specific Components	Other Generic Components	Other NSPIS Components
Ref1	App Spec Compt 1			
Ref2	App Spec Compt 2			
Ref3	App Spec Compt 3			
Ref4	App Spec Compt 4			
etc.				

Suppliers indicate by a tick whether they interoperate with the other components. If they do not interoperate directly but through another (intermediate) component listed, then the reference number of that intermediate component is inserted in the box. Where they do not interoperate, a cross is inserted.

Design templates for the Interoperability Processes in each application will be developed in conjunction with the application project teams before full proposals. Suppliers indicate the components involved in providing interoperability with other NSPIS applications, that is:

- Desktop-to-application interoperability
- Application-to-application interoperability
- Application-to-database interoperability
- Database-to-database interoperability

35.8.8 Technical Requirements and Views

Suppliers will be asked to respond to technical requirements under business, information, application, and engineering headings for each of the number of views.

The Requirement Views are a definition of the architecture in terms of the requirements that they set out to satisfy. Each requirement is broken down and considered under four headings: Business requirement, Information requirement, Application requirement, and an Engineering requirement. Within each of these requirements it will specify if it is:

M Mandatory: suppliers must conform to a constrained or specified solution set.

R Required: suppliers must provide a solution.

O Optional: suppliers may provide and state how or give reasons for omission.

There are 10 views, each with the four requirements. They are: User, Organization, Management, Operations, Processing Platform, Integration, Data Management, Security, Contract, and Service Delivery. This produces an 4 X 10 matrix. (See below.)

	Business	Information	Application	Engineering
User				
Organization				
Management				
Operations				
Processing Platform				
Integration				
Data Management				
Security				
Contract				
Service Delivery				

Table 35.2: Requirements Matrix

As well as taking account of all the requirement views when selecting, implementing, and using the components of the application platform, the selection must take account of how well the components work together and what effect the choice one might have on the freedom of choice of another service. To assist in this choice, the application platform before and after each choice is compared using the metrics generated from each analysis. The analyses include gap analysis, value analysis, and risk analysis.

Whilst suppliers and integrators have necessarily to be constrained in their choice of application platform to ensure interoperability and portability, it is important to its relevance over time that suppliers are given every opportunity to comment on and submit alternative preferred or more appropriate components. This is particularly important where standards are immature, difficulties of component interoperability are being experienced, or mandated and preferred components are nearing obsolescence or irrelevance. Similarly suppliers, IT departments, and users must be able to exploit new methods and technology paradigms and incorporate them into the architecture without compromising the current applications or architectures.

35.8.9 The Architecture in Action

Suppliers respond to the technical architecture at specific stages within the NSPIS application procurement and implementation cycle. Each differs in detail depending on the procurement route adopted for each application and the type of product sought.

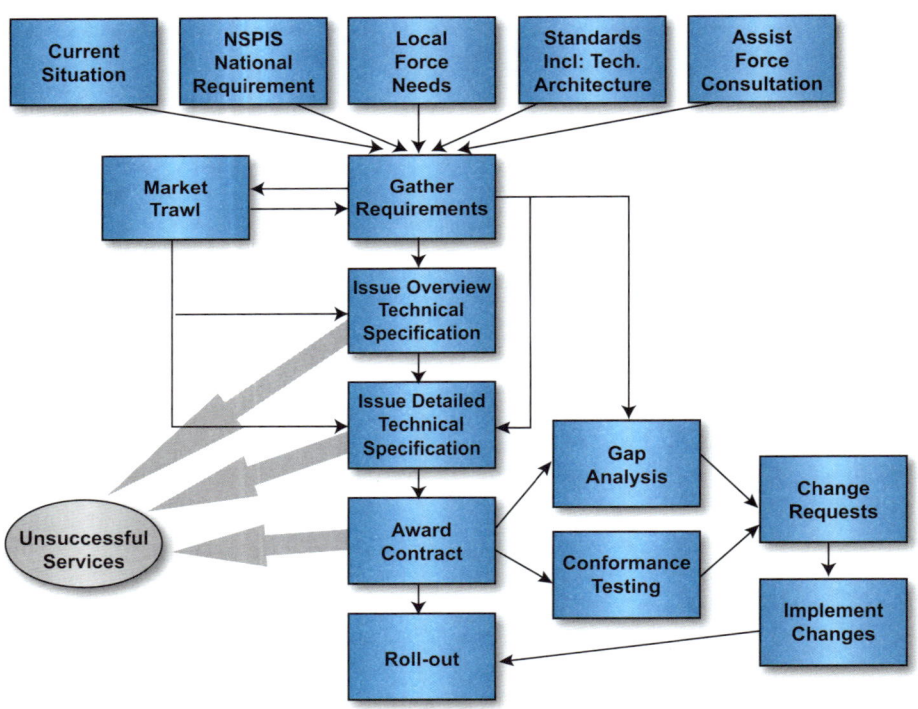

Figure 35.19: Procurement using the NSPIS Technical Architecture

All NSPIS suppliers need details of each other's application-specific architectures to enable interoperability and consistency of change control. Mechanisms to achieve the desired level of co-operation and visibility of design are required from the NSPIS supplier community, PITO, and NSPIS application projects. These mechanisms are set up and further developed in conjunction with existing NSPIS suppliers and those suppliers short-listed and subsequently awarded NSPIS contracts. The selection and subsequent implementation of each NSPIS application platform informs subsequent selections and direction. NSPIS suppliers and the conformance testing agency are contributors to the debate with PITO and the Technical User Group.

35.9 QA Consulting

QA Consulting are a UK consultancy and training company whose mission is to improves IT effectiveness within large organizations. The company's focus is on enhancing the skills of people - optimizing human capital investment, and providing IT expertise that complements in-house skills. The company is the UK's No.1 IT Trainer, with 400+ Courses, both Instructor-lead and Internet-based, covering both technical and business skills.

The QA Case Study[19] explains the company's approach to using TOGAF, and gives an example of a recent client engagement in the Travel industry using TOGAF.

35.10 Statskonsult (Norway)

Statskonsult is the Department of IT Planning & Co-ordination, in the Directorate for Public Management, within the Norwegian Government. It used parts of the TOGAF Architecture Development Method (ADM) to develop an architecture for an IT infrastructure for the public sector in Norway.

The Case Study explains the general background to the project. The use of the TOGAF ADM is explained in a separate presentation.[20]

35.10.1 Norway Streamlines Government Processes by Going Online

In Norway, over 35% of the population are experienced in navigating the Internet. The Norwegian government intends to leverage this knowledge by using the Internet to deliver more effective and cost-efficient public administration services. Termed the Public Sector Network, this initiative is a joint venture between Norway's Ministry of National Planning and Co-ordination and the Norwegian Association of Local and Regional Authorities. The objective is to create a national Internet-based infrastructure that will enable the public administration (both local and central government) to transform from a traditional paper-based, bureaucratic organization into an easily-approached, responsive online body. Initially, over 100 paper-based reporting mechanisms between public bodies are being targeted for conversion to online systems. The aim is to convert every applicable service by 2001.

Through the Public Sector Network, the Norwegian people will be able to manage their relationship with the public administration in the fields of taxation, welfare, and other public administration functions. As a result, the Norwegian government will deliver improved service levels and significantly reduce its costs on currently labor-intensive, paper-based tasks. Consequent savings can then be allocated to furthering the public good in areas such as health care and education.

---

19. Available at *www.opengroup.org/architecture/togaf8-doc/arch/p4/cases/qa/qa.pdf*.
20. *www.opengroup.org/arcitecture/togaf8-doc/arch/p4/cases/sk/garotnes.pdf*.

35.10.2 Working with The Open Group to Plan the Future

In helping to establish the Public Sector Network, an ongoing relationship has been established between the Norwegian Ministry of National Planning and Co-ordination and The Open Group.

The Open Group will serve as a central resource that tests, brands, and guarantees compatibility with IT DialTone specifications, products, and technologies. In this capacity, The Open Group will contribute substantially to the Norwegian Public Sector Network and similar projects around the globe.

35.10.3 An Internet DialTone Framework as Easy-to-Use as the Telephone

Creating a national infrastructure such as the Public Sector Network poses a number of challenges. There are currently many point-solutions, technologies, and products from a growing number of suppliers. But how do companies wishing to utilize the Internet understand the benefits and risks associated with each one? Which ones work with each other, conform to agreed standards, or will remain relevant in five years' time? How do companies avoid making proprietary decisions that could erode the required benefits of the Internet?

"The more common approach to this project would have been to build one big government network that is planned, constructed, and managed centrally. However, this approach is not very flexible and would almost certainly have required the costly duplication or replacement of existing infrastructure - in fact it would probably have failed. It's really a challenge to match the formal, juridical framework with the needs of the marketplace, especially under the European Union rules for public procurement," says Gard Titlestad, Head of the Secretariat for IT Standardisation.

"The alternative is to adopt a more "open" approach that protects the vast investment of public money in existing infrastructure and enables the ongoing integration of new technology from a broad range of suppliers. To do this we identified the need for a common framework - an industry-agreed reference point by which to identify standards, products, and technologies that provide consistent features and attributes, such as security and reliability - now and in the future. A solution is to work closely with The Open Group to assist in the delivery of its IT DialTone architecture."

To ensure that the Public Sector Network remains flexible and maximizes the use of the latest market developments in technology and service, the project is based on a framework agreement. The IT DialTone set of technologies provides the framework with a reference point and an agreed approach to the development and implementation of Internet standard specifications, technologies, and products. In turn, this framework guides the procurement policies of each municipality and government department, guaranteeing a consistent approach to the network implementation. Yearly re-negotiation of the framework will consistently reflect market development dynamics.

Joseph De Feo, Former President & CEO of The Open Group said: "The Norwegian Government is leading Europe in the charge to realize the true social potential of the Internet.

As part of this process they have identified the benefits of basing their future infrastructure development on robust, industry-agreed standards not on proprietary solutions, which they realize could eventually erode the country's ability to communicate freely with the world if alternative, non-compatible decisions are made by other governments, companies, or organizations."

With the Public Sector Network, Norway leads the world in creating a national, Internet-based infrastructure to administer public services and improve government operational efficiency. The country's proactive steps guarantee the construction of an effective, supplier-independent, and flexible national online resource.

35.11 Westpac (Australia)

Westpac is a major Australian bank who have used TOGAF in collaboration with IBM, in much the same way as the UK Department of Social Security; i.e., as the basis of managing the technology components of a major outsourcing relationship.

The Westpac Case Study[21] gives an overview of the approach used and reactions.

---

21. www.opengroup.org/architecture/togaf8-doc/arch/p4/cases/westpac/westpac.pdf

Chapter 36: Glossary

The TOGAF Glossary is intended to define terms essential to the understanding of TOGAF. It is not intended as a general-purpose open systems glossary and does not contain terms considered to be in common use.

AC	Access Control
ACSE	Association Control Service Element
Ada	High-level computer programming language developed by the US Department of Defense (DoD). Ada is used as the standard programming language for the DoD. It is used for real-time processing, is modular in nature, and includes object-oriented features.
ADM	Architecture Development Method
ANSI	American National Standards Institute
API	See Application Program Interface.
APP	See Application Portability Profile.
Application	A classification of computer programs designed to perform specific tasks, such as word processing, database management, or graphics.
Application Platform	The collection of hardware and software components that provide the services used by support and mission-specific software applications.
Application Portability Profile (APP)	The NIST APP is the structure that integrates US federal, national, international, and other specifications to provide the functionality necessary to accommodate the broad range of US federal information technology requirements.
Application Program Interface (API)	1. The interface, or set of functions, between the Application Software and the Application Platform. 2. The most common means by which a software programmer invokes other software functions.
Application Software	Software entities which have a specific business purpose.
APSE	Ada Programming Support Environment

Architecture	Architecture has two meanings depending upon its contextual usage: 1. A formal description of a system, or a detailed plan of the system at component level to guide its implementation. 2. The structure of components, their inter-relationships, and the principles and guidelines governing their design and evolution over time.
Architecture, Baseline	The existing system architecture before entering a cycle of architecture review and redesign.
Architecture Continuum	A part of the Enterprise Continuum. The Architecture Continuum provides a repository of architectural elements with increasing detail and specialization. This Continuum begins with foundational definitions like reference models, core strategies, and basic building blocks. From there it spans to Industry Architectures and all the way to an organization's specific architecture.
Architecture, Database	The logical view of the data models, data standards, and data structure. It includes a definition of the physical databases for the information system, their performance requirements, and their geographical distribution.
Architecture, Target	Depicts the configuration of the target information system.
Architecture Framework	A tool for assisting in the production of organization-specific architectures. An architecture framework consists of a Technical Reference Model, a method for architecture development, and a list of component standards, specifications, products, and their inter-relationships which can be used to build up architectures.
Architecture View	A perspective from which an architecture may be viewed in order to ensure that a specific topic is considered in a coherent manner; e.g., security.
ASN	Abstract Syntax Notation
ASP	Active Server Pages
Availability	The probability that system functional capabilities are ready for use by a user at any time, where all time is considered, including operations, repair, administration, and logistic time. Availability is further defined by system category for both routine and priority operations.

Base-Level Functions	Initial or basic functions.
Baseline	A specification or product that has been formally reviewed and agreed upon, that thereafter serves as the basis for further development and that can be changed only through formal change control procedures or a type of procedure such as configuration management.
Batch Processing	Processing data or the accomplishment of jobs accumulated in advance in such a manner that each accumulation thus formed is processed or accomplished in the same computer run.
Business System	Hardware, software, policy statements, procedures, and people which together implement a business function.
CCITT	Consultative Committee on International Telegraph and Telephone
Client	An application component which requests services from a server.
CMIS	Common Management Information Service
CMIP	Common Management Information Protocol
COBIT	Control OBjectives for Information and related Technology
COBOL	Acronym for Common Business-Oriented Language. COBOL is a computer programming language used extensively in mainframes and minicomputers for business applications.
Communications Mechanism	Hardware and software functions which allow Application Platforms to exchange information.
Communications Network	A set of products, concepts, and services that enable the connection of computer systems for the purpose of transmitting data and other forms (e.g., voice and video) between the systems.
Communications Node	A node that is either internal to the communications network (e.g., routers, bridges, or repeaters) or located between the end device and the communications network to operate as a gateway.
Communications System	A set of assets (transmission media, switching nodes, interfaces, and control devices) that will establish linkage between users and devices.

Configuration Management	A discipline applying technical and administrative direction and surveillance to: a. Identify and document the functional and physical characteristics of a configuration item b. Control changes to those characteristics c. Record and report changes to processing and implementation status
Connectivity Service	A service area of the External Environment entity of the Technical Reference Model (TRM) that provides end-to-end connectivity for communications through three transport levels (global, regional, and local). It provides general and application-specific services to platform end devices.
CORBA	Common Object Request Broker Architecture
Data Dictionary	A specialized type of database containing metadata, which is managed by a data dictionary system; a repository of information describing the characteristics of data used to design, monitor, document, protect, and control data in information systems and databases; an application of data dictionary systems.
Data Element	A basic unit of information having a meaning and that may have subcategories (data items) of distinct units and values.
Database	Structured or organized collection of information, which may be accessed by the computer.
Database Management System	Computer application program that accesses or manipulates the database.
Data Interchange Service	A service of the Platform entity of the Technical Reference Model that provides specialized support for the interchange of data between applications on the same or different platforms.
Data Management Service	A service of the Platform entity of the Technical Reference Model that provides support for the management, storage, access, and manipulation of data in a database.
DBMS	Database Management System
DCE	Distributed Computing Environment
DDL	Data Definition Language
Default	Command which is automatically executed if none is specifically indicated.

Directory Service	Part of the network services of the Application Platform entity of the Technical Reference Model (TRM) that provides locator services that are restricted to finding the location of a service, location of data, or translation of a common name into a network-specific address. It is analogous to telephone books and supports distributed directory implementations.
DISA	US Department of Defense Information Systems Agency
Distributed Database	1. A database that is not stored in a central location but is dispersed over a network of interconnected computers. 2. A database under the overall control of a central Database Management System (DBMS) but whose storage devices are not all attached to the same processor. 3. A database that is physically located in two or more distinct locations.
DMF	Data Management Facility
ECMA	European Computer Manufacturers Association
EDI	Electronic Data Interchange
EEI	External Environment Interface
End User	Person who ultimately uses the computer application or output.
Enterprise	The highest level in an organization; includes all missions and functions.
Enterprise Continuum	Comprises two complementary concepts: the Architecture Continuum and the Solutions Continuum. Together these are a range of definitions with increasing specificity, from foundational definitions and agreed enterprise strategies all the way to architectures and implementations in specific organizations. Such coexistence of abstraction and concreteness in an enterprise can be a real source of confusion. The Enterprise Continuum also doubles as a powerful tool to turn confusion and resulting conflicts into progress.
Enterprise Model	A high-level model of an organization's mission, function, and information architecture. The model consists of a function model and a data model.
ERP	Enterprise Resource Planning
ES	End System
Expand	Ability to resize objects to produce better organization of on-screen material, usually a graphic or a window.

External Environment Interface (EEI)	The interface that supports information transfer between the Application Platform and the External Environment.
File	Any specifically identified collection of information stored in the computer.
FIPS	Federal Information Processing Standard
FORTRAN	Acronym for FORmula TRANslator, which is a high-level computer language used extensively in scientific and engineering applications.
FTAM	File Transfer, Access, and Management
Function	A useful capability provided by one or more components of a system.
GNMP	Government Network Management Profile
GOSIP	Government Open System Interconnection Profile
GSS	General Security Service
GUI	Graphical User Interface
Hardware	1. Physical equipment, as opposed to programs, procedures, rules, and associated documentation. 2. Contrast with software.
Human Computer Interface (HCI)	Human Computer Interface hardware and software allowing information exchange between the user and the computer.
IEC	The International Electrotechnical Commission, the international standards body which is responsible for electrical standards.
IEEE	Institute of Electrical and Electronic Engineers
III	Integrated Information Infrastructure
III-RM	Integrated Information Infrastructure Reference Model
Information	Any communication or representation of knowledge such as facts, data, or opinions, in any medium or form, including textual, numerical, graphic, cartographic, narrative, or audio-visual forms.
Information Domain	A set of commonly and unambiguously labeled information objects with a common security policy that defines the protections to be afforded the objects by authorized users and information management systems.
Information System	The computer-based portion of a business system.

Chapter 36: Glossary

Information Technology (IT)	The technology included in hardware and software used for information, regardless of the technology involved, whether computers, communications, micro graphics, or others.
Interface	Interconnection and inter-relationships between two devices, two applications, or the user and an application or device.
Interoperability	1. The ability of two or more systems or components to exchange and use information.
	2. The ability of systems to provide and receive services from other systems and to use the services so interchanged to enable them to operate effectively together.
IS	Information System
ISA	Information Systems Architecture
ISO	International Standards Organization
IT	Information Technology
ITIL	Information Technology Infrastructure Library
JTC1	A Joint Technical Committee established by ISO and IEC to take responsibility for their shared interests in IT standardization.
LAN	Local Area Network
Lifecycle	The period of time that begins when a system is conceived and ends when the system is no longer available for use.
MAN	Metropolitan Area Network
Metaview (also known as a Viewpoint)	A specification of the conventions for constructing and using a view. A metaview acts as a pattern or template of the view, from which to develop individual views. A metaview establishes the purposes and audience for a view, the ways in which the view is documented (e.g., for visual modeling), and the ways in which it is used (e.g., for analysis).
MIS	Management Information Systems
MLS	Multi-Level Security
MTA	Message Transfer Agent
Multimedia Service	A service of the Technical Reference Model (TRM) that provides the capability to manipulate and manage information products consisting of text, graphics, images, video, and audio.
NIST	US National Institute of Standards and Technology
NLSP	Network Layer Security Protocol
ODA	Office Document Architecture
ODIF	Office Document Interchange Format
OECD	Organization for Economic Co-operation and Development

OIW	OSI Implementors' Workshop
OODBMS	Object-Oriented Database Management System
Open Specifications	Public specifications that are maintained by an open, public consensus process to accommodate new technologies over time and that are consistent with international standards.
Open System	A system that implements sufficient open specifications for interfaces, services, and supporting formats to enable properly engineered Application Software:
	a To be ported with minimal changes across a wide range of systems
	b To interoperate with other applications on local and remote systems
	c To interact with users in a style that facilitates user portability
Open Systems Environment (OSE)	The comprehensive set of interfaces, services, and supporting formats, plus user aspects for interoperability or for portability of applications, data, or people, as specified by IT standards and profiles.
Operating System Service	A core service of the Application Platform entity of the Technical Reference Model (TRM) that is needed to operate and administer the Application Platform and provide an interface between the Application Software and the Platform (e.g., file management, input/output, print spoolers).
ORB	Object Request Broker
OS	Operating System
OSE	Open System Environment
OSI	Open Systems Interconnection
PEX	PHIGS Extension to X Windows
PHIGS	Programmer's Hierarchical Interactive Graphics System
Platform	See Application Platform.
Portability	1. The ease with which a system or component can be transferred from one hardware or software environment to another.
	2. A quality metric that can be used to measure the relative effort to transport the software for use in another environment or to convert software for use in another operating environment, hardware configuration, or software system environment.
	3. The ease with which a system, component, data, or user can be transferred from one hardware or software environment to another.
POSIX	Portable Operating System Interface (for Computer Environments)

Profile	A set of one or more base standards and, where applicable, the identification of those classes, subsets, options, and parameters of those base standards, necessary for accomplishing a particular function.
Profiling	Selecting standards for a particular application.
RAS	Remote Access Services
RDA	Remote Database Access
RDBMS	Relational Database Management System
Repository	A system that manages all of the data of an enterprise, including data and process models and other enterprise information. Hence, the data in a repository is much more extensive than that in a data dictionary, which generally defines only the data making up a database.
RM	Reference Model
RPC	Remote Procedure Call
Scalability	The ability to use the same Application Software on many different classes of hardware/software platforms from PCs to super-computers (extends the portability concept). The capability to grow to accommodate increased work loads.
Security	Services which protect data, ensuring its confidentiality, availability, and integrity.
Server	An application component which responds to requests from a client.
SGML	Standard Generalized Markup Language
SIB	Standards Information Base
SMAP	Security Management Application Process
SMTP	Simple Mail Transfer Protocol
SNA	System Network Architecture
SNMP	Simple Network Management Protocol

Solutions Continuum	A part of the Enterprise Continuum. The Solutions Continuum contains implementations of the corresponding definitions in the Architecture Continuum. In this way it becomes a repository of re-usable solutions for future implementation efforts.
SQL	Structured Query Language
SWG	Special Working Group
System	A collection of components organized to accomplish a specific function or set of functions (taken from Draft Recommended Practice for Architectural Description IEEE P1471/D5.2).
System and Network Management Service	A cross-category service of the Application Platform entity of the Technical Reference Model (TRM) that provides for the administration of the overall information system. These services include the management of information. processors, networks, configurations, accounting, and performance.
System Stakeholder	An individual, team, or organization (or classes thereof) with interests in, or concerns relative to, a system (taken from ANSI/IEEE Std 1471-2000).
TAFIM	Technical Architecture Framework for Information Management
Taxonomy of Architecture Views	The organized collection of all views pertinent to an architecture.
TCP/IP	Transmission Control Protocol/Internet Protocol
TCSEC	Trusted Computer System Evaluation Criteria
Technical Reference Model	A structure which allows the components of an information system to be described in a consistent manner.
TFA	Transparent File Access
TLSP	Transport Layer Security Protocol
TNI	Trusted Network Interpretation
TP	Transaction Processing
Transaction	Interaction between a user and a computer in which the user inputs a command to receive a specific result from the computer.

Transaction Sequence	Order of transactions required to accomplish the desired results.
TRM	Technical Reference Model
TSIG	Trusted Systems Interoperability Group
UIDL	User Interface Definition Language
UIMS	User Interface Management System
UISRM	User Interface System Reference Model
User	1. Any person, organization, or functional unit that uses the services of an information processing system. 2. In a conceptual schema language, any person or any thing that may issue or receive commands and messages to or from the information system.
User Interface Service	A service of the Application Platform entity of the Technical Reference Model (TRM) that supports direct human-machine interaction by controlling the environment in which users interact with applications.
View	A representation of a whole system from the perspective of a related set of concerns.
Viewpoint (also known as a Metaview)	A specification of the conventions for constructing and using a view. A metaview acts as a pattern or template of the view, from which to develop individual views. A metaview establishes the purposes and audience for a view, the ways in which the view is documented (e.g., for visual modeling), and the ways in which it is used (e.g., for analysis).
WAN	Wide Area Network

Chapter 37: Other Architectures and Frameworks

37.1 Introduction

TOGAF is one of a number of architectures and architecture frameworks in use today. Many of the other architectural initiatives have a good deal in common with TOGAF. In the following sections these initiatives are briefly described and their relationships to the TOGAF elements are explored.

37.2 C4ISR Architecture Framework

37.2.1 Overview

The acronym C4ISR stands for Command, Control, Computers, Communications (C4), Intelligence, Surveillance, and Reconnaissance (ISR). The C4ISR Architecture Framework Version 2.0 is a framework giving comprehensive architectural guidance for all of these related US Department of Defense (DoD) domains, in order to ensure interoperable and cost-effective military systems. It has emerged in recent years as a successor to the Technical Architecture Framework for Information Management (TAFIM), which was officially withdrawn in January 2000.

The C4ISR Architecture Framework is under revision to generalize it to apply to all functional areas of the DoD. It is already being used in government areas beyond the Defense sector.

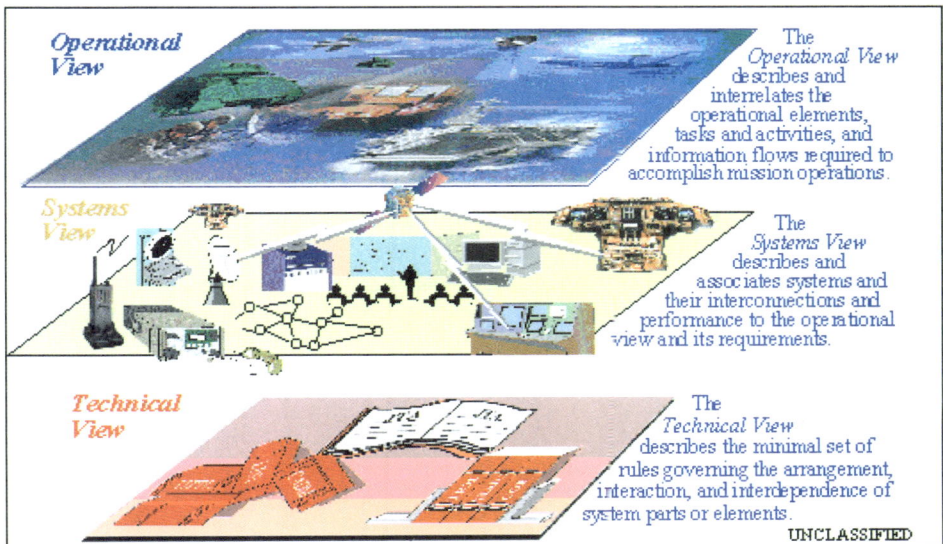

Figure 37.1: C4ISR Architecture Framework - Three Views of an Architecture

The impetus for the C4ISR Architecture Framework was the realization within the DoD that Defense organizations across the world were developing architectures representing specific contributions and relationships with respect to overall DoD operations, but that significant differences in content and formats were inhibiting the ability to rationalize or compare different architecture descriptions. In turn, disparate and unrelatable architecture products were leading to non-integrated, non-interoperable, and non-cost-effective capabilities in the field.

The C4ISR Architecture Framework is intended to ensure that the architecture descriptions developed by the various commands, services, and agencies within the DoD are inter-relatable between and among each organization's operational, systems, and technical architecture views, and are comparable and integratable across joint and multi-national organizational boundaries.

In particular, the C4ISR Architecture Framework:

- Assures that architectures are integratable across the Defense community
- Establishes linkages or threads that tie together the operational, systems, and technical views of an architecture
- Provides the basis for an audit trail that relates current and postulated systems to measures of effectiveness for mission operations

37.2.2 Relationship to TOGAF

Whereas the Architecture Development Method (ADM) forms a core part of TOGAF, guidance in the C4ISR Architecture Framework concerning the process of describing an architecture - i.e., what steps to perform and in what order - has intentionally been kept to a minimum. There are several reasons for this:

- The decision as to which products to build, beyond the essential ones, depends on the purpose of the architecture description.
- The sequence in which the products are built likewise depends on the purpose of the architecture description, and on other programmatic factors as well.
- Many DoD organizations use their own tailored processes, which the C4ISR Architecture Framework can complement.

The most critical aspect of the guidance is that the purpose for building the architecture description should be clearly understood and articulated up front. This purpose will influence the choice of what information to gather, what products to build, and what kinds of analysis to apply.

A major structural concept in the C4ISR Architecture Framework is the three sets of "views" (Operational, System, Technical). The use of the term "view" in the C4ISR Architecture Framework is different from the use of the term in TOGAF, although there is a rough correspondence:

- Between the Operational view in the C4ISR Architecture Framework, and the Business Architecture in TOGAF ("operations" in the military sphere is the "business" being undertaken by the military "enterprise")

- Between the System view in the C4ISR Architecture Framework, and the Information Systems Architectures (Data and Applications Architecture) and Technology Architecture in TOGAF

- Between the Technical view in the C4ISR Architecture Framework, and the standards view of the Technology Architecture in TOGAF

A number of the products (deliverables/artifacts) defined in the C4ISR Architecture Framework have no equivalent in the TOGAF ADM because the ADM does not go down to the level of detail that these particular C4ISR products address. These C4ISR products are at the level of system design rather than architecture. Specific organizations tailoring the ADM to their own needs might decide to go to this level of detail, however (typically, by including them in the Target Architecture step in Phases B, C, and D).

37.3 CORBA

37.3.1 Overview

The Object Management Group's (OMG) Object Management Architecture (OMA), often loosely referred to as the CORBA architecture, is an object-oriented Applications Architecture centered on the concept of an Object Request Broker (ORB) (see *www.omg.org/gettingstarted*). The ORB acts as a switching center, locating objects, storing interface definitions and object implementations, and relaying messages between objects in a distributed heterogeneous environment.

CORBAservices are a low-level set of common object services available to all objects, covering functions like object creation and deletion, naming, security services, and many others.

Horizontal CORBAfacilities are higher-level functions such as distributed documents or printing, suitable for use in a wide variety of market sectors.

Domain CORBAfacilities are vertical market-specific interfaces which will provide common facilities for applications within a particular market sector.

37.3.2 Relationship to TOGAF

The CORBA architecture, or OMA, is an application-level architecture which focuses exclusively on issues affecting distributed object-oriented systems. It is entirely consistent with TOGAF, and depends on the presence of lower-level facilities such as those described by TOGAF for operating system support, communications, and so on.

Object-based service categories in TOGAF are called out in Object-Oriented Provision of Services .

37.4 Enterprise Architecture Planning (EAP)

Steven Spewak's Enterprise Architecture Planning (EAP) is a set of methods for planning the development of Information, Applications, and Technology Architectures (the recommended approach being to develop them in that order), and for aligning the three types of architecture with respect to each other. The goal is to ensure that such architectures form the blueprints for sound, implementable systems that solve real business problems.

The overall EAP methodology involves the following "steps":

1. Planning Initiation: defining scope, objectives, roles, and responsibilities and deciding which methodology to use, who should be involved, and what toolset to use. This leads to producing a workplan for the enterprise architecture planning activity and securing management commitment to go through all of the following phases.
2. Principles: developing the core principles to support the effective governance of information and technology. These principles form the basis for making architectural decisions, accepting the results, and managing the migration. They are based on industry best practice and the enterprise's purpose, vision, and values and are implemented through policies, procedures, and standards.
3. Business Modeling: modeling the current business activities and the information used, and identifying business process improvement opportunities.
4. Current Systems & Technology: defining what is in place today for application systems and supporting technology platforms. This is a summary-level inventory of application systems, data, and technology platforms to provide a baseline for long-range migration plans.
5. Data Architecture: developing the Data Architecture, including defining the major business activities and data objects needed to support the business.
6. Applications Architecture: defining the major kinds of applications needed to manage the data and support the business functions.
7. Technology Architecture: defining the platforms needed to provide a technological infrastructure for the applications that manage the data and support the business functions.
8. Implementation/Migration Plans: defining the sequence for implementing applications, a schedule for implementation, a cost/benefit analysis, and a clear step-by-step path for migration. Executive-level recommendations are made for implementing the plan, and a plan is developed for the transition period after following the enterprise architecture planning activity.
9. Planning Conclusion: final report and presentation of the results to management.

The EAP methodology thus positions the four types of "architecture" in the sequence: Business Architecture, Data Architecture, Applications Architecture, and Technology Architecture as the recommended sequence.

37.4.1 Comparison with TOGAF

Spewak's EAP methodology is analogous to the TOGAF ADM:

- Steps 1, 2, and 3 map to the development of a Business Architecture and the underlying business and technical requirements in Phase B of the TOGAF ADM.
- Step 4 maps to the first step, Baseline Description, in ADM Phases C and D.
- Steps 5, 6, and 7 map directly to the Target Architecture-related steps of ADM Phases C and D.
- Step 8 maps to ADM Phase E and Phase F.

EAP does not have a taxonomy of the various viewpoints and views, or a Foundation Architecture (Technical Reference Model (TRM) and Standards Information Base (SIB)).

37.5 Federal Enterprise Architecture: Practical Guide

37.5.1 Overview

The US Federal CIO Council published A Practical Guide to Federal Enterprise Architecture (Version 1.0) in February 2001, in a cooperative venture with the General Accounting Office (GAO) and the Office of Management and Budget (OMB). The purpose of this document is to provide guidance to US federal agencies in initiating, developing, using, and maintaining their enterprise architectures. This guide offers an end-to-end process to initiate, implement, and sustain an enterprise architecture program, and describes the necessary roles and responsibilities for a successful enterprise architecture program. The guidance presented in the practical guide should be tailored by each federal agency according to its needs.

This guide focuses on enterprise architecture processes, products, and roles and responsibilities. The guide addresses how enterprise architecture processes fit within an overall enterprise lifecycle; namely, by describing in detail how the enterprise architecture processes relate to enterprise engineering, program management, and Capital Planning and Investment Control (CPIC) processes, as summarized in figure 37.2.

At the initiation of its enterprise architecture program, each agency should establish the scope of its enterprise architecture and formulate a strategy that includes the definition of a vision, objectives, and principles. The figure 37.3 summarizes the enterprise architecture processes.

Executive buy-in and support should be established and an architectural team formed within the organization. The team defines an approach and process tailored to agency needs. The architecture team implements the process to build both the Baseline and Target Architectures. The architecture team also prepares a sequencing plan for transitioning systems, applications, and associated business practices, based on gap analyses and business drivers. Projects are selected and controlled in the CPIC and the enterprise engineering and program management processes and are guided by, and compliant with, the enterprise architecture. Lastly, the architecture is maintained through a continuous modification to reflect the agency's baseline and target business practices, organizational goals, visions, technology, and infrastructure.

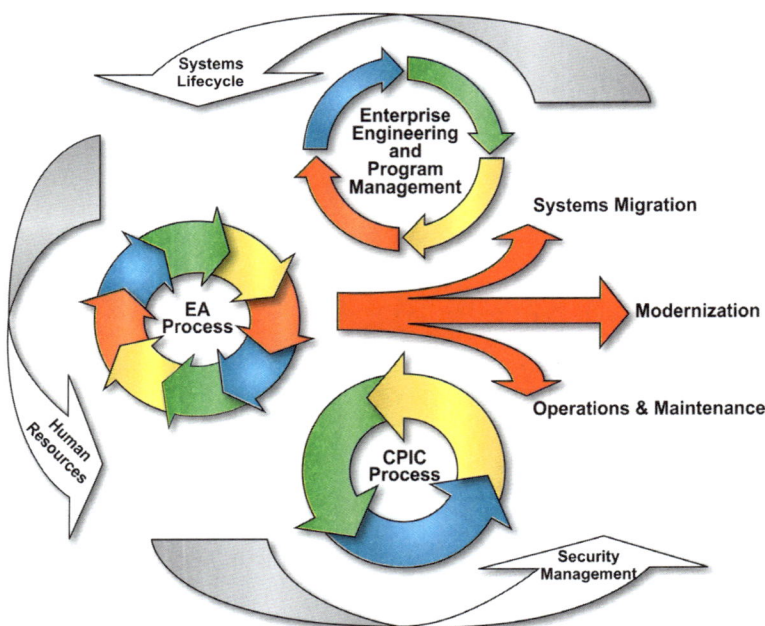

Figure 37.2 The Enterprise Life Cycle

Figure 37.3 The Enterprise Architecture Process

37.5.2 Relationship to TOGAF

The Practical Guide's enterprise architecture processes closely align with the lifecycle phases of the TOGAF ADM. In addition, the Practical Guide adds steps such as establishing an enterprise architecture policy and principles.

37.6 FEAF

37.6.1 Overview

The US Federal CIO Council published the Federal Enterprise Architecture Framework (FEAF) (Version 1.1) in September 1999. The FEAF promotes shared development for US federal processes, interoperability, and sharing of information among US federal agencies and other governmental entities. The FEAF provides direction and guidance to federal agencies for structuring an enterprise architecture. The FEAF describes eight components of an enterprise architecture:

- Architecture Drivers
- Strategic Direction
- Baseline Architecture
- Target Architecture
- Transitional Processes
- Architectural Segments
- Architectural Models
- Standards

The FEAF also provides direction for establishing "federal segments", which are cross-agency business areas (such as international trade, grants, common patient records) that transcend federal agency boundaries. These federal architectural segments collectively constitute the Federal Enterprise Architecture.

The FEAF partitions a given architecture into Business, Data, Applications, and Technology Architectures, as shown in the figure 37.4. The FEAF currently includes the first three columns of the Zachman Framework and the Spewak Enterprise Architecture Planning (EAP) methodology.

The figure 37.5 shows the FEAF Architecture Matrix, which names the enterprise architecture products to be developed for each cell. Version 1.1 of the FEAF does not prescribe the contents or approach for developing these work products.

37.6.2 Relationship to TOGAF

The FEAF contains guidance analogous to the TOGAF Foundation Architecture and

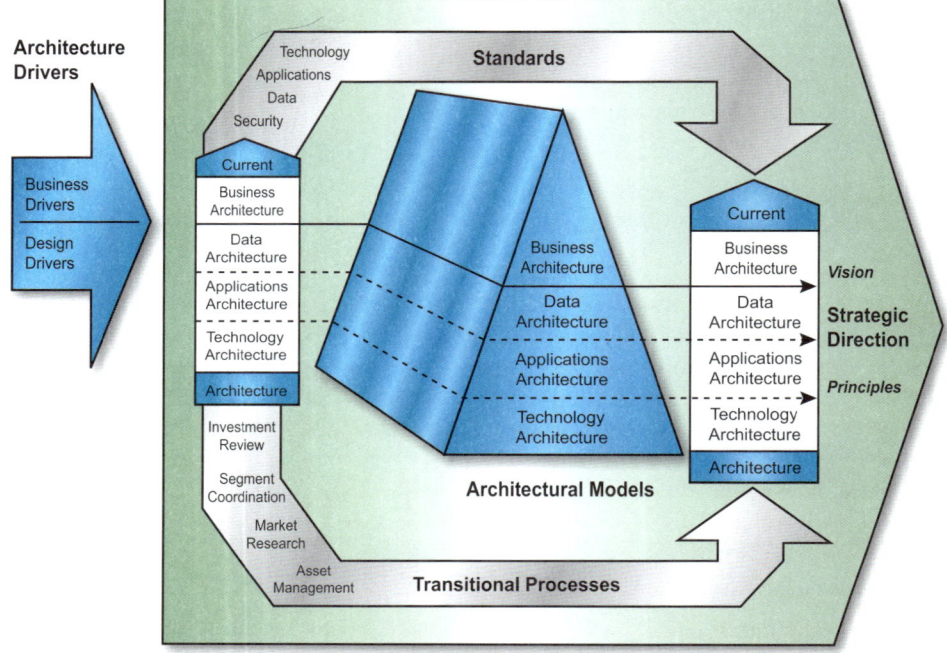

Figure 37.4

architecture viewpoints and views. The rows of the FEAF matrix (which correspond to the Zachman Framework) do not directly map to the TOGAF structure, although the ADM mapping to the Zachman Framework supports a close correlation between the FEAF and TOGAF. The columns of the FEAF matrix correspond directly to three of the four architecture domains covered by TOGAF (TOGAF also covers Business Architecture).

	Data Architecture	Applications Architecture	Technology Architecture
Planner Perspective	List of Business Objects	List of Business Processes	List of Business Locations
Owner Perspective	Semantic Model	Business Process Model	Business Logistics System
Designer Perspective	Logistic Data Model	Applications Architecture	System Geographic Deployment Architecture
Builder Perspective	Physical Data Model	Systems Design	Technology Architecture
Subcontractor Perspective	Data Directory	Programs	Network Architecture

Figure 37.5 The Enterprise Architecture Process

37.7 ISO/IEC TR 14252 (IEEE Std 1003.0)

Note: IEEE Std 1003.0-1995 is administratively withdrawn by IEEE.

37.7.1 Overview

ISO/IEC TR 14252:1996, Guide to the POSIX Open System Environment, is a direct line ancestor of TOGAF. TOGAF was originally based on the US DoD Technical Architecture Framework for Information Management (TAFIM), which was itself a development of ISO/IEC TR 14252.

37.7.2 Relationship to TOGAF

At the topmost level, ISO/IEC TR 14252, TAFIM, and TOGAF share a very similar high-level reference model. ISO/IEC TR 14252 does not include a diagram giving a detailed breakdown of the Application Software, Application Platform, or external environment entities, but the remainder of the document breaks down the Application Platform into a number of similar, though not identical, areas.

TOGAF includes a considerable amount of material on architecture development which is lacking from ISO/IEC TR 14252, while ISO/IEC TR 14252 includes a considerable amount of detail in service category definition and in the recommended lists of standards and specifications.

The architectural approach taken in ISO/IEC TR 14252 is broadly similar to that of TOGAF, in that the architecture reference model diagram implies no structure among the service categories, leaving that to individual system architectures and real-world implementations.

37.8 NCR Enterprise Architecture Framework

The description of the NCR Enterprise Architecture Framework, including a comparison with TOGAF, is hosted on NCR's own web site (see *www3.ncr.com/architecture/togaf*).

The NCR Enterprise Architecture Framework is based on NCR's architecture practice Global Information Technology Planning (GITP), and NCR's architecture model Open Cooperative Computing Architecture (OCCA 6). The Enterprise Architecture Framework was created to guide the development of systems, industry, and customer-specific architectures.

37.9 ISO RM-ODP

37.9.1 Overview

The ISO Reference Model for Open Distributed Processing (ITU-T Rec. X.901 | ISO/IEC 10746-1 to ITU-T Rec. X.904 | ISO/IEC 10746-4), commonly referred to as RM-ODP, provides a framework to support the development of standards that will support distributed processing in heterogeneous environments. It is based, as far as possible, on the use of formal description techniques for specification of the architecture.

RM-ODP uses an object modeling approach to describe distributed systems. Two structuring approaches are used to simplify the problems of design in large complex systems: five viewpoints provide different ways of describing the system; and eight transparencies identify specific problems unique to distributed systems which distributed system standards may wish to address. Each viewpoint is associated with a language which can be used to describe systems from that viewpoint.

The five viewpoints described by RM-ODP are:

1. The enterprise viewpoint, which examines the system and its environment in the context of the business requirements on the system, its purpose, scope, and policies. It deals with aspects of the enterprise such as its organizational structure, which affect the system.
2. The information viewpoint, which focuses on the information in the system. How the information is structured, how it changes, information flows, and the logical divisions between independent functions within the system are all dealt with in the information viewpoint.
3. The computational viewpoint, which focuses on functional decomposition of the system into objects which interact at interfaces.
4. The engineering viewpoint, which focuses on how distributed interaction between system objects is supported.
5. The technology viewpoint, which concentrates on the individual hardware and software components which make up the system.

37.9.2 Relationship to TOGAF

RM-ODP is very tightly focused on problems relating to interactions between the objects making up distributed information processing systems, while TOGAF embraces the full spectrum of systems, whether distributed or not. As such, TOGAF coverage is a superset of that provided by RM-ODP. However, the relationship between the viewpoints described by RM-ODP and the TOGAF views is not an obvious one, and there is some danger of confusing the two.

In fact, each RM-ODP viewpoint is an examination of a distributed system at a different level of detail, while TOGAF adopts the ANSI/IEEE Std 1471-2000 approach to views as representations of a whole system from the perspective of a related set of concerns. This makes it impractical to try to compare the set of TOGAF views with RM-ODP viewpoints.

A better comparison can be made between the RM-ODP viewpoints and the different levels of detail used by TOGAF in the examination of building blocks. In Building Blocks and the ADM, Iteration between the Four Levels of Modeling shows how the iterative process of building block definition can be divided into the Business Process level, the Technical Functionality and Constraints level, the Architectural Model level, and the Solution Model level.

The mapping between the building blocks example and ODP viewpoints is as follows:

Business Process level	<==>	Enterprise and Information viewpoints and Technical Functionality and Constraints level
Architectural model level	<==>	Computational viewpoint
Solution level	<==>	Technology and Engineering viewpoints

37.10 SPIRIT Platform Blueprint Issue 3.0

37.10.1 Overview

The Service Providers' Integrated Requirements for Information Technology (SPIRIT) Platform Blueprint is a specification that was developed within the Network Management Forum, now known as the TeleManagement Forum (TMF) - www.tmforum.org. The SPIRIT Platform Blueprint Issue 3.0 is published by The Open Group (see *www.opengroup.org/bookstore/catalog/sp.htm*).

SPIRIT is a joint effort between telecommunication service providers, computer system vendors, and independent software vendors, with the goal of producing a common, agreed set of specifications for a general-purpose computing platform. The objective is to provide a core set of specifications for use in each company's purchasing of software components for general-purpose computing platforms. The SPIRIT specifications are based predominantly on widely accepted industry standards.

37.10.2 Relationship to TOGAF

SPIRIT defines a practical, tested selection of specifications, most of which are referenced within the TOGAF Standards Information Base (SIB), that achieves portability and interoperability for largescale systems. The focus of SPIRIT is on ensuring that the SPIRIT selections are agreed upon by the vendor side for implementability and on the user side for procurability.

37.11 TAFIM

37.11.1 Overview

The US Department of Defense (DoD) Technical Architecture Framework for Information Management (TAFIM) was developed from ISO/IEC TR 14252:1996, Guide to the POSIX Open System Environment (IEEE Std 1003.0), and was used as the basis of TOGAF Version 1. As a result, there is a strong resemblance between the three.

Note: IEEE Std 1003.0-1995 is administratively withdrawn by IEEE.

On January 7th, 2000 TAFIM was officially canceled by the DoD. The TAFIM web site has been archived at *www-library.itsi.disa.mil/tafim.html*, where it will continue to be available for information and reference purposes only. A number of new documents have been developed that supersede specific TAFIM subject areas. These are:

- C4ISR Architecture Framework, Version 2.0, 18 December 1997
- JTA, Version 3.0, 15 November 1999
- DoD Technical Reference Model (TRM), Version 1.0, 5 November 1999

37.11.2 Relationship to TOGAF

TAFIM was the parent of TOGAF, and the US Defense Information Systems Agency (DISA) contributed extensively to the development of TOGAF, with the result that the two architecture frameworks have much in common. The TOGAF Technical Reference Model (TRM) was largely derived from TAFIM, and the TOGAF Architecture Development Method (ADM) was originally based on parts of TAFIM.

37.12 TEAF

37.12.1 Overview

In July 2000, the Department of the Treasury published the Treasury Enterprise Architecture Framework (TEAF). The TEAF provides:

1. Guidance to Treasury bureaus concerning the development and evolution of Information Systems Architecture
2. A unifying concept, common principles, technologies, and standards for information systems
3. A template for the development of the enterprise architecture

The TEAF describes an architecture framework that supports Treasury's business processes in terms of work products. This framework guides the development and redesign of the business processes for various bureaus in order to meet the requirements of recent legislation in a rapidly changing technology environment. The TEAF prescribes architecture views and a set of essential and supporting work products to portray these views. The following figure illustrates the TEAF framework.

The TEAF's functional, information, and organizational architecture views collectively model the organization's processes, procedures, and business operations. By grounding the architecture in the business of the organization, the TEAF defines the core business procedures and enterprise processes. Through its explicit models, a TEAF-based architecture enables the identification and reasoning of enterprise and system-level concerns and investment decisions.

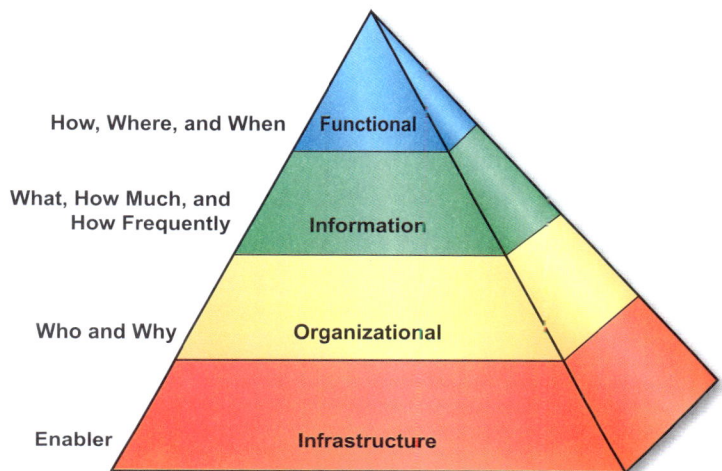

The TEAF separates enterprise architecture information into Enterprise Architecture Direction (drivers, policies, program roadmap), Enterprise Architecture Description, and Enterprise Architecture Accomplishment (transition strategy, technical forecasts, and insertion). The Enterprise Architecture Description is a matrix, with columns being views (functional, information, organizational, and infrastructure) and rows being perspectives (planner, owner, designer, builder). Many of the TEAF work products are also in the C4ISR Architecture Framework. However, TEAF introduces the Information Assurance Trust Model, Information Assurance Risk Assessment, and the Enterprise Architecture Roadmap. The Enterprise Architecture Roadmap summarizes the scope of the bureau's enterprise architecture, the drivers, governance plan, approach and methodology, and program plan.

37.12.2 Relationship to TOGAF

Many of the observations made in describing the relationship of the C4ISR Architecture Framework to TOGAF apply also to the TEAF. Namely, the TEAF is prescriptive as to what work products should be produced, and the term view/perspective is used differently.

37.13 Zachman Framework

The Zachman Framework is a framework providing a view of the subjects and models needed to develop a complete enterprise architecture. This framework is described in detail at the ZIFA web site (see *www.zifa.com/zifajz02.htm*).

An alternative source is the University of Nebraska at Omaha, which gives a very detailed and highly readable description of the Zachman Framework.

The Zachman Framework is a widely used approach for developing and/or documenting an enterprise-wide Information Systems Architecture. Zachman based his framework on practices in traditional architecture and engineering. This resulted in an approach which on the vertical axis provides multiple perspectives of the overall architecture, and on the horizontal axis a classification of the various artifacts of the architecture.

The purpose of the Framework is to provide a basic structure which supports the organization, access, integration, interpretation, development, management, and changing of a set of architectural representations of the organization's information systems. Such objects or descriptions of architectural representations are usually referred to as artifacts.

The framework, then, can contain global plans as well as technical details, lists, and charts as well as natural language statements. Any appropriate approach, standard, role, method, technique, or tool may be placed in it. In fact, the Framework can be viewed as a tool to organize any form of metadata for the enterprise.

37.13.1 Relationship to TOGAF

The ADM mapping to the Zachman Framework (see ADM and the Zachman Framework) supports a close correlation between the Zachman Framework and the TOGAF ADM.

The Zachman Framework provides a very comprehensive and well-established taxonomy of the various viewpoints, models, and other artifacts that an enterprise may want to consider developing as part of an enterprise architecture. (The recommendation of the Zachman Framework itself is that all the cells be covered.)

The current recommended set of viewpoints in TOGAF does not cover all 30 cells of the Zachman Framework. However, with TOGAF it is possible to develop viewpoints and views to cover other aspects of the Zachman Framework as necessary.

TOGAF recommends some viewpoints that are not included in the Zachman Framework; for example, the security and manageability viewpoints. The selection of viewpoints needs to be determined by the purpose of the architecture, and the TOGAF ADM defines a process for driving that selection.

The vertical axis of the Zachman Framework provides a source of potential viewpoints for the architect to consider. The horizontal axis could be regarded as providing a generic taxonomy of concerns.

The Zachman Framework says nothing about the processes for developing viewpoints or conformant views, or the order in which they should be developed. It does not provide a method such as TOGAF's ADM, or a Foundation Architecture (Technical Reference Model (TRM) and Standards Information Base (SIB)).

Chapter 38: Tools for Architecture Development

This section discusses tools and techniques helpful in using TOGAF.

38.1 Overview

As an enterprise architecture framework, TOGAF provides a basis for developing architectures in a uniform and consistent manner. Its purpose in this respect is to ensure that the various architecture descriptions developed within an enterprise, perhaps by different architects or architecture teams, support the comparison and integration of architectures within and across architecture domains (Business, Data, Applications, Technology), and relating to different business area scopes within the enterprise

To support this goal, TOGAF defines numerous deliverables in the form of architectures, represented as architecture models, architecture views of those models, and other artifacts. Over time, these artifacts become a resource that needs to be managed and controlled, particularly with a view to re-use. This concept is referred to in TOGAF as the Enterprise Continuum.

Architecture models and views are discussed in detail separately in Developing Architecture Views . This section discusses considerations in choosing automated tools in order to generate such architecture models and views, and to maintain them over time.

38.2 Issues in Tool Standardization

In the current state of the tools market, many enterprises developing enterprise architectures struggle with the issue of standardizing on tools, whether they seek a single "one size fits all" tool or a multi-tool suite for modeling architectures and generating the different architecture views required.

There are ostensible advantages associated with selecting a single tool. Organizations following such a policy can hope to realize benefits such as reduced training, shared licenses, quantity discounts, maintenance, and easier data interchange.

However, there are also reasons for refusing to identify a single mandated tool, including reasons of principle (endorsing a single architecture tool would not encourage competitive commercial innovation or the development of advanced tool capability); and the fact that a single tool would not accommodate a variety of architecture development "maturity levels" and specific needs across an enterprise. Successful enterprise architecture teams are often those that harmonize their architecture tools with their architecture maturity level, team/ organizational capabilities, and objectives or focus. If different organizations within an enterprise are at different architecture maturity levels and have different objectives or focus (e.g., Enterprise versus Business versus Technology Architecture), it becomes very difficult for one tool to satisfy all organizations' needs.

38.3 Evaluation Criteria and Guidelines

TOGAF does not require or recommend any specific tool. However, in recognition of the problems that enterprise architects currently face in this area, this section provides a set of proposed evaluation criteria for selecting architecture tools to develop the various architecture models and views that are required.

Individual enterprises may wish to adapt these generic evaluation criteria to their particular circumstances and requirements. In particular, such an exercise would typically produce weightings of the various criteria that can be used to produce a "score" for the specific tools evaluated.

38.3.1 Tool Criteria

38.3.1.1 Functionality

Key Features and Functions

- Does it support the framework that your organization has chosen to use?
    - Does it support production of the deliverables required?
    - If not, does it support some of the known frameworks; e.g., TOGAF or Zachman Framework out-of-the-box?
- Glossary:
    - Glossary extendible to become a taxonomy?
    - Active Glossary to enforce a taxonomy?
- Ability to represent architecture models and views in a way meaningful to non-Technology Architecture stakeholders
- Does it support meta-models; e.g., ability to configure and tailor models?
- Does it support enterprise use; e.g., multi-user collaboration support?
- Does it allow drill down; e.g., conceptual, logical, physical, etc.?
- Does it provide a mechanism for linking requirements to the resulting enterprise architecture; i.e., requirements traceability?
- Security features:
    - Does it facilitate access control; e.g., different permissions for different roles?
    - Does its security design support corporate security policies?
- Does it natively support report generation?
- Does it support a common language and notation?

Intuitiveness/Ease-of-Use Factors

- An easy to follow "process map" guiding use of the tool
- Online help
- Relevant out-of-the-box architecture constructs, be it Business, Data, Applications, or Technology
- Relevant out-of-the-box templates or patterns for constructs, which can be used to help organizations "jump start"
- Support for visualization modeling; e.g., drag-and-drop and lines that equate to links
- Can it be extended or customized and does it provide utilities to do that?
- Does it track and audit changes?
- Does it provide a way for consistently naming and organizing those artifacts?
- Can those artifacts/components be easily viewed, used, and re-used?
- What requirements are there for use of programmatic languages?

Organizational Compatibility Factors

- Internationalization/localization capability:
    - Can the tool be used in all the geographic locations and/or language domains in which architecture work is done?

Tool Capacity/Scalability Constraints

- Does the tool have capacity constraints?
    - Size of data
    - Number of files
    - Number of data entries/records?
- What are the tool's design "sweet spots" (i.e., optimal design configuration parameters), and how scalable is it around those optima?
    - Is there an upgrade path beyond the capacity constraints of the tool?

38.3.1.2 Architecture of the Tool

- Repository distributed or central?
- Dynamic repository?
- Does the tool function with multiple industry standard data stores (e.g., Oracle, Sybase) or is storage proprietary?
- Backwards-compatibility with prior releases of the tool?
- Does it allow integration and consolidation of data into a central repository?

- Does it include version control?
- Is it accessible through a web client?
- What platforms (hardware, OS, DBMS, network) does it run on?

38.3.1.3 Full Lifecycle Support

- Does it provide full lifecycle support?
- Does it support various relevant views out-of-the-box; e.g., Business Process, Data, Applications, Technology?
- Does it support the creation of custom views?
- Does it use modeling methods and techniques relevant to this enterprise's architecture practice?
- Does is support simulation?
- Is the model that it produces executable?

38.3.1.4 Interoperability Factors

- Import/Export:
    - Can it create an artifact inside the tool and export it to other commonly used tools, and have the users of those tools use the artifact intact?
    - Can it import an artifact created in another tool, and use the artifact intact?
- Does it integrate with other tools?
- Does it provide and support industry standard APIs?
- Does it use relevant industry standards; e.g., XML, HTML, produce hypertext, UML, other industry standard?

38.3.1.5 Financial Considerations

- What is the acquisition cost?
- What is the total cost of ownership?
    - Maintenance
    - Equipment costs
    - Support costs
    - Number of resources required to keep it up-to-date
    - Administration responsibilities/time constraints
    - Will there be any impacts of introducing the tool into your environment; e.g., does it require some unique infrastructure?
    - Training
    - Licensing models

38.3.1.6 Vendor Factors

- Will vendor remain viable?
- How long has vendor existed in this arena?
- Do they have large customers?
- Do they have professional services?
- Third-party support?
- Does the tool have history at the organization and, if so, what is its reputation?
- Training factors:
    - Availability
    - Costs
    - Amount required to become productive
    - Style of learning (CBT, classroom)

38.3.2 General Pointers

- Value of the tool is dependent upon the architecture maturity of the organization.
- Need to match the tool to the capability of your organization; i.e., where it is architecturally?
- Trade-off between tactical considerations (competency, familiarity, etc.) and strategical considerations (overall organization's standards and directions).
- Teaming can positively or negatively affect a tool's success.

Chapter 39: ADM and the Zachman Framework

This chapter provides a mapping of the TOGAF Architecture Development Method (ADM) to the Zachman Framework.

39.1 Introduction

A number of architecture frameworks exist, each of which has its particular advantages and disadvantages, and relevance, for enterprise architecture. Several are discussed in Other Architectures and Frameworks .

However, there is no accepted industry standard method for developing an enterprise architecture. The Open Group goal with TOGAF is to work towards making the TOGAF ADM just such an industry standard method, which can be used for developing the products associated with any recognized enterprise framework that the architect feels is appropriate for a particular architecture. The Open Group vision for TOGAF is as a vehicle and repository for practical, experience-based information on how to go about the process of enterprise architecture, providing a generic method with which specific sets of deliverables, specific reference models, and other relevant architectural assets can be integrated.

To illustrate the concept, this section provides a mapping of the various phases of the TOGAF ADM to the cells of the well-known Zachman Framework.

39.2 The Zachman Framework

The Zachman Framework for Enterprise Architecture, sometimes simply referred to as the ``Zachman Framework'', has become a de facto standard for classifying the artifacts developed in enterprise architecture. It is a logical structure for classifying and organizing the design artifacts of an enterprise that are significant to its management. It draws on a classification scheme found in the more mature disciplines of architecture/construction and engineering/manufacturing, used for classifying and organizing the design artefacts relating to complex physical products such as a building or an aircraft. Zachman adopts this classification scheme to the design and construction of information systems.

The Zachman Framework comprises a 6x6 matrix.

The columns represent various aspects of the enterprise that can be described or modeled; and the rows represent various viewpoints from which the aspects can be described. Thus each cell formed by the intersection of a column and a row represents an aspect of the enterprise modeled from a particular viewpoint. The architect selects and models the cells that are appropriate to the immediate purpose, with the ultimate objective of modeling all the cells.

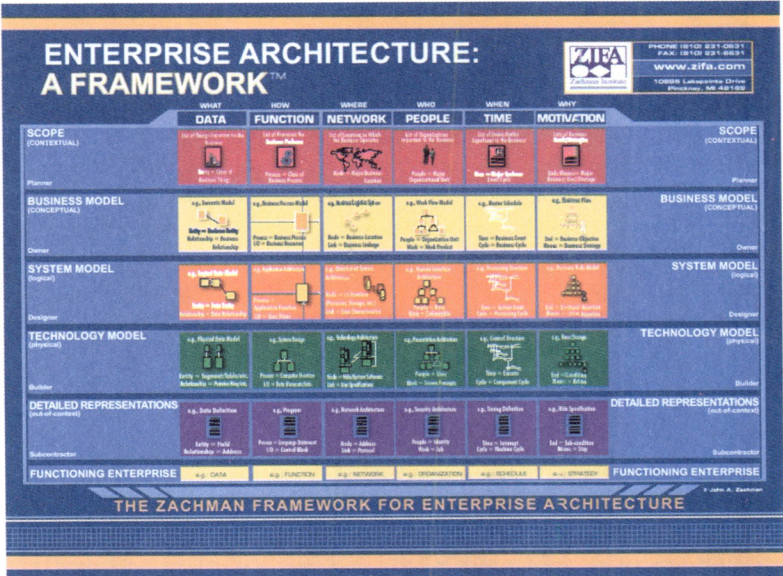

The six viewpoints are:

1. The Scope (Contextual) viewpoint - aimed at the planner
2. The Business Model (Conceptual) viewpoint - aimed at the owner
3. The System (Logical) viewpoint - aimed at the designer
4. The Technology (Physical) viewpoint - aimed at the builder
5. The Detailed Representations (Out-of-Context) viewpoint - aimed at the subcontractor
6. The Functioning Enterprise viewpoint

The six aspects - and the interrogatives to which they correspond - are:

1. The Data aspect - What?
2. The Function aspect - How?
3. The Network aspect - Where?
4. The People aspect - Who?
5. The Time aspect - When?
6. The Motivation aspect - Why?

Although the Zachman Framework applies to enterprises, the Framework itself is generic. It is a comprehensive, logical structure for the descriptive representations (i.e., models or design artefacts) of any complex object, and it does not prescribe or describe any particular method, representation technique, or automated tool.

The strength of the Framework is that it provides a way of thinking about an enterprise in an organized way, so that it can be described and analyzed. It also enables the individuals involved in producing enterprise information systems to focus on selected aspects of the system without losing sight of the overall enterprise context. In designing and building complex systems, such as enterprise systems, there are simply too many details and relationships to consider simultaneously. At the same time, isolating single variables and making design decisions out of context results in sub-optimization, with all the attendant costs and risks. The challenge is the same whether the system is physical (like an aircraft) or conceptual (like an enterprise system). How do you design and build it, piece by piece, and step by step, such that it achieves its purpose without losing its value and raising its cost by optimizing the pieces and sub-optimizing the overall?

39.3 Mapping TOGAF to the Zachman Framework

The scope of the four architecture domains of TOGAF align very well with the first four rows of the Zachman Framework, as shown in the following mapping of these domains.

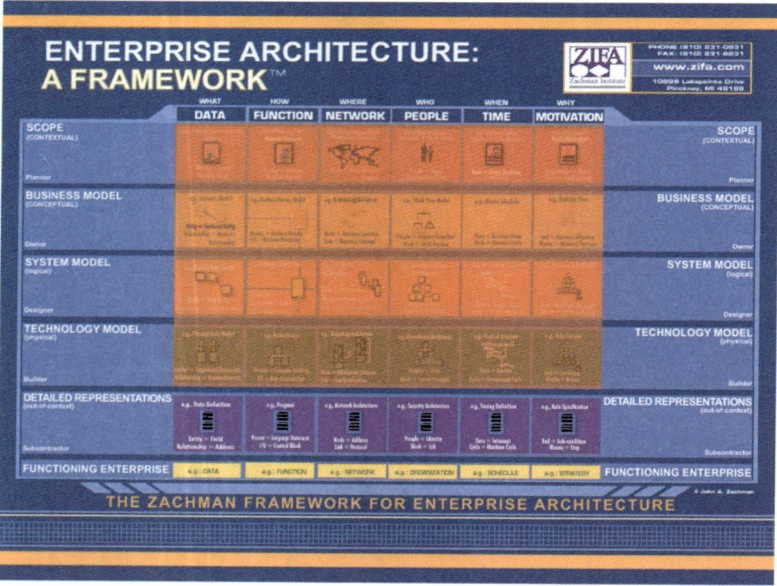

Scope of TOGAF ADM

Several domains overlap in the above diagram: the earliest domain to address a cell has precedence in the coloring scheme.

The mappings of the individual phases of the ADM are shown in detail below.

Note: In addition to the mappings to specific cells given below, the detailed representations and functioning enterprise viewpoints (the lowest two rows) of the Zachman Framework are also addressed and represented in TOGAF, through the Architecture Governance Framework (see Architecture Governance Framework), and through ADM deliverables such as the various Architecture Contracts (see Architecture Contracts). These ensure the validity and viability of the delivered solutions to meet the business needs.

39.3.1 Preliminary Phase: Framework and Principles

The outputs of this phase are:

- Framework Definition
  ZF: Business/Function (model of the architecture development process) [R2,C2]

- Architecture principles
  ZF: Scope/Data, Scope/Function, Scope/Network, Scope/People, Scope/Time, Scope/Motivation [R1,C1; R1,C2; R1,C3; R1,C4; R1,C5; R1,C6]

- Restatement of, or reference to, business principles, business goals, and business drivers
  ZF: Composite of: Scope/Motivation, Business/Motivation [R1,C6; R2,C6]

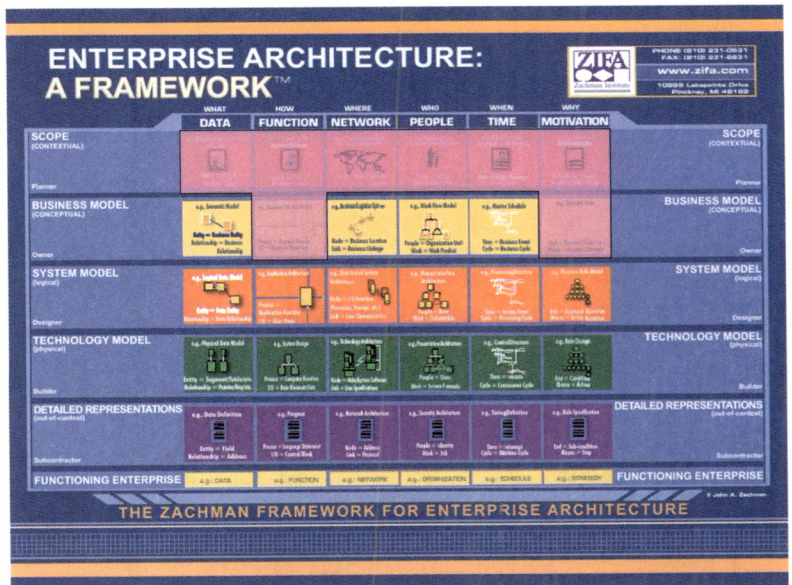

Scope of Preliminary Phase: Framework and Principles

39.3.2 Phase A: Architecture Vision

The outputs of this phase are:

- Approved Statement of Architecture Work, including in particular:
    - Scope and constraints
      ZF: Scope/Data, Scope/Function, Scope/Network, Scope/People, Scope/Time [R1,C1; R1,C2; R1,C3; R1,C4; R1,C5; R1,C6]

Note: The Scope/Motivation cell is presumed to be addressed by strategic business planning activities outside the scope of the Architecture Vision.

- Plan for the architecture work

- Refined statements of business principles, business goals, and strategic drivers
  ZF: Scope/Data, Scope/Motivation [R1,C1; R1,C6]

- Architecture principles (if not previously existing)
  ZF: Scope/Data, Scope/Function, Scope/Network, Scope/People, Scope/Time, Scope/Motivation [R1,C1; R1,C2; R1,C3; R1,C4; R1,C5; R1,C6]

- Architecture Vision/Business Scenario, including:

  - Baseline Business Architecture, Version 0.1
    ZF: Business/Data, Business/Function, Business/Network, Business/People, Business/Time, Business/Motivation [R2,C2; R2,C2; R2,C3; R2,C4; R2,C5; R2,C6]

  - Baseline Technology Architecture, Version 0.1
    ZF: System/Data, System/Function, System/Network, System/People, System/Time, System/Motivation [R3,C2; R3,C2; R3,C3; R3,C4; R3,C5; R3,C6]

  - Target Business Architecture, Version 0.1
    ZF: Business/Data, Business/Function, Business/Network, Business/People, Business/Time, Business/Motivation [R2,C2; R2,C2; R2,C3; R2,C4; R2,C5; R2,C6]

  - Target Technology Architecture, Version 0.1
    ZF: System/Data, System/Function, System/Network, System/People, System/Time, System/Motivation [R3,C2; R3,C2; R3,C3; R3,C4; R3,C5; R3,C6]

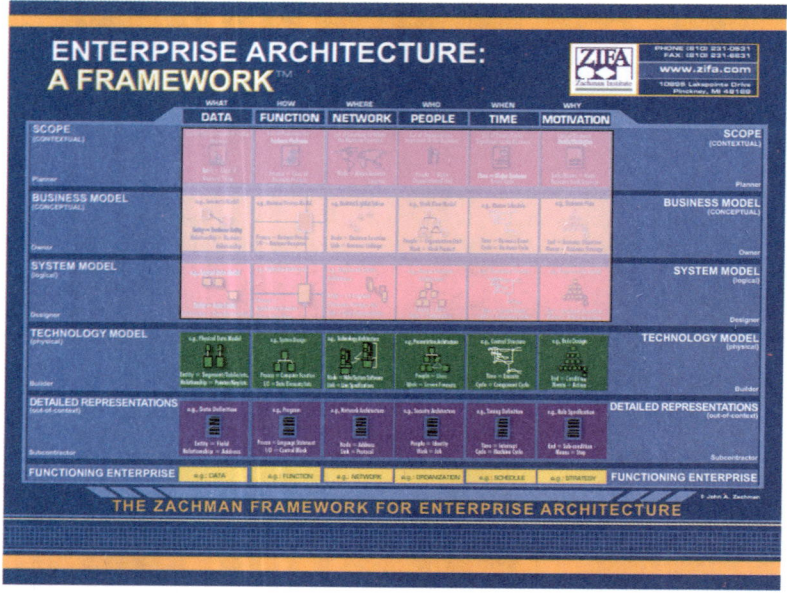

Scope of Phase A: Architecture Vision

39.3.3 Phase B: Business Architecture

The outputs of this phase are:

- Statement of Architecture Work (updated if necessary)
- Validated business principles, business goals, and strategic drivers
  ZF: Scope/Data, Scope/Function, Scope/Network, Scope/People, Scope/Time [R1,C1; R1,C2; R1,C3; R1,C4; R1,C5; R1,C6]
- Target Business Architecture, Version 1.0 (detailed)
    - Organization structure, identifying business locations and relating them to organizational units
      ZF: Scope/Network, Scope/People, Business/Network, Business/People [R1,C3; R1,C4; R2,C3; R2,C4]
    - Business goals and objectives, for each organizational unit
      ZF: Scope/Network, Scope/Time, Business/Network, Business/Time, Business/Motivation [R1,C3; R1,C5; R2,C3; R2,C5; R2,C6]

      Note: The Scope/Motivation cell is presumed to be addressed by strategic business planning activities outside the scope of the Business Architecture.
    - Business functions - a detailed, recursive step involving successive decomposition of major functional areas into sub-functions
      ZF: Scope/Function, Business/Function [R1,C2; R2,C2]
    - Business services - the services that each enterprise unit provides to its customers, both internally and externally
      ZF: Business/Function, System/Function [R2,C2; R3,C2]
    - Business processes, including measures and deliverables
      ZF: Business/Function, Business/Time [R2,C2; R2,C5]
    - Business roles, including development and modification of skills requirements
      ZF: Scope/People, Business/People [R1,C4; R2,C4]
    - Correlation of organization and functions; relate business functions to organizational units in the form of a matrix report
      ZF: Scope/Function, Scope/Network, Scope/People, Business/Function, Business/Network, Business/People [R1,C2; R1,C3; R1,C4; R2,C2; R2,C3; R2,C4]
- Baseline Business Architecture, Version 1.0 (detailed), if appropriate
- Views corresponding to the selected viewpoints addressing key stakeholder concerns
- Gap analysis results
- Technical requirements (drivers for the Technology Architecture work): identifying, categorizing, and prioritizing the implications for work in the remaining architecture domains; for example, by a dependency/priority matrix (e.g., guiding trade-off between speed of transaction processing and security); list the specific models that are expected to be produced (e.g., expressed as primitives of the Zachman Framework)

ZF: System/Motivation [R3,C6]

- Business Architecture Report
- Updated business requirements

Note: The Business/Data cell is covered by the Data and Applications Architectures.

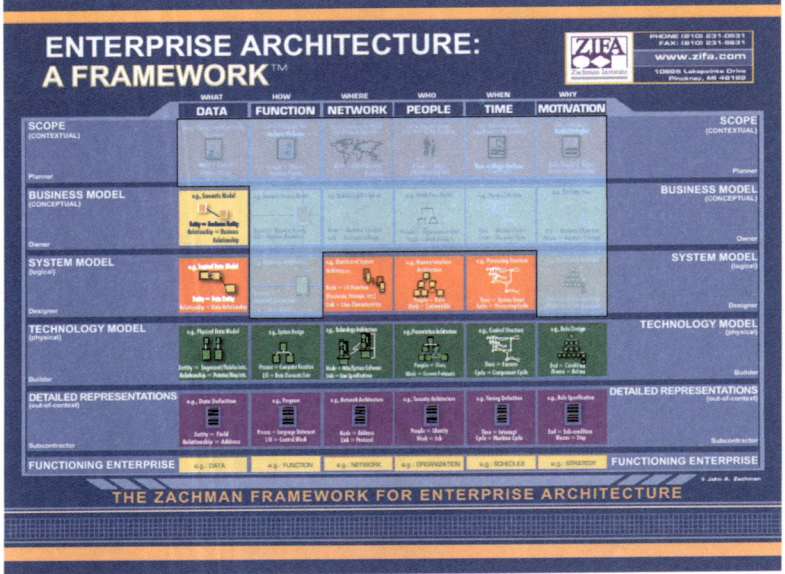

Scope of Phase B: Business Architecture

39.3.4 Phase C: Informations System Architectures: Data Architecture

The outputs of this part of Phase C are:

- Statement of Architecture Work (updated if necessary)
- Baseline Data Architecture, Version 1.0, if appropriate
- Validated principles, or new data principles (if generated here)
  ZF: Scope/Data, Scope/Network, Scope/People, Scope/Time [R1,C3; R1,C4; R1,C5]
- Target Data Architecture, Version 1.0
    - Conceptual data model
      ZF: Business/Data [R2,C1]
    - Logical data model
      ZF: System/Data [R3,C1]
    - Data management process models
      ZF: System/Function, System/People [R3,C2; R3,C3]
    - Data entity/business function matrix
      ZF: Composite of Business/People, System/Data, System/Function [R2,C4; R3,C1; R3,C2]
    - Data interoperability requirements
      ZF: Composite of System/Data, System/Function, System/Network, System/People [R3,C1; R3,C2; R3,C3; R3,C4]
- Viewpoints addressing key stakeholder concerns
- Views corresponding to the selected viewpoints; for example:
    - Data dissemination view
      ZF: Composite of System/Data, System/Function, System/Network, System/People [R3,C1; R3,C2; R3,C3; R3,C4]
    - Data lifecycle view
      ZF: Composite of System/Data, System/Function, System/Time
    - Data security view
      ZF: Composite of System/Function, System/Data, System/Network, System/People, System/Time
    - Data model management view
      ZF: Composite of Business/Data, System/Data, Business/Time, System/Time
- Gap analysis results
- Relevant technical requirements that will apply to this evolution of the architecture development cycle
  ZF: System/Motivation
- Data Architecture Report, summarizing what was done and the key findings
- Impact Analysis
- Updated business requirements, if appropriate

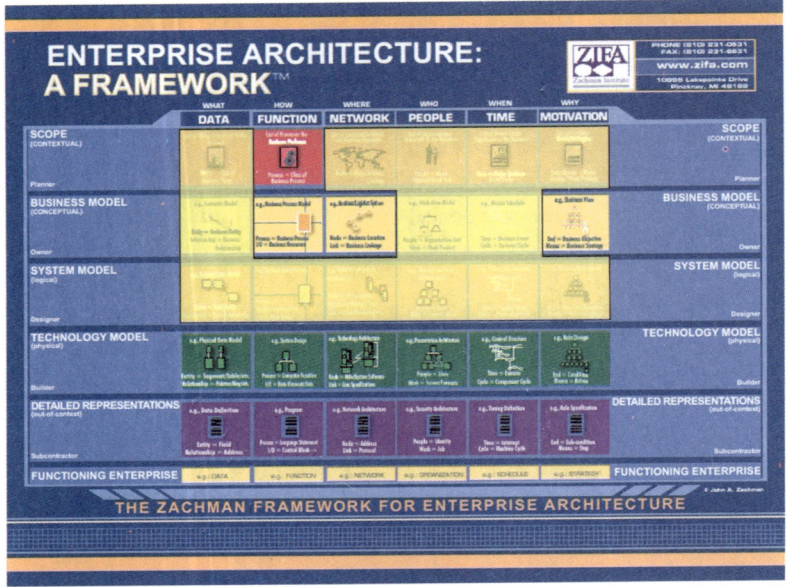

Scope of Phase C: Data Architecture

39.3.5 Phase C: Informations System Architectures: Applications Architecture

The outputs of this part of Phase C are:

- Statement of Architecture Work (updated if necessary)
- Baseline Applications Architecture, Version 1.0, if appropriate
- Validated application principles, or new application principles (if generated here)
  ZF: Scope/Function, Scope/Network, Scope/People, Scope/Time
- Target Applications Architecture, Version 1.0

    - Process systems model
      ZF: System/Function

    - Systems/place model
      ZF: System/Network

    - People/systems model
      ZF: System/People

    - Systems/time model
      ZF: System/Time

    - Applications interoperability requirements
      ZF: Composite of System/Data, System/Function, System/Network, System/People, System/Time, System/Motivation

- Viewpoints addressing key stakeholder concerns

- Views corresponding to the selected viewpoints; for example:
    - Common applications services view
    ZF: Composite of System/Data, System/Function, System/Network, System/People, System/Time
    - Applications interoperability view
    ZF: Composite of System/Data, System/Function, System/Network, System/Time
    - Applications/information view
    ZF: Composite of System/Data, System/Function, System/Network, System/Time
    - Applications/user locations view
    ZF: Composite of System/Network, System/People
- Gap analysis results
    - Areas where the Business Architecture may need to change to cater for changes in the Applications Architecture
    ZF: Composite of Business/Data, Business/Function, Business/Network, Business/People, Business/Time
    - Identify any areas where the Data Architecture (if generated at this point) may need to change to cater for changes in the Applications Architecture
    ZF: Composite of Business/Data, Business/People, Business/Time
    - Identify any constraints on the Technology Architecture about to be designed
    ZF: System/Motivation
- Applications Architecture Report, summarizing what was done and the key findings

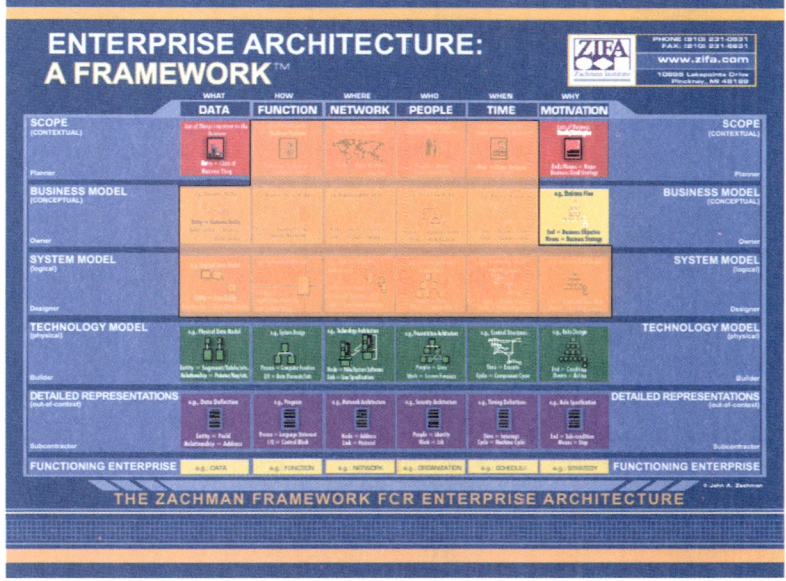

Scope of Phase C: Application Architecture

- Impact Analysis
- Updated business requirements, if appropriate

39.3.6 Phase D: Technology Architecture

The outputs of Phase D are given below, first by relevant individual step, and then as a composite for the whole phase.

Step 1: Create a Baseline Description in the TOGAF Format

The outputs of this step are:

- Technology Architecture principles (if not existing)
  ZF: Scope/Data, Scope/Function, Scope/Network, Scope/People, Scope/Time, Scope/Motivation
- Target Technology Architecture, Version 0.2
    - Technology Architecture - Constraints
    - Technology Architecture - Architecture Principles
    - Technology Architecture - Requirements Traceability, key questions list
    - Technology Architecture - Requirements Traceability, criteria for selection of service portfolio
    - Technology Architecture Model, Version 0.1
      ZF: Technology/Function, Technology/Network

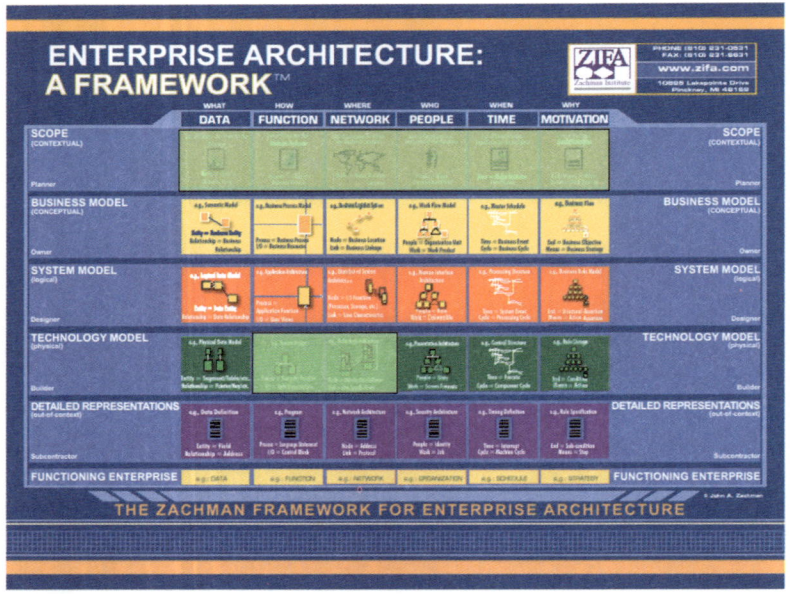

Scope of Phase D: Technology Architecture - Step 1

Step 2: Consider Different Architecture Reference Models, Viewpoints, and Tools

The outputs of this step are:

- Target Technology Architecture, Version 0.3
    - Technology Architecture - Architecture Viewpoints
        - Networked computing/hardware view
          ZF: System/Network, Technology/Network
        - Communications view
          ZF: Composite of: System/Network, System/People, Technology/Network, Technology/People
        - Processing view
          ZF: System/Data, System/Function, System/Network, System/People, System/Time, Technology/Data, Technology/Function, Technology/Network, Technology/People, Technology/Time
        - Cost view
          ZF: Technology/Motivation
        - Standards view
          ZF: Technology/Motivation
    - Technology Architecture - Constraints
      ZF: System/Motivation

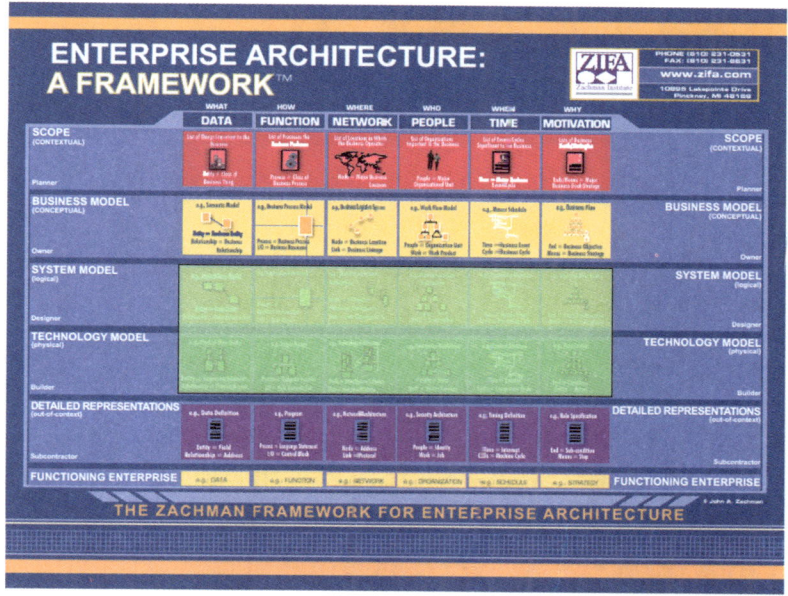

Scope of Phase D: Technology Architecture - Step 2

Chapter 39: ADM and the Zachman Framework 485

Step 3: Create an Architectural Model of Building Blocks

The outputs of this step are:

- Target Technology Architecture, Version 0.4
    - Technology Architecture Model
        - Networked computing/hardware view
          ZF: Technology/Network, System/Network
        - Communications view
          ZF: Composite of: Technology/Network, Technology/People, System/Network, System/People
        - Processing view
          ZF: Technology/Network, Technology/Time, Technology/People, Technology/Data, Technology/Function, System/Network, System/Time, System/People, System/Data, System/Function
        - Cost view
          ZF: Technology/Motivation
        - Standards view
          ZF: Technology/Motivation
    - Technology Architecture - change requests and/or extensions or amendments to be incorporated in an organization-specific Architecture Continuum

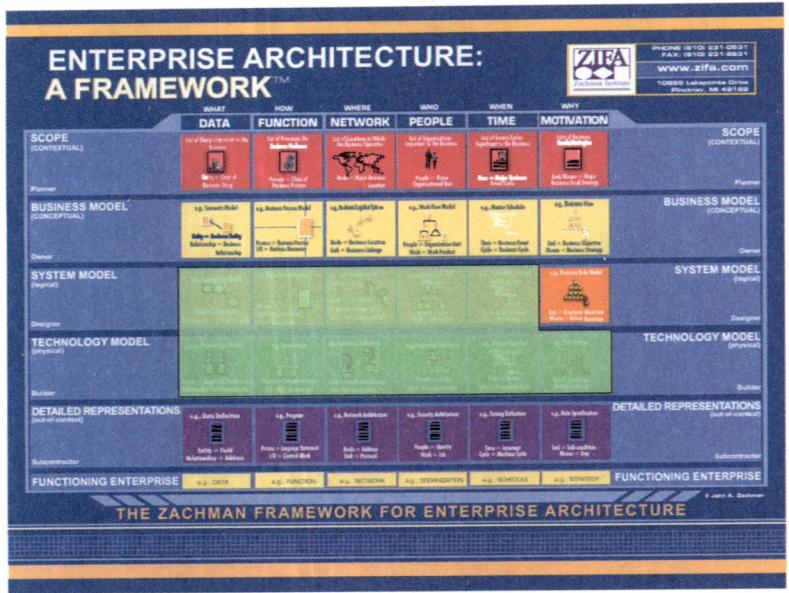

Scope of Phase D: Technology Architecture - Step 3

Step 4: Select the Services Portfolio Required per Building Block

The outputs of this step are:

- Target Technology Architecture, Version 0.5
    - Technology Architecture - target services (a description of the service portfolios required also known as an Organization-Specific Framework)
    ZF: Technology/Network, Technology/Time, Technology/People, Technology/Data, Technology/Function, Technology/Motivation
    - Technology Architecture - change requests and/or extensions or amendments to be incorporated in an organization-specific Architecture Continuum

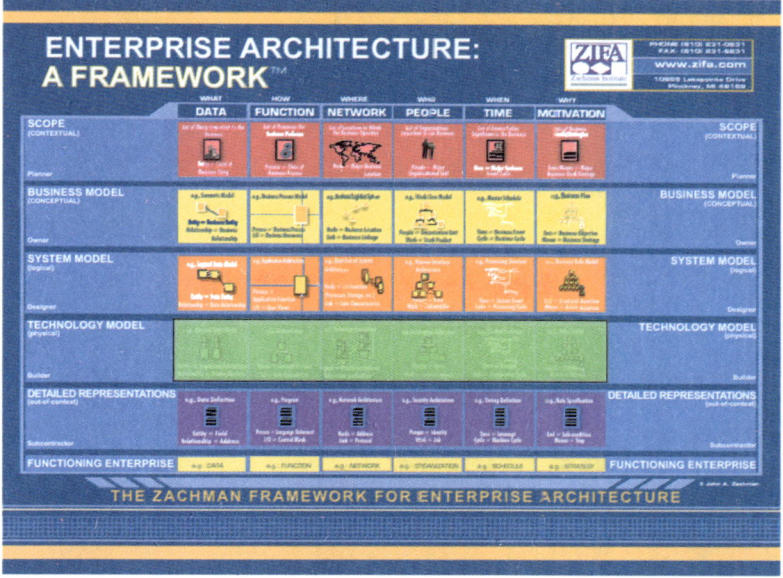

Scope of Phase D: Technology Architecture - Step 4

Step 8: Conduct a Gap Analysis

The outputs of this step are:

- Target Technology Architecture, Version 1.0
    - Technology Architecture - gap report
    ZF: Composite of Technology/Data, Technology/ Function, Technology/Network, Technology/People, Technology/Time, Technology/Motivation

Composite Mapping for Phase D

For more detailed information on the Zachman Framework, refer to any of John Zachman's publications, or the Zachman Institute for Framework Advancement (ZIFA) (*www.zifa.com*).

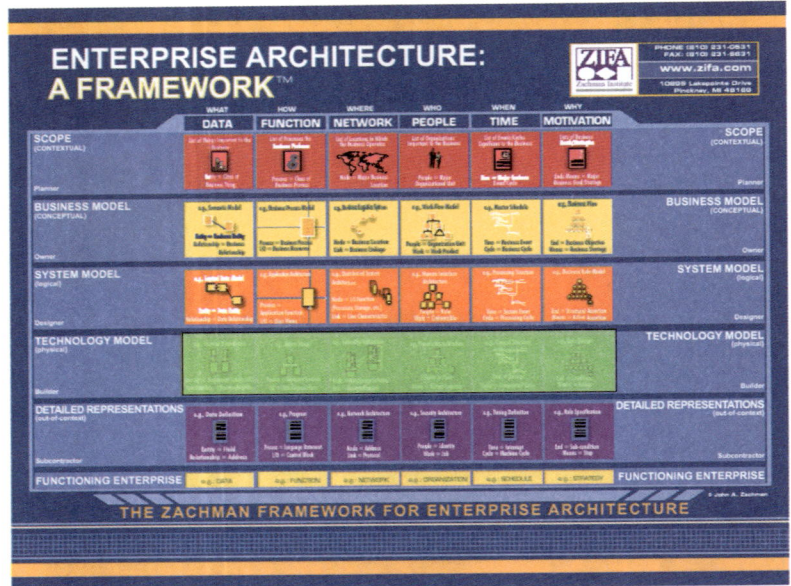

Scope of Phase D: Technology Architecture - Step 8

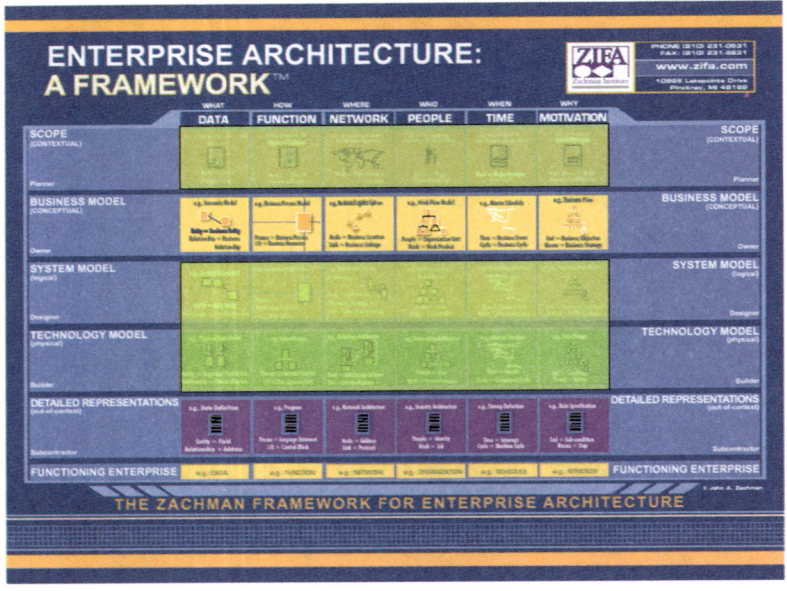

Scope of Phase D: Technology Architecture

488

INDEX

A5 interoperability 318
ABB 79, 85-86, 350-351, 354
AC 444, 451-454
ACMM . . . . xii, 251-252
Acknowledgements . . . . iii, xxii, 269
ACLs 312
ACSE 444, 453-454
Active Store 133
Ada 340, 444
ADM . . . . iii, vii, xiv-xvi, xix, 2-3, 6-3, 10-13, 15-22, 27-28, 30, 33-35, 38, 40-41, 45, 50, 78, 106, 108, 110, 113-120, 128-129, 132, 138-140, 149, 175, 186, 213, 215, 233-236, 241, 245, 257, 260, 294, 300-301, 307, 349-353, 356-357, 362, 375, 387-388, 392, 409-410, 420, 428, 441, 444, 456-457, 459, 461-462, 464, 466, 468, 474, 476-477
  requirements management . . . . . vii, 113-119
ANSI . . . . xxiii, 4, 67, 82, 296-298, 301-302, 309, 374, 444, 453, 464
ANSI X.12 67
ANSI/IEEE Std 1471-2000 . . . . . xxiii, 4, 82, 296-298, 301-302, 309, 453, 464
API 146-147, 161, 192, 327, 342, 420, 444
APP 88, 438, 444
Application . . . . viii, x-xi, xiii, 7, 13, 45, 56-57, 63-64, 66-73, 79, 83, 86, 88, 101, 121, 140-149, 151, 153-154, 156, 158-160, 162, 164-166, 169-170, 172, 185, 187, 189-193, 195, 197-199, 201, 212-213, 220, 222, 224-229, 234, 236, 249, 256, 264, 270-271, 273-280, 292, 294, 302, 311, 315-317, 320-323, 326-328, 331, 334-336, 339-340, 345, 350, 363-364, 369-371, 374-376, 378-380, 392-393, 395, 397, 405, 407, 412-413, 418-420, 422, 424-425, 431, 433-434, 436-440, 444, 446-454, 458, 463, 482
application logic 56, 159, 225, 320-323, 363
Application Platform . . . . viii, x, 140-143, 145-149, 153-154, 156, 158-159, 162, 165, 169-170, 185, 189-190, 192, 198-199, 335, 379, 407, 412-413, 420, 434, 436-440, 444, 448-449, 451, 453-454, 463
  service qualities . . . . viii, 153-154, 212, 379

taxonomy	viii-x, xiv, 8, 11, 130, 132, 139-140, 146-149, 154, 156, 175, 180, 185-186, 192-193, 261, 296, 302-304, 404, 407, 453, 459, 468, 470
Application Platform Interface	viii, 141, 143, 146-147
application portability	88, 140-141, 147, 397, 422, 424, 444
Application Portability Profile	88, 444
Application Portability Profile (APP)	88, 444
application principles	xiii, 57, 68-69, 73, 121, 276-279, 482
Application Program Interface (API)	444
Application Software	viii, 141, 143, 145-147, 154, 156, 158-159, 162, 164-165, 170, 185, 190, 192, 279, 302, 335, 422, 437, 444, 451-452, 463
Applications Architecture	v, xix, 7, 10, 40, 42, 50, 56-58, 63-69, 71-73, 76, 79, 84, 91-92, 97, 102, 190, 199, 228, 234, 287, 291, 297, 302, 305, 457-459, 482-483
APSE	444
Architectural Building Blocks	78
Architecture Framework	iii, xvii-xviii, xxi, xxiii-xxiv, 2, 4, 6, 9-12, 21, 25, 29, 32, 34, 62, 77, 89, 112, 140, 218-219, 237, 240, 261, 269, 352, 399-400, 402-403, 420, 424, 427, 432, 434, 445, 453, 455-457, 461, 463, 465-467, 469
architectural segments	25, 461
Architecture Board	x, 22, 111-112, 204-209, 216-219, 231, 248, 267, 286, 409
Architecture Compliance	x-xi, 105-106, 205, 207, 209, 211, 213-219, 231, 248, 269
checklists	xi, 16-17, 215, 218-219, 221-222, 224, 227, 231
guidelines	vii, xi, xiv, xvi, xviii, 4, 7-8, 11-13, 16-17, 26, 53, 61, 69, 75, 78, 80, 108, 110-111, 121, 123, 133, 138, 158, 204, 211, 219, 225, 231, 233, 237, 240, 247, 257-258, 260, 265-266, 275, 280, 292, 300, 305, 316, 325, 343-344, 379-380, 388, 390-392, 421, 427, 432-433, 445, 469-470
review process	x, 207, 211, 215-217, 221, 248, 254
Architecture Compliance review	x-xi, 207, 211, 213-219, 231, 248
Architecture Continuum	v, viii, xii, 30, 45, 51-52, 61, 63-64, 69-72, 75, 79, 82-86, 90-91, 121, 129-132, 134-138, 174, 260, 350, 357, 445, 448, 453, 486-487
Architecture Contract	vii, 105-106, 108, 124-125, 205, 209, 233-236, 247

architecture development	iii, ix, xii, xvii-xviii, xxiv, 2, 6-7, 9-10, 13, 15-22, 24, 26-27, 34, 37-38, 41, 44-45, 50, 65, 94, 108-110, 119-120, 124, 129, 138-139, 146, 154, 174-175, 186, 213, 217, 233, 235, 241, 245, 252, 254, 257, 261, 294, 300-301, 307, 309-310, 344, 349-350, 354, 369, 373, 378, 380, 387, 398, 404, 406, 409, 441, 444-445, 456, 463, 466, 469, 474, 477, 481
Architecture Development Method	iii, 2, 6-7, 10, 13, 15-16, 34, 108, 120, 129, 138-139, 175, 186, 213, 233, 241, 245, 257, 294, 300-301, 307, 349, 387, 409, 441, 444, 456, 466, 474
architecture domains	iii, 23-24, 26-28, 40-41, 45, 53-54, 115, 233, 235, 380, 462, 469, 476, 479
Architecture Forum	iii, xx-xxii, 2, 9, 399
architecture governance	iii, xi-xii, 11-12, 22, 34, 40, 105-106, 108-109, 128, 204, 207, 209-211, 213, 216, 233, 236-237, 240-248, 252, 265, 269, 292, 477
implementation	iv, vi, 4, 7-8, 16, 23, 28-29, 41, 47-48, 56, 69, 75, 91, 94-98, 100-106, 108, 115, 117-118, 121, 123-124, 130, 134-136, 144, 148, 153-154, 158-159, 163, 169, 171, 176-178, 197, 204-205, 207-209, 211, 214-215, 233-234, 239-241, 243, 245, 247-248, 250, 260, 262, 264-265, 267, 273, 281-282, 292-293, 295, 312-315, 322, 324, 331, 335, 342, 347, 349, 351-352, 354, 379, 407, 420, 426-428, 440, 442, 445, 447, 453, 458
Architecture Governance Framework	xii, 207, 209, 237, 241-242, 244-247, 477
structure	iii, vii, x, xii, xvi, 2, 4-5, 7, 18, 51, 53, 78, 122, 130, 139-140, 143, 145, 147, 149, 178, 180, 185, 207, 212, 221, 224, 231, 238-239, 242, 244-246, 258-262, 264, 325, 333, 339, 342, 356, 378-379, 388, 409, 420, 422, 424, 444-445, 453, 462-464, 468, 474-475, 479
architecture pattern	260-262
content	xii, xv, 47, 120, 136, 176, 191, 193, 208, 224, 231, 242-245, 257-258, 261, 269, 276, 279, 298, 339, 342-343, 350-351, 353, 385, 456
architecture principles	vii, xiii, 21, 33-35, 37-40, 42, 50, 53, 61, 69, 78, 80, 121-122, 248, 265-269, 357, 362-363, 366, 477-478, 484
Architecture Skills Framework	xiii, 251, 283-286, 288, 295
proficiency levels	xiii, 284-285, 288
skills	xiii, 51, 53-54, 186-187, 247, 251, 263, 283-292, 294-295, 381, 441, 479
Architecture View	xiv, 305, 310-314, 445

architecture views	xiv, xvii, 4, 7, 11, 26, 41, 57-58, 81-82, 260, 292, 296, 298-307, 365, 369-370, 378, 406, 408, 428, 430, 453, 456, 466, 469
taxonomy	viii-x, xiv, 8, 11, 130, 132, 139-140, 146-149, 154, 156, 175, 180, 185-186, 192-193, 261, 296, 302-304, 404, 407, 453, 459, 468, 470
Architecture Vision	iv, vii, xix, 21, 24, 28, 36-42, 45, 50, 57, 60, 68, 75-76, 79, 115, 121-122, 234, 354, 357, 380, 387, 409, 477-478
Architecture, Baseline	76-77, 108, 445
Architecture, Database	445
Architecture, Target	86, 445, 487
ARTS	59, 62, 128
ASN	445
ASP	264, 445
ATA method	52, 63, 70, 82, 84
Availability	18, 23, 37, 71, 102, 136, 144, 152, 154, 166, 170, 175-179, 182, 198-199, 208, 229, 247, 264, 267, 278, 305-306, 309, 314, 324, 326, 333, 343-344, 353, 357, 360-361, 374-375, 378, 397, 408, 445, 452, 473
Base-Level Functions	446
Baseline	iv, 4, 21, 25, 28, 37-42, 44-45, 49-52, 54, 57, 60-61, 63, 65, 67-68, 70-71, 73, 76-81, 83, 92, 108, 111, 116-118, 122-123, 253, 282, 301, 354, 356-357, 365, 416, 426, 429-430, 445-446, 458-461, 478-479, 481-482, 484
Baseline Description	iv, 45, 50-51, 61, 68, 70-71, 76, 78, 83, 111, 354, 365, 459, 484
Batch Processing	151, 164, 338, 446
brokerage applications	x, 193, 195-196
building blocks	vii, xv-xvi, 4, 7-8, 13, 17, 26, 48-49, 51-53, 60-61, 63-64, 68-73, 76-79, 83-85, 87, 89-90, 94, 96-97, 121-124, 129-135, 140, 146, 154, 175, 178, 211-212, 257, 293, 305-306, 346-357, 361-367, 370-377, 379, 421-422, 428, 430, 445, 464-465, 486

example	ix, xii-xiv, xvi, xx, 3-4, 11, 16, 18, 20-21, 25, 27-28, 33, 39, 44, 46-49, 52, 54, 56, 59-60, 62-67, 69-70, 72-73, 75, 77, 79, 83, 87-89, 92, 96, 101, 109-111, 115, 120, 128-129, 133, 137-138, 140, 145, 148-149, 159, 172, 177-182, 186-187, 211, 215, 222-223, 231, 233, 251-252, 257-258, 266-267, 269, 279, 284-285, 292, 294, 296-300, 303-304, 306-309, 317-318, 320-324, 329, 331, 339-341, 349, 356-358, 360, 363, 373, 382-383, 390, 392-393, 424-425, 441, 464-465, 468, 479, 481, 483
business applications	viii, x-xi, 7, 48, 143-145, 178, 185, 190-191, 193, 222-223, 234, 446
Business Architecture	iv, vii, xiv, xix, 6, 10, 16, 21, 25, 27, 38, 40-47, 49-54, 56-58, 61-66, 68, 70-73, 76, 78-79, 81, 83-84, 86-88, 90-92, 97, 102, 122-123, 129, 138, 286-287, 291, 297, 302, 305, 310-311, 357-358, 380, 384, 428, 457, 459, 462, 478-480, 483
Business Architecture view	xiv, 305, 310-311
business modeling	iv, 46, 51, 197, 458
business principles	xiii, 21, 33-35, 37-39, 42, 44, 50, 53, 121, 269, 357, 477-479
business process domain	xvi, 378-379
Business Process Management Initiative	46
business requirements	7, 17, 26, 28, 37-38, 40-41, 44-45, 51, 54, 58, 63, 65, 72-73, 78, 90, 114, 122, 124, 131, 135, 145-146, 215, 217-219, 222, 236, 310, 351, 358, 361, 368-369, 378, 380, 387-388, 398, 425-426, 464, 480-481, 484
business scenario	vii, xvi, xxiii, 41-42, 45, 50, 57, 60, 68, 70, 76, 79, 96, 115, 122, 188, 378, 380-388, 390-391, 478
business scenario descriptions	385
business scenario models	xvi, 385, 391
business scenario workshops	382-384, 388
business scenarios	iv, vii, xii, xvi, 38-42, 45, 51, 87, 114, 116-118, 260, 293, 300, 310-311, 343, 378, 380-383, 386-388, 397-398
Business System	120, 446, 449
C2STA	xxiv, 296
C4ISR	xviii, 11, 62, 427, 429, 455-457, 466-467
C4ISR/DoD Framework	11
capability maturity model	xxv, 250-251, 255
Catalyst	109

CCITT	413, 417, 446
CDE	320
change management	vii, 107-111, 117-118, 125, 153, 169, 172, 230, 281
class model	46-47
Client	xi, xv, 83, 144-146, 152, 162, 166, 171, 191, 193, 195, 197, 220, 228-229, 292, 320-321, 324, 326-329, 331, 412, 418-419, 432, 441, 446, 452, 472
client/server model	xv, 83, 326-329
CMIP	446
CMIS	446
CMM	250, 255
CMMI	xii, xxv, 250, 255-256
COBIT	xi, 23, 208, 240, 246, 446
COBIT framework	208, 240
COBOL	446
CODASYL	340
COM	xxiv, 115, 210, 263-264, 297, 324, 463, 467, 487
common object services	153, 172, 457
Common Systems Architecture	133, 135, 137, 185
communications engineering view	xv, 306, 332-333
communications framework	334-337
Communications Infrastructure	viii, xv, 141-143, 147-148, 333-334, 336
Communications Infrastructure Interface	viii, 141, 143, 147-148
Communications Mechanism	446
communications network	312, 314, 333, 446
Communications Network	312, 314, 333, 446
Communications Node	446
Communications System	335, 446
Configuration Management	152, 158, 169, 172, 230, 433, 446-447
Connectivity Service	447
CORBA	xviii, 324, 331, 447, 457
corporate governance	21, 237-238, 240
COTS	xi, 115, 128, 144, 214, 218-219, 224, 229, 279, 302, 319-320, 346, 352, 381, 416-418, 420-421

CRUD	62, 101
DAI	321-323
data access interface	xv, 321-323
data administration	xv, 158, 277, 338, 342
Data Architecture	iv, xix, 6-7, 10, 40-42, 50, 56-66, 71-73, 76, 79, 84, 91-92, 97, 101-102, 234, 286-287, 291, 302, 305, 342, 428, 458-459, 481, 483
data dictionary	xv, 150, 157-158, 171-172, 338, 341, 447, 452
Data Dictionary	xv, 150, 157-158, 171-172, 338, 341, 447, 452
Data Element	158, 276-277, 447
data encapsulation	320
data encryption	343
data flow view	xv, 305, 337
Data Interchange Service	447
data interchange services	ix-x, 149-150, 153, 156, 172, 181, 201, 413
data management	ix-x, 7, 61-62, 64-65, 71, 150, 157-158, 171-173, 192, 201, 222, 224-225, 234, 275, 287, 326-327, 338, 341-342, 370, 406-407, 410, 412-413, 418, 420, 439, 447-448, 481
Data Management Service	447
data management services	ix-x, 150, 157, 171-173, 201, 225, 338, 341-342
data principles	xiii, 57, 60-61, 65, 121, 271-273, 481
data security	xv, 61-62, 65, 170, 275, 278, 338, 342, 481
data standardization	276-277, 320
Database	xv, 8, 59, 64, 72, 97, 136, 139, 145, 149-150, 158-159, 162, 165, 173-175, 179, 181, 198, 201, 215, 222, 224-225, 232, 302, 305, 309, 318, 320, 322-323, 329, 337-343, 350, 369, 373, 376, 396, 413, 417-418, 420, 444-445, 447-448, 451-452
database administration	342
Database Management System	150, 158-159, 338-340, 413, 447-448, 451-452
database services	337
database system	337, 341, 343
DBMS	150, 158-159, 173, 309, 338-342, 447-448, 472
flat files	340
hierarchical model	339
network model	340

object-oriented model	340
relational model	339
DCE	374, 447
DD/DS	341-342
DDL	339, 342, 447
Default	324, 370, 447
design pattern	260, 262
development tools	x, 192, 197
Directory Service	448
directory services	ix-x, 150, 158, 160, 162, 199-200, 407
DISA	448, 466
dispensation	23, 26, 110, 208-209, 243, 269
Distributed Database	341, 448
distributed DBMS	340-341
distributed object management model	xv, 329, 331
DMF	448
DML	339
domain views	xvi, 378-379
DRDA	320, 322
EAP	xviii, 56, 458-459, 461
ebXML	67
ECMA	448
EDI	448
EEI	448-449
End User	160, 200, 313, 448
enterprise architecture	iii, xiii, xviii, xxiii-xxiv, 2-13, 16-17, 21, 23-27, 29-31, 34, 37, 47-48, 56, 101, 108-110, 114, 125, 129, 134, 136, 138, 185, 204-206, 211-216, 233-237, 240-241, 247, 249-251, 253-254, 256, 265, 269, 279, 281, 283, 286-287, 289, 291, 295, 297, 373, 378, 380-381, 387, 398, 425, 458-463, 466-470, 474
Enterprise Continuum	iii-v, vii-viii, xiii, 2, 7, 13, 16-18, 22-23, 39-40, 47-48, 50, 57, 59, 66, 68, 76, 79, 90, 97, 106, 121, 124, 127-131, 136-138, 174, 185, 232, 235, 242, 245, 293, 445, 448, 453, 469

detail	iii, v, viii, 12, 16, 18, 20-21 24, 27-30, 35, 40-41, 45-47, 50-52, 61, 68, 75-78, 81, 83, 105, 114, 130-132, 134, 140-143, 148-149, 161-162, 174, 182-183, 185, 188, 193, 210, 213, 241, 252, 259, 262, 287, 291, 300, 303, 307, 309, 350, 356, 358, 368, 373, 377, 382, 391, 407, 437, 440, 445, 457, 459, 463-464, 467, 469, 476
enterprise manageability view	xv, 69, 306, 311, 343-344
Enterprise Model	448
Enterprise principles	265
enterprise security view	xiv, 306, 311-312
enterprise solution	136
ERP	48, 56, 223, 448
ES	448
ESC	xxiv, 296
evaluation criteria	xviii, 230, 268, 453, 469-470
tools	vii, x-xi, xiv, xviii, 2-4, 7, 10-11, 20, 33, 44, 46-47, 49, 51, 53, 61-62, 64, 69, 72, 77, 80, 82, 90, 115, 120, 140, 144-145, 147, 151, 156, 158, 164-165, 175, 179, 192, 197-198, 221, 223-224, 226-227, 229-230, 240, 247, 250, 275, 287, 298, 307-310, 318, 350, 469-470, 472, 485
Expand	193, 255, 293, 342, 448
External Environment Interface (EEI)	449
FEAF	xviii, xxiii, 11, 25-26, 269, 461-462
Federal Enterprise Architecture	xviii, xxiii-xxiv, 11, 25-26, 47-48, 269, 459, 461
federated architecture	24, 33
File	3, 145, 148, 150-151, 156, 158, 161-165, 193, 198, 201, 225-226, 319, 338, 340-341, 343, 449, 451, 453
FIPS	88, 449
FORTRAN	449
foundation architect	294
Foundation Architecture	viii-ix, 2, 8, 13, 16-17, 78, 80, 83, 90, 111, 129-130, 132-133, 137-139, 174-175, 185, 459, 461, 468
FTAM	449
Function	xi, 26, 33, 49, 52, 60-65, 70-71, 92, 100, 108-109, 128, 132, 144-145, 162, 164-165, 211, 214-215, 233-236, 264, 271, 273, 298, 305-306, 310, 316, 326, 328, 367, 378, 414, 446, 448-449, 452-453, 471, 475, 477-479, 481-487
gateway	97, 175, 179, 341, 435-436, 446

GITP 463

global transaction 165

GNMP. 449

GOSIP. 449

GOTS 279

governance characteristics. . . . . .xii, 240

graphics services 159

GSS 449

GUI 151, 165, 413, 449

Hardware . . . . .xi, 7, 69, 76, 82, 84-85, 89-90, 135, 147, 170, 219-220, 227, 229, 246, 260, 271, 278-279, 282, 302, 305-306, 309, 314-315, 317, 326, 334, 341, 343, 345-346, 351, 395-396, 410-412, 415-417, 433, 444, 446, 449-452, 464, 472, 485-486

hierarchic model 328-331

Hillside Group. . . . . .xxiv, 264

Human Computer Interface (HCI) . . 165, 449

human interaction services . . . . . x, 200

ICAM 46

ICD 319

IDEF. 46, 62

idiom 260

IDL 325

IEC . . . . .xviii, xxiii-xxiv, 140, 179, 420, 449-450, 462-463, 465

IEEE . . . . .xviii, xxiii-xxiv, 4, 82, 134, 140, 174, 179, 296-298, 301-302, 309, 420, 428, 449, 453, 462-465

IEEE 1003.0 140

IEEE Std 1003.0 . . . . .xviii, xxiv, 140, 179, 462-463, 465

IEEE Std 1003.23 . . . . .xxiii, 134, 179

III . . . . .vii, 2, 13, 16, 51-53, 61-64, 69-73, 77, 90, 97, 106, 127, 130, 174, 182, 449

III-RM . . . . .x, 2, 8, 67, 70, 75, 129-130, 133, 185-186, 188-193, 199, 449

taxonomy . . . . .viii-x, xiv, 8, 11, 130, 132, 139-140, 146-149, 154, 156, 175, 180, 185-186, 192-193, 261, 296, 302-304, 404, 407, 453, 459, 468, 470

498

III-RM graphic	x, 186, 190, 192-193
imaging services	ix, 150, 159
Impact Analysis	vii, 58, 64-65, 72-73, 91, 98, 102-103, 106, 124, 481, 483-484
implementation governance	vi, 104-106, 234, 241, 245
IMS	340
industry architect	294
Industry Architecture	133, 136
industry solution	136
industry standards	8, 149, 174, 183, 282, 465, 472
information consumer applications	x, 191, 193, 195-196
Information Domain	47, 313, 315-316, 449
information domains	xiv, 312-313, 315
information exchange matrix	47
information provider applications	x, 191, 193-196, 199
Information System	xvi, xxiv, 4, 47, 57, 101, 129, 133, 139, 143, 149, 159, 167, 169, 224, 239, 261, 296, 312-314, 316, 326, 352, 360, 371, 373, 375, 421, 425, 436, 445, 449-450, 453-454
Information System Architecture	xxiv, 261
Information Technology (IT)	265, 450
information-intensive software	xiv, 317-318
infrastructure applications	viii, x, 143-145, 185, 190-192, 196-197
inheritance	317, 340
input and output	vii, 120, 163, 418-419
integrated information infrastructure	ix, 2, 8, 30, 67, 70, 75, 129-130, 133, 185, 187-190, 192, 197, 199, 449
Interface	viii-ix, xv, 106, 141-143, 146-148, 150-153, 156-158, 161, 165-166, 172, 175, 177-178, 187, 194, 221-222, 224-225, 262, 277, 308, 311, 316-325, 329, 331, 339, 342, 373, 392-393, 395, 397, 405, 413-414, 420, 444, 448-451, 454, 457
international operation services	ix, 150, 159-160
Internet Society	174
interoperability	viii, xiv, xvii, xix, 5, 24-25, 29, 47-48, 64-65, 70, 73, 97-98, 133, 139-142, 144, 148, 155, 158, 161, 282, 307, 311, 316-318, 325, 333-335, 350, 362, 370, 372, 396, 406, 408, 410, 418, 420-422, 424-425, 427-428, 430-431, 433, 438-440, 450-451, 454, 461, 465, 472, 481-483

Interoperability . . . . viii, xiv, xvii, xix, 5, 24-25, 29, 47-48, 64-65, 70, 73, 97-98, 133, 139-142, 144, 148, 155, 158, 161, 282, 307, 311, 316-318, 325, 333-335, 350, 362, 370, 372, 396, 406, 408, 410, 418, 420-422, 424-425, 427-428, 430-431, 433, 438-440, 450-451, 454, 461, 465, 472, 481-483

IPD-CMM xxv

IS . . . . ix, xx-xxii, xxiv-xxv, 2-13, 16-18, 20-31, 33-34, 37-41, 44-53, 55-56, 59-60, 63-64, 66-68, 70-72, 75-89, 91-92, 94-97, 99-103, 105-112, 114-115, 117-120, 125, 128-149, 153-154, 157-167, 169-190, 192-193, 195, 197, 199, 201-202, 204-217, 219-222, 224-245, 247, 249-256, 258-264, 266-284, 286-287, 291-302, 304-324, 326-329, 331-333, 335-350, 352-354, 356-358, 360-363, 365, 367, 369-373, 375-378, 380-386, 388-393, 397-403, 405-410, 412-414, 416-422, 424-439, 441-452, 454-460, 463-465, 467-469, 471-476, 478-480

ISA 450

ISACF 240

ISAM 158, 340

ISO . . . . xviii, xxiii-xxiv, 48, 140, 174, 179, 255, 323-324, 420, 450, 462-463, 465

ISO RM-ODP . . . . xviii, 463

ISO/IEC TR 14252 . . . . xviii, xxiii-xxiv, 140, 179, 462-463, 465

Key Characteristics of an IT Architect 294

role of . . . . iii, viii-ix, xiv, xvii, 6, 10, 44, 139, 142, 148, 174, 211, 274, 286-287, 291-293, 295-296, 322, 386, 399, 427, 434

IT governance . . . . xi, 17, 26, 34, 37, 39, 207-208, 211, 214-215, 218-219, 233-234, 236-237, 239-241, 244, 248

IT Governance Institute 240

IT principles 122, 265, 267, 385

ITIL 23, 109, 450

Java . . . . xxv, 279, 320

JTC1 450

JVM 320

LAN 319, 329, 334, 450

LCS 314

Lifecycle . . . . xix, 28, 38, 44, 61-62, 65, 117-118, 153, 172, 213, 215, 219-220, 223, 245, 255, 316, 387-388, 396, 417, 450, 459, 461, 472, 481

LISI	70
local subscriber environment	312
location services	151, 161
MAN	450
manageability	xv, 13, 69, 89, 128, 133, 148, 153-154, 306, 311, 343-344, 351, 374, 397, 408, 468
management utilities	x, 192, 197-198
master/slave model	328-329
maturity model	xxv, 250-251, 255
MDA	69
Metaview (*also known as a Viewpoint*)	450
middleware	xi, 7, 220, 279, 319, 324, 436
migration	vi, xiv, xvii, 11, 24, 29, 89, 96, 98-103, 106, 109, 124, 139, 156, 158-159, 162, 170, 185, 253, 287, 311, 316-317, 324, 326, 375, 379, 417, 420, 422, 426, 435, 458
MIS	407, 425, 437, 450
MLS	450
Model-Driven Architecture	69
MTA	313, 407-408, 450
Multimedia Service	450
NCR Enterprise Architecture Framework	xviii, 463
network management services	ix, 152, 169-172, 181
network services	ix, xiv, 71, 92, 151, 161, 172-173, 315, 342, 374, 396, 448
NIST	88, 444, 450
NLSP	450
node connectivity diagram	47
OAG	48
OASIS	67
object management	xv, 47-48, 66, 69, 150, 159, 171, 174, 329, 331-332, 418-419, 457
Object Management Group	47-48, 66, 69, 174, 331, 457
OCCA	463
ODA	450

ODBC	320, 322
ODIF	450
OECD	xxiv, 238, 450
OIW	451
OLE	331
OMA	457
OMG	47-48, 66, 69, 174, 331, 457
OODBMS	150, 158, 173, 340, 451
Open Brand	ix, 175-176, 178-179
Open Group Architecture Forum	iii, xx-xxii, 2, 9, 399
Open System	xxiii-xxiv, 132, 134, 169, 312, 314, 416, 418, 421-422, 424, 449, 451, 463, 465
Open Systems Environment (OSE)	422, 451
Operating System Service	314, 451
operating system services	ix-x, xiv, 148, 151, 158, 163, 172, 182, 201, 315-316, 413
operational-level agreements	243
ORB	153, 171, 173, 331, 451, 457
ORB services	153, 171
organization architect	294
Organization-Specific Framework	34, 86, 487
OS	451, 472
OSE	xxiii-xxiv, 134, 421-422, 451
OSI	171, 315, 333-336, 451
OSI Reference Model	333-336
pattern resources	xii, 264
patterns home page	xxiv, 264
patterns-discussion FAQ	xxiv, 264
peer-to-peer model	xv, 329, 331
PEX	159, 451
Phase A	iv, xix, 36-40, 42, 45, 76, 78, 233-234, 353-354, 361, 477
Phase B	iv, xvi, xix, 40, 43-45, 47, 49-50, 53, 63, 71, 117-118, 357-358, 459, 478-479
Phase C	iv-v, xix, 55-57, 59, 66, 234, 301, 480-482
Phase D	v, xix, 20, 49, 60, 67, 74-77, 96-97, 234, 484, 487

Phase E	vi, xvi, 95-98, 213, 354, 356-357, 375, 459
Phase F	vi, 99-100, 102-103, 459
Phase G	vi, 104-106, 108, 234, 236, 241, 245
Phase H	vii, 107-108, 111-112, 117-118, 125, 236
PHIGS	159, 451
Platform	viii-x, xviii, 8, 69, 76, 130, 139-143, 145-149, 153-154, 156, 158-160, 162-165, 169-170, 185-186, 189-192, 198-199, 306, 317, 325-326, 328, 335, 341-342, 370, 376, 379, 407, 410-413, 417, 420, 432-434, 436-440, 444, 447-449, 451, 453-454, 463, 465
platform taxonomy	viii-ix, 130, 139-140, 147-148, 156
Portability	viii, xiv, 5, 88, 139-141, 145, 147, 155, 279, 316-317, 333, 396-397, 406, 418, 421-422, 424, 439, 444, 451-452, 465
POSC	59, 62, 128, 133
POSIX	xxiii-xxiv, 416, 420, 451, 463, 465
Preliminary Phase	iv, xix, 32-35, 37-40, 108, 235, 477
PRINCE 2	109
Product Line Architecture	22
Product Standard	176, 179, 182-183
Project Impact Assessment	213
project slice	212
qualities	viii, x, xiii, 63, 72, 148, 153-154, 156, 190, 192, 202, 212, 258, 267, 379, 408
RAS	369, 452
RDA	452
RDBMS	339, 341, 413, 416, 418, 452
REA	48
Red Books	xxiv, 261, 263
Referenced Documents	iii, xxii-xxiii
Registered Product	182
relay system	313-314
repository	2, 4, 7, 11, 16-17, 22, 33, 52, 64, 72, 79, 90, 115-119, 125, 128, 138, 150, 153, 157-158, 160, 171-172, 197, 224, 244, 275, 342, 374, 401, 414, 416-417, 445, 447, 452-453, 471, 474
Repository	2, 4, 7, 11, 16-17, 22, 33, 52, 64, 72, 79, 90, 115-119, 125, 128, 138, 150, 153, 157-158, 160, 171-172, 197, 224, 244, 275, 342, 374, 401, 414, 416-417, 445, 447, 452-453, 471,

Request for Architecture Work	vii, 37, 39, 50, 57, 60, 68, 75, 79, 97, 102, 105, 111-112, 120, 357
Requirements Impact Statement	vii, 116-119, 125
Resource-Event-Agent	48
RM	452
RM-ODP	xviii, 324, 463-464
RosettaNet	48
RPC	162, 374, 452
SA-CMM	xxv
SANS Institute	273
SBB	347, 351, 354
Scalability	155, 258, 264, 351, 389, 396, 408, 421, 431, 433, 452, 471
SCAMPI	xii, xxv, 255-256
SE-CMM	xxv
Security	ix-xi, xiv-xv, xvii, 5, 13, 47, 54, 61-65, 71, 89, 133, 136, 148, 152-154, 158, 161-163, 167-170, 173, 195, 199, 219, 224-225, 240, 246, 252-255, 258, 269, 273, 275, 278-279, 287, 292, 294, 296, 298, 300, 305-306, 309, 311-316, 323, 337-339, 342-345, 351, 363, 369-370, 374-375, 395, 397, 400-402, 406-408, 415, 422, 424, 439, 442-443, 445, 449-450, 452-453, 457, 468, 470, 479, 481
security association	315
security context	315
security management	xiv, 152, 168, 170, 315-316, 452
security mechanisms	313, 315, 415
security services	ix-x, xiv, 148, 152-153, 167-170, 173, 195, 199, 312-316, 374, 452, 457
SEI	xxv, 52, 63, 70, 82, 84, 249, 255-256
Server	xi, xv, 8, 83, 145-146, 152, 162, 166, 191, 193, 197, 220, 225, 228-229, 262, 320-329, 331, 412, 416, 418-419, 432, 445-446, 452
service qualities	viii, 153-154, 212, 379
Application Platform	viii, x, 140-143, 145-149, 153-154, 156, 158-159, 162, 165, 169-170, 185, 189-190, 192, 198-199, 335, 379, 407,

	412-413, 420, 434, 436-440, 444, 448-449, 451, 453-454, 463
TRM	viii, x, 8, 75, 78, 80, 82-83, 85-86, 128-130, 132, 138-143, 145-146, 148-149, 154, 171, 174-175, 180, 185-186, 189-192, 199, 253, 327, 329, 335, 368, 404-405, 407, 421-425, 427-428, 436-438, 447-448, 450-451, 453-454, 459, 466, 468
SIB	ix, 8, 86, 88, 90, 129-130, 132, 138-140, 149, 174-176, 178-182, 184, 373-375, 400, 404-406, 452, 459, 465, 468
SLA	125, 236
SMAP	452
SMART	xvi, 299, 380-381, 392-393
SMTP	452
SNA	335, 452
SNMP	452
software engineering services	ix-x, 151, 154, 164, 199, 413
software engineering view	xiv, 69, 305, 316, 324-325
software modularity	xiv, 316
software portability	139, 317, 406
software re-use	317, 395
software tiers	xiv-xv, 317, 319
Solution Building Block	106
Solutions Continuum	viii, 79, 106, 129-130, 134-137, 351, 448, 453
SPE 68794	xxiii, 101
SPIRIT	xviii, 213, 265, 268, 407, 465
SQL	158, 320, 322, 340, 374, 418, 420, 453
stakeholder	xiv-xv, 11, 28, 38, 44, 49, 51, 54, 58-59, 62, 65, 67, 69, 73, 77, 81-84, 91, 110, 116-118, 125, 240, 271, 298, 302, 307-310, 312, 326, 332-333, 337, 358, 453, 479, 481-482
Standards Information Base	ix, xvii, 8, 86, 88, 90, 129-130, 132, 138-139, 174, 373, 400, 404-405, 409, 452, 459, 465, 468
Statement of Architecture Work	vii, xi, 39, 41-42, 50, 53, 57, 60, 64-65, 68, 72-73, 75, 77, 79, 81, 91, 97, 102, 105-106, 121, 234, 357, 477, 479, 481-482
STEP Framework	48
steward	274, 276
SW-CMM	xxv

SWG 453
System. . . . . .ix-xi, xiv-xvi, xix, xxiii-xxiv, 3-6, 21-22, 24, 28, 41, 47, 57, 66, 71, 77-78, 80-81, 83-84, 87-89, 91, 96-98, 101, 105-106, 111, 120, 122-123, 129, 132-136, 138-139, 143-152, 154-155, 158-160, 162-165, 167-173, 181-183, 191-193, 197-198, 201-202, 212, 214-215, 218-221, 224, 226-233, 238-240, 247, 257-258, 260-261, 271-272, 275, 278, 280-281, 294-296, 298-299, 301-302, 305-319, 321, 324-326, 333, 335, 337-345, 347-348, 350, 352, 354, 356-360, 362-363, 365, 367, 369-376, 379, 384-385, 388, 390-391, 397, 400-401, 406-408, 410, 413-414, 416-422, 424-428, 430, 434, 436, 445-454, 456-457, 463-465, 475-476, 478-483, 485-486

System and Network Management Service 453

system architect 294

system engineering view. . . . . .xv, 305, 325-326, 344

system management services 315

system solution 135

System Stakeholder 453

TADG . . . . .xii, xxiv, 261-262

TAFIM . . . . .xviii, xxi, 2, 140, 453, 455, 463, 465-466

Target Architecture descriptions . . .28

taxonomy . . . . .viii-x, xiv, 8, 11, 130, 132, 139-140, 146-149, 154, 156, 175, 180, 185-186, 192-193, 261, 296, 302-304, 404, 407, 453, 459, 468, 470

Taxonomy of Architecture Views. . .xiv, 296, 302-304, 453

TCP/IP 325, 335, 369, 413, 420, 436, 453

TCSEC 453

TEAF . . . . .xviii, 11, 466-467

Technology 72

Technology principles . . . . . . .xiii, 75, 77, 79-80, 121, 266, 279-280, 389

Technical Reference Model . . . . .viii, xvii, 8, 75, 86, 128, 130, 132, 138-139, 141-143, 148, 171, 174, 185, 253, 294, 327, 368, 404-405, 421, 436-437, 445, 447-448, 450-451, 453-454, 459, 466, 468

Technology Architecture . . . . . .v, vii, xix, 7, 10, 16, 19-21, 40-42, 50, 56, 58, 63-65, 72-77, 79-92, 94, 97, 102, 110-111, 123, 129, 143, 145-147, 175, 185, 247, 287, 291, 297, 301-302, 306, 317, 358, 428, 457-459, 469, 478-479, 483-487

detail	iii, v, viii, 12, 16, 18, 20-21, 24, 27-30, 35, 40-41, 45-47, 50-52, 61, 68, 75-78, 81, 83, 105, 114, 130-132, 134, 140-143, 148-149, 161-162, 174, 182-183, 185, 188, 193, 210, 213, 241, 252, 259, 262, 287, 291, 300, 303, 307, 309, 350, 356, 358, 368, 373, 377, 382, 391, 407, 437, 440, 445, 457, 459, 463-464, 467, 469, 476
technology governance	xi, 237-239
TeleManagement Forum	48, 66, 69, 75, 465
TFA	453
The Open Group	ii-iii, ix, xviii, xx-xxiii, xxv, 2, 6, 8-9, 11, 66-67, 70, 75, 90, 132, 138, 149, 175-183, 186-188, 219, 285, 299-300, 373-375, 399, 403, 405, 422, 426, 432, 441-442, 465, 474
membership	xxi-xxii, 9, 172, 188, 206, 313
standards	ix, xiv, xvii, 4, 6-8, 26, 29-30, 45-46, 52-53, 63, 70, 72, 78, 82-85, 88-90, 100, 109-111, 123, 129-130, 132-134, 138-139, 143, 148-149, 158-159, 165, 171, 174-183, 188, 192, 197-198, 211, 213, 218-220, 228, 230, 233, 240, 243, 252-255, 266-268, 275, 279, 282, 296-297, 306, 320, 324-325, 331, 335, 346-347, 349, 351-352, 354, 373, 381, 389, 395-396, 400, 402, 404-406, 409, 420-425, 427, 431-434, 438-439, 442-445, 449-452, 457-459, 461, 463-466, 468, 472-473, 485-486
technical process	176
TLSP	453
TMF	48, 66, 69, 75, 128, 465
TNI	453
TOGAF	ii-iii, vii, ix, xii-xiv, xvi-xxii, xxv, 2-4, 6-13, 16-17, 21, 30, 34, 42, 45, 75, 78, 80, 82-83, 85, 114, 120, 128-133, 138-140, 143, 145-146, 148-149, 174-175, 178, 180, 184-186, 188-190, 199, 207, 216, 237, 240-241, 245-247, 249, 256-257, 260, 284-288, 294-298, 301-302, 309-310, 314-315, 324, 327, 333, 335-336, 342, 349-350, 365-368, 387-388, 392-393, 399-400, 403-407, 409, 412, 428, 430, 437, 441, 443-444, 455-470, 474, 476-477, 484
TOGAF ADM	vii, xvi, 3, 7-8, 11-13, 16-17, 30, 34, 45, 120, 128-129, 132, 140, 149, 241, 245, 387-388, 428, 441, 457, 459, 461, 468, 474
TOGAF Foundation Architecture	2, 8, 13, 16, 78, 129-130, 132, 139, 174-175, 461
TOGAF Licensing Terms	iii, xx
TOGAF Resource Base	3, 8, 16-17
TOGAF SIB	149

TOGAF Standards Information
    Base 8, 400, 465

TOGAF Technical Reference Model 8, 75, 174, 185, 327, 368, 466

TOGAF TRM 80, 82-83, 85, 132, 139-140, 145-146, 148-149, 175, 180,
                                   185, 189-190, 199, 405, 437

TP 165, 374, 453

Trademarks . . . . iii, xxiv-xxv

Trademark License Agreement 179

Transaction . . . . ix, 54, 71-72, 83, 136, 145, 151-153, 165-166, 173, 221,
                                   225, 280, 324, 341, 407, 413, 420, 453-454, 479

transaction processing services . . . ix, 151, 165, 173

Transaction Sequence 454

Transitional Architecture 28-29, 89, 426-427

TRM . . . . viii, x, 8, 75, 78, 80, 82-83, 85-86, 128-130, 132, 138-143,
                                   145-146, 148-149, 154, 171, 174-175, 180, 185-186, 189-
                                   192, 199, 253, 327, 329, 335, 368, 404-405, 407, 421-425,
                                   427-428, 436-438, 447-448, 450-451, 453-454, 459, 466,
                                   468

detail . . . . iii, v, viii, 12, 16, 18, 20-21, 24, 27-30, 35, 40-41, 45-47,
                                   50-52, 61, 68, 75-78, 81, 83, 105, 114, 130-132, 134, 140-
                                   143, 148-149, 161-162, 174, 182-183, 185, 188, 193, 210,
                                   213, 241, 252, 259, 262, 287, 291, 300, 303, 307, 309,
                                   350, 356, 358, 368, 373, 377, 382, 391, 407, 437, 440,
                                   445, 457, 459, 463-464, 467, 469, 476

TRM graphic 139-140, 149, 191-192

trustee 276-277

TSIG 454

UIDL 454

UIMS 454

UISRM 454

UML 46-47, 67, 472

UN/CEFACT 67

US DoD 250, 428, 463

use-case 46-47, 51, 358-361, 369

use-case model 46

User . . . . ix, xxi, xxiii, 11-12, 22. 26, 48, 71, 73, 88, 97, 100, 134,
144, 151-152, 159-160, 162, 164-169, 173, 175, 191, 193,
200, 202, 219, 224-228, 244, 276-277, 279-282, 305, 308-
311, 313, 315, 318, 320-321, 324, 335, 340-341, 351, 390,
392-393, 395-397, 406, 413-416, 418, 420-421, 430, 433,
439, 441, 445, 448-451, 453-454, 465, 483

User Interface Service 454

user interface services . . . . ix, 152, 166

View . . . . ix-x, xiv-xv, xvii, 24-25, 28, 46-47, 51, 61-62, 65, 69-70,
73, 82-85, 130, 141-143, 148, 169, 175, 180, 183, 189,
201, 238, 278, 283, 236, 293, 297-302, 305-314, 316, 318,
322, 324-326, 332-333, 337, 343-346, 361, 367, 370, 372,
378, 390, 406, 410-411, 414-415, 422, 428, 436, 445, 450,
454, 456-457, 467, 469, 481, 483, 485-486

Acquirer's views 306

communications engineering . . . . xv, 306, 332-333

data flow . . . . xv, 305, 337

enterprise manageability . . . . xv, 69, 306, 311, 343-344

enterprise security . . . . xiv, 306, 311-312

software engineering . . . . ix-x, xiv, xxv, 69, 144-145, 151, 154, 164, 199, 223, 249,
287, 305, 316, 324-325, 413, 420

system engineering . . . . xi, xv, 24, 219, 227, 229-230, 305, 325-326, 344

Viewpoint (also known as a
Metaview 454

viewpoints . . . . xiv, 44, 51, 54, 58, 61-62, 65, 69, 73, 77, 80-84, 135, 298-
299, 301-302, 307-308, 357-358, 390, 428, 459, 461-462,
464-465, 468, 474-476, 479, 481-483, 485

Volere . . . . vii, 114-115

W3C 181

WAN 319, 454

wrapping process 315

X device 179

XML 64, 67, 222, 224, 319, 472

Zachman Framework . . . . xviii-xix, 11, 18, 21, 30, 54, 61, 304, 461-462, 467-468,
470, 474-476, 479, 487